Artist-to-Artist

Independent Art Festivals in Chiang Mai 1992–98

David Teh

With additional texts by Patrick D. Flores, May Adadol Ingawanij, David Morris and Rosalind C. Morris; and an extended oral history with contributions from participating artists, organisers and others.

Exhibition Histories

Exhibition Histories

Afterall Books presents *Exhibition Histories*, a series dedicated to shows of contemporary art that have – since the first documenta in Kassel, Germany in 1955 – shaped the way art is experienced, made and discussed. Each book in the series draws on archival material, bringing together numerous illustrations, texts from the time and newly commissioned essays to provide detailed exploration and analysis of selected exhibitions. The shows under consideration have all responded to and influenced artistic practice whilst provoking debates about the meaning and importance of art within culture and society more broadly.

The history of modern art has conventionally focussed on artistic production, emphasising the individual artist in the studio and the influences on his or her practice. *Exhibition Histories* complicates this approach by arguing for an examination of art in the moment and context in which it is presented to a public. Exhibitions offer art its first contact with an audience, and in so doing they place art within explicit or implicit narratives and discursive frameworks. Every decision about the selection and installation of work, the choice and use of the venue, the marketing strategy and the accompanying printed matter informs our understanding of the art on display. The various agents and diverse factors that give form to an exhibition and determine its subsequent influence are addressed in these books from multiple standpoints: the voices of artists, curators and writers are all brought to bear. In some instances the shows selected for study already have established reputations and our work involves analysing why this is so and whether it is justified. In other cases the opportunity is taken to illuminate lesser-known exhibitions that have, nonetheless, suggested new paradigms and that can stake an equal claim to historical importance.

This series is the result of a research project initiated by Afterall at Central Saint Martins and currently benefitting from collaboration with Asia Art Archive and the Center for Curatorial Studies, Bard College. Through archival study, interviews, symposia and seminars, we have amassed the materials to allow us to select exhibitions for examination and to give shape to the resulting books. The findings, analyses and narratives we propose are by no means exhaustive; rather, we see these books as a spur to further research into the exhibition form, and ultimately as a contribution towards a better understanding of contemporary art and its histories.

Front cover image:
Sunthorn Meesri, *bot bat sommut* (*role play*) performance at Tha Pae Gate, Chiang Mai, 1993

Back cover image:
Montien Boonma, *Body Temple*, Wat Suan Dok, Chiang Mai, 1996

Edited by David Teh and David Morris

First published 2018 by Afterall Books in association with Asia Art Archive and the Center for Curatorial Studies, Bard College

***Exhibition Histories* Series Editors**
Lauren Cornell, Tom Eccles, Charles Esche, Pablo Lafuente, Lucy Steeds, John Tain and Michelle Wong

Assistant Editor
Louis Hartnoll

Research Assistant
Manuporn Luengaram

Copy Editor
Deirdre O'Dwyer

Design
Andrew Brash, based on an original design by A Practice For Everyday Life

Print
Die Keure

Afterall
Central Saint Martins
Granary Building
1 Granary Square
London N1C 4AA
www.afterall.org

Afterall is a Research Centre of University of the Arts London, located at Central Saint Martins. Centre Directors: Charles Esche and Mark Lewis; Publishing Director: Caroline Woodley; Research Coordinator: Beth Bramich; Researchers/Editors: Ana Bilbao, Louis Hartnoll, David Morris, Lucy Steeds; Research Assistant: Rose Thompson; AWP Intern: Ella Sweeney

Distribution
Koenig Books, London
c/o Buchhandlung Walther König, Köln
Ehrenstr. 4, 50672 Köln
Tel. +49 (0) 221 / 20 59 6 53
Fax +49 (0) 221 / 20 59 6 60
verlag@buchhandlung-walther-koenig.de

UK & Eire
Cornerhouse Publications
HOME, 2 Tony Wilson Place
Manchester, M15 4FN
+44 (0) 161 212 3466
publications@cornerhouse.org

Outside Europe
D.A.P. / Distributed Art Publishers, Inc.
155 6th Avenue, 2nd Floor
USA-New York, NY 10013
Tel. +1 212 627 1999
Fax +1 212 627 9484
www.artbook.com

British Library Cataloguing-in-Publication Data
A catalogue record for this book is available from the British Library

ISBN 978-3-96098-229-6 (Koenig Books, London)
ISBN 978-1-84638-191-1 (Afterall Books, London)

Exhibition Histories was initially developed with Teresa Gleadowe as Research Consultant and as a Series Editor with Stephan Schmidt-Wulffen and Sabeth Buchmann. It was launched in 2010 with the support of the following institutions: Academy of Fine Arts Vienna, Van Abbemuseum and Musée d'Art Moderne Grand-Duc Jean

Artist-to-Artist

Independent Art Festivals in Chiang Mai 1992–98

Exhibition Histories

Contents

Introduction: Artist-to-Artist
— David Morris and David Teh

The urge to compose histories of 'Asian contemporary art' has recently reached an intensity that those committed to the mission could scarcely have imagined when they began it. The demand issues from the same powers who demand it elsewhere – the market, collecting institutions (state and private) and, to a lesser extent, academia – yet the conditions shaping such initiatives in Asia differ from those where art's twentieth-century 'master' discourses were formulated. Among these differences we should note, first, the paucity and irregularity of literature and archival resources on the *modern* art from which, and in tension with which, that contemporary art emerged. Second, the breakneck pace of institutional and infrastructural development in certain parts of Asia has both stimulated and scrambled a relatively immature research workforce. And third, the proper means of *writing* such histories is nowadays a matter of contention, with not just scholarly accounts but also oral histories, archival exhibitions and art works being considered seriously as historiographical instruments. In most of Asia, art history is not a well-entrenched academic discipline, however the lack of settled methods and vocabularies may be as much a blessing as a curse.

The present volume undoubtedly answers this rising demand, yet it is atypical inasmuch as it carries a certain circumspection regarding the disciplinary apparatus of art history now seeking its global footings and bearings. Our central object, a series of artist-initiated festivals held in northern Thailand, is surely a strange attractor for the new imperatives to historicise, and epitomises some regional specificities – an emphasis on ephemerality and sociality being perhaps the most notable of these qualities from an outsider's perspective. These festivals certainly lend themselves to an art history that would de-privilege the work of art in favour of the moment it encounters a public. Their most significant exchanges were by all accounts the moments of communion between artists, encounters that would not conventionally be regarded as 'exhibition'.

Siting the Chiang Mai festivals at a moment of emergent contemporaneity in Southeast Asia, David Teh's central essay addresses the local, regional and transnational conditions that gave rise to them, approaching their challenges to established modes of historiography as a set of speculative coordinates for future research – an approach shared by this volume as a whole.[1] As noted in the essay's epilogue, the existing historicisation of Chiang Mai Social Installation has been largely dialogic, passed on piecemeal through art-scene word of mouth. As with any storytelling worthy of the name, these tales are embellished and filtered according to their relevance to the particular moment of telling. When considering the question of how to produce a publication about CMSI, it seemed important to us to emphasise the oral dimension of historicisation, in keeping with the festivals' spirit of performativity, ephemerality and interpersonal connection. At

—

[1] See David Teh, 'Artist-to-Artist: Chiang Mai Social Installation in Historical Perspective', in this volume, pp.12–47.

the same time, this was to no small extent a pragmatic decision – in the absence of extensive written discourse on the festivals, there simply was little else to go on. With the invaluable research assistance of Manuporn Luengaram, innumerable conversations with the festivals' instigators, participants and other interested parties shaped the resulting 'oral history' here, a multivocal account of the festivals following the themes and threads that emerged in the telling.[2] This verbal archive runs in parallel to several others, from scattered moments captured on VHS camcorders during various festivals, to the extensive collection of documentation and ephemera kept by organiser Uthit Atimana, to personal photographs shared by participants.[3]

Rosalind C. Morris's personal account of Chiang Mai in the 1990s offers a perspective deeply informed about the cultural and political context of the festivals, albeit from the relative distance of a non-participant.[4] Morris was at the time conducting her own investigations into the paradox of a 'new city' that was 'saturated with the ethos of the market', in which 'signs of antiquity [were] constantly being produced anew and where the monumental aspirations of newly empowered classes produce[d] ruins of glass and cement much more quickly than did the builders of stone and brick fortresses of earlier eras'.[5] Suffused with signs of the premodern kingdom of Lanna, which had Chiang Mai at its centre, the now provincial city manifests a complex tension in the modernity of the comparatively young Thai nation. Morris notes the 'odd continuity in the discontinuity of Chiang Mai's history, in the impossible tradition of disintegration and disruption that afflicted the city so regularly and rendered it the ruinous memory of another era's aspiration to futurity'.[6]

If an emphasis on region offers a strategic middle way between the traps of a regressive nationalism and the countervailing tendencies of a one-size-fits-all globalism, it is not without its difficulties – not least, in the case of 'Southeast Asia', the region's formative history in Cold War geo-politics and US 'area studies' departments. Morris's keen analyses qualify Chiang Mai as a peri-urban geography heterogenous and complex enough to demand focussed study in itself, and suggest a framework of enquiry at least as illuminating as 'nation' or 'region'. Rather than an exercise in fixing new borders, this approach calls for a more speculative kind of history, grounded in instability and discontinuity. And, in what is perhaps another of the inexplicit theses of this volume, 'that profoundly ambiguous entity, the regional center', inspires a local or translocal rejoinder to the question of regionality.[7]

—

[2] See 'Oral Histories of Chiang Mai Social Installation', in this volume, pp.50–85.
[3] See *ibid.* and pp.86–243.
[4] See Rosalind C. Morris, 'Chiang Mai: Looking Back at the Nineties', in this volume, pp.244–51.
[5] See R. C. Morris, *In the Place of Origins: Modernity and Its Mediums in Northern Thailand*, Durham, NC: Duke University Press, 2000, in particular its second chapter, 'Ruin, or, What the New City Remembers', pp.55–79.
[6] *Ibid.*
[7] *Ibid.*

In search of an alternative narrative of the festivals, May Adadol Ingawanij turns to the practice of Araya Rasdjarmrearnsook, whose involvement with and reflections upon CMSI offer ways of sidestepping a melancholic-nostalgic reminiscence bound up with the social-political anomie in Thailand since the 1990s.[8] Could the festivals' ethical potential be recaptured, and reactivated at another juncture? Any duly sceptical take on the progressivist claims of CMSI must take account of the gendered nature of its organisation – as a 'boys' club', no less.[9] Araya's influence and her reserve, also in evidence in the oral history, bear witness to important counter-narratives immanent to the festivals and their history. Seen alongside other artist-led initiatives such as Womanifesto[10] and the vital organisational and curatorial work done by a younger, predominantly female post-CMSI generation in Thailand, such practices moot the 'condition of possibility for [female] artistic autonomy: a ... resistant, evasive, perhaps even anarchistic potential' which May associates with 'a "matriarchal" practice yet to be named'.

Finally, from a region-wide standpoint, Patrick D. Flores offers a genealogy of the 'installative' as a specifically Southeast Asian mode of practice, seen in 'the desire of the artist to convene an art world, or a relational or transpersonal world of art, by creating conditions for people to assemble along the various axes of dissent, development, nationalism and solidarity'.[11] Forerunners to the confluence of social and installative tendencies at CMSI are detectable in contemporary art practices emerging in the Philippines, Malaysia, Thailand, Indonesia and Singapore from at least the 1970s; and in artist-curator Raymundo Albano's estimation, Flores notes, installation is akin to indigenous rituals of the Philippines and may be seen as 'natural-born'. Albano's nativist spin on installation foreshadows what may be a far more radical proposition: that certain localised, always-already-present and life-giving practices – 'installative' practices – do not merely expand the framework of 'exhibition' but decentre and recentre it. What is the encounter that really matters when artists share their work? Is it not the social more than any material exchange? Or as Albano puts it: 'Maybe the most fitting art form is *fiesta*.'[12]

—

A note from the Series Editors: A refrain of this book is *process* – and this volume should be seen in light of a larger project of research, collectively undertaken. In this regard, the fact that this volume is the first in an ongoing research collaboration with Asia Art Archive, who join our existing partners Center for Curatorial Studies, Bard College, is also a matter for celebration.

—

[8] See May Adadol Ingawanij, 'Art's Potentiality Revisited: Araya Rasdjarmrearnsook's Late Style and Chiang Mai Social Installation', in this volume, pp.252–63.

[9] Araya Rasdjarmrearnsook, quoted in *ibid.*, p.252.

[10] See pp.31 and 82–83.

[11] See Patrick D. Flores, 'A Changing World: Phases of the Installative in Southeast Asia', in this volume, pp.264–78.

[12] Raymundo Albano, 'Installations: A Case for Hangings', *Philippine Art Supplement*, vol.2, no.1, January–February 1981, p.3.

Artist-to-Artist: Chiang Mai Social Installation in Historical Perspective
— David Teh

At some point in the last few decades, the term *contemporary*, which had long tagged certain modern art with a temporal connotation, took on an ideological one. That is, it became a source and an indicator of value. What makes artworks contemporary? It seems the possible answers to this question are – like art's histories, or its modernities – multiple, and endlessly diverse. Sceptics may say this contemporary is a matter of publicity and spin, yet the art of the present increasingly mobilises values once reserved for the art of the past, like those accrued through public sale and collection, or through academic criticism and historicisation. Moreover, *contemporary* may be defined differently in different places; even as it comes to stand for an inclusive, worldwide system, it is less and less clear which criteria, if any, may be considered general or universal. And as art's forms also continue to proliferate, is contemporaneity even visible any more? Or does it consist otherwise, in the social encounters in which art is produced and exchanged?

Such queries have become acute and far-reaching as modern art's histories have begun to overflow and route around the bottlenecks, both geospatial and intellectual, of disciplinary Art History. The present volume locates a singular and timely case study in an experimental, artist-initiated festival series held in northern Thailand in the 1990s – a context that was nothing if not peripheral to the international circuit forming at the time, and yet in many ways was exemplary of a new *proximity* experienced amongst people and practices considered 'local' and others considered 'foreign'.[1] Though considerable attention has recently been devoted to the Chiang Mai Social Installation (CMSI) festivals, they have been the subject of precious little scholarly literature. They comprised mostly live or otherwise ephemeral art-works, difficult if not impossible for even aggressive collections to acquire, and never given market value. Indeed, it cannot be taken for granted that exhibition *per se* was their main event, the most significant exchange that should be historicised. This essay is a tentative step in rendering their history, with consideration given to the challenges ahead.[2] I will begin with an account of the festivals' background, establishing the key players and interests whose convergence gave rise to them. Then I will try to historicise the kinds of art and exhibition that resulted, situating these in both a national and a larger, transnational historiography of contemporary art. With reference to both contexts, I hope also to reflect on problems of theory and method that complicate the historiography of contemporary art in Asia, and to consider what the festivals, and others like them, might tell us about sensible ways of proceeding.

—

[1] Okwui Enwezor, 'Intense Proximity: Concerning the Disappearance of Distance – Negotiating the Near and the Far', in *Intense Proximity: An Anthology of the Near and the Far – La Triennale 2012* (exh. cat.), Paris: Centre national des arts plastiques, 2012.
[2] The Chiang Mai festivals collectively became a historiographical object around 2011, first in the doctoral dissertation of Thasnai Sethaseree, then in doctoral research and archival exhibitions by Gridthiya Gaweewong centred on the archive of Uthit

The Round-up: Siting the Contemporary

In early 1992, a group of young artists made the first of several road trips from Chiang Mai, in Thailand's north, to its capital city, Bangkok. At first glance, their missions seem unexceptional. Bangkok was the country's undisputed art centre, as it is today – the location of the key exhibition spaces, training institutions and promotional opportunities, and the nexus of modern art's production and patronage. As is often the case for emerging provincial artists in developing countries, such journeys to the national centre were prospective, a chance to catch up on new trends, to meet peers, share ideas and take the temperature of the metropolis. The Chiang Mai artists' visits were purposeful, then, but their purposes by no means singular. They did the rounds of the city's galleries, made a nuisance of themselves at some openings, and visited art colleges including Silpakorn University, the national academy set up in the 1930s and still today Thai art's institutional centre of gravity.

Bangkok's concentration of intellectual, bureaucratic and financial resources also made it Thailand's chief portal to the wider world. The city was still swelling after decades of heady economic growth initiated by US military investment during the Cold War, and brought to a peak by the export-driven economic boom of the 1980s. Chiang Mai, by contrast, was a small, picturesque city some 700 kilometres upcountry. The entire province's population was only 1.5 million, less than a quarter of Bangkok's. Though it had a storied premodern history – Chiang Mai dated its founding as capital of the Lanna Kingdom to 1296 – it had not been an important symbolic or economic centre since the eighteenth century. Yet with its fertile hinterland and cool highland climate (making it a favoured retreat of Thailand's royal family since the 1960s), Chiang Mai had long been relatively affluent by provincial standards, and was identified as a site for cultural tourism as early as the mid-1970s. It was also home to the first art school outside the capital, the Faculty of Fine Arts at Chiang Mai University (CMU), only ten years old at the time of the students' Bangkok missions.

These trips to the capital bore tangible fruit. The prospectors landed a series of exhibition opportunities at a range of venues including the Goethe-Institut and several small independent galleries, and even a group show at the National Gallery on Chaofa Road. Located just off the royal Ratchadamnoen Avenue – close to the

—

Atimana. The first of these was part of the grand national survey 'Art in the Reign of King Rama IX: Thai Trends from Localism to Internationalism' (2012), organised by Apinan Poshyananda at the Bangkok Art and Culture Centre in 2012. The same year, a presentation was considered for inclusion in a show at a university museum in the US, but it was never realised. Gridthiya's efforts were also sponsored by the Asia Culture Center in Gwangju, South Korea, where an exhibition was mounted in 2015. Another display was configured for the largest ever Southeast Asian survey show, 'Sunshower: Contemporary Art from Southeast Asia, 1980s to Now' (2017), at the Mori Art Museum and the National Art Center in Tokyo. This still-developing archive richly informs the present volume. See Thasnai Sethaseree, 'Overlapping Tactics and Practices at the Interstices of Thai Art', unpublished doctoral thesis, Chiang Mai: Chiang Mai University, 2011; and Gridthiya Gaweewong, 'Curatorial Practices and Small Narratives: A Case Study of Chiang Mai Social Installation and Its Trajectory', *Thammasat University Journal of Sociology and Anthropology*, vol.34, no.2, July–December 2015.

Grand Palace and the historic, touristic and bureaucratic centre of Bangkok – the National Gallery was hardly a crucible of contemporary or experimental practice. Inaugurated in 1977 and occupying the former Royal Thai Mint, it housed a somewhat lacklustre collection of Thai modern art and offered some spaces for temporary rental, as is typical of Southeast Asia's national galleries. It had, however, hosted a string of solo exhibitions by some of Thailand's most innovative artists, including, in 1987, Araya Rasdjarmrearnsook and Apinan Poshyananda, and, in 1989, Montien Boonma – all freshly returned from graduate studies overseas.

Bangkok was a thriving metropolis, but setting aside the many picture shops catering to tourists and well-to-do decorators, its 'contemporary' spaces were few and far between. Prospects for aesthetic risk-taking were brighter across town at the Visual Dhamma Gallery, the city's most lively and unpredictable exhibition space, located in the busy and cosmopolitan Sukhumvit Road business district and run by Austrian expatriate Alfred Pawlin, an enthusiastic promoter of the emerging contemporary scene. In 1992, Pawlin hosted a group project called 'Magic Set', initiated by Chiang Mai artist Mit Jai Inn. The title was lifted from a stage-hire company run by one of the artists' friends, from whom they borrowed temporary flooring that they laid down like duck-boards to control the audience's passage through the space. In the upstairs gallery, Pawlin was obliged to introduce four unclothed male artists while playing congas – an unusual bout of libertinage in socially conservative Thailand – as Thai-born art historian Helen Michaelsen nailed her theses on a 'new art movement' to the gallery wall.[3]

If the presence of a manifesto suggested organisational intent, it did not foreshadow aesthetic cohesion. A second iteration of 'Magic Set' was held the following year, occupying eight rooms of the National Gallery and deliberately uncurated, with each artist assigned a room in which to do whatever they wanted. Yet the event did signal a certain generational change. This artist-led, group initiative was formally permissive – a platform for experiment featuring ephemeral works and nonobjective practices before the domestication of installation and performance as exhibition formats. A far cry from both academic norms and the egoism promoted by a booming art market, it was in all respects a rejection of the superficial 'consensus art' that was rapidly becoming a 'status symbol' for Bangkok's nouveau riche.[4]

Navin Rawanchaikul, then a CMU freshman, took part in most of these group
p.16 shows, including the second 'Magic Set' (in 1993) and two at Visual Dhamma, 'Melancholic Trance', which opened in May 1992, and a follow-up show called 'Social Contract: New Art from Chiang Mai', which opened in February 1993.[5] The connection was made by Navin's mentor, Montien, who also participated in 'Melancholic Trance'. After studying in France, Montien's star was on the rise: he had exhibited on five continents in two short years, a staggering feat for

—

[3] Alfred Pawlin, correspondence with the author, 14 December 2017.
[4] Apinan Poshyananda, 'Smile-a-while Campaigns for Cultural Correctness', *Behind Thai Smiles: Selected Writings, 1991–2007*, Bangkok: Office of Contemporary Art and Culture, 2007, p.86; originally published in *Art & Asia Pacific*, vol.2, no.3, July 1995.
[5] For more information on the former, see https://www.artdesigncafe.com/alfred-pawlin-visual-dhamma-gallery-1992 (last accessed on 5 July 2018).

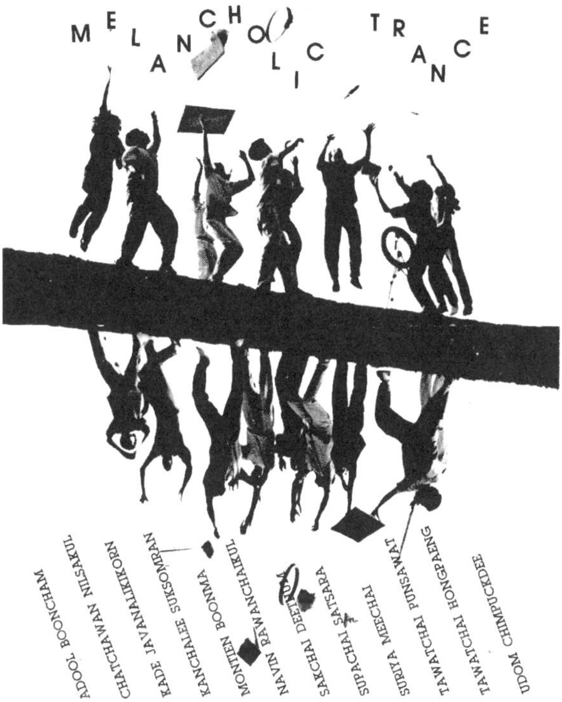

Invitation card for 'Melancholic Trance', Visual Dhamma Gallery, Bangkok, 1992
Courtesy Alfred Pawlin

an artist still in his thirties, especially one from a developing country. He had taken a teaching job at CMU, where most of the group (including Supachai Satsara, Udom Chimpakdee and Tawatchai Puntusawasdi) were enrolled as students, and had been working with Pawlin since 1990. The decision to accommodate Montien's students, while unorthodox, was easy for the gallerist, who clearly sensed a changing of the guard. 'The future belongs' to these young artists, he wrote in the exhibition brochure for 'Melancholic Trance'. Formal experimentation was the index of change: 'Installation, mixed media, fluxus, beyond the frame, virtual reality, video art, performance, sound sculpture, all these forms of expression do not belong to some esoteric (avant-garde) circles. They have become the mainstream.' It was a viewpoint that only an outsider – probably only a *farang,* the Thai word for a white or Western foreigner – could have held.[6] Few Thais would have agreed, or been as sanguine, for this expansive

—

[6] A possible exception would be the well-travelled artist Chumpon Apisuk, who observed in 1993 that '[s]treams of universal culture have begun to flow in'. Chumpon, 'Unpredictable Repercussions', *Artlink*, vol.13, no.3–4, November 1993–March 1994, p.23. *Farang* critic David Johnson saw the Chiang Mai scene as a 'new wave ... burning with fresh, positive ideas'. D. Johnson, 'Earth Works', *Metro*, c.1995, p.33 (copy held in the archive of Uthit Atimana).

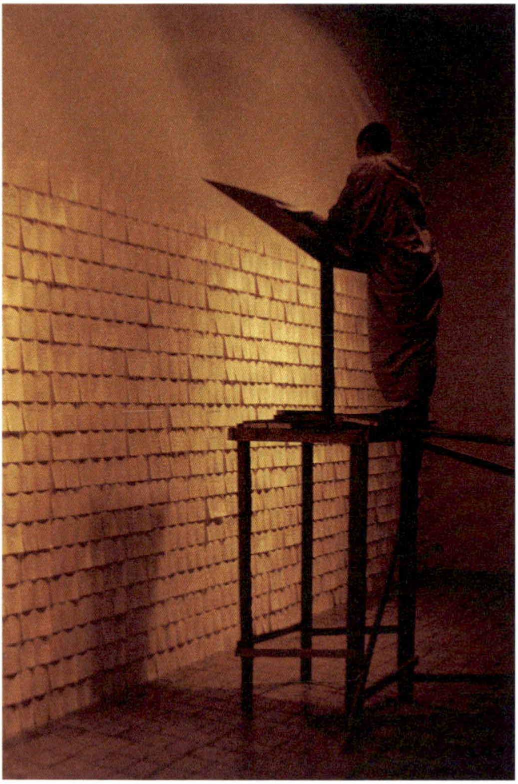

Navin Rawanchaikul, *Please Donate Your Ideas for A Dispirited Artist*, as shown in 'Magic Set 2', National Gallery Bangkok, 1993
Courtesy Navin Production

approach to techniques and materials stood in stark contrast to both institutional and market norms at the time.

Thai contemporary art in the early 1990s consisted of two loose but distinct camps. The incumbents were the 'artist-civil servants' of the elite national academy, Silpakorn University, and the larger patronage system of which it was the mainframe. Its gatekeepers controlled the national art curriculum and the country's only master's degree – a prerequisite for academic employment – as well as access to the annual National Exhibition, prestigious state commissions and major prizes sponsored by banks and insurance companies.[7] They included modernist painters and sculptors, sometimes dismissively called 'formalists' by the more experimentally inclined (though Clement Greenberg would have winced at the characterisation). But the mainstream, and the imagination of pundits, had been decisively claimed by neo-traditionalists, celebrants of the three ideological 'pillars' of bourgeois nationalism: religion, monarchy and the nation state itself.

—

[7] Even into the 1990s, it was still the only place one could obtain a master's degree and thus be qualified to teach.

These purveyors of national-cultural essence (*kwampenthai*, Thai-ness) were more inventive and more enterprising than the modernists. Their hallmarks were the motifs and moral dictates of Siamese Theravada Buddhism.[8]

Meanwhile, an alternative scene had emerged since the mid-1980s, driven by recent returnees from Western art schools on the one hand and groups of less-travelled outsiders and activists on the other.[9] Operating outside the art market, these more experimental artists pushed modern art's formal envelope, employing the very formats and styles Pawlin would later list as signals of a new wave. They engaged with pressing issues on the civil society agenda, like the litany with which critic Thanom Chapakdee described the confusing 'flux' of globalisation: poverty, prostitution, moral decline, rootlessness and environmental degradation due to unfettered development.[10] We will revisit this alternative scene later, but for now it will suffice to note briefly two of their affinities, which point to national context, but also beyond it. First, while they were united by no explicit political position or ideology, a salient point of convergence was their rejection of the rising consumerism Thailand's already large middle class had unabashedly embraced. The anti-materialist high ground would later be claimed by a more conservative Buddhist moralism, channeled effectively by the political elite's monarchist old guard[11] – as a unifying cause it had a shelf life – but in the early 1990s it still broadly underwrote artists' eschewal of the market and their pursuit of ephemeral new forms, especially performance. This ethos was moreover shared by independent and critical artists everywhere in Asia where consumerism had taken root; it was a key ingredient of a *contemporaneity* clearly discernible across national boundaries.

A second affinity also points to the interface between national and transnational currencies. Both camps' claims to contemporaneity were secured by international points of reference, albeit according to very different criteria. The re-engineering

—

[8] Not all the neo-traditionalists were Silpakorn functionaries. The firebrands Chalermchai Kositpipat and Thawan Duchanee, both Silpakorn graduates, were based in the northern city of Chiang Rai and styled themselves as outsiders. Yet despite their claims to independence, their work dovetailed with ideological imperatives of the state and the Silpakorn system, which took pains to absorb and celebrate them.

[9] For example, the Ruang Pong Art Community formed in the busy Chatuchak Weekend Market around 1984, which gave rise to the Uggabat and Bon Fai performance art groups (Vasan Sitthiket was pivotal in both). From 1993, this activist community staged a series of annual festivals under the Bangkok Outsider banner, with each year dedicated to a particular civil society cause. From 1988–90, Chumpon organised the experimental theatre group Tap Root Society in Chiang Mai; beginning in 1993, he worked with his wife, Chantawipa Apisuk, on the Concrete House, which combined experimental art with HIV advocacy. He notes the importance to the alternative art scene of former radicals who returned from the jungle after the 1982 amnesty and were absorbed into the NGO sector. See Jay Koh, 'Art Activism and Cross-cultural Projects in Thailand and Myanmar: The Need to Open Up Structures for Engagement', *focas (Forum on Contemporary Art & Society)*, no.2, Singapore, 2002; and 'What Mind Not Mine', *Wai* [zine], no.1, 1995.

[10] Thanom Chapakdee, 'Chiang Mai Changes', *Metro*, c.1995, p.73 (copy held in the archive of Uthit). See also Apinan, 'Modern Art in Thailand: A Glimpse', *Artlink*, vol.13, no.3–4, November 1993–March 1994, p.23.

[11] See Duncan McCargo, 'Network Monarchy and Legitimacy Crises in Thailand', *Pacific Review*, vol.18, no.4, December 2005, pp.499–519.

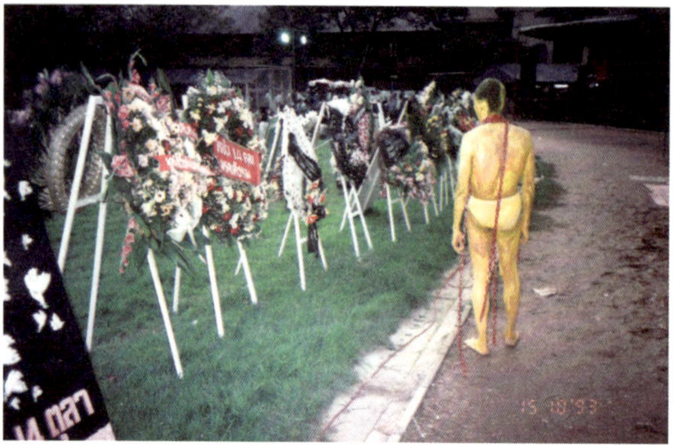

Lee Wen, *Journey of a Yellow Man No.4*, Thammasat University, Bangkok, performance as part of the exhibition 'Sense Yellow', Concrete House, Nonthaburi, 1993
Courtesy the artist and Koh Nguang How

of foreign styles for local purposes was a process with long-standing precedents at Silpakorn, commencing with its Italian founder, Corrado Feroci (1892–1962, also known as Silpa Bhirasri). So, while the 'alternative' artists were also bearers of international trends, their distinction lay less in their foreign credentials than in their lack of personal debts to the national institution or its senior functionaries. The latter had international credentials too, however parochial their concerns. And they had recently scored two triumphs in the West: a large group show, 'The Integrative Art of Modern Thailand', organised by Herbert Phillips at the Lowie Museum of Anthropology at the University of California, Berkeley in 1991; and the eight-year mission by a rotating group of 28 mural painters to decorate the *ubosot* (ordination hall) of Wat Buddhapadipa, a Buddhist temple in south-west London, concluded in 1992.[12]

Back in Thailand, their foreign currency was readily converted into local ones by royal, bureaucratic and corporate patrons eager for association with an 'export-grade' national art product.[13] On the other hand, the formal currency of the alternative artists (styled 'critical', 'postmodern' and even 'conceptual') proved harder to parlay. If the latter were destined to become the Thai 'mainstream', as Pawlin

—

[12] See Herbert Phillips, *The Integrative Art of Modern Thailand* (exh. cat.), Berkeley: Lowie Museum of Anthropology, University of California, Berkeley, 1992; and Sandra Cate, *Making Merit, Making Art: A Thai Temple in Wimbledon*, Honolulu: University of Hawaii Press, 2003. One might imagine the Californian mission, initiated and funded by a foreign agency, was the more prestigious, but the opposite was true. The mustering of Thai patronage for the projection of 'international grade' Siamese culture abroad was far more decisive for artists' careers, propelling several of the muralists (e.g. Chalermchai and Panya Vijinthanasarn) to stardom. Meanwhile, Apinan decried Phillips's 'exotic and politically correct' survey as an instance of neocolonial appropriation and essentialism, and for overlooking artists' social and political concerns. Apinan, 'The Future: Post-Cold War, Postmodernism, Post-Marginalia', in Caroline Turner (ed.), *Tradition and Change: Contemporary Art of Asia and the Pacific*, Brisbane: University of Queensland Press, 1993, pp.3–20.
[13] See also the 'export-grade' heritage films historicised in May Adadol Ingawanij, 'Hyperbolic Heritage: Bourgeois Spectatorship and Contemporary Thai Cinema', unpublished doctoral thesis, London: University of London, 2006.

claimed, this hadn't happened yet. By the late 1990s, they had become the bread and butter of a rapidly expanding global exchange, of which biennials were the main exhibitionary outlets, but art's promotional apparatus in Thailand – collectors and dealers, mass-media coverage, the government's Fine Arts Department – was still heavily lopsided in favour of the Silpakorn establishment, who derided the experimental fringe for its 'strange' practices.

For artists from the provinces it was even harder to achieve visibility. But the young Chiang Mai artists had other notions of professional advancement. In the course of their sorties to Bangkok, an idea took shape that would change the geography of art in Thailand profoundly, if only temporarily. Little did our travellers know they were in step with a wider renovation of modern art and its institutions, happening simultaneously within and far beyond its traditional centres. Little did they know of brewing initiatives to redraw the map of contemporary art into a 'global' one through recurring transnational surveys in Australia, Cuba, South Africa, Japan and Korea.[14] Few of them had ever seen a biennial. Nor would they have known of the independent groups forging alternative platforms nearby – like the Baguio Arts Guild (BAG) in the Philippine highlands or The Artists Village (TAV) in Singapore.[15] They could not have anticipated that in the ensuing years their diminutive hometown would be hosting its own transnational interdisciplinary art festivals, which would easily eclipse any international exhibition programme in Bangkok at the time. Despite scant resources and an ad hoc organisational structure, their festivals would be a beacon for experimental practices, drawing hundreds of participants from Thailand and far beyond.

pp.43 and 40

Finding a Public: Black May and the Genesis of a Festival

One of our travellers, Mit Jai Inn, was a member of the Yong ethnic minority from the town of Lamphun, just south of Chiang Mai. A disaffected Silpakorn dropout, Mit was something of an adventurer: in 1987 he had taken off for Germany without a plan ('like a hippie'), loitering for months in Kassel during documenta 8, selling his paintings in the street, then gaining admission to the Academy of Fine Arts in Vienna before working in the studio of Franz West. Charming, worldly and outspoken, Mit quickly gained a reputation as a rabble-rouser after returning to Thailand in early 1992. On a visit to Bangkok in 1994, he caused a stir at the opening of a group exhibition of leading neo-traditionalists called 'Ha Salaa Lan Na' ('Five Northern Artisans'). A heritage-themed shopping mall annex of the luxurious Oriental Hotel was the setting for an elaborate

—

[14] See Anthony Gardner and Charles Green, '1989: Asian Biennialization', *Biennials, Triennials, and Documenta: The Exhibitions that Created Contemporary Art*, Malden, MA and Oxford: Wiley Blackwell, 2016, pp.111–44; and John Clark, 'Contemporary Asian Art at Biennales and Triennales', *caa.reviews* [online journal], 7 September 2006, available at http://www.caareviews.org/reviews/884 (last accessed on 11 June 2018).

[15] Apinan's reportage at the time reflected the regional upturn in artist-run activities, but apart from Montien and Chumpon, who had seen some of these platforms first-hand, he was probably the only Thai mobile enough to have a clear sense of the global picture. See Apinan, 'The Future: Post-Cold War, Postmodernism, Post-Marginalia', *op. cit.* Pawlin had made several visits to the Philippines and his Bangkok gallery served as a de facto portal for foreign visitors engaging with the Thai scene.

spectacle, complete with 'traditional' parade, dancing angels in 'ancient' Siamese garb and a charity auction capped off by the attendance of Prime Minister Chuan Leekpai. In this perverse theatre for bourgeois aspiration and the national encompassment of provincial culture and history, Mit distributed flyers attacking the superstar painter Thawan Duchanee as a sell-out. Not one to mince his words, Mit accused Thawan of abusing both charity and northern culture, serving them up for appropriation by the Bangkok nouveau riche as badges of a bogus national ideology.[16] On any sober assessment of the art historical facts, Thawan was guilty as charged. But it was Mit who was arrested and, refusing to apologise, was eventually prosecuted for defamation. The ensuing scandal eventually died down, but no incident could have crystallised more dramatically the impasse between contemporary art's opposing camps. It faithfully reflected a larger schism in middle-class identification being played out at the time in what Rosalind Morris called Thailand's national 'economy of appearances'.

On an earlier trip to the capital, Mit had narrowly avoided much more serious trouble. Pawlin's upbeat brochure for 'Melancholic Trance' was clearly penned some weeks in advance of the show, for just six days before it opened, Bangkok was brought to a standstill by a general strike in protest of the entrenchment of General Suchinda Kraprayoon as Prime Minister a year after he had unseated the corrupt (but elected) government of Chatichai Choonhavan in a coup d'état. For days the old town's central administrative precinct and the royal field (Sanam Luang, in front of the Grand Palace) heaved with hundreds of thousands of protestors. A state of emergency was declared late on the night of 17 May 1992. Protesters were dispersed and their leaders arrested as the crowds shifted to a university in the city's east. The following day, English-language broadsheet *The Nation* carried a photograph of two protesters in action, pulling down a barbed-wire barricade blocking the historic Phan Faa Bridge: in a loud patterned shirt, Mit lunges at the offending barrier with a comrade, while rows of security personnel in combat boots and helmets look on, batons at the ready. So began the three days of violent repression by Thai authorities that would come to be known as Black May. Scores were killed or disappeared, hundreds injured. Mit recalls joining the swelling crowd as vehicles were overturned and set ablaze. He recounts the events in the first-person plural, but says he slipped through a military cordon before the worst of the violence, and that he is grateful he was not more involved. Few artists were.

It was not the first such showdown. Since the overthrow of absolutism in 1932, Thailand had endured a steady cycle of coups and standoffs, and the army was far and away the dominant political institution. For the protesters and their fretful parents, Black May brought back the indelible but unspeakable trauma of Cold War polarisation in the 1970s, when civic and student uprisings were brutally put down by military and paramilitary groups leaving thousands dead and a whole generation of thinkers exiled to the wilderness. But Black May was new in other ways. The first broad mobilisation of Bangkok's large middle class, united under moral crusader (and former city governor) Chamlong Srimuang, it has sometimes been called the 'mobile phone revolution'.[17] It was the first campaign to feature real-time coordination between protests in the capital and in provincial centres, including Chiang Mai and the northeastern city of Khon Kaen. And it was the first in which the simultaneity of transnational information networks would be decisive. The generals' censorship of print media achieved partial containment of the unfolding drama, but they could not prevent images and updates from reaching a global audience via satellite and feeding back into local circulation. The political impasse itself was defused by way of a bizarre, televised spectacle on the evening of 20 May, in which Suchinda and his foe – the populist Chamlong – prostrated themselves before a grim-faced King Bhumibol. Suchinda resigned as Prime Minister four days later.[18]

With the return to democracy and relative stability under Chuan's government, elected in September, younger artists would be galvanised less by political urgency than by their rejection of rampant consumerism and their frustration with the academic status quo.[19] The more restless students at CMU were meeting informally, to discuss art world trends and share reports and opinions on Thailand's topsy-turvy political drama. Their visits to Bangkok had amplified their sense of both the possibilities and the limitations facing emerging artists at the time. Chief amongst the latter was a lack of suitable venues. In Chiang Mai, there was almost nowhere for contemporary artists to show their work. Exhibitions had from time to time been held at the Buddhasathan, a Buddhist 'practice centre' on Tha Pae Road, and in the library of the non-profit American University Alumni Language Center.[20] The CMU Faculty of Fine Arts, lacking a gallery, improvised with interstitial spaces on the campus.

Yet there was no particular urge amongst the students to reproduce the kinds of spaces they had seen in the capital, public or private. Plans were hatched to stage a festival. From the outset, Navin assumed a central logistical role, tapping his family's connections to local merchants and other small-business people, securing free accommodation and transport, and manning the phone and fax line that

—

[16] The architect of this bizarre spectacle was Chalermchai Kositpipat, himself an iconoclastic presence on the art scene, known for his theatrical bravura and unstinting self-promotion (more recently, he was the guru-host of a reality TV show for aspiring artists). Mit was eventually bailed out by friends, and after a year on trial, served a suspended sentence for defaming Thawan. See S. Cate, *Making Merit, Making Art*, *op. cit.*, pp.127–29; and Apinan, 'Smile-a-while Campaigns for Cultural Correctness', *op. cit.*, pp.86–87. For a more colourful and partisan account, see issue 2 of the collectively authored art zine *Wai* (c.1996).

[17] It is notable that the election that sparked the crisis and the election that followed in September were the first in which Thai voters were offered relatively clear choices between pro-military and pro-democracy coalitions. See Daniel E. King, 'The Thai Parliamentary Elections of 1992: Return to Democracy in an Atypical Year', *Asian Survey*, vol.32, no.12, December 1992, pp.1118–20.

[18] See Rosalind C. Morris, 'Photography and the Power of Images in the History of Power: Notes from Thailand', in R.C. Morris (ed.), *Photographies East: The Camera and Its Histories in East and Southeast Asia and Klima*, Durham, NC: Duke University Press, 2009; and Alan Klima, *The Funeral Casino: Meditation, Massacre, and Exchange with the Dead in Thailand*, Princeton, NJ and Oxford: Princeton University Press, 2002.

[19] If the early festival editions had a politics, Araya recalls, it was the politics of newly emerging art practices in tension with those 'that already dominated the existing art education system'. Interview with May Adadol Ingawanij and Manuporn Luengaram, 21 July 2017.

[20] See Thanom, 'Chiang Mai Changes', *op. cit.*

constituted the group's communication base. In addition to exhibiting his own art, he would serve as the festivals' bilingual compere, leading walking tours from site to site with mic in hand and a portable public address system. Mit's friend and erstwhile Silpakorn classmate Uthit Atimana (nicknamed 'Russia' for his bolshie attitude), who had taken a job at CMU, became a key organiser and de facto spokesman, authoring the group's statements of purpose. As a lecturer, he conferred the institution's imprimatur on their unorthodox initiatives and requests to use various spaces and resources. Mit showed the group a brochure from a project in which he had participated in late 1991 in Vienna, for which works were exchanged and mounted in private homes, with a map to guide visitors from place to place. But in Chiang Mai, modern art would have been an alien intrusion into domestic spaces, so the group gave the idea a local twist, setting their first festival in 'temples and cemeteries'. The terrain would expand in subsequent years to include 'private residences, public buildings, streets, bridges, walls, rivers and canals, open spaces'.[21]

The initial selection of locations was not as loaded as it might seem in light of Buddhism's thematic preponderance in Thai art since the 1970s. A certain Buddhist ethos was palpable, indeed unconcealed, in the group's stated agenda, but they were not driven by religious motivations. Rather, the goal was to find and engage a public consisting of 'ordinary' people, from whom modern art had long stood aloof. As Uthit would later put it, the choice of setting was about 'the consciousness of freedom, of citizenship, of everyone's right to speak of public issues'.[22] Temples and cemeteries were inclusive, relatively class-neutral and democratic sites, in contrast to the burgeoning spaces of consumption and commercial recreation. Indeed, as elsewhere in Southeast Asia, temples had long been important vectors of modernisation – of modern ideas, administration, education and, thus, social mobility. Buddhist temples were not exclusively religious, nor even exclusively Buddhist; traditionally they were porous, multifunctional spaces. These 'cultural centres' of the past, as Uthit would have it, accommodated communal celebrations, civic meetings and various kinds of entertainment.[23] Beyond a few large cities, for example, seasonal temple fairs were the primary venues for the diffusion of film in Thailand, serving as way stations for a mobile cinema still common through the 1980s.

Mit, himself a beneficiary of temple schooling, cites the model of the *pha pa* ritual, which he distinguishes from the more salubrious *kathin* ceremony. In both, the community makes donations to a temple, including robes for the monks. But whereas the latter happens only once a year, at the end of the rains retreat, and is usually led symbolically by a moneyed benefactor, *pha pa* is locally initiated and can happen at any time. It derives from the practice of leaving used cloth on the branches of trees for monks to collect to make their robes. As Mit recalls the

—

[21] These are the site categories enshrined in the official title of the second edition in 1993.
[22] Uthit, interview with Gridthiya, 10 February 2015. Navin recalls the group's desire to 'connect our art to our society, to our community' and their excitement at later discovering similar efforts in neighbouring countries. Navin, interview with Atikom Mukdaprakorn, 23 June 2015.
[23] Interview with Gridthiya, 10 February 2015.

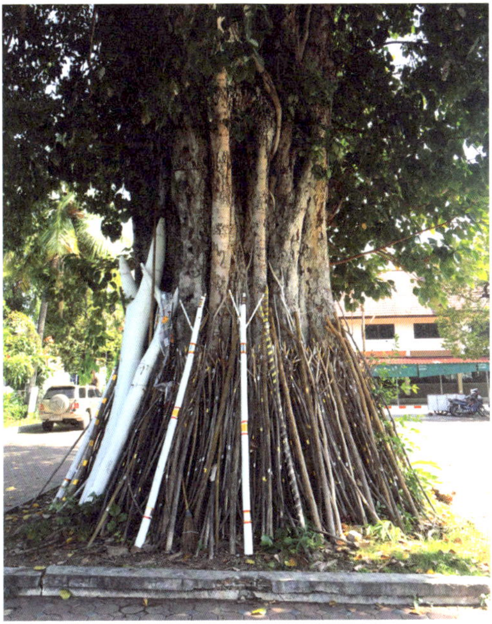

Tree at Wat Suan Dok, Chiang Mai, 2017
Photography: David Morris

ritual of his childhood, it also serves as a kind of informal monitoring system, by which villagers might satisfy their curiosity about the monks, who often hail from elsewhere. We should not be surprised, then, that the young artists' engagement with religious sites and communities, while broadly respectful, was not without a certain irreverence that helped set the festivals' tone. Nor were these collaborations always harmonious – on several occasions works were damaged or removed by the faithful or by monks, offended by what they saw as disrespectful or sacrilegious intrusions.

Buddhist faith was an important aesthetic ingredient of the Chiang Mai festivals, as it has been for much Thai modern art. Buddhist forms and rituals, and the religious sites used as venues, were suggestive 'local' material for foreign participants with varying levels of religious understanding. But the point, at least for the organisers, was not to imbue the events with spiritual significance. Their principal aim was to set up encounters between contemporary art and a largely uninitiated general public, in places where the latter were accustomed to having everyday social and aesthetic experiences.

A Short History of Fission

Sixteen artists, all Thai, participated in the first festival in 1992, which was marked by disagreements with their clerical hosts. There were some site-specific installations, but many works were simply transposed from the CMU studios to the four temples and four cemeteries used as venues. Participants and audiences toured the venues together, with each artist delivering a short talk about their pp.86–93 contribution. While the scale of this first edition was modest, word quickly spread of a successful foray beyond art's conventional architecture and social pp.94–123 limitations. Participation almost doubled for the second edition, in late 1993, which saw the addition of women artists and foreigners (one Indian artist, three Europeans and several from Australia who had come to Thailand for residencies p.109 at art schools); Mit also inserted purportedly 'delegated' installations attributed to high-profile US artists Lawrence Weiner, David Hammons and James Lee Byars.[24] The range of public spaces was expanded to include bridges, canals and streets. These early editions received modest funding from a few Bangkok collectors, including stockbroker Chongrux Chantaworrasut (a major collector of Montien's work) and the Chaiyong Foundation of Sino-Thai media tycoon (and later conservative ideologue) Sondhi Limthongkul. As publisher of *Phujadkaan* (*Manager Daily*), Sondhi had, since the early 1980s, controlled one of the liveliest channels of Thailand's bourgeois public sphere; the newspaper featured columns by outspoken public intellectuals, many of whom participated in the festivals' discursive events. These funds, while far less than sufficient for mounting the events professionally, at least allowed the artists to print the festival map-cum-brochure. The great majority of support was in kind, in the form of volunteer labour and venues offered rent-free. Artists were responsible for bringing their own materials and did not receive fees.

pp.124–35 The first week of 1995 saw the advent of a spin-off gathering called the Week of Cooperative Suffering. Concerned that the platform was becoming too exhibition-centric, Mit redoubled his efforts to stimulate inclusive public engagement, this time situating events squarely in civic space.[25] A nightly 'Midnight Socrates' gathering fell somewhere between a town hall meeting and a kind of pop-up Speakers' Corner. From midnight until around 5am, leading intellectuals such as Buddhist social critic Sulak Sivaraksa and historian Nidhi Eoseewong shared the dais with artists, shift workers and passers-by, on the paved plaza in front of Tha Pae Gate, a touristic hotspot where the city's main commercial axis meets the eastern wall of the historic town centre.[26] At the end of that year, CMSI's pp.136–79 third edition – from an organisational standpoint, the peak of the festival series –

—

[24] Though women were better represented in Chiang Mai than in previous Thai art gatherings, the core group could fairly be described as a boys' club. One artist, a CMU undergraduate during the early editions, recalls being excited by the 'strange' new art forms but acutely aware of where her engagement stopped. The conviviality would often end in the kinds of nocturnal venues young women could not enter without bringing alarm, or even shame, to their families. Female curator Somporn Rodboon, a Silpakorn graduate who went on to teach at CMU, organised an International Women's Art Exhibition in Bangkok in 1992 and hosted numerous residencies (at both institutions) for Melbourne-based foundation Asialink. Joan Grounds and Noelene Lucas, both guests of Somporn, participated in the second edition of CMSI.

[25] There were some artists for whom an exhibitionary thrust was a good thing. Chumpon, for example, participated in CMSI but not the Week of Cooperative Suffering. Suspicious of the latter's aesthetico-religious framing, he has noted that it was 'too enlightened' for him. Interview with Manuporn, 12 August 2017.

[26] Two more Week of Cooperative Suffering programmes were staged, in the first week of 1996 and of 1997. 'Midnight Socrates' later took on a life of its own, evolving into the seminal online civil society forum 'Midnight University'.

saw not only an expansion of scale, but also a dramatic internationalisation. The brochure listed 62 artists and collaborations, of whom less than half were Thai. pp.138–41 Fifteen participants were from Europe, nine from Southeast Asian countries other than Thailand, nine from Japan, three from North America, two from South Asia and two from Australia. This edition coincided with Chiang Mai's hosting of the Eighteenth Southeast Asian Games, and in early 1996, with celebrations for the seven hundredth anniversary of the city's founding. These festivities marked Chiang Mai's debut in a wider image economy, as the city was put on show as a destination for national and global television audiences. The expansive use of civic and other non-art spaces continued into the festival's fourth and final edition, pp.216–43 launched in late 1997 in the midst of the Asian Financial Crisis and popular political mobilisation around the ratification of Thailand's new constitution (ill-fated but historically its most democratic instrument by far). The following years saw several attempts to revive the platform, but there was no organisational structure to replace the energy and charisma of its prime movers, who were by then either busy exhibiting abroad or had moved on to other projects.

Apart from their innovative use of non-art locations, what distinguished the festivals from contemporary art's mainstream in these years? Summing up the different outlook of Chiang Mai's new wave, Uthit stresses the artists' assertion of their conceptual and intellectual credentials over formal, practical ones, of an artistic competence properly detached from craft. This put them at odds not only with the modernist establishment in the art schools, but also with new state investment in – and bourgeois consumption of – images of 'tradition', of which craft was a key signifier.[27] Chiang Mai's makeover had seen cottage industries ramped up for the growing tourist trade; prominent northern artists, particularly the virtuosi Thawan and Chalermchai, had shown how the performance of provincial, 'traditional' craftsmanship could generate lucrative currency in the national economy of appearances.[28] The CMSI group's intellectual confidence became a hallmark of the festivals, indexed in the events' frequent punctuation by discussion and debate, whether organised or spontaneous.[29]

The CMU students strove to escape the habits of practice and thinking formed and monitored by the Silpakorn system, as Gridthiya Gaweewong and others have argued.[30] The faculty and its curriculum were established in 1982 by Silpakorn alumni mostly from the Art Education stream – that is, not by

—

[27] Summing up the contrast, David Johnson noted that CMSI was 'a far cry from corporate sponsored exhibitions in hotel lobbies by Merc-driving *ajarn* artists in Bangkok'. D. Johnson, 'Earth Works', *op. cit.*

[28] There is no better emblem of this semiotic arbitrage than Chalermchai's Wat Rong Khun, in nearby Chiang Rai, which opened in 1997.

[29] Between festival editions, the organisers grazed voraciously across CMU's faculties, attending lectures and engaging with teachers from other fields. Such transdisciplinary forays were unusual in Thailand's bureaucratic universities.

[30] Gridthiya, 'Curatorial Practices and Small Narratives', *op. cit.*; Thasnai, 'Overlapping Tactics and Practices at the Interstices of Thai Art', *op. cit.*; and Araya Rasdjarmrearnsook and Supachai Satsara, interview with Manuporn and David Teh, 21 December 2016. Supachai, a member of the festival's original core group, underscores the significance of 'students coming together as a group to brainstorm and to challenge the teachers'.

professional artists. Some were open-minded, but the prevailing pedagogy was doctrinaire and conservative. Navin recalls tensions between them and returnees like Montien and Araya, both Silpakorn Fine Arts graduates who had studied in Europe and taken teaching jobs in Chiang Mai in the late 1980s.[31] By 1992, room to manoeuvre outside the Silpakorn system had been won through overseas study and the emergence of competing programmes at Chulalongkorn University and the Prasarnmit teachers' college, both in Bangkok, and at CMU, with another being instituted at the time at Khon Kaen University. Opportunities for artists without the Silpakorn pedigree were multiplying, in small independent galleries and foreign cultural institutes, and increasingly overseas.

Montien was already thriving on a nascent international circuit; widely respected, he became a key mediator, endorsing the students' experiments with unorthodox forms of exhibition and participating himself in the festivals. His success opened networks, and glimpses of international activity, to members of the younger generation who travelled overseas to assist him. The faculty's imprimatur was moreover essential for negotiating access to spaces around the city. The position of university lecturer and its honorific term of address (*ajarn*) carry high status in Thai society, and CMU was a large institution in a small city. The core group fondly recall that the mere utterance of the university's name worked like a shibboleth, overcoming bureaucratic obstacles, placating obstructive officials and opening the doors of public, institutional and religious spaces alike.

So the independent initiatives which culminated in CMSI cannot be regarded as a clean break from the national-academic system, nor a partisan rejection of it, but rather as a kind of *fission* by which some autonomy was achieved at the fringes, without forgoing all the advantages the system conferred.[32] Though mostly 'outsiders' – provincial students like Navin, conscientious objectors like Mit and Uthit – the Chiang Mai group deliberately engaged with Silpakorn circles, albeit socially rather than officially, laterally rather than hierarchically. They encouraged Silpakorn students to join their gatherings, which constituted a kind of 'temporary autonomous zone', free from academic regulation.[33]

—

[31] When she returned from Germany in 1990, Araya was the only female *ajarn* on CMU's faculty. See John Clark, 'The Thai Avant-Garde and Araya Rasdjarmrearnsook's Visual Work', in *Araya Rasdjarmrearnsook: Storytellers of the Town* (exh. cat.), Sydney: 4A Centre for Contemporary Asian Art, 2014, pp.14–15.

[32] I borrow 'fission' from James C. Scott, who uses it to characterise 'fugitive' group formation proper to the upland political geography of the Southeast Asian massif, known as Zomia; Chiang Mai sits on its southern fringe. See J. C. Scott, *The Art of Not Being Governed: An Anarchist History of Upland Southeast Asia*, New Haven: Yale University Press, 2009, p.215; and 'A Short Account of the Deep History of State Evasion', presentation at the conference 'Flights from the Empire', Haus der Kulturen der Welt, Berlin, 17 June 2017, available at https://www.hkw.de/en/programm/projekte/veranstaltung/p_134071.php (last accessed on 16 June 2018).

[33] Araya recalls that her relationship to the group was that of an *ajarn*, but that they interacted more like friends. This was far from typical in Thai university contexts. Interview with Manuporn and May Adadol, 21 July 2017.

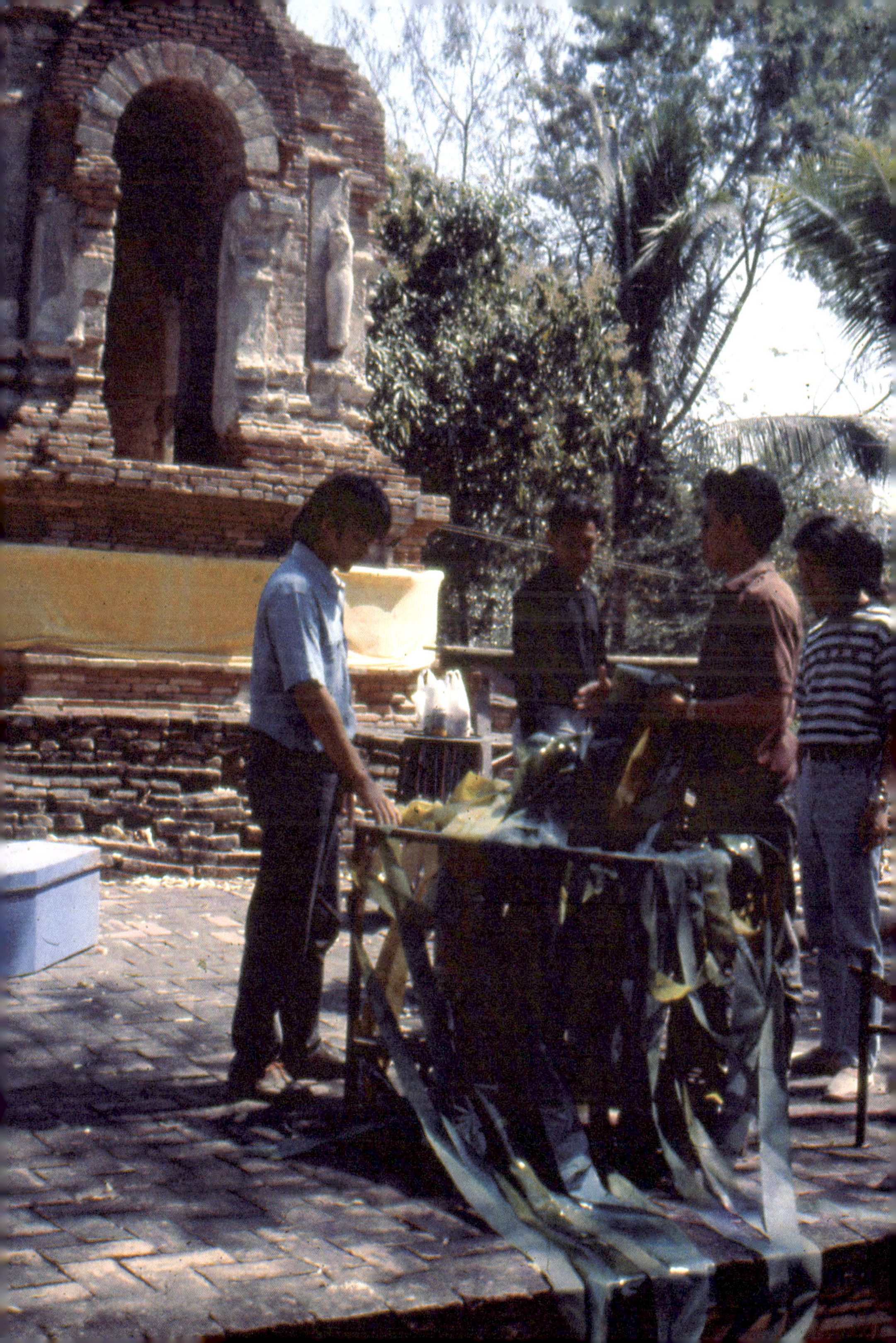

Precedents: Experiment and Independence

It bears remembering that the vocation of the artist in Thailand was plainly artisanal into the 1930s and still not particularly respectable as late as the 1960s. But with the rapid expansion of tertiary education during the Cold War, it drew in more black sheep of the burgeoning middle class, on whom Silpakorn at least conferred bureaucratic respectability. This status could be enhanced, or even transcended, with international credentials. Thai modern art was anything but a closed discourse – it was inaugurated by an Italian, after all, and like Thai culture generally, was permeable to outside influences. A period of study abroad had been an important rite of passage since Feroci's first cohort graduated in the 1940s.[34] But there was often nowhere for the exogenous methods thus acquired to be practiced by returnees, who mostly returned to the institutional fold for job opportunities and patronage. Any absorption was administered by the Silpakorn authorities, who determined what could be recognised and what would be ignored.[35]

In the 1980s, it remained difficult to become a professional artist without status in that system. Silpakorn's dominance was legible not only in patterns of taste and style, but throughout the cycle of artistic production – education and training, access to facilities, opportunities to exhibit, inclusion in the national art history. But more recently the globalisation of art and the gravitational shift from national to international markets have made success abroad more material, guaranteeing promotion even for non-Silpakorn graduates; meanwhile the artist-bureaucrats' seniority has gotten them nowhere on the global circuit. Thailand's most prominent 'international' artists (e.g. Navin, Surasi Kusolwong, Apichatpong Weerasethakul, Arin Rungjang) have outgrown the local institutional framework through sustained exposure abroad; they enjoy global profiles unthinkable for previous generations and owe nothing to Silpakorn for that success. This scenario has parallels all over Southeast Asia, where art education has broadly been dominated by authoritarian states and their 'national schools'.

Our historical picture of what lay *outside* Thailand's national academic sphere is spare indeed, hence the importance of the Chiang Mai festivals. Yet to appreciate fully their significance, we would need at our disposal a history that has not yet been written – an alternative art history, a history of artistic alternatives – in the absence of which we might at least venture a brief survey of the autodidacts, dropouts and castaways from the institutional mothership of Thai modern art. This list could even accommodate the early *haute bourgeoise* modernist Misiem Yipintsoi, who was made an honorary member of the Silpakorn club but wasn't formally trained there. It would certainly include Paiboon Suwannakudt – first recognised as a choreographer, later encouraged to paint by Feroci – who left

—

[34] Before the 1960s, most went to Europe. An interesting exception was Fua Haripitak, who spent several years at the college-cum-ashram set up by Rabindranath Tagore at Santiniketan, West Bengal, renowned for its 'pan-Asian' philosophy of art (later Visva-Bharati University).

[35] In 1991, Chalermchai could brag of being the only artist under forty to have joined the ranks of the 'independents' (i.e. those not reliant on Silpakorn), a category which included only Thawan, Angkarn Kalayanapong and self-taught painter Pratuang Emjaroen. See S. Cate, *Making Merit, Making Art*, *op. cit.*, p.130.

Silpakorn to revive a threatened mural tradition and mentored many young artists; and the Sino-Thai modernist Chang Sae-tang, who deliberately kept his distance from the institution even after fellow self-taught innovators, including his friend Pratuang Emjaroen, had been recuperated.[36] It would include émigrés like the painter Somboon Hormtientong, who studied informally with Chang before relocating to Germany; and print and installation artist Prawat Laucharoen, an orphan from Ratchaburi Province who, after training at Silpakorn, left for New York in 1967 and has stayed put ever since. The subsequent generation that came of age in the 1980s were more numerous. They included fine art photographers Pramuan Burusphat and Itthi Khongkakul, and such experimental figures as Apinan, Araya, Montien, Kamol Phaosavasdi and Chumpon Apisuk. These artists enjoyed the benefits of overseas study and found, upon their return, more latitude in paid work and exhibition opportunities.

This outsiders' history is more visible now that the art market seeks under-capitalised names from outside the national canon, and as the flattening designation 'global' has come to name the dominant sector of the art economy and demand historicisation. However sceptical we may be about such motives, they make an alternative genealogy all the more urgent. Its common thread will be a more inclusive approach to both media and the public. The outsiders took up new methods, and sought not simply viewers but active participants, anticipating the formal and social concerns of 1990s contemporary art: the time-based and ephemeral modes that would be entrenched in installation and performance; the seeds of 'relational' and socially engaged practices; an interest in moral and civic education; and the move beyond modern art's socially exclusive architecture towards engagement with specific public spaces and everyday life. If one had to synthesise these traits in a single term, 'social installation' would not be a bad summation. CMSI belongs squarely to this alternative genealogy, which describes a shift away from studio-bound notions of technical prowess and the moral authority conferred by institutions, towards a 'post-medium' condition in which production is outsourced and material choices followed the artist's concept rather than technical training – what Thasnai would later suggestively gloss as 'alternative creative competencies'.[37]

With this alternative history in mind, we are better placed to identify precedents and parallels of the kind of gathering that took place, and the kind of art that was made, in Chiang Mai's 1990s festivals. For clarity, I will attempt this in two steps, dealing first with the Thai context and then considering the larger regional one. The festivals' deliberate activation of diverse public spaces – their signature innovation – was a bold departure from Thai modern art's exhibitionary norms. This was not the first time artists had taken their work to the streets – Simon

—

[36] See Phaptawan Suwannakudt and John Clark, 'A History of Paiboon Suwannakudt', unpublished manuscript, 2018.

[37] In the 1960s, it was common for visual artists to be writers too, a versatility killed off by the academy's bureaucratic studio structure and the depoliticised atmosphere in the 1970s. The CMSI group were not exactly poets, but their facility with language allowed the incorporation of discursive public events and spontaneous critique and discussion in the festival programmes.

Soon has aligned the festivals with activist art manifestations of the 1970s – but connections between the two eras, either genealogical or aesthetic, are hard to discern.[38] The repressions of the first, especially in October 1976, crippled progressive cultures and inaugurated a systematic depoliticisation of educational institutions (as in contemporaneous dictatorships elsewhere in Asia). Progressive art initiatives of the 1980s remained bound by Bangkok's institutional proprieties and morally conservative force fields. The most salient experimental node had arisen amid the upheaval of the 1970s, at arm's length from Silpakorn, but was nonetheless institutional, and even named in honour of the academy's founder. The Bhirasri Institute of Modern Art (BIMA) was conceived in the early 1960s by a group of patrons around Princess Pantip Paribatra Chumbhot, on whose land it was eventually built.[39] It foreshadowed a certain elite-cosmopolitan patronage that is still pivotal today, which included both Thais and expatriate foreigners – self-assured in their wealth and royal and state connections – with their eyes on developments overseas. A foundation was set up, and after more than a decade of sporadic fundraising, BIMA was finally inaugurated in 1974, during the flirtation with democracy between bouts of unrest in 1973 and 1976, a unique and anomalous interlude in the Cold War military-authoritarian order.[40]

Though its slated modern art collection never materialised, BIMA's exhibition and public education programmes were lively and inclusive, and not monopolised by Silpakorn players. It promoted artists experimenting with new trends encountered abroad, amongst them Damrong Wong-Upparat, a student of Feroci's who was instrumental in BIMA's founding and sat on its board. The institution's importance lay in its openness to younger returnees such as Apinan and Kamol, neither of whom had attended Silpakorn, and stalwart of Thai performance art Chumpon, who was a Silpakorn alumnus but had also studied informally with Chang in the late 1960s and in Boston in the 1970s. All three were cross-artform pioneers. Landmark shows at BIMA included Apinan's daring debut after his studies in the UK, 'How to Explain Art to a Bangkok Cock' (1985), which saw the annual national prize awarded to a non-Silpakorn artist for the first time, and 'Folk-Thai-Time: the first conceptual art exhibition' (1986), curated by Chumpon and featuring 'installation, Process Art and performance Art' by Pramuan, Itthi, Kamol, Vasan Sitthiket and others.[41] BIMA was progressive and nonconformist enough for neither its cosmopolitan

—

[38] See Simon Soon, 'Images Without Bodies: Chiang Mai Social Installation and the Art History of Cooperative Suffering', *Afterall*, no.42, Autumn/Winter 2016, pp.36–47. It is hard to discern continuities between, on the one hand, Somchai Hatthakitkoson and Thammasak Booncherd, two leftists cited in Ahmad Mashadi's gloss on 1970s activist art, and, on the other, the CMSI generation. See A. Mashadi, 'Framing the 1970s', *Third Text*, vol.25, no.4, 2011, p.413. See also Chumpon, 'Unpredictable Repercussions', *op. cit.*, pp.23–24.

[39] Pantip was married to a grandson of the fifth king. Her circle included expatriates from the diplomatic community and members of Bangkok's new technocratic elite including the Sino-Thai economist Puey Ungphakorn, long-time Governor of the Bank of Thailand.

[40] At one point a donation was made, for instance, by the John D. Rockefeller III Fund, but the bulk of support came from local patrons. The patrons' efforts had stalled in 1969 when land allotted by the Palace was given over to the ruling military kleptocracy instead. See John Clark, 'Decoration and Distance: The Work of Damrong Wong-Upparaj', *Art and AsiaPacific*, vol.2, no.3, July 1995, pp.50–57.

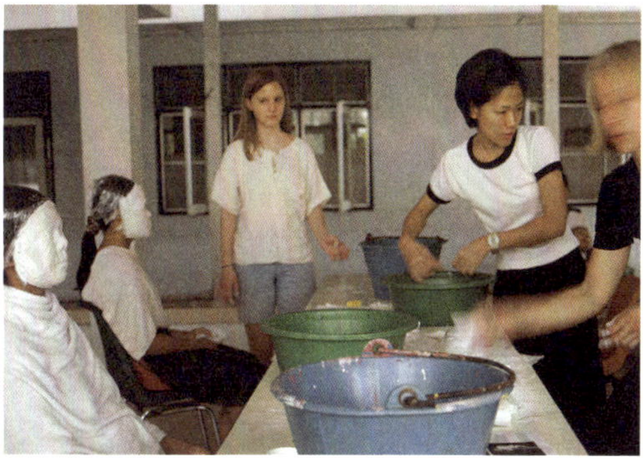

Sanja Iveković workshop at a womens' shelter, Womanifesto II, Bangkok, 1999 © Womanifesto

patrons nor Silpakorn grandees to get fully behind it. It closed in 1988, after Pantip's passing. For all its well-heeled supporters, institutional appearances were often kept up by volunteer labour, donations and goodwill – indeed, by a collaborative spirit not unlike that of many artist-run initiatives. And anticipating much of Southeast Asia's art infrastructure, the hardware was built long before the software was ready. In Damrong's account, staffing was almost an afterthought.[42]

BIMA's significance for contemporary art's history is hard to overstate, and rests in two precedents: first, it provided a site and an audience for experimental and non-traditional practices, including photography; second, while neither antagonising nor ignoring the national institution, it operated at arm's length from the latter's dominant cliques.[43] The Chiang Mai festivals took up both these mantles, and helped to inspire an extraordinary efflorescence of independent activity through the 1990s that was increasingly focussed on the capital, in one-off and recurring festivals such as the Bangkok Outsider platform (from 1993), Huay Kwang Mega City (1996), the Bangkok Experimental Film Festival, and Womanifesto (both from 1997).[44] The openness to new art forms and discourses was enshrined in

—

[41] 'Folk-Thai-Time' poster, 1986. Chumpon was already quite active in a curatorial capacity, initiating in the same year a series of monthly events at BIMA called 'Wethi-Samai', with an explicitly multidisciplinary agenda. Apinan, who has called BIMA 'the most exciting art space Bangkok ever had', remembers some consternation at his opening on the part of then director Chatvichai Prommadhattavedi, who before the arrival of local dignitaries closeted a bust of Feroci that stood like a sentinel at the entrance (as does his statue at Silpakorn). Interview with Apinan, 25 February 2013. See also Apinan, 'Modern Art in Thailand', *op. cit.*, p.23.

[42] See J. Clark, 'Decoration and Distance', *op. cit.*

[43] Clare Veal, 'The Photographic Conditions of Contemporary Thai Art', *Journal of Taipei Fine Arts Museum*, no.34, 2017, available at https://www.tfam.museum/Common/editor.aspx?ddlLang=zh-tw&f=sys&id=229 (last accessed on 11 June 2018).

[44] This pioneering women's art group had its origins in the 1995 exhibition 'Tradisexion' at Concrete House (see n.9). See www.womanifesto.com (last accessed on 11 June 2018); Asia Art Archive's 2009 interview with Varsha Nair, available at https://aaa.org.hk/en/ideas/ideas/interview-with-varsha-nair (last accessed on 11 June 2018); and V. Nair, 'Womanifesto II – jogging ahead', *n.paradoxa*, vol.4, July 1999, pp.91–94.

independent spaces such as Project 304 and Tadu Contemporary Art (both from 1996), and About Art Related Activities with its Chinatown venue, About Café (from 1997). All welcomed international styles and artists. For a developing country in the throes of financial crisis, Thailand had become a surprisingly busy crossroads on the global art map by the time 'Cities on the Move', a rolling resumé of Asian urban culture conceived by Hans Ulrich Obrist and Hou Hanru, alighted there in 1999.[45]

Regionality and Contemporaneity

The festivals were undoubtedly a bellwether for contemporary art in Thailand, yet their historical importance may ultimately lie in their synchronicity and confluence with developments elsewhere. They coincided with a sharp upturn in the intensity of international art circulation, since naturalised as a feature of a global system called 'contemporary' and commonly understood to have emerged after 1989.[46] Several CMSI participants became exemplars of that circulation, notably Navin and Rirkrit Tiravanija. And while the platform did not endure beyond the 1990s, it gave Chiang Mai international visibility at a pivotal time as a haven for certain trending practices; it also served as a template for later artist-led initiatives with similarly transnational horizons, for instance The Land Foundation and the performance art festival Asiatopia, both founded in 1998. But if the festivals' immediate effect was to plug Thais into emerging global networks, the real aesthetic or intellectual convergence, more legible with hindsight, suggests a different geography.

The stylistic and ethical affinities with Western artists were to prove less substantial and less enduring than those amongst Asian ones, though the regional simpatico was not self-evident at the time. Asian participation in Chiang Mai was neither very deliberate on the part of organisers nor all that extensive – East Asia was as well represented as Southeast Asia thanks to the support of the Japan Foundation.[47] In the early 1990s, Southeast Asian artists' knowledge of each other's scenes was patchy and there was little discussion of the region as such.

—

[45] While undoubtedly another watershed for Southeast Asian contemporary art's opening towards the global, 'Cities on the Move' was not really comparable with CMSI. Rather than globalist, the latter was locally initiated and entirely artist-run, and took place far from the cosmopolitan capital. It was the more deliberate excursion beyond the conventions and spaces of art.

[46] Emerging histories of this globalisation of art exchange range from the celebratory to the more circumspect. See, for instance, Hans Belting, Andrea Buddensieg and Peter Weibel (ed.), *The Global Contemporary and the Rise of the New Art Worlds* (Cambridge, MA: The MIT Press, 2013); and past titles in Afterall Book's *Exhibition Histories* series such as *Making Art Global (Part 1): The Third Havana Biennial 1989* (2011, ed. Rachel Weiss et al.) and *Making Art Global (Part 2): 'Magiciens de la Terre' 1989* (2013, ed. Lucy Steeds).

[47] The brochure for the third edition of CMSI lists only seven non-Thai Southeast Asian participants and eight Japanese. Though Japanese exhibitors were notably absent from the second edition, its brochure lists a seminar featuring two Japanese artists and influential curator Tani Arata, a co-organiser of 'New Art from Southeast Asia', held at the Fukuoka Art Museum the previous year. See Seng Yu Jin, 'The Primacy of Exhibitionary Discourses: Contemporaneity in Southeast Asian Art, 1992–2002', in *Intersecting Histories: Contemporary Turns in Southeast Asian Art* (exh. cat.), Singapore: Nanyang Technological University, 2012, pp.116–29.

Yet browsing the archives today, one is struck by the presence of many key artists and artist-organisers, particularly at the third festival in 1995, which included Arahmaiani from Indonesia; Noel Soler Cuizon from the Philippines; Vincent Leow, Tang Da Wu, Lee Wen, Amanda Heng and Jay Koh from Singapore; and US artist, critic and videographer Ray Langenbach (then living in Singapore, later based in Malaysia).[48]

As noted in the introduction to this volume, the historiography of modern art in Southeast Asia has recently accelerated, but most research is still conceived within national frames of reference. These are often illuminating, but they have the effect of concealing parallels, or what Ahmad Mashadi calls 'horizontal-synchronic references', across national histories clearly shaped by transnational forces.[49] To date, few academic studies have adopted a regional frame, and fewer still offer reflexive theorisation of regionality.[50] This leaves art history with a kind of structural deficit: its methods and vocabulary are geared in favour of national historiography, against the recognition of extra-national sources of artistic meaning and value. The bias presents acute problems for historians of *contemporary* art, which has, since the 1990s, been shaped more by transnational markets and currents (e.g. styles, themes, modes of organisation, institutional affirmation) than by national ones.

Globalisation poses opportunities and challenges for artistic and political regionalism alike. In the words of one historian, the thawing of the Cold War strengthened the appeal of regions as 'intermediate zone[s] between the deterritorializing impulses of capitalism and the territorial limits of nationalism'.[51] As academic and curatorial appetites have been piqued for older models of regionalism, we see a striking convergence of art historical and political historical interests, for instance in the 1955 Asia-Africa Conference in Bandung, and an earlier pan-Asianism associated with figures like Okakura Tenshin and Rabindranath Tagore. But while political regionalism has been dealt some serious setbacks of late – with signs of fission in Europe, tensions around the South China Sea, a resurgence of US exceptionalism – contemporary art may have passed its point of no return. Its commercial and institutional circuits thrive as a global system in which national identification may persist, but national isolation is

—

[48] Arahmaiani became a familiar presence in the Thai scene, basing herself there in virtual exile after receiving death threats in Indonesia for her progressive views and work. CMSI exemplified a freedom of expression she was denied at home. She also collaborated with Apinan, Chumpon, Manit Sriwanichpoom and the Womanifesto group. Amongst the Thais, Montien and Chumpon had the most friends and experience elsewhere in Southeast Asia. Montien also proposed a deliberately regional art initiative – a 'Mekong Biennale' – in the late 1990s, but it never materialised.
[49] A. Mashadi, 'Framing the 1970s', *op. cit.*, p.409.
[50] Examples include the July 2011 special issue of *Third Text* on 'Contemporaneity and Art in Southeast Asia', guest edited by Joan Kee and Patrick D. Flores; Nora A. Taylor and Boreth Ly, *Modern and Contemporary Southeast Asian Art: An Anthology*, Ithaca, NY: Cornell Southeast Asia Program Publications, 2012; and the recently launched journal *Southeast of Now*.
[51] Prasenjit Duara, 'Asia Redux: Conceptualizing a Region for Our Times', *Journal of Asian Studies*, vol.69, no.4, November 2010, p.974.

unthinkable. We need to historicise this transnational exchange with reference to national and wider contexts, without being blinkered by one or the other.

If region has been the primary optic through which Southeast Asian contemporary art has been exhibited, it is not in spite of national identifiers but by virtue of them. This curatorial habit has its roots in Cold War area studies, a discourse predisposed to treat modern art as an expression of a universal if not 'Western' modernity – administered principally by the nation state – in tension with customs conceived as local and 'traditional'.[52] Its underlying assumptions are that contemporary art has generally been progressive with respect to national politics (usually a sound idea) and that the nation has been, and remains, the ultimate horizon of artistic meaning (more dubious). One needs national context to qualify the first assumption; one can't moderate the second without some reading of artworks beyond national frames. Yet 'global art history' has proven less coherent than the global art market. This may explain the enduring desire for 'Southeast Asia'; but too often its geography is a given, and the assumptions may be getting stronger rather than weaker.[53] The regional frame can offer critical purchase on both national and global ones, provided it is deconstructive rather than cumulative – not by merely gathering national stories but by comparing, queering and complicating them.[54] Unfortunately, this reflexivity is not prevalent in museums and academia, nor in large-scale exhibitions of Southeast Asian contemporary art. The latter is typically made to illustrate tales of national

—

[52] See, for example, Claire Holt, *Art in Indonesia: Continuities and Change*, Ithaca, NY: Cornell University Press, 1967; and Caroline Turner (ed.), *Tradition and Change: Contemporary Art of Asia and the Pacific*, Brisbane: University of Queensland Press, 1993. Prominent exhibitionary iterations of this dialectic include Apinan's travelling exhibition 'Contemporary Art in Asia: Traditions/Tensions' (1996), organised by the Asia Society Galleries, New York; the Asia Pacific Triennial of Contemporary Art, in Brisbane since 1993; and the programme of the Singapore Art Museum (SAM), founded in 1996.

[53] Duara applauds the art world's expansive and experimental notion of Asia, but recent institutional initiatives suggest the entrenchment of an unreflexive geography, among them 'Sunshower' (see n.2). P. Duara, 'Asia Redux', *op. cit.*, p.977. Meanwhile, the US funders of a recent art history colloquium held in Singapore, Indonesia and Australia, 'Ambitious Alignments: New Histories of Southeast Asian Art', insisted arbitrarily that contemporary art be excluded, removing a valuable basis for comparative thinking across national lines. See 'Ambitious Alignments' website, http://www.ambitiousalignments.com (last accessed on 5 July 2018). It is hard to fathom why a regionally framed conference should deliberately ignore the one historical period in which art's regional circulation has been deliberate and brisk.

[54] For example, the work of internationally celebrated film-maker Apichatpong Weerasethakul, who grew up in northeastern Thailand, launched his career in the 1990s via Chicago and Bangkok and now lives in Chiang Mai. Starting with his early films, his work evokes multiple layers of non-national identification which irritate the national imaginary but which cannot be understood without acknowledging and reckoning with transnational, subnational and, indeed, pre-national histories and experiences – a complexity embodied throughout his oeuvre by working-class storytellers (*Mysterious Object at Noon*, 2000), *sans-papiers* (*Blissfully Yours*, 2002; *Mobile Men*, 2008), itinerant labourers (*Unknown Forces*, 2007) and the borderland descendants of Cold War combatants (*Primitive*, 2009; *Uncle Boonmee Who Can Recall His Past Lives*, 2010). On Thai contemporary art's ethnopolitical nuances, see David Teh, *Thai Art: Currencies of the Contemporary*, Cambridge, MA: The MIT Press, 2017.

modernity; an impression of gradual democratisation has even been offered as a kind of regional template, a discursive hangover of the Cold War with little basis, sadly, in political fact. Future research must be more exacting, its vocabulary more nuanced, in order to moot systematically any continuities between art since the 1990s and that of earlier periods.

To this end, nationality can scarcely be put aside, but nor should it be presumed to be the primary axis of artistic subjectivity. There is no doubt that after World War II, many of Southeast Asia's influential modern artists saw themselves as protagonists in decolonisation and nation-building projects; but few didn't also see themselves as part of some larger culture and intellectual history, whether progressive-socialist, liberal-individualist, something more spiritual or apolitical, or a mixture of these. Asian modernism was mostly neither derivative nor doctrinaire, and what makes it such fertile ground for researchers today is precisely its complexity, its unresolved blends of worldliness and particularism.[55] Locating the seeds of artistic regionalism in Southeast Asia, Mashadi suggests that an earlier internationalism, expressed in the putatively universal language of abstraction, gave way in the 1970s to a heightened focus on local contingencies, an 'introspection' that generated 'new grounds for critique' and 'new points of departure'.[56] Citing the 1974 exhibition 'Towards a Mystical Reality' in Kuala Lumpur, and the near contemporaneous formation of the Gerakan Seni Rupa Baru (New Art Movement) in Indonesia and the Kaisahan (Solidarity) group in the Philippines, Mashadi grounds this turn in the urgency of immediate sociopolitical conditions and constraints that were specific to each country.[57] Following him, we could identify cognate gestures towards a dawning contemporaneity before or after this in the Shop 6 group initiated by Roberto Chabet in Manila in 1970, in progressive projects such as the 1985 environmental exhibition 'Proses '85' in Jakarta, and in the 'Folk-Thai-Time' show p.36
at BIMA the following year. No doubt these were all important developments, but it is hard to align them politically, iconographically or organisationally. Art history is bound to reveal as much divergence as convergence in that regional picture; few of the artists involved had any knowledge of contemporary art in neighbouring countries. This is not to deny their contemporaneity but to recognise that though they were independent, experimental and internationally informed, in each case their currency was circumscribed by nationally specific situations and art histories, and for good reason – most were working under authoritarian conditions, with limited mobility.

—

[55] See D. Teh (ed.), *"Misfits": Pages from a loose-leaf modernity* (exh. cat.), Berlin: Haus der Kulturen der Welt, 2017.

[56] A. Mashadi, 'Framing the 1970s', *op. cit.*, p.411. See also his *Telah Terbit (Out Now): Southeast Asian Contemporary Art Practices During the 1970s* (exh. cat.), Singapore: Singapore Art Museum, 2006.

[57] A. Mashadi, 'Framing the 1970s', *op. cit.*, pp.413–16. Mashadi's analysis of Malaysian art after the 1969 race riots is compelling. The conceptual turn instigated by Redza Piyadasa and Sulaiman Esa uncovered a 'mystical' tendency that clearly anticipated a 1990s preoccupation with identity, but in the meantime proved susceptible to ethnonationalism. Their conceptualist credentials would wait decades to be appreciated. See also T.K. Sabapathy, 'Intersecting Histories: Thoughts on the Contemporary in Southeast Asian Art', in *Intersecting Histories, op.cit.*

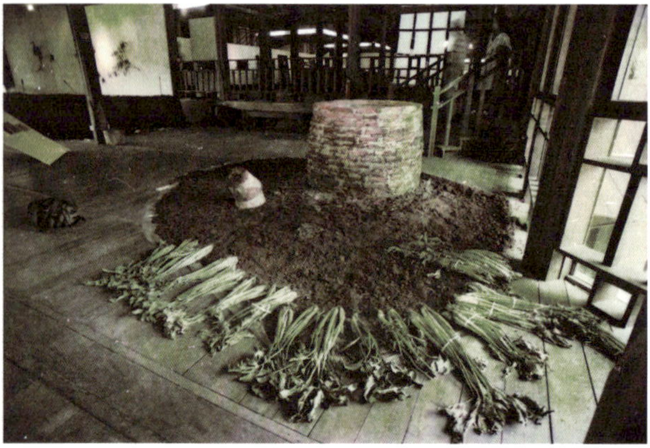

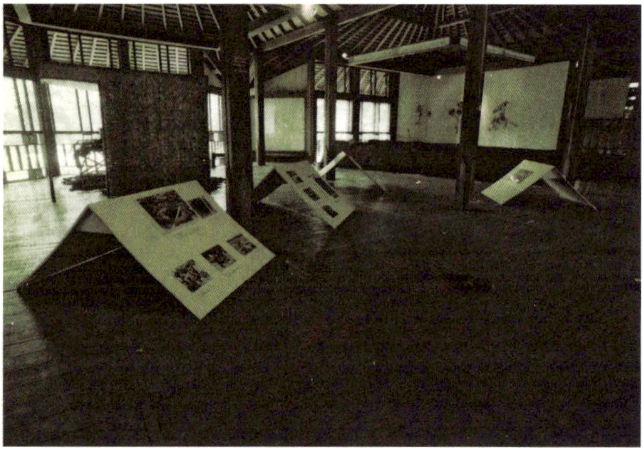

Installation views, 'Proses '85', Galeri Seni Rupa Ancol, Jakarta, 1985
Courtesy Indonesian Visual Art Archive (IVAA), Hyphen — and the artists

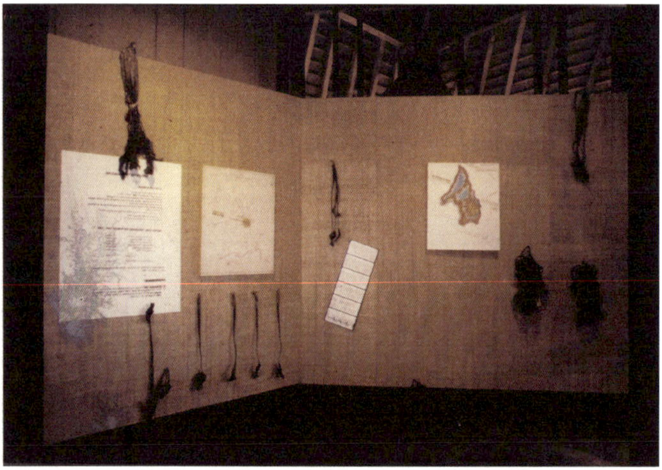

Regular intra-regional circulation of art kicked off in the 1970s, but was mediated by the diplomatic machinery of the postcolonial state. When this 'consular' model was struck in an earlier phase, as in the exhibition Sukarno staged during the Bandung Conference, it was both more progressive and more worldly.[58] But by 1981, when the Association of Southeast Asian Nations (ASEAN) began its annual rotating and touring exhibitions, with Japanese funding, the Cold War's geo-political faultlines were all too obvious. Restricted to painting, sculpture and photography, the ASEAN shows promoted a staid and academic modernism. Responding to the fourth one, held in Singapore in 1985, critic and historian T.K. Sabapathy found the series too diplomatic and lacking in any curatorial point of view. *Contemporary* exhibitions, he objected, ought to occasion 'cultural persuasion', 'critical attitudes' and 'new ways of seeing'.[59] By the late 1980s, a motley group of critics and artist-curators had begun to cross paths with some frequency, including Sabapathy; Malaysians Syed Ahmad Jamal and Redza Piyadasa; Emmanuel 'Eric' Torres from the Philippines; and later, Apinan, Somporn Rodboon and Jim Supangkat. Most of these figures were artists who, as Patrick D. Flores puts it, had 'settled within the discourse of the "avant-garde" and wavered at the threshold of a curatorial future'.[60] But it is striking that none were drivers of transnational art platforms. Why not? One is tempted to infer that their assumption of the curatorial function removed them from the lateral, artist-to-artist plane of collaboration and exchange. They became gatekeepers, working with national bureaucracies though without surrendering their critical credentials – an ambivalence astutely described by Flores, and which they carried into a wider sphere of operation.[61]

—

[58] Mashadi notes that the excursions of Filipino modernists reflected 'notions of national "progressiveness"' and a 'drive towards internationalism and international recognition', but with disappointing results. A. Mashadi, 'Framing the 1970s', *op. cit.*, pp.410–11.
[59] T.K. Sabapathy, *Writing the Modern: Selected Texts on Art & Art History in Singapore, Malaysia & Southeast Asia, 1973–2015*, Singapore: Singapore Art Museum, 2018, p.237.
[60] P.D. Flores, 'Turns in Tropics: Artist-Curator', in N.A. Taylor and B. Ly, *Modern and Contemporary Southeast Asian Art*, *op. cit.*, p.171. By 1992, Apinan had published his seminal art history, was writing newspaper and magazine criticism, and was no longer a practicing artist. He rapidly became the doyen of Southeast Asian curatorship, his stature easily surpassing that of the other pathfinders identified by Flores. Apinan, *Modern Art in Thailand: Nineteenth and Twentieth Centuries*, Oxford: Oxford University Press, 1992. For more detailed studies of Apinan and Supangkat in particular, see P.D. Flores, *Past Peripheral: Curation in Southeast Asia*, Singapore: National University of Singapore Museum, 2008.
[61] These curators 'either supplemented the fraught aspirations of nation-building ... or rendered them untenable. ... They interact with each other, the political with the aesthetic, the institutional with the agitating, the disciplinal with the ludic, caught up in the process of national formation and imaginative expansion.' P.D. Flores, 'Turns in Tropics', *op. cit.*, pp.175–76. Flores's poetics invites us to see this last pair as opposites, yet his characterisation of the curatorial function demands of us something much harder: to acknowledge that the curatorial state was not a priori – perhaps not even typically – pitted against the opening up of art's formal and conceptual possibilities, even where its academy was; and that the production of national form, in which artists were conspicuous and usually willing collaborators, must itself be read as an artistic and 'imaginative' production. See also his 'The Curatorial Turn in Southeast Asia and the Afterlife of the Modern', in Melissa Chiu and Benjamin Genocchio (ed.), *Contemporary Art in Asia*, Cambridge, MA: The MIT Press, 2011, pp.197–210.

By the 1990s, contemporary art's circulation was becoming more demonstrably regional thanks to institutions being set up in Japan, Australia and Singapore. These efforts yielded three recurring, and competing, survey vehicles for building
p.265 regionally framed collections: the quinquennial Asian Art Show in Fukuoka, first held in 1980, became a triennial with the opening of the Fukuoka Asian Art Museum in 1999; the Queensland Art Gallery in Brisbane launched the first
p.45 Asia-Pacific Triennial (APT) in late 1993; and the Singapore Art Museum (SAM) opened in 1996 with 'A Century of Art in Singapore' and the first in a long line of regional surveys, Sabapathy's 'Themes in Southeast Asian Art'. These institutions gave visibility and legitimacy to activity that was not exactly 'modern art', laying foundations for a regional market and contemporary art history. They stimulated artistic networks and friendships, and sketched a career destination that was to be, for many artists of the time, the ceiling of international recognition. And while all three catered to ministerial appetites for a regionalism transparently shaped by trade and investment policies, behind each lay more interesting intellectual agendas and histories.[62]

Translocal: Modes, Structures and Geography of the Contemporary

Recent knowledge production around Southeast Asian art betrays a tendency to consolidate, rather than challenge, the putative regional canon composed over two decades by these institutions.[63] The newer paradigm of exhibition history is being put to quite traditional art historical ends, even giving the impression that a regional contemporaneity emerged at the point of institutionalisation rather than in independent projects run by artists.[64] The institutions have been recipients and promoters of contemporaneity but rarely its authors, and no extant public collection or state-backed survey has seriously challenged that view.[65] Their preponderance in regional historiography must therefore be weighed against the less formal histories of individuals and groups like CMSI.

—

[62] Fukuoka has generated the most sustained curatorial research on Southeast Asia, led by Ushiroshoji Masahiro and Kuroda Raiji. The early editions of APT, in 1993 and 1996, convened a formidable network of advisors and artist-curators, developed in part through the Artists Regional Exchange (ARX), a government-funded but artist-initiated programme begun in 1987 in Perth. And long before SAM's inauguration, the region's experimental tendencies had been tracked in the programme of Singapore's National Museum Art Gallery (NMAG), which gradually integrated international trends, positioning itself between the diplomatic imperatives of the ASEAN shows (which it hosted) and emerging regional 'undercurrents'. See Shabbir Hussain Mustafa, 'We Made Space: In Conversation with Choy Weng Yang', in *Earth Work 1979 – Tang Da Wu* (exh. cat.), Singapore: National Gallery Singapore, 2016, pp.47–48.

[63] Distinctions should be observed, in any case, between the various institutional views. From Fukuoka and Brisbane, Southeast Asia was framed by a broader geography ('Asia' and 'Asia-Pacific', respectively), whereas Singapore invested more assiduously in the notion of 'Southeast Asia' as such.

[64] Seng Yu Jin, 'The Primacy of Exhibitionary Discourses', *op. cit.*

[65] With the possible exception of the 'developmental art' advanced through the Cultural Center of the Philippines. Though few made it to Chiang Mai, Filipinos were especially adventurous. Early pathfinders included David Medalla and film-maker Kidlat Tahimik; Lani Maestro emigrated to Canada in the early 1980s and participated in the second and fifth Havana biennials and the third APT; Noel Soler Cuizon showed in Havana and Fukuoka in 1994 and in the third CMSI the following year. Santiago Bose was one of six Filipinos in the Fukuoka show and three in the third Havana biennial in 1989, the year his Baguio

Two kindred platforms suggest themselves: the Baguio Arts Guild, founded in 1987, and its international festival, begun in 1989; and Singapore's The Artists Village, initiated in 1988, which stepped up its international activities in the early 1990s. Though relatively small-scale, it was in these encounters that departure from the constraints of academic modern art became possible and regional friendship and awareness could take root. Just as crucial as any transnational understanding was *self*-recognition – artists saw in each other reflections of their own ambitions and inhibitions, recognising a contemporaneity that overran national boundaries, not to mention shared heritages whose overlaps nationalism had effectively but only recently obscured. The consolidation of such networks into quasi-institutional formations was to leave lasting imprints on what came to be called 'Southeast Asian' contemporary art.[66] p.265

Several factors distinguish this ground-up, artist-to-artist regionalism from the institutional kind. In the Chiang Mai, Baguio and Singapore platforms, the energy and resources – the sense of a shared *currency* – came from fellow artists and the public, not from officials, collectors or gallerists. Quarantine from the market did not ensure moral purity, but did allow these platforms to be incubators for practices and styles that would be recognised as 'contemporary' and later valorised by institutions. The platforms' affinities may be summarised according to three parameters. First, they shared a set of *formal and thematic* preferences. All accommodated activities that were self-consciously different from academic 'modern art'. All were marked by formal permissiveness, encouraging cross-media experiments that could be described as ephemeral, performative, site-specific, 'installative', socially engaged or participatory. Art met its public on substantially altered terms as audiences local and foreign were engaged in ordinary public spaces. Meanwhile, the groups' thematic sympathies were obvious and their concerns resonant Asia-wide: struggles against dictatorship and censorship, corruption and poverty; protest against the testing and proliferation of nuclear weapons; critiques of irresponsible development and environmental degradation, of consumerism and conformism.[67] These groups took up progressive positions

—

Arts Guild mounted the first of its seminal festivals in the Philippine Cordillera. Bose later participated in the first APT alongside his friend Roberto Villanueva, also a veteran of both Havana and Fukuoka. Others followed work opportunities, including Jose Tence Ruiz, who participated in Singapore's artist-run scene in the early 1990s while working as a cartoonist for a state-run newspaper. For an overview of Asia's recurring exhibitions, see C. Green and A. Gardner, '1989: Asian Biennialization', *op. cit.*, pp.111–44.

[66] This perspective will highlight pivotal moments at which independent players gained reflexive understanding of their importance and growing power, for example the exhibition 'Pause' at the fourth Gwangju Biennale (2002); SENI Singapore (2004), a pilot project for that city's biennial (begun in 2006); and the wave of self-historicisation by art collectives in Java starting around 2008. The latter process included the conversion of Cemeti Art House's resource centre (Cemeti Art Foundation) into Indonesian Visual Art Archive, a process initiated as early as 1995 with the decision of Mella Jaarsma and Nindityo Adipurnomo to step back from directorial duties at Cemeti Art House, but which came to fruition with a physical archive site in 2007.

[67] These formal and thematic parallels even cross the Cold War divide. Comparison could be made with both Para Site in Hong Kong (founded 1996) and Big Tail Elephant group in Guangzhou (active from 1991). See Nikita Yingqian Cai and Hou Hanru

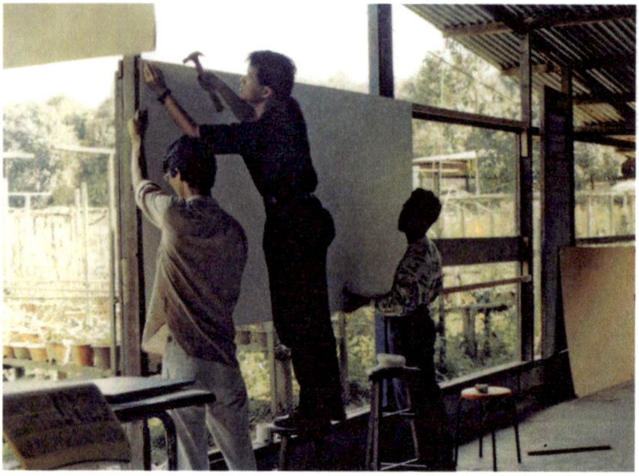

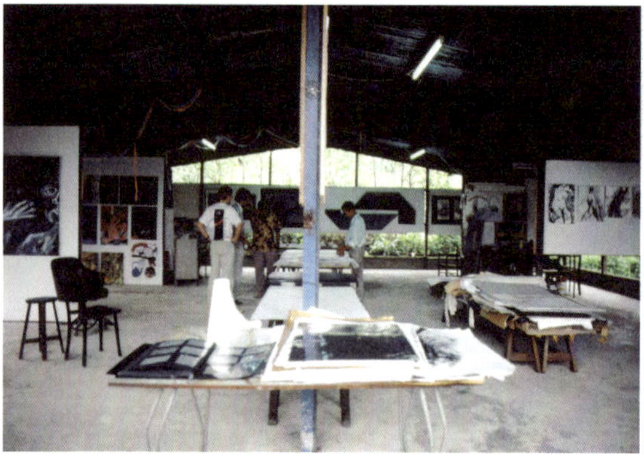

Views of a chicken coop during conversion for the first 'Open Studio Show', The Artists Village, Singapore, 1989
Courtesy and photography: Koh Nguang How

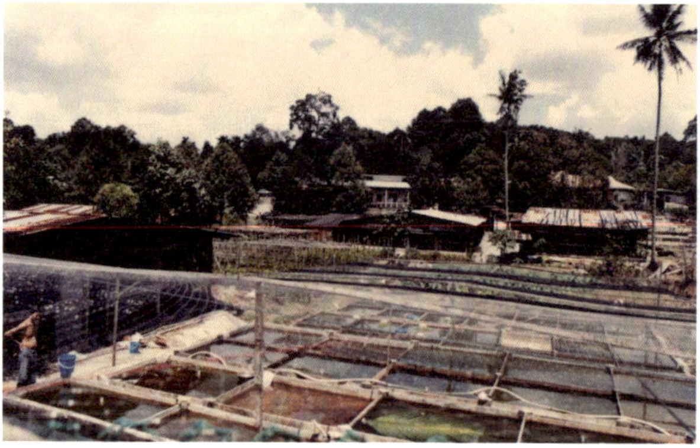

Agricultural buildings and plots surrounding Tang Da Wu's studios in Sembawang, Singapore
Courtesy and photography: Koh Nguang How

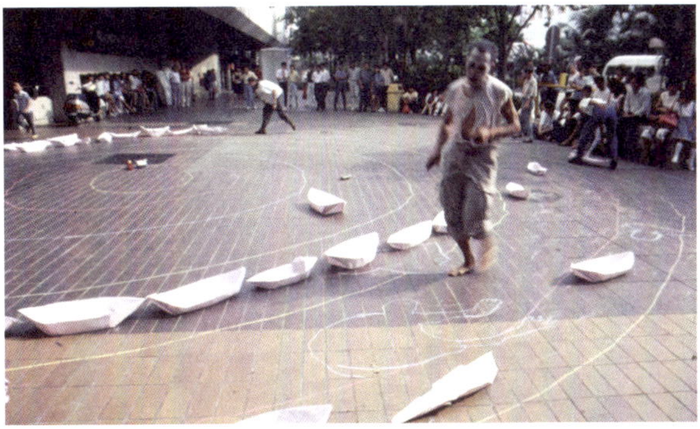

Tang Da Wu, *Life Boat*, performed at 'Art Mart: Singapore International Shopping Festival', 1989
Courtesy and photography: Koh Nguang How

in emerging civil societies, though without giving up art's autonomy – they maintained some distinction between their art and their activism.

Second, clear *structural and organisational* similarities are to be noted. All three platforms were artist-initiated and artist-run, wrought collectively by artists practising as artists and neither mediated by curators nor affirmed by the state and its academicians. Santiago Bose's description of the first Baguio festival could easily apply to CMSI: 'It was run on a shoe-string budget of less than 200,000 pesos (approx. [US]$20,000) and was sustained largely through the energy of participating artists' who shouldered their own expenses. The informal, lateral structure was a deliberate choice, integral to the event's rationale and endurance. The 'initial concept', Bose wrote, 'was a celebration of artists by artists for artists and the city of Baguio'.[68] Those assuming organisational responsibilities performed as *hosts*, not as authors of exhibitions. TAV founder Tang Da Wu was famously suspicious of curators; CMSI's principals stress that their roles were those of coordinators and facilitators, their demurral with respect to curatorial agency the result of frequent discussion.

Yet while non-authorial, the remit of these hosts was nonetheless *discursive*, a fact which might productively displace our conception of the curatorial function more generally. Though they proposed no theme to unite disparate artworks, they clearly communicated their platforms' values and took responsibility for framing contemporary art within prevailing discourses and circuits of exchange (local, national, transnational) – a role since assumed by curators.[69] The groups' relations with national institutions varied, but were in each case ambivalent. CMSI was an escape route from the Silpakorn system, but its Thai participants did not need to

—

(ed.), *Operation PRD – Big Tail Elephants: One Hour, No Room, Five Shows* (exh. cat.), Guangzhou: Guangdong Times Museum, 2016.

[68] Santiago Bose, 'No Water, No Books, No Materials, No Money: Cultural Organisations in a Third World Country (A History of the Baguio Arts Guild)', *Artlink*, vol.13, no.3–4, November 1993–March 1994, p.97.

[69] Compare with Rachel Weiss's discussion of the 'decisive innovations' of the third Havana biennial, in *Making Art Global (Part 1)*, *op. cit.*

burn bridges. In the case of Baguio, the national picture was dominated by the 'state vanguardism' of the Cultural Center of the Philippines in Manila, initiated by the repressive Marcos regime yet aesthetically progressive. The Center's inclusive ethno-nationalism often dovetailed with the localist inclinations of artists, as in the Baguio festival series, which it supported. In land-scarce Singapore, meanwhile, TAV was officially registered as an 'art society' in early 1992, allowing its members to apply for limited funding and subsidised spaces in which to work and exhibit. Direct negotiation and collaboration with state agencies were essential to securing venues and visibility.

A third, *geographical* affinity is more suggestive, if less than clear-cut: all three platforms began at some remove from the national centre: Chiang Mai and Baguio in upland retreats, both modernised during the Cold War; and TAV on the fringe of a small, rapidly urbanised island city-state. This centrifugal inclination deserves further research, and must be carefully qualified. In his account of the Baguio Arts Guild's formation, Bose underscores the importance of attracting the attention of the national-institutional centre, whereas Uthit cites coverage in foreign print publications (e.g. articles by Apinan in Australia and Japan in 1993 and 1994) as important early affirmation of the Chiang Mai initiative.[70] Writing alongside Apinan in the Australian journal *Art and Asia Pacific*, Sabapathy described TAV's semi-rural compound as a dynamic alternative centre and a physical and spiritual 'oasis', but hailed the group's 1992 (downtown) collaboration with the National Arts Council on the city's Fringe Festival as a 'breakthrough'.[71]

These three platforms each had one foot in the provinces or countryside, yet their distancing from national centres was not anti-urban – the groups engaged earnestly with city life and urban publics. (They can therefore be distinguished from the harder provincialist postures of, for example, the artist Moelyono's village-embedded pedagogical projects in Indonesia; Paiboon's mural restorations in far-flung provincial temples; or the biennial VIVA EXCON on the Visayas islands, which, after its first and transnational second editions in 1990 and 1992, adopted a more defensive localism.[72]) It was de rigueur for artists of the period to advert to the materials, artisanal values and sociality of premodernity, indexing an experience of urbanisation in train and recognisable everywhere in

—

[70] See, within a section of *Artlink* edited by Apinan, Chanyaporn Chanjaroen, 'Strange Encounters', *Artlink*, vol.13, no.3–4, November 1993–March 1994, pp.32–33; Apinan, 'The Future: Post-Cold War, Postmodernism, Post-Marginalia', *op cit.*, and 'The Potential of Asian Thought: Asian Art in the Post-Hegemonic World' in *Playing with Slippery Lubricants: Apinan Poshyananda, Selected Writings 1993–2004*, Bangkok: Office of Contemporary Art and Culture, 2010.

[71] In another text, Sabapathy underscored the strict limitations on 'alterity' and public critique in Singapore. He mistakenly dates the Fringe Festival collaboration to 1991. See 'Trimurti: Contemporary Art in Singapore' (1993) and 'The Space: An Introduction' (1992), in T.K. Sabapathy, *Writing the Modern*, *op. cit.*, pp.86 and 259.

[72] The Visual Art Exhibition and Conference on the Visayas was initiated by artists-advocacy group Black Artists in Asia, founded in 1986 and spearheaded by Norberto Roldan. With CCP funding, it expressed a different, intra-national sense of 'regionality', gathering and promoting artists from the central band of the Philippine archipelago, initially alongside others from Manila and Baguio. See Ma. Cecilia Locsin-Nava, 'The

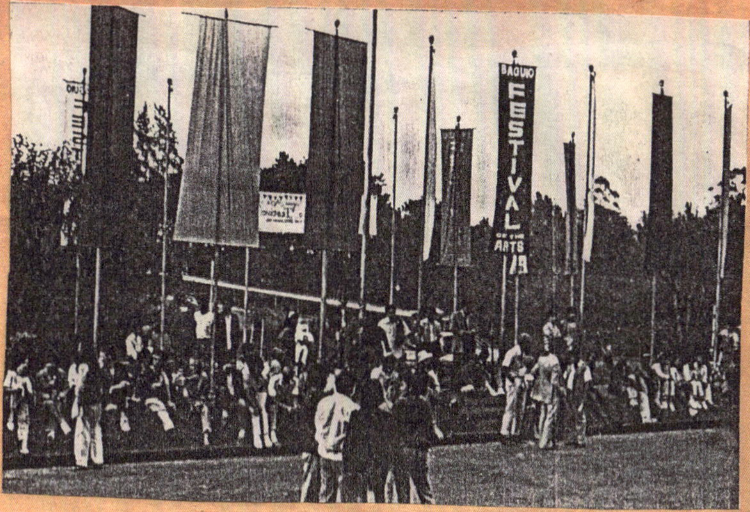
BAGUIO
FESTIVAL
OF THE
ARTS

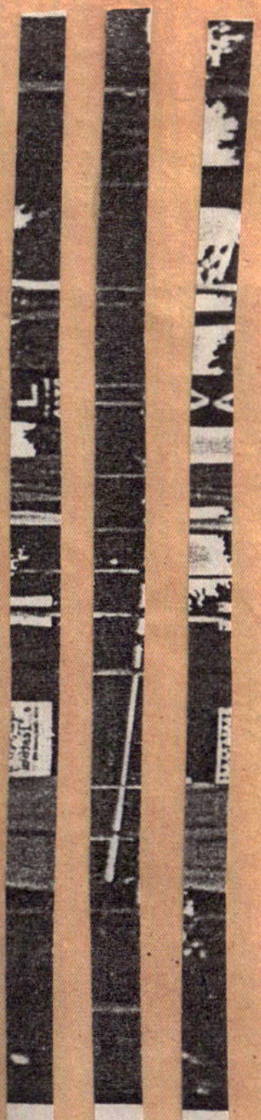

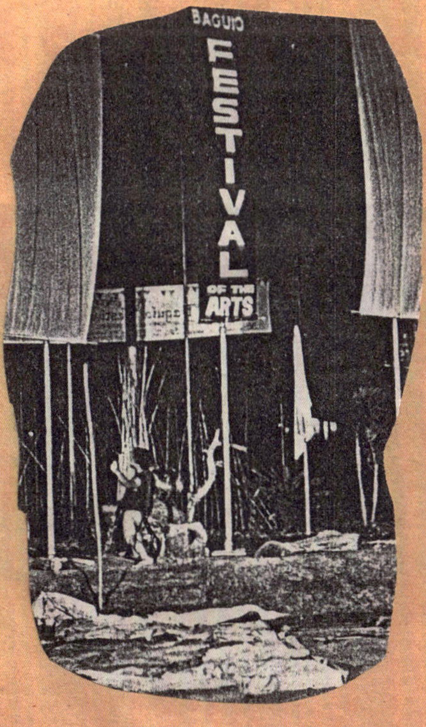
BAGUIO
FESTIVAL
OF THE
ARTS

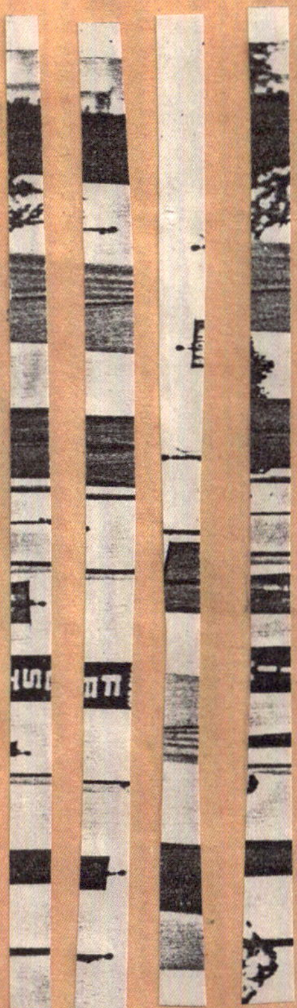

the region. In Chiang Mai, such appeals were often framed by religious sites and practices. In Baguio, they were epitomised by the guild's *dap-ay*, an outdoor circular space where Cordilleran villagers would customarily gather for meetings, storytelling and knowledge-sharing. TAV began amid the last vestiges of peri-urban agriculture, in a disused poultry farm, evoking the *kampong* culture fast being erased by Singapore's public housing juggernaut.[73]

These settings underscore the importance of the *local*, then being enshrined as an unimpeachable virtue in contemporary art. The artists' gatherings may have been transnational but their guiding ethos was *translocal*, an affirmative localism that did not limit their broader, international outlook, but on the contrary was an important footing of their cosmopolitanism. To what extent was this translocalism informed by a shared politics, or concerned with larger, global problems? And as it was not dictated by state institutions, did it articulate an aesthetics to which national form and national experience were no longer central? These should be focal questions for future studies. Flores has hinted that the surpassing of postcolonial academic modernism may have called somehow for dialogical and 'relational' solutions, and certainly, Southeast Asia has seemed disproportionately well represented in these styles on the global circuit. As Flores suggests, these solutions were responsive to local social histories and spatial dynamics, not to Euro-American theories of art. Were they also part of a broader effort to engage publics in more lateral or even democratic national conversations?[74] Much work remains to be done in gathering evidence for and testing such propositions.

The challenge facing us as researchers today is to illuminate the emergence of a distinctively *regional* contemporaneity whose aesthetic and political address was translocal. To this end, compelling models for describing art's globalisation may be found in earlier, pre-national histories. Much recent research by artists and curators has explored the contested and liminal borderlands created arbitrarily by the region's colonisers. Inspiration has been found in the archipelagic cultures of the Malay world and the sprawling upland region known as Zomia, vast geographies in which stable, centralised state administration has been the historical exception

—

Viva Story', in *VIVA EXCON 1990–1996: The Contemporary Visual Arts Movement in the Visayas*, Manila: National Commission for Culture and the Arts, 1998, pp.3–8; and P.D. Flores, 'A Changing World: Phases of the Installative in Southeast Asia', in this volume, pp.264–78.

[73] *Kampong* is the word for 'village' throughout the Malay world. This nostalgia has strong echoes in the region's national art histories before and after the period in question. The appeal of traditional and indigenous modes of sociality is apparently undiminished amongst Baguio artists today, judging by the transposition of the *dap-ay*, made by Bose, into the archive section of 'Sunshower' in Tokyo in 2017 (see n.2). TAV's *kampong* nostalgia had pre-national precedents in the nativism mooted by Singapore's (immigrant Chinese) modern artists after their formative fieldtrip to Bali (1952) and later forays onto the Malay peninsula. See Kevin Chua, 'Painting the Nanyang's Public: notes toward a reassessment,' in J. Clark, M. Peleggi and T.K. Sabapathy (ed.), *Eye of the Beholder: Reception, Audience, and Practice of Modern Asian Art*, Sydney: Wild Peony, 2006, pp.72–93; and Kwok Kian Chow, 'Ten Men Art Group and Field Trips in Southeast Asia', available at http://www.postcolonialweb.org/singapore/arts/painters/channel/18.html (last accessed on 18 July 2018).

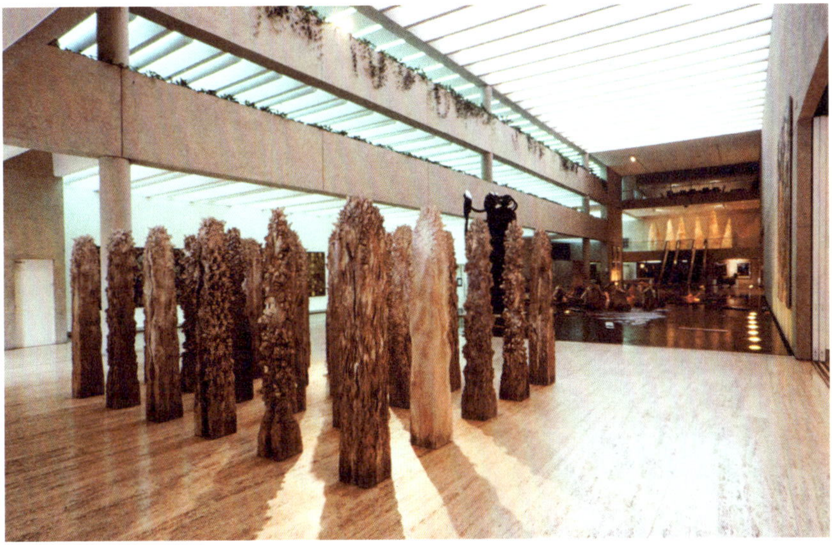

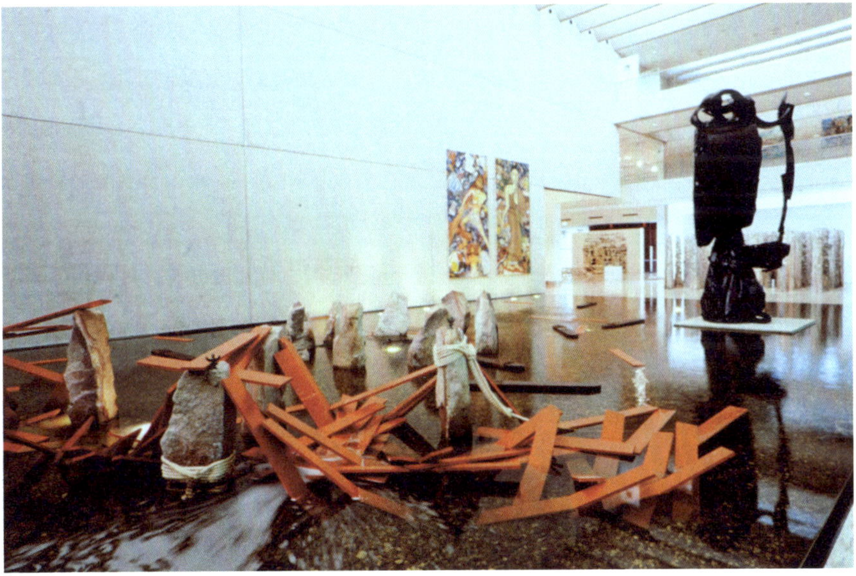

Installation view, 'The First Asia-Pacific Triennial of Contemporary Art' (APT1), Queensland Art Gallery, Brisbane, 1993
Courtesy Queensland Art Gallery | Gallery of Modern Art

Previous spread: Baguio Arts Festival, 1989

rather than the norm – spaces characterised by the coexistence, interdependence and mixing of different identities. Historian Prasenjit Duara even ascribes an innate tolerance to Asia's 'pre-nationalist' societies, in which there was 'non-congruence' between state and culture.[75] Though some of these societies could be called 'fugitive' (following James C. Scott), that is not to say they were isolated.[76] All were the result of sustained migration and vigorous trade with counterparts (including states) within what is now called Southeast Asia as well as beyond the region – exponents of a worldliness yet to be narrowed by national particularism. This pre-national perspective could materially alter our view of the contemporary. For one thing, the globalisation of art in the region might no longer seem like a recent evolution sparked by new, deterritorialising forces. For another, the convergence of autonomous, transnational artist networks after the Cold War may no longer seem so novel. Both might rather be considered reversions to a very old rhythm of encounter and exchange – a dynamic more and more discoverable in the multicentred regional art world of the present – to which the exclusive, centralising logic of national modernity was but a brief and anomalous interruption.[77] Self-organised platforms like CMSI may not have laid explicit claim to premodern or pre-national models; and perhaps their initiators did not ultimately escape the professional and discursive orbit of the nation. But they did manage to communicate local experience to a much larger world, finding palpable sympathies and even solidarities, artist to artist, outside the order of national representation. They were thus able to articulate and renew a fundamental promise of contemporary art, even if they could not fulfil it – that despite the unkept promises of the modern, art might still be a vehicle of progressive social and aesthetic transformation.

—

Epilogue

When I started visiting Thailand in the early 2000s, I tried to meet as many contemporary artists, and see as many of their exhibitions and spaces, as possible. I fast got a sense of what was going on, but like any newcomer to a foreign scene, I wanted to know about people's backgrounds and formative experiences – about the past. From the outset, Chiang Mai Social Installation loomed as a pivotal episode in a largely unwritten collective history. More gradually, I came to understand two things about the Thai past. First, it was seldom composed with reference to material documentation; even when the latter existed, Thais were inclined to elaborate, filter or forget the past, not to record or study it. Yet their reflections could not be deemed less valuable or less telling, or even less accurate, than the documentation one might dig up.[78] A second lesson was more general, and more compromising for the would-be art researcher: it wasn't just young

—

[74] P.D. Flores, 'Actually Existing: Aesthetic Effect and Effective Relations in Southeast Asia', in H. Belting, A. Buddensieg and P. Weibel (ed.), *The Global Contemporary and the Rise of the New Art Worlds*, *op. cit.*, pp.272–76.
[75] P. Duara, 'Asia Redux', *op. cit.*, p.982.
[76] See J.C. Scott, *The Art of Not Being Governed*, *op. cit.*
[77] Oliver W. Wolters, *History, Culture, and Region in Southeast Asian Perspectives*, Ithaca, NY: Cornell Southeast Asia Program and ISEAS, 1999, pp.216–21.

artists living cash-poor, non-archival lives who were accessing the past in this way. It was far more general, a 'total social fact' or *episteme*. It was my first swim against the tides of oral memory and culture. Little did I know how many places, how many histories, how many cultures posed this kind of challenge to an evidence-based scholarship.

The paucity of critical literature was confounding, but also liberating. Research for me was not a forensic process anyway. After years of learning in an imprecise dialogical manner, I had discussed the Chiang Mai festivals with dozens of artists – with older ones who had participated or watched events unfold, with most of the principal organisers, and with younger ones who recalled a watershed they had observed, with excitement, as students. I felt I knew the story pretty well. On visits to Chiang Mai, I developed a relatively solid idea of when, where and how it had unfolded. I knew it had been an attempt to get modern art out of its academic rut and into 'real' social spaces. I had some notion of its non-Thai inspirations, and of the overseas experiences of some of its prime movers before and during the 1990s. I knew it had been a milestone in Thai art's integration into the global circuit, but that it stood out for its abiding localism. Only many years later did it occur to me that nobody, in any of those conversations, *had ever mentioned a single work of art*. At no point did anyone produce a document of an event, nor was it ever suggested that I should look for any. The notion that the Chiang Mai festivals belonged to a kind of spoken lore, no less substantial for being immaterial, was a matter of unexamined and very broad consensus.

If the study of art has too long privileged individuals and their tangible, collectible products, these festivals lend themselves to another kind of history, one in which the encounter between artists and the public takes precedence. If the exhibition of artworks was the pretext for this encounter, it was not necessarily the main point. More crucial, it seems, was the moment of public communion between artists; their coming together from near and far; and their mutual recognition, unmediated by the institutions that had long governed their work and determined its value.

—

[78] Thais are notoriously vague with chronologies, not only because some don't straightforwardly inhabit modern, linear, teleological time, but also because pinning Buddhist dates to Gregorian ones requires an unwieldy, on-the-spot calculation – a subtraction of 543 years – to which the convivial contexts of art conversation in Thailand are not conducive.

Independent Art Festivals in Chiang Mai, 1992–98

'Art Festival: Temples and Cemeteries', November 1992–February 1993

'Chiang Mai Social Installation: Second Art Festival: Temples, Cemeteries, Private-Residences, Public Buildings, Streets, Bridges, Walls, Rivers and Canals, Open Spaces', November 1993–February 1994

Week of Cooperative Suffering, 1–7 January 1995

'Chiang Mai Social Installation: Third Art and Cultural Festival: Temples, Cemeteries, Private-Residences, Public Buildings, Streets, Bridges, Walls, Rivers and Canals, Open Spaces', November 1995–February 1996

Week of Cooperative Suffering, 1–7 January 1996

Week of Cooperative Suffering, 1–7 January 1997

'Chiang Mai Social Installation: Fourth Art and Cultural Festival: Temples, Cemeteries, Private-Residences, Public Buildings, Streets, Bridges, Walls, Rivers and Canals, Open Spaces', December 1997–January 1998

Oral Histories of Chiang Mai Social Installation

> *Many stories go round in the old city. People have been sitting telling stories together without the slightest sigh of boredom for generations. For the old stories, it is easy to combine different fragments or add distortions in various ways, to make the story-telling more interesting. Perhaps this is the reason why these stories are still around. But the city also has more recent stories. Sometimes it is quite difficult to talk about because the people involved may still be sensitive to them or to some details, especially to the final phrase of a story that says: '...and so it all ended.' This is such a story.*
> Araya Rasdjarmrearnsook[1]

Chiang Mai Social Installation has largely been remembered and understood through word of mouth. Oral culture is characterised by performativity, presence, collectivity and non-fixity, all terms that could equally be applied to CMSI; it is also an anarchistic form of remembrance, resistant to governance and control.[2] If storytelling is an appropriate way to remember the events

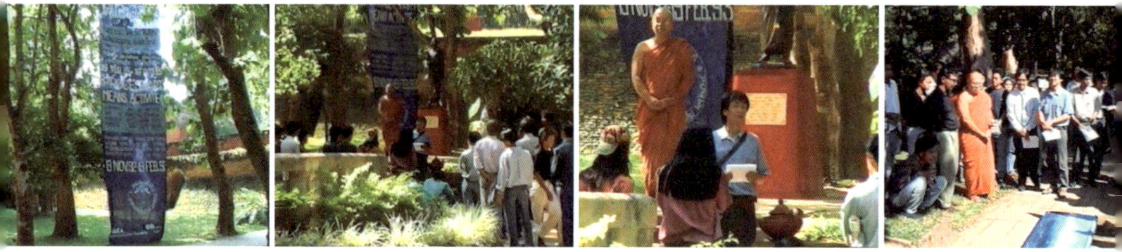

Stills from video footage held in the archive of Uthit Atimana

of CMSI, this is not without complication. Certain tendencies within the festivals offer resistance to the usual methods of historical study, as do certain participants. Some claim that archiving is a Western practice that they do not need, and that CMSI was 'a Buddhist concept, that you can let happen, and let go; we don't archive anything'. Its aims were expansive – a situation in which any activity from any discipline may contribute to *social installation* – while its material traces were few. CMSI was 'kind of a sand palace', as one participant puts it.

—

[1] Araya Rasdjarmrearnsook, 'A narrative of an event that has just come to an end', *Journal of Fine Arts* (Chiang Mai University Faculty of Fine Arts), vol.1 no.1, 2000, p.14.

[2] James C. Scott notes that 'oral tradition is, in most respects, inherently more democratic than a written tradition for at least two reasons. First, the ability to read and write is typically less broadly distributed than the ability to tell stories. Second, there is rarely any simple way to "adjudicate" among variant tellings of oral history; certainly there is no fixed, written text to which the variants can be compared for veracity.' He also notes oral culture's 'inalterable presentness', noting that it 'exists and is sustained only through each unique performance at a particular time and place for an interested audience'. J.C. Scott, *The Art of Not Being Governed: An Anarchist History of Upland Southeast Asia*, New Haven: Yale University Press, pp.229–30.

If this text fixes events in a particular way, it does so to open up the conversation around CMSI, and in the knowledge that it will remain an unruly object of study. Indeed, the increased attention given to CMSI today has caused its historiographic complexities to multiply. Thasnai Sethaseree, a core participant and early chronicler of CMSI, reflects on some of the problems it poses: 'CMSI had several layers of displacement which overlapped one another'; each participant only had a partial view, since 'the scale of operation covered the whole city'; and 'even those who witnessed the same moment in history came out telling different tales'. Participants also have a tendency to expand or revise their tales, with interviewees telling 'one thing the first time, but another thing the second'. An exchange between Santiphap Inkong-ngam and Manuporn Luengaram reflects the general condition: 'I am surprised that I can hardly remember any works'; 'our conversation is very much about the vibe of the festival rather than the work exhibited'.

Such accounts correspond with the experience of producing the present text: rather than converging on a set of singular figures, works or events, CMSI has tended to multiply in the retelling. What follows is by no means comprehensive or definitive or without contradiction, but is offered in the hope that something

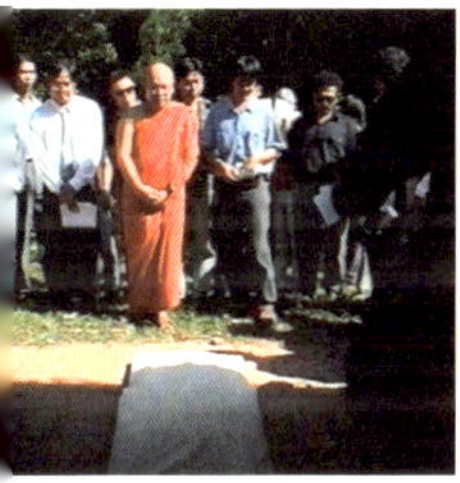
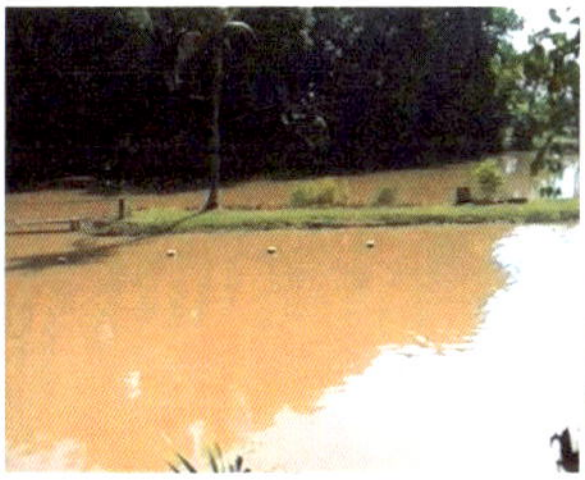
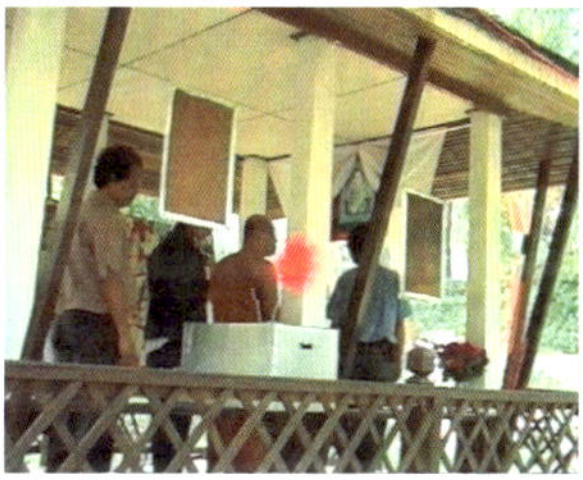
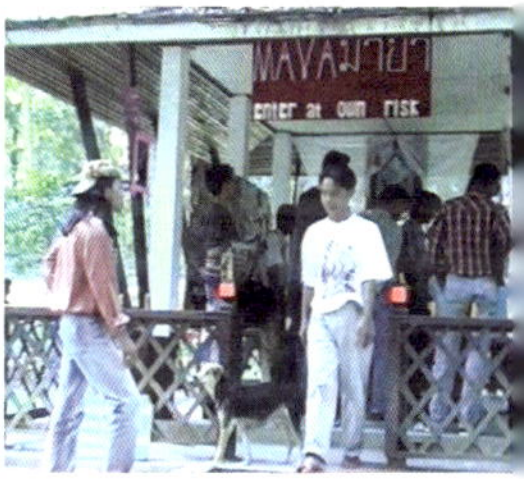

of the spirit of the festivals may emerge. This oral history builds on four extended research interviews conducted by Gridthiya Gaweewong with the assistance of Penwadee Nophaket Manont and Atikom Mukdaprakorn in 2015; around twenty newly commissioned interviews conducted by Manuporn Luengaram and by May Adadol Ingawanij, David Morris and David Teh in 2017–18; and many hundreds of informal conversations.[3] The concepts and themes that

—

[3] 2015 interviewees were Mit Jai Inn, Navin Rawanchaikul, Thasnai Sethaseree and Uthit Atimana; they were conducted in Thai and translated by Inkdot Translation House, Bangkok. 2017–18 interviewees were Angkrit Ajchariyasophon, Arahmaiani, Araya Rasdjarmrearnsook, David Blamey, Chumpon Apisuk, Gridthiya Gaweewong, Koh Nguang How, Kade Javanalikhikara, Kamin Lertchaiprasert, Tei Kobayashi, Jay Koh, Kosit Juntaratip, Ray Langenbach, Mit Jai Inn, Varsha Nair, Narumol Thammapruksa, Navin Rawanchaikul, Alfred Pawlin, Phaptawan Suwannakudt, Rirkrit Tiravanija, Santiphap Inkong-ngam, Supachai Satsara, Sutthirat Supaparinya, Tawatchai Puntusawasdi, Thanom Chapakdee, Thasnai Sethaseree, Thatree Pokawanich, Thepsiri Sooksopa, Uthit Atimana and others; interviews in Thai with Angkrit, Araya, Chumpon, Kade, Kamin, Rirkrit, Supachai, Tawatchai, Thanom, Thatree and Thepsiri were translated by Manuporn, and Narumol and Santiphap by Nuttha Isaraphitakkul. Unless noted, quotations are taken from these interviews or archival materials held by Uthit, with Thai text translated by Chanon Kenji Praepipatmongkol. The text was written and composed by David Morris.

emerged are what shape this text: 'Beginnings / False Starts / Interruptions'; 'Temples and Cemeteries'; 'Social Installation'; 'Culturalists / Inter-Expression'; 'Artist-to-Artist'; 'Non-Artists / Midnight University / Cooperative Suffering'; 'Arrivals / Influx of Global Dynamic Torrent / Disappearance'; 'Afterlives'. It is not expected that readers will proceed systematically from start to end. Above all, what follows is an attempt to populate the memory of these festivals – to articulate CMSI through its participants and to collect some of its stories.
– David Morris

Beginnings / False Starts / Interruptions
'Chiang Mai is a city of custom and tradition. In addition, it is a place with many beautiful girls (according to the "owners" of these Northern Thai girls), and lots of nature. All of these are attractive for tourists, landscape-lovers (who mostly come from other places to the mountains of Chiang Mai), craftsmen and people interested in tradition. This brings together many different interpretations of the town. Some may get along quite well, but others, like beer combined with cake, may be proof of bad taste. At night, while long rows of candles in small clay trays are lighted in front of the houses as a token of respect for the place's spirits,

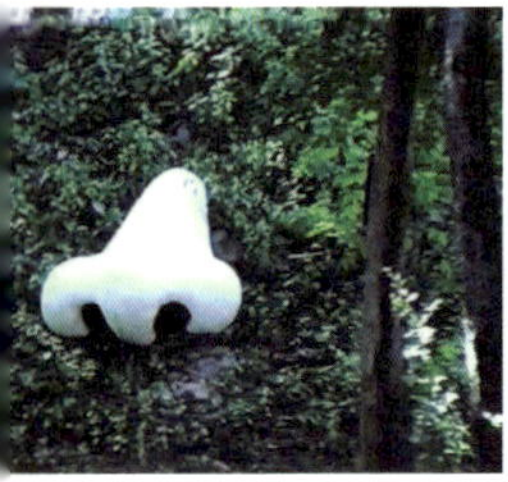
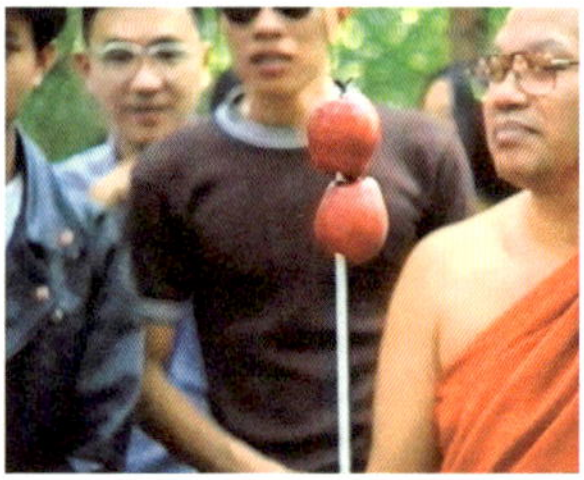
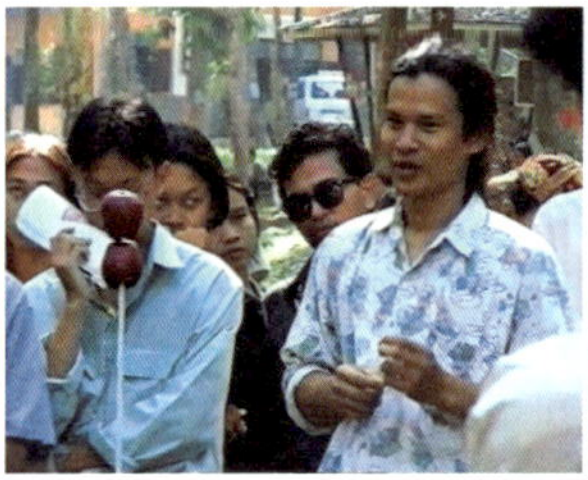
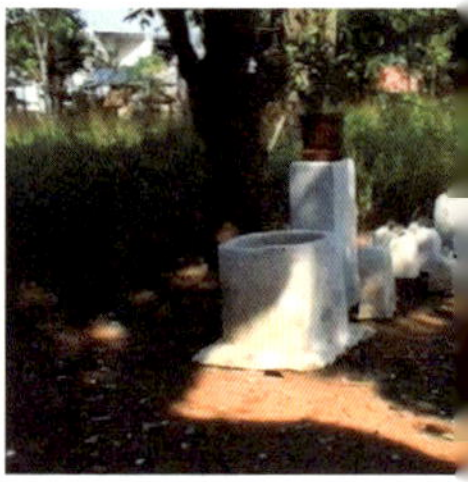

the daughters of the houses are working in karaoke clubs and bars under the artificial lights of night. On some white painted walls of old Buddhist temples in town, one finds fixed labels with the names of guesthouses in English. On Friday, working people sit in traditional outfits in front of their computers in the bank, the airport or in their offices. They go back home in the evening through the well-lit tourist scene. As for the arts, traditional art has dominated this city for many generations and deals mainly with beliefs, rituals and things that are familiar to the local people, mostly located within the temple compounds. But finally, space and time had to be divided to provide the possibility for the emergence of contemporary art.'[4]

Accounts vary as to the beginning of CMSI and rarely recall events in strict sequence. In the digital archive assembled under the guidance of core CMSI members from the materials of Uthit Atimana, a performance-installation led by Supachai Satsara from one of the middle festivals is indexed as 1991, a year before the first festival, 'Art Festival: Temples and Cemeteries'. If the timeline is not fixed, this reflects little more than the fact that, in the shared memory of CMSI, chronology is not of great importance. Supachai recalls various gatherings

—
[4] Araya, 'A narrative of an event that has just come to an end', *op. cit.*, pp.14–15.

of artists and friends at that time, for discussions of art, life and social issues, but CMSI's *beginning* is not something he remembers. For him, there was something like a 'group spirit'. 'I'm not interested in whose ideas started CMSI, I'm interested in the process – that students came together as a group to brainstorm and to challenge the teachers. In fact, it is not possible to say who started CMSI. … Anyone can say anything to take credit for it. But I'm interested in the process that shook this place – shook it like an earthquake. Even people from Bangkok recognised what was happening in Chiang Mai.'

'CMSI in its early years was the operation of a small group of students', says Thasnai Sethaseree. 'The most active and enthusiastic were the juniors – Navin [Rawanchaikul]'s class, Kosit [Juntaratip]'s class, Adul Boonsham's class. They were the main force behind the operation. Early on, there was nothing with such a distinctive structure as a *social installation*; mostly it was just classwork that was moved to be displayed at Wat Umong and other places.' 'Uthit saw potential in me, as I was a student brimming with questions, always ready to learn. Mit [Jai Inn] had just came back from abroad, and Uthit told me I needed to meet him. Mit was also burning with enthusiasm. We talked about philosophy and social

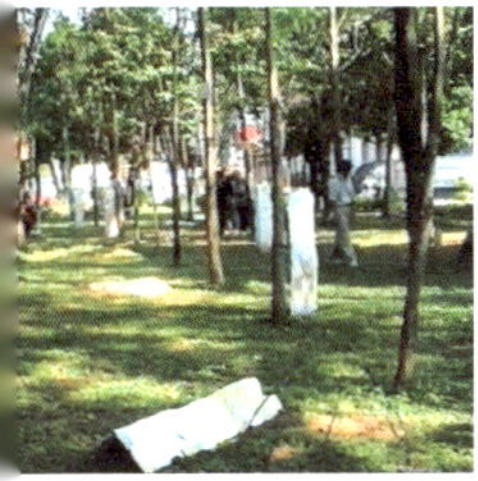
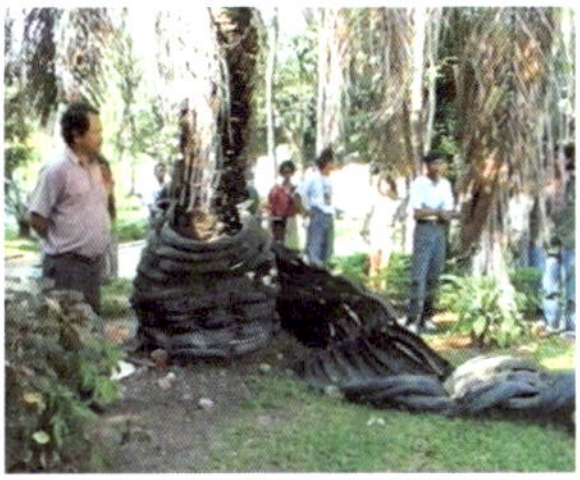
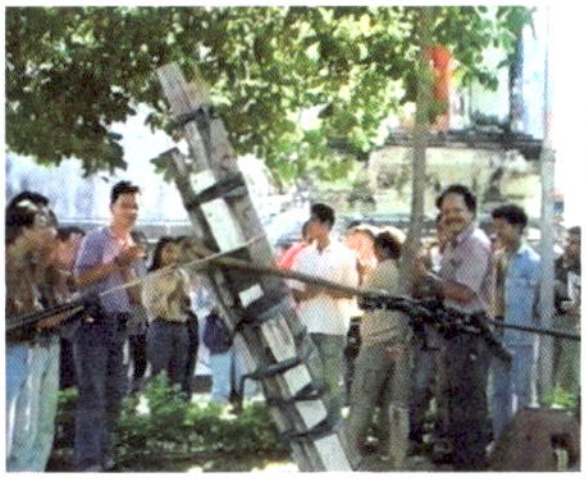
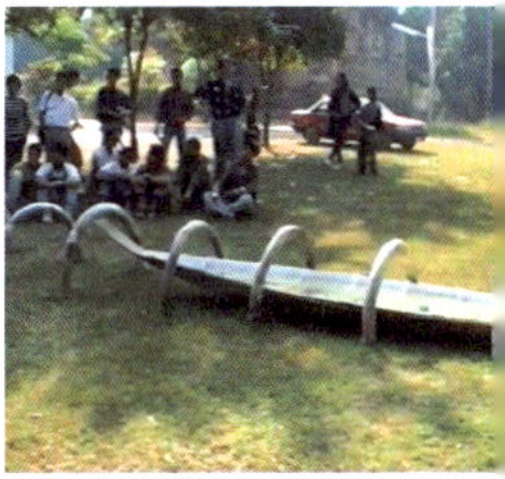

issues. Then, both of them started talking about Chiang Mai Social Installation. I was still a freshman. They recruited me on the spot. … But when I joined, I didn't work alone. I brought fellow freshmen with me.'

'It was our desire that started it all', says Uthit. 'I felt that, hey, I was teaching contemporary art and talking about Joseph Beuys and Marcel Duchamp in classes, while other people – parents out there – knew nothing about all this. So I felt a little ashamed about what I was doing. It was like an alien culture. It wasn't serving the society. … Then Mit Jai Inn came back from abroad, an ambitious man full of exotic ideas. We started to talk about what we wanted to do, about the Venice Biennale, documenta, socially [engaged] art, about how to get the audience's attention … that sort of stuff. But the problem was, our talks often ended with us having to wait for government support, infrastructure and things of that nature. When Mit joined the conversation, we discussed and realised we didn't have to wait that long to start cultural activities. We just needed to understand the pressing issues and limitations, to then transform the issues and limitations into an activity. This is what we believed. There was no need to wait, we could do it right away. Saying something that benefits the public could happen on a daily basis, and shouldn't have to wait for funding or anything else.'

Having left Thailand in the late 1980s to go travelling and in the hope of making a living as a street artist – 'like all the Thai boys, I was just a hippy at that time, I knew nothing' – Mit returned in 1992. 'I had to come back home. As a former communist, what caught my interest at the time was social class. There was a huge gap between people in Bangkok and rural areas. Even today, it persists. And the accessibility of resources and spaces was similarly limited. Just like today, it was in the hands of one group. I wasn't really interested in art. Once I came back to Chiang Mai, I met Uthit Atimana and Montien Boonma. I could sense that they felt frustrated. Lots of students began to graduate, but their futures looked gloomy. No art facilities were available. Uthit was also interested in social issues, but there was no space available for him.'

Araya notes that CMSI emerged in the 1990s following a series of shifts in Thailand's art-institutional landscape, suggesting that the starting point 'may have been the creation of an art academy – at Chiang Mai University – more than fifteen years ago'. Bangkok had long been the centre of the Thai art world. A 1993 guide by Apinan Poshyananda, for the Australian magazine *Artlink*, lists around forty venues in which art might be seen, from galleries and cafes to hotels and

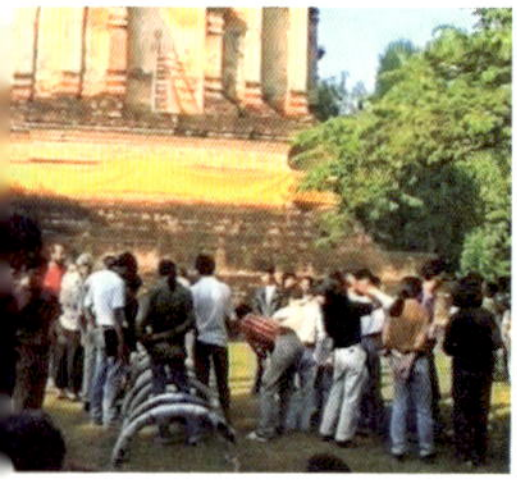

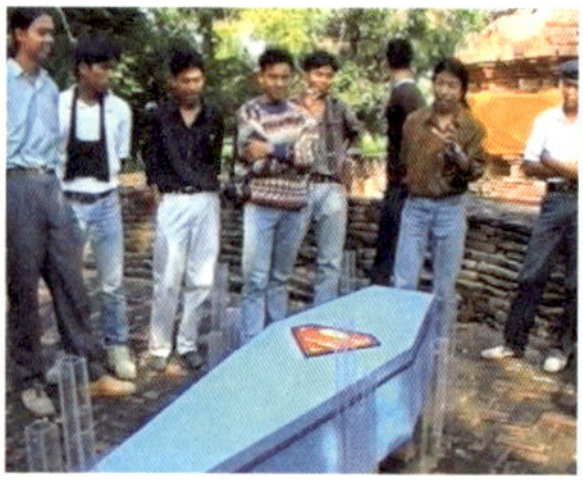

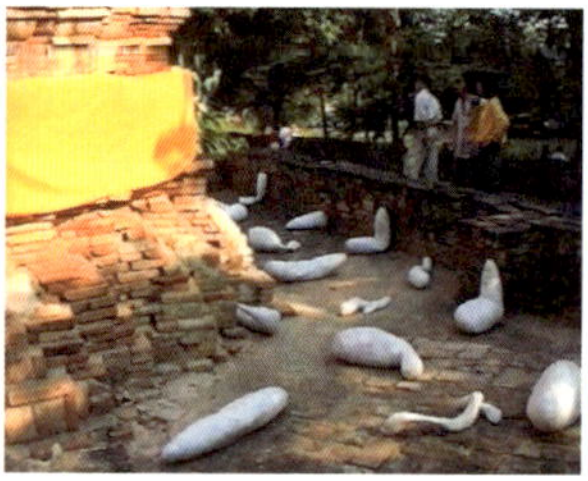

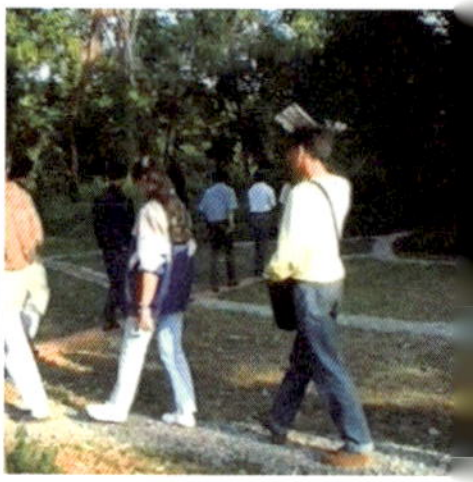

banks, only four of which were outside the capital. Until the 1980s, Silpakorn was Thailand's only fine arts university. With close links to national, religious and corporate institutions and systems of patronage, it was the main route for young artists looking to make their way into the system. (Mit and Uthit had both left Silpakorn on bad terms – expulsion, in Mit's case.) But alternatives emerged when several new art schools opened in the 1980s, including Chiang Mai, where certain faculty members were recognised as establishing a site for alternative practices. 'We should give credit to Montien. He was like a magnet, and laid the foundations for a contemporary art environment', says Uthit. 'Araya Rasdjarmrearnsook was there as well. She's been another progressive professor, introducing a new academic model in which technical skill is not the only focus, instead focussing on art as a cultural concept. This situation gave birth to the new generation of our students.' And the situation was particular to the Chiang Mai province. 'Those with a progressive mindset, who rejected mainstream education and wished to create an alternative, they would come to teach at Chiang Mai.'

'At the time,' says Kamin Lertchaiprasert, 'there was no art centre. But there was a plan to build one. Mit opposed it – he said, "Why have the art centre? It's like driving a Mercedes-Benz in the middle of rice fields, on dirt roads."' What little artistic scene there was locally was quite traditional, says Kade Javanalikhikara, then a faculty member at Chiang Mai University. 'There was an artist group called Lanna Group, which existed before the Faculty of Fine Arts. Most of them graduated from Silpakorn and Poh Chang Academy of Arts and moved to Chiang Mai. Their works were rather traditional in style – landscape and portrait painting. They exhibited together at a public library.' Chumpon Apisuk had exhibited at an old library building of the Faculty of Fine Arts (since destroyed). 'I was working with students on the issue of waste disposal at the university. At that time, many old historical buildings in Chiang Mai were torn down to make way for new buildings. I brought the stones from demolished buildings to show in my installation.' Tap Root Society, established by Chumpon in Chiang Mai in 1988, was a short-lived outlier in the institutional landscape then, 'an art centre where artists and community-development workers can meet and join together to organise events, exhibitions and workshops on various subjects and mediums'. Having coordinated a residency programme at the Bhirasri Institute of Modern Art (BIMA) in Bangkok in the 1980s, Chumpon was experienced in bringing artists to Thailand. Via initiatives such as Concrete House (from 1993) and the annual Asiatopia Performance Art Festival (from 1998), he fostered a network of artists, especially ones working with performance (though 'at that time in Thailand, there weren't so-called performance artists').

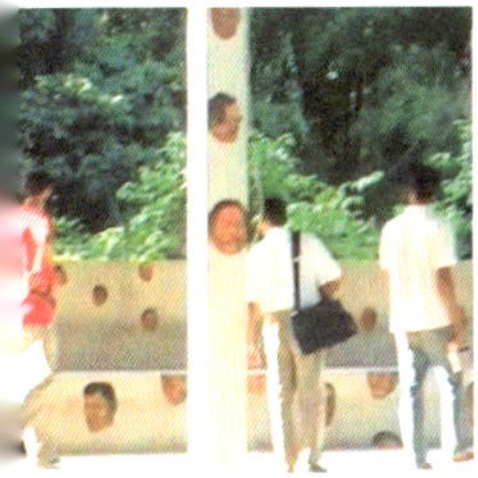
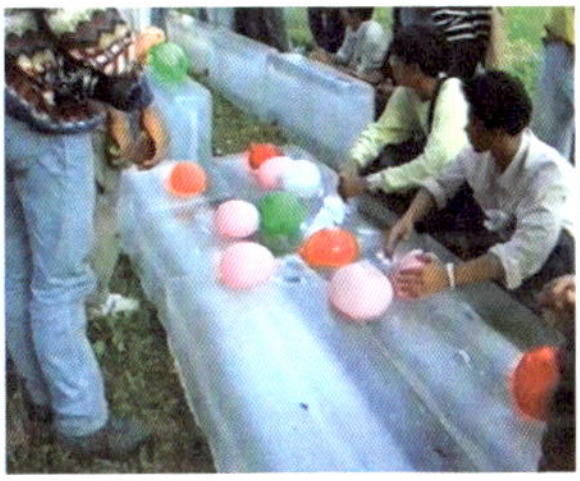
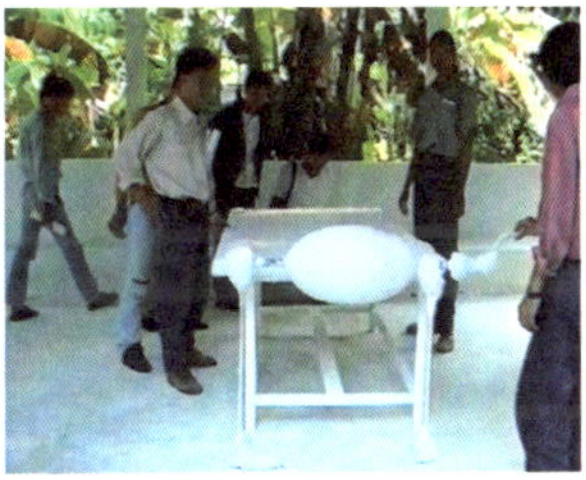
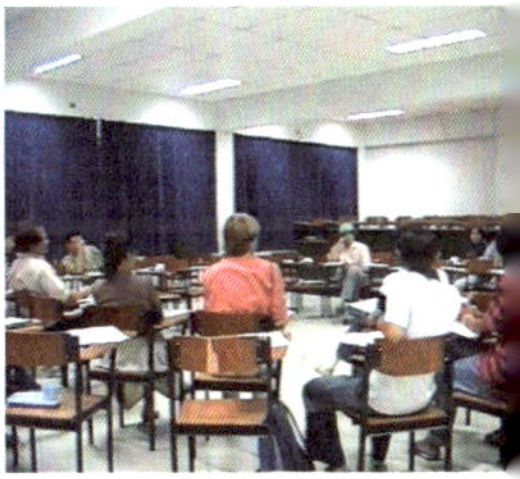

Koh Nguang How, one of the founders of Singapore artists' initiative The Artists Village, says that his 'introduction to Thai contemporary art started in 1989, which was the year The Artists Village was officially named. I had personally tried to connect The Artists Village with Tap Root Society in Chiang Mai, but Tap Root had closed due to flooding and evolved into the Concrete House in Nonthaburi, near Bangkok. In 1993, Chumpon and I initiated "Sense Yellow" p.18
– an exhibition and performance event of Thai, Singaporean and German artists in Bangkok and Nonthaburi.' In 1992–93, a small number of exhibitions were organised in Bangkok by artists in the CMSI circle, including Montien Boonma and his students, who travelled down from Chiang Mai. Several took place at Visual Dhamma Gallery, run by Alfred Pawlin, and one at a space of the pp.15–16
National Gallery. Uthit describes the latter as an 'ugly' and 'anti-art' gesture – 'We invite our friends and say "you can do what you want".' 'Sense Yellow' originally drew from a somewhat separate circle of artists – 'the Asiatopia artists' according to one observer's retrospective point of view – but overlapped with CMSI once it gained momentum. The exhibition took place as part of 14 October commemorations, associated with the brief moment of optimism for Thailand's political future that came after the 1973 student uprising that ended Thanom Kittikachorn's military dictatorship, which abruptly ended with the Thammasat University massacre in 1976.

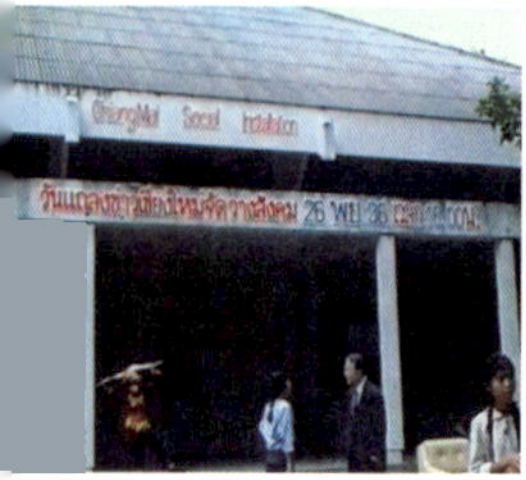

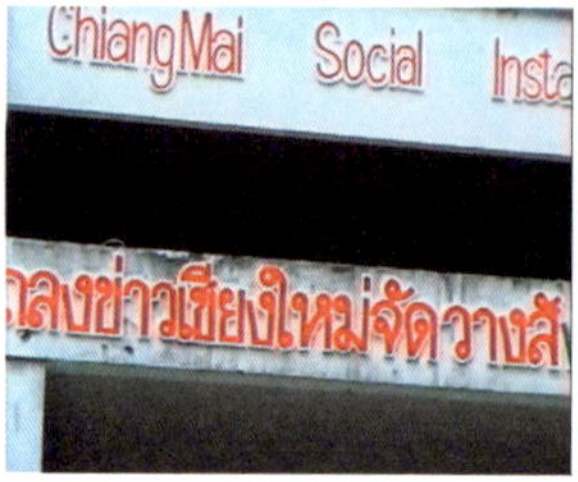

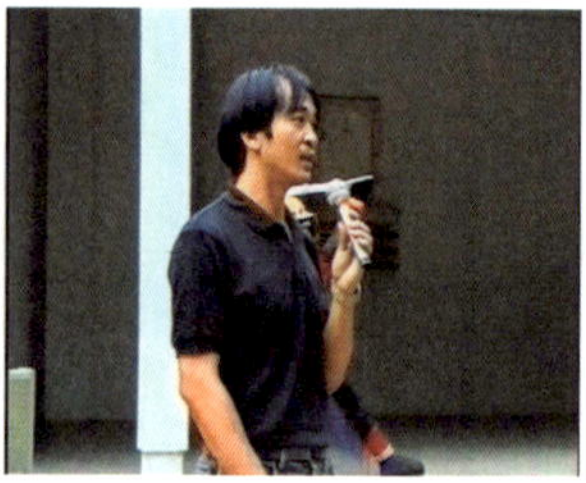

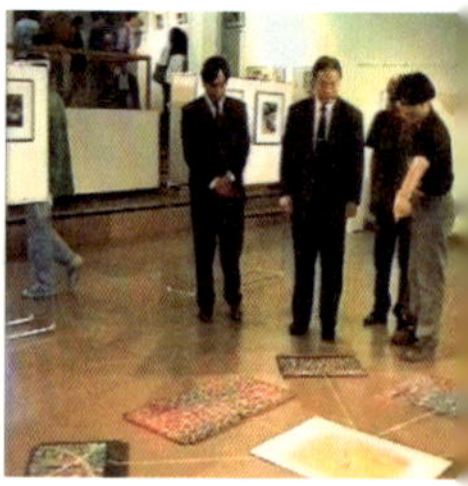

In the 1980s, Chiang Mai received an influx of progressive intellectuals and activists who had gone into hiding following the events of 1976. Chumpon notes that the loosening of the political situation under army commander-in-chief cum Prime Minister Prem Tinsulanonda (in office 1980–88) allowed 'intellectuals and former students, who had fled to the jungle, to return to the city. At the same time, people who had studied abroad also returned. They met, collaborated and organised together. Old friends reunited to create movements; social and cultural movements began to harmonise. One group, after leaving the jungle, worked in NGO jobs, while another worked in the cultural field. As a result, a cultural movement started to take shape. However, I am not certain whether [CMSI was] a continuation of these little things that happened earlier. Or perhaps it might relate to the political situation after Black May 1992, which made people want a release. … Artistic and cultural movements in Thailand took place periodically, during times of distress. Our movement was the sign of this period.'

Thasnai's account of the anti-government protests of 1992, preceding Black May's violent crackdown, picks up on a mix of festivity and peer-to-peer communication, and a certain mobilisation of the sacred. 'People from different classes and walks of life joined the protest, but the majority was comprised of white collar, urban residents. Unlike the rigid top-down hierarchy of the Thai student movement of the 1970s, the organization of the middle class demonstrators was made possible by modern telecommunication technology – mobile phones. Initially, the rallies had a playful sense of festivity, where theater and dance mingled with free speech, music, food-vendors and spectators. Traffic in and around Rajadamnern area was totally disrupted. Ribbons attached to the trees along the avenue marked it as a sacred place, creating a surreal atmosphere on this corridor of power.'[5] Following the shock of Black May, artists began to identify with progressive causes, and also began to incorporate previously suspect 'Western' influences into their work. 'Such phenomena are not the fallout or the after-effect of political developments. Rather, these are two streams of events running parallel, depending on each other and giving each other strength.'[6]

'Before CMSI there were already various groups seeking new possibilities to express their artistic ideas', says Supachai. 'During Black May there were many

—

[5] Thasnai Sethaseree, 'Overlapping Tactics and Practices at the Interstices of Thai Art', unpublished doctoral thesis, Chiang Mai: Chiang Mai University, 2011.
[6] Chumpon Apisuk, 'Unpredictable Repercussions', *Artlink*, vol.13, no.3–4, November 1993–March 1994, p.23.

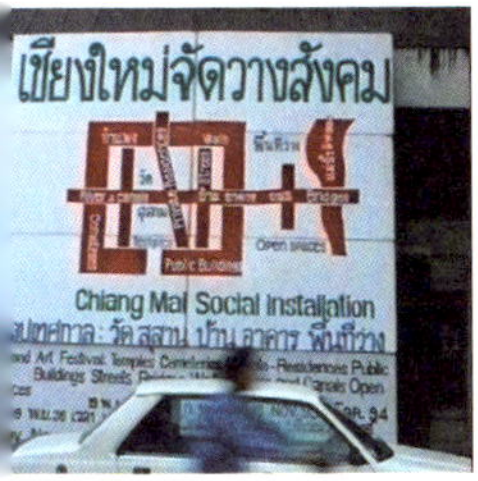

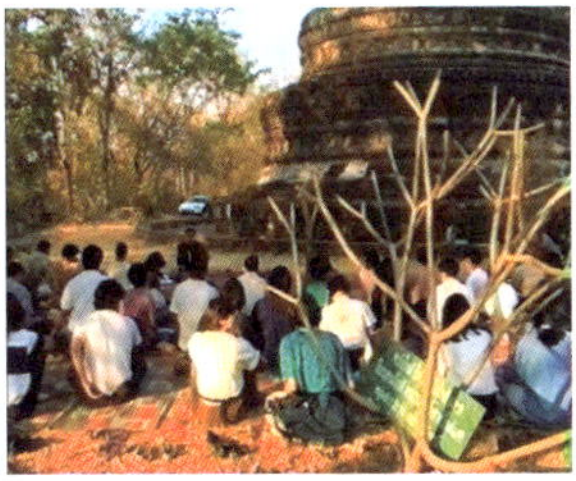
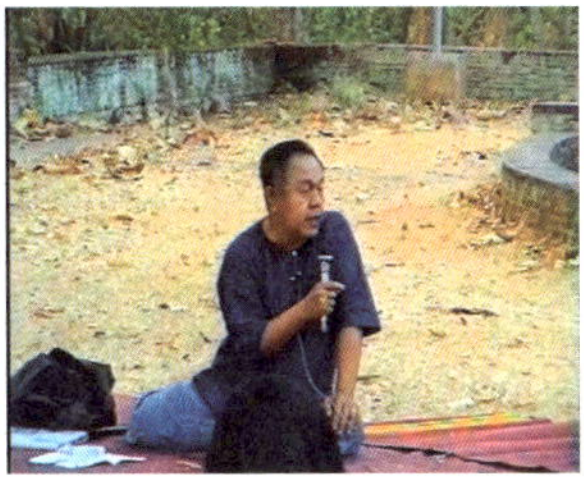
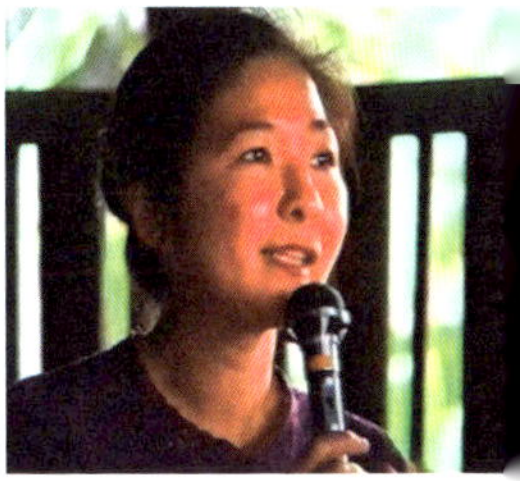

teachers, thinkers and activists – not only artists – who gathered and formed a group at Chiang Mai University. This was the same time that the first [CMSI] event, "Temples and Cemeteries", began.' Mit, upon his return to Chiang Mai in 1992, 'showed us brochures and a map of an exhibition they'd had in Vienna', says Navin. 'You had to knock on the door and go into different private residences to see the artworks. I don't know what the content of the show was, but Mit had this map, and he said it would be a good idea to do something. And then suddenly, he talked with Uthit and they decided to use temples and cemeteries – temples as connected to Thai *life*, from birth, education, etc., and cemeteries as *death*.'

Temples and Cemeteries
'Why temples and cemeteries? "Thai people are more familiar with temples than art galleries, as it's purely a part of Western culture to view art in galleries", says Uthit Atimana. ... "This has made it hard for Thai contemporary artists to communicate with the public. So we are bringing art to places which people are already familiar with." Artists who are exhibiting also believe art is somehow related to religion, which makes the place more suitable as an art venue. "Temples and cemeteries have unique characteristics which encourage people to contemplate life. Unlike ordinary galleries, these places have their own spirit."'[7]

'Art Festival: Temples and Cemeteries' opened in November 1992. The abbot of Wat Umong welcomed the intervention. 'I am very happy to have art exhibited in the temple. Because professors, students and artists have always learned that art, over the course of history, has migrated from temples into other spaces. ... Art slowly disappeared from temples and became the expertise of civilians. ... But this current exhibition shows that the temple, once again and as always, is at the heart of social life in Thailand, no matter what region. Wat Umong accepts art into its spaces because this is an opportunity to promote mutual understanding that is beneficial for everyone.' He also noted that the temple 'does not only exhibit art. I explained to the festival organisers that in this space we have shown horror films, Thai and Chinese films. We have even projected films in the tunnels – anything that is not pornographic, anything that is morally edifying.'[8]

pp.86–93

—

[7] Chanyaporn Chanjaroen, 'Art is a Temple', *The Nation*, 19 January 1993. A few years later, quoted in another news report, Uthit was more pragmatic: 'We first thought of temples as venues because Chiang Mai has plenty and it would be easy to ask permission to place artworks in them.' Pattara Danutra, 'Up, up, and away', Bangkok Post, 5 September 1997.

[8] Video documentation (trans. Chanon), c.1992, from Uthit's archive.

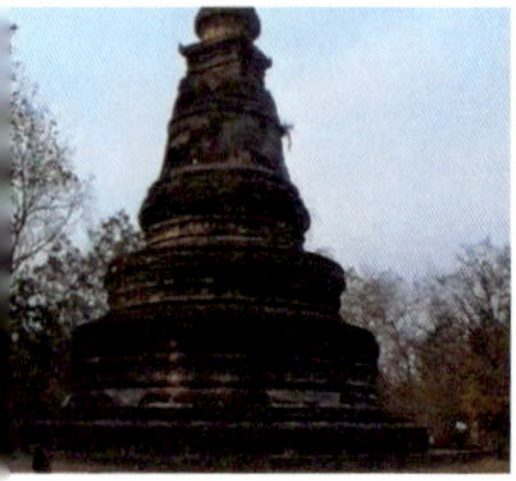
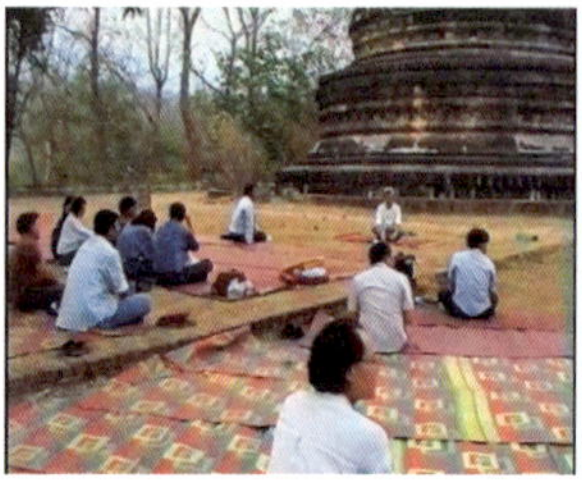
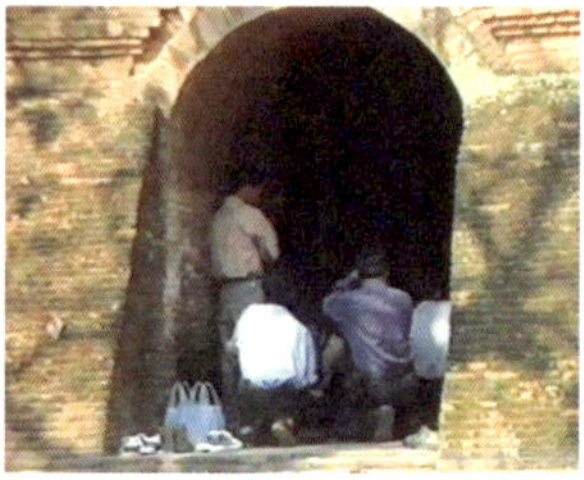
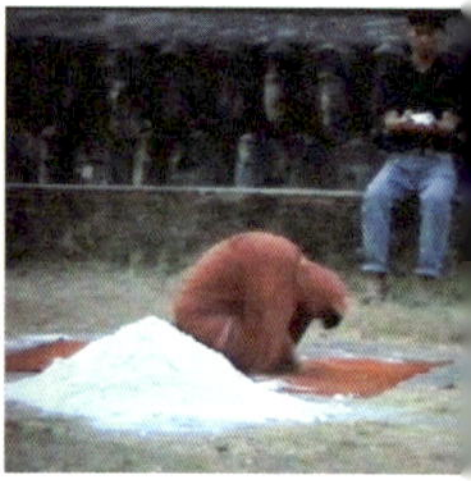

'The first year was about friends.' Navin Rawanchaikul was appointed as a kind of project manager, responsible for organising the installation of works. 'They used my home address, phone number and everything. At that time we had no mobile phones, so the address and phone number was my dad's house.' (Other participants also tell the same story of their homes being used as the main point of contact for CMSI.) 'It was like a class, one student would say, "I'll do this", and we'd give comments. Uthit and Mit [Jai Inn] or Montien [Boonma] mostly gave the feedback, whereas my role was more like management. I had to connect with the temples, ask permission from the monks, install the works. I had a truck, so I'd do the transport. But after the opening, my work was pulled down, damaged. And I asked the monks who did it – "just people who came here, they were angry".' Thai English-language broadsheet *The Nation* reported that 'many of these creative art works "disappeared" quite early on during the period of exhibition. Some were destroyed, due to misunderstanding, greed and ignorance.'

p.92

The group was not fazed by these hostile reactions. Navin's work, a Buddhist-inflected assemblage of objects and photographs around the water-filled wood form of a canoe, was demolished within a week of the opening, apparently at the order of a senior monk in Bangkok and a lecturer from Chiang Mai University. Yet, '"we expected this from the start. … We know that there are still many people who don't understand contemporary art. The abbot told me that those who ordered the demolition think my works are disrespectful to Wat Chet Yod." Wat Chet Yod houses the relics of the king who founded Chiang Mai 700 years ago. "We don't mind at all if our works are destroyed or stolen", said Uthit. "One of our ideas is that artworks have no material value. We didn't create these works for sale or any other commercial reason. Just the fact that we have created them and worked accordingly to our concepts is enough."'[9]

'At the end of the first year, we wanted it to be local and accessible to rural people', says Mit. 'The title wasn't defined yet. We just didn't want to display art in a white cube, or mix it with other projects. We just wanted a small and temporary exhibition. Even the documenting process, Uthit loved to do it. But for me, once it ended, I just let it go; we just packed up and went home. Then a new day began, and we went on living our lives. For a social context, we made use of local traditions which saw people gathering in one place. You could call it a "public sphere". … Back then, we just wanted to do something that wouldn't pile up

—
[9] Chanyaporn, 'Art is a Temple', *op. cit.*

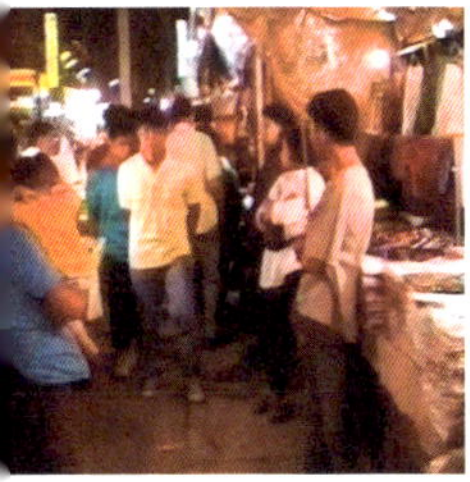
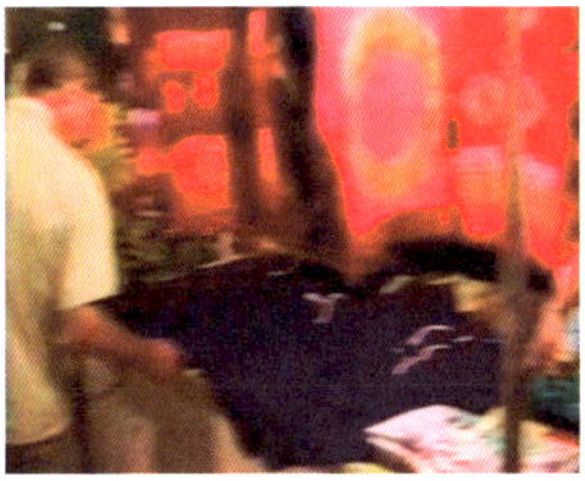
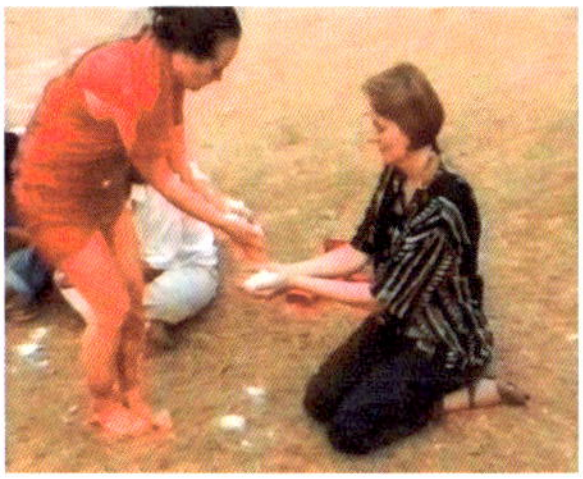
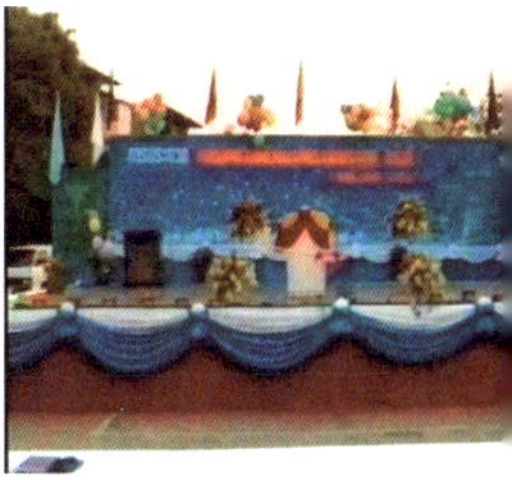

in a conventional box, that didn't follow social norms or formalities. We didn't want anything to be formal at all.' Referring to the strength of anti-establishment sentiment and institutional critique during the 1990s, Mit sums up the general feeling: 'Like the idea of burning down a museum.'

Social Installation

According to Uthit Atimana, 'there are two types of installation: one is confined to the gallery; the other is site-specific, fixed to a certain space. This form of art-making was becoming well known. So, we thought using "installation" in the title was a suitable way to explain [what we were doing]. The word "social" was clear in itself – it emphasised the society. We agreed that not only artists should have the right to discuss social issues. Everyone could contribute. So in the second year, pp.94–123 the concept and the logic of Chiang Mai Social Installation were rather clear.' This next festival was the first to be named Chiang Mai Social Installation – *Chiang Mai jat wang sang khom* – presented in both English and Thai. *Jat wang* ('social installation') is an unusual turn of phrase in Thai. For Thasnai Sethaseree, 'it is a form of "making space for the public"'; and Mit Jai Inn emphasises it as an ephemeral act connected to daily practice, to putting something into a particular order and then letting it be.

The idea of 'social installation' is remembered as originating from various participants, not least Mit. 'Uthit always complained that we couldn't do much; that we were just side dishes in our society. How could we engage in or encourage social dynamics? Then the words "social installation" popped into my head – for it to suit Thai society, we could just install it, and then discard it. Each project was meant to be ephemeral. We must admit that we can't truly establish society. Thailand has always been an authoritarian society. As witnessed today, once we can't fight for more, arts have to fade out and become disorderly, scattered.'

The group issued a kind of mission statement or manifesto to 'promote the pp.96–97 essence of an ideal society', 'balance the effects of materialism and consumerism', 'promote the value of cooperation, and to encourage communal thoughts and actions', 'expand the scope and influence of *art activities* to enter the realm of all *creative activities*'. They were also to pursue 'other activities such as speech, discussions, statistical research and other forms of research', as well as 'provid[ing] services and promot[ing] social information through lectures at centres of education, pamphlets and brochures, etc.'. Noting that 'social installation' is something distinct from 'art & environment' or 'public art', they announced: 'Society will be changed into a new social installation.' The second festival had more than double the participants of the previous edition, and around fifty artist projects. Its budget remained minimal; while Montien Boonma and Araya Rasdjarmrearnsook attempted to solicit help from collectors, Uthit remembers that finding sponsors was difficult 'because of the project's eccentric nature'. Artists funded their own projects, with logistical support provided by CMSI's organising group plus a network of friends and family. In Araya's words, 'We used our private connections to build a group.'

'It was a great leap forward in the second year', says Uthit, with the framework of installation extending into the space of Chiang Mai in its entirety. As the third pp.138–39 edition announced, 'Any activity, any topic, any means of expression from any social discipline can become a creative activity that contributes to *Social installation*'; it was all part of an attempt to '"rouse" an atmosphere' and promote values of 'being in the "present"', of 'peaceactivity' and 'cooperative consciousness'. 'Participants at CMSI made use of every space in the city, and they transformed their original functions', says Thasnai. 'Spaces of state authority/power, for instance Tha Pae Gate, became areas of cultural activity. Commercial spaces and hospitals had their functions polluted and changed. Public space was disrupted, some works stopped the traffic. ... I mean, the boundary of a road, a space reserved for car users, was contravened by alien objects; this paved the way for other things to happen.'

If temples and cemeteries were originally chosen as sites of everyday social and aesthetic experience where the people of Chiang Mai could be introduced contemporary artworks, by this time it was also clear that everyday temple practices were sure to resonate for the art-inflected bystander. This was true for visitors from afar as well as more local spectators. *The Nation*'s account of the first festival concludes: 'Given the unusual nature of the "galleries", unexpected and rather spiritual incidents can happen. This writer visited Wat Padaeng cemetery,

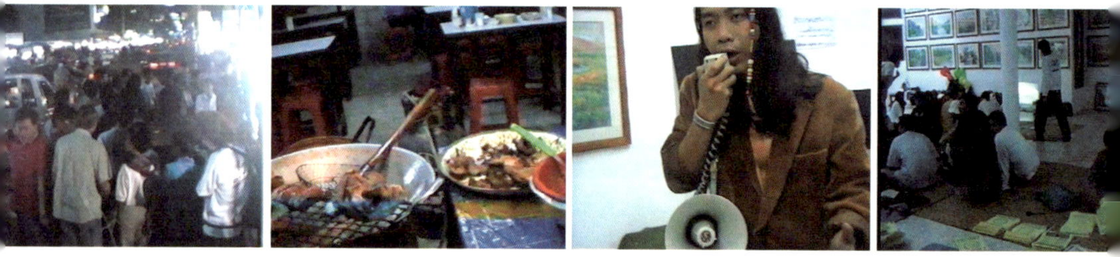

quite late in the evening. There was a simple funeral pyre, on which a body was being burned, outside a coffin, without ceremony. A very rare sight indeed.'[10]

Visitors were appreciative of CMSI's unboundedness. 'It was a social installation all the time', notes one Thai returnee, and 'difficult to know what's the art and what isn't', as a journalist put it at the time. For David Blamey, who arrived as part of a delegation of artists from London in 1996, this was all part of the experience. 'Over the course of the week's public art production and consumption, it wasn't

---

[10] Chanyaporn, 'Art is a Temple', *op. cit.*

always clear how much of other people's work we had seen, or indeed, how much of an audience – if any – our own work had gained. In the wake of the YBA [Young British Artists] phenomenon in the UK, the absence of sensationalism and egoism in the Chiang Mai situation was a joy. There were situations where people just sat around in groups talking, installations of commonplace objects arranged to resemble temple shrines, and actions where, for example, hundreds of paper lanterns were silently launched into the fragrant night sky. In Thailand the social, cultural and religious boundaries placed to separate various spheres of public life in the UK were allowed to dissolve to the point of non-existence. After a while, I no longer cared about what was art and what wasn't. Perhaps the omnipresent influence of Buddhism had helped to liberate my mind? The organisation may have been intangible, the formalities casual, but the effect was truly magical.'

Culturalists / Inter-Expression

> *A period has been allocated for any activity in which anybody may participate using any means of expression that deals with the notion of Culture in a creative manner. … We basically believe that 'everybody has the potential to be a Culturalist'.* '
> 7 Collective Principles from Friends', CMSI brochure, 1995 pp.138–41

During the second festival, Uthit Atimana opened his home daily to the public, between 5 and 6 p.m., under the title *My Family is Art*. Over the course of numerous interviews and conversations during the research for this book, Uthit never mentioned this, which is consistent with how CMSI has been remembered by its participants – in terms of neither individual artists nor individual works. Indeed, the project was intended to extend its scope beyond the activities of self-identified artists. 'We planned to allow everyone to display their works. The

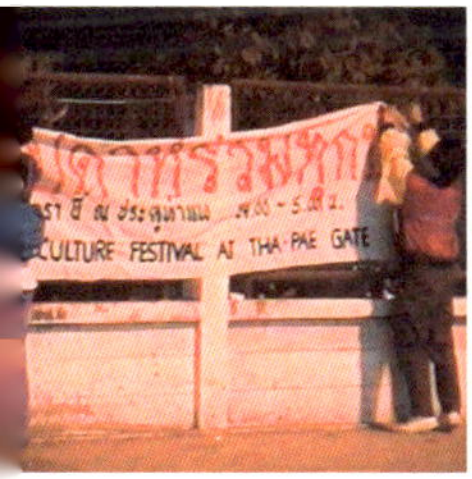

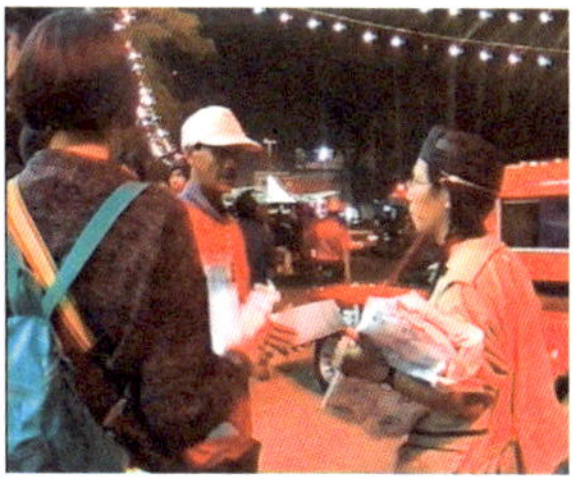

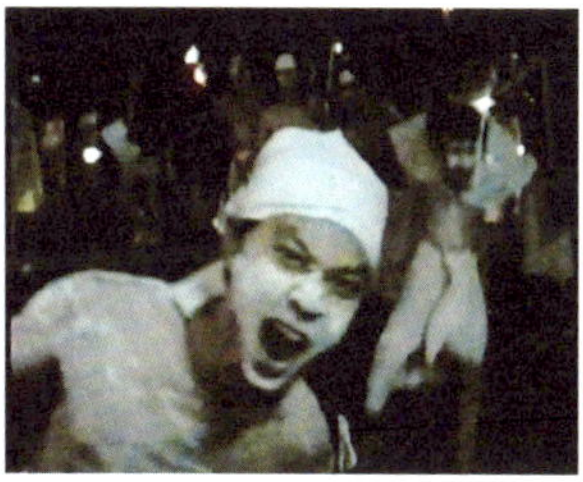

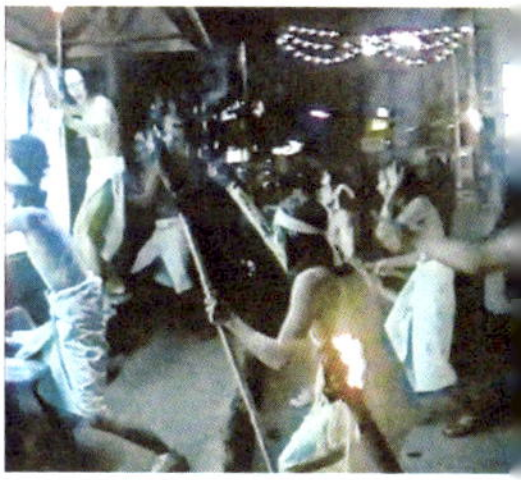

showcase wouldn't be limited to artists only. … The general public should have the right to express themselves through artistic activity.' Uthit recalls a doctor p.184 who turned up at one edition having had heard about CMSI in the news. 'He said, "Artists are a bunch of dangerous people!" … He claimed that he needed to inject them with a dose of morality. And he injected them. I asked about the medicine. He told me not to worry, that it was just glucose. Imagine the doctor. Was that art? Was he an artist? For me, he'd get an A+ for his key message, up there with Joseph Beuys. For me, this is a great example of Art.' 'Around that time we invented the term "Culturalist" – we avoided using the word "artist". … We began to declare this wasn't an Art Festival but a Cultural Festival.'

'By that time, I began to see CMSI as another form of art.' After the second edition, Thasnai Sethaseree stopped participating in CMSI. 'It was nothing like I thought it would be. … I questioned if CMSI was actually a social operation.' Thasnai's contribution to the second edition, with the help of some of his classmates, was to put up signs around the city with screen-printed questions – 'What is truth?', 'What is beauty?', 'What is art?' – that provoked strong reactions from participants. 'The signs caused a stir by questioning the other artworks' authenticity, and appearing at sites claimed to be "prohibited". … It erupted into an argument the night before the opening. Imagine the whole class, around twenty or thirty of us. … In the end, the lead organisers said we couldn't do it – they banned our work. If we continued our project, the authorities wouldn't let them organise it next year. We had a long talk that night. In the end, my question on CMSI was answered. The truth is, the so-called "social installation" didn't actually inspire a social movement. It was just another festival. So I decided to quit. The whole class quit. Mit [Jai Inn] and Uthit [Atimana] had no clue we quit. They learnt that later.'

'Public response to the Chiang Mai Art and Culture Festival has ranged from indifference to delight, from bewilderment to disgust', reported Khetsirin Knithichan and Phatarawadee Phataranawik in *The Nation* in 1995, under the headline 'But is it Art?'. 'Though the festival is intended to raise awareness about social ills and to promote a better understanding of contemporary art, the organizers appear to be a long way from achieving these goals. Indeed, the only people who seemed interested in the whole affair were foreign artists, Chiang Mai-based artists and Bangkok reporters – many of them familiar faces from the previous years' events. Although many of those who did attend seemed to genuinely appreciate seeing art outside the confines of a gallery, for others the concept may still be a bit difficult to grasp. "What are they doing?" and "Is this art?" were the two most common questions heard at installation sites around

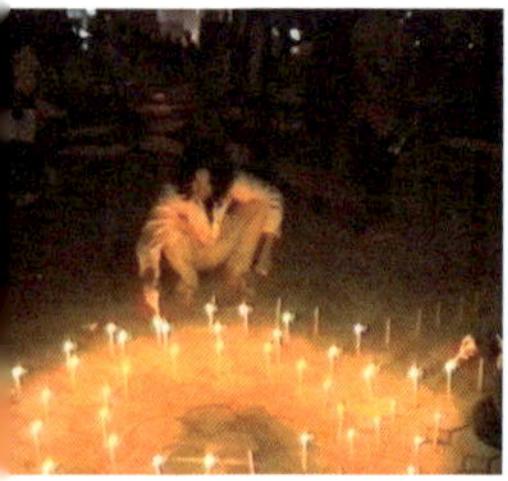

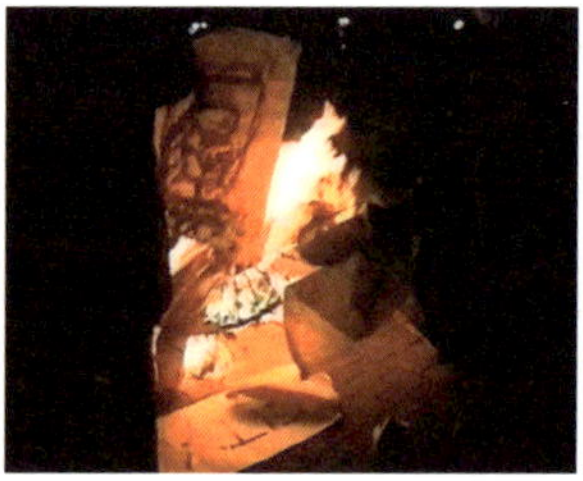

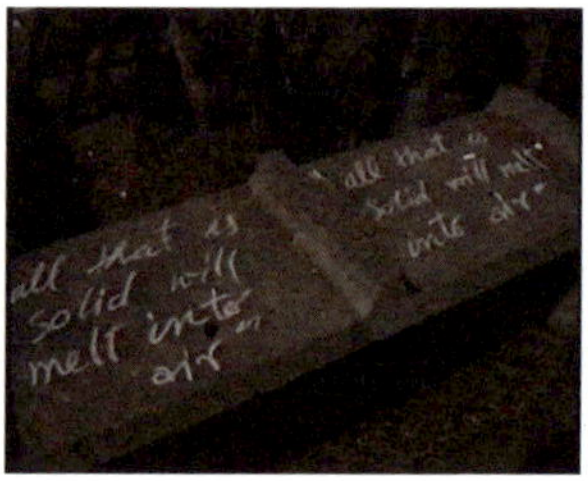

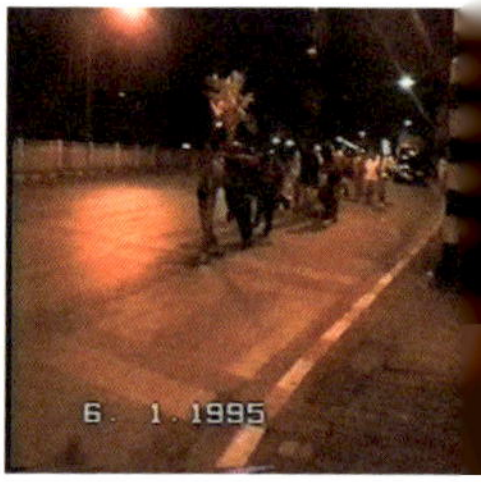

the city.'[11] The lack of comprehension was also shared by artists such as Thatree Pokawanich, who was a student at the time. 'The art I knew was painting. When I experienced these other kinds of artwork in Chiang Mai, I was excited, but puzzled. Something stuck to a tree – is that art? I tried to understand it. Mostly we spent time talking and eating together.' Other, more experienced artists, invited by Montien Boonma, were wary of participating, asking, 'What is this art festival?' Or, 'Is it a standard art exhibition?'[12] Organisers at the third edition

—

[11] Khetsirin Knithichan and Phatarawadee Phataranawik, 'But is it Art?', *The Nation*, 4 December 1995.

referenced factional disagreements within the Thai scene as a source of CMSI's mixed reactions; they also noted their limited funding, and acknowledged that 'local residents don't fully understand contemporary art yet'.[13]

The local radio call-in show *Sawasdee Chiang Mai* (on 107.95 FM) reported the following reactions during February 1994: 'Khun Surasak suggests that the bird sculpture in the moat be replaced, because the current one has turned green and is accumulating moss'; 'Agrees with Khun Surasak, and suggests that replacing the sculpture with lotuses would be a better way of bringing nature into the city'; 'Would like to pass along a question to the municipality about what will happen to the "bird" installation in the moat. Personally wishes that it be removed. Hopes for the municipality to start a water treatment program, after which it can be decided again what should be installed in the moat'; 'Shares the opinion that art exhibitions for the public are good, because other cities in other countries also mount such exhibitions. Would like to suggest that the art is changed over time to create a sense of dynamism and novelty. Don't wait for things to get old before changing them'; 'Passed by Suan Prung Hospital and inquired whether the installation is part of the exhibition taking place in temples and cemeteries. All one can notice right now is that there is moss everywhere. Please take care of this'; 'Suggests that the birds be removed, and the wooden stilts completely uninstalled because they could pose a danger to maintenance workers whose job is to clean the moat'; 'Tried to figure out the meaning of the bird and the art installation (arch shaped) in the moat in front of Suan Prung Hospital, but failed to understand. Suggests that there be explanatory texts or captions alongside the artworks. Or, actually, would prefer the moat be filled with lotuses as it originally was'.

Organisers were nonetheless optimistic about the gradual integration of contemporary art into Chiang Mai's daily life. 'If the festival continues to

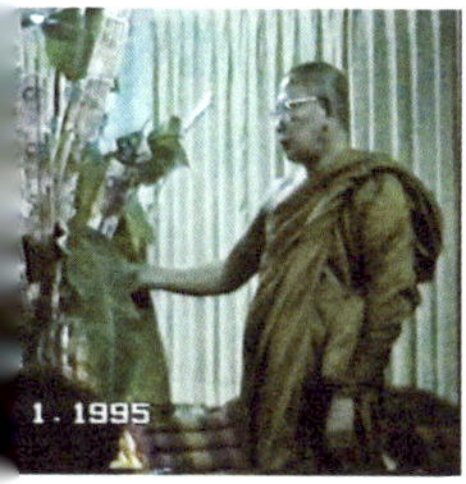

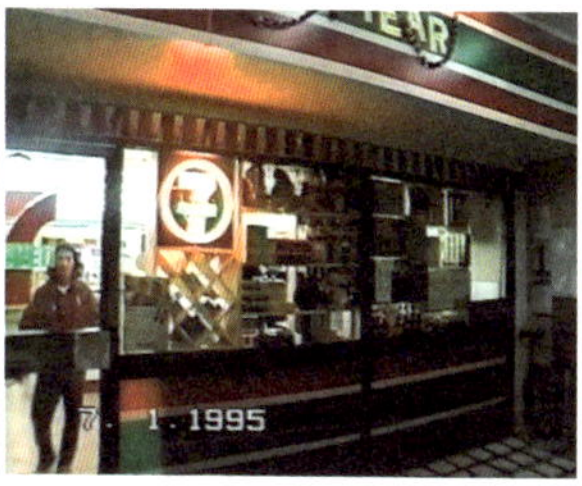

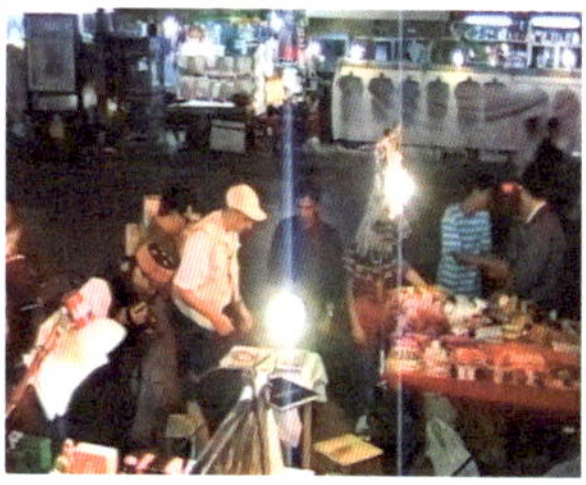
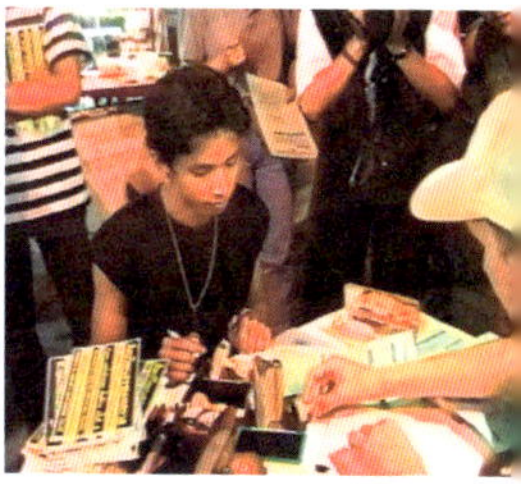

take place each year, it will become part of the local fabric, and locals will take an increasingly active role in it', as one organiser told the *Bangkok Post* in 1995. The interview included mentions of the cooperation of local residents in allowing artists to install works in their homes and businesses, albeit framed as 'indirect exposure' to contemporary art rather than direct participation or

—

[12] Montien Boonma, quoted in Khetsirin, 'Turning galleries inside out', *The Nation*, 29 November 1993.

[13] Khetsirin and Phatarawadee, 'But is it Art?', *op. cit.*

co-production. And although some would explain the lack of understanding among Chiang Mai residents as resulting from their unfamiliarity with new cultural ideas from abroad, in this article organisers position CMSI as an attempt to reconnect increasingly Westernised Thais with a culture of localism. 'Thais have followed Western culture so blindly in recent years that we have failed to develop our own contemporary culture. We've jumped directly from our traditional roots into Western ways. This event, then, is an attempt to enrich local contemporary culture.'[14]

According to Mit Jai Inn, non-artists – including the nuns in the Buddhasathan, a religious practice centre and CMSI venue – were able to appreciate certain of its actions as forms of party or celebration. 'People in Chiang Mai were so

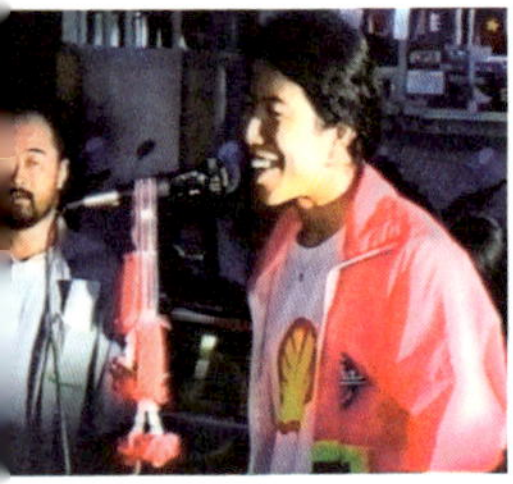

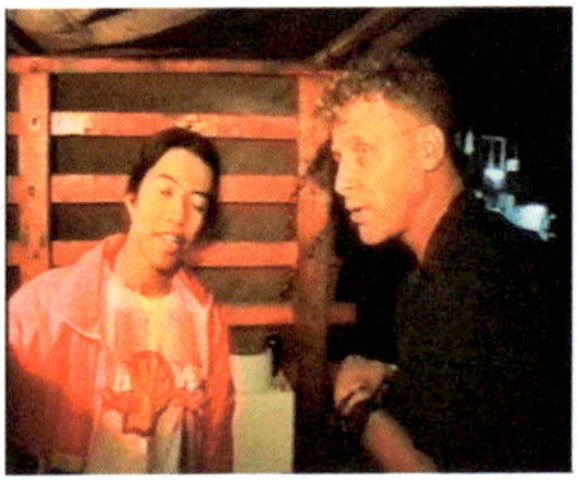

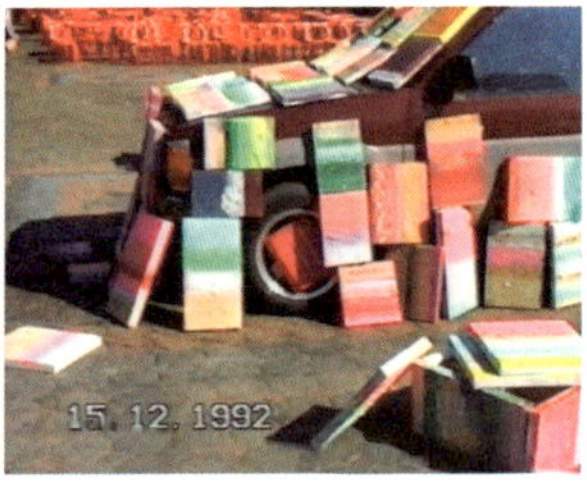

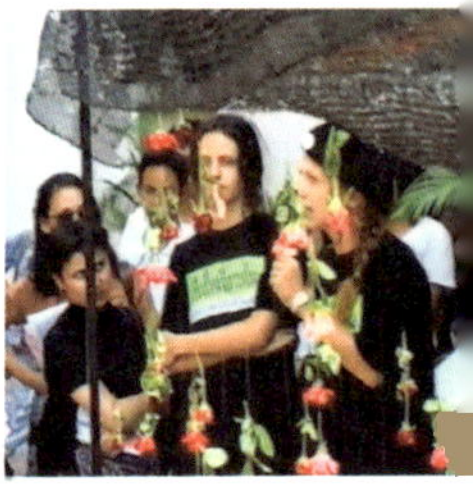

active. The local people outside the art circle also participated. We occupied public spaces, such as temples, and the abbots were so happy about it. We held a midnight robe-offering ceremony [at the third CMSI] that has now become a tradition. At midnight, people go to temples to offer robes to monks. Chiangrai adopted this tradition as well. We tried to penetrate every space: religious, social and academic.' Some participants recall a monk who became a film-maker following his experience of CMSI. 'They liked it, the monks, especially Montien Boonma's works', says Navin Rawanchaikul. 'They got inspired.' Also inspired by the festivals, Santiphap Inkong-ngam, an artist and film-maker who participated in the festivals as a student, would later go to Phra Singh temple 'to do a film-making workshop for monks during the holidays – scriptwriting, cinematography and editing. The monks would shoot footage and it would be made into a film.' Araya Rasdjarmrearnsook notes that works from the first festival gave 'gentle encouragement towards understanding aspects of life in relation to the beliefs of Buddhist religion/philosophy within the rounds of temples and cemeteries. After the first CMSI, groups of interested monks could be witnessed constantly going in and out of the temples and cemeteries. Those among them who were therefore closest to the artworks concluded that "Art is a riddle on life's mystery."'[15]

pp.168–70 Arahmaiani recalls lengthy negotiations around a 'problematic' 1995 performance at Wat Umong. 'I had a debate with Uthit and Navin because I wanted my

—

[14] Karnjariya Sukrung, 'Art, art everywhere', *Bangkok Post*, 27 November 1995.
[15] Araya, 'A narrative of an event that has just come to an end', *op. cit.*, p.16.

performance to be done in the temple, and in particularly sacred places. They were like, "You're a foreigner, you don't understand. For us it's very difficult." "You're right – because I'm a foreigner I want to know!"' After some discussion they agreed to ask permission together from the head monk. 'I was amazed. He was very knowledgeable. I was bringing up social-political issues, a feminist approach, but he was responding in a very interesting way. Later I learnt that it was a forest-monk monastery – not your average monks. So that's how I got to learn also about them.' With warning that ordinary Thais would probably find the performance very strange, the monks gave permission. Various interviewees describe how CMSI afforded access to certain, otherwise inaccessible spaces. For instance, for Phaptawan Suwannakudt, entering the *viharn* (assembly hall) of Wat Phra Singh to view a work was the highlight of her visit to the third

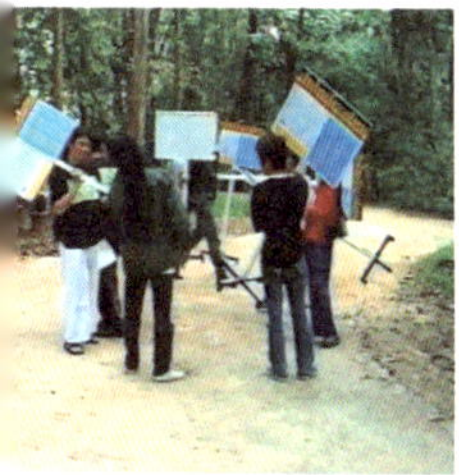

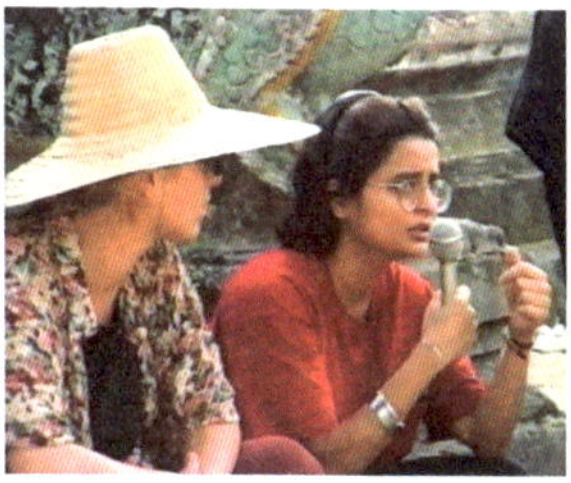

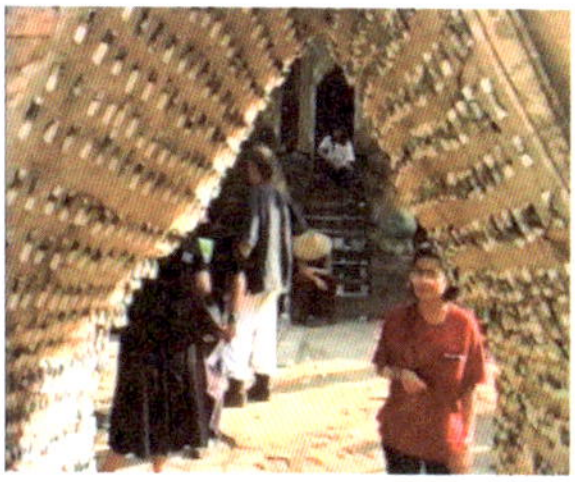

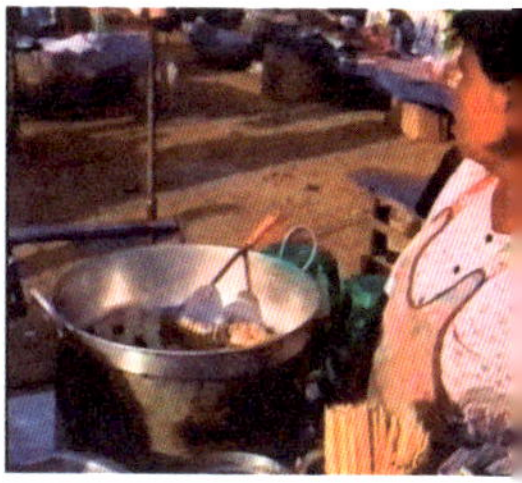

festival. 'It was the first and only time I was going to be allowed to go in. This temple had placed a sign in front of the entrance that women were not allowed to enter, and it may have been the only time the temple let in the public who included women.'

'I like the saying of the abbot of Wat Umong', says Uthit. 'I tried to explain contemporary art to him in different ways. He responded that he didn't understand it, but that it made sense to him. He compared contemporary art to a Dharma puzzle, just in a different framework or form. This, as I tried to explain to many people, was a success [of CMSI]. ... Asking for permission in different venues allowed us to explain the project in detail, so that people began to understand how this form of art was important to society.' Arahmaiani remembers the experience as a 'communication with the community'. She was happy to have monks and visitors discussing her work, and to in turn learn something about the local situation – 'a real exchange'.

'The interface between classes, made possible by placing the installations throughout the city rather than in gallery spaces, became for me one of the most radical and significant aspects of the festival', wrote Ray Langenbach of his first impression of the third CMSI. 'As the days wore on, though, I realized that very little real interaction was actually taking place between the classes. For example, a sidewalk *roti canai* seller did a bit of brisk business when our group came by to see an installation on the railing next to his stall, and his opinion was solicited during the discussion, but he had business-as-usual on his mind and clearly had never been involved in the work by the artist.' A local dentist who participated 'was really a bit amazed that we liked the work so much and seemed to find the whole project a curiosity. He allowed the piece in his clinic in deference to his acquaintance with one of the Festival organizers, rather than any deep feeling for the motives or work of the artist. I left wondering if he and the foreign artist had ever gone out drinking together, or if the two would stay in touch after the Festival ended.'[16]

The most effective projects followed a 'non-art methodology', according to Langenbach, who gives the example of Tang Da Wu's nonchalant, low-p.160 key conversations with locals (*Meeting With the Chiang Mai People*), a 'non-performance' in which little more happened than 'making the acquaintance of the local shop owners, and advertising their establishments to the gathered artists and others passing by'. According to the artist, as quoted by Langenbach, 'This

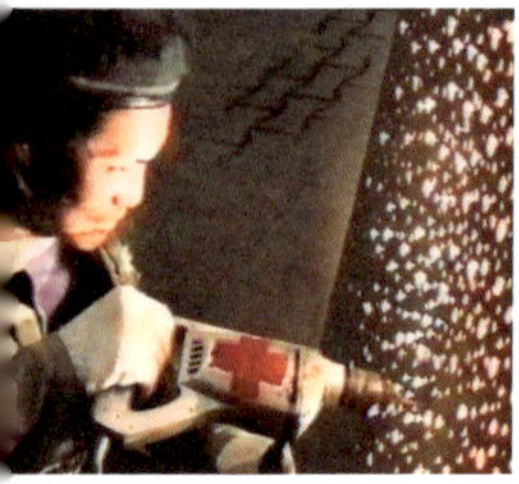

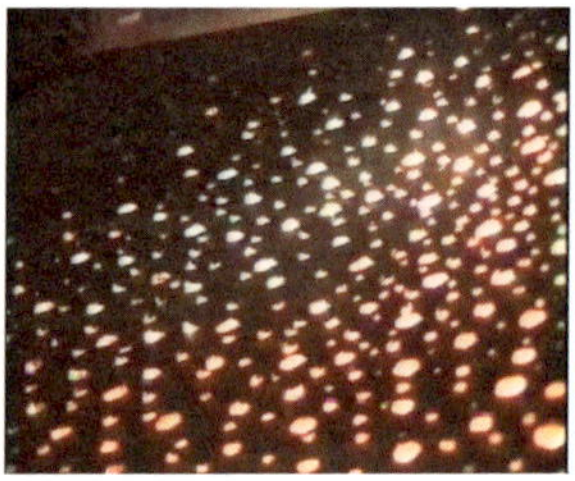

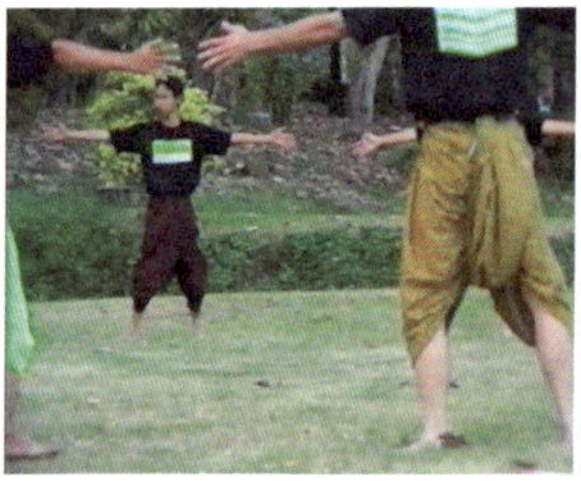

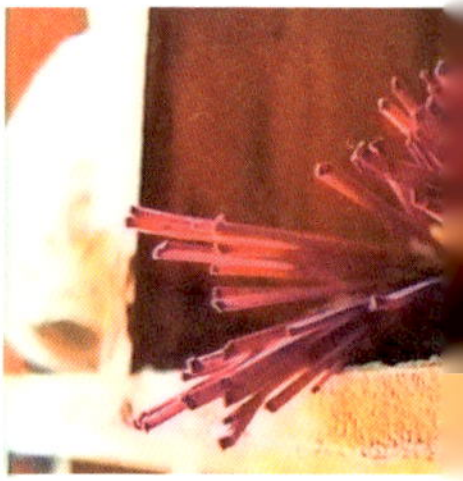

idea came from my own direct experiences. Since I don't know any Thai, it's hard for me to ask local people where to buy something, even a newspaper. Language is the most important barrier. So I wanted to have a board indicating these items.' Given their closer connection to the context, local artists (and perhaps regional artists, in the case of Tang Da Wu) were more suited to this 'non-art' approach. 'Many of the foreign artists, who arrived just before the Festival began, conceived, created or designed their works in their respective countries and then placed them in Chiang Mai. The works appeared dressed in concerns that couldn't always translate to Chiang Mai. Transposed from a specific social context they could be read only for their formal qualities, rather than social concerns.'

'They told me CMSI was to bring modern or contemporary art to the people. Very simple.' Jay Koh came to the festival as a visitor in 1994–95 and returned in pp.161-63 1995–96 as a participant, with his project, *E.T. (Exchanging Thoughts)* based on the exchange of items from different artists living abroad with locals in markets around the city. 'Artists whose works that I saw in the earlier edition behaved like "gallery artists" – they didn't engage with the residents, they didn't engage them in a conversation, they didn't get input from them. They just put a work somewhere and expected the public to see it. ... So when I came to do my work, I asked, "How can I get the people to participate?"' Koh retrospectively feels he was ill-equipped to step back as an author, to allow the collaboration to happen; that both CMSI and his work within it were flawed by a residual modernism. 'If I work as a modernist artist, or within a modernist trajectory, it means the artist determines everything.

—

[16] Ray Langenbach, early draft of 'Through the Keyhole: The third Chiangmai art and culture festival', *ArtAsiaPacific*, vol.3, no.3, 1996.

… All this public work is still very much based on the idea of artist as leader, artist as author. I thought that I could have more participation with my work [at CMSI], but I was still the author of it. I discussed with my Thai collaborators how they could engage the participating public through the interview processes and data collections, but not with the public directly as I could not speak Thai.' Nonetheless, the relationship-building at the core of his participation may offer a more localised alternative to imported art methodologies. 'I don't have to be nice to everyone – but if I want to work with someone, I *do* have to be nice.[17] Otherwise the person won't talk to me. An agonistic approach, the kind Claire Bishop writes about, doesn't work in Thailand. Because if I antagonise you – you're a stranger, I'm a stranger – you won't want to talk to me again. That kind of Western theory doesn't work here. So we have to find our own way and our own theory to work with.'

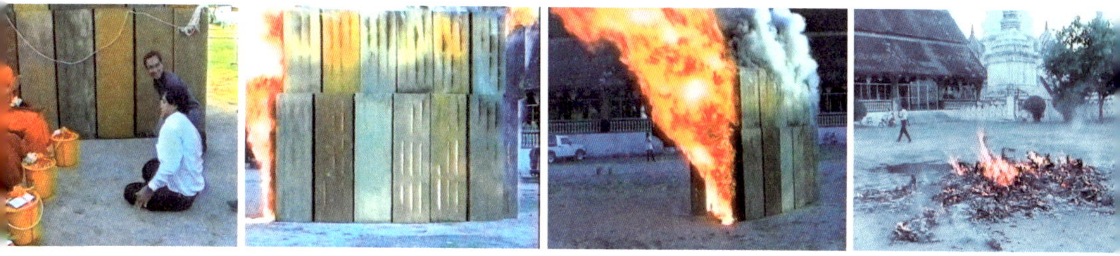

Artist-to-Artist
'In my feeling, everyone helped each other in CMSI, to organise our own works and to organise things that needed to happen', says Rirkrit Tiravanija, who returned to Thailand in 1996 after many years abroad. 'In those days, people got together and talked a lot. They visited Kamin [Lertchaiprasert]'s place, cooked together and talked with each other. In fact, it was a social installation all the time, not only during CMSI events. Everything blurred together. … I recall everyone sitting outside in the evening, drinking local rice whiskey. Passers-by stopped to look, listen, talk and ask questions; some people didn't like it. Meanwhile, Uthit walked around and passed a microphone to passers-by to speak. I gave a lecture, 'The Mat is the Message', on the mat as a platform for everybody to sit together. p.203
It's about community.'

If CMSI did not always connect with its intended publics, it produced some remarkable mechanisms for exchange among its visitors and participants. The approach was direct, assertive and self-reflexive; groups were led around festival sites and encouraged to discuss performances and other works as they happened, often with the artists themselves. Organisers 'walked the audience through the festival like a guided tour', says Santiphap Inkong-ngam, a student at the time.

—

[17] Koh notes: 'The concept of "being nice" is how I would have explained my action at the time. Today, I would refer to my cross-disciplinary artistic research on building relationships; from strangers to acquaintances to participants to collaborators.' See Jay Koh, *Art-Led Participative Processes: Dialogue and Subjectivity within Performance in the Everyday*, Kuala Lumpur: SIRD/Gerakbudaya, 2016.

'Uthit [Atimana] would walk around with a megaphone, telling everyone where the performance would take place. … And when the performance was over he would come and talk to us: "How do you feel? What were you thinking while performing?"' For some of the students there could be a comical aspect to such exchanges ('artists would be performing in the street and he would shout, "This is art, this is art, don't touch them – be careful!"'), but most observers recall more in-
p.178
depth conversations emerging; for example, the response to a work by young Thai artist Toeingam Srisubut: 'A group of foreign women artists interpreted the piece as a protest against the religious institution's exclusion of women; its presence turned the temple grounds into a forum to discuss the issues of feminism and Buddhism in Thailand.' An observer noted that 'the artist herself seems indifferent to its sociopolitical connotations, or perhaps she is simply too clear about the

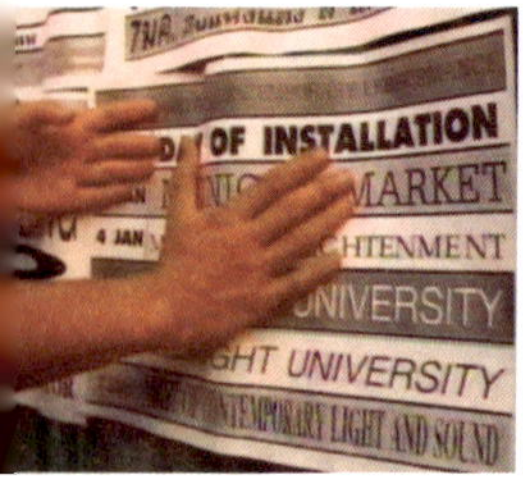

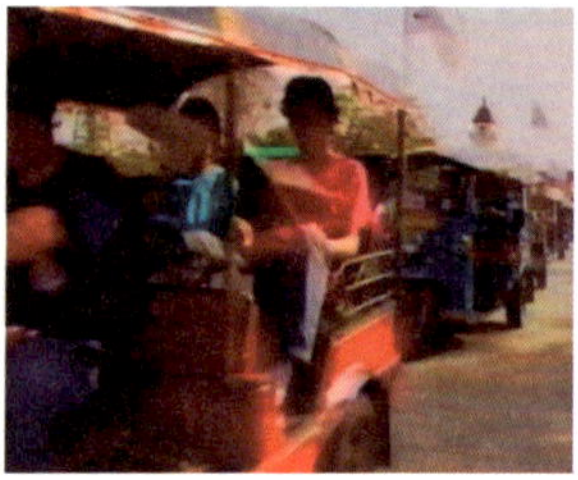
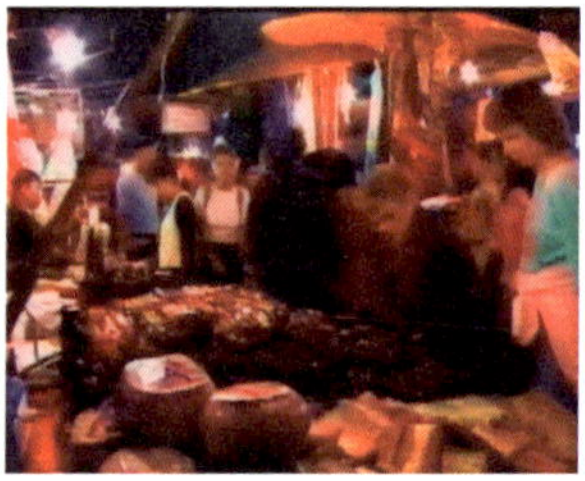
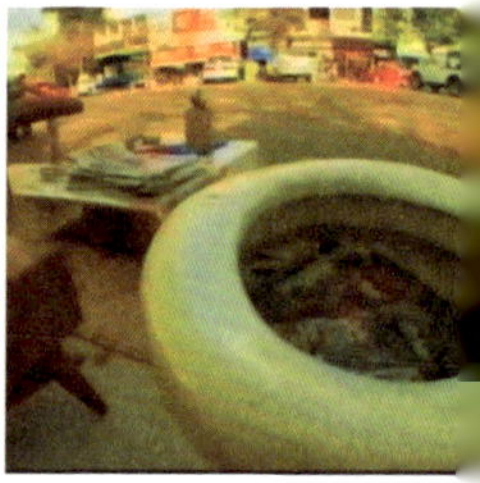

issues. She denied a feminist stance and simply said, "It's just an idea of art which works in its own right."'[18]

Such exchanges 'had the effect of coalescing the entire festival into a singular performance', producing 'an interactive structure of infinite surface and zero volume, in which group interpretations and critiques were immediately folded back into the artworks and to the event, thereby providing a template for the festival itself to function as a meta-discourse on the notion of the art festival and the temple festival'. For Ray Langenbach, this was one of the most remarkable features of CMSI. 'The pedagogical process cohered with the governing ideology of the festival: the need to inquire, to critique, to learn, to create social interaction. During the succeeding days, the audience was bussed to particular sites, which were then followed immediately by a critical dialogue, during which the artist was questioned on motives, aesthetics, materials and contradictions perceived in the work. I have never seen this unusual and courageous process of immediate feedback, because I have tried to institute this several times since and found it very difficult to do.'

Participants are unanimous in feeling that there was nobody taking on a curatorial role at CMSI. 'There was no word "curator" in Thailand at the time.' Kade Javanalikhikara was a participating artist and also helped with logistics. 'We helped each other in organising the event. … There were red pickup trucks taking people around the city to see artworks, and then in the evening we had dinner together.' Santiphap confirms that 'since the management was quite loose, it was

—

[18] Karnjariya, 'Art, art everywhere', *op. cit.*; and Tei Kobayashi (writing as T.J. McGuire), 'A Week of Suffering in Chiang Mai', *Asiana*, February 1996.

very hard to tell who did what. … There wasn't any proper selection process, neither was there a curatorial process, nor censorship. If someone wanted to do something they could just give their name to Uthit, and he would put their name in the programme, which would later be followed by a festival tour [to see the work]. Whatever happened, the mess would be cleaned up later.'

'We were not curators. We didn't have any experience. We artists played different roles, which made CMSI lively.' Supachai Satsara also assisted with the festivals' organisation in the early years. 'I hardly had time to do my own artworks. I had to manage spaces, take care of artists and assist them in working with these spaces. I had to visit the police station, the courts. Navin [Rawanchaikul] had other responsibilities and Kosit [Juntaratip] was responsible for producing printed

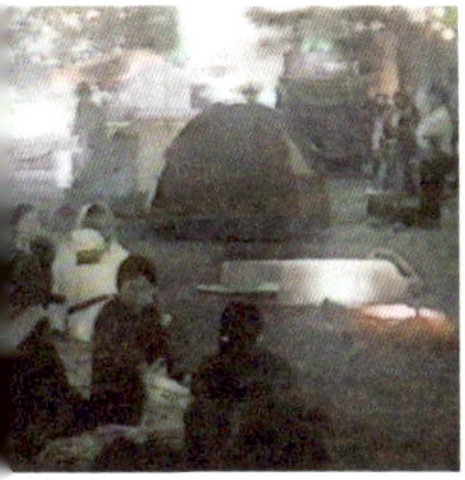

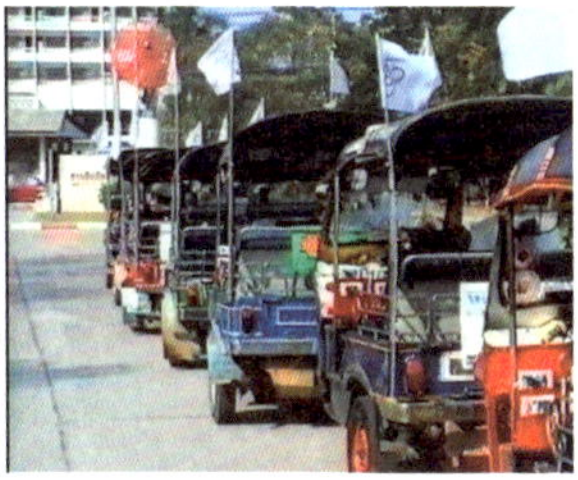

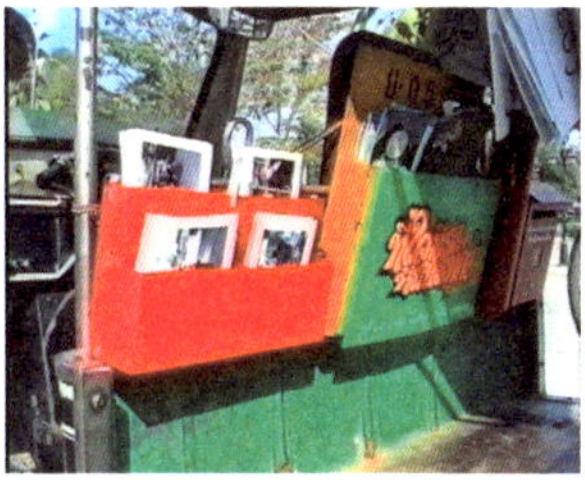

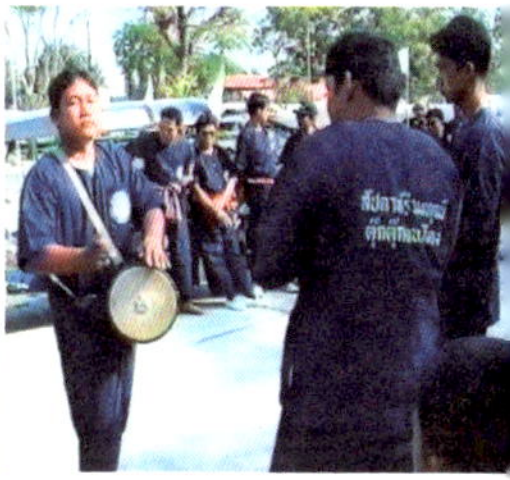

materials.' Chumpon Apisuk sees CMSI's mode of organising as a reflection of the local situation. 'For a long time in Thailand it has been the case that artists organise everything by themselves. And as well as exhibiting, artists also need to explain their works to audiences. We have to be both organisers and publicists – to do everything by ourselves, just like farmers.'

'It was very badly managed and chaotic', says Angkrit Ajchariyasophon, another participant-organiser. 'We didn't know when or where each work would be shown. I think many foreign artists got headaches. They had to rely on assistants like me and my friends, who couldn't communicate effectively in English. Nevertheless, it was organic, and this was a good thing. There was no selection. Anyone could do anything. It reached out to society.' The open selection could be surprising even for local participants like Sutthirat Supaparinya. 'Everyone could propose something. But then I found out that if you wanted to participate you needed to organise your own contribution. I thought they could manage some of that for me – at least the contact with the city. But there was nothing like that.'

Thepsiri Sooksopa hosted performances and events at his home near Wat Umong, which also provided CMSI visitors a place to stay. 'They said my door was always open.' He was able to acquaint visitor-participants with the local situation and help facilitate their projects. 'Because I knew Chiang Mai communities – institutions, universities, villages, etc. – I could connect participants to the local communities. … My house was often a gathering place for art and cultural activities – literature, performing arts, sometimes political events. People from other provinces and foreign artists always stayed at my place. Sometimes I'd see a group with backpacks leaving in the morning and I'd ask myself, "When did they come to sleep here

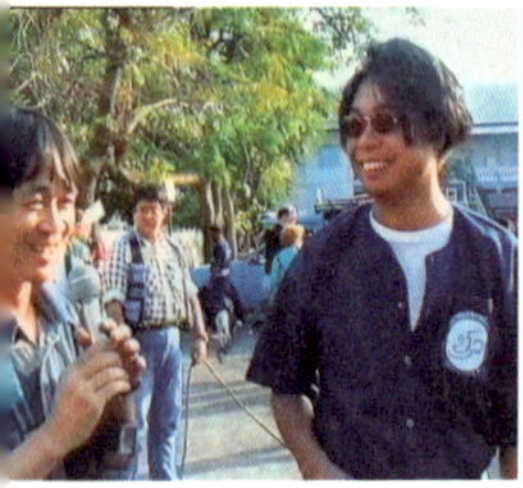
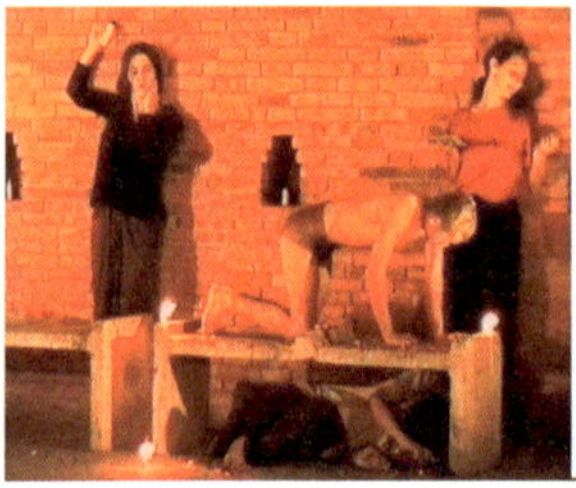
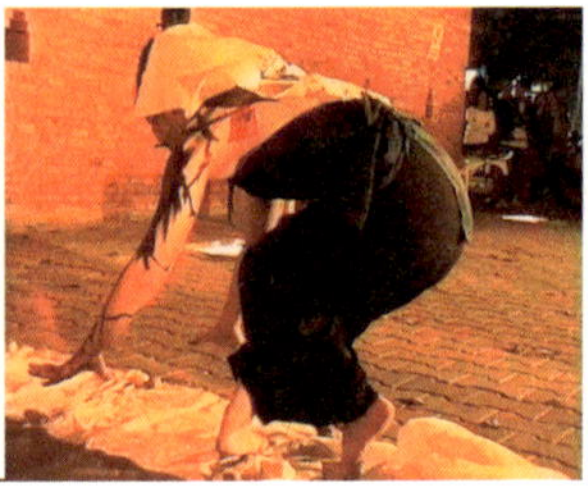
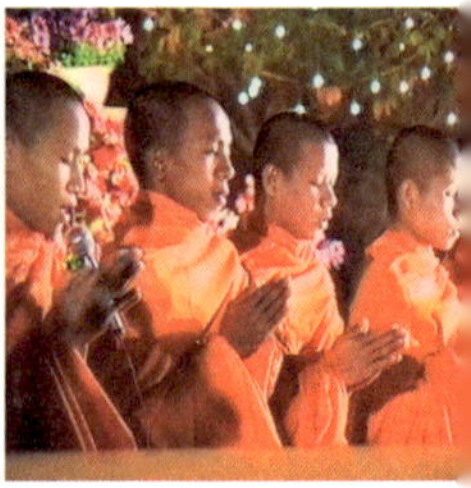

last night?" … There were a lot of performances by foreign artists, some of which I liked. There was a performance by a *farang* [Western/foreign] couple, drinking straight Mekhong whiskey, shouting the names of national heroes – Che Guevara, George Washington – and throwing glasses at the wall. After a while, the audience began to shout the names of their own heroes. I had to call an ambulance to pick up one of the artists who had drunk too much.[19] A Japanese couple's performance was to stand naked in the middle of my pond, facing the street. … Passers-by just kept looking at them. There was no problem, no one bothered me about it.'

Organisers describe their roles variously: 'representative', 'filter', 'facilitator', 'teacher', 'chauffeur', 'host of the party'. They agree that nothing close to the concept of 'curator' existed at that time; or if it did, it did not fit the ethos of CMSI. For Araya, 'the word *pantarak* [curator] in Thai is very sad. It's like an old man sitting in an old museum like the National Museum in Bangkok.' In publicity materials, individuals are rarely credited and group statements such as '7 Collective Principles from Friends' are presented without attribution. The group transformed over time as core members departed and returned and others joined. In some cases, and particularly in early editions, artworks were presented without information on their makers or otherwise. Mit Jai Inn refers to the *pha pa* tradition of community-organised but generally spontaneous collections for monks' robes (which he also connects to the midnight timing of certain CMSI events). 'In the village, everybody helps and no one gets credit at all.' This was not particular to CMSI. An anonymous exhibition of Mit's work had taken place in private apartments throughout Vienna the year before the first CMSI edition; he brought back a brochure to show his fellow artists in Chiang Mai (as described above). In the case of CMSI, he recalls names only ever being used out of legal necessity – never authorially. 'In Thailand, when you printed something, you would have to give the name of the person with legal responsibility [for the printed material]. I would say, "Put my name. But not as an artist."'

'Thai culture, in terms of uniting/coming together to help, was expressed strongly [in CMSI]. There was no hierarchy.' Araya says she stopped participating when the project began to be associated with particular individuals, an ambivalence shared by others. Uthit, who became one such prominent figure, explains that projects like CMSI need strong leaders, and that while if a 'leader' is named publicly nobody will join, it was nonetheless necessary to have hierarchy in order make CMSI

—

[19] According to Chumpon Apisuk, this was part of an event organised by Asiatopia in 2004.

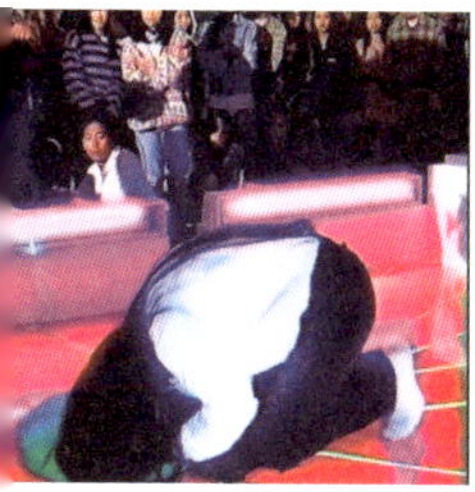
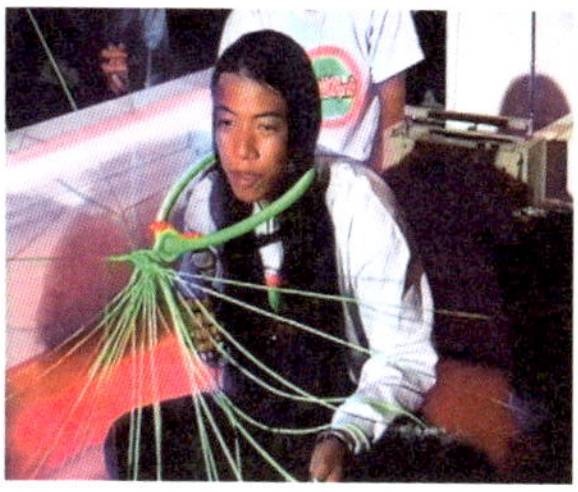
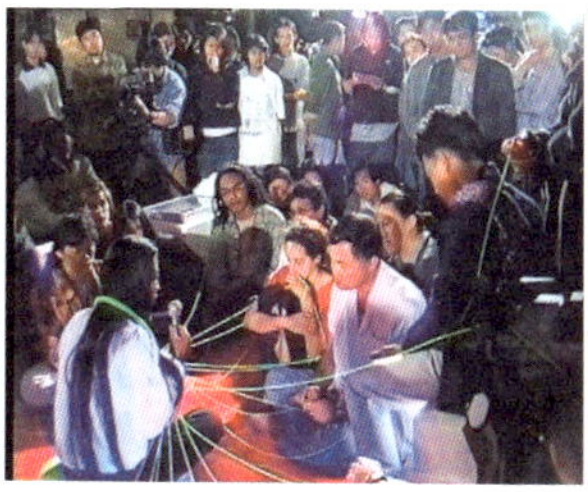
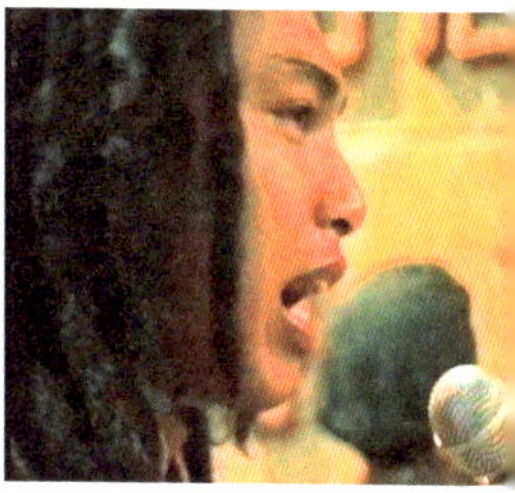

happen. 'We tried to organise without a formal organisation, in order to leave a space for *spirit*. I never used my own name. For myself, for all the organisers, I always said, don't use our names. I would only appear as a co-ordinator.' In a *Bangkok Post* article from 1997, he is quoted as saying 'The organisers believe in participation and open space. Viewers will be the curators themselves.'

Araya was one of the few members of CMSI's organising group to have participated in large-scale exhibitions and biennials abroad; she had 'seen the works of several artists [participating in CMSI] installed in famous exhibitions in big cities. Their names and interviews have appeared in various art magazines. Some have participated in major international exhibitions, had their airfare sponsored by commissioning bodies, been escorted from the airport to luxurious hotels, been in the limelight of openings with hundreds of attendees, basked in applause and praise. Today in Chiang Mai, they have all travelled here on their own dime – no complimentary airfare, no hotel accommodation, no grand opening event. As for applause, we clap for one other, providing encouragement and support among us artists. This is a showing of art workers, a voluntary sacrifice on the part of the artists, to realise – and realise in excellence – a spirit of generosity.'[20]

Non-Artists / Midnight University / Cooperative Suffering
'The week of cooperative suffering was another important aspect of CMSI that took the emphasis off the value of art objects. Although it was apparent that night workers like tuk tuk drivers (the tuk tuk is the local form of motorised tricycle for ferrying passengers around Chiang Mai) enjoyed themselves very much during this week of cooperative suffering, it was also apparent that professional artists from abroad looked worried when they saw people doing yoga work-outs at the plaza near a main street in town. Throughout the week the question 'but is this really art?' seemed to float in the air of the city. Another component of the week of cooperative suffering was the Midnight University. This aspect of the events was designed especially for non-artists: people like students, labourers, and those who work and return back home late at night like entertainers and singers were welcome to participate in the Midnight University.'[21]

The first Week of Cooperative Suffering – also called 'Angst Week' – took place in 1995 during in a break between editions of CMSI. According to Kosit Juntaratip, pp.124–35

—

[20] Araya, 'Bao bao thang sara lae mai mee sara jaak "chiang mai jad wang sangkhom"', *Krungthep thurakij jood prakai*, 27 November 1995, p.8.
[21] Araya, 'A narrative of an event that has just come to an end', *op. cit.*, p.16.

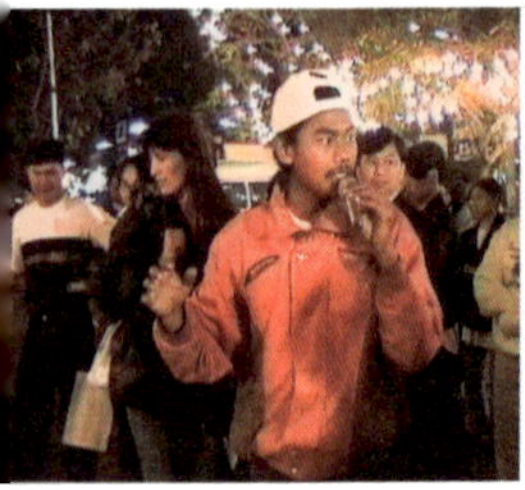 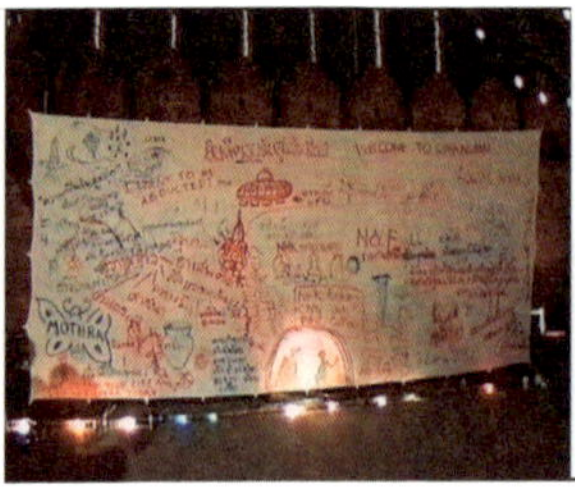 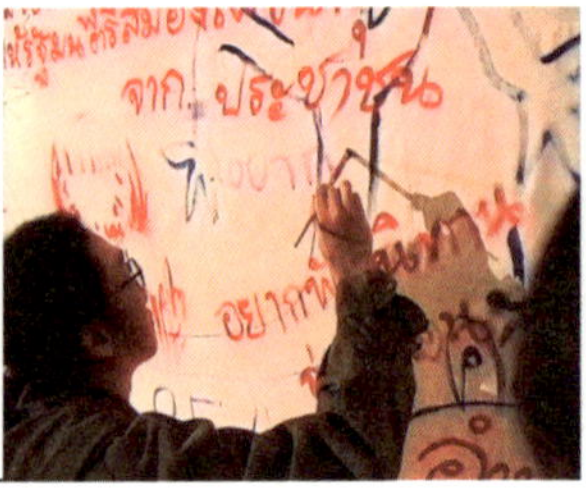 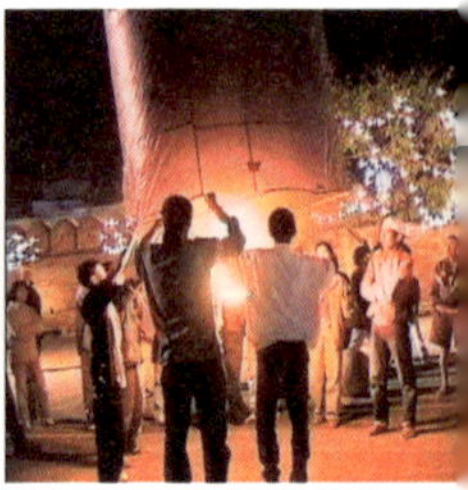

'We are born in Buddhism. When we say "suffer" this already includes our birth. Being human also includes our suffering. For me, the meaning of "suffering" is to enjoy life. ... The Week of Cooperative Suffering wasn't directed towards anything in particular. It was more about how to collaborate, and to bring people to the meetings. Midnight University happened because of the Week of Cooperative Suffering. We could share and enjoy ourselves equally. We brought art to the public space. ... we sat on the ground, in kind of a circle. And everyone could handle the microphone and say anything. This is good – equal and in balance with the whole society. For Midnight University, the idea was chained more to politics [in contrast to the Week of Suffering]. Most of the people came from the social sciences. It was in a democratic spirit – no heroes – to open up and try to be equal.'

Arranged over a series of nights (1–7 January 1995) in the public square at Tha Pae Gate, the week announced itself as 'a cultural activity for the masses focussing attention on the notion that we are all trapped "in a pool of suffering". There will be musical performances by visually disabled people, contemporary experimental music, folk dancing, a discussion on how and why people suffer, a "buy-sell-donate" event of art, antiques and other commodities, and lots of installations and seminars.' Archival documents reveal unrealised plans for an ambitious and popular programme, to take place in multiple provincial locations and with Thai stars such as Jaran Manopet and folk-rock band Caravan. The initial plan was to initiate parallel events in Ubon Ratchathani, in the northeastern Isan region, a great geographical and cultural distance from Chiang Mai. The documents detail that it was hoped that the event would spread to 'every province except Bangkok', explaining that semi-village, semi-urban situations – where real life and tradition are still coherent – are the best places to develop community-centric culture.

'"Because suffering is a collective state of everyone in society"' this festival can only be complete with your participation. Please propose activities you think feasible, from your perspective, and which promote the spirit of creative practice.' Registration forms were distributed with a checklist for proposals: 'Painting, Sculpture, Mixed Media, Performance, Installation Art, Music, Dance, Poetry, Travelling Theater Troupe, Outdoor Film Screening, VDO, Writer, Seminar, Lecture, Acrobatics, Fortune Telling, Divination of Lottery Numbers, Mor Lam, Folk Music, Lae Song, Comedy, Sermon, Human Rights Activist, Second-hand Sales, Street Vendor, Bureaucrat, Soldier, Police, Doctor, Thief, Prostitute, Lawyer, Magician, Other (please specify)'. Although Mit Jai Inn is generally

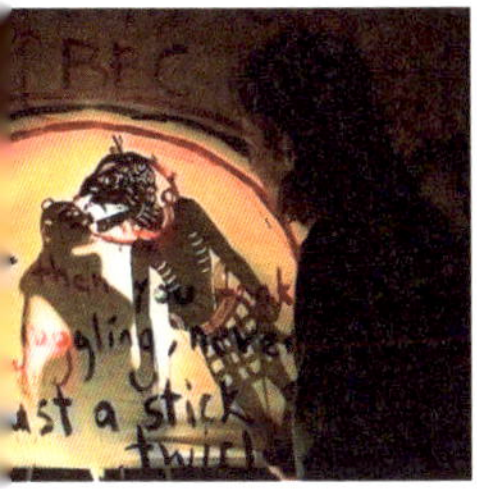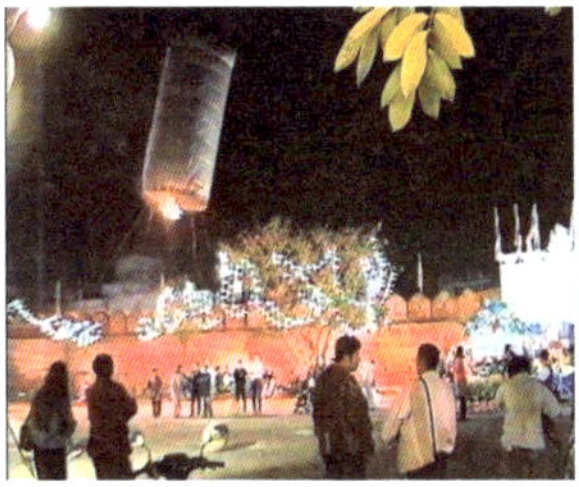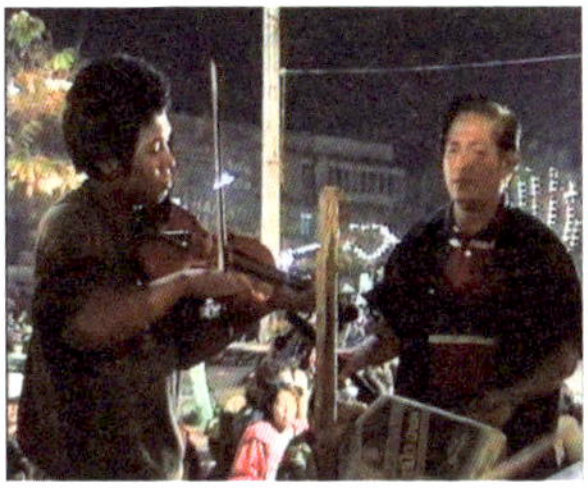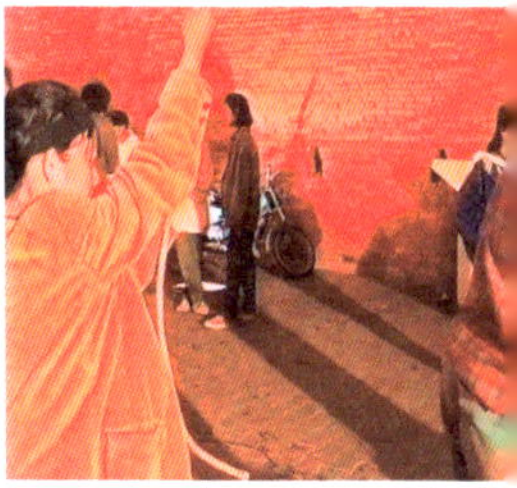

seen as the instigator, Supachai Satsara says that it 'was not really Mit's project. I don't want to say that this project was owned by anyone.' According to Narumol Thammapruksa, 'I think it mainly came from Uthit [Atimana] and Mit, probably Somkiat [Tangnamo] and friends. Or maybe Nidhi [Eoseewong] as well – though this was before Midnight University was formed. It was like a gathering around the bonfire. In the first year we saw how difficult the lives of people in that area were. So we decided to be their friends, since we were chatting already. We decided to learn more about their lives.'

Midnight University, known in its early stages as 'Midnight Socrates', began p.213 as part of the first Week of Cooperative Suffering as a public seminar around a campfire at Tha Pae Gate, with academics from Chiang Mai University alongside the popular public square's late-night crowd of rickshaw drivers, drug dealers, police, sex workers, tourists, stall-holders, students and unauthorised city guides. This would become an ongoing and semi-regular public gathering with sessions taking place overnight, between 6 p.m. and 6 a.m., underwritten by coffee and cheap whiskey. 'The situation allowed that anything could happen', and, according to Mit, its timing derived from the fact that 'the Buddha said that between midnight and 2 a.m. is a good time, not for human beings, but for devas [gods], who would come from heaven or hell, to gather and debate, mostly against the Buddha'. At the early iterations of Midnight University, 'we got drunk, became more quiet, and then people started to think quite big at that moment, around midnight'. At this stage, 'we had no platform, there was no internet yet', but Midnight University would become much better known in Thailand for its subsequent online iteration, a site of 'alternative higher education' and critical discourse that 'receive[d] over 2.5 million unique visits per month and offer[ed] users from around the world access to over 1500 scholarly articles'.[22] Uthit describes the Midnight University website as 'the target of mainstream politics for quite some time', and it has been shut down repeatedly by successive Thai military governments – notably after the 2006 and 2014 coups. At the time of writing, the main site is blocked, though its imprint may be found by alternative routes.

According to Thasnai Sethaseree, Midnight University's roots are in regular academic gatherings, since the early 1990s, in room 1307 at Chiang Mai University's Faculty of Fine Arts. 'The meetings took place on Fridays, with

—

[22] See 'Archive / Midnight University', Arte Útil website, http://www.arte-util.org/projects/midnight-university/ (last accessed on 8 August 2018).

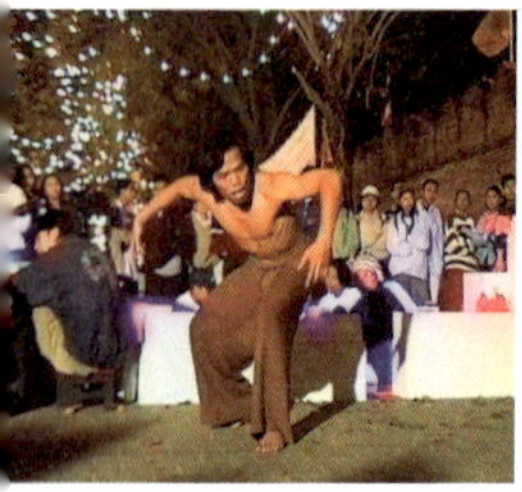
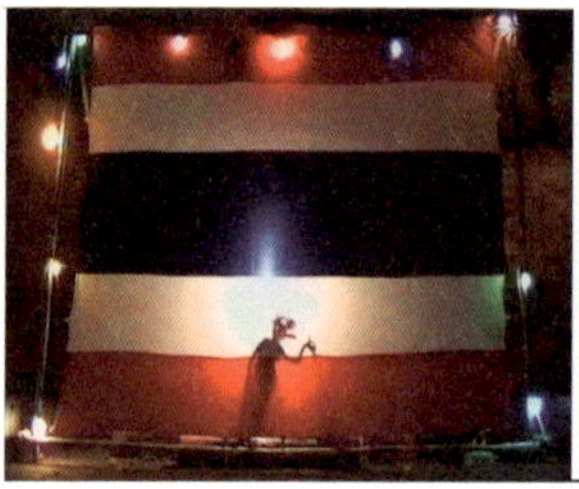
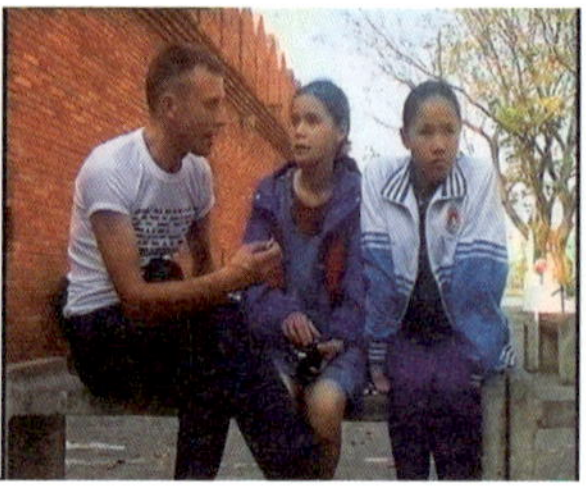
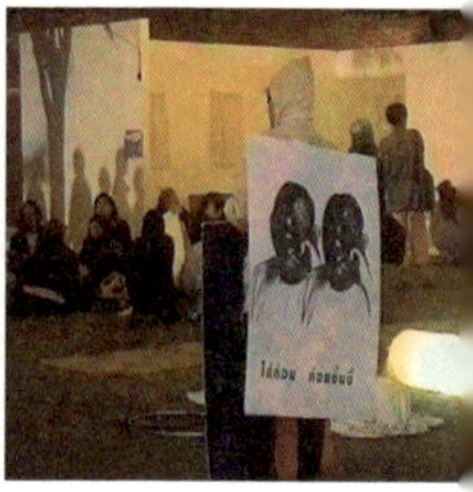

scholars from art, sciences, humanities, social sciences, philosophy and law departments.' Most of the CMSI group were not part of these gatherings, but Uthit and Mit were amongst those who attended regularly. 'Later, NGOs, social activists and local intellectuals were also invited, which expanded the network of Midnight University and increased the political involvement of the platform – most significantly, during the constitutional reform of 1996–97, when room 1307 became a hub of ideas, discussion and public gatherings, of yearning for a democratic era in Thailand. I think this process was then reflected in the emergence of Midnight University as a non-hierarchical online platform.'

In the context of widespread activities around Thailand's adoption of a new 'people's' constitution in 1997, with a reformist and pro-democratic agenda, 'Poi Luang Constitutional Installation' was planned – a two-day event in which some of the CMSI organising group were involved.[23] '"Poi Luang" in its original meaning refers to a Northern Thai tradition of collaboration without coercion. Whoever has betel, rice, medicine or roasted fish brings their bounty to contribute in an act of communal merit-making. Poi Luang Constitutional Installation is a continuation of the aforementioned tradition, but modifying its aims from merit-making to a collective expression of the people's "pure intention". The aim is to make this constitution a constitution for the people, so that "Thai politics will be a politics of quality and moral virtue"'. Publicity materials promised: debates with community leaders, academics, politicians, businessmen and civilians; breakout discussion groups led by academics and various non-governmental organisations; legal advice consultation sessions by lawyers; an exhibition on Thai political and constitutional history and the development of various political issues; a video projection about how different forms of political power have positively or negatively affected civilians; an exhibition of essays and drawings by children and civilians under the topic 'Thai Politics in Your Dreams'; an arts exhibition with folk music, experimental music, performance and visual art; a marketplace; and a public procession. Angkrit Ajchariyasophon, a participant, recalls that 'Politicians came on stage to deliver speeches at Tha Pae Gate. Some university lecturers, academics and students joined the campaign, such as Somkiat and Uthit. I joined them. We wanted to contribute through art. There were a lot of performance activities

—

[23] Despite its ambitions, what followed was a consolidation of Thaksin Shinawatra's power, ultimately preparing the ground for the 2006 military coup.

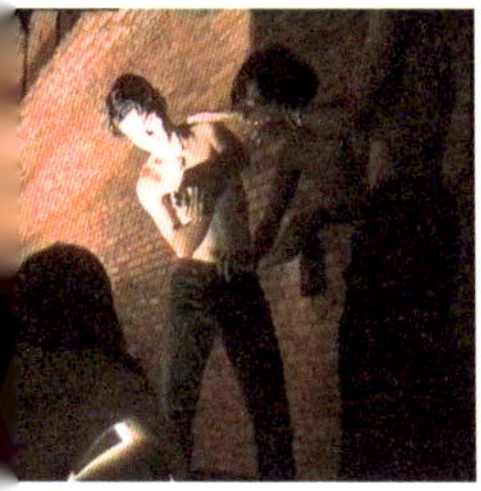
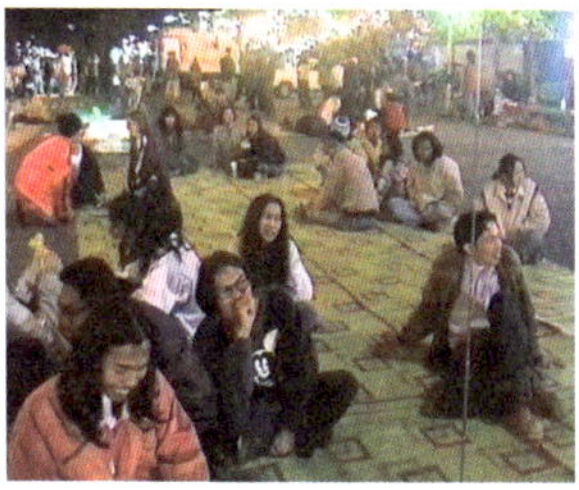
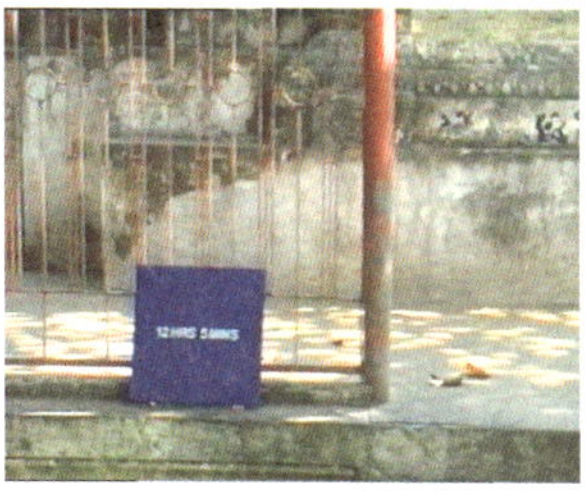
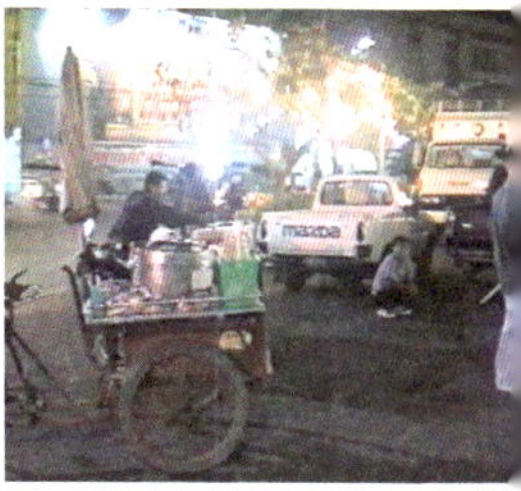

taking place in front of the stage. … I blew soap bubbles during one of the politicians' speeches. Every time he finished a sentence I blew bubbles.'

A driving force behind the Midnight University's online platform was the late Somkiat Tangnamo, who translated and transcribed much of the material hosted by the site. Thasnai recalls that 'Somkiat was a scholar who was always hungry for knowledge. He constantly translated English texts and books into Thai. … He told me that although his capacity in English was limited, he felt it necessary to create a capsule of thought in Thailand. … After Somkiat passed away, Midnight University continued. Some of the group left, and some stayed. They carry on the spirit of political endeavour that persists for democracy in Thailand.'

'It was basically a group of people conversing very late at night', says Santiphap Inkong-ngam. 'The compelling thing about it was the diversity of people. There were homeless people and prostitutes who joined in. It was all done very casually. Even I didn't know who the organiser was. The gathering seemed almost coincidental, just some people coming together and chatting – like a temple fair.' For some art students, such as Angkrit, Midnight University also offered a wider, parallel curriculum. 'It offered us a new way of thinking. We learned that art is not isolated from social contexts. In the early days of Midnight University, there were discussions organised every Saturday. Students like myself had a chance to meet students from other faculties who were interested in alternative education, outside the classroom. Some of those friends now work in the NGO sector. Nidhi gave the first talk for Midnight University, "Poverty 101", and set the rule that he was a janitor, not a teacher. Everyone had an equal right to raise their hand, and we were there to exchange ideas. It gave the courage to ask questions – normally in school we didn't dare. We gained knowledge beyond art. Compared to that, what I learned in art school was quite boring and narrow.'

Arrivals / Influx of Global Dynamic Torrent / Disappearance

'Streams of universal culture have begun to flow in', wrote Chumpon Apisuk of Thailand's early 1990s scene, in an edition of *Artlink* that also featured a review of the first CMSI. Such coverage was one factor in the growing number of international visitors to Chiang Mai in subsequent years. 'The peak moment was in 1996', says Uthit Atimana. 'Media is such a weird and powerful thing. Just a single journal could spread the word, domestically and internationally. I'm still amazed by how far we reached.' By the middle of the decade, CMSI's international participants outnumbered local ones, and it had received press attention in Thailand and far beyond – in the Netherlands and Japan, for instance. Santiphap Inkong-ngam says that by this time 'the festival was packed with visitors. Many had flown in just for the event, along with those who wanted to exhibit. It was something people just knew about. ... Basically the news spread by word of mouth.'

Tei Kobayashi, who heard about the festival via fellow artists, recounts her midnight arrival in 1996 (writing at the time for *Asiana* magazine): 'I step through the ancient wooden portico. Someone is there. He looks Mongolian. He holds a paintbrush, not a weapon, dipped in red paint, not blood. Artists are ambassadors of peace. He paints a red line across the wooden gate, slowly, with intent. I approach him, he smiles, I question, "Social Installation?" He gestures to the bonfires in the distance. He asks me to join them. ... I notice that J.J. [Jian Jun Xi] is using oil-based paint. He initiates me: a bright, red dash of a line (a bindi) on my forehead and one on my hand are carefully painted in. At
p.185 the end of the Week of Cooperative Suffering everyone else will paint J.J. using his paint (primary colours only) and brushes in a ritualistic performance. ... An
p.187 installation of blocks of ice filled with kerosene and lit was an intense work that spattered the centre of town around Tha Pae Gate with fire and ice. The blocks burst and fire filled the air. The danger was obvious, but everything was accepted as an experiment in reality.'

'Like other tourists, I arrived at the airport in Chiang Mai around midnight on 18 November 1995, accompanied by a bevy of retirees from eastern Europe, *Lonely Planet* guide – the backpacker bible – under my arm.' Ray Langenbach's account, like Tei Kobayashi's, proceeds from an arrival at Chiang Mai Airport from afar and foregrounds the 'tourist' position. David Blamey arrived at the same edition as part of a delegation of UK-based artists whose contributions to the festival, under the shared title 'Backpacker', were characterised by a keen, self-reflexive awareness of their 'outsider' status, 'made with degrees of reference to the problematics of our sudden British Council-funded presence in the Thai cultural scene'. He recalls

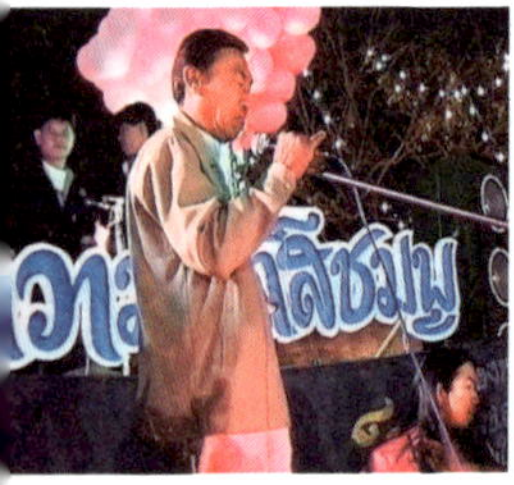
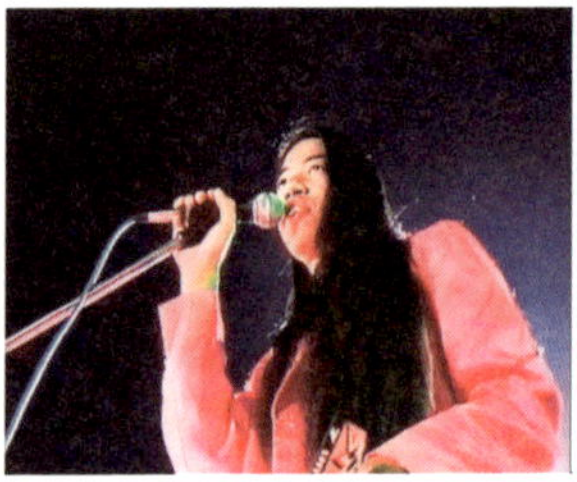
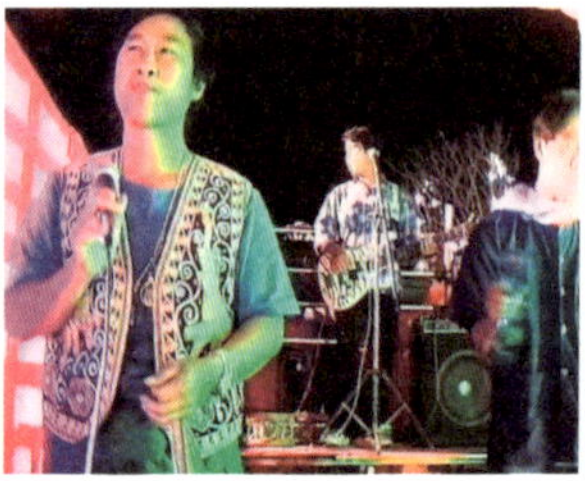
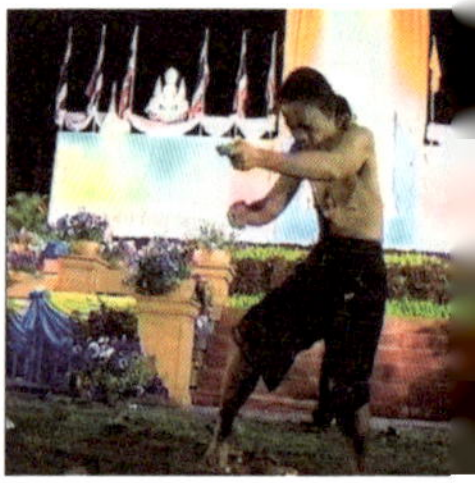

his arrival: 'I can distinctly remember that some sort of incident had just taken place by the time we got to the university grounds. Someone told us that all the teachers were on strike because they hadn't been paid and that students had spent the day protesting against the administration of their school. This information offered a plausible rationale for why the campus was pretty much deserted. Only a partially dislodged banner on a handrail in the central courtyard still fluttered in the warm breeze and a few discarded handouts remained on the floor. There was an invigorating whiff of art and politics in the air, but our enigmatic host was nowhere to be found. It was immediately apparent that we had stumbled into a sensitive local situation from an international perspective in a way that was exciting to witness, but which raised some searching questions about why we were even there at all. In hindsight it has been possible to see this initial brief encounter as a microcosmic forewarning of the mythical and mysterious Week of Cooperative Suffering that was about to unravel around us over the next seven days.'

Describing a magical and intense week of performances and exchanges in this 'ocean of cultural signifiers', Blamey notes wryly that, 'as a group of foreigners who had miraculously found ourselves a part of this exceptional event, we were ultimately unable to discard our attachment to all conventions of the Western art world. We made the mistake of organising a traditional closing party in a downtown bar to mark the conclusion of our project. After distributing invitations and stocking up on cold beers, we installed ourselves in preparation for our guests. Sadly, I can only recall two people turning up: Rirkrit Tiravanija and a friend. We played a few games of pool together and caught up on international art world gossip. After that, everyone went their separate ways. It was as if the whole thing had never happened. But I can assure you it did.'

Rirkrit was, by 1996, well travelled on the international contemporary art circuit but 'unknown in Thailand. People thought I was an alien because I was born and grew up outside of Thailand. Senior artists dismissed me. I was not in the Thai art circle.' In New York he had met Navin Rawanchaikul, who invited him to Chiang Mai. 'I was surprised to learn that there were so many artists working in Thailand and expressing their ideas. They invented different methods for survival, such as CMSI. Meanwhile, globalisation was taking shape, in my opinion as a result of the West's need to benefit from developing regions such as Asia and Southeast Asia, whose economies were growing. I was interested in the ideas and energies that were emerging in Thailand at that moment. There are different institutions in Thailand, but these institutions hadn't dominated our thinking

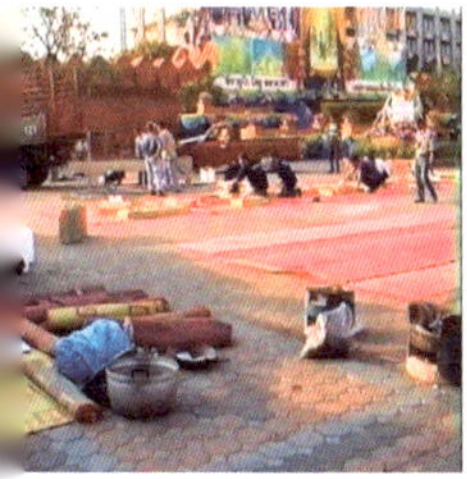
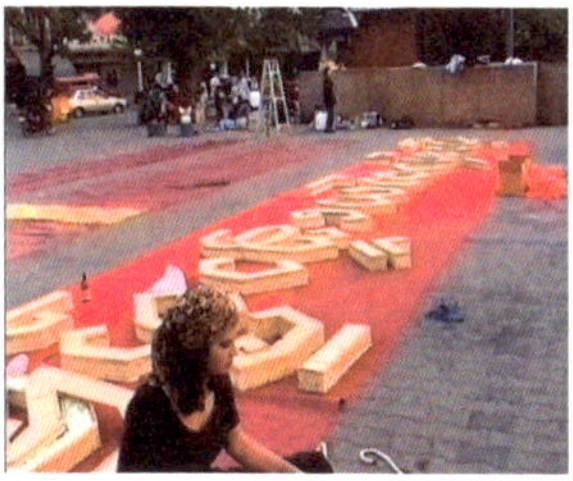
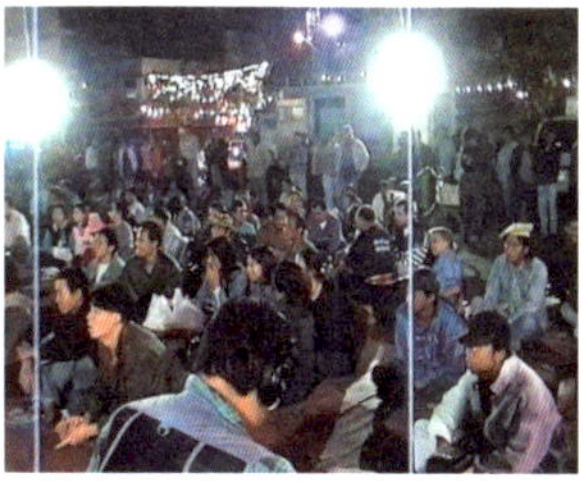
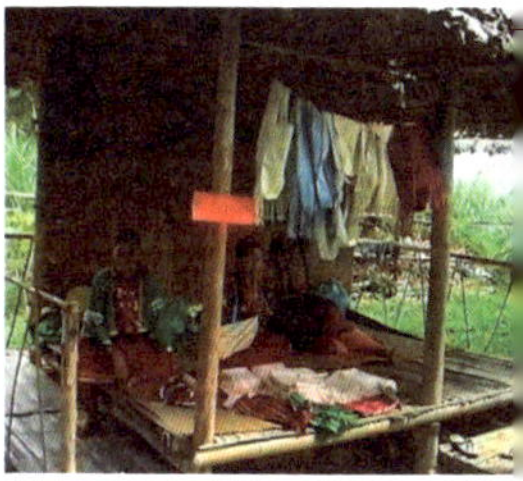

completely. It was a highly creative space. … People had to be creative to be able to survive in the existing system – or in a place where there is no system at all.'

'I think *farang* who came at that time tried to adjust themselves to the Asian lifestyle', says Araya Rasdjarmrearnsook. For Supachai Satsara, the shared creative vocation of Southeast Asian and *farang* participants was enough to outweigh any differences. 'Artists' ways of life are rather strange. They have a lot of privacy, while at the same time travelling widely and connecting with many different people.' Writing in *Artlink* of her experience of artist residencies in Thailand in the 1990s,

US-born and Australia-based CMSI participant Joan Grounds notes that local debates pitching local against imported culture were lost on her, whether due to language barriers or other reasons, and that her rapport with fellow artists tended to be strongest with those educated in Europe, North America or Japan. Nonetheless, the experience was 'not unlike being born into a culture, nation, city, family. I usually say, Thailand chose me.'[24]

Various participants note that CMSI produced freedoms that would have been unavailable in their home countries. Juan Jun Xi said: 'I could never do anything like this in London. They would arrest me before the paint was on my brush. Defacing public property or some such regulation would inhibit the freedom of expression the artist thrives on.'[25] Another observer noted that CMSI 'was too radical for the German government', relating the fact that no German artists were able to get support to participate.[26] The free use of public space was in no small part due to the status of the *ajarn* (professor) in Thai society. 'One thing that amazed some of the Japanese participants was our permission to use public spaces', says Uthit. 'The charm of this place is, we can get permission pretty easily. In Thai society, the status of university professors and the sacredness of Chiang Mai University are still strongly felt.'

Araya notes the contradictory forces that shaped CMSI: 'While one of the objectives was to support individuality and reject Thai traditional art, the exhibition itself, because of the interest of the national and international press, was taken into the main current of the art world. Although the second CMSI supported individuality in favour of upholding traditional Thai values, at the same time it fell into another trap in its emphasis on globalised values such as international fame and reputation.'[27] The festivals partook in Thailand's entry into global circuits of commerce and tourism, and also reflected a growing anti-globalisation and anti-Western feeling in Thailand that overlapped with less-than-

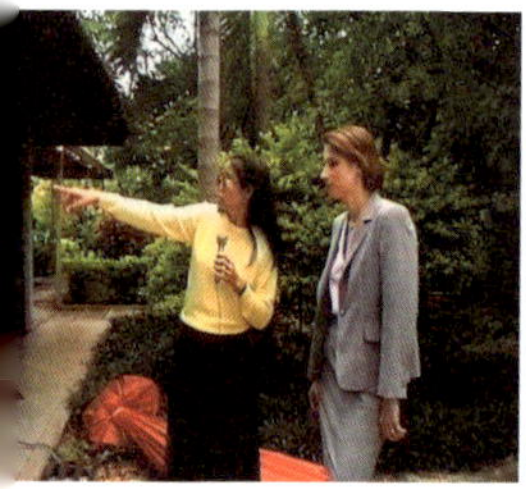
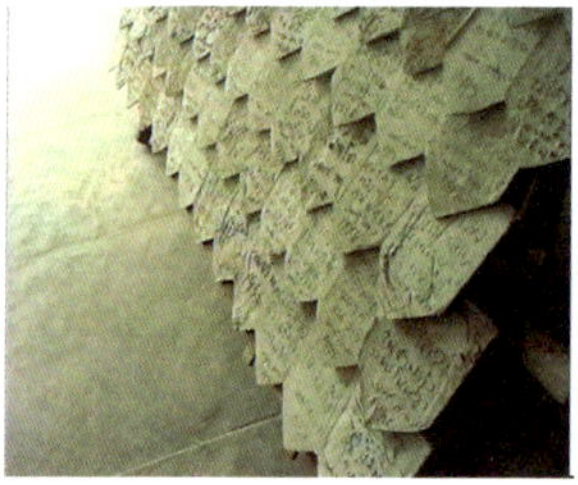
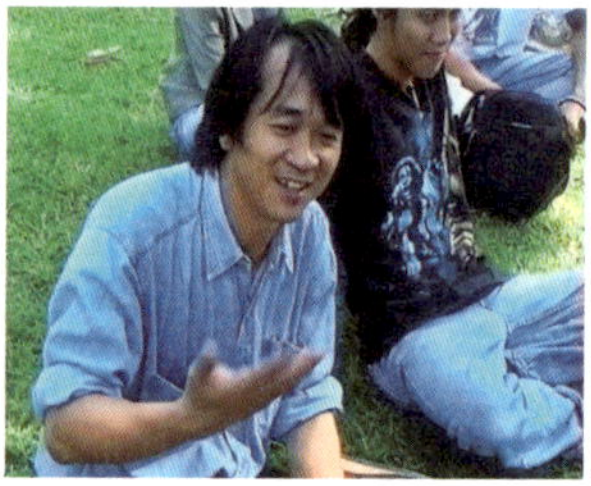
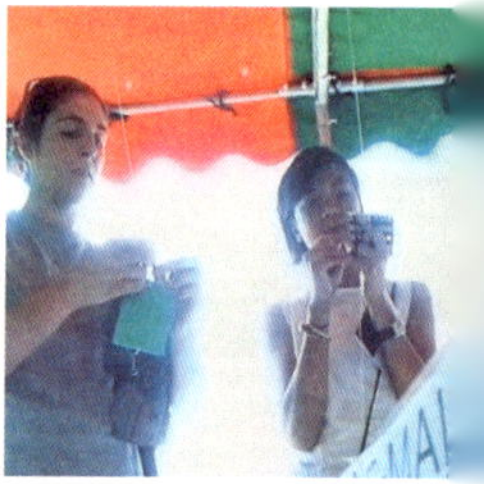

progressive political, religious and nationalist tendencies. According to Thasnai Sethaseree, the first edition 'perfectly embodied the characteristics of Thai society. Even Midnight University had a strong Buddhist aura. Anti-Western feeling was very distinct. It was a trend of opposition, the swing back from globalisation. ... Localism was built up to attack anything that wasn't [Thai]. It opposed Westernism, Americanism and globalisation.'

—

[24] Joan Grounds, 'Learning About Difference', *Artlink*, vol.13, no.3–4, December 1993.
[25] Quoted in T. Kobayashi (T.J. McGuire), 'A Week of Suffering in Chiang Mai', *op. cit.*

In the end, as Araya writes, CMSI 'quietly disappeared from the town's future'. Its end is remembered variously as a natural decline, a falling apart due to administrative pressures and organisational incapacity, and a deliberate strategy of withdrawal. Most participants agree that the end was around the fourth edition, in 1997–98, though events in continuation of CMSI, with many of the same protagonists, have appeared since, such as 'Eukabeuk' (November 2001–March 2002) and 'Chiang Mai Social Installation: Mok Muan' (October 2002–January 2003). Angkrit recalls that 'the last one that I participated in had a theme – "the poverty of the artist" – because we didn't have money to organise the event'. Uthit's involvement in CMSI projects has been fairly continuous, but he agrees that the energies dwindled around 1997–98, and that a transition to a younger generation occurred, including curators such as Gridthiya Gaweewong (the driving force behind Project 304, founded in Bangkok in 1996) and initiatives such as The Land Foundation (founded in 1998 by Uthit, Rirkrit and Kamin Lertchaiprasert in Chiang Mai). 'I began to realise that CMSI was being institutionalised. It started to have a pattern. It was becoming an art activity like any other. Its popularity had turned against itself, turning it into an undersized documenta.' For Uthit, whose energies began to be redirected into his work as director of Chiang Mai University Art Gallery, CMSI was failing to connect to wider publics even as it gained popularity – 'only artists joined', which was 'not my concept'.

Navin, who says there was 'always a question of how this could continue', recalls the 'chaos' of CMSI's later years. 'They did not plan. It was more like a party or a get-together than a social intervention. … Since '96 it was really chaos. I think Uthit liked that kind of chaos.' According to some, CMSI's undoing was also the absence of key supporting figures such as Navin, Kosit Juntaratip and their peers who had long helped with planning and organisation. By the late 1990s, this student cohort had graduated and were moving on to other projects. Some 'had become famous already', or they were keen, says Uthit, to do 'their own thing. They don't want a part of cooperation like mine.' For Sutthirat Supaparinya, a member of the student cohort, it was clear by the early 2000s that the project had run its course and that the older generation 'could not continue on their own. Without Kosit and Navin, how could they run it? It's a lot of work.' For Jay Koh, the organisers' 'critical position had no cohering value. That's why after the fourth time they collapsed. Because there was no continuum. We are supposed to learn, from one stage to the next, but the festivals didn't build on the ones before.

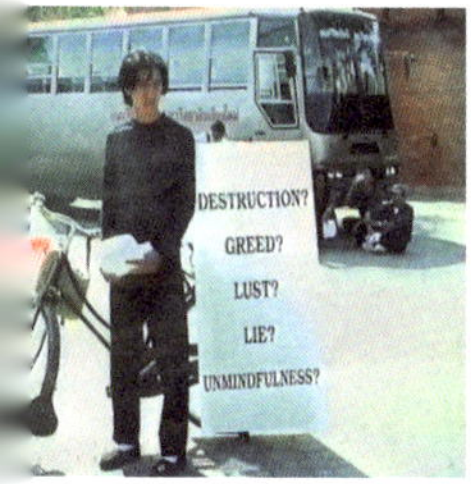

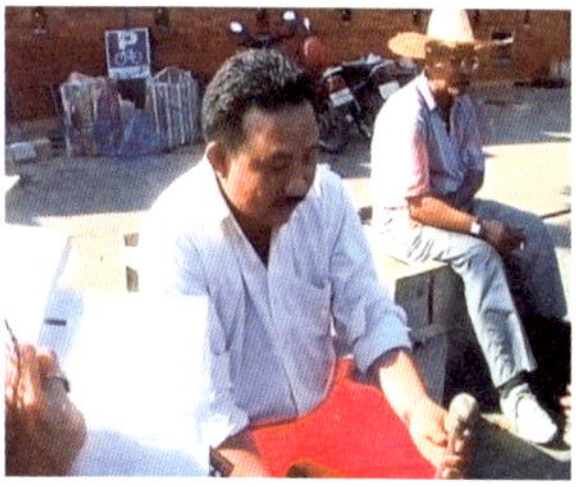

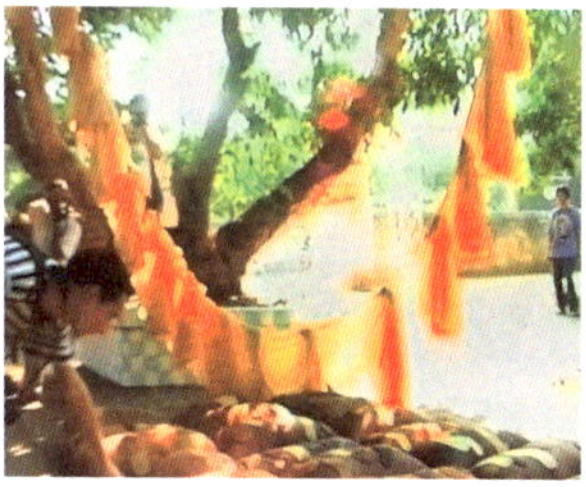

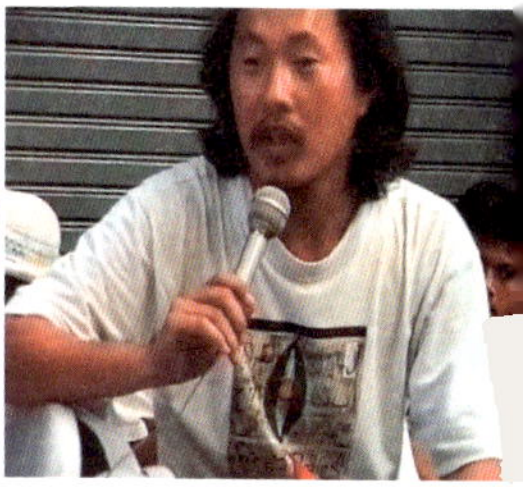

—

[26] *Ibid.*

… That's why it was no surprise to me that they stopped. If you have no vision, how do you survive with mere repetition? How do you work if there is no sense of development?' Supachai also suggests that later, when the project had drifted from its founding ethos of collectivity, CMSI was felt to 'belong to' certain organisers, whereas 'in the beginning, it didn't belong to anyone. It was a group.' 'The reasons for the end of CMSI are people themselves [the organisers of the event], ideas and management. Maybe the scale of the event became too big, or difficult to control in terms of management and funding. It ended by itself.'

From CMSI, Uthit 'learned that we could create social environments. But [many of] the people who joined, especially the artists, did not come with the right mindsets. They proved very difficult to change and only served to exacerbate the problems in society. There was an overemphasis on artistic beauty and a perfunctory approach to academic issues. That's another reason why I dedicated myself to establishing the media art and design department [at Chiang Mai University] as a pillar of art and cultural education, which I've been experimenting with for almost ten years. And now I'm rather confident that new graduates from this institution will be an entirely different group of artists – artists who are well balanced in both academic mindset and public performance. This is what I hope could fix the problem at its root. And after fixing the problem at its root, I've been thinking that CMSI should be renewed once more.'

Afterlives

At the same time that CMSI's energies were diminishing, the *Bangkok Post* reported that 'So-called "alternative art" is taking off in Thailand now that it has escaped from the galleries. You'll find it in cafes, in condos, even on the street.' The article lists 'at least three longterm positive results for the Thai art scene: it has broken down the gallery fence that kept art firmly inside, it has created new informal academic communities in Chiang Mai, and it has set a precedent for other nongallery art

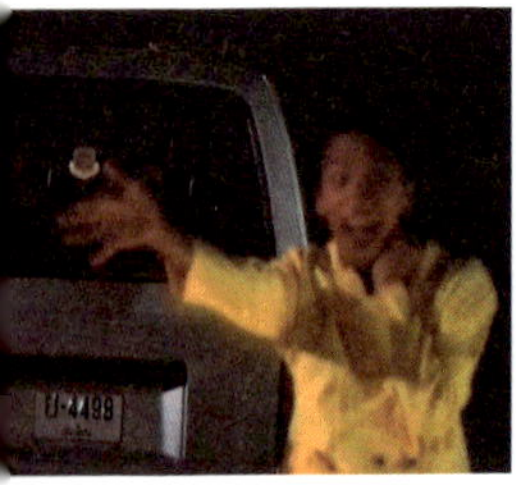

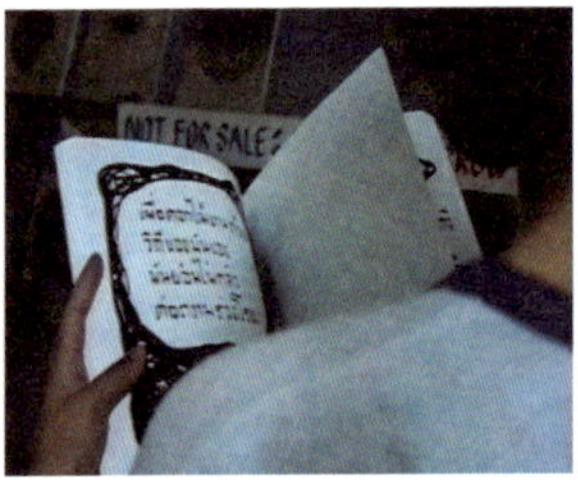

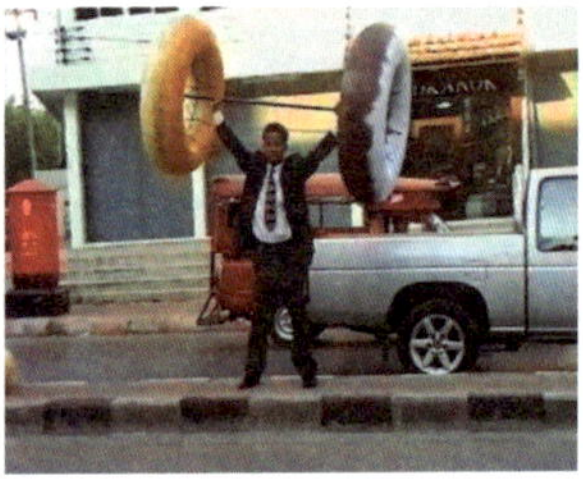

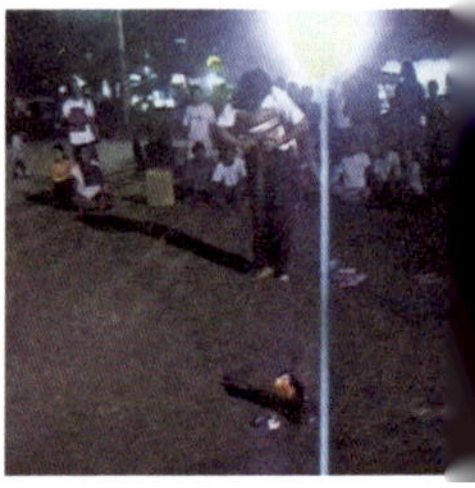

activities to follow.'[28] Writing a few years later, Araya Rasjarmrearnsook saw the after-effects of CMSI in the fact that 'many Thai artists and others who returned from their art studies in the USA and Europe have increasingly taken their art into public spaces'. Araya sees its most lasting legacy in having 'reversed the normal trend where the provinces follow Bangkok's cultural initiatives. … This is may be the most positive contribution of CMSI to the art world of our nation.'[29]

—

[27] Araya, 'A narrative of an event that has just come to an end', *op. cit.* p.16.

[28] Pattara Danutra, 'Up, up, and away', *Bangkok Post,* 5 September 1997.

'The early 1990s open a new chapter for contemporary art in Thailand. Political instability, social unrest, AIDS, child prostitution [and] the May massacre of 1992 are some of the issues which have jolted the artists out of their comfortable boredoms', noted Apinan Poshyananda in 1993, observing that artists were now more willing to go 'against the grain of the money-spinning whirlwind that will make them rich but perhaps not so famous'.[30] Visual Dhamma, directed by Alfred Pawlin, was one of only a handful of art spaces in Bangkok that supported such artists, hosting several exhibitions of various members of the CMSI circle in 1992–93. 'It's funny that this public art approach, that had also appeared in the West, where people protested against galleries – "the gallery system is sick, full of greedy people…" – would also emerge in Thailand, where there was only one gallery – me!' Pawlin identifies a strong resonance between CMSI and art events happening in the Philippines from the late 1980s. He recalls Filipino artists' reactions to the restrictive 'stiffness' of the Bangkok art scene, for instance, 'in the Philippines we dance and drum, and we have parties!' In particular, Pawlin cites the festivals held in Baguio from 1989. 'Baguio is like Chiang Mai, more or less. p.43
Its climate is cooler through the whole season compared to Manila, very similar to Chiang Mai. … And then many artists moved there because life was cheaper. And the Baguio festivals were certainly an influence.' In the words of Santiago Bose, Baguio was a 'celebration of artists by artists for artists'.

'CMSI was not like biennials or other art events', says Kamin Lertchaiprasert. 'It was a cooperative social activity. Everyone invited their friends, students and acquaintances to participate. There was no process of submissions and no selection of works from proposals. Everyone just got together, like a temple fair, which had both advantages and disadvantages. For me, I see it as an advantage. It provided opportunities for young artists and non-artists to express their ideas. It didn't focus on quality or on featuring famous artists. If people expected a biennial, they would be disappointed. But it actually contributed to learning,

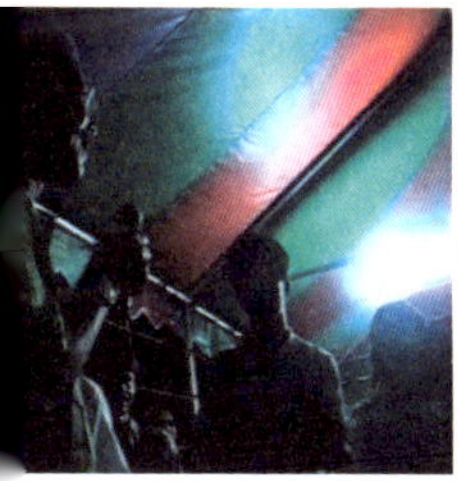
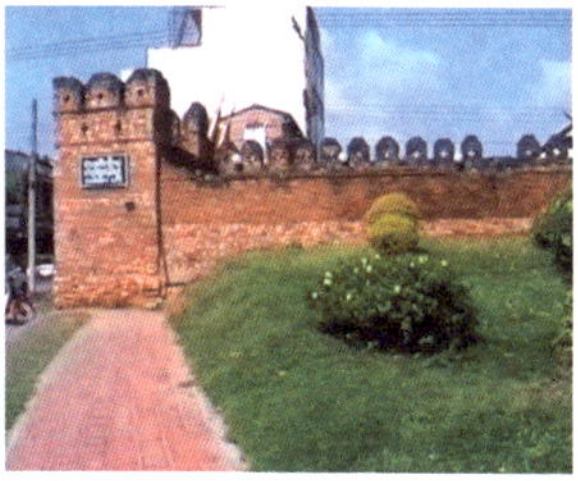
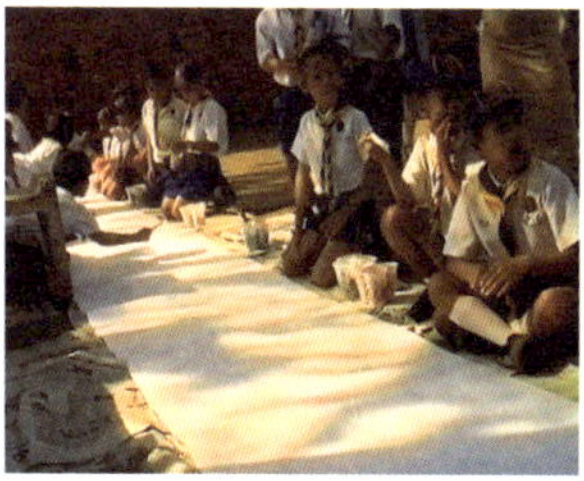
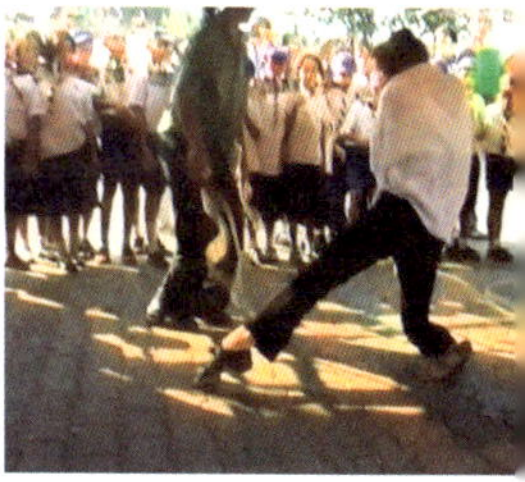

sharing and reaching out to the community. This was a strength of CMSI that other art events don't have.'

CMSI's afterlives are perhaps most apparent in the experience of its participants. For Tawatchai Puntusawasdi, 'it affected my art practice in that I began to think

—

[29] Araya, 'A narrative of an event that has just come to an end', *op. cit.*, p.16.

[30] Apinan Poshyananda, 'Modern Art in Thailand: A Glimpse', *Artlink*, vol.13, no.3–4, December 1993.

about site and space first when I began to make work'. For Thatree Pokawanich, 'participating in CMSI enabled me to expand my ideas about art. In terms of an interaction with the public, I don't think they had anything like the experience I did. ... Nowadays I work with the community, as a facilitator doing community art projects. I feel better about this than my contributions to CMSI, because the people I work with are so happy and proud of the art they produce. There is no "me" in the project, and I feel it has affected the public more than what I did in CMSI.' Navin Rawanchaikul notes the organisers' disconnection from commercial art circuits. 'I say this to young artists, today. Even before they've made an artwork they've thought about how they're going to sell it. [Whereas in the case of CMSI] there weren't art fairs – we didn't think about artworks being for sale, we had no idea. And that gave us a certain freedom, you know, separate from any art market. Montien [Boonma] had an installation and in the end he burned it – it was really freedom.'

Supachai Satsara connects CMSI to the spread of certain forms of art practice. 'It made an impact because you could see artworks and performances around the city, everywhere. ... In Southeast Asia, people didn't really know what performance art was at that time – but Asiatopia I think started soon after.' Chumpon Apisuk, who founded Asiatopia Performance Art Festival in 1998, sees CMSI in the context of a

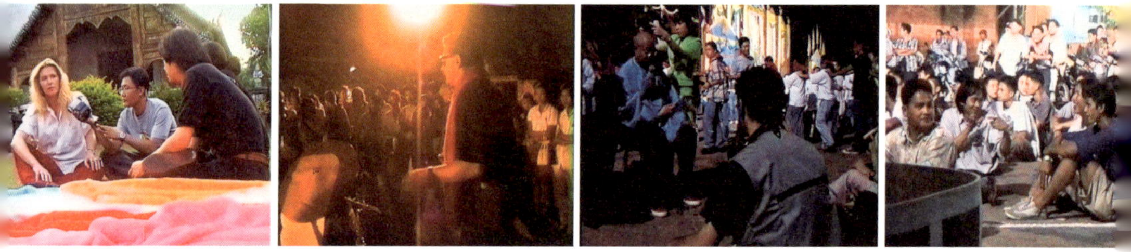

wider emergence of like-minded practices in Thailand since the early 1990s: 'There were small groups of people who created movements in unusual spaces that were not art spaces, such as Ruangpeung, founded by Jutha Sucharit.' Chumpon was also part of Bangkok-based group City Art League, formed around 1993, who would present their works 'in performance and multimedia formats', in 'streets, shopping centres, parks or other public places'.

For Arahmaiani, the festivals created a context in which artistic autonomy felt possible. 'We would discuss whether people would see what we're doing as art, within an art world context. But since we felt we were part of a group, we had more confidence – like, "they can call it whatever, I just do it. That's how I feel and that's what I want to express."' Like other participants, Arahmaiani describes how she was involved in what others would later describe as 'performance art', but before it was ever named as such. For her it was 'very important that we, as an artistic community,
p.31 could support each other so that everyone could express themselves. ... I just felt there was a kind of freedom there at that time.' Another important gathering in this regard was the women artists' network and festival Womanifesto, featuring CMSI participants including Arahmaiani, Nilofar Akmut, Amanda Heng, Ingrid Klauser and Tei Kobayashi, and organised by a group including Nitaya Ueareeworakul and

Varsha Nair. It grew out of the exhibition 'Tradisexion', held at Concrete House in response to the ban on women in temples in Thailand; Nair recalls that 'there were no women's art gatherings taking place in the region. So Womanifesto was very much set up from thinking, why don't we do something? … It took place biannually from 1997 all the way to 2005–06. … As a woman artist, I really feel that we are being erased – like we are being made invisible. Because no one talks about [Womanifesto]. … CMSI was like a stepping stone. And I really give it credit for having that open format where all these artists were able to come and meet each other – things come out of that. It really is an amazing model [and] ran on a different energy, in a way. I recognise it because that was how Womanifesto was run – on your own energy, your own passion.' There was very little money, but 'it didn't really matter. Artists came, they stay in our homes. We met at each other's homes. We cooked together. We lived together. We exhibited together. We talked about each other's work. And we exchanged. That was really the core energy.'

Navin says at the time artists did not think in terms of region. 'We didn't call it Southeast Asia. … We just thought, Philippines, neighbours.' In his opinion, Southeast Asian artists gathering at CMSI 'felt a sense of freedom. Of course, they had fun, getting together with friends, but there was also a feeling of opening up.'

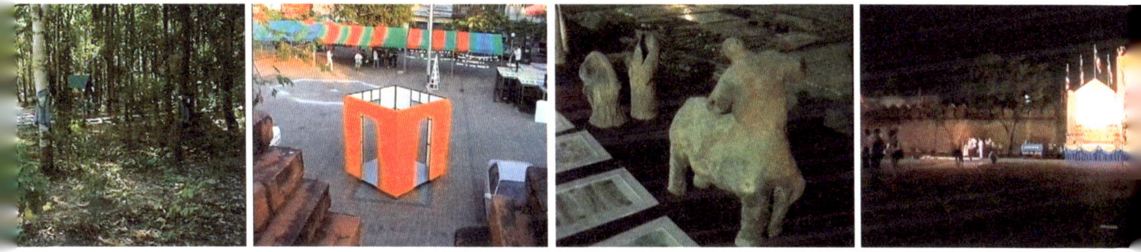

Kosit Juntaratip references a complicated sense of autonomy, for him particular to Thailand, that meant they were able to access 'other layers, other dimensions of Thai society'. 'To feel free while knowing you are controlled – even though you are aware of this control, you feel free.' Arahmaiani recognises certain similarities with other parts of the region, particularly her native Indonesia. 'Although they believe in different religion, the way they instrumentalise religion is not so different. And the military regime – although there is no king [in Indonesia] the president behaves like a king anyway.' Thasnai Sethaseree says that 'people always believe art is free. They don't realise they are part of the matrix of political discourses.' 'The main argument in my thesis is that the artist is not central to the work but is part of the whole matrix that they build up, which is also part of the social setting. … I tried to argue against the egoism in the artists' mindset of the time.' In Thasnai's opinion, CMSI was ultimately not able to produce the 'social installation' it intended. 'It neither really changed the social situation nor questioned it. It was just another "form" of art exhibition in the 90s.' Political developments in Thailand, and the positions of CMSI participants in the artistic community, have since led him to see the project in a different light. 'After the latest coup, I couldn't help but notice that the main force behind 1990s CMSI, who tried to criticise the existing traditional art, and who called for freedom of expression and new languages of art, turned to relinquish their hard-fought freedom … [and ran into the arms of] dictatorship.' 'The freedom that I saw – if explained by Marxists, would be "false consciousness". It's a misled consciousness, an ideology they don't truly believe, a faith they don't truly have, I mean, a faith in their freedom. … It is a conflict that reflects a general problem of the art world today.'

'We tried to prevent institutionalisation', says Uthit. 'This became a source of conflicts later on. When the project became popular, many people wanted to take control and make it look good. I told them that it was already self-sufficient. We only needed people to join us and present their works.' The idea of selection was a particular bone of contention in later years, with some arguing for a more curated approach, whereas others, such as Uthit, felt that such ideas of selection and artistic quality went against the basic ethos of CMSI. 'Imagine if we, the organisers, were looking at some works and saying, "Oh, that's so professional" or "that's so amateur". People with the old paradigm of what an exhibition should be like come with an expectation to see all the chosen masterpieces. They just want to see the "best" works within a limited time. But Chiang Mai Social Installation was more like a tropical forest.'

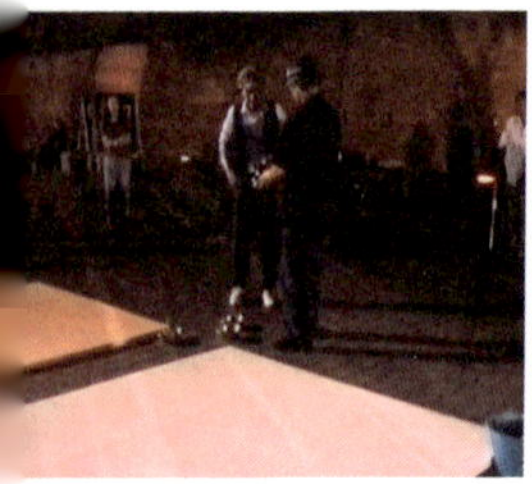
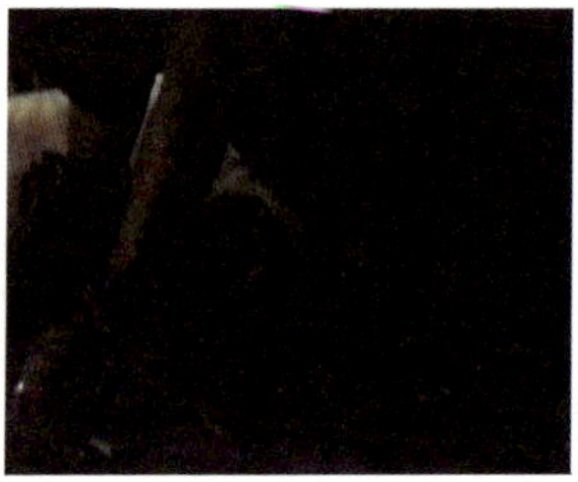
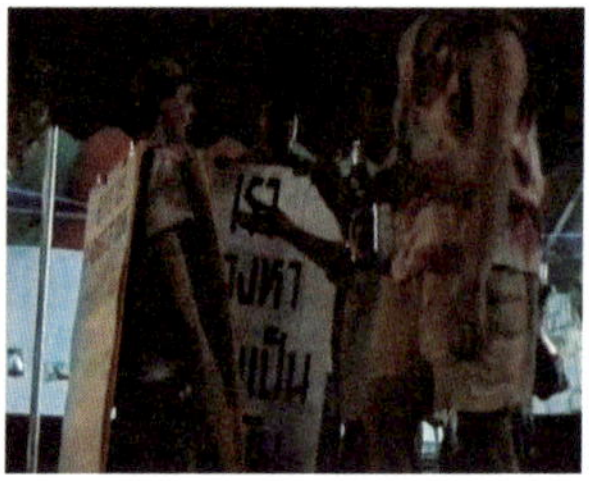
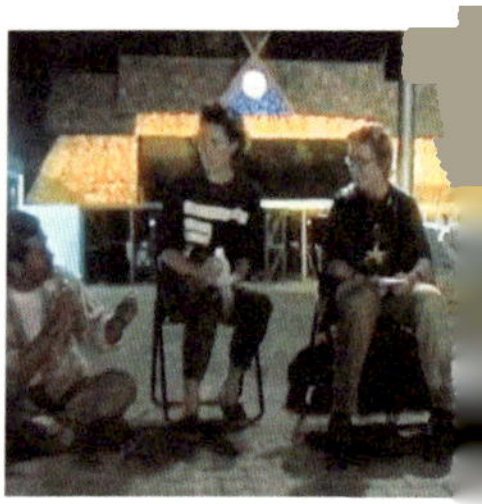

Araya says CMSI was the meeting of 'two opposite kinds of energies – a young group's energies and permanent energies that were very slow. … The important question is how we can build a new wave of that ambient energy again.' For Jay Koh, for the festivals to return 'they would have to build a critical structure or process to look at how an artist goes into a community, and how an artist operates in public space. Because now, after twenty years, the world has changed.' For Gridthiya Gawaeewong, CMSI was part of a 'new generation of art movements that challenged the status quo and shook the scene for six years in the early 90s. During this transitional period, it managed to redefine the idea of art in relation to the public, becoming an early Thai contemporary art platform and posing a set of problems of contemporaneity – and deciding to end itself before it could be historicised.'[31]

Thasnai 'took it as a movement, not a festival. I believe that people who were engaged in the project thought the same thing. They were trying to criticise other festivals, mainly documenta or biennales. They didn't want to reproduce that kind of festival in Asia, but it inevitably turned into that later on. It morphed into an institution by itself. Nevertheless, it dissolved, because it had grown too much and had become just another festival. People who joined took it as an open space that was more accessible than other festivals. No permission was needed. Everyone did their own thing. They took it as a stepping stone, leading towards something more official. You can see that many Thai artists thrived elsewhere and left CMSI behind. There are also international artists from that generation, now famous, who actually originated from CMSI. These people didn't come for "social installation" in the sense of bringing about change or social revolution. They came for an art project. That's easy with an open space.'

'Many people, I don't want to name names, benefitted from CMSI – became professors, became well-known artists, and so on', says Uthit. 'For me, this is human. We can learn. We cannot make people become good people. For me, CMSI is only a space in which you can show something together. And in this space you can have many kinds of people. People liked this a lot. They came and participated, again and again, without caring much about the project itself. Some became old friends, too. Any group of people can become friends. That's why, when I want to do something in Chiang Mai, there are many friends I can ask. To this day.'

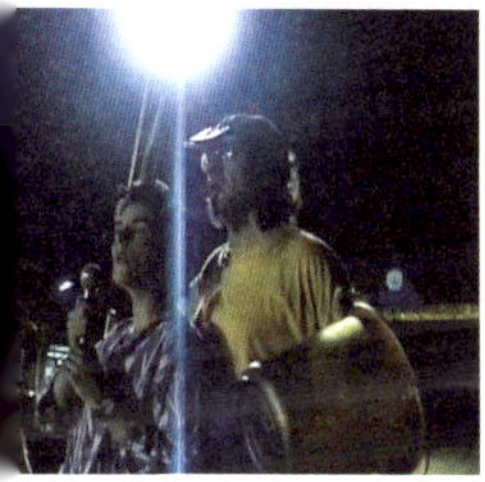

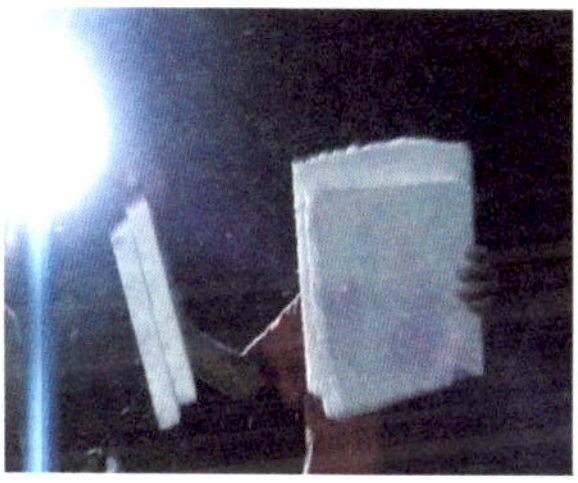

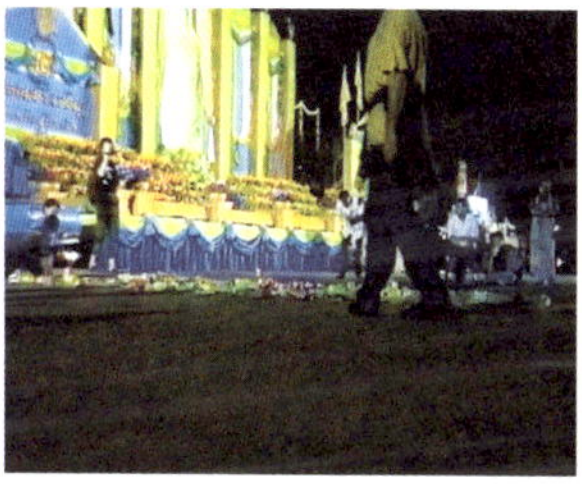

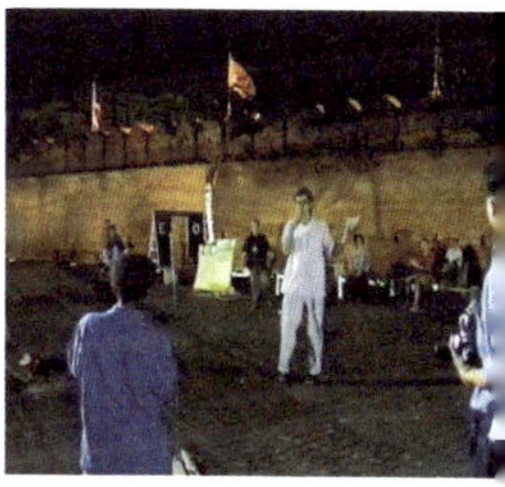

—

[31] Gridthiya Gaweewong, 'Curatorial Practices and Small Narratives: A Case Study of Chiang Mai Social Installation and Its Trajectory', *Thammasat University Journal of Sociology and Anthropology*, vol.34, no.2, July–December 2015.

'Art Festival: Temples and Cemeteries'
Chiang Mai
November 1992–February 1993

'Art Festival: Temples and Cemeteries'

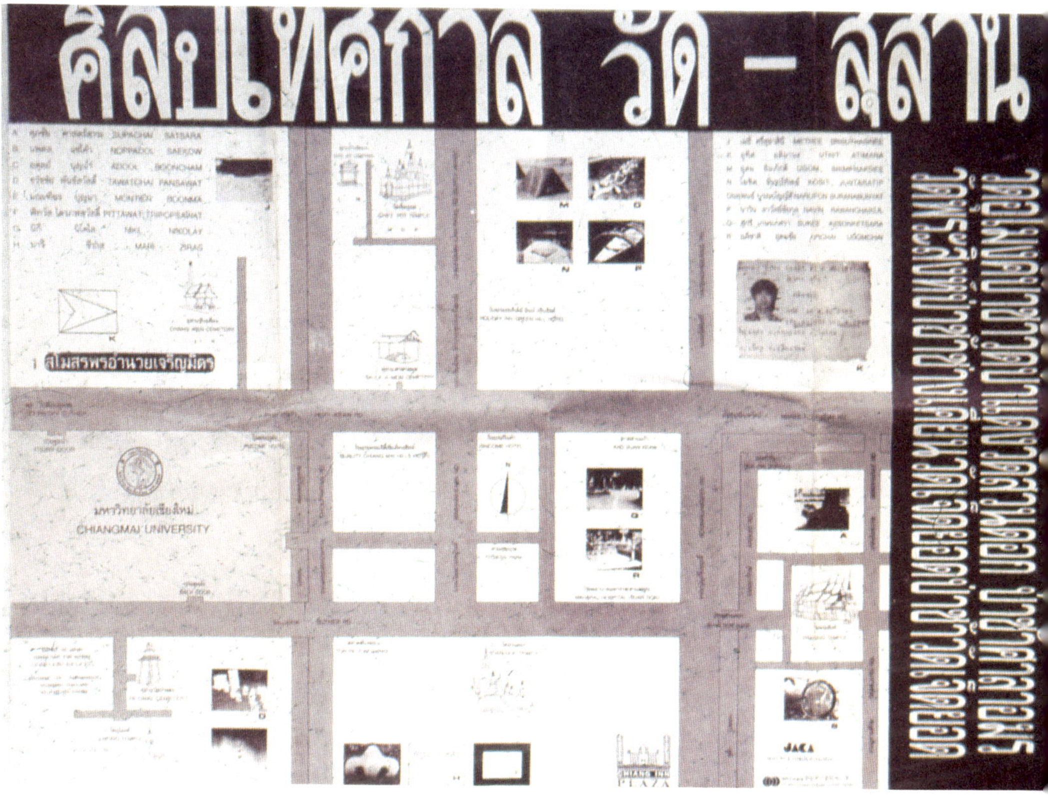

Information brochure for 'Art Festival: Temples and Cemeteries'. It involved sixteen artists (including art students at Chiang Mai University), who worked at eight sites throughout the city: four temples (Wat Umong, Wat Phra Singh, Wat Suan Dok and Wat Chet Yod) and four cemeteries (Chang Kien, Amorn, Wat Padaeng and Wat Chet Yod).

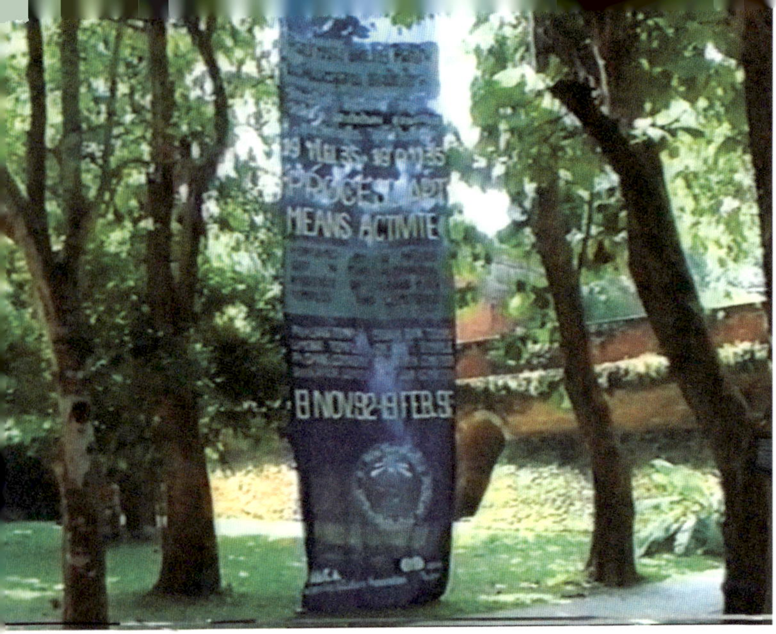

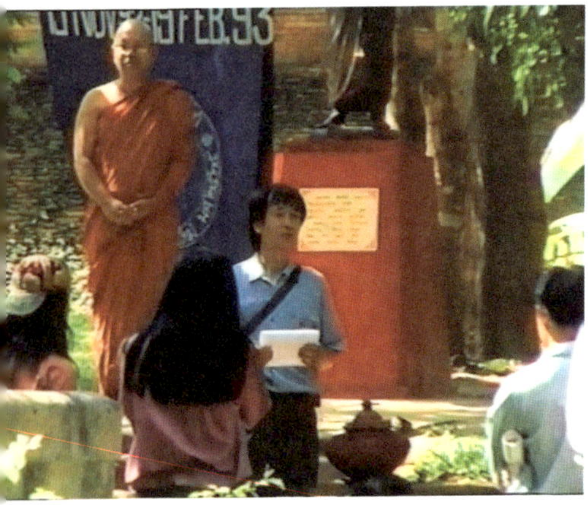

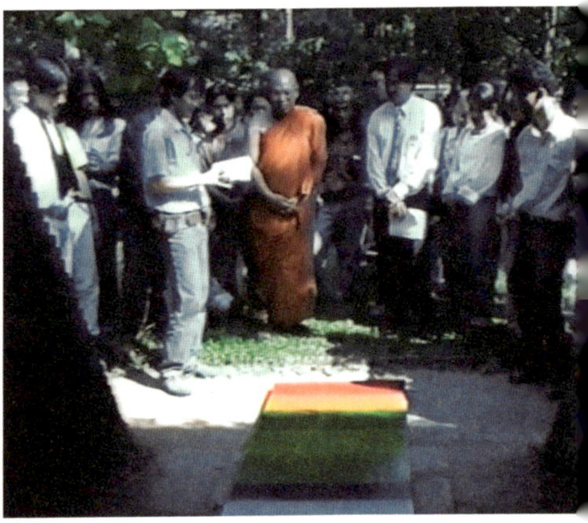

The opening of the festival, with introductions by Uthit Atimana (left) and work by Mit Jai Inn (right).

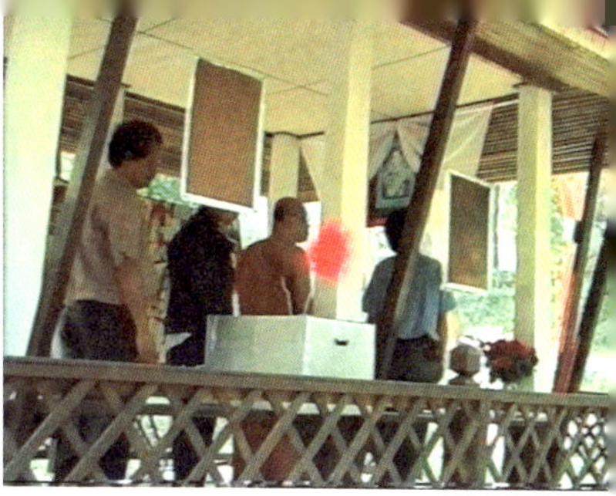

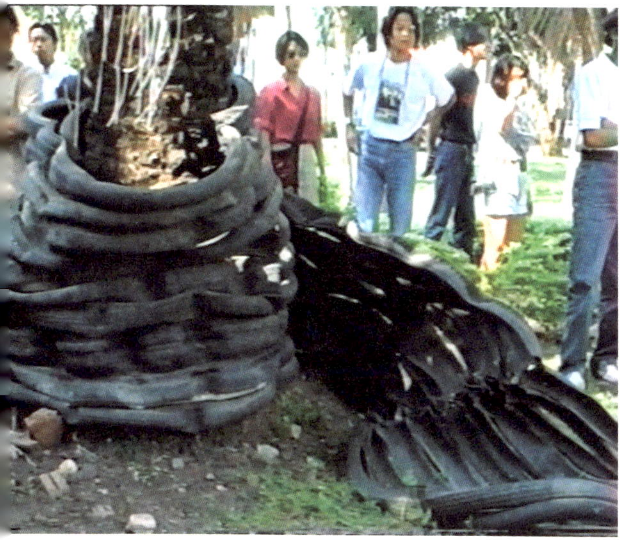

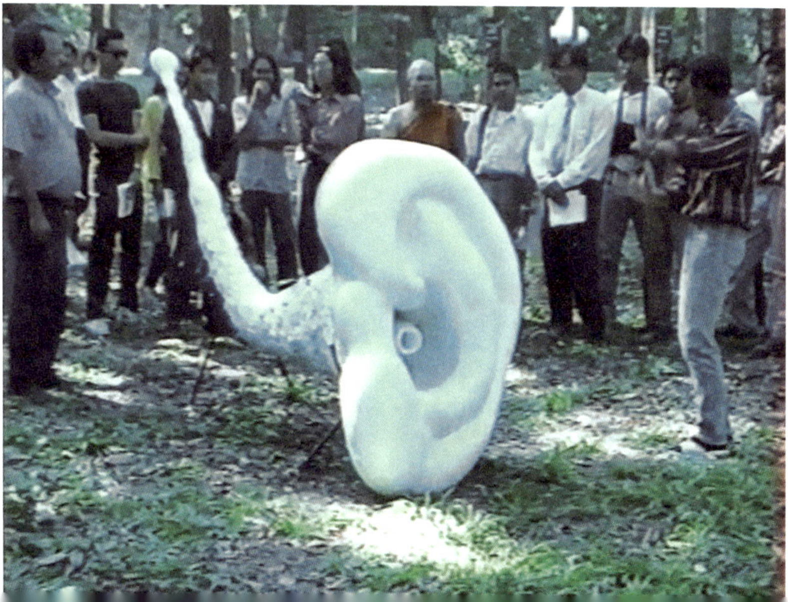

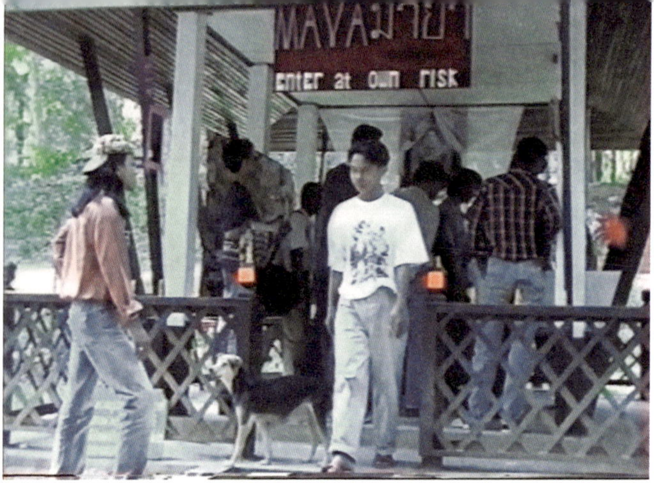
MAYA มายา
enter at own risk

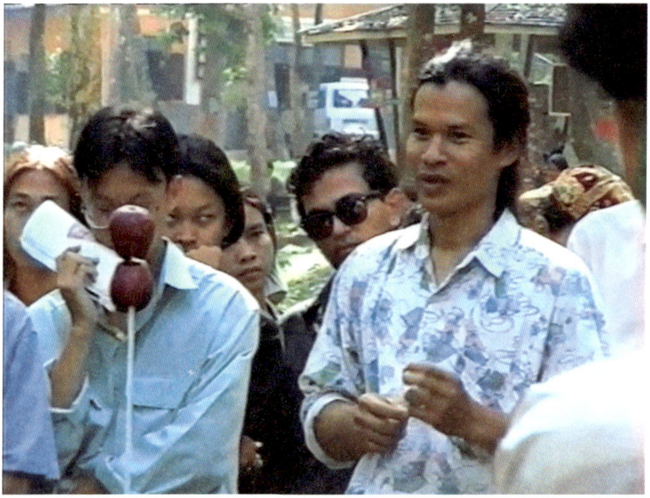

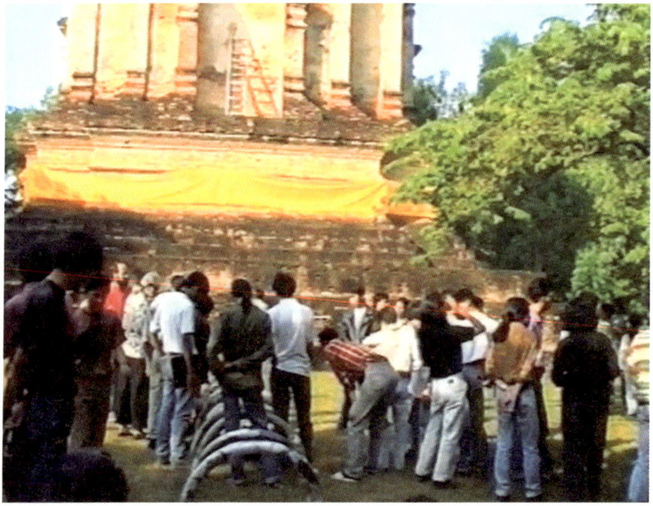

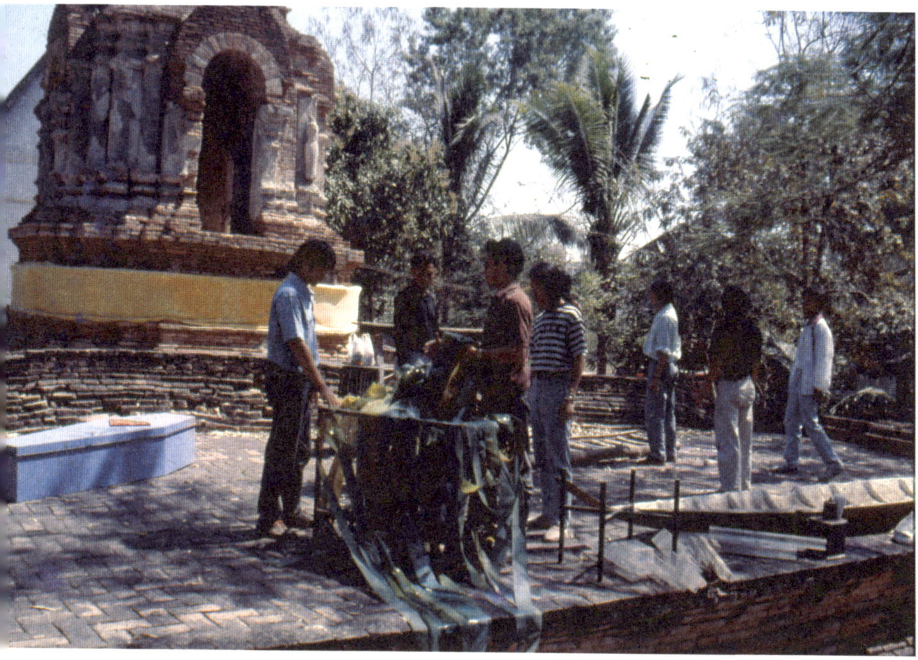

Uthit Atimana, Kosit Juntaratip and Navin Rawanchaikul preparing to install works at Wat Chet Yod.

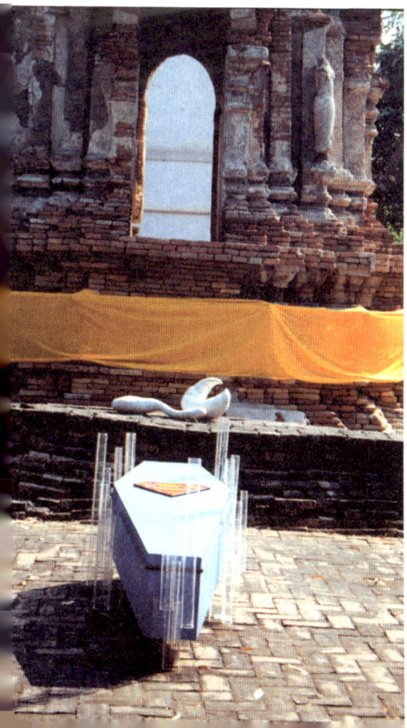

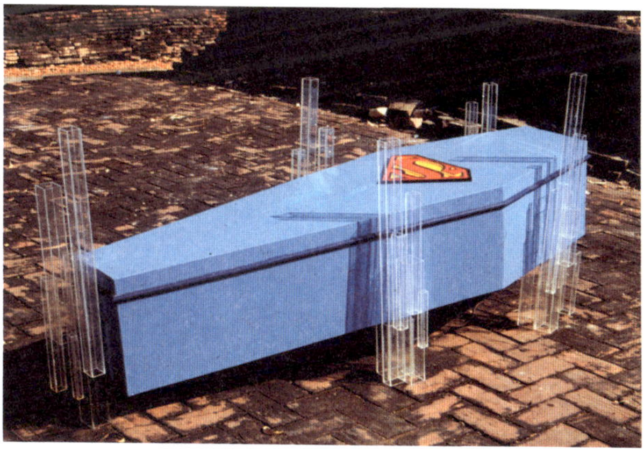

Work by Kosit Juntaratip at Wat Chet Yod. 'What Kosit wanted to present in his work, he said, was the idea of anti-heroism. He mocks Superman, a fictitious immortal hero, comparing him with the ancient pagoda which symbolises religion. The art student thinks the former is unreal, while religion is the only truth of life and lasts forever' (*The Nation*, 19 January 1993).

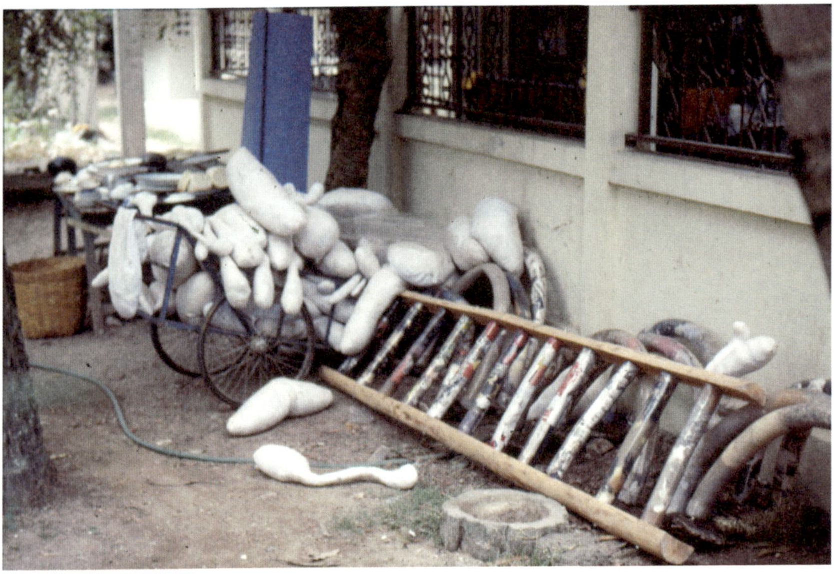

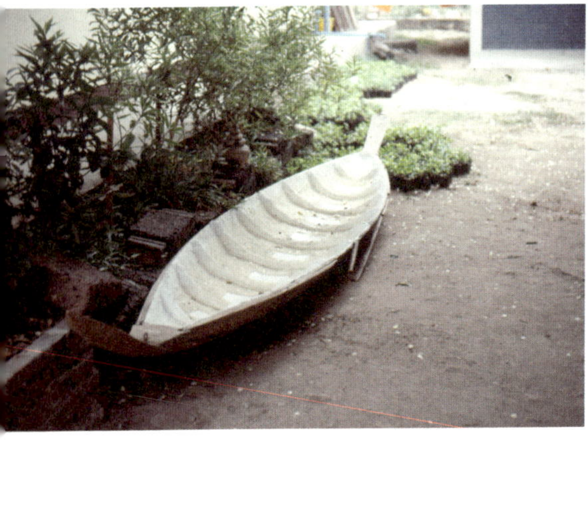

Work by Navin Rawanchaikul after its removal from its original installation (see p.58). He said at the time: 'I want to talk about journeys – spiritual and worldly ones. ... Normally, our transportation takes us to our destination in a horizontal way, like a boat taking us from one place to another, but spiritual, or religious journeys take us in vertical ways, like from earth up to heaven, or from heaven down to hell. The boat and the pagoda represent these two worlds, the earth and heaven, or you could say nirvana, the utmost goal of Buddhism. The stairs on the pagoda are like a two-way medium; they can take you upward to the pinnacle or downward to reach the earth' (*The Nation*, 19 January 1993).

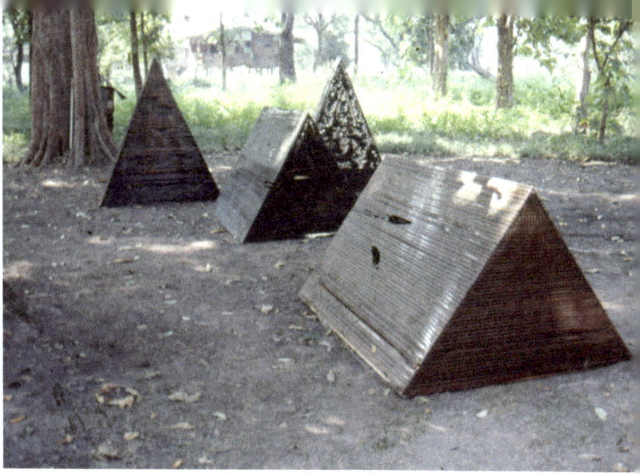

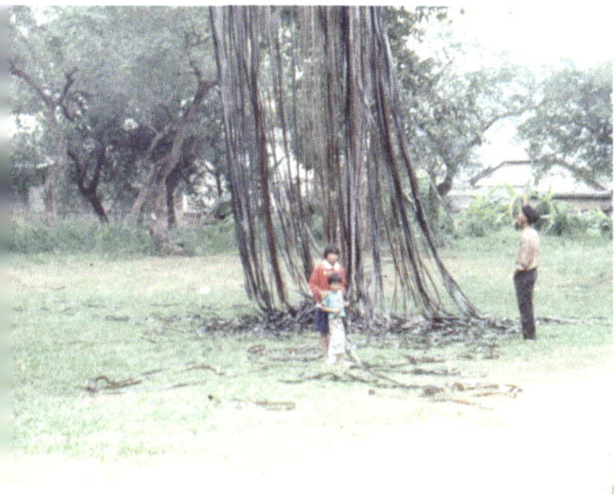

Work by Udom Chimpakdee at Wat Chet Yod.

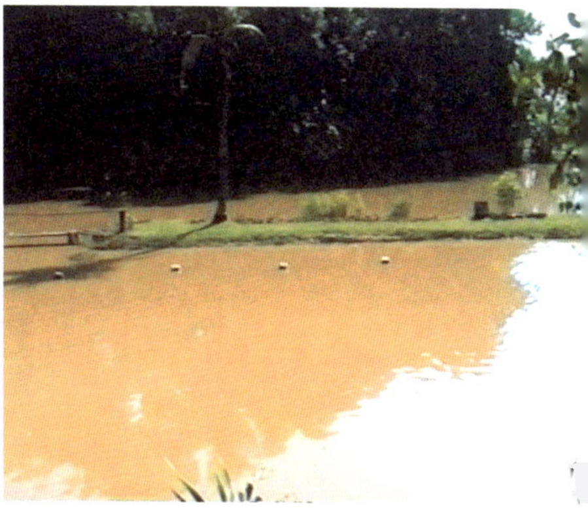

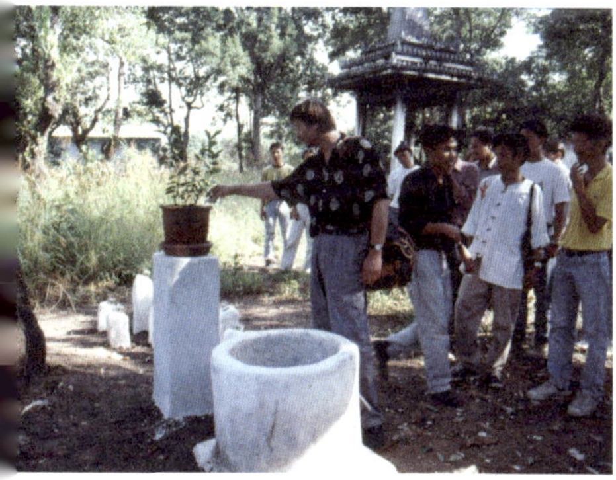

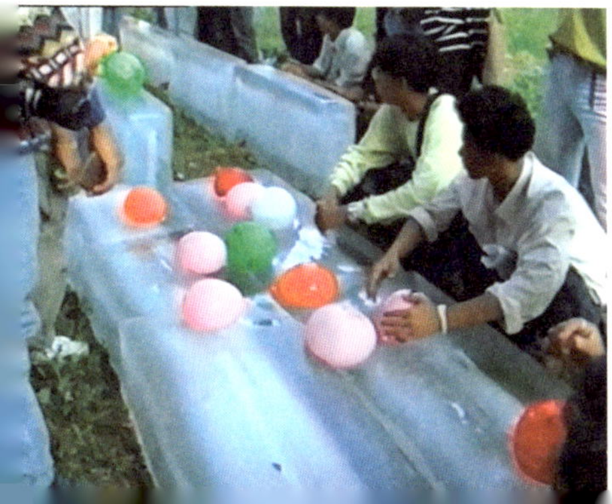

Araya Rasdjarmrearnsook wrote of the first festival: '[T]wo works of note must be mentioned: the first from Uthit himself: a group of large blocks of ice placed on the grass field in front of the cremation pedestal. On the blocks of ice were placed many pink balloons. During the process of melting, the balloons gradually sank into the ice, and when a cremation took place on the cremation pedestal, a voice could be heard complaining: "This corpse does not catch fire: it will take us a long time." Eventually, when the ice had finally melted, little children came to collect the leftover balloons. In another work by Tawatchai Pansawat, the artist planted small trees in flowerpots and placed them around the crematorium. In the eyes of the local villagers, who certainly would not recognise them as art, they looked like decorative trees. Back at the Umong temple a group of young monks could [be] seen laughing and joking about their alms bowls (the work in which artist Montien Boonma had set the bowls adrift on the lake)' (*Journal of Fine Arts*, 2000). For Montien's work *Vipassanā-Vessel*, eight terracotta vessels were floated in the temple's pond in front of a statue of Buddhadasa Bhikkhu.

‘Chiang Mai Social Installation: Second Art Festival: Temples, Cemeteries, Private-Residences, Public Buildings, Streets, Bridges, Walls, Rivers and Canals, Open Spaces’
November 1993–February 1994

‘Chiang Mai Social Installation: Second Art Festival: Temples, Cemeteries, Private-Residences, Public Buildings, Streets, Bridges, Walls, Rivers and Canals, Open Spaces’

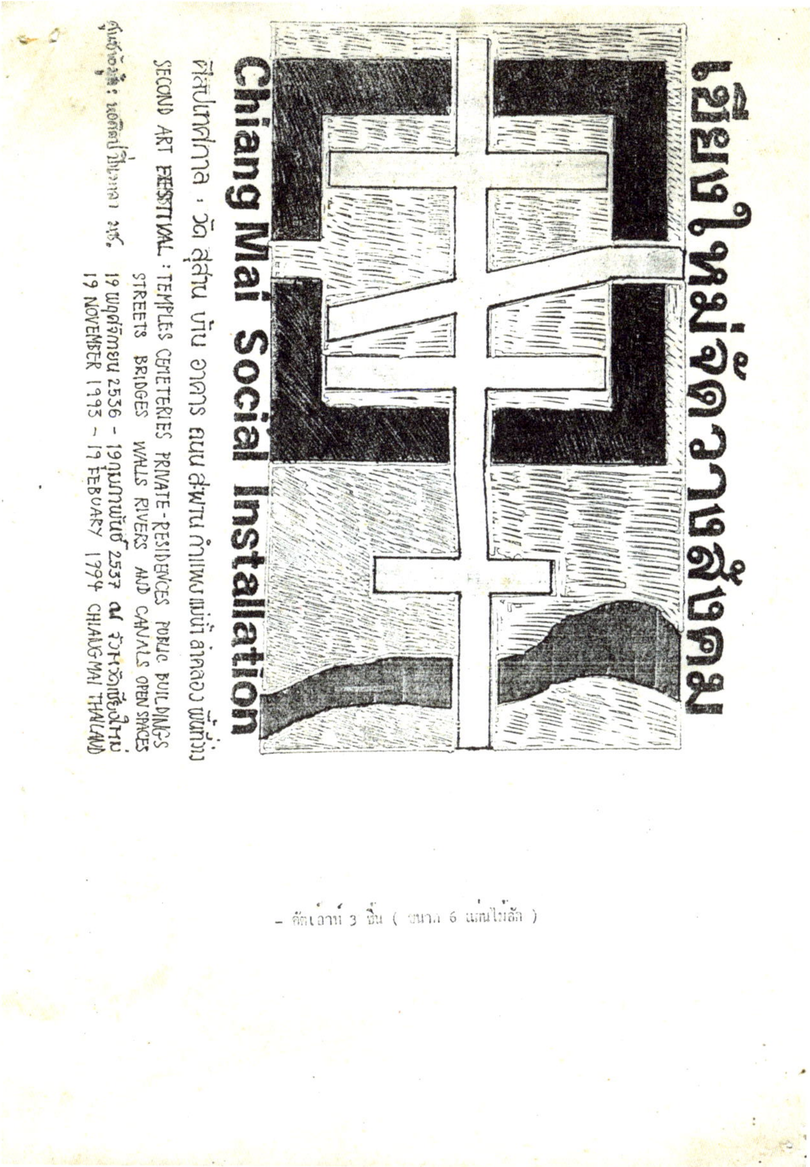

The next edition was the first to be named Chiang Mai Social Installation. Around fifty artists participated, largely self-funding their projects. They were aided by the logistical support of CMSI's organisers, and a budget reported to be around 100,000 baht (approximately €3500), supported by the Chaiyong Limthongkul Foundation, Japan Cultural Centre, Toshiba, Chiang Mai University and Chiang Mai Municipality.

ศิลปเทศกาล วัด สุสาน บ้าน อาคาร ถนน สะพาน กำแพง แม่น้ำลำคลอง พื้นที่ว่าง ครั้งที่ 2

Second Art Festival : Temples Cemeteries Private-Residences Public Buildings Streets Bridges Walls Rivers and Canals Open Spaces

19 พฤศจิกายน 2536 - 19 กุมภาพันธ์ 2537 ณ จังหวัดเชียงใหม่ 19 November 1993 - 19 February 1994 at Chiang Mai, Thailand

คนส่วนใหญ่ในสังคมได้ถูกกล่อมและมอมเมาจากลัทธิความเชื่อเศรษฐกิจแบบทุนนิยมเสรี ให้กลายเป็นบุคคลที่มองอะไรเพื่อตัวเอง......ในลักษณะที่เป็นปัจเจกบุคคลลดขอบ......จนกลายเป็นการพัฒนาที่ไม่ได้ดุลยภาพของความเป็นมนุษย์

ศรีศักร วัลลิโภดม

พระภิกษุเป็นการจำลองอุดมคติของพระพุทธศาสนา.....เป็นประจักษ์พยานว่า ความเป็นอยู่ที่ไม่เห็นแก่ตัว ไม่สะสมวัตถุและเกียรติยศยศ เป็นชีวิตที่ไม่เศร้าหมอง และเป็นไปได้จริงในโลก

นิธิ เอียวศรีวงศ์

การสวนทางกันระหว่าง ความรู้ความสามารถในการควบคุมพิชิตธรรมชาติแวดล้อมกับควบคุมพิชิตธรรมชาติในตัวมนุษย์เอง เป็นจุดวิกฤติที่มีอันตรายยิ่งนัก

เอกวิทย์ ณ ถลาง

เป็นที่รวมของคนมีความคิดในแนวทางคล้ายคลึงกัน อ่อนน้อม ถ่อมตน ยอมรับความคิดเห็นของกันและกัน พิจารณาสิ่งต่างๆ อย่างเชื่อมโยงไม่แยกส่วน

คำแถลง มูลนิธิ ภูมิปัญญา

วิสัยทัศน์ที่ตระหนักถึงการเปลี่ยนแปลงของโลก......ในลักษณะของการเกิดกระบวนการโลกานุวัตร (GLOBALIZATION) ซึ่งทำให้เกิดสภาวะการพึ่งพาต่อกัน (INTERDEPENDENCE) อย่างใกล้ชิดมากขึ้นระหว่างนานาชาติ......
ทุกภาคส่วนของสังคมจะต้องช่วยกันในการยึดโยงรักษามรดกวัฒนธรรมเดิม พร้อมกับหนุนนำจิตสำนึกของชาวไทยให้เปิดกว้างสู่สังคมโลกแห่งศตวรรษใหม่.....

ถ้อยแถลงบางส่วน มูลนิธิไชยยง ลิ้มทองกุล

น่าแปลกใจในช่วงทศวรรษนี้ ปัญญาชนในหลายๆ สาขาพูดถึงปัญหาที่ใกล้เคียงกัน อันเป็นผลมาจากพัฒนาการสังคมโลกในแนวบริโภค-วัตถุนิยมอย่างเช่นปัจจุบัน เมื่อกลับมาพิจารณาโลกศิลปะร่วมสมัยในบรรยากาศของ "ทุนนิยมศิลป์" ปัญหาเหล่านั้นก็เป็นปัญหาร่วมเช่นกัน บนรากฐานของความหลงเชื่อ "ตัวกู ของกู" (สาเหตุของความเสื่อม : พุทธทาส) เหล่าศิลปินต่างมุ่งแข่งขัน (ลงทุน) แสวงหาเพียง (กำไร) ความสำเร็จส่วนตัวในการสร้างผลงานจนดูเหมือนว่า กิจกรรมทางศิลป์กับวิถีชีวิตของคนส่วนใหญ่ดำเนินอยู่คนละเส้นทาง

ปัญหาดังกล่าวกลายเป็นแรงบันดาลใจผลักดันให้มีการรวมกลุ่ม "เชียงใหม่จัดวางสังคม" (Chiang Mai Social Installation) เป็นกลุ่มเอกชน ประกอบด้วยบุคคลหลากหลายอาชีพ ส่วนใหญ่มีภูมิลำเนาหรือปฏิบัติหน้าที่ในเชียงใหม่ รวมตัวขึ้นโดยคาดหวังจะเห็นกิจกรรมทางศิลปะ และวัฒนธรรมของปัจจุบันเป็นแก่นสารของอารยสังคม มีส่วนเชื่อมโยงกับชีวิตของคนส่วนใหญ่อย่างแท้จริง (โดยเฉพาะท้องถิ่น) บนหลักการของ(ก) การแสวงหาความร่วมมือ (ข) วิทยาการก้าวหน้า และ (ค) เข้าถึงมหาชน โดยในขั้นต้นเห็นว่า จังหวัดเชียงใหม่ในฐานะเมืองศิลปวัฒนธรรมดั้งเดิมแห่งหนึ่ง เหมาะสมในหลายๆ กรณีที่จะเป็นเมืองศิลปวัฒนธรรมร่วมสมัยอีกด้วย สำหรับแนวทางของกิจกรรม ได้นำเสนอความเป็นไปได้ใหม่ๆ ดังนี้

เทศกาลศิลปและวัฒนธรรมร่วมสมัย : เป็นความพยายามที่จะแสวงหาความร่วมมือในวงกว้างจากศิลปินทุกรุ่น ทุกสาขาศิลปะ ทุกสาขาอาชีพ นานาชาติ ร่วมกันสร้างกิจกรรมทางศิลปะและวัฒน-ธรรมปัจจุบันในช่วงเวลา-สถานที่แห่งหนึ่งที่ใกล้เคียงกัน เพื่อสร้างความเชื่อมโยงต่อมหาชนอย่างเป็นรูปธรรม ส่งเสริมค่านิยมการร่วมมือ การคิดและการกระทำในแบบ "องค์รวม" วางรากฐานอนาคตสำหรับการมีวัน "เทศกาลศิลปและวัฒนธรรมร่วมสมัย" ในสังคมไทย ซึ่งจะเป็นแก่นสารของอารยสังคมสมัยใหม่และสร้างดุลยภาพต่อสังคม บริโภค-วัตถุนิยมในปัจจุบัน

กิจกรรมสร้างสรรค์ : มีความคิดริเริ่มที่จะขยายขอบเขตสัมฤทธิผลของ "ศิลปกิจกรรม" ไปสู่ "กิจกรรมสร้างสรรค์" ซึ่งหมายถึงยังคงสร้างศิลปกิจกรรมตามแบบขนบดั้งเดิมของโลกศิลปะ และยังรวมเอากิจกรรมทางปัญญาในวิธีการอื่นๆ เท่าที่จะเป็นไปได้จากทุกๆ ศาสตร์ (เช่น ปาฐกถา เสวนา การสำรวจทำสถิติ การทำข้อมูลวิชาการ ฯลฯ) รวมทั้งการให้บริการและการเผยแพร่ข้อมูลต่อสังคม (บรรยายตามสถานศึกษา สิ่งพิมพ์ ฯลฯ) โดยเห็นว่ากิจกรรมทั้งหมดที่เกิดในช่วงเวลาที่กำหนดเหล่านั้น ถือเป็นกระบวนการของ "กิจกรรมสร้างสรรค์"

จัดวางสังคม : ออกจากค่านิยมการแสดงศิลปวัตถุเพียง "หอศิลป์" (GALLERY) ซึ่งได้ผลน้อยมากในบริบทของสังคมไทย ด้วยความคิดใหม่ที่ว่า ทุกๆ พื้นที่ในสังคมมีประวัติศาสตร์และความหมายที่น่าสนใจในตัวเอง ศิลปินเพียง "เลือก" และ "แต่งตั้ง" ทุกๆ พื้นที่ในสังคมด้วยกลวิธีทางศิลปะให้กลายเป็นรูปของ "ศิลปวัตถุ" เป็น "หอศิลป์มหาชน" (เป็นกระบวนการเปลี่ยนบทบาทสังคม (และมนุษย์) ไปสู่รูปศิลป์) สิ่งนั้นไม่ใช่ "ศิลปะกับสิ่งแวดล้อม" ไม่ใช่ศิลปะและสังคม หากคือ "การจัดวางสังคม"

อนึ่ง ศิลปเทศกาลในครั้งที่ 1 กำหนดสถานที่เพียง วัด และสุสาน โดยเห็นว่ากิจกรรมทางศิลปะของปัจจุบัน ควรเริ่มต้นบนรากฐานและสิ่งแวดล้อมของศิลปวัฒนธรรมดั้งเดิม สำหรับศิลปเทศกาล ครั้งที่ 2 นี้ เป็นอีกก้าวหนึ่งของความพยายามที่จะสร้างกิจกรรมทางศิลปะภายในพื้นที่ที่มีประชากรอยู่อย่างหนาแน่น สังคมจะถูกเปลี่ยนบทบาทไปสู่ "ศิลปวัตถุ" การมีส่วนร่วมจากมหาชนมีมากขึ้น และการทำให้กิจกรรมทางศิลปะและวัฒนธรรมร่วมสมัยกับวิถีชีวิตของคนส่วนใหญ่ดำเนินอยู่ร่วมกันมากยิ่งขึ้น

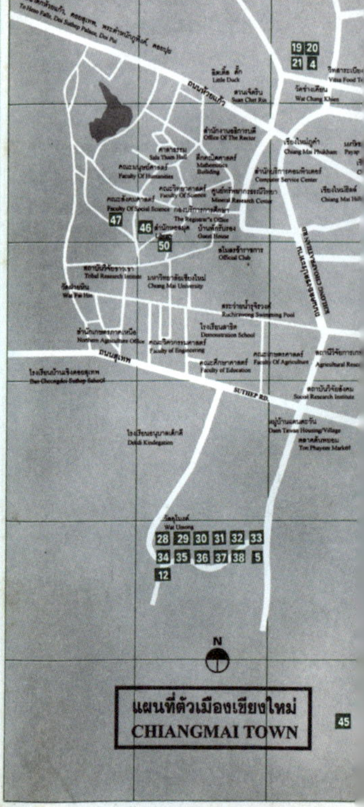

● ชื่อผลงาน TITLE ■ สถานที่ SITE SPECIFIC ◆ วัสดุ MATERIAL ▲ วัน, เวลา

ost people in society are influenced and pursuaded by the tenets of capitalism. As a esult, they become highly individualized and alienated from society. Eventually this ourse of personal development causes a loss of balance in the nature of being human.

By : Srisak Wanleephodom

---

monk represents the ideal of Buddhism. He is a model of unselfishness, onmaterialism, and high honor. It is not a sad life. This life is truely possible in this orld.

By : Niti Ieawsriwong

---

here is conflict between mans' knowledge and ability to control and destroy nature, nd the ability to control and destroy man's spirit. This represents an extremely angerous crisis.

By : Ekkawit Na Thalang

---

he Bhoombhanya Foundation is a group of people with similar thoughts and humble elings that accepts each member's thoughts. We analyze various subjects omprehensively.

By : Bhoombhanya Foundation

---

obalization and interdependence constitute two major components of the world's hanging nature that includes closer international relations. Every segment of society ust work together not only to preserve traditional culture but also to encourage onscience, among Thai people, of progress into a new century of the world's ommunity.

By : Chaiyong Limtongkul Foundation

---

this decade, intellectuals from all disciplines have become concerned with similar sues relating to the increasing consumerism and materialism of society. If we analyze ontemporary art in the era of the commercialization of art, we can see similar oblems. If we perceive the world through ideas of 'Myself is my Own' (cause of egration: Buddhadasa Bhikkhu), artists invest in the creations only to make profit nd gain personal fame. Consequently, artists pursue personal interests and ignore eater issues.
s a result of the above concerns, the 'Chiang Mai Social Installation' group was unded. This group hopes to encourage creative activities that promote the essence an ideal society. These activities will be related to the lifestyle and concerns of ost people, especially local Chiang Mai residents, by emphasizing on cooperation, dvanced Knowledge and public interaction.
t first, it becomes clear that Chiang Mai, as one of the original art centers in hailand, was suitable to become a center of contemporary culture and to host eative activities. The following are new possibilities for the group to consider:

ontemporary Art and Culture Festival

he 'Chiang Mai Social Installation' group hopes to create a Contemporary Art and ulture Festival in Thai society that will represent the ideal contemporary society and ill balance the effects of materialism and consumerism.
order to create an abstract relationship with the public, to promote the value of ooperation, and to encourage communal thoughts and actions, the festival will include tists from all generations, disciplines, occupations and nationalities, who will be orking in a specific area during a certain period of time, in order to have a concrete fect on the public.

reative Activities

he group would like to expand the scope and influence of art activities to nter the realm of all creative activities. While preserving the original ontent of art objects, the group would also pursue other activities such as speech, scussions, statistical research and other forms of research. In addition, they will rovide services and promote social information through lectures at centers of ducation, pamphlets and brochures, etc.

ocial Installation

rtists generally present their creations in art galleries. However, this creates few enefits for the population at large, a few people are able to view art in galleries. ather than hold exhibitions in galleries, this group decided to select pre-existing tes. Each location already possesses a history and meaning. Artists will "select" nd "appoint" locations which will become 'Art objects' and 'public art centers.' his method changes social and human roles and leeds them towards the art works. hanging from galleries to public art centers will create a 'Social Installation', rather an 'Art & Environment' or 'Public Art.'

he group decided that the first art exhibition would be held at temples and emetaries because creative activities of the present time should begin at the base nd with the atmosphere of traditional art and culture. As for the 2nd festival, it will present the next phase of the group's attempt to bring art to highly populated eas. Society will be changed into a new social installation.

40 กลุ่มระคน ละคร RAKON LAKON GROUP

P● ลานกามารมณ์
■ ลานเอนกประสงค์ ประตูท่าแพ
▲ เฉพาะวันที่ 24 พฤศจิกายน 2536 เวลา 19:10 - 19:40 น.
* ความต้องการทางเพศ เป็นแรงปรารถนาพื้นฐานของมนุษย์เป็นมโนภาพที่แจ่มชัดในอารมณ์ของทุกคน สำหรับบางคนมันเป็นเสมือนภาพหลอนที่สร้างความเร่าร้อนใจต่อผู้ตกอยู่ในวังวนของกามารมณ์

P● แม้จะเป็นเพียงเงา แต่เราก็เชื่อฟัง
▲ เฉพาะวันที่ 24 พฤศจิกายน 2536 เวลา 19:40 - 20:10 น.
* สัญญาณไฟจราจรเป็นเพียงระบบอิเลคทรอนิคที่ไร้วิญญาณแต่กลับมีสิทธิ์อำนาจสั่งการ ถ้าไฟจราจรกลายเป็นสิ่งมีชีวิตจะเป็นเช่นไร

P● First Performance : Sexual square.
■ Tha - Pae Gate
▲ November 24, 1993 only (7:10 p.m. - 7:40 p.m.)
* Sexual desire creates an illusion in man.

P● Second Performance : 'We're to rely on a shadow".
▲ November 24, 1993 only (7:40 p.m. - 8:10 p.m.)
* Traffic light, although lifeless, can give order. What would happen if they become alive?

42 ดนตรีร่วมสมัยโดย สุรัตน์ เขมาลีลากุล CONTEMPORARY MUSIC BY SURAT KEMALEELAKUL

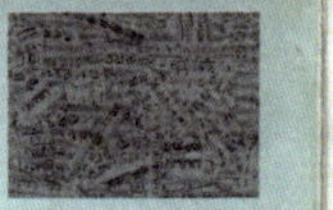

M● New music ensemble and solo
■ ห้องสาระนิเทศ มหาวิทยาลัยพายัพเชียงใหม่ วิทยาเขตแม่คาว
▲ เฉพาะวันที่ 1 กุมภาพันธ์ 2537 เวลา 17:30 - 21:00 น.
* เขาเป็นคีตกวีหนุ่มพึ่งจบการศึกษามาจาก CHICAGO MUSICAL COLLEGE OF ROOSEVELT UNIVERSITY สำหรับผลงานในครั้งนี้เขาละทิ้งทฤษฎี HARMONY แบบโบราณ หรือเชิงคิดโดยการกำหนดเป็น MELODY AND CHORD แต่หันมาใช้การเรียบเรียงเสียงแบบใหม่โดยใช้ทฤษฎี 12th - tone, mode และวัตถุดิบพื้นเมือง

M● New music ensemble and solo.
■ Payap University, Mae - Kao Campus.
▲ February 1, 1994 only (7:30 p.m. - 9:00 p.m.)
* A graduate of the Chicago Musical College of Roosevelt University. His music, abandons the traditional theories on harmony and bases his composition on the 12th tone theory.

43 ดนตรีร่วมสมัย โดยกลุ่มคีตกวีเชียงใหม่ CONTEMPORARY MUSIC BY A GROUP OF CHIANG MAI COMPOSERS

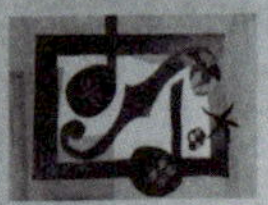

M● คืนของดนตรีร่วมสมัย
■ หอประชุมคณะแพทยศาสตร์ มหาวิทยาลัยเชียงใหม่
▲ เฉพาะวันที่ 5 กุมภาพันธ์ 2537 เวลา 15:30-21:00 น.
❖ นำเสนอความคิดใหม่ในการประพันธ์ดนตรีร่วมสมัย โดยเน้นการใช้เครื่องเคาะต่างๆ ทั้งเครื่องดนตรีของไทยและตะวันตกมาผสมผสานกัน เพื่อให้เกิดสีสันแบบใหม่ๆ

M● A Night with Contemporary music.
■ The Hall of Faculty of Medicine, Chiang Mai University.
▲ February 5, 1994 Only (7:30-9.00 p.m.)
❖ To demonstrate new ideas in contemporary music, focussing on the mixture of Thai & Western percussion.

มโน บุพพ์ คมา THOUGHTFORM - THE

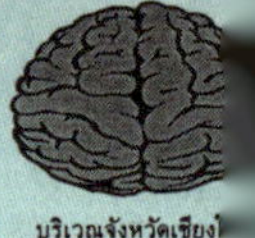

■ บริเวณจังหวัดเชียง
◆ อากาศธาตุ - มโน
* ศิลปะควรเป็นเพียง อยู่เหนือไปจากอ ความปรารถนา จากตัวตน-บุคคล-เ

■ Chiang Mai Provin
◆ Space thoughtform
* Thinking without Thoughts and des Beyond feeling an

เสวนาโดย โกวิท เขม SEMINAR BY KOVIT KEM เทพศิริ สุขโสภา THEPSIRI SUKSOPHA ศิริชัย นฤมิตรเรขก SIRICHAI NARUMITRRA

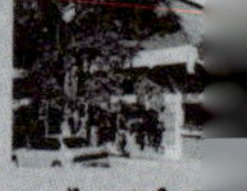

S● ตรงไหนหัวใจศิ
■ เรือนไทลื้อ สถาบันวิจั วิทยาลัยเชียงใหม่
▲ วันที่ 28 มกราคม 16:00 น.

S● Where is the esse
■ Ruen Thai-Lua, Soc Institute, C.M.U.

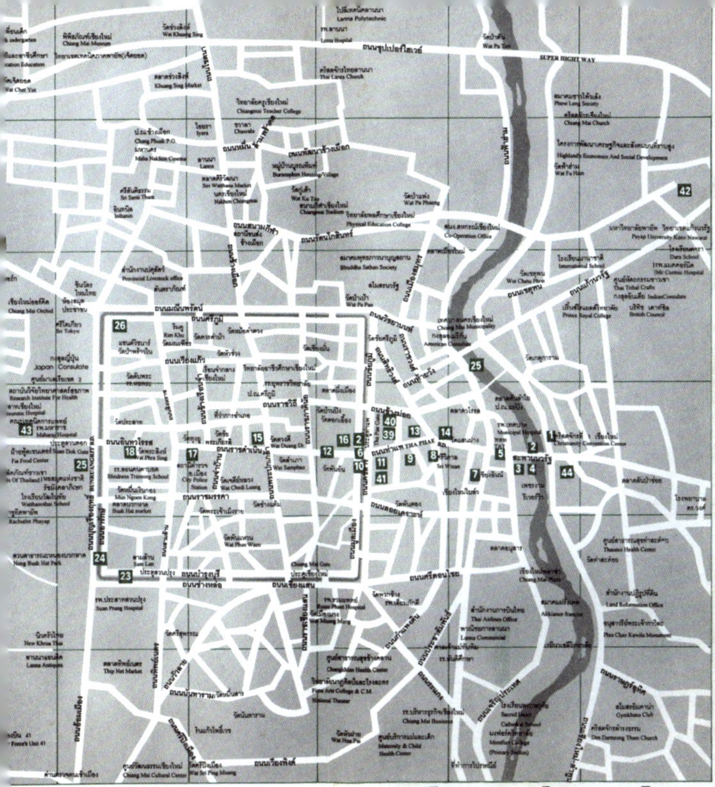

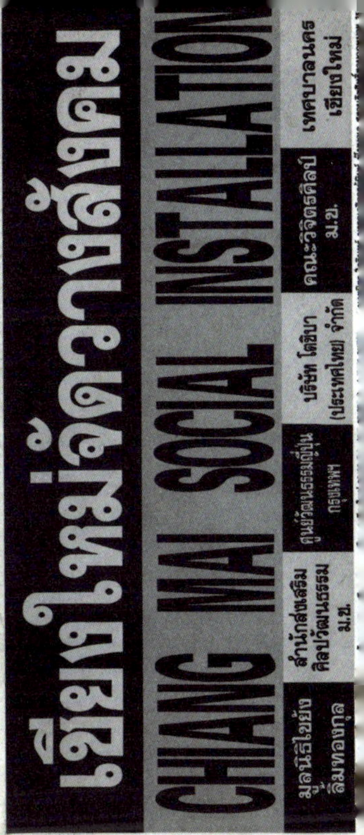

ของศิลปิน ARTIST STATEMENT ❖ บทคัดย่อ ABSTRACT **P** การแสดง PERFORMANCE **M** ดนตรี MUSIC **D** ถกปัญหา DISCUSSION **L** ปาฐกถา LECTURE **S** เสวนา SIMINAR

46

...ศิลปเทศกาล
...ON CENTER

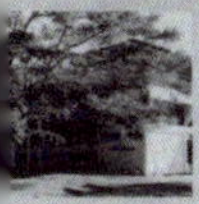

...ลปปิ่นมาลา มหา-
...าลัยเชียงใหม่
...ศูนย์ข้อมูลวันที่
...พฤศจิกายน 2536
... 16:00 น.
...ศูนย์จัดแสดงภาพ
...และภาพร่างผลงาน
...ร่วมโครงงานครั้ง
... และ 2 รวมทั้งมี
... และสิ่งพิมพ์
... ที่เกี่ยวข้องกับ
...งาน จะเปิดแสดง
... จนถึงวันที่ 19
...พันธ์ 2537

...ala Art Gallery,
...ng Mai Univer-
...
...mber 26, 1993 -
...ary 19, 1994.
...ning reception
... November 26,
...4:00 p.m.)
...des all informa-
... of the 2nd
...ng Mai Art
...al. The sketches
... every Projects
... also on view

49

ปาฐกถา โดย ศ.ดร.ชัยอนันต์ สมุทวณิช
LECTURE BY Prof.Dr.CHAIANAN SAMATTAVANIT

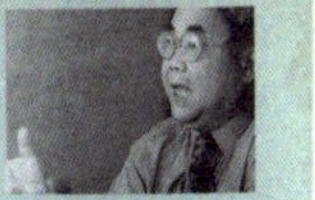

S● **ความจริง ความงาม จินตนาการ และการเมือง**

■ สถานที่จะประชาสัมพันธ์ต่อไป

▲ วันที่ 3 กุมภาพันธ์ 2537 เวลา 16.00-19.00 น.

✱ มนุษย์ในฐานะที่เป็นสัตว์ช่างคิดช่างฝัน และมีพลังทั้งสร้างสรรค์และทำลาย ได้จัดความสัมพันธ์ทางอำนาจต่อกันในลักษณะต่างๆ มานับหมื่นนับแสนปี การเมืองเป็นกิจกรรมที่สานสัมพันธภาพอันแตกต่างหลากหลายระหว่างมวลมนุษย์ เพื่อทำให้มนุษย์สืบทอดความทรงจำทางศิลปะวัฒนธรรมอย่างต่อเนื่องมาได้ ความจริง ความงาม และจินตนาการทั้งปวงของเรา ต่างเกี่ยวพันกับการเมือง ซึ่งกำหนดคุณค่าโดยอาศัยการให้คุณ-ให้โทษทั้งสิ้น

S● **Truth, beauty, imagination and politics**

■ Detailed information about location will be advertised later on.

▲ February 3, 1994 (4:00-7:00 p.m.)

✱ Man is a being who thinks, dreams, has energy to create or destroy, and has arranged power-relations in various ways. For many centuries, politics has been an activity that weaves human relations in order to convey a continuous artistic and cultural memory. Truth, beauty and imagination, however, are all linked to politics. Politics stipulates its values by relying on the motto "to give and take".

50

บรรยายประกอบสไลด์และเสวนาโดย
SEMINAR AND SLIDES PRESENTATION BY :
TANI ARATA (Art Critic) (JAPAN)
KIMIO TSUCHIYA (Artist) (JAPAN)
CHIEO SENZADI (Artist) (JAPAN)

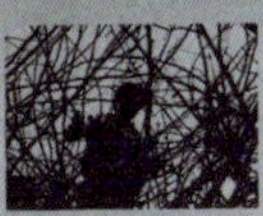

S● **ศิลปร่วมสมัยในญี่ปุ่นและเอเชีย**

■ สำนักหอสมุด มหาวิทยาลัยเชียงใหม่

▲ วันที่ 17 กุมภาพันธ์ 2537 เวลา 9:30-12:00 น.

❖ ARATA เป็นผู้เชี่ยวชาญคนหนึ่งเกี่ยวกับศิลปะร่วมสมัยในญี่ปุ่นและในเอเชียอาคเนย์ เคยจัดแสดงผลงานให้มณเฑียร บุญมา และนิทรรศการ NEW ART FROM SOUTHEAST ASIA 1992 ในประเทศญี่ปุ่น
TSUCHIYA ผลงานของเขาแสดงออกถึงความรักต่อธรรมชาติ ผ่านการนำไม้หิน จัดเรียงจากหน่วยย่อยๆ ไปสู่รูปทรงเดี่ยวที่ดูเรียบง่าย ประณีต และมักแฝงความหมายเชิงปรัชญา
SENZADI ผลงานมักแสดงรูปที่ขัดแย้งกันระหว่างธรรมชาติและเทคโนโลยีใหม่ อย่างไรก็ตามสิ่งที่น่าจับตามองสำหรับการบรรยายครั้งนี้ คือพัฒนาการและเอกลักษณ์ของศิลปะญี่ปุ่นร่วมสมัย

S● **Contemporary Art in Japan and Asia.**

■ Chiang Mai University Library Auditorium.

▲ February 17, 1994, 9:00-12:00 a.m.

❖ Arata is an expert in contemporary Japanese and Southeast Asian art, in addition he has organized an exhibition for Thai artist Montien Boonma, and also curated the exhibition "New Art from Southeast Asia 1992" in Japan.
Tsuchiya is an artist whose works manifest the love of nature through the assemblage of wood and pebbles into unity.
Senzadi's works frequently demonstrates the conflict between nature and modern technology.

51

ปาฐกถา โดย ผศ. ดร.อภินันท์ โปษยานนท์
LECTURE BY Dr.APINAN POSHYANANDA

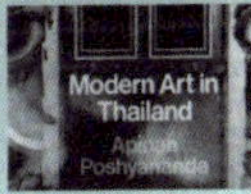

L● **ศิลปะไทยร่วมสมัย... ก้าวไกลหรือหยุดนิ่ง ?**

■ สถานที่จะประชาสัมพันธ์ต่อไป

▲ วันที่ 17 กุมภาพันธ์ 2537 เวลา 13:00-15.00 น.

❖ อาจารย์อภินันท์เป็นนักประวัติศาสตร์ศิลปร่วมสมัยชาวไทยคนแรกที่เขียนประวัติศาสตร์ศิลปของไทยอย่างมีมาตรฐานที่สูง โดยเฉพาะหนังสือ MODERN ART IN THAILAND พิมพ์โดย OXFORD UNIVERSITY PRESS และเผยแพร่ในปี 2535 หลังจากนั้น เขาได้ก้าวไปสู่บทบาทสำคัญทางวิชาการศิลป์ในระดับนานาชาติ โดยเฉพาะศิลปะร่วมสมัยในเอเชีย

L● **Thai Contemporary Art... Progress or Stand Still?**

■ Detailed information about location will be advertised later on.

▲ February 17, 1994 (1:00-3:00 p.m.)

❖ Apinan is the first Art historian in Thailand who has, documented contemporary Thai Art in a highly standardized manner. His book "Modern Art in Thailand" printed by Oxford University Press, was first published in 1992. Since then he has emphasised the importance of art theory on an international level, featuring contemporary art in Asia.

48

สุลักษณ์ ศิวรักษ์
SULUK SIVARAK

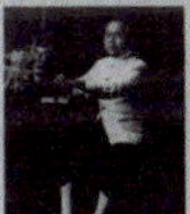

L● **พุทธทัศนะในการสร้างสรรค์สังคมสมัยใหม่**

▲ วัน เวลา สถานที่ จะประชาสัมพันธ์ต่อไป

L● **Buddhist Vision on Creating New Society.**

▲ Date and location will be advertised later on.

52

เอกวิทย์ ณ ถลาง
EKKAWIT NA THALANG

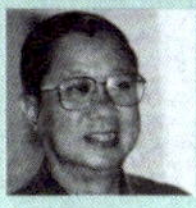

L● **การศึกษาของอนาคต**

▲ วัน เวลา สถานที่ จะประชาสัมพันธ์ต่อไป

L● **Future education system**

▲ Date and location will be advertised later on.

53

ถกปัญหาโดย DISCUSSION BY
ALFRED PAWLIN (AUSTRIA)
HELEN MICHAELSON (GERMANY)
MICHAEL WRIGHT (NOT CONFIRMED)

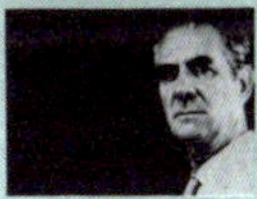

D● **ฝรั่งมองไทย**

▲ วัน เวลา สถานที่ จะประชาสัมพันธ์ต่อไป

D● **Discussions Centre on the Foreigner's vision of Thai Art and Culture.**

▲ Detailed information about date, time and location on each lecture, will be advertised later.

54

ปาฐกถา โดย นิธิ เอียวศรีวงศ์
LECTURE BY NITHI EAWSRIWONG
เสน่ห์ จามริก
SANAE JAMRIK
เสกสรรค์ ประเสริฐกุล
SEAKSUN PRASERTKUL

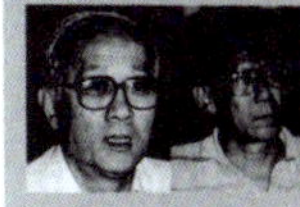

▲ วัน เวลา สถานที่ และหัวข้อ จะมีการประชาสัมพันธ์ให้ทราบต่อไป

▲ Detailed information about date, time, location and the topic of each lecture will be advertised later on.

KADE JAVANALIKIKORN

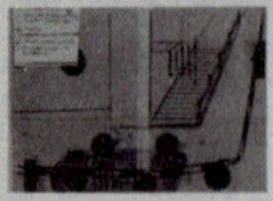

● เจ้ารถสกปรกกับเจ้าคนสกปรก
■ ด้านหลังห้างสรรพสินค้าเชียง-อินทร์พลาซ่า
◆ ล้อรถ
* การจอดรถในที่ห้ามจอดสามารถทำให้รถยนต์ของท่านถูกล็อคล้อไม่สามารถเคลื่อนย้ายได้ แต่ในกรณีนี้ เจ้าของรถได้ย้ายรถกลับบ้านไปแล้ว เหลือเพียงล้อและเงา ที่ผู้รักษากฎหมายสามารถเอาผิดได้ลงโทษได้ นี่คือความเจ้าเล่ห์ของคนที่มีต่อกฎหมาย

● A dirty autumo-bile and a dirty man.
■ Back of Chiang Inn Plaza.
◆ Car-Wheels.
* When you park your car in a no-parking zone, you risk having the wheels of your car locked, so that car cannot be moved. But in this case, the owner of the car has taken his car home and left just the wheels and a shadow for the guardian of the law to fine. This is one of the cunning ways in which people behave towards the law.

UDOM CHIMPUKDEE

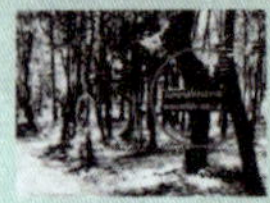

● รุ้งกินน้ำ [1]
■ ราวถนนท่าแพ หน้าพุทธสถาน
* สีฟ้า หมายถึง ท้องฟ้า
สีแดง เกี่ยวข้องกับ เลือด ความกล้าหาญ
สีดำ หมายถึง ความตาย ขลฯ สังคม คือ สีสันที่หลากหลายของปัจเจกชน

■ ลานกวีวัดอุโมงค์ [2]
◆ เหล็กแผ่นทาสี
* ดวงตา ผัสสะสำคัญที่ทำให้เราเข้าใจความหมายของชีวิต และอาจไปเข้าใจอะไรเลย แม้แต่บริเวณนี้ ที่ที่ข้าพเจ้าต้องการจะเน้นให้เห็น

● Rainbow [1]
■ Tha-Pae Road, front of Buddhasatan.
* Blue refers to the sky.
Red refers to blood and courage.
Black refers to death.
Society is a colourful variety of individuals.

■ Poet garden in U-Mong Temple [2]
◆ Coloured steel plate.
* Eyesight is an important sense that enables us to understand the meaning of life; yet may be the eye understands nothing which can be seen, even in this environment.

THEERAPONG TAKERD

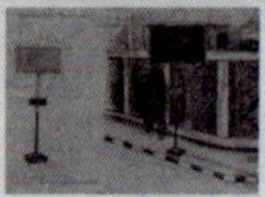

● อาหารจิตวิญญาณ
■ ถนนท่าแพ ตั้งแต่ริมสะพานคลองแม่ข่า ถึงประตูท่าแพ
◆ ป้ายจราจรทาสี
* โดยลักษณะและตำแหน่งของป้ายจราจรที่บังคับสายตาให้ผู้ใช้ถนนต้องดูและอ่าน 'เพื่อชี้ทิศทาง' มันจะถูกเปลี่ยนหน้าที่มาเป็นข้อความที่มีคุณค่าในการจุดประกายความคิดและความเข้าใจที่ดีงามสำหรับมนุษย์ 'เพื่อชี้แนวทางชีวิต'

● Spiritual Food.
■ Tha-Pae road to Tha-Pae Gate.
◆ Coloured tax-plates.
* The characteristics and position of traffic sign are such that they force their significance upon the driver's eyes; to show the way. Here, their significance is changed to incite the viewer to ponder things like goodness and beauty; to show the way of life.

KOSIT JUNTARATIP

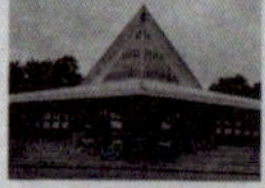

■ คริสตจักรที่หนึ่ง เชียงใหม่
▲ วันที่ 14 กุมภาพันธ์ 2537 เวลา 18:00 น.
* สภาพจิตวิญญาณของมนุษย์ปัจจุบันกลับหาไม่พบ สัญชาติญาณแห่งการสร้างเพื่อทดแทนก็เกิดขึ้น นำไปสู่การแสวงหาความรักจากสิ่งที่ไร้จิตวิญญาณ

■ Chiang Mai First Church.
▲ February 14, 1994 6:00 p.m.
* Nowadays people don't have the spirit for things anymore. Instinctively, the need for compensation erects; and leaves us searching for love from things that have no soul.

SUPACHAI SATSARA

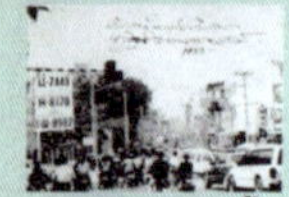

● จราจร; สายน้ำ;700 ปี เชียงใหม่.
■ บริเวณสะพานนวรัฐ, สี่แยกพุทธสถาน ประตูท่าแพ
◆ ป้ายทะเบียนรถ, ไม้อัด, น้ำแข็ง, ลูกโป่ง และเชือก
* ปัญหาจราจร; บนลำน้ำชีวิต; ดำเนินไปจนสูญสลาย.

● Traffic River 700 years Chiang Mai.
■ Nawarat bridge, Buddhasatan intersection, Tha-Pae Gate.
◆ License plates, plywood, ice, balloon and rope.
* The traffic Jam is declining of the concious.

KITTI MALEEPA

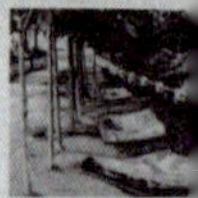

● เตียง
■ บริเวณหน้าสวนหย่อม
* จากสนามหญ้าหรือส เป็นที่พักผ่อนในขณะ เสริมบทบาทและคว สำนึกของมนุษย์ที่ ครอบครัว

● Bed.
■ Park near Governor
◆ A grass-field.
* A place to rest along its role and me increased. For members of "family" to consider

13 DAVID HAMMONS (U.S.A.)

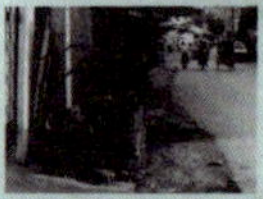

■ ทุกเสาไฟฟ้าถนนท่าแพ
◆ เศษวัสดุและโลหะ
* สัมพันธภาพระหว่างสุนัขกับเนยแข็ง

■ Electricity poles on Tha-Pae Road.
◆ Found objects and stool.
* The dog that take the cheese as a girlfriend.

14 ทัศนัย เศรษฐเสรี TATSANAI SEDSAEREE

WHAT IS ART

WHAT IS VALUE

WHAT IS REALITY

● ศิลปะ คุณค่า ความจริง
■ ตั้งแต่สะพานนวรัฐถึงประตูท่าแพ
◆ สีบนกระดาษ
* เป็นกระบวนการแสวงหาคุณค่าที่แท้ กำหนดจากตัวเอง มิใช่การยัดเยียด

● Art-Value-Reality.
■ From Nawarat bridge to Tha-Pae Gate.
◆ Colour on papers.
* The search for real values should be determined by each individual and not by the others.

พิทักษ์ สง่า PITAK SA-NGA

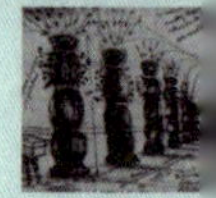

● ปาร์ตี้ชาวน
■ ตลอดเส้นทางจากสะพา สิงห์ และวัดเจ็ดยอด
◆ ฟาง, แผ่นโลหะ, ล้อโลห
* ระบบของธรรมชาติทำให้ เงื่อนไขทางสังคมขึ้น ความเชื่อที่มีต่อวัดอุโม ความอยู่รอดของสังคม

● The Farmer's
■ The route from Naw Pra-Singh Temple Temple.
◆ Straw, metal sheets,
* Man is part of the sy This forces man to c ditions. According to his b human race to survive

22 จราวุธ ทองคำภา ARAWUT TONGKOMPHA

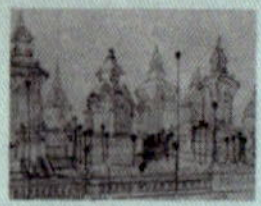

■ วัดสวนดอก
▲ แสดงเฉพาะวันที่ 19 พฤศจิกายน 2536 เวลา 8:00 - 18:00 น.
◆ ลูกโป่ง, ปูนพลาสเตอร์, เชือก
* มุมมองของมนุษย์ในสังคมปัจจุบัน มองสิ่งที่ดีกลับกลายเป็นสิ่งเลว และคิดว่าสิ่งเลวคือสิ่งที่ดี

■ Suan Dok Temple.
▲ November 19, 1993 only (8:00 a.m. - 6:00 p.m.)
◆ Balloons, plaster, rope.
* From the point of view of people in today society, the right is wrong and the wrong is right.

23 นพรัตน์ โชคขัยชุติกุล MINK NOPPARAT

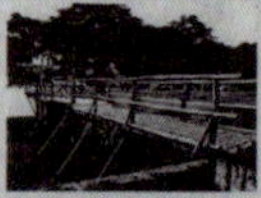

● ทางเลือก
■ คูเมืองหน้าโรงพยาบาลสวนปรุง
◆ ไม้ไผ่ทาสี, ผ้า, ไฟนีออน
* เมื่อโลกที่หมุนเวียนเปลี่ยนไปถูกทำให้หยุดนิ่ง เพื่อให้ผู้คนได้มีโอกาสมองสำรวจและคิดไตร่ตรองให้มากขึ้น

● The choice.
■ Canal across Suan Phung Hospital.
◆ Painted bamboo, clothes, neon.
* When the world comes to a stand-still, giving people a chance to look around with more attention and think twice about.

24 สุทธิศักดิ์ ภูธรารักษ์ SUTTHISAK PHUTHARARAK

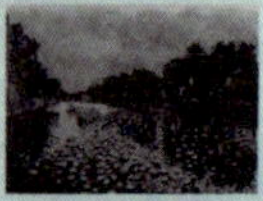

■ คูเมืองหน้าโรงเรียนวัฒโนทัยพายัพ
◆ ปูนพลาสเตอร์
* การสอดใส่อะไรท่านองนั้นของผู้ชายเข้าไปในตัวผู้หญิงเป็นการให้กำเนิดสายพันธุ์ที่หลายหลาก เป็นกระบวนการตามธรรมชาติ จากสองคนกลายเป็นสังคม

■ Canal across Wattanotai Payap school.
◆ Plaster.
* The story goes that a man once inserted something into another thing of a woman and fertilized her. She gave birth to a large and various lineage of descendants. This is a very natural process. From two people up to a whole society.

25 พงษ์เดช ไชยคุตร PONGDEJ CHAIYAKUT

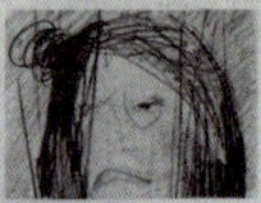

● หุ่นชัก
■ หอสมุดแห่งชาติ รัชมังคลาภิเษก ริมแม่น้ำปิงเยื้องสะพานนครพิงค์ สี่แยกรินคำ
▲ ติดตั้งผลงานวันที่ 1 มกราคม 2537
◆ วาดเส้นบนคัตเอาท์ (ไม้อัด 16 แผ่น)
* มนุษย์ถูกชักด้วยกิเลส ตัณหา และความอยาก

● Puppet
■ Ratchamangkala Pisek National Library.
An area near Nakorn Ping bridge.
Rincome intersection.
▲ January 1, 1994.
◆ Drawing on billboard.
* "Man is tempted by physical desires."

26 METTE CAMILLA SKADBERG (NORWAY)

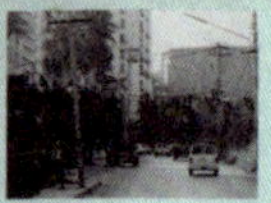

■ แจ่งหัวรินด้านใน
▲ ติดตั้งวันที่ 15 ธันวาคม 2536 - 15 มกราคม 2537
* การโต้เถียงทางวัฒนธรรมระหว่างเก่า - ใหม่ ผ่านรูปทรงของสถาปัตยกรรมทั้งสอง ความจริงแล้ว ทั้งสองก็คือร่องรอยของวัฒน-ธรรมเดียวกัน

■ Back of Hua-Rin corner.
▲ December 15, 1993 - January 15, 1994.
* Old and new traditions are actually the same trace of culture.

LAWRENCE WE (U.S.A.)

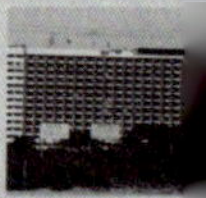

● สี่เหลี่ยมผืนผ้าหน จากสี่เหลี่ยมผืนผ
■ อาคารฮิลล์ไซด์พลา เทล 4
▲ เฉพาะเวลา 17:00 - วัน
◆ แผงไฟโฆษณาคอมพ
* ลุกขึ้นแล้วจงนั่งลงส

● One rectangle Away from anot
■ Hill Side Plasa and
▲ 5:00 p.m. - 6:00 p
◆ Electric billboard.
* Stand up for all and then sit down

32 JOELENE LUCAS AUSTRALIA)

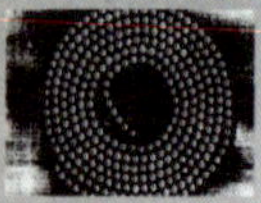

■ วัดอุโมงค์
◆ ไข่มุก
* มีความเชื่อว่าที่บนสวรรค์ของพระอินทร์มีไข่มุกมากมายเรียงรายอย่างมีแบบแผน ถ้าเราเพ่งมองไข่มุกหนึ่งลูกจะสามารถเห็นภาพสะท้อนของไข่มุกอื่นๆ ทั้งหมด

■ U - Mong Temple.
◆ Pearls.
* In the heaven of Indra, there is said to be a Network of pearls, so arranged that if you look at one you see all the others Reflected in it.
Flower Gerland Seetry.

33 JACQUELINE CLAYTON (AUSTRALIA)

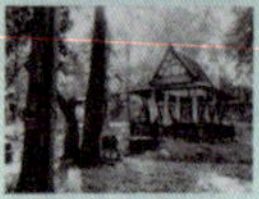

● ใบเสี่ยงทาย
■ วัดอุโมงค์
◆ กระดาษ
* ฉันได้ส่งบุคลิกภาพแบบชาวออสเตรเลียมากับใบเสี่ยงทายนี้

● Prayer Slips.
■ U-Mong Temple.
◆ Papers.
* I have sent 'prayer slips' with an Australian Character.

35 ธาตรี โภควนิช THATREE POKAVANICH

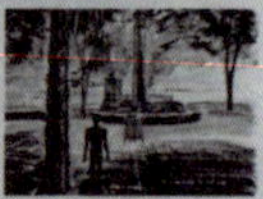

● ภายนอก - ภายใน
■ วัดอุโมงค์
◆ กรงนกไม้ไผ่, กิ่งไม้ และรอก
* ความศรัทธาในความรู้สูงสุดภายใน ภายนอก ที่มนุษย์ควรจะตัดสินใจเลือกว่าอะไรเป็นปัญหาเร่งด่วน

● Inside - Outside.
■ U - Mong Temple.
◆ Bamboo bird - cage, wood stick and pulley.
* The faith of Knowledge, inside and outside, is what we must consider urgent.

36 CHERKOORI (INDIA)

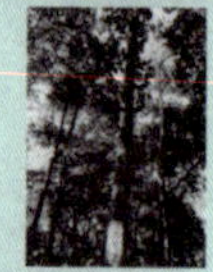

■ วัดอุโมงค์
◆ โลหะ และพลาสติก
* ลิงฝูงหนึ่งบนต้นไม้เกิดความละอายใจทุกครั้งที่มองลงมายังพื้นดินเห็นผู้คนกลุ่มหนึ่งเฝ้าแหงนหน้าขึ้นจ้องมองอยู่

■ U-Mong Temple.
◆ Metal and Plastic.
* Up up on the tree and shame on you.

37 MARI ZIRAS (DENMARK)

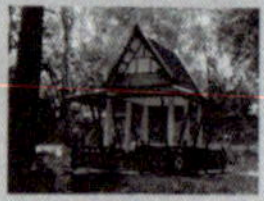

■ ศาลาในวัดอุโมงค์
* ระเบียบโลกใหม่ได้กลายเป็นการจัดการระบบเพื่อการบริโภคโลกและธรรมชาติ เปรียบเสมือนกับตัวสัตว์เลื้อยคลานที่กำลังหันกลับมากลืนกินหางของตัวเอง

■ Pavilion in U-Mong Temple.
* The waterlizard that eats its own tail until Nothing remains of the body.

ธวัชชัย หอมท TAWATCHAI HOMT

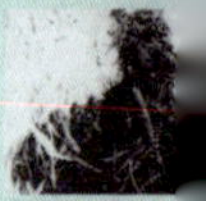

P ● เดิน - ยืน บ
■ วัดอุโมงค์และที่ว่าง
▲ เฉพาะวันที่ 19 พฤ
* ความสำนึกในธรรม ของมนุษยชาติ แห่งการสร้างสรรค์ บทบาทร่วมกัน และอริยบทต่างๆ

P ● To walk - on the road
■ U-Mong Temple space.
▲ November 19, 1993
* Awareness of Na of mankind, and creation are show various time, space

ราษฎร์จำเริญสุข
RASDJARMREARNSOOK

ล ลาภก่อเกียรติ์
วี เพชรรุ่ง
า สัมฤทธิ์

ังหนึ่ง เธอเคยเป็นแม่บ้าน
ังหนึ่ง เธอเคยเป็นพยาบาล
ังหนึ่ง เธอเคยเป็นโสเภณี
นสาธารณะข้างจวนผู้ว่าฯ
านช่างเคี่ยน
พ์บนผ้ายาง, น้ำ, โลหะ
ลรำลึกเหตุการณ์สะเทือนใจ
ๆ ในสังคมไทยที่สตรีเพศเป็นผู้
กระทำ

ce she was housewife.
ce she was nurse.
ce she was prostitute.
k near Governor's Residence.
ng-Kien Cemetery.
ber sheet, Water and Steel.
ollecting a series of tragic
nts in Thai society when
nen were taken advantage of.

พิทวัส ไตรภพสวัสดิ์
PITTAWAT TRIPOPSAWAT

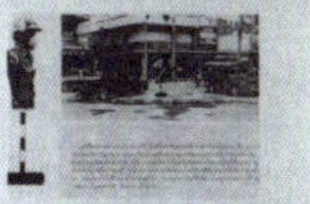

■ หน้าลานอเนกประสงค์ ประตูท่าแพ
◆ ผ้า, ฟาง, ไฟเบอร์, กระดาษ
* เป็นการสะท้อน ประชดประชัน เตือนสติ ต่อพฤติกรรมของมนุษย์ในวิถีชีวิตปัจจุบันที่ขาดความพอดีเพื่อความพอดี

■ Tha-Pae Gate.
◆ Clothes, Straw, fibre and paper.
* Reflecting and satirising man's current way of life in his lack of moderation.

NIKI NIKOLAY (AUSTRIA)

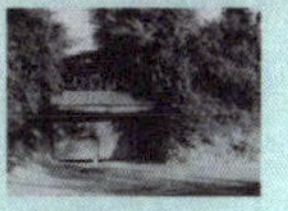

■ กำแพงดิน ลอยเคราะห์ซอย 3
◆ ภาพพิมพ์บนผ้าฝ้าย
* ผู้หญิงเป็นผู้ชาย ผู้ชายเป็นผู้หญิง

■ Kampheangdin Loi-Kroe Soi 3.
◆ Print on cotton.
* Man is woman, woman is man.

NIGEL HELYER (AUSTRALIA)

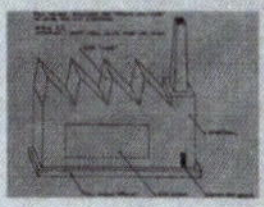

● โรงงานของจิตวิญญาณ
■ หน้าวัดมหาวัน
◆ โลหะ, กระจก, ทาสีบนผนัง
* นำเสนอความขัดแย้งหรือความตรงข้ามอย่างรุนแรงระหว่างความคิดทางพุทธศาสนา และทุนนิยมอุตสาหกรรมในปัจจุบัน

● The Factory of spirits.
■ Outside Mahawan Temple.
◆ Metal, glass, Wall texts.
* Presenting the contradictory tensions between traditional Buddhist thought and contemporary industrial capitalism.

คมสัน หนูเขียว
KOMSAN NUKEAW
ขัชวาล นิลสกุล
CHATCHAWAN NILSAKUL
วรพจน์ เพรียบจริยวัฒน์
WORAPOJ PREABJARIYAWAT

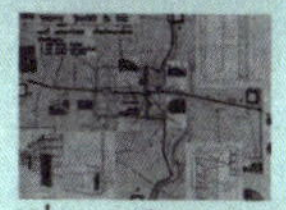

● สิ่งเหลือใช้ศิลป์
■ รอบลานเอนกประสงค์ ประตูท่าแพ
* เป็นโครงงานสำรวจพัฒนาการของสังคมปัจจุบันโดยพิจารณาผ่านสิ่งเหลือใช้ (ขยะ) ตามจุดต่างๆ ในสังคม

● Junk-Art.
■ Tha-Pae Gate.
* Reflecting Social development through Junk-Art.

นฤพนธ์ บูรณะบัญญัติ
NARUPON BURANABANYA

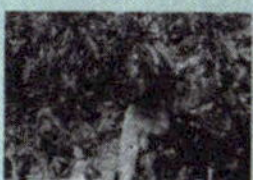

■ ถนนราชดำเนิน [1]
◆ ผ้าหลากหลายสี
* เมื่อเราคิดว่ามีสิ่งนั้นอยู่
เมื่อเรารู้สึกว่าได้สัมผัสแล้
เมื่อเราเชื่อว่าคนอื่นติดตามเร
เมื่อเราตัดสินว่า สิ่งนั้น
อำนาจที่ยิ่งใหญ่
เมื่อเราสรุปว่า เราทั้งหลา
ต้องศรัทธา

■ วัดอุโมงค์ [2]
▲ เฉพาะวันที่ 19 พฤศจิกาย
2536 เวลา 9:00 น. - 18:00
◆ ผ้า, กระดาษ, นุ่น, ขนสัตว์
ยม ,กิ่งไม้, เถาวัลย์
* ธรรมชาติมีการเปลี่ย
แปลง โครงสร้างของสิ
ต่างๆ ในธรรมชาติเป
ตัวแทนความหมายของกา
ดิ้นรนเพื่อคงอยู่

■ Ratchadanneam road [2]
◆ Different kinds
coloured textile.
* When we think it
truly there.
When we feel we hav
touched it.
When we believe w
are being followed.
When we have decide
it is enormously powe
ful.
When we conclude th
we ought to have faith.

■ U-Mong Temple [2]
▲ February 19, 1993 only.
◆ Clothed, Papers, Cotto
Woods.
* As nature changes, th
structure of things in na
ture are the will to live

17
เกษรเกศรา
E KAESORNKASARA

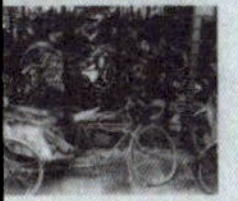

านีตำรวจภูธรอำเภอเมือง
ยงใหม่
งพารา
ลึกถึง กฎความเป็นเช่นนี้
งธรรมชาติ ชีวิต วัฒนธรรม
รพลิ่ง

Muang Police Station,
iang Mai.
bber sheets.
flecting the law of
permance.

18
JAMES LEE BYARS (U.S.A.)

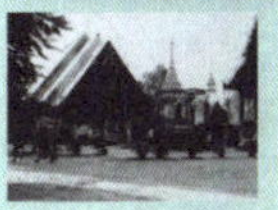

■ วัดพระสิงห์ หน้าวิหารลายคำ
◆ ทองคำเปลว เชือกไนล่อน
* ช.ม.ม.ก.ม.จ.ช.ม.ม.ม.ค.

■ Prasingh Temple (Front of Vihara Laikam).
◆ Gold leaves, rope.
* C.M.H.T.M.P.

19
อภิชาติ อุดมชัย
APICHAT UDOMCHAI

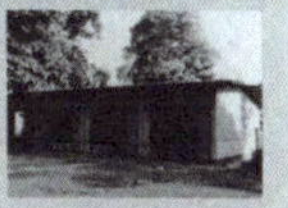

■ สุสานช่างเคี่ยน
◆ ปูนปั้น, ซีเมนต์, กระดาษ
* สุสานคือสถานที่พักพิงของสังขารมนุษย์ทั้งหมด ในบั้นปลายของชีวิต บทบาทของศิลปะในสถานที่ดังกล่าวจึงเป็นการบันทึกสะท้อนถึงวิถีชีวิตและพฤติกรรมของมนุษย์ในยุคนั้นๆ

■ Chang-Kien Cemetery.
◆ Stucco, cement, paper.
* A cemetery is a resting place for every human being. It reflects man's behaviour and his way of life in a certain era.

20
KARYN KAPLAN (U.S.A.)

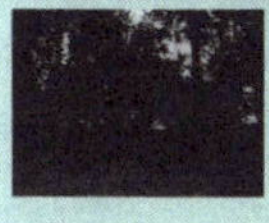

■ สุสานวัดช่างเคี่ยน
◆ โลหะ
* แท่นนั่งสำหรับสามัญชนในสุสาน เพื่อใช้ร่วมกัน

■ Chang-Kien Cemetery.
◆ Metal.
* The seat for all ordinary.

21
เมธี ศรีสุทธาสินี
MAETHEE SRISUTTHASINEE

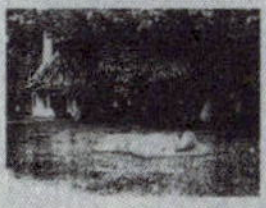

● หยดน้ำ
■ สุสานวัดช่างเคี่ยน
◆ ซีเมนต์, เชือกสลิง
* หยดน้ำ แสดงถึงการหลุดร่วง ซึ่งสอดคล้องกับสุสานซึ่งเก็บรักษาความหลุดร่วงของมนุษย์

● Waterdrop.
■ Chang-Kien Cemetery.
◆ Cement, String.
* A waterdrop refers to decline. Corresponding with the notion of a cemetery that conserves the remmants of man's decline.

28
เทียร บุญมา
IEN BOONMA

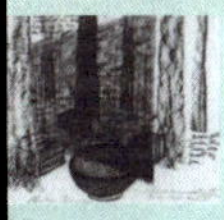

ปัสสนา–ภาชนะ (2536)
ดุโมงค์
ขี้เถ้า, ชามดินเผา 600 ใบ,
เหลือง-ดีบุก
ของสัตว์เหมือนภาชนะดิน ซึ่ง
มีความสลายเป็นที่สุด (จาก
รภาษิต)

passana-Vessel. (1993)
ong Temple.
ds, excretions, 600 terra-
a plates, brass-tin.
lives of sentients being
like the clay-pots, which
destinated to break sooner
ater (from Buddha Proverb).

30
กมล เผ่าสวัสดิ์
KAMOL PAOWSAWAT

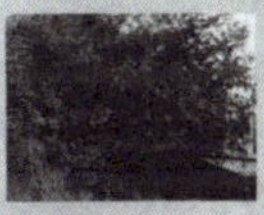

● ศาลพระภูมิ
■ วัดอุโมงค์
◆ สังกะสี หวาย เชือก และไม้เลื้อย
* คำไข – เศรษฐกิจฟองสบู่ สามล้อถูกหวย คาราโอเกะวัฒนธรรมและศาลพระภูมิ ไฮเทค

● Spirit House.
■ U-Mong Temple.
◆ Zinc, rattan, rope, climber.
* Bubble economic; karaoke cult; Hightech-Spirit House = keyword

31
JOAN GROUNDS (AUSTRALIA)

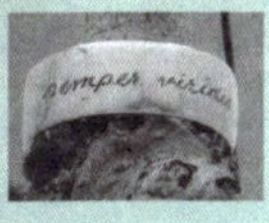

● นกในพุ่มไม้มีคุณค่าเท่ากับนก 2 ตัวในมือ
■ วัดอุโมงค์
◆ แหวนโลหะ, สายสิญจน์
* ผลงานของฉันเกี่ยวข้องกับความซับซ้อนของสิ่งแวดล้อมที่เราอาศัยอยู่ และความเป็นไปของพืชต่างๆ

● A Bird in the bush is worth two in the hand.
■ U-Mong Temple.
◆ Rings, white monk's strings.
* This installation is located within my continuing concerns with the complex issues surrounding the environment in which we live and the living beings of this planet.

16
นาวิน ลาวัลย์ชัยกุล
NAVIN RAWANCHAIKUL

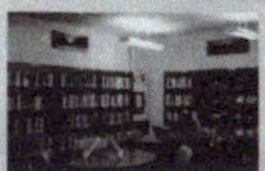

◆ คนแก่, หนังสือ, ห้องสมุด
■ ห้องสมุดสำนักข่าวสารอเมริกัน (USIS)
* ห้องสมุดในฐานะแหล่งข้อมูลวิทยาการทุกแขนงของมนุษยชาติในอดีตจะทำหน้าที่ใหม่ในฐานะศิลปวัตถุ

* ในช่วง 19 พ.ย. 36 - 19 ก.พ. 37 นาวินจะทำหน้าที่เป็นหน่วยวิจัยทางสังคมของกลุ่มเชียงใหม่จัดวางสังคม โดยแสวงหาความรู้เกี่ยวกับรสนิยมทางความงามสังคมชาวเชียงใหม่ ดังนั้น ท่านอาจเป็นผู้หนึ่งที่ได้รับการติดต่อทางจดหมายหรืออื่นๆ หวังว่าทางกลุ่มจะได้รับความร่วมมือจากทุกท่าน

◆ Used peoples, Books, Library.
■ USIS Library.
* Library seen as an artistic object.

* During the 19th Nov. 36 -19th Feb. 37. Navin will work in the Social Research Organization of the "Chiang Mai Social Installation Group" In search of artistic taste of the Chiang mai residents. Consequently, you might be the one who is being contacted by mail or other voies. Navin is attending for your cooperation.

29
NELIA JUSTO (AUSTRALIA)

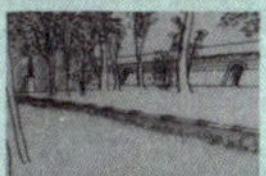

● WAT U-KNOW
■ วัดอุโมงค์
◆ ปูนปั้น
* มนุษย์สามารถแยกออกเป็น 4 กลุ่ม
(ก) เป็นคนมีความรู้ที่รู้ว่าเขามีความรู้ ซึ่งมนุษย์ต้องไปหาความรู้จากเขา
(ข) เป็นคนมีความรู้แต่ไม่รู้ตัวว่าเขามีความรู้ คนประเภทนี้ควรปลุกเขา
(ค) คนไม่มีความรู้และรู้ตัวว่าไม่รู้ คนเหล่านี้ต้องถูกสอน
(ง) คนไม่มีความรู้แต่คิดว่ารู้ คนแบบนี้คือคนโง่ คนบ้า ต้องเชิญออกไป (SALOMOD IBN GABIROL)

● WAT U-KNOW.
■ U-Mong Temple.
◆ Stucco.
* Man are divided into 4 groups :
a) Those who know that they know.
b) Those who don't know that they know.
c) Those who know that that they don't know.
d) Those who don't know that they don't know.

34
อนุรักษ์ ชัฎอนันต์
ANURAK CHATANAN

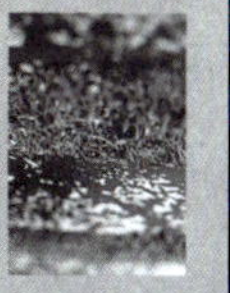

● พฤติกรรมของ
มนุษย์ และร่ม
เงาแห่งชีวิต
■ วัดอุโมงค์
◆ ไม้, ตะปู, ใบเลื่อย
ลวด, มุ้งลวดและอื่นๆ
* สะท้อนภาพพฤติกรรม
บางอย่างของมนุษย์ใ
ด้านบวกและลบต่
ต้นไม้ ในฐานะชีวิต
กระทำต่อชีวิต

● Man's
behavio
and the
shadow
of life.
■ U - 'Mong Temple.
◆ Woods, nails, saw
blades, wire, an
wire netting, etc.
* Reflecting some
man's behavior, bot
positive and nega
tive, towards trees
Trees are compare
with a nice, coo
shelter along the jour
ney of life.
An interactio
between two lives.

39
มีศรี
ORN MEESRI

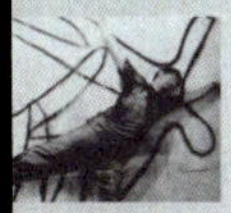

ณลานเอนกประสงค์ ประตูท่าแพ
าะวันที่ 24 พฤศจิกายน 2536
18:45 - 19:10 น.
ภาทสมมุติ คือวิถีของชีวิต
มลวงเป็นสารัตถะแห่งศิลปะ
ย่าประหลาดใจอันใดเลย หาก
เจ้าได้เลือกสื่อศิลปะเพียงเงา

-Pae Gate.
ember 24, 1993 only (6:45
- 7:10 p.m.)
is but an illusory role.
ion is the essence of art
se do not be surprised if I
se "shadow" as artistic
ium.

41
ปรีชา ปั้นกล่ำ และคณะ
PREECHA PUNKLAM AND COLLEAGUE

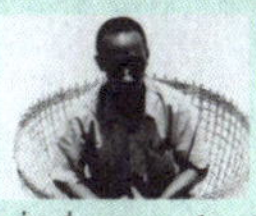

P■ เริ่มต้นที่ลานเอนกประสงค์ประตูท่าแพถึงวัดพระสิงห์
▲ เฉพาะวันที่ 24 พฤศจิกายน 2536 เวลา 20:10 - 20:40 น.
* อะไรเอ่ย เป็นสัญลักษณ์ของเชียงใหม่
อะไรเอ่ย คือวัฒนธรรมลานนา
อะไรเอ่ย ควันลอยปกคลุมเชียงใหม่
อะไรเอ่ย เพิ่งจะมาถึง

P■ From Tha-Pae Gate to Pra-Singh Temple.
▲ November 24, 1993 only (8:10-8:40 p.m.).
* What is the symbol of Chiang Mai ?
What is the Lanna culture ?
What pollutes Chiang Mai ?
What has just arrived ?

44
อุทิศ อติมานะ
UTHIT ATIMANA

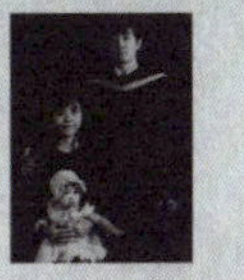

■ 48/4 ถ.ท่าสะต้อย อ.เมือง เชียงใหม่ โทร. (053) 242098
▲ เฉพาะเวลา 17:00-18:00 น. ทุกวัน -30 พฤศจิกายน 2536
* ครอบครัวผมคือศิลปะ

■ 48/4 Tasatoy Road, A.Muang Chiang Mai,
▲ Daily 5:00-6:00 p.m. only, Tel (053) 242098 - until Nov. 30, 1993.
* My family is Art.

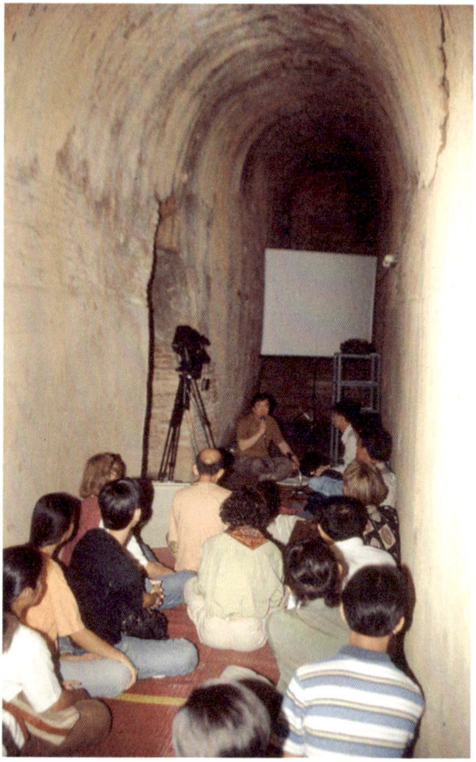

At Wat Umong: a discussion on contemporary art in Japan and Asia with Tani Arata, Kimio Tsuchiya and Chieo Senzaki (left); and a talk by Sulak Sivaraksa on a Buddhist vision of creating a new society (right and below).

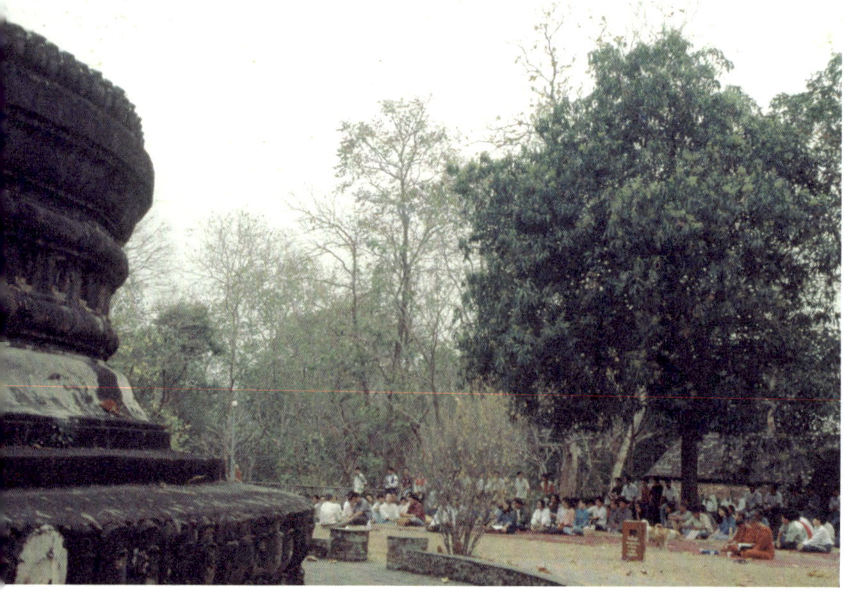

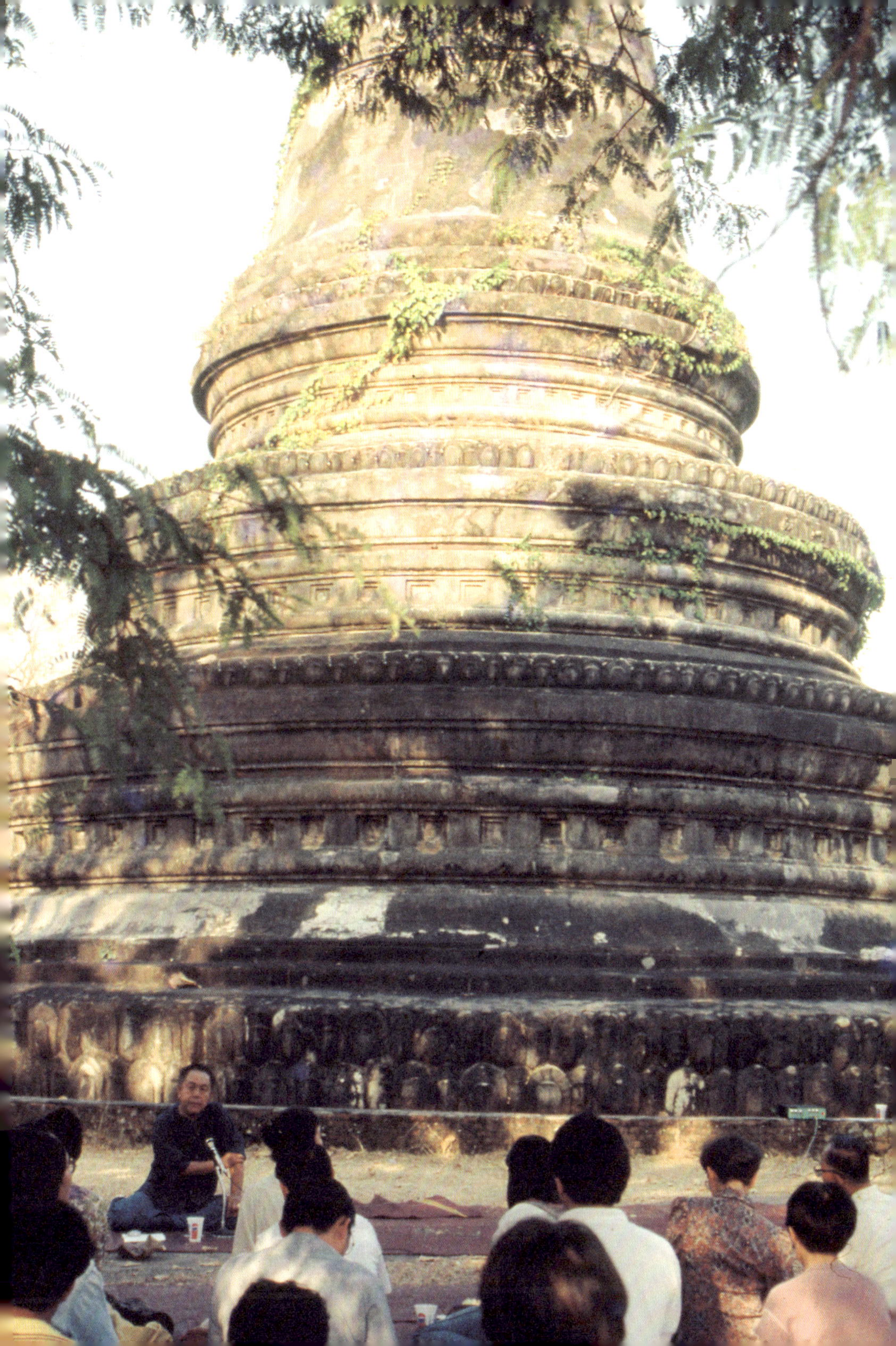

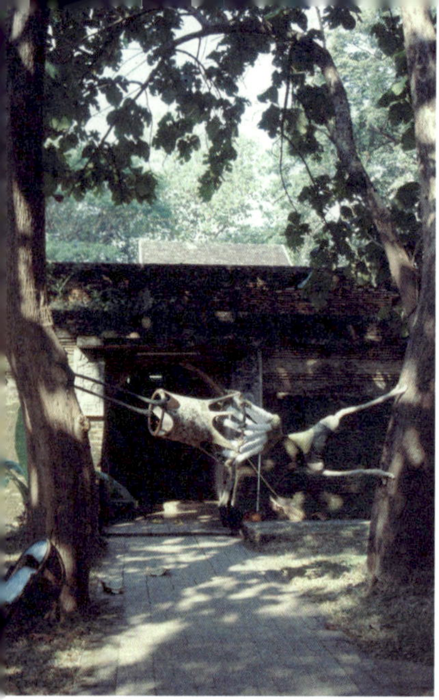

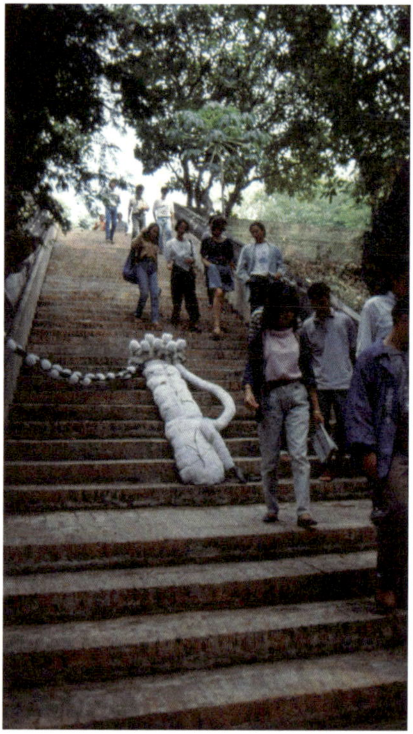

Works by Narupon Buranabanyat.

Performance by Tawatchai Homthong.

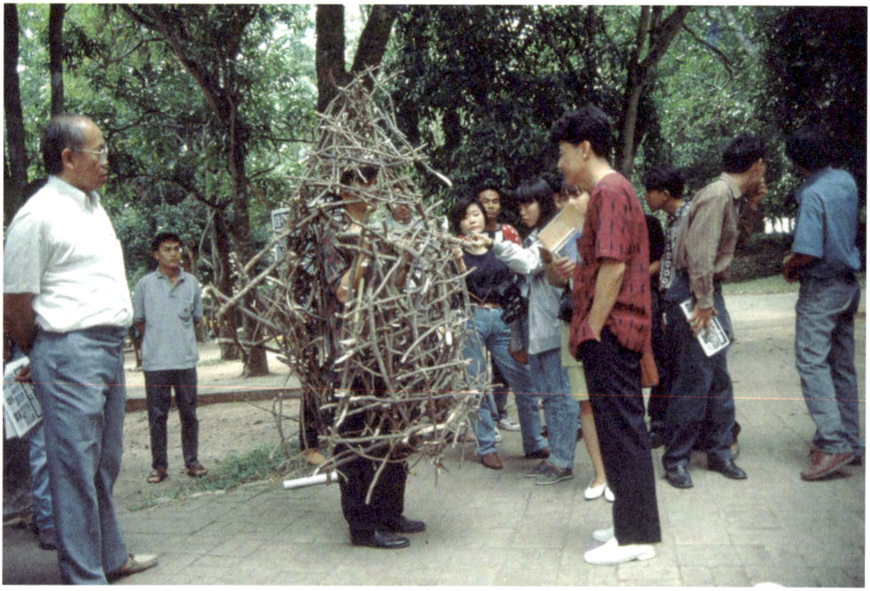

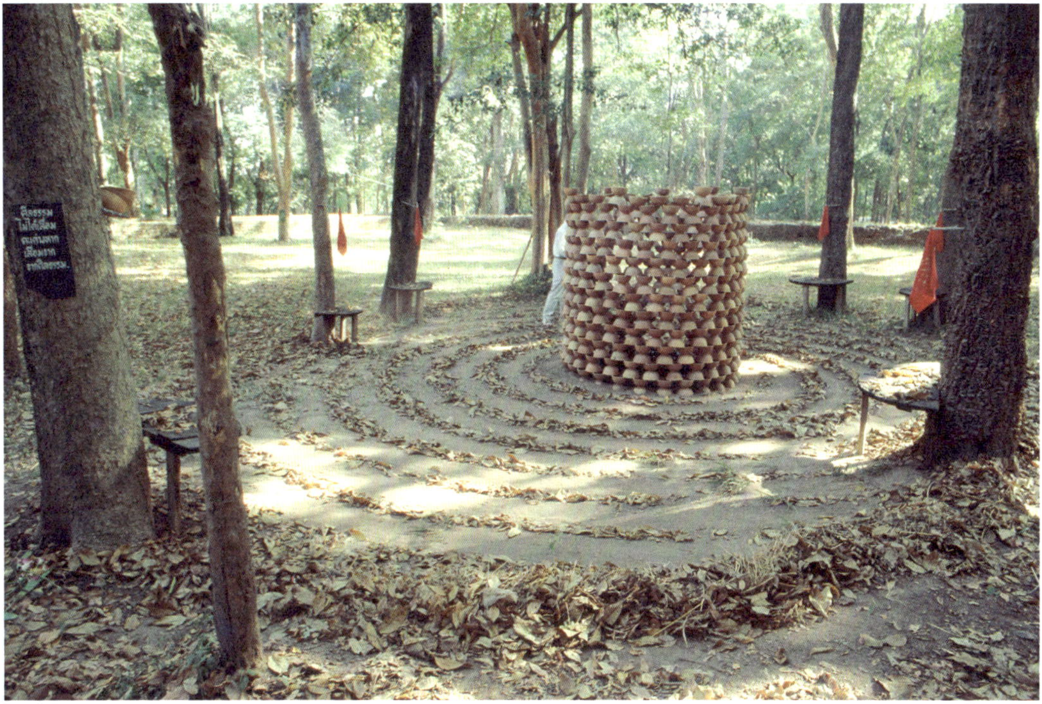

Montien Boonma's *Vessel – Meditation* set an arrangement of terracotta vessels amid trees that had jawbone- and teeth-imprinted cloths attached to them with metal chopsticks. It resembled the artist's *The Pleasure of Singing, Crying, Dying and Eating*, which had been displayed at the National Gallery, Bangkok earlier in 1993. 'I chose to set my work here surrounded by trees because it brought to mind the place the Buddha tortured himself when searching for the truth of life,' he explained. 'The pottery symbolizes the burning of lust in our minds' (*The Nation*, 29 November 1993).

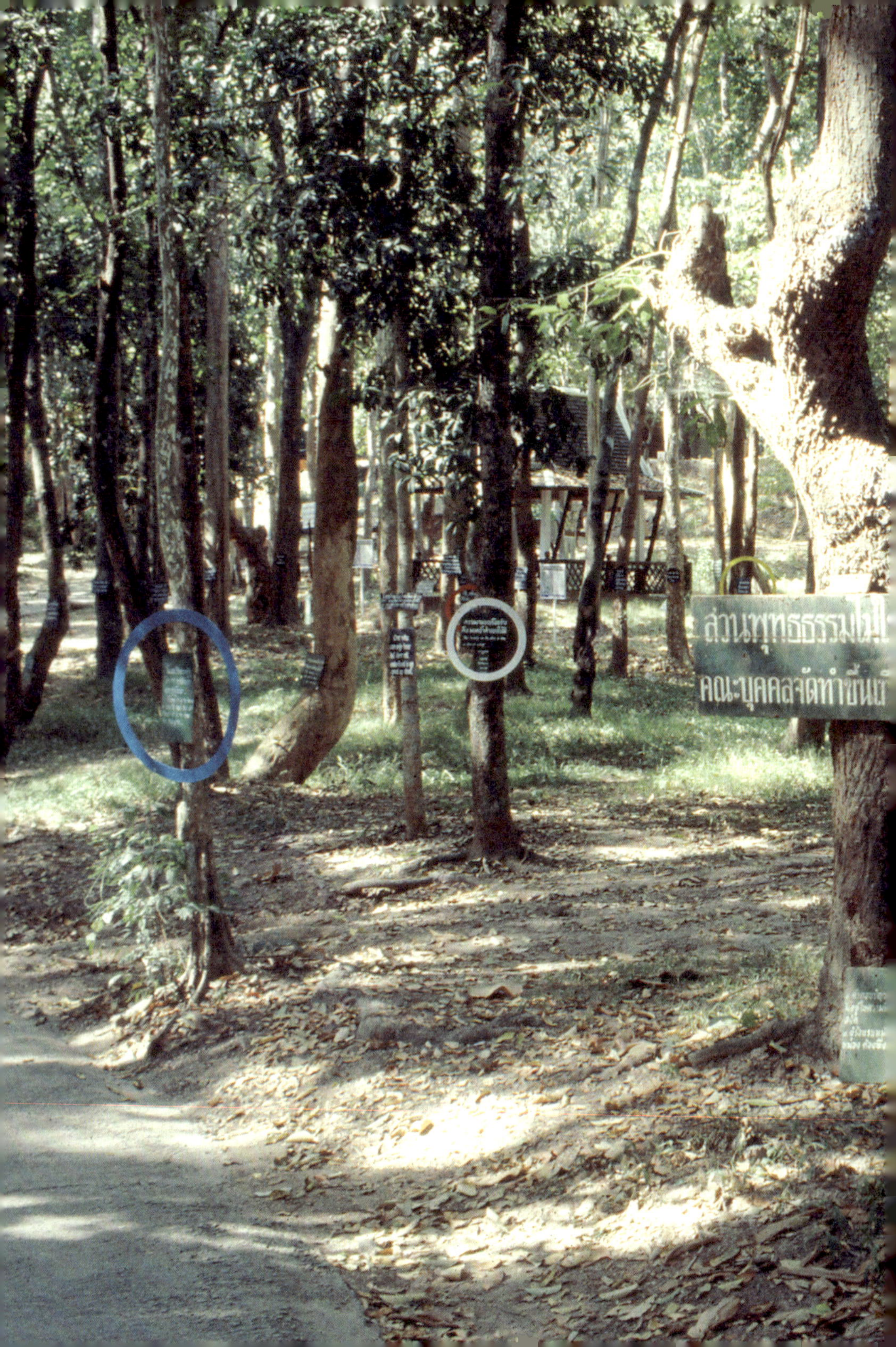
สวนพุทธธรรม
คณะบุคคลจัดทำขึ้นนี้

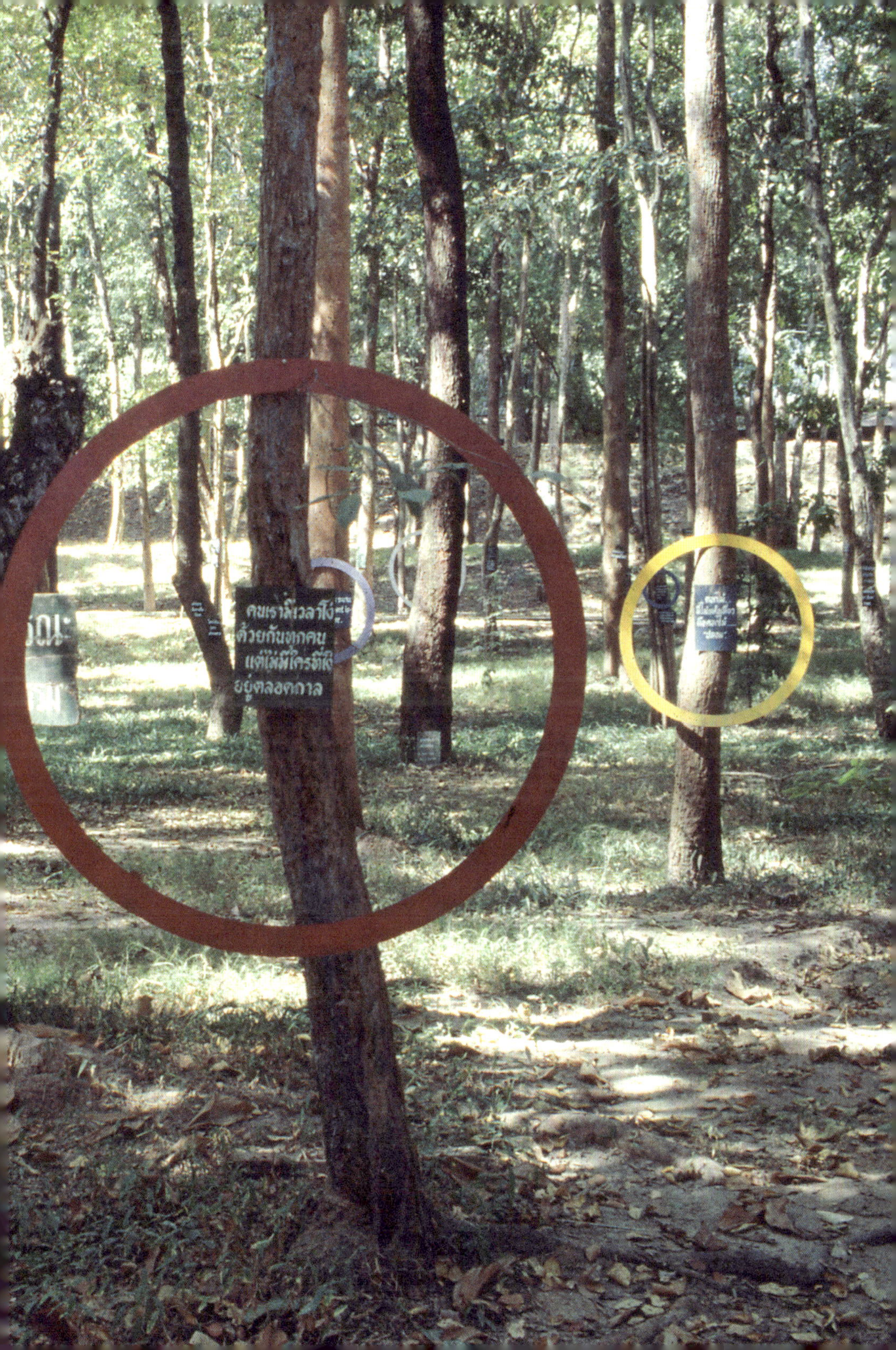
คนเรามีเวลา
ด้วยกันทุกคน
แต่ไม่มีใครที่ได้
อยู่ตลอดกาล

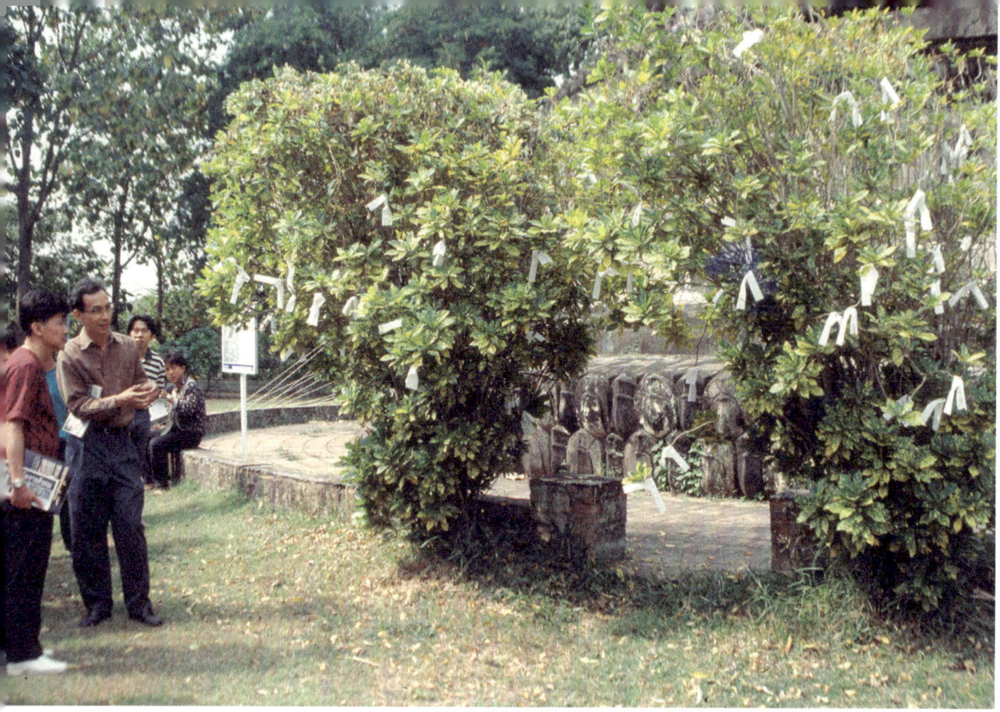

Onto trees around Wat Umong temple, Udom Chimpakdee added circular constructions with Buddhist texts, 'megaphones to spread the Buddha's teachings (see previous spread). For her work *A Bird in the Bush is Worth Two in the Head,* Joan Grounds hung fabric printed with birds from trees in the temple and 'used holy threads to express the suffering of birds at the hands of humans' (*The Nation*, 29 November 1993).

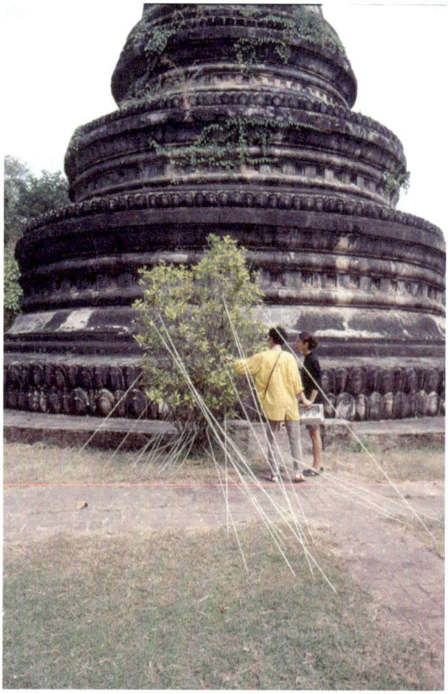

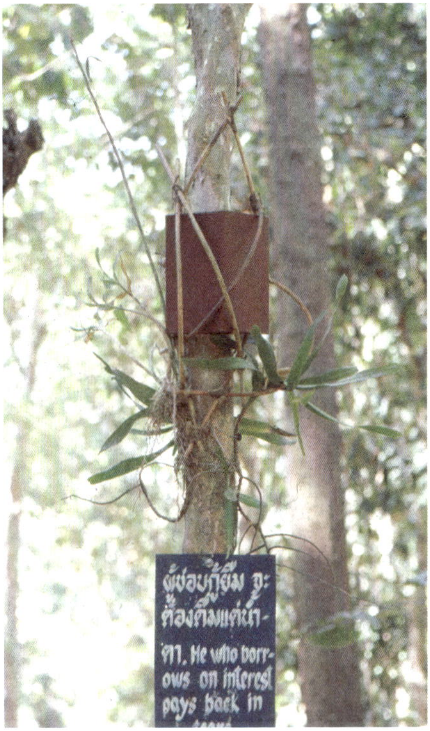

Also hanging on trees around the temple were Thatree Pokavanich's bamboo bird cages with bells inside them. He explained: 'Bells are like the minds of human beings and the cages are symbols of houses. ... When we live surrounded by extremely luxurious things, it's easy to be convinced of the importance of these things. It depends on each individual, whether they choose to live inside the cages or outside' (*The Nation*, 29 November 1993).

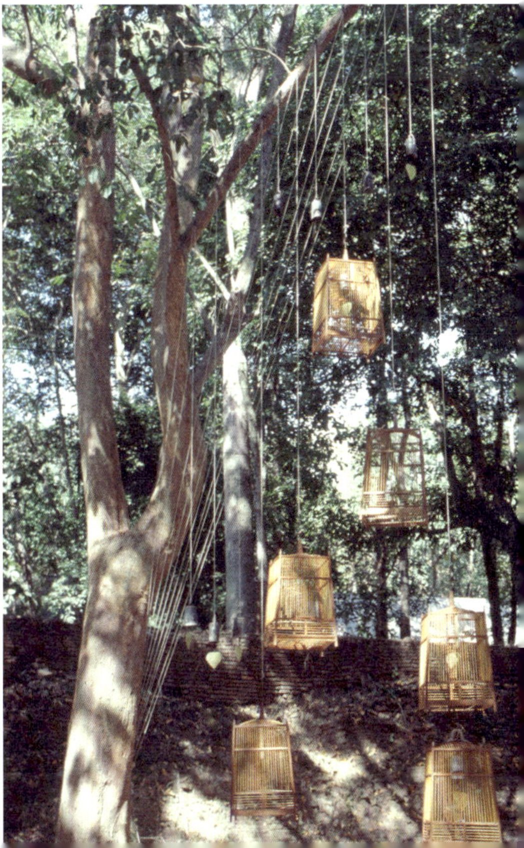

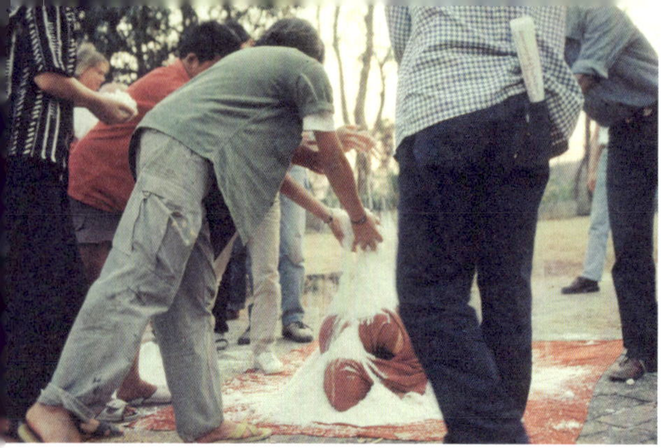

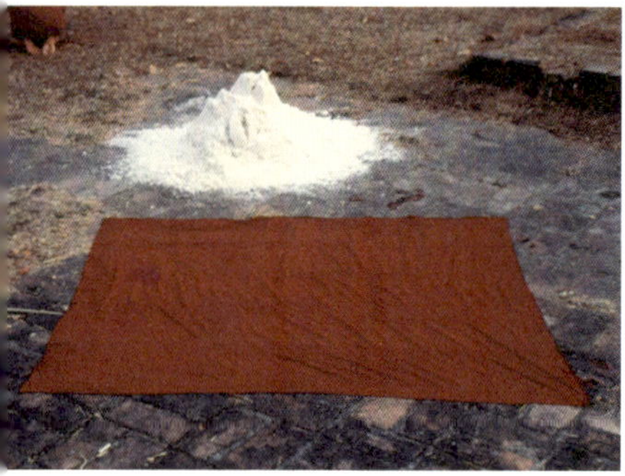

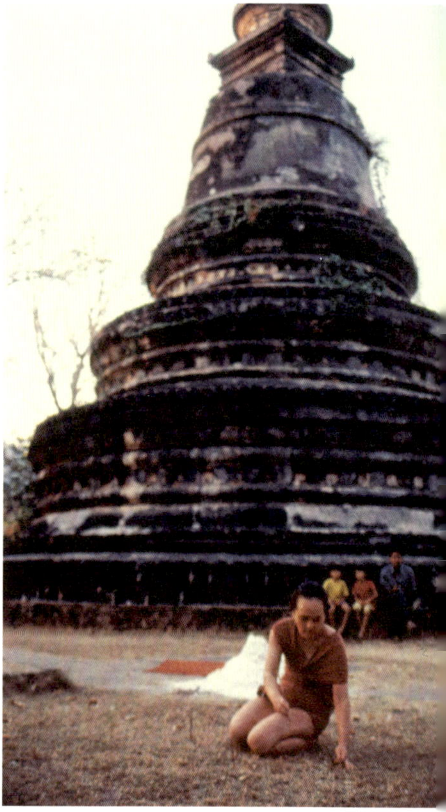

Performance by
Tei Kobayashi.

Visitors in front of a work by Apichat Udomchai.

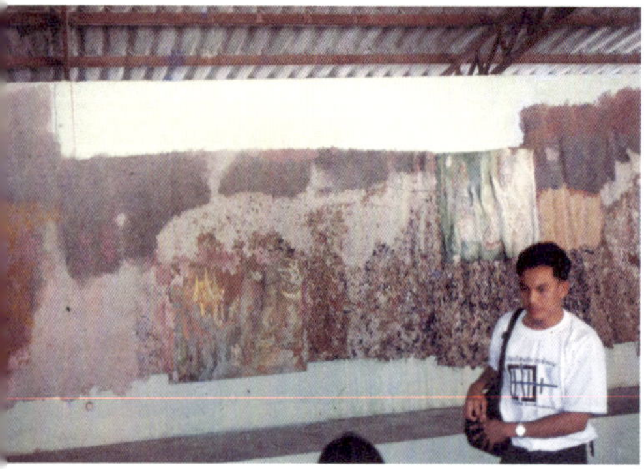

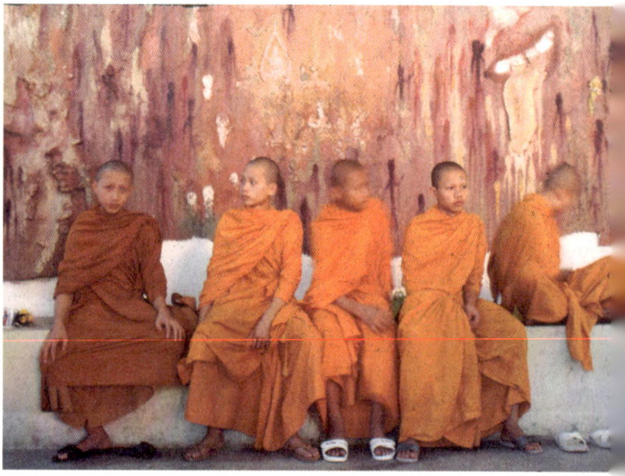

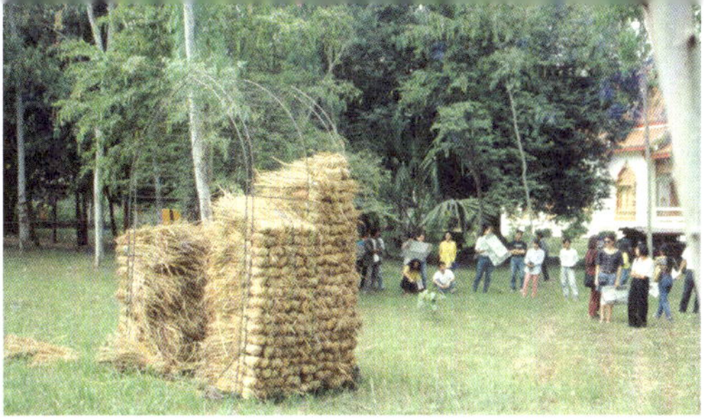

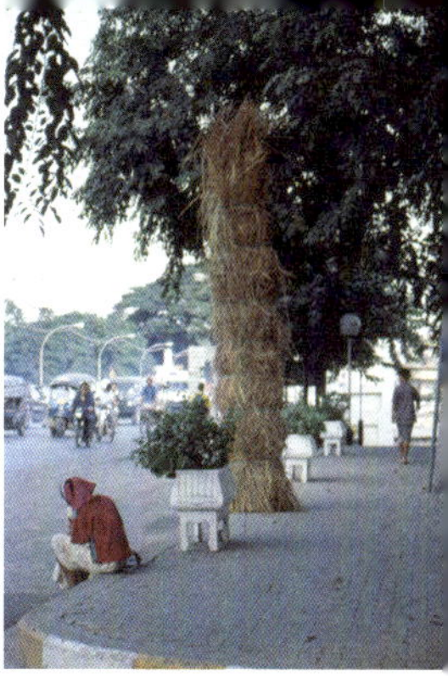

Work by an unidentified artist at Wat Chet Yod and a second location.

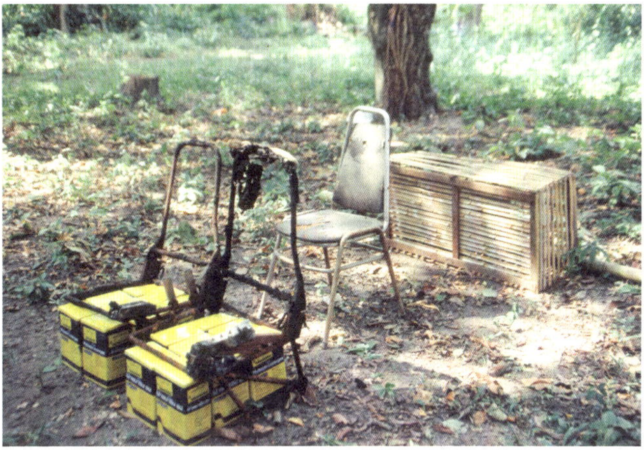

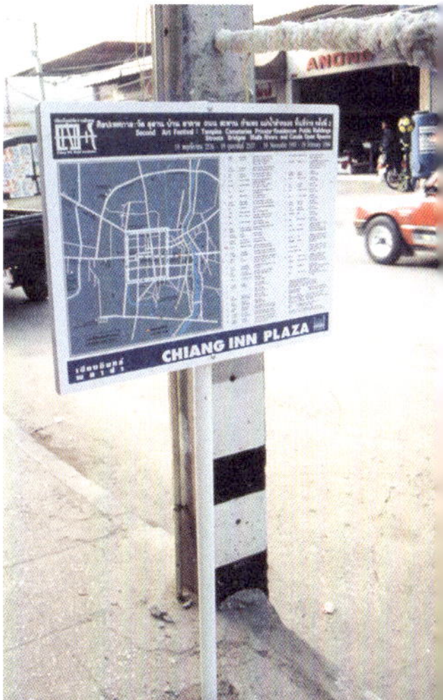

Among several 'copycat' works created by Mit Jai Inn for this edition of CMSI was a work attributed to Lawrence Weiner that appeared on the digital display of Hillside Plaza & Condotel 4. Other works were said to be by James Lee Byars, David Hammons and Nik Nikolai.

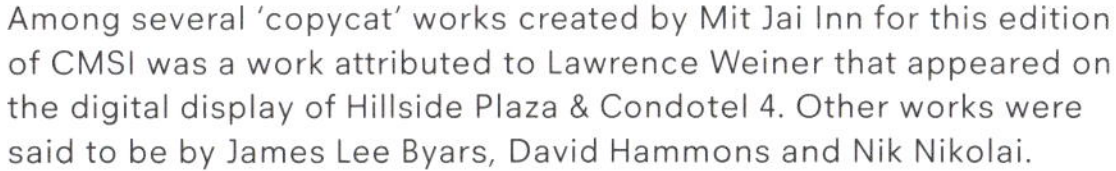

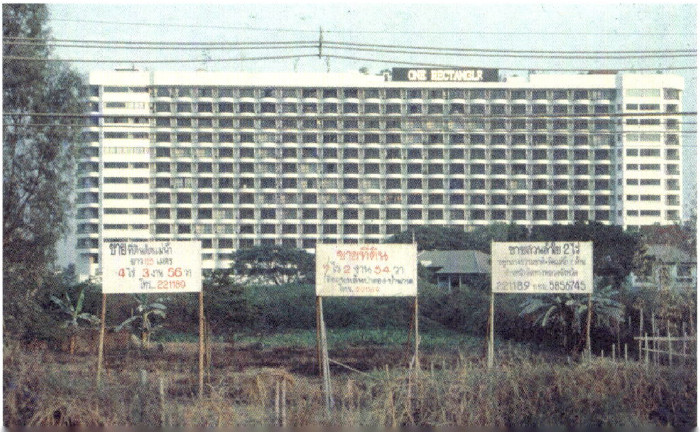

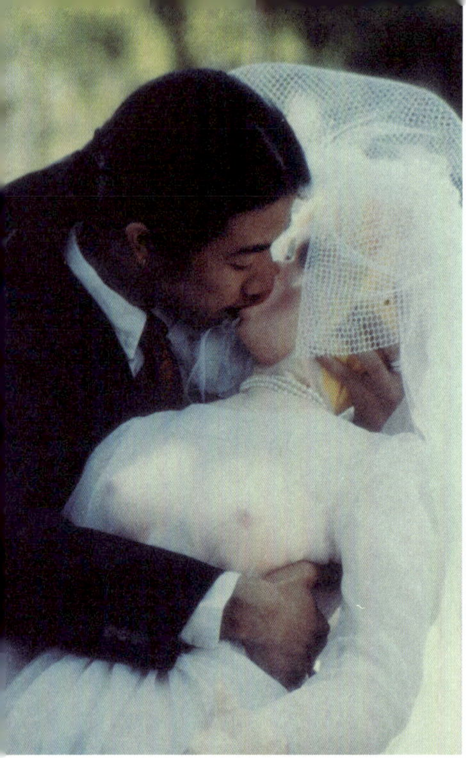

Work by Kosit Juntaratip, Chiang Mai First Church.

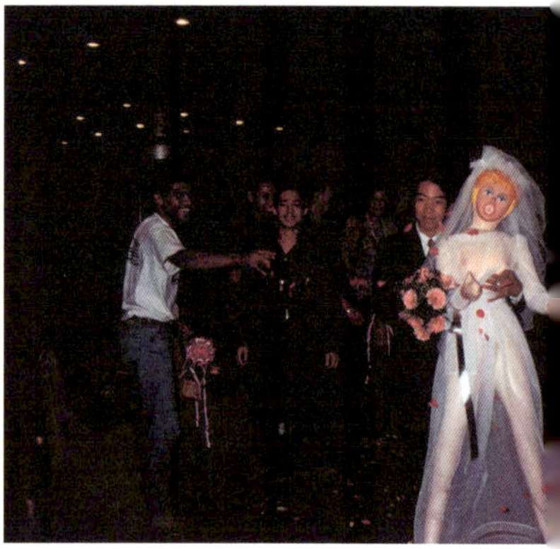

Work by Sarawoot Tongchampa, Wat Suan Dok. The installation 'lasted just one day before the pieces disappeared overnight' (*The Nation*, 29 November 1993).

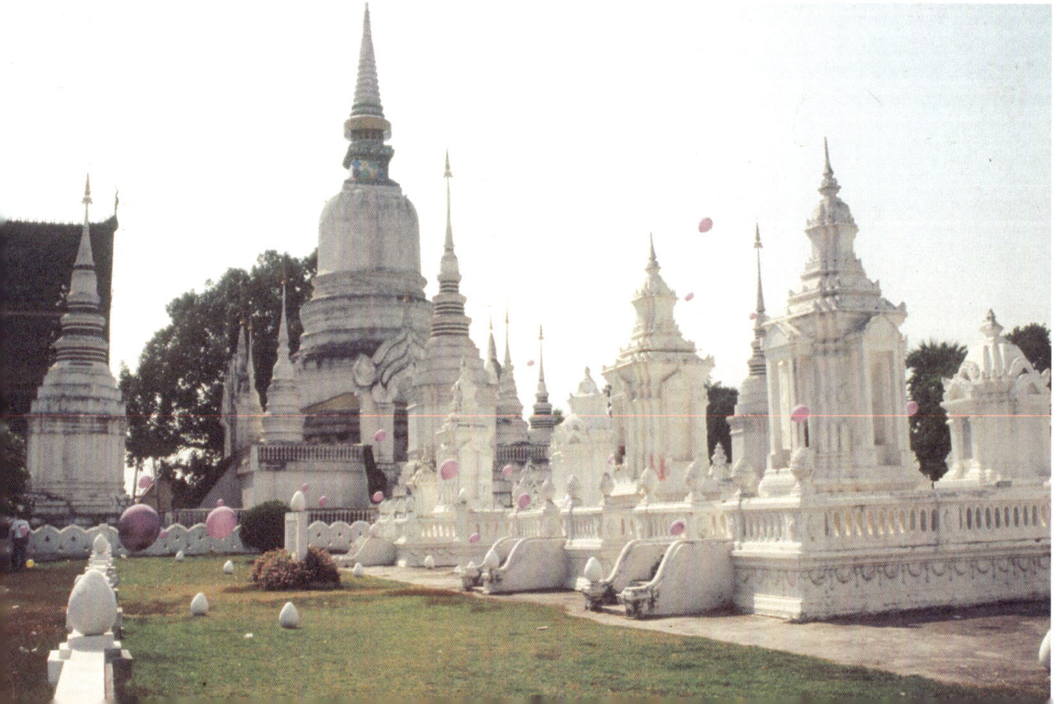

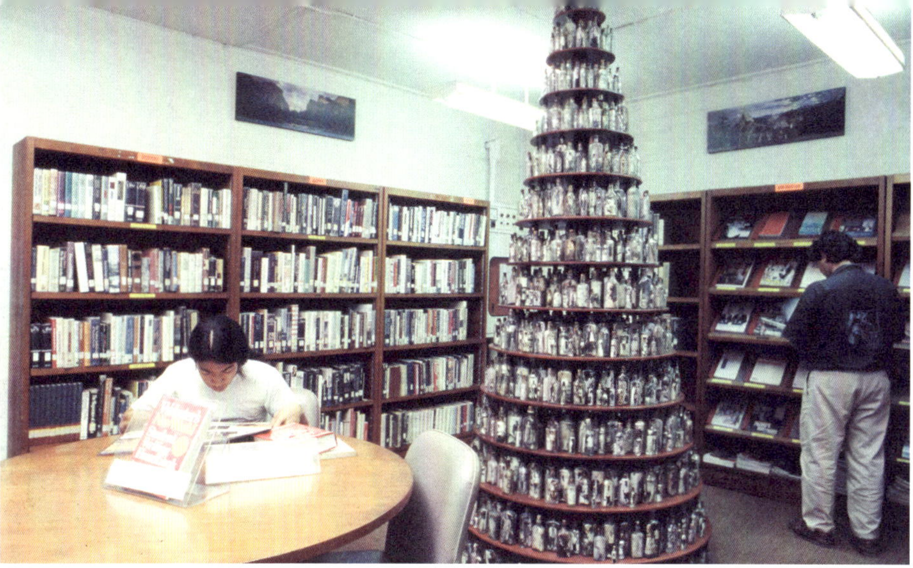

Navin Rawanchaikul, *There is No Voice*, United States Information Service (USIS) library.

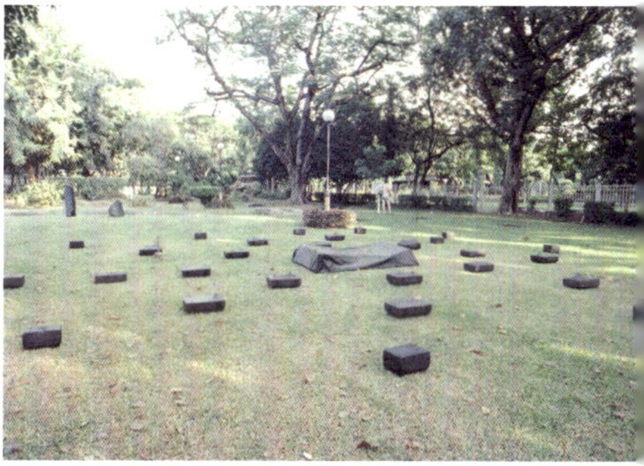

Kitti Maleepan, *Bed*.

Araya Rasdjarmrearnsook, *Once she was housewife, Once she was nurse, Once she was prostitute*.

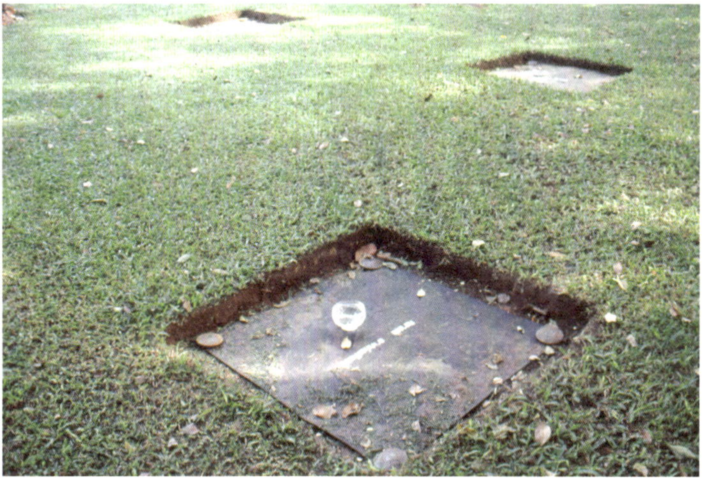

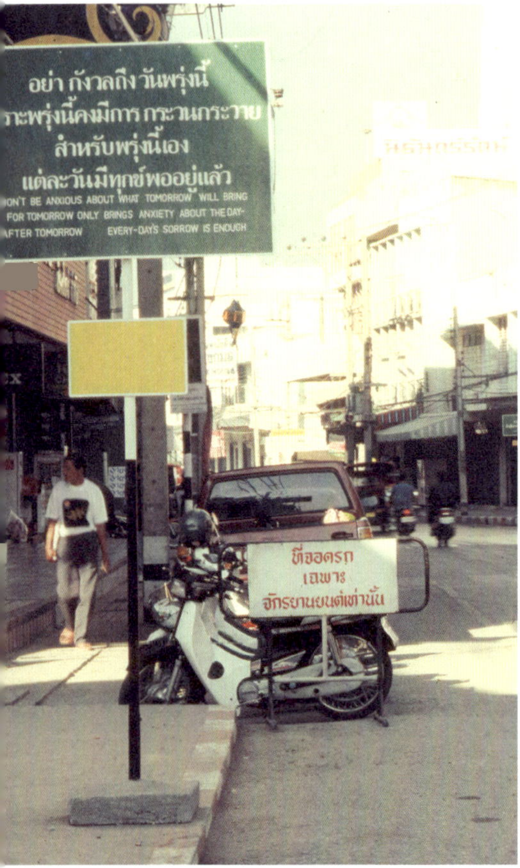

Theerapong Takerd, *Spiritual Food*.

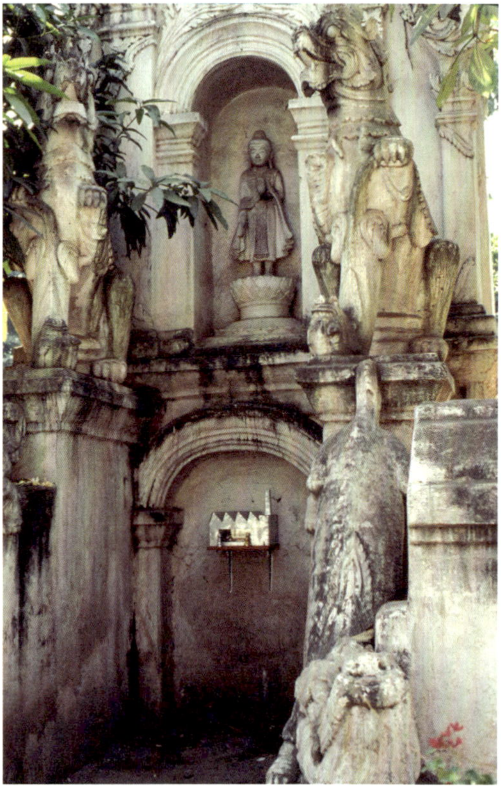

Nigel Helyer, *Inside – Outside*.

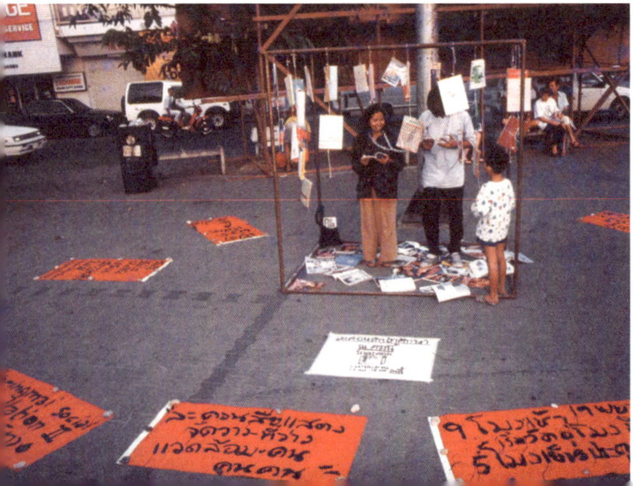

Works by Vasan Sitthiket appeared at both Tha Pae Gate and Wat Umong. There were three works at the former, 'each reflecting current social issues. For the work *Hilltribe*, the outspoken artist has utilized six wooden boxes. Inside each box he has placed hilltribe dolls. "The six boxes refer to six hilltribe groups", he said. "People who call themselves 'civilized' always think the people in these tribes are uncivilized. They bring things and ways that they consider 'civilizing' to the hilltribes instead of trying to learn about the lives of these people." The work *Education* reflects what he sees as a current frivolous approach to education by students, while *Prostitute* is a reflection on the numerous brothels in Chiang Mai' (*The Nation*, 29 November 1993).

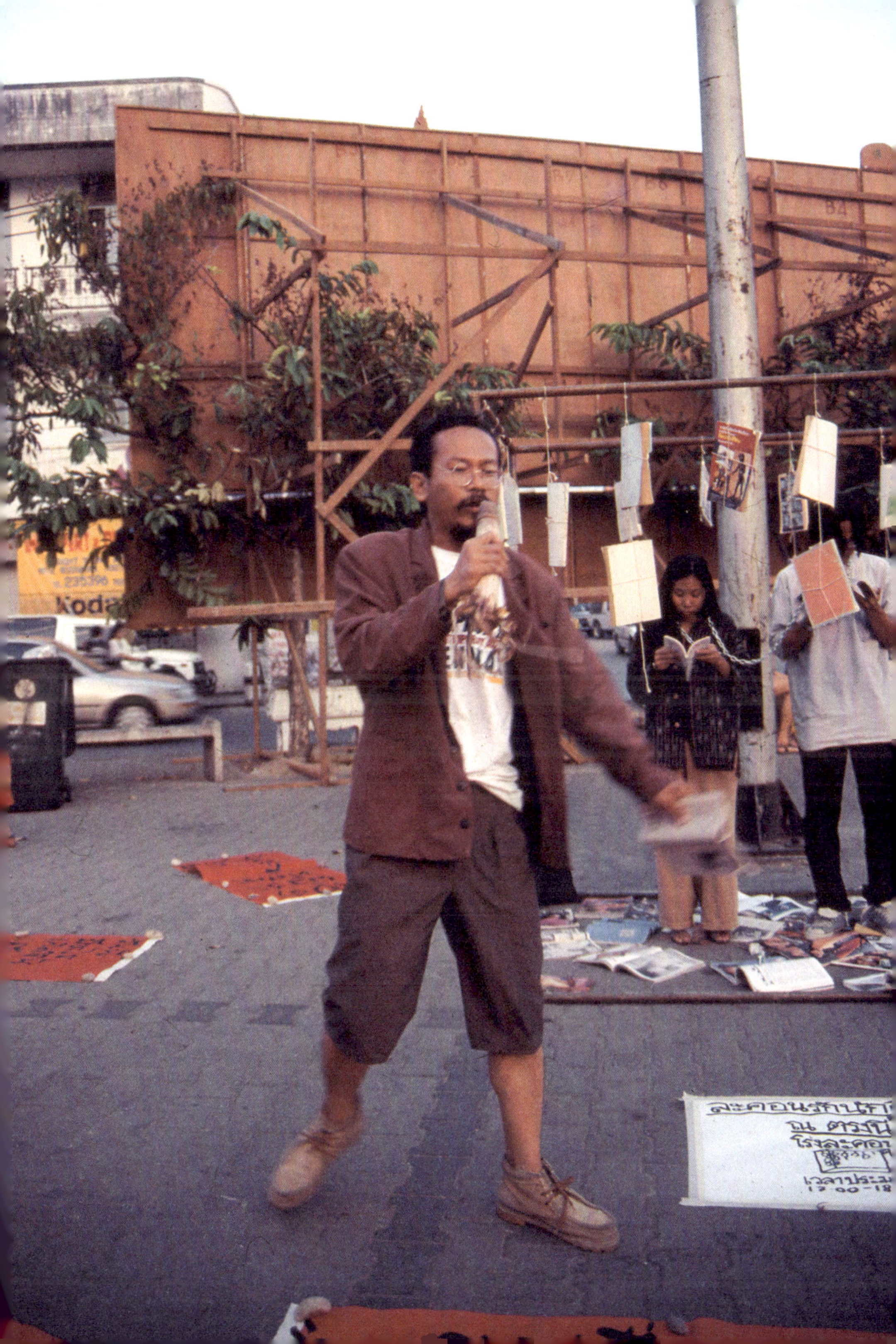

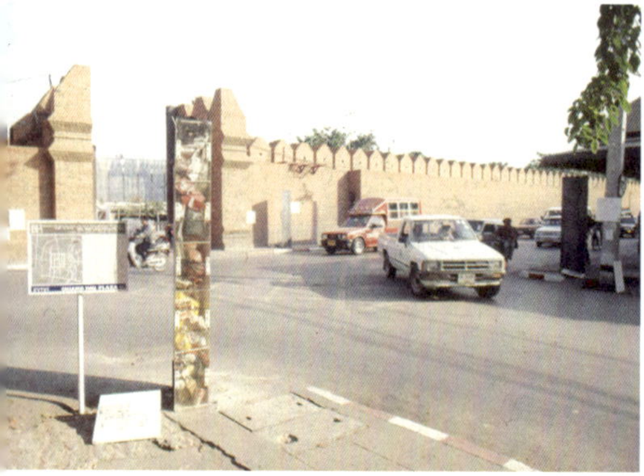

Komsan Nookaew, Chatchawan Nilsakul and Worapoj Preabjariyawat presented works based on a survey of discarded items and rubbish around Tha Pae Gate.

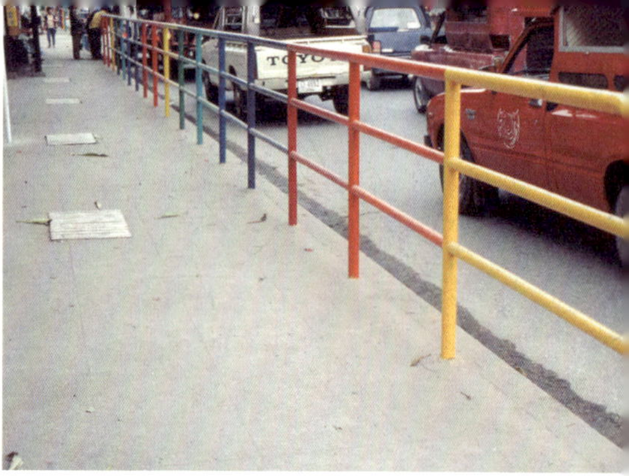

Work by Udom Chimpakdee, who 'painted parts of town gaudy colours just to brighten things up'. He said: 'I sometimes go to observe people's feedback at various spots. ... They often ask what we are doing. When I told them we create art for society's sake, some shot back that it might be more worthwhile to work on other things. But I'm not angry. Our concept of beauty and perceptions are different. It doesn't matter to me who's right or wrong. The point is that we can exchange ideas and people become more familiar with contemporary art, which focuses on concepts' (*Bangkok Post*, 15 December 1993).

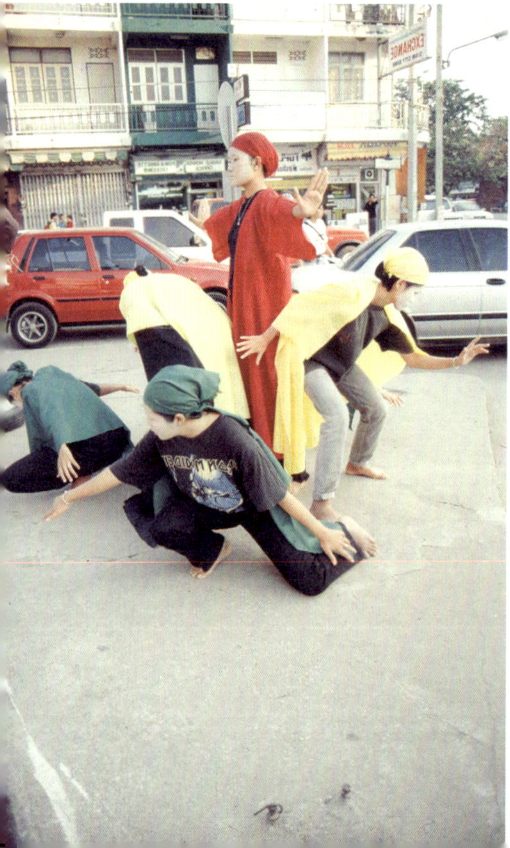

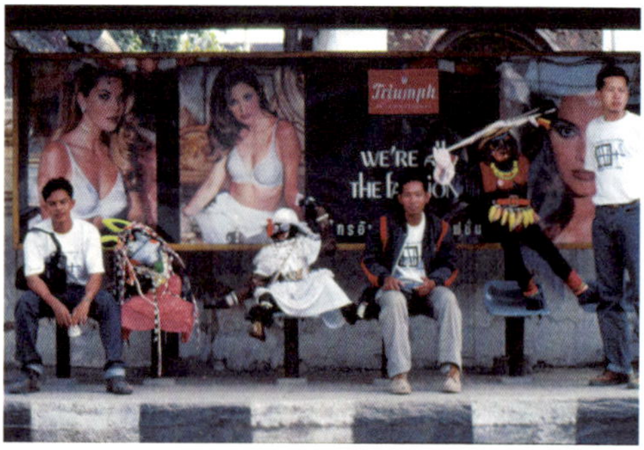

Works by Pittawat Tripopsawat and a performance by Rakon Lakon Group, near Tha Pae Gate.

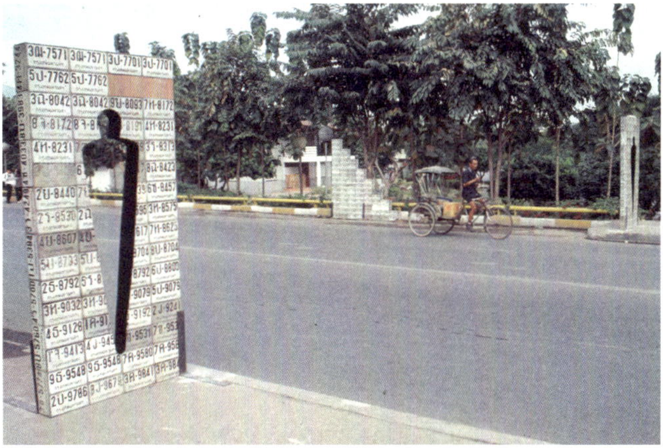

Supachai Satsara, *Traffic River 700 Years Chiang Mai*. The artist recalls: 'During the event, some licence plates were stolen because they could be sold on as fakes. The Department of Land Transport was looking for me for three days, asking how I was able to acquire these plates. Also, this work was publicised in *Plak* magazine [a local publication on strange phenomena], which claimed that my work made people see ghosts or caused a family breakup/divorce. ... People who lived nearby said they saw ghosts.'

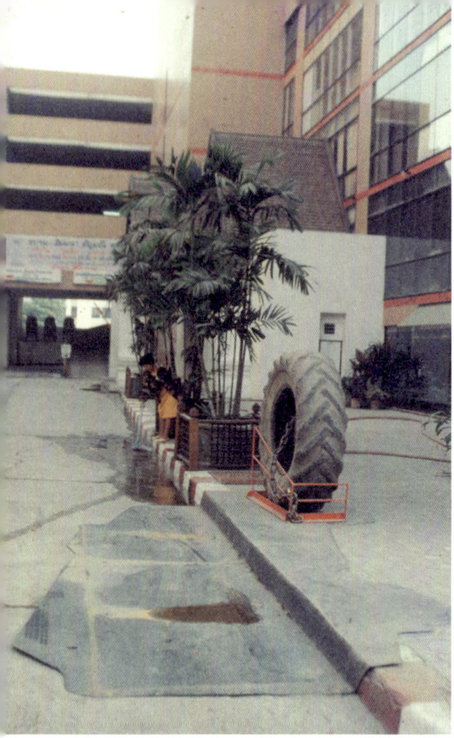

Kade Javanalikhikara, *A Dirty Automobile and a Dirty Man*, Chiang Inn Plaza.

Preecha Punklam, *The Arrival of Mr X*, performance that began at Wat Phra Singh and proceeded to Tha Pae Gate.

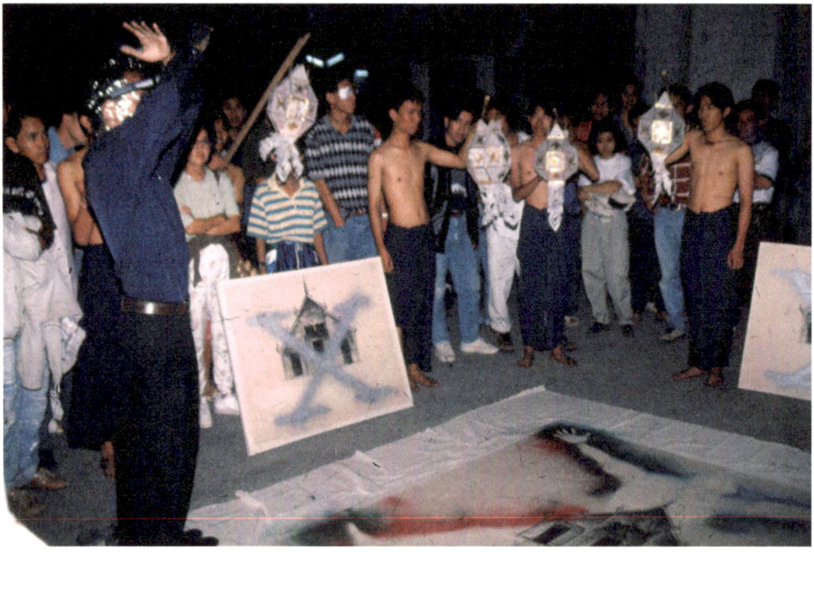

Sunthorn Meesri, *bot bat sommut* (*role play*), performance at Tha Pae Gate.

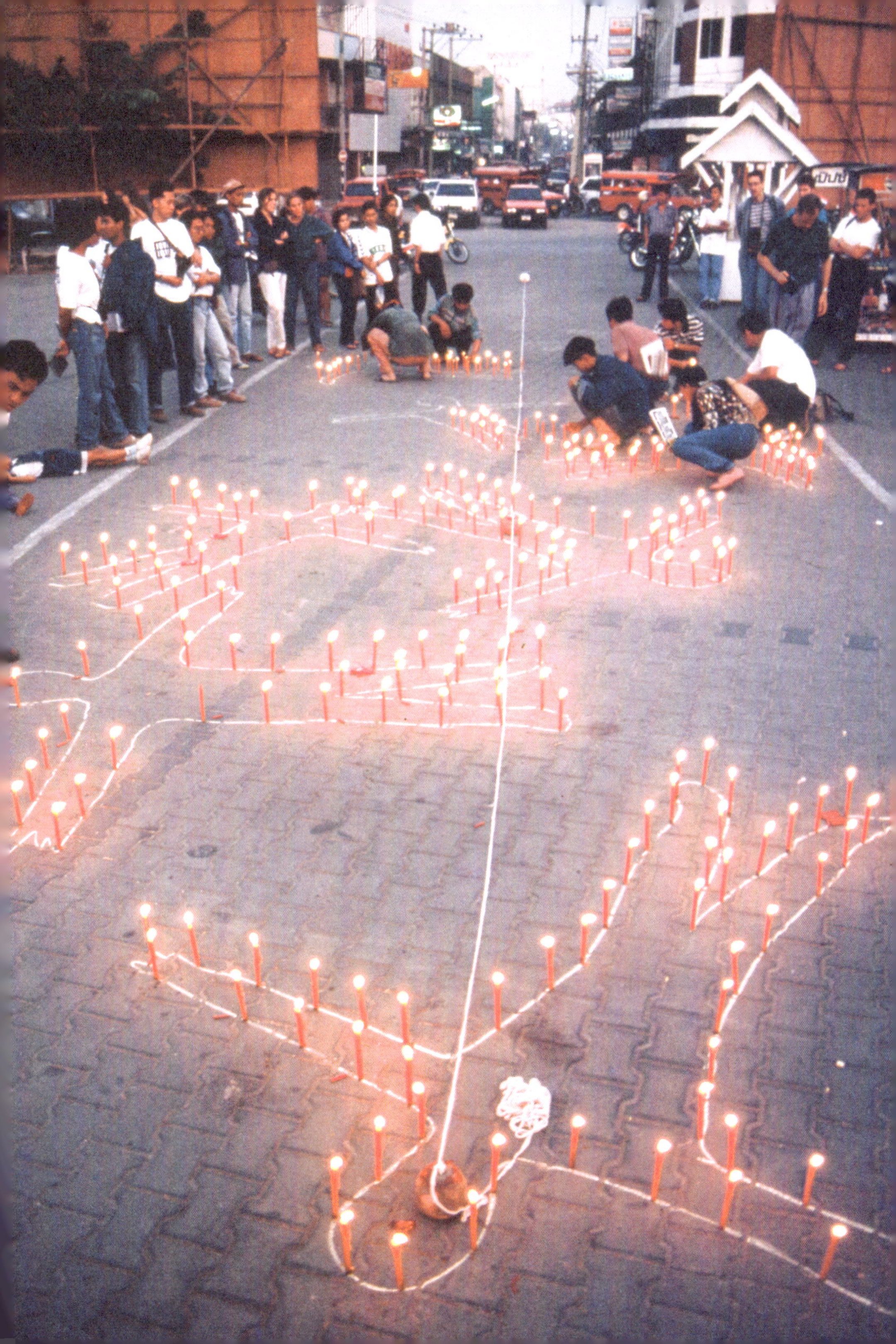

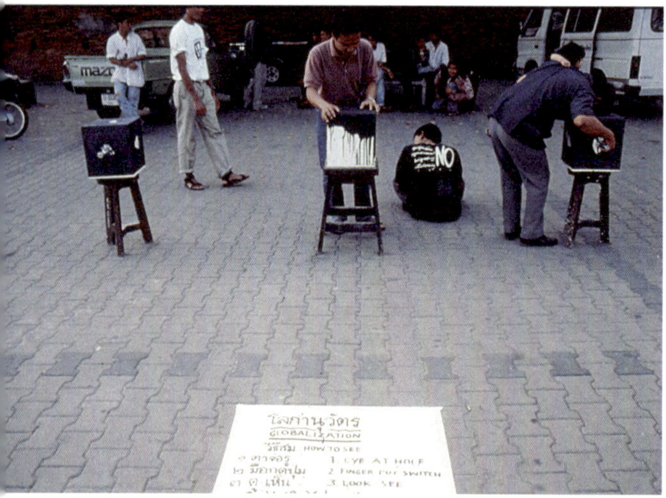

โลกาภิวัตร
GLOBALIZATION
HOW TO SEE
1. EYE AT HOLE
2. FINGER PUT SWITCH
3. LOOK SEE

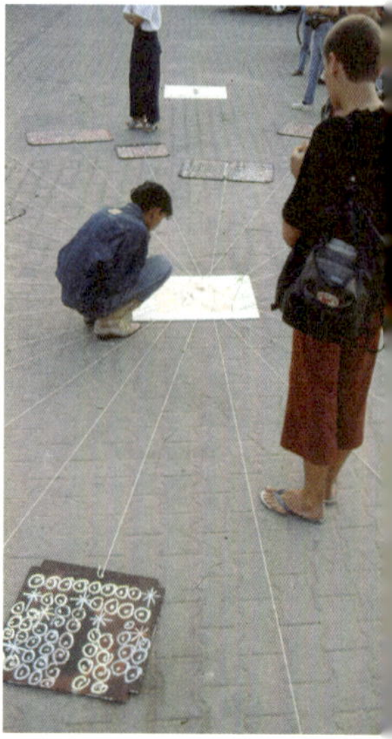
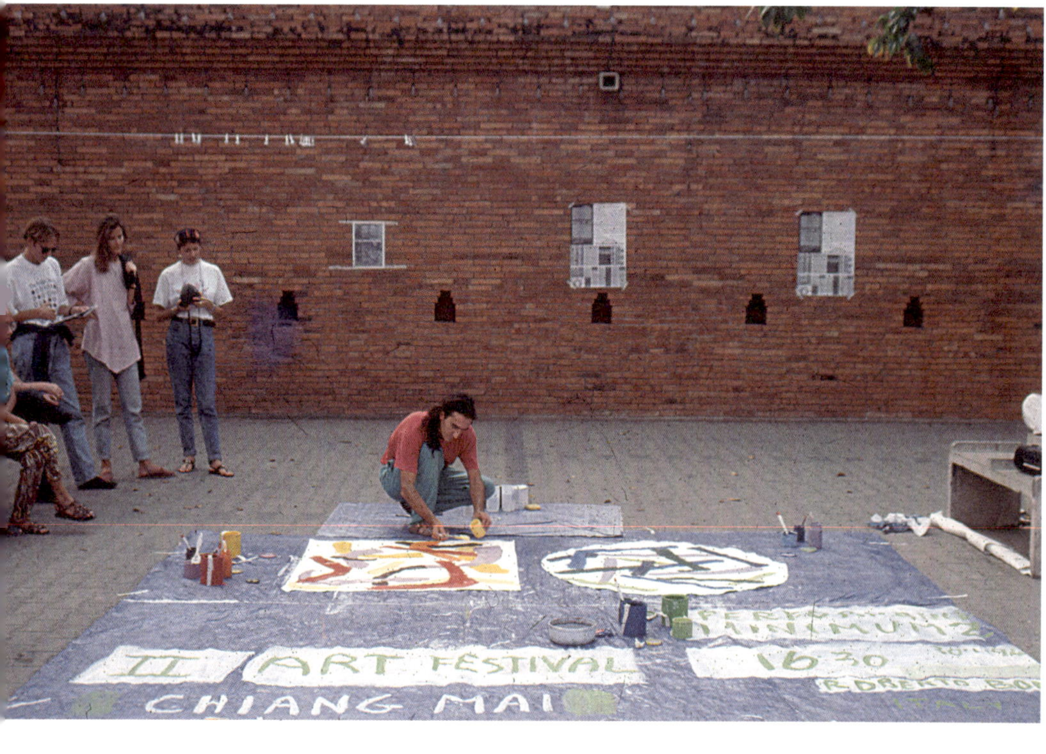

II ART FESTIVAL
CHIANG MAI
16 30

Work by Tei Kobayashi. She recalled it as 'a performance at the Buddhist Center in the middle of the town of Chiang Mai, backed by lecturing and chanting by one of the more illustrious Buddhist monks ... I scrubbed the platform located at the top of the stairway leading into the expansive lecture hall. On this platform, on the forbidden-to-women monk's surplice, I experience[d] a purification and rebirth of woman, symbolically lifted above all religious and social taboos. Theravada Buddhism in Thailand forbids women to touch the monk's robes as well as places within the sacred grounds of Buddhism. This taboo has been taken to such an extreme that a male dressed as a female worshipper, a transvestite, performs the sacred temple dances. Taboos manipulate much of woman's sacredness. The Thai woman faces a paradoxical position in this land of Buddha, which has recently become shrouded in the veils of sexual oppression and AIDS. Although it is an economic, albeit spiritual, issue, there is something else involved here. Woman is entitled to a respectable position in society and should be allowed her own integrity. Mit [Jai Inn] was there two years ago at the Buddhist Center taking my hand after my rebirthing performance. All the people present were asked to join hands and grasp a rope, which provided another tie, or rather link, to the group' (*Asiana*, February 1996).

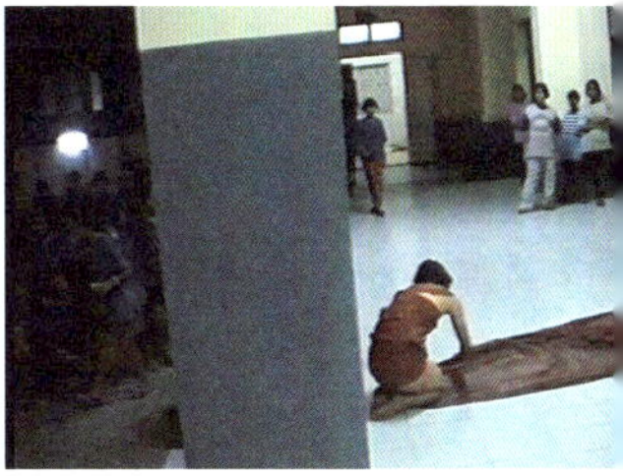

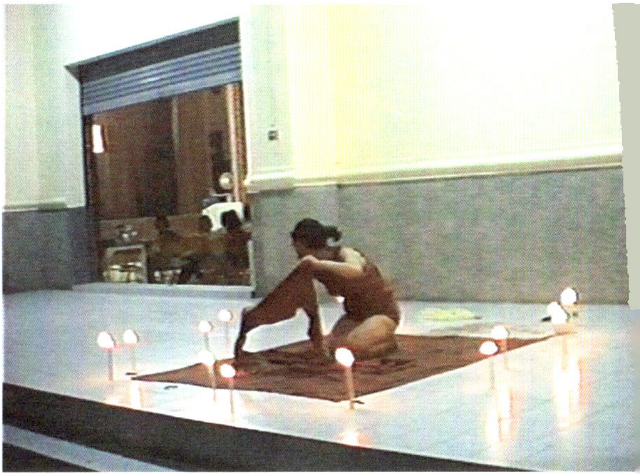

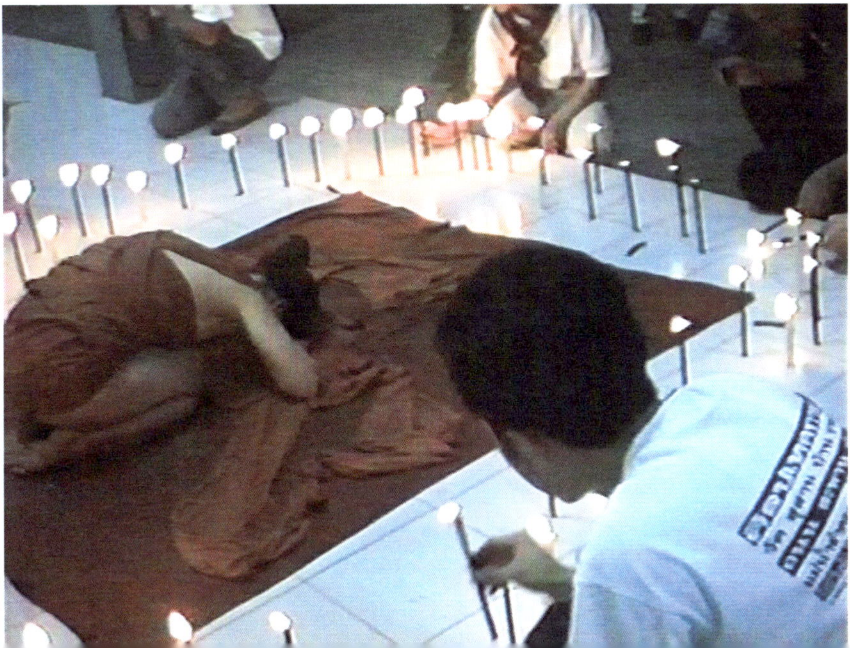

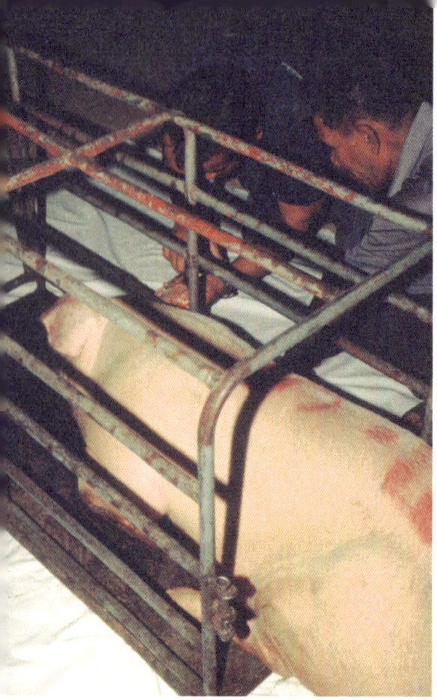

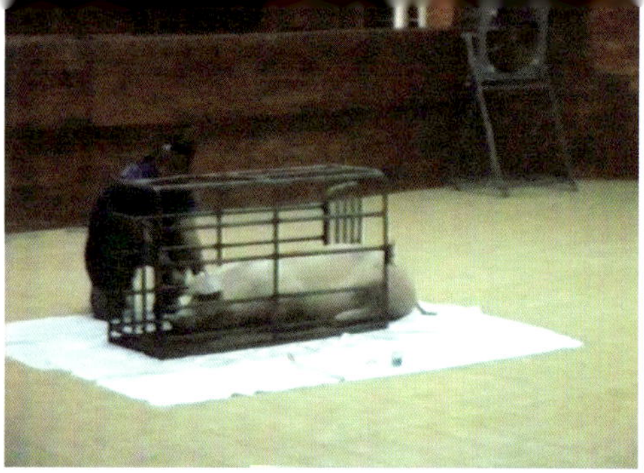

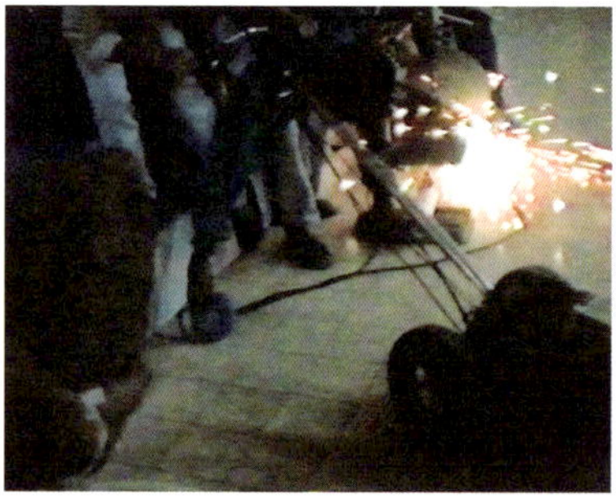

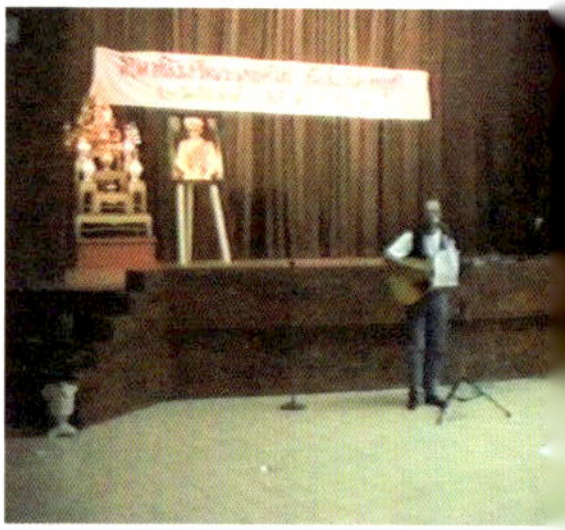

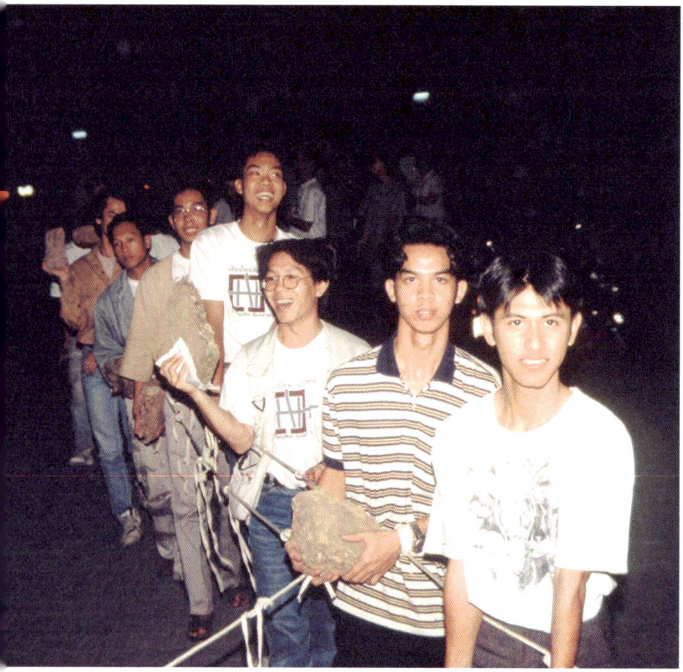

The final day of the festival featured talks and performances at the Buddhasathan, also known as the Chiang Mai Religion Practice Centre. Video footage taken at the time shows a musical performance interrupted by a live pig being led into the room and the operation of a circular saw. Mit Jai Inn is seen attaching audience members together with a length of rope, in preparation for a 'participatory walkabout', as he recalls. 'Everyone who joined the tour was made to carry a large object and participants were bound together for the duration of the walk by a rope. We walked from the Buddhasathan to the night bazaar, a short distance away. There were about seventy to one hundred of us. We walked past a luxury hotel where a wedding celebration was taking place. We then walked past the red-light district and solicitous bar girls. We proceeded through the slum where many Cambodian refugees were trying to rebuild their lives, and then through the various neighbourhoods that make up Chiang Mai. We finally ended our walk at the municipal abattoir, where pigs and cows are slaughtered. We stayed on and observed the scene. It was a narrative of great suffering – from dancing and celebration to death.'

Events included lectures by Nidhi Eoseewong, Saneh Jamarik and Seksan Prasertkul, and a symposium.

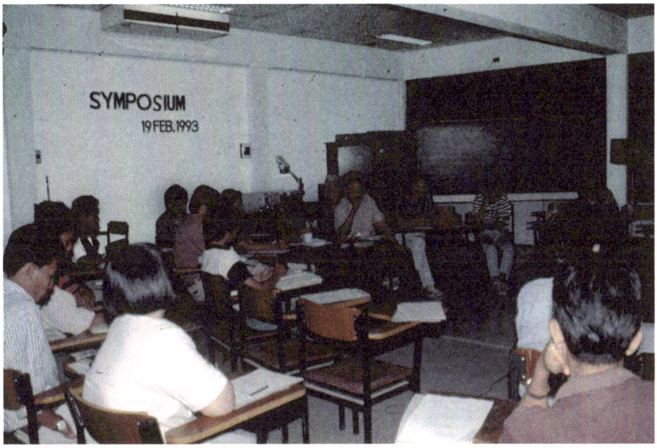

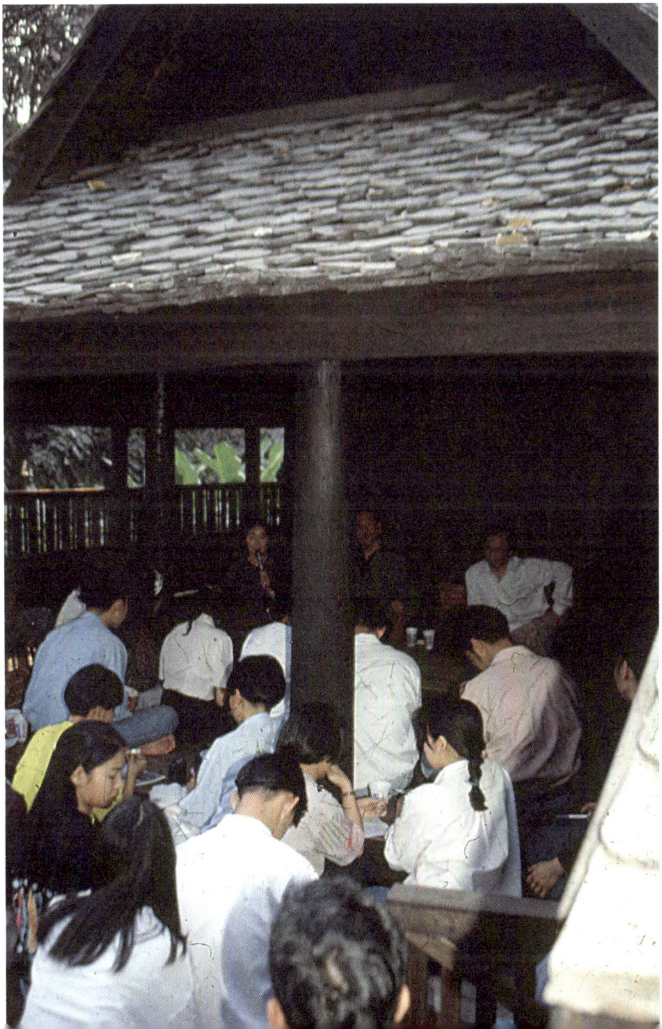

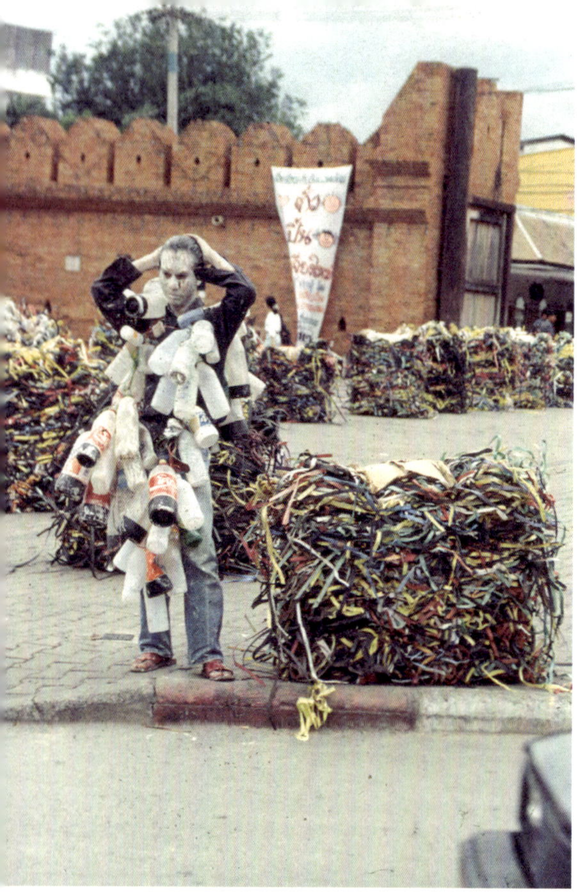

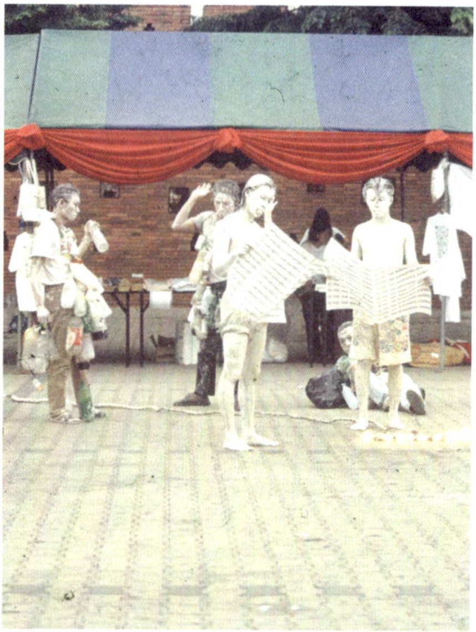

Supachai Satsara, *Junk*, installation and performance at Tha Pae Gate.

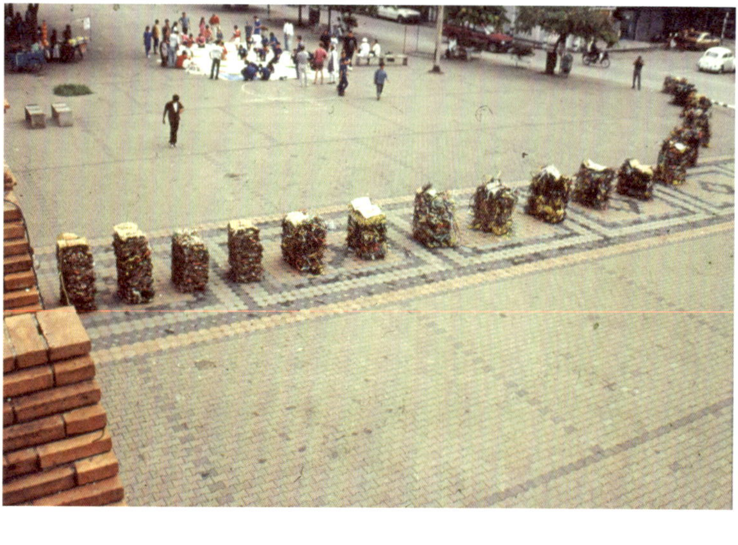

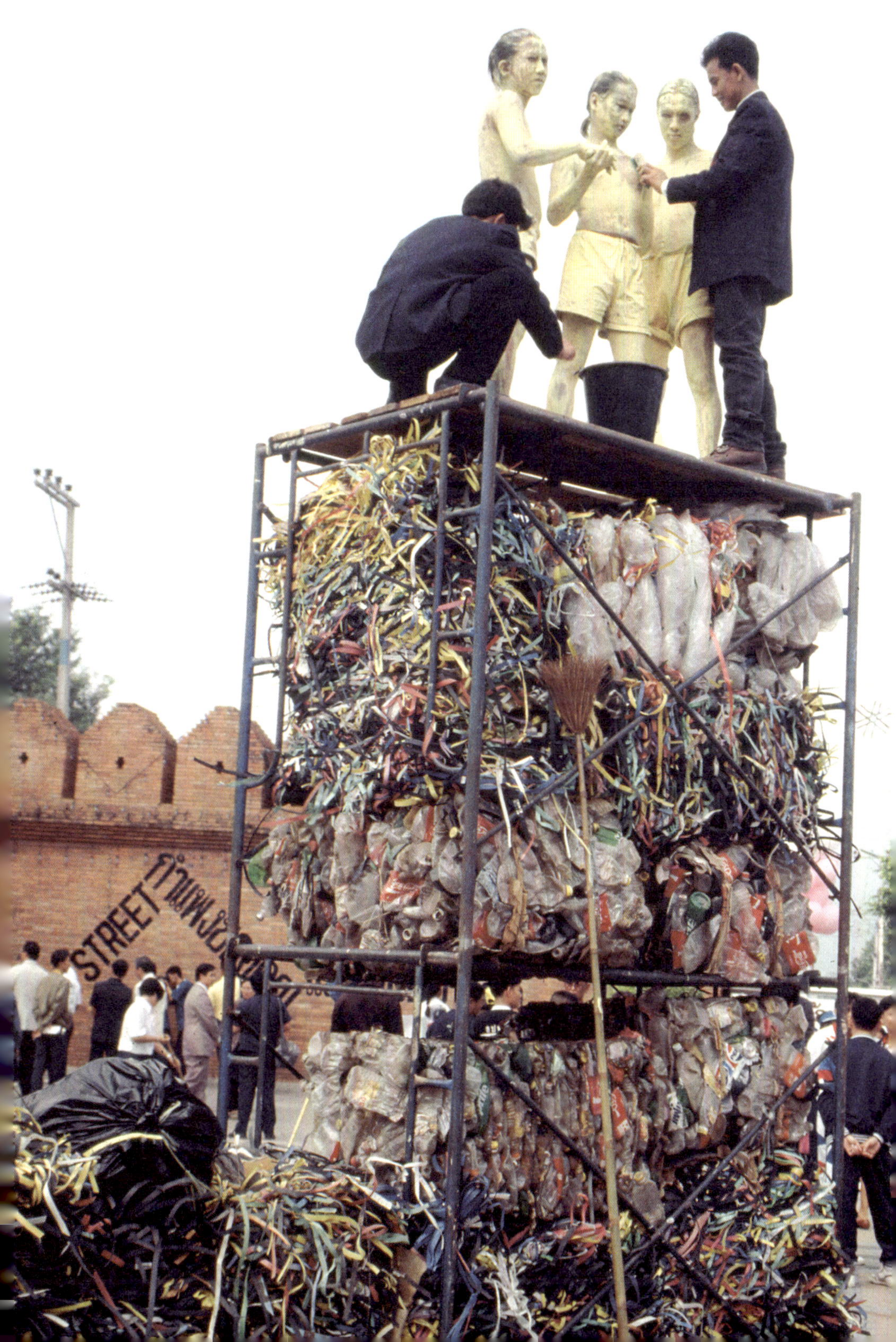
STREET

Week of Cooperative Suffering
1–7 January 1995

Week of Cooperative Suffering

สัปดาห์ร่วมทุกข์

เที่ยงคืน → ตีห้า ๑-๗ มกราคม ๒๕๓๘ สะพานนวรัฐ → ประตูท่าแพ

■ วัน เวลา สถานที่ ▲ ลักษณะกิจกรรม ● นักวัฒนธรรม

การแสดงร่วมสมัยเที่ยงคืน
(NIGHT OF CONTEMPORARY PERFORMANCE)

■ อาทิตย์ 1 ม.ค. 38; เที่ยงคืนเป็นต้นไป; เริ่มต้นสะพานนวรัฐถึงลานประตูท่าแพ

▲ คืนแห่งการใช้ร่างกาย, การแต่งตัว กิริยาอาการของมนุษย์เป็นสื่อแสดงออกทางวัฒนธรรม

●

ไสว วงศ์ษาพรม *(แหลโสเหล)*
เทพศิริ สุขโสภา *(นิทานและสื่อการแสดง)*
นาวิน ลาวัลย์ชัยกุล *(ห้องไร้เสียง)*
โฆษิต จันทราทิพย์ *(รักเธอเสมอ)*
อารยา ราษฎร์จำเริญสุข *(แสดง ณ คณะวิจิตรศิลป์ มช.)*
จิตติ เกษมกิจวัฒนา *(......)*
กลุ่มคนรุ่นใหม่ *(จิตรกรรมกลางถนน)*
ไพบูลย์ ธรรมเรืองฤทธิ์ *(ดนตรี ปากเปล่า หยิบข่าวมากล่าวทำนอง)*
พิภพ พรแสงศิลป์ *(ลำนำแห่งความรัก)*
ทรงศักดิ์ แซ่ตั้ง *(TV)*
เดชา พรหมรัตน์ *(โต๊ะจีนกลางเมือง)*
สุทิน สายหยุด, เนตรชนก วรรณจิการ์ *(แด่มนุษย์ผู้ผยอง)*
ศิวดล สิทธิพล *(ชีวิต-แรงงาน-เสียง)*
นายพลากร ใจสงัด *(พลาด)*
อาคม ทองโปร่ง *(I.C.U.)*
คน 100 คน *(วัตถุร้อยอย่าง/กิจกรรมร้อยเสียง)*
ทรงวิทย์ พิมพะกรรณ์ *(การระบาดของวัฒนธรรมใหม่*

คืนแห่งแสง-เสียงร่วมสมัย
(NIGHT OF CONTEMPORARY LIGHT & SOUND)

■ จันทร์ 2 ม.ค. 38; เที่ยงคืนเป็นต้นไป; ณ ลานประตูท่าแพ

▲ โดยใช้เสียงทุกรูปแบบ ทั้งจากธรรมชาติ เครื่องดนตรี ฯลฯ เป็นสื่อ และใช้แสงเป็นสื่อแสดงออกทางวัฒนธรรม

หนังทดลองร่วมสมัย
เกษมสันต์ พรหมสุภา *(ภาณายักษา)*
มานิต ศรีวานิชภูมิ *(ดินแดนเสียงหัวเราะ)*
เจิดศักดิ์ พูลทรัพย์ *(UNDER TABOO)*
นิดา กาญจนเวชกุล *(พันธาติ)*
วัฒนพันธุ์ ครุฑะแสน *('โซ่ เอ่ย ... ฝรั่ง)*
โกศล ตรงต่อศักดิ์ *(CITY DOG)*
ฮาเมอร์ ซาลวาลา *(บุญทิ้ง)*
สมชาติ บางแจ้ง *(ฟิล์มบำบัด)*
ภาพยนตร์จากมูลนิธิญี่ปุ่น
MUDDY RIVER *'แม่น้ำโคลน'*
DUMP FACTORY *'โรงงานนรก'*
HOME VILLAGE *'บ้านเกิดเมืองนอน'*

วิดีโอ โปรเจกเตอร์ บนกำแพงวัด
ปกากะญอ *(บทกวีแห่งขุนเขา)*
พิพัฒน์ ธนาภิวัฒนกูร *(หมาเห่า)*
ธาตรี โภควนิช *(สำหรับมนุษย์ 2538 (จิตหนึ่ง) ธาตรี โภควนิช)*
ชมรมอนุรักษ์ธรรมชาติและสิ่งแวดล้อม ม.รามฯ *(แง่มุมธรรมชาติในรูปแบบศิลปะ)*
วัลลภ แม่นยำ *(เชียงใหม่พาโนรามา)*
กิตติ บุญมี และคณะ *(ผมคือกีตาร์)*

มหาวิทยาลัยเที่ยงคืน (MIDNIGHT UNIVERSITY)

■ อังคาร 3 ม.ค. 38; เที่ยงคืนเป็นต้นไป; ณ ลานประตูท่าแพ

▲ สนทนาโต๊ะกลมจากบุคคลทุกสาขาอาชีพ เพื่อสะท้อน ปัญหาและร่วมกันหาทางออกในประเด็น ***"ความทุกข์ ท่ามกลางวิถีชีวิตร่วมสมัย"***

ตลาดค้าวัตถุร่วมสมัยเที่ยงคืน
(MIDNIGHT MARKET : ART FOR SALE)

■ พุธ 4 ม.ค. 38; เที่ยงคืนเป็นต้นไป; ณ ไนท์บาร์ซา

▲ ชุมนุมสินค้าทางวัตถุร่วมสมัย เพื่อซื้อ-ขาย แลกเปลี่ยนความคิดผ่านวัตถุทางวัฒนธรรม อาทิ ศิลปวัตถุ ของเก่า พระเครื่อง คน สัตว์ ฯลฯ

สุทธิศักดิ์ ภูธรารักษ์ *(ส.ค.ส. 2538)*
อภิศันส์ มูลมะโน *(แผงเบอร์ศิลปะ)*
ภุชงค์ บุญเอก *(บรรพบุรุษ)*
ปานทิพย์ จันทะนาม, นริสา วงษ์วรรณา *(SALE)*
ชาตรี ศรีเจริญ *(ร้านค้าวัฒนธรรม)*
ธงชัย ยุคันตพรพงษ์ *(ศิลปะกินได้)*
พิทักษ์ สง่า *(กลิ่นควาย-สาบโคลน)*
บุญสิทธิ์ เจริญจิต *(ศิลปะสื่อผสม : สินค้าอนุรักษ์ หัตถกรรมสัญจร)*
อนุรักษ์ ชัฏอนันต์, นิเวศ รักษาสัตย์ *(ทุกข์ของคนนอนไม่หลับ)*
ศิวชัย เดชะ *(ปฏิกิริยาร่วมจากภาพรวมเชียงใหม่)*
วสันต์ สิทธิเขตต์ *(ชาวเขา ≠ ชาวเมือง, ชาวมึง ≠ ชาวกู)*

ผ้าป่าเที่ยงคืน (MIDNIGHT PAH-PA)

■ พฤหัสบดี 5 ม.ค. 38; เที่ยงคืนเป็นต้นไป; เริ่มขบวนที่สะพานนวรัฐเดินรอบเมืองเชียงใหม่

▲ เชิญมวลชนทุกสาขาอาชีพร่วมทำบุญกุศล ทอดผ้าป่าเที่ยงคืน 9 วัด เป็นขบวนผ้าป่าสามัคคีที่เงียบที่สุด มุ่งแต่กุศล มงคล เพื่อมวลชนผู้ทุกข์ยาก จากเที่ยงคืนเป็นต้นไป จตุปัจจัยไม่จำกัด

คืนแห่งศิลปะจัดวาง
(NIGHT OF INSTALLATION ART)

■ ศุกร์ 6 ม.ค. 38; เที่ยงคืนเป็นต้นไป; ณ สะพานนวรัฐถึงลานประตูท่าแพ

▲ นำเสนอศิลปะจัดวางกับสถานที่จริงตามจุดต่าง ๆ ตั้งแต่สะพานนวรัฐถึงลานประตูท่าแพ

มณเฑียร บุญมา *(ศาลาสติ)*
สุทธิศักดิ์ ภูธรารักษ์ *(LOGO)*
กลุ่ม SHADE *(นอนกลางเมือง)*
ยุวนัจ วงศ์สายันห์ *(สังขาร-เชียงใหม่)*
สมศักดิ์ ยินดี *(ตู้ปัญญาสาธารณะ)*
กิติพงษ์ สุริยทองชื่น *(......)*
ฤทธี หอมสิน *(กุ๊ก-ไก่)*
วันเอก จันทรทิพย์ *(ไม่มีชื่อ)*
วัชชนะ ประสิทธิชัย *(GET UP)*
พยุง เกิดพุฒ *(เสี่ยงทาย)*
ปรีชา ราชขันธ์ *(ความสัมพันธ์เร้นแห่งสังคม)*
เบญจรงค์ โควาพิทักษ์เทศ *(สิ่งที่มาทดแทน)*
นพรัตน์ โชติชัยชุติกุล *(ต้นไม้วัฒนธรรม)*

ปาร์ตี้วัฒนธรรมเที่ยงคืน (คืนแห่งความกระจ่าง) (CULTURAL PARTY NIGHT)

■ เสาร์ 7 ม.ค. 38; เที่ยงคืนเป็นต้นไป; ณ ลานประตูท่าแพ

▲ ชุมนุมสังสรรค์ เสวนาแลกเปลี่ยนทัศนคติเพื่อสรุป กิจกรรมทางวัฒนธรรมที่ผ่านมา และควรเกิดขึ้นในอนาคต สัมพันธ์กับระบบวิถีชีวิตร่วมสมัย โดยผู้เข้าร่วมโครงงานและผู้สนใจทุกท่าน

ANGST-WEEK CHIANG MAI SOCIAL INSTALLATION

CULTURAL ACTIVITY : MIDNIGHT → 5.00 AM.; JANUARY 1-7, 1995; NAVARUT BRIDGE → THA-PAE GATE.

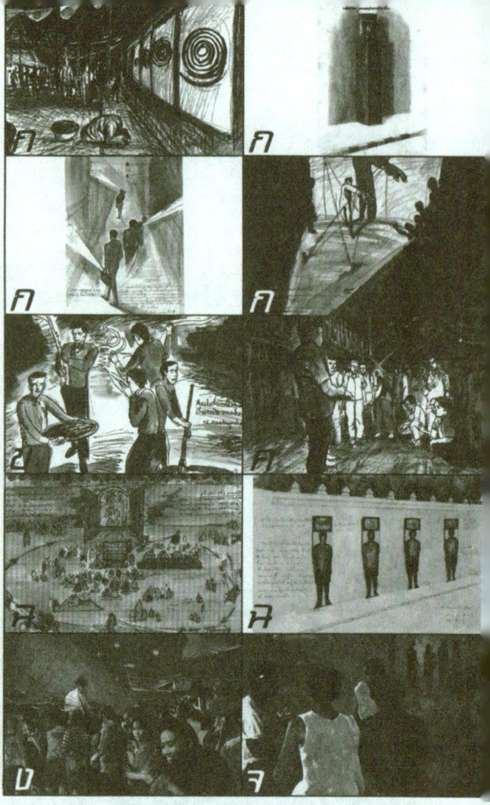

วัฒนธรรมที่สูญเปล่า

❑ รัฐและราชการไทย ได้บิดเบือนให้วัฒนธรรมเป็นเครื่องมือแห่งอำนาจ ด้วยการรณรงค์ห้เป็นปีแห่งวัฒนธรรม ทั้งโดยการทุ่มงบประมาณเกือบร้อยล้านบาท กับการโฆษณาตามสื่อ่างๆ และสอดแทรกกิจกรรมอย่างฉาบฉวย ปราศจากเป้าหมายที่ชัดเจน ด้วยการดำเนินารอย่างขาดความเข้าใจ

❑ ชุมชนและประชาชน จะต้องเป็นผู้สร้างคำนิยาม และเป็นผู้รับผิดชอบในการสร้างสรรค์จกรรมทางวัฒนธรรม โดยที่รัฐต้องเอื้อเฟื้อ สนับสนุน และตอบรับความต้องการของชุมชนละประชาชนในการแสดงออกทางวัฒนธรรม

❑ เราได้ก้าวมาถึงจุดหนึ่งซึ่งควรตระหนักและสำนึกได้แล้วว่า เรากำลังเผชิญกับวิกฤตทางฒนธรรมและการสร้างภาพลักษณ์ทางสังคมอันว่างเปล่า (1.เพราะถูกบิดเบือนโดยหน่วยงานงเป็นเครื่องมือของรัฐหรือ2.จากระบบทุนนิยมที่นำเอาสื่อสารมวลชนมาเป็นกลไกทางผลประโยชน์หรือ 3.จากการขาดสำนึกและการศึกษาทางวัฒนธรรมของประชาชน)

❑ เมื่อแก่นแท้ของกิจกรรมทางวัฒนธรรมและการรณรงค์ทางวัฒนธรรมที่ผ่านมาเป็นเพียงงายาทัศน์ การตระหนักในภาระแห่งการรับผิดชอบทางวัฒนธรรมของชุมชนโดยประชาชนอย่างเท่าทันนั้นคือการมีเวทีทางวัฒนธรรมของตนเอง (โดยไม่ต้องรอให้มีผู้หยิบยื่น) จึงน่าจะเป็นางออกในภาวะวิกฤตโดยที่ทุกหน่วยในสังคมล้วนมีสิทธิและหน้าที่ในการ 'จัดวางสังคม' ร่วมน (ทั้งนี้โดยไม่หวังว่าจะเป็น 'สังคม ในอุดมคติ' หากแต่เป็นสังคมที่สามารถแบ่งปันสารทุกข์ุกดิบได้ถ้วนหน้า)

เมื่อความสุขเป็นเพียงความหวัง

❑ - ความสุขที่เป็นสัจธรรมที่มนุษย์แสวงหา แต่น้อยคนที่จะมีความสุขสมบูรณ์ การแบ่งปันวามสุขจึงเป็นไปได้ยาก ความทุกข์จึงกลายเป็นของจริงแท้ ที่ทุกคนล้วนมีไม่ว่ามากหรือน้อยละไม่สามารถปฏิเสธได้

❑ - ความทุกข์กลายเป็นต้นทุนของชีวิตที่ทุกคนมีร่วมกัน ตั้งแต่กำเนิดและสะสมต่อเนื่องามิได้ขาด

❑ - เมื่อความสุขสมบูรณ์เป็นเพียงความหวังลมๆ แล้งๆ ความทุกข์สาหัสเป็นสัจธรรมละแก่นแท้ของชีวิตจึงเป็นการแสดงออกทางวัฒนธรรม เป็นสิ่งที่ชุมชน ประชาชน สามารถร้างร่วมกันได้ โดยเฉพาะการนำประสบการณ์ความทุกข์ที่แต่ละคนเผชิญอยู่มาเป็นแรงดลใจื้นฐาน ในการสร้างสรรค์กิจกรรมจัดวางสังคมใน 'สัปดาห์ร่วมทุกข์'

ความทุกข์ยามค่ำคืนกับวัฒนธรรมชุมชน

❑ สัปดาห์ร่วมทุกข์ เป็นแนวคิดและแนวทางหนึ่งของกิจกรรมซึ่งสามารถแสดงออกได้หลากหลายรูปแบบ ในนิยามของการจัดวางสังคม(เป็นการนำเสนอแนวคิดและแนวทางปฏิบัติี่พอจะเป็นไปได้สำหรับสังคม ด้วยวิธีการต่างๆ อย่างสันติ ในประเด็นปัญหาต่างๆ หรือกรณีื่นๆ ตามความสนใจและวิสัยทัศน์ของ ประชาชนและปัจเจกชน ทุกสาขาอาชีพ) ซึ่ง กำหนดห้มีขึ้นระหว่าง 1-7 มกราคมนี้ ที่จังหวัดเชียงใหม่ โดยมีศูนย์กลางอยู่ในย่านชุมชนบริเวณประตูท่าแพ

เพียง 7 ใน 365 วัน

❑ เจตนารมย์ในกิจกรรม สัปดาห์ร่วมทุกข์ ไม่ได้มุ่งหวังจะเป็นกิจกรรมของการคลายทุกข์หรือเพิ่มสุขแต่อย่างใด หากแต่หวังให้สัปดาห์ร่วมทุกข์เป็น 7 วันแห่งการแลกเปลี่ยนและแบ่งปันาระแห่งทุกข์โดยแสดงออกตามวิถีทางของแต่ละบุคคลเป็นกิจกรรมทางวัฒนธรรมโดยมีความทุกข์เป็นแรงบันดาลใจจากการเผชิญชีวิตในรอบ 365 วัน

กลางคืนกับความทุกข์

❑ กลางคืนกับความทุกข์ ช่างเป็นสิ่งที่สอดคล้องและจะกลมกลืนยิ่งขึ้น หากมีการชุมนุมทุกข์มาก ทุกข์น้อย ทั้งเพื่อชมและนำเสนอความทุกข์อย่างมีวัฒนธรรม โดยปราศจากภาระกิจการนัดหมายและกิจกรรมบันเทิงเริงรมย์อย่างอื่น

เชียงใหม่-อุบลราชธานี (หรือทุกจังหวัดยกเว้นกรุงเทพฯ)

❑ วัฒนธรรมเป็นสิ่งที่เกิดขึ้นได้ทุกชุมชน ทุกเชื้อชาติ ทุกศาสนา ในหมู่ชนผู้มีสติปัญญาโดยเฉพาะการมีเวลาให้กับชีวิตด้วยกิจกรรมทางศิลปวัฒนธรรม ซึ่งนับว่าเป็นไปได้ยากมากสำหรับชุมชนที่เต็มไปด้วยค่านิยมแบบแปลกๆ ที่เป็นปัญหาสังคมและปัญหาทางวัฒนธรรมท่ามกลางกระแสทุนนิยมสุดขั้ว แม้จะมีความพร้อมทางด้านบุคคลและทรัพยากร แต่เชื่อว่าบรรยากาศของชุมชนในต่างจังหวัดที่เป็นเมืองกึ่งชนบท น่าจะเป็นสิ่งแวดล้อมที่เหมาะสมกว่า

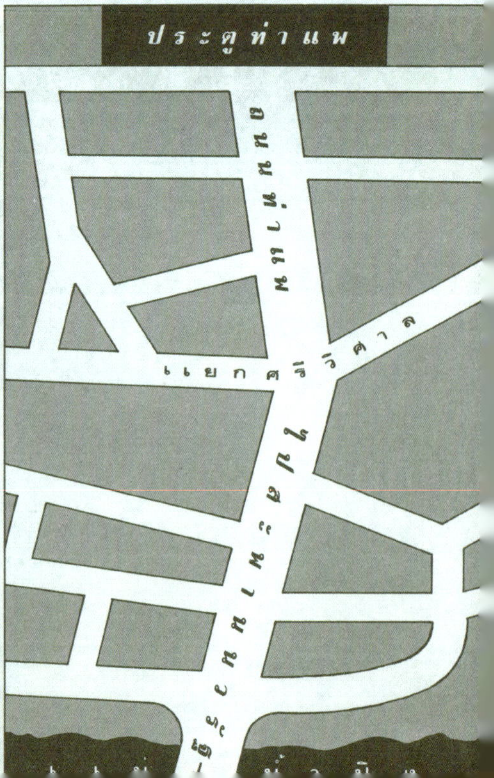

...รรม–เหตุการณ์

...าง วันที่ 29-30 ธันวาคม 2537 จากกรุงเทพมหานคร
จากหอพักนิสิตจุฬาฯตรงข้าม ร.ร.เตรียมอุดมฯ
สะพานนวรัฐ ถึงลานประตูท่าแพ จ.เชียงใหม่
เที่ยงคืนถึงตีห้า วันที่ 1-7 มกราคม 2538

...ลา	รายการกิจกรรม
...538 .	<u>ศิลปธรรมเที่ยงคืน</u> คืนแห่งการผสมผสานศิลปะและการแสดงทุกรูปแบบ โดยเน้นอุบายในการมองโลกร่วมสมัย ซึ่งจะแสดงและนำเสนอแบบสร้างสรรค์ (ศิลปะวัตถุ , ศิลปะติดตั้ง , สื่อการแสดง)
...ที่ ...538 .	<u>ราตรีแห่งเสียงร่วมสมัย</u> สื่อดนตรี และเสียงของการ ประกอบกิจกรรมทุกประเภทที่ผ่านการเรียบเรียงและจัดวาง เพื่อเป็นตัวแทนแห่งภูมิปัญญาและจิตวิญญาณชุมชน (โสตศิลป์ , การแสดง , ละคร)
...ี่ ...538	<u>มหาวิทยาลัยเที่ยงคืน</u> การระดมภูมิปัญญาจากผู้เชี่ยวชาญอาชีพในสาขาต่างๆ มาหาทางออกร่วมกันในประเด็น 'จัดการความทุกข์โดยจัดวางสังคม' โดยมีออาชีพ รุ่นอาวุโส และ รุ่นหนุ่มสาว (สนทนา , ประติมากรรม , ปาฐกถา)
...ี่ ...538 .	<u>ตลาดค้าวัฒนธรรมเที่ยงคืน</u> ชุมนุมสินค้าศิลปะวัฒนธรรม, ผลิตภัณฑ์แปลกๆ ใหม่ๆ ทุกประเภท ทุกราคา เพื่อแลกเปลี่ยนรูปแห่งความคิดผ่านรูปแห่งวัตถุวัฒนธรรม (ซื้อ , ขาย , แลกเปลี่ยนศิลปะวัตถุทุกรูปแบบ)
...38	<u>คืนแห่งปัญหา</u> เป็นการชุมนุม มวลชนที่ประสพปัญหาเพื่อหาทางออกร่วมกัน โดยเน้นสันติวิธี เช่น ผ้าป่าเที่ยงคืนและการเดินขบวนต่อต้านความไม่ยุติธรรมของรัฐ และสังคม (กิจกรรมสะท้อนปัญหา)
...ดีที่ ...38	<u>คืนแห่งวัตถุร่วมสมัย</u> ทำอย่างไรมนุษย์จึงจะสามารถทำการปฏิสัมพันธ์กับวัตถุ และสื่อร่วมสมัยได้อย่างสอดคล้องกลมกลืน และเท่าทันแต่ไม่เพลี่ยงพล้ำและควรมีปฏิกิริยาโต้ตอบในเชิงวิพากษ์ วิจารณ์ โดยเน้นสื่อและเทคโนโลยี (วีดีโอ , สื่อการแสดง , ประชามติ)
...38	<u>คืนแห่งความกระจ่าง</u> ร่วมสังสรรค์ เสวนาแลกเปลี่ยนทัศนคติ ความคิด ผลงานและประเมินผลทุกกิจกรรมที่ผ่านมา

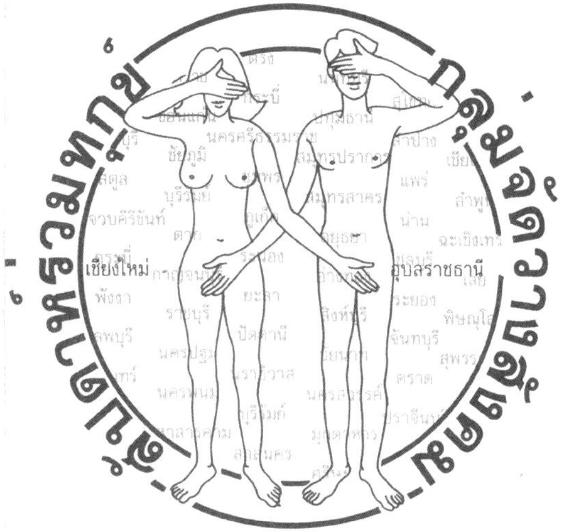

MOVING CULTURAL
CHIANGMAI - UBONRAJATHANEE

กิจกรรมเคลื่อนไหวทางวัฒนธรรม
เชียงใหม่ – อุบลราชธานี

...สังคม
...วัฒนธรรม
...นเชียงใหม่–อุบลราชธานี

ติดแสตมป์
2
บาท

ตู้ปณ.210
ปทจ.คลองจั่น
กรุงเทพฯ
10240

...ความทุกข์เป็นสภาวะร่วมกันของทุกคนในสังคม"กิจกรรมนี้จะสมบูรณ์...ร่วมเสนอแนวทางและแนวปฏิบัติที่พอจะเป็นไปได้ ในทรรศนะ...เป็นการแสดงเจตนารมย์ในการสร้างสรรค์กิจกรรม

สำหรับผู้ที่มีความสุขดี หรือทุกข์สาหัส

กราบเรียนเชิญเข้าร่วม งานสัปดาห์ร่วมทุกข์ กิจกรรมเพื่อปรับทุกข์และเข้าใจวิถีของโลกที่ผันผวนและซับซ้อน โดยการนำเอาภูมิปัญญา ความรู้ความเข้าใจของท่านมาเสนอร่วมกัน ซึ่งเป็นกิจกรรมทางวัฒนธรรมของทุกสาขาอาชีพ ทุกเพศ ทุกฐานะ โดยท่านที่มีความสนใจ สามารถเลือกเข้าร่วมในฐานะผู้นำเสนอกิจกรรมและผู้เข้าร่วมชมในเหตุการณ์ดังกล่าว ในฐานะและบทบาทต่างๆ กันตามความสนใจและถนัด โดยการกรอกข้อความตามรายละเอียดดังนี้

ข้าพเจ้า ______
อาชีพ ______ อายุ ______
ที่อยู่ ______
โทรศัพท์ ______

มีความสนใจต้องการเข้าร่วมกิจกรรม 'สัปดาห์ร่วมทุกข์' โดยจะนำกิจกรรมมาเข้าร่วมดังนี้

☐ จิตรกรรม	☐ ประติมากรรม	☐ สื่อผสม
☐ สื่อการแสดง	☐ ศิลปะจัดวางกับพื้นที่	☐ ดนตรี
☐ เต้นรำ	☐ กวี	☐ ละครเร่
☐ หนังกลางแปลง	☐ วีดีทัศน์	☐ นักเขียน
☐ เสวนา	☐ ปาฐกถา	☐ เกมส์ปาหี่
☐ ทำนายโชคชะตา	☐ ใบ้หวย	☐ หมอลำ
☐ ดนตรีพื้นเมือง	☐ ร้องแหล่	☐ ตลกอาชีพ
☐ สอนศาสนา	☐ นักสิทธิมนุษยชน	☐ ขายของเก่า
☐ หาบเร่แผงลอย	☐ ข้าราชการ	☐ ทหาร, ตำรวจ
☐ หมอ	☐ มิจฉาชีพ	☐ โสเภณี
☐ ทนาย	☐ มายากล	☐ อื่นๆ ระบุ

ผู้ตอบรับเข้าร่วมกิจกรรม สามารถดำเนินกิจกรรมตามที่ให้ข้อมูลกับคณะผู้จัดกิจกรรมได้ฟรีโดยไม่เสียค่าใช้จ่ายและได้รับความคุ้มครองตามกฎหมาย

The initial Week of Cooperative Suffering took place at Tha Pae Gate over the first nights of 1995, in between the second and third editions of CMSI. Its published schedule was as follows:

Saturday, 1 January 1995, 24:00h: Night of Art:
A night when art and all kinds of performance meet. Introducing new strategies to see the contemporary world anew, exhibited and presented creatively (object art, installation art, performance art).

Sunday, 2 January 1995, 24:00h: Night of Contemporary Sound:
Music and sonic media performed alongside various compositional and installation activities, all representing the collective wisdom and spirit of the community (sound art, performance, theatre).

Monday, 3 January 1995, 24:00h: Midnight University:
Assembling the wisdom of specialists in various fields and vocations to find a collective solution to the issue of 'managing suffering through social installation'. Professionals, elders and young people welcome (conversation, sculpture, lecture).

Tuesday, 4 January 1995, 24:00h: Midnight Cultural Market:
Display of cultural objects, strange new products of all kinds and prices, with the goal of transforming thought through the forms of cultural objects (buy, sell, exchange cultural objects of all kinds).

Wednesday, 5 January 1995, 24:00h: Night of Problems:
Public gathering to find collective solutions to social problems by peaceful means, such as midnight pha pa, demonstration against state-inflicted injustices and activities that critically reflect on social issues.

Thursday, 6 January 1995, 24:00h: Night of Contemporary Objects:
How can humans enter into relations with contemporary objects and media in harmony? How can humans engage critically through media and technology (VDO, performance, referendum)?

Friday, 7 January 1995, 24:00h: Night of Clarity:
Get-together to exchange perspectives, ideas and works. Evaluate every activity conducted.

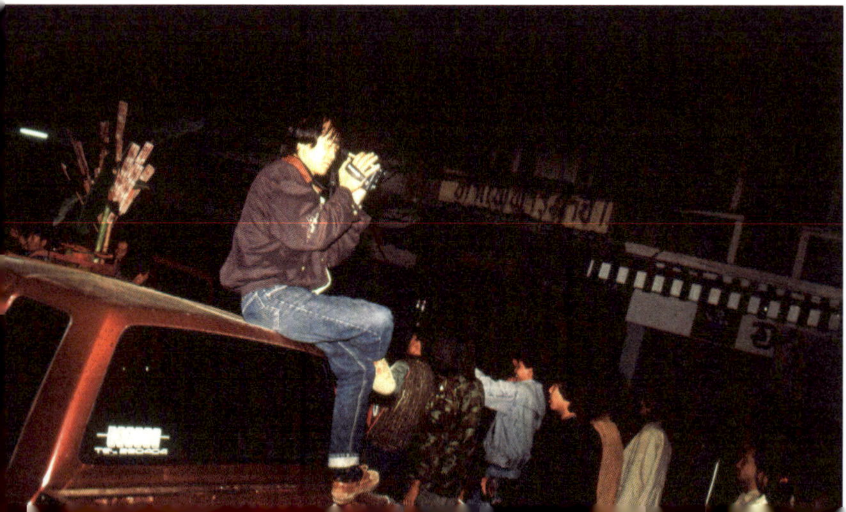

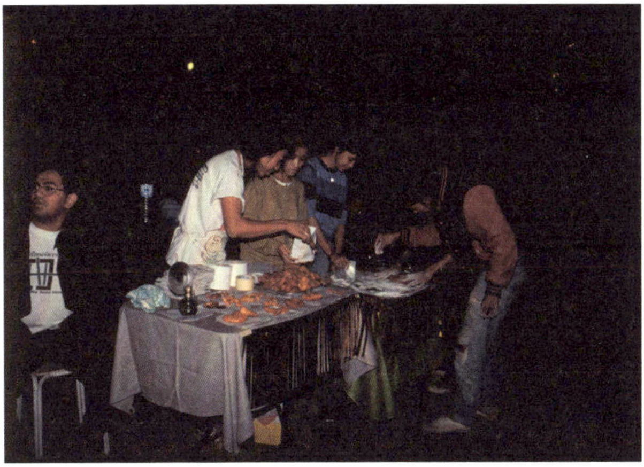

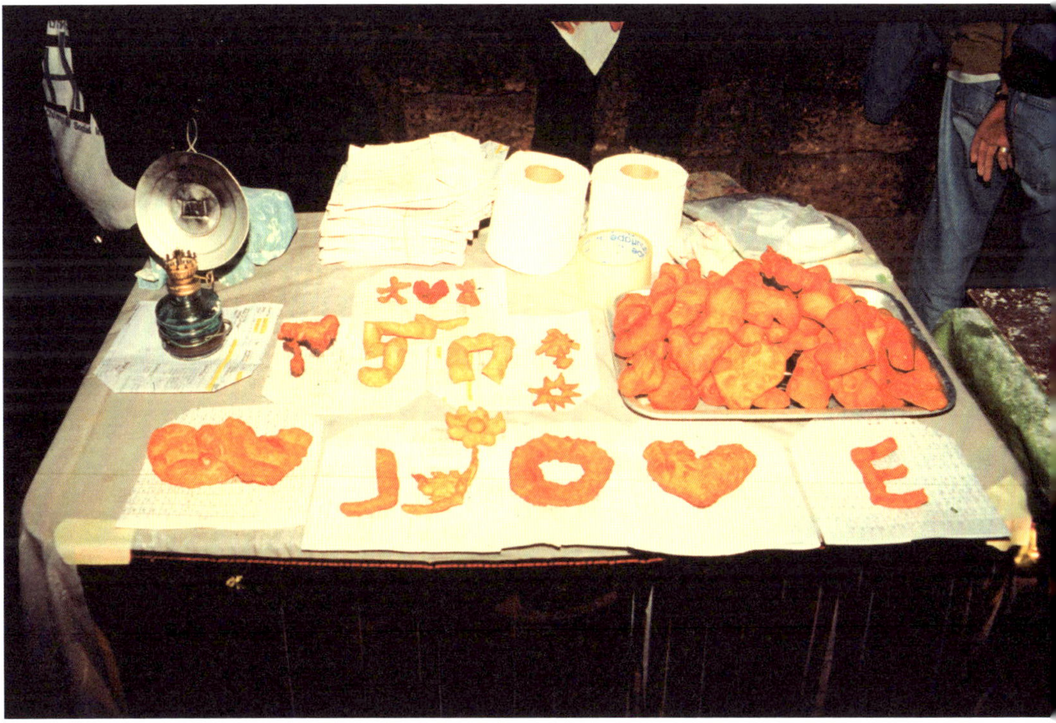

Kosit Juntaratip, *Sweet in the Beautiful Night*, Tha Pae Gate.

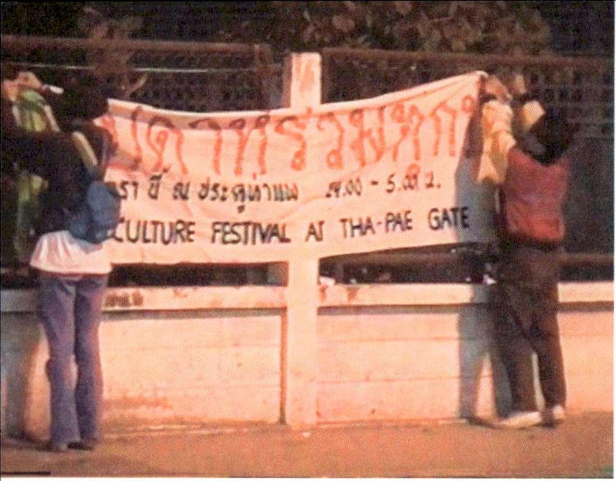
CULTURE FESTIVAL AT THA-PAE GATE

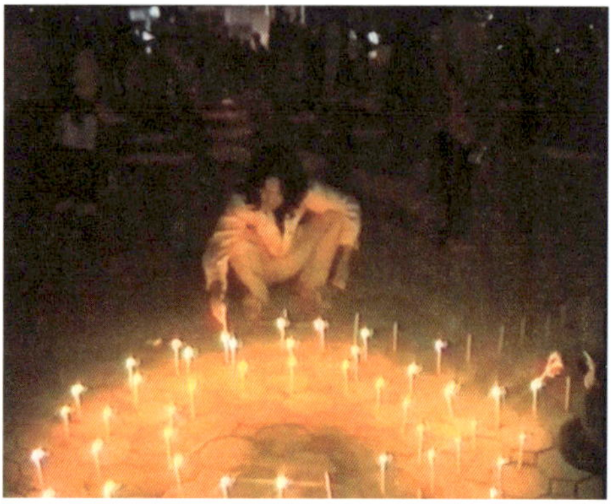

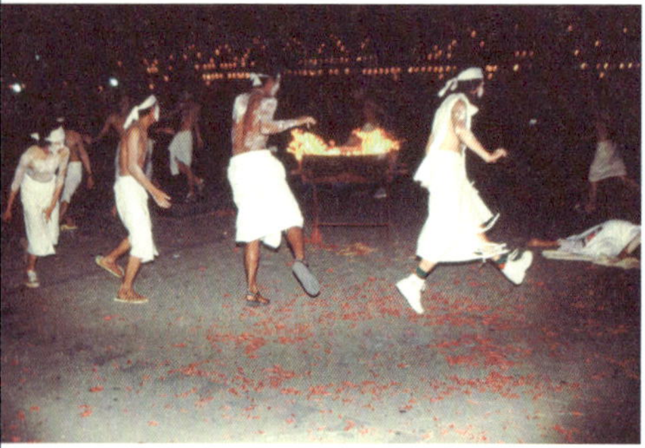

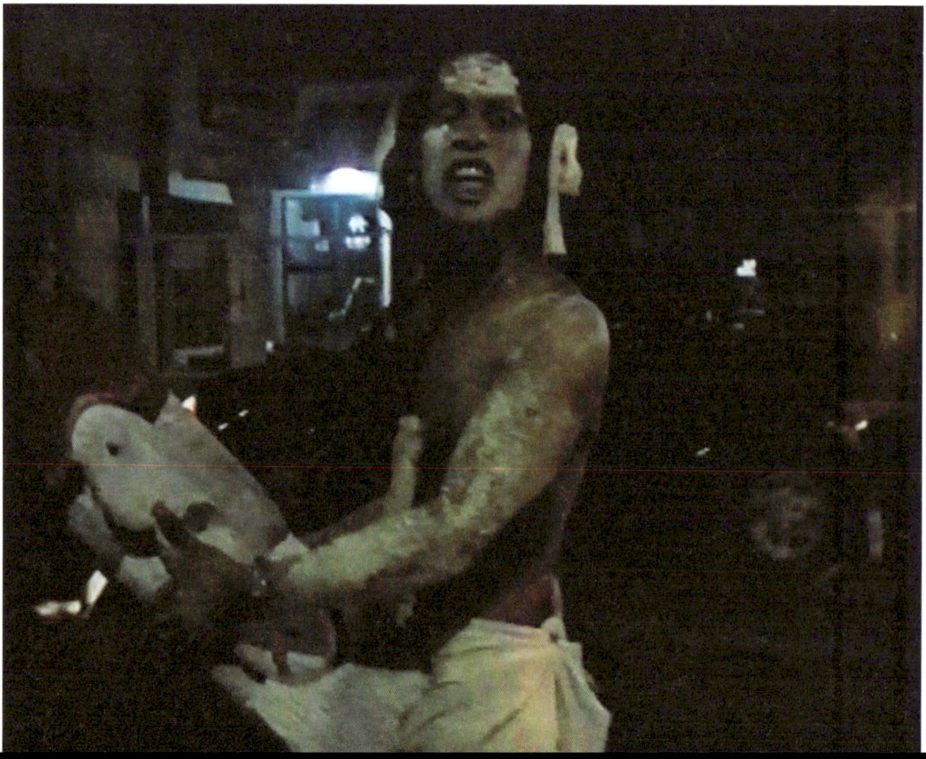

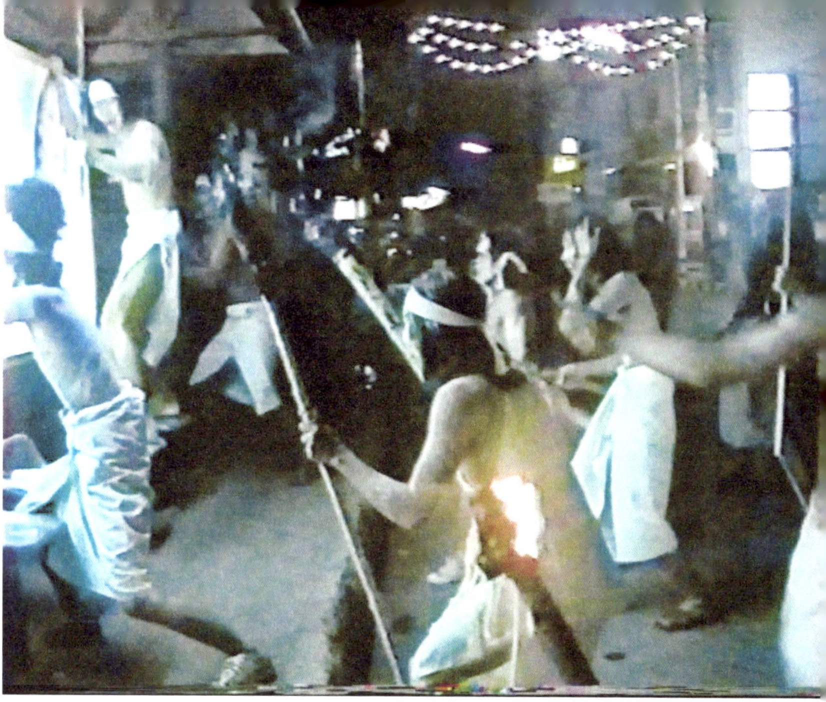

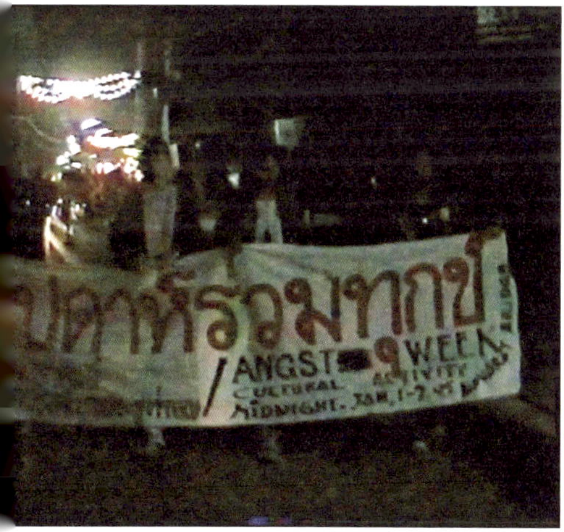
ANGST
WEEK
CULTURAL
ACTIVITY
MIDNIGHT.

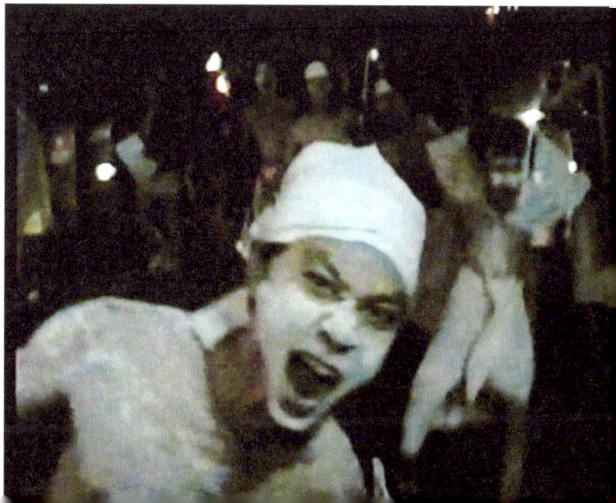

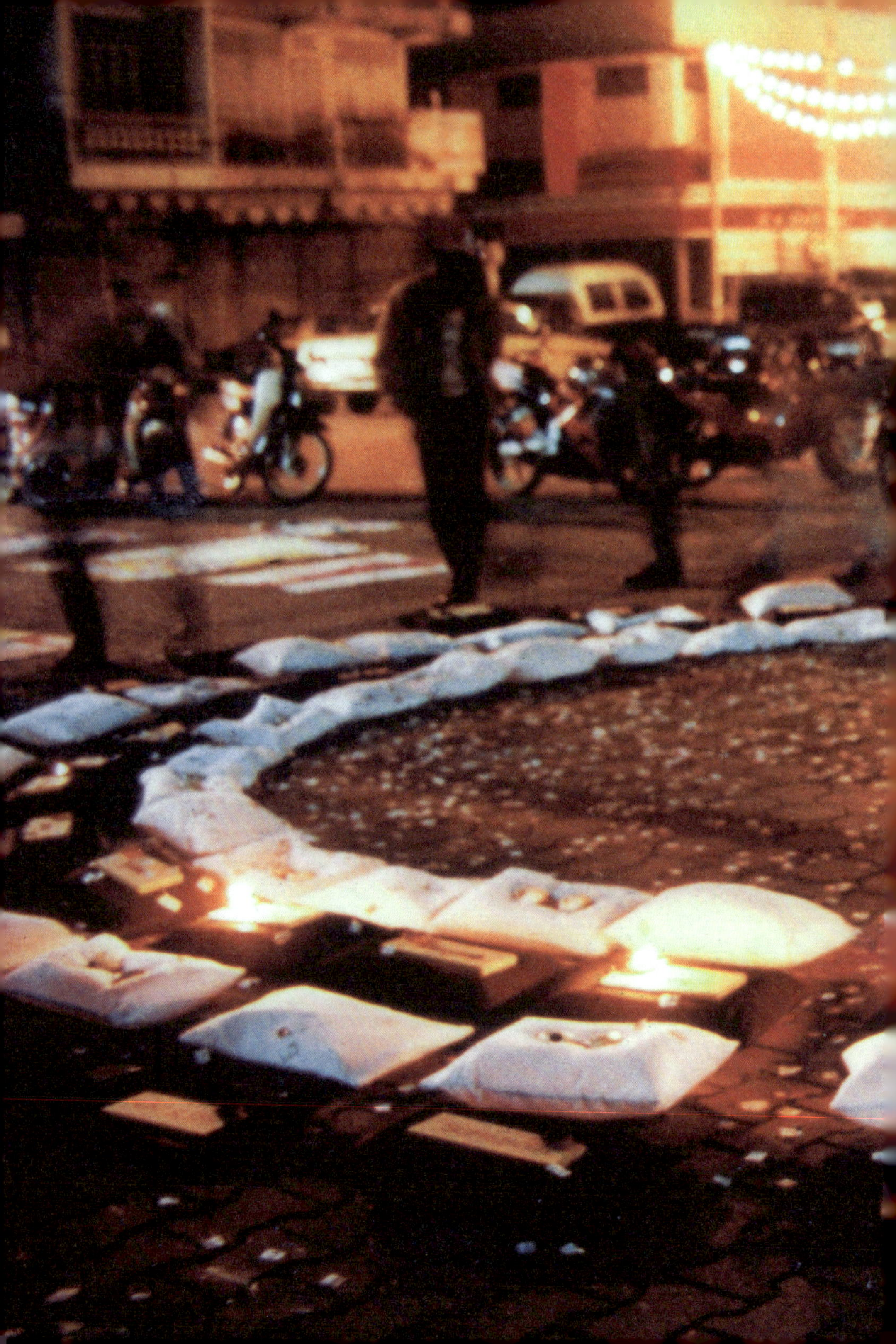

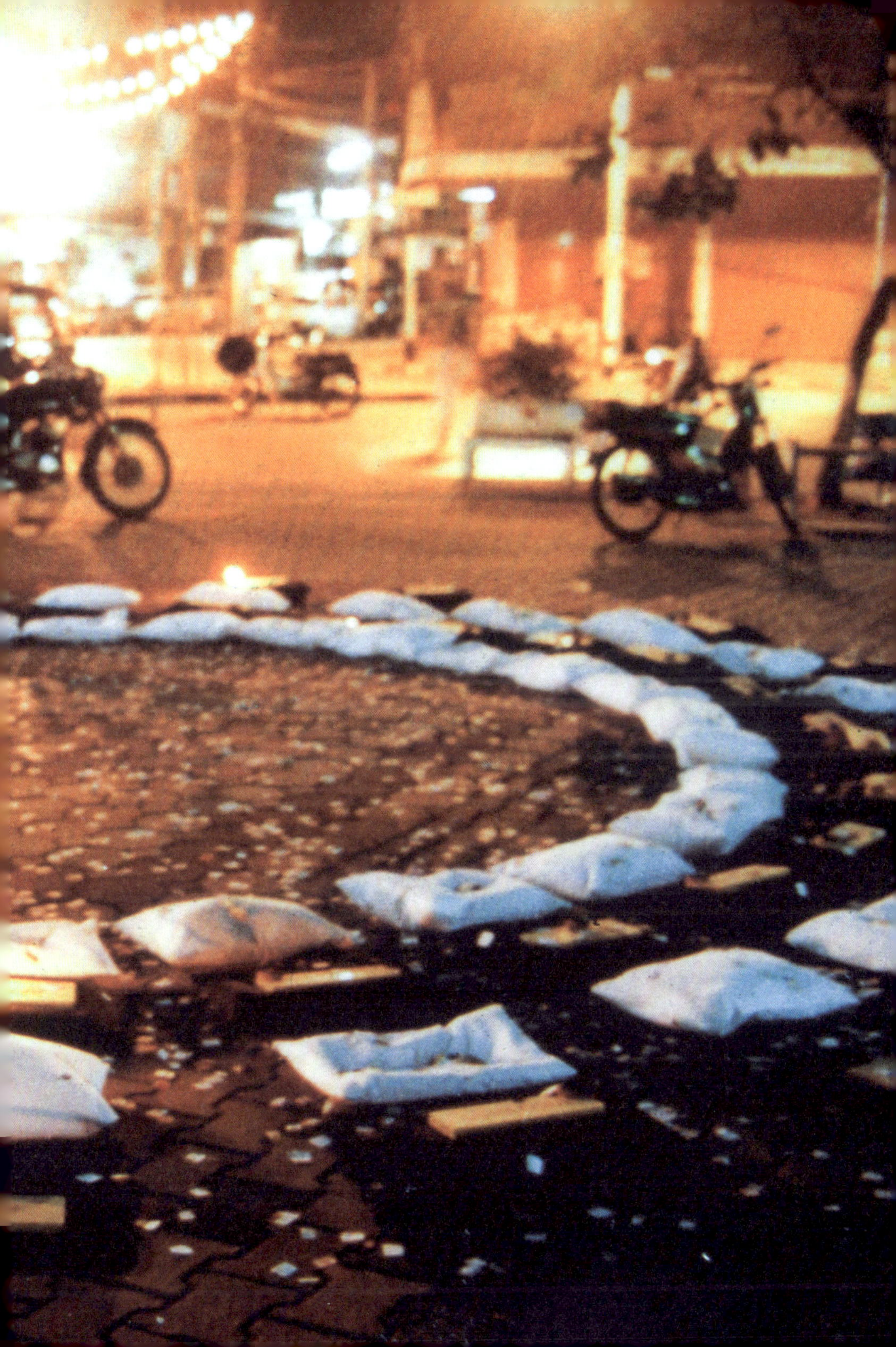

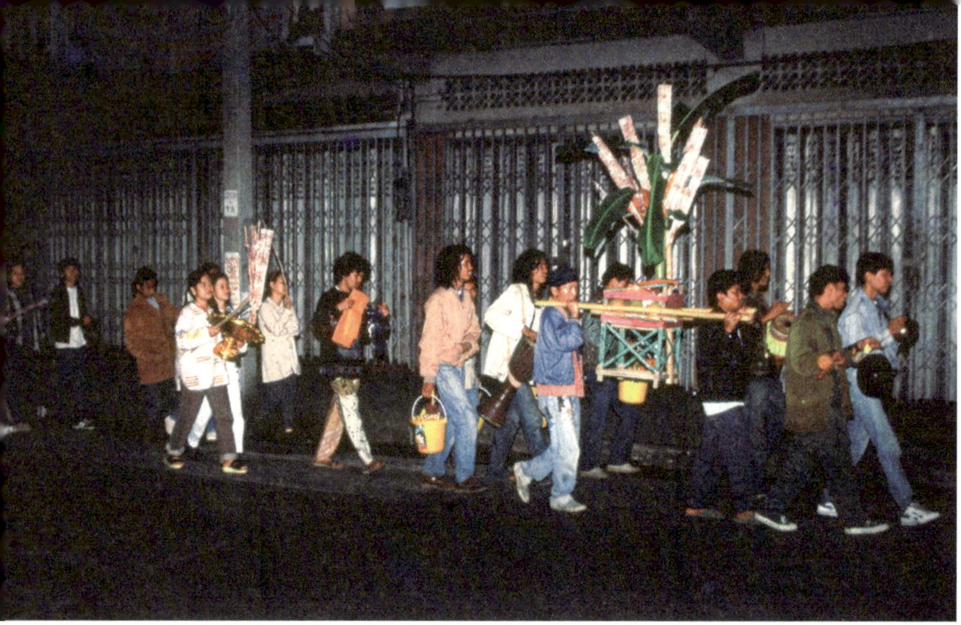

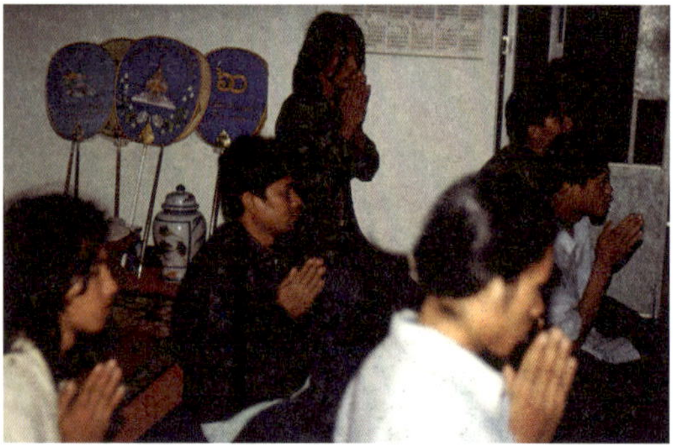

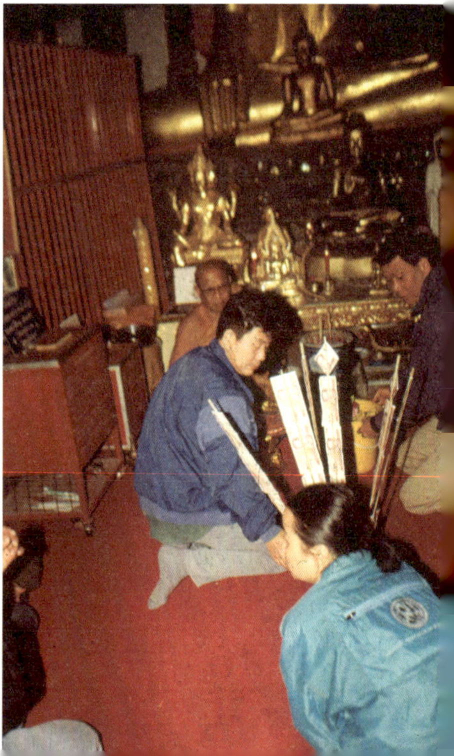

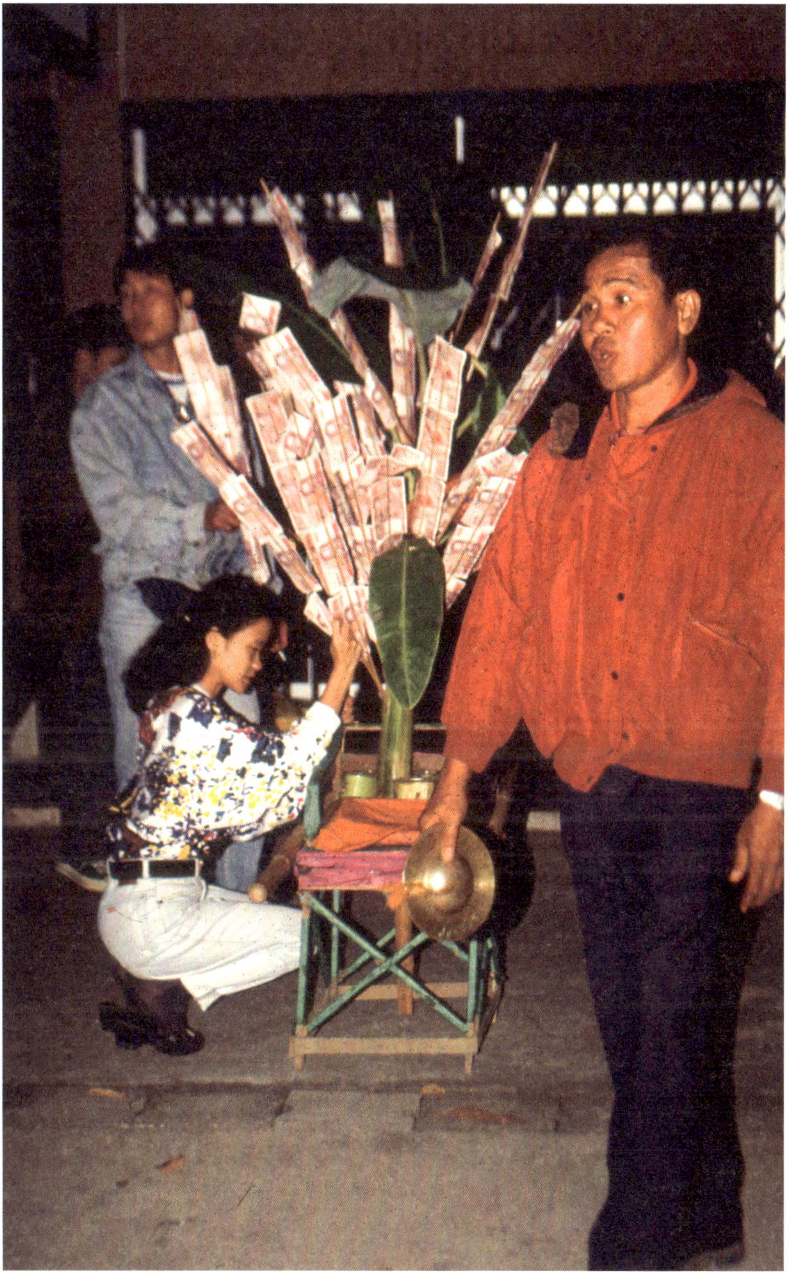

Midnight *pha pa* procession.

‘Chiang Mai Social Installation: Third Art and Cultural Festival: Temples, Cemeteries, Private-Residences, Public Buildings, Streets, Bridges, Walls, Rivers and Canals, Open Spaces’
November 1995–February 1996

‘Chiang Mai Social Installation: Third Art and Cultural Festival: Temples, Cemeteries, Private-Residences, Public Buildings, Streets, Bridges, Walls, Rivers and Canals, Open Spaces’

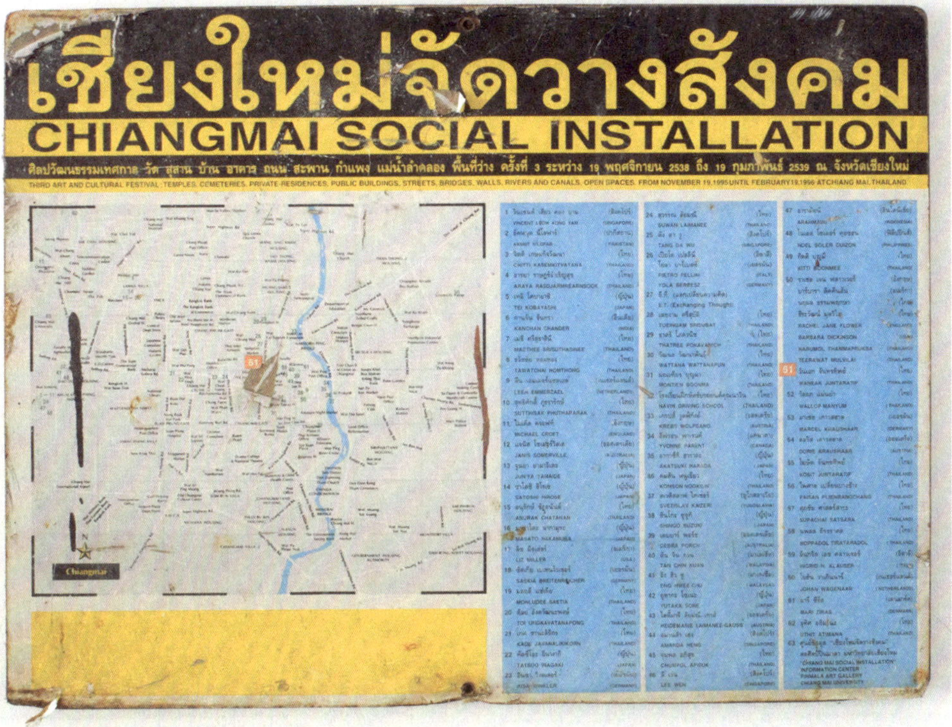

Signs with information were placed around the city.

CHIANGMAI SOCIAL INSTALLATION

เชียงใหม่จัดวางสังคม

ที่อยู่ร่วม: "เชียงใหม่จัดวางสังคม" คณะวิจิตรศิลป์ มหาวิทยาลัยเชียงใหม่ เชียงใหม่ 50200 โทร./โทรสาร (053) 211724

ADDRESS : "CHIANG MAI SOCIAL INSTALLATION" C/O FACULTY OF FINE ARTS CHIANG MAI UNIVERSITY, CHIANG MAI 50200 THAILAND. TEL./FAX. (6653) 211724

7 สาระรวบรวมจากเพอน

1. วัฒนธรรมอุดมคติ

"**เรา**" ดั้งเดิมนั้นเหมือนกัน ต่อมาค่อยๆ แตกต่างและไม่เข้าใจกันมากยิ่งขึ้น มีแนวโน้มการยึดถือ "**อัตตา**" ทั้งระดับบุคคล อาชีพ ชนชาติ และเผชิญหน้าต่อกันด้วยกลอุบาย และความรุนแรง ฯลฯ เมื่อ "**พวกเรา**" เติบโตขึ้นภายใต้วิถีชีวิตส่วนตัว และระบบสังคมวัฒนธรรมที่ต่างกาละ-เทศะกัน ดูเหมือนว่ากระบวนการของกิจกรรมทางวัฒนธรรมอุดมคติที่แสวงหาคุณค่า "**ความจริง-ความดี-ความงาม**" เกิดขึ้นตามมาส่วนใหญ่ ล้วนเป็นความพยายามที่ทำให้ "**พวกเรา**" พัฒนา วิธีคิด ความรู้ และจิตวิญญาณกลับไปสู่ "***ภาวะดั้งเดิม***" ของเราร่วมกัน

2. จัดวางสังคม

(เชียงใหม่) จัดวางสังคม เป็นเทศกาลประจำปีด้านวัฒนธรรมทุกสาขาอาชีพ เพื่อ "**ปลุก**" กิจกรรม สาระและบรรยากาศทางวัฒนธรรมอุดมคติร่วมสมัย ซึ่งเป็นกิจกรรมที่ถูกส่งเสริมน้อยมากในบริบทสังคมเสรีทุนนิยม เป็นสังคมที่สุดโต่งภายใต้กิจกรรมเพื่อตอบสนองอัตตา ลัทธิโลภนิยม การแข่งขันเบียดเบียนเสรี และวัฒนธรรมบันเทิง

3. คุณค่าธรรม (ธรรมะ-ธรรมชาติ-ธรรมดา)

"**คุณค่าธรรม**" คือคุณค่าหลักของเทศกาลจัดวางสังคม ในที่นี้คือ คุณค่าที่มนุษย์นำเสนอกิจกรรมสร้างสรรค์ร่วมกัน การที่ประชาชน "**นำ**" ความคิด ความเชื่อ ความรู้ จิตวิญญาณ ผลงานศิลปะ ฯลฯ มาแสดงออกปฏิสัมพันธ์ร่วมกันในบรรยากาศแห่งความเสียสละ ถ่อมตน ได้เรียนรู้แลกเปลี่ยน และเคารพจุดยืน ความคิดความเชื่อซึ่งกันและกัน เป็นคุณค่าที่ได้รับขณะกระทำ เป็น "**สันติกิจกรรม**" เป็นรูปทรงแห่ง "**สหกรณ์จิตสำนึก**"

4. วิสัยทัศน์ทางสังคม

เทศกาลนี้ส่งเสริมประชาชนให้มีจิตสำนึกในการรับผิดชอบต่อสังคมร่วมกัน โดยส่งเสริมผลงานและกิจกรรมที่แสดงความคิดริเริ่มสร้างสรรค์ ความเป็นไปได้ใหม่ๆ จากทุกคนและทุกศาสตร์ ที่พัฒนาชีวิตและสังคมไปสู่ความจริง-ความดี-ความงาม มันเปรียบเสมือนเป็น "**สติของสังคม**" ซึ่งจะเป็นกลไกและกระบวนการพื้นฐานเพื่อพัฒนาระบบวัฒนธรรมแต่ละสังคมให้มีการปรับตัว มีชีวิตยืดหยุ่น และนำไปสู่การแก้ไขปัญหาสังคมวัฒนธรรมโดยมวลชนอย่าง **พร้อมเพรียง มีความต่อเนื่อง** และ **เป็นไปเองตามธรรมชาติ**

5. วัฒนธรรมสถานร่วมสมัย

ทุกๆ พื้นที่ในจังหวัดเชียงใหม่ในช่วง 3 เดือน จะถูกเปลี่ยนบทบาทเดิมของสถานที่ที่มีอยู่แล้วในสังคมให้มาทำหน้าที่ใหม่ เป็นพื้นที่เพื่อการแสดงออกทางวัฒนธรรม โดยนักวัฒนธรรมทั้งหลาย "**เลือก**" สถานที่ ช่วงเวลา รูปแบบกิจกรรมแล้ว "**แต่งตั้ง**" ให้ทำหน้าที่เป็น "**วัฒนธรรมสถานร่วมสมัย**"

6. นักวัฒนธรรม : นานาการแสดงออก

เป็นช่วงเวลาที่เปิดพื้นที่เพื่อกิจกรรมสำหรับทุกคน ทุกสาขาอาชีพ ทุกประเด็น และทุกกลวิธีการแสดงทางวัฒนธรรมในเชิงสร้างสรรค์ และทุกชนชาติ เสมือน "**งานวัดร่วมสมัยนานาชาติ**" ที่เชิญชวนผู้คนจากหลากหลายจุดยืนทางวัฒนธรรมมาแสดงออกในช่วงเวลาเดียวกัน เพื่อให้สังคมได้รับรู้และเห็นภาพรวมแต่ละประเด็นทางวัฒนธรรมในปัจจุบันอย่างชัดเจน โดยมีความเชื่อพื้นฐานที่ว่า *"ประชาชนทุกคนมีศักยภาพเป็นนักวัฒนธรรม"* และ *"ทุกกิจกรรม ทุกประเด็น และทุกกลวิธีการแสดงออกแต่ละศาสตร์ของมนุษย์ที่ดำเนินอยู่ในสังคมสามารถกลายเป็น**กิจกรรมสร้างสรรค์**เพื่อการจัดวางสังคม"*

7. อดีตปัจจุบันอนาคต

(เชียงใหม่) จัดวางสังคม ในชื่อย่อ (ชม)จส. เป็นกลุ่มเอกชนรวมตัวกันอย่างยืดหยุ่นและเป็นไปเองอย่างสมัครใจ มีความคาดหวังถึงการเกิดเทศกาลทางวัฒนธรรมอุดมคติร่วมสมัย (งานวัดร่วมสมัยนานาชาติ) ที่จะทำให้ระบบสังคมเสรีทุนนิยมมีจุดอ่อนน้อยที่สุด และเห็นว่า (ชม)จส. เป็นเพียงโครงงานตัวอย่างที่จะขยายไปสู่จังหวัดหรือสังคมอื่นๆ ต่อไป เริ่มต้นกิจกรรมครั้งแรกเมื่อปี 2535-2536 ในนามศิลปเทศกาลวัดและสุสาน ต่อมาในครั้งที่ 2 ปี 2536-2537 ศิลปเทศกาล วัด สุสาน บ้าน อาคาร ถนน สะพาน กำแพง แม่น้ำลำคลอง พื้นที่ว่าง และสัปดาห์ร่วมทุกข์ ต้นปี 2538 นอกจากกิจกรรมประจำปีดังกล่าว (ชม)จส. ยังเข้าร่วมกิจกรรมกับชุมชนหลายครั้ง สำหรับศิลปวัฒนธรรมเทศกาล ครั้งที่ 3 นี้ โครงงานจะพยายามแสวงหาความร่วมมือจากมวลชนทุกสาขา ทุกกลุ่มเอกชนมากยิ่งขึ้น รวมทั้งขยายความร่วมมือกับบุคคลและสถาบันทางวัฒนธรรมนานาชาติ เพื่อให้ (ชม)จส. เป็นเทศกาลทางศิลปวัฒนธรรมร่วมสมัยเพื่อจัดวางสังคมโดยมวลชนทั่วโลกอย่างแท้จริง

7 COLLECTIVE PRINCIPLES FROM FRIENDS

1. Culture with a capital "C"

Originally "**we**" were all the same. Gradually we started to differ and to understan other less and less. Emphasis on '**ego**' has lead to trickery and confrontation. W up in our respective socio-cultural systems which are determined by different time references. We believe that most processes in a Culture with a capital 'C' are a for the values **Goodness, Truth, Beauty**, and an attempt to develop our w thinking, our knowledge and our spirits towards an "**original condition**" ba equality.

2. Social Installation

(Chiang Mai) Social Installation is an annual Cultural Festival open for all discip society, that want to "**rouse**" an atmosphere and stimulate activities on a Conten Cultural level. The capitalist market economy does not encourage such activ rather promotes egotistical greed, competition, exploitation and commercial en ment.

3. Natural Value

Natural Value is the main value of this Festival. Natural Value originates where present creative activities together; when people convey their ideas, beliefs, know spirits, art works, etc.., to one another in an atmosphere of sacrifice and modesty we respect, acknowledge and exchahge each other's point of view. This is the being in the '**present**'; '**peaceactivity**'; it is a form of "**co-operative consciou**

4. New Social Vision

The Festival encourages works and activities that deal with originality, creativity a possibilities from all disciplines (Goodness, Truth, Beauty). It may be likened to " **Consciousness"** which will be the basic mechanisms and processes for devel and adjustment of each and every people's culture, towards a more flexible l Social and Cultural problems cound be solved by the masses continously a "natural spontaneity".

5. Contemporary Cultural Location

During a 3 month period, the function of existing locations within Chiang Mai provi be altered into locations, for cultural expression. Every Culturalist will "**choose**" th time and nature of his or her activity, and will thereby set up a Contemporary Location.

6. Culturalists ; Inter-Expression

A period in time has been allocated for any activity in which anybody may par using any means of expression that deals with the notion of Culture in a creative r This can be likened to an '**International Contemporary Temple Fair**' where peo different cultural opinions are invited to participate in contemporary Cultural discu in order for society to acknowledge a clear collective picture of Contemporary topics.

We basically believe that *"everybody has the potential to be a Culturalist"*. *" Any any topic, any means of expression from any social discipline can become a activity that contributes to **Social Installation.**"*

7. Past-Present-Future

(Chiang Mai) Social Installation (CM.)SI. is a flexible and spontaneous co-operat organizes this Contemporary Cultural Festival (International Contemporary Fair), as a counterweight to the free market economy of capitalist society.It hope an example to be followed by other provinces in Thailand or elsewhere in the w

(CM.)SI. originated in 1992-93, under the name "**Art Festival : Temple Cemeteries**". The second festival was organized in1993-94, and the w "**Co-operative Suffering**", at the begining of 1995. Besides these yearly a (CM.)SI. also participated in many community activities. For the 3rd Festival, the will attempt to enlarge the Co-operation will extend to private organizations International artists and Cultural Instititutions all over the world, to make this a f of Contemporary Art and Culture that works on a Social Installation.

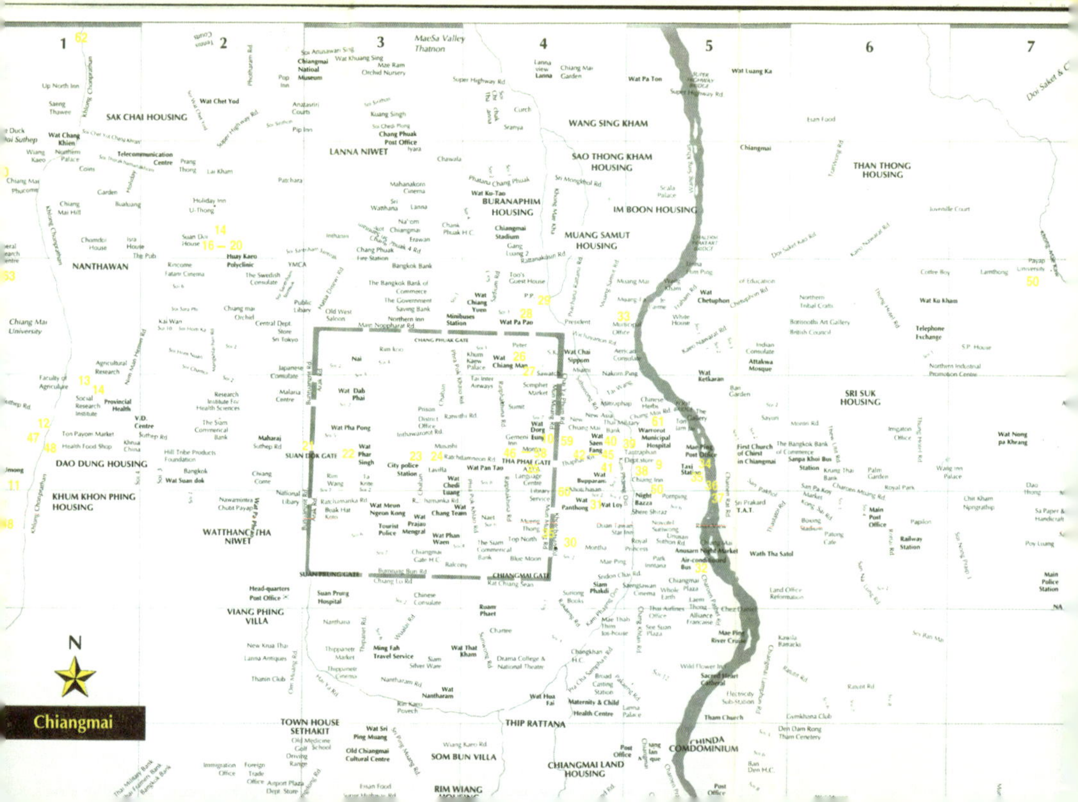

ศิลปวัฒนธรรมเทศกาล
วัด สุสาน บ้าน อาคาร ถนน สะพาน กำแพง แม่น้ำลำคลอง พื้นที่ว่าง ครั้งที่ 3

THIRD ART AND CULTURAL FESTIVAL : TEMPLES, CEMETERIES, PRIVATE-RESIDENCES, PUBLIC BUILDINGS, STREETS, BRIDGES, WALLS, RIVERS AND CANALS, OPEN SPACES.

19 พฤศจิกายน 2538 ถึง 19 กุมภาพันธ์ 2539 ณ จังหวัดเชียงใหม่

NOVEMBER 19, 1995 - FEBRUARY 19, 1996 AT CHIANG MAI, THAILAND

...ทุกข์

7 มกราคม 2539

มนุษย์ถูกธรรมชาติสาบมาให้มี **"ความหวัง"** ถึงชีวิตที่ดีกว่าปัจจุบัน นั่นหมายถึง **"ความสุข"** แต่ความสุขก็เป็นเพียงความหวังที่ไม่เคยอิ่ม **"ความทุกข์"** จึงกลายเป็นความจริงแท้ในชีวิตที่มิอาจปฏิเสธได้ กล่าวได้ว่า **"ความทุกข์"** เป็นประสบการณ์ร่วมของมนุษยชาติ ดังนั้น **"สัปดาห์ร่วมทุกข์"** จึงเป็นช่วงเวลา-สถานที่เพื่อการนำเสนอกิจกรรมวัฒนธรรมจากมวลชนทุกรูปแบบ โดยแรงบันดาลใจจากความทุกข์ เพื่อให้เราตระหนักร่วมกันว่า เราต่างอยู่ร่วมกันในวังวนแห่งทุกข์ อย่างเสมอภาคเท่าเทียมกัน

ประชาชนทุกคน ทุกสาขาอาชีพ และทุกชนชาติสามารถเข้าร่วมกิจกรรมได้ฟรี โดยไม่มีเงื่อนไขและจำกัดจำนวน ทุกๆ กิจกรรม อาทิ ดนตรีคนตาบอด ดนตรีทดลองร่วมสมัย ฟ้อนรำ กลอนสด จิตรกรรมบนถนน ประติมากรรมกับเสาไฟฟ้า มายากล หมอดู ตลก เสวนา วีดิทัศน์ ฯลฯ รวมทั้งเป็นเพียงผู้ชม

แบ่งออกเป็นดังนี้

- **การแสดงร่วมสมัยเที่ยงคืน**
  ใช้ร่างกาย กิริยาอาการ การแต่งกายของมนุษย์เป็นสื่อการแสดงออกทางวัฒนธรรม
- **คืนแห่งแสง-เสียงร่วมสมัย**
  ใช้แสง-เสียง ทุกรูปแบบเป็นสื่อการแสดงออกทางวัฒนธรรม
- **มหาวิทยาลัยเที่ยงคืน**
  วงสนทนาจากบุคคลทุกสาขาอาชีพ เกี่ยวกับ "ความทุกข์"
- **ตลาดค้าวัฒนธรรมวัตถุเที่ยงคืน**
  ชุมชนสินค้าทางวัฒนธรรมเพื่อการซื้อ-ขาย และแจกฟรี อาทิ ศิลปะ พระเครื่อง ของเก่า สัตว์ ฯลฯ
- **วันแห่งศิลปะจัดวาง**
  นำเสนอทัศนศิลป์ ติดตั้งสถานที่ต่างๆ ในจังหวัดเชียงใหม่
- **ปาร์ตี้วัฒนธรรมเที่ยงคืน**
  ชุมนุมสังสรรค์ เสวนาทุกๆ ประเด็นทางวัฒนธรรมที่สนใจ

...งปัญหา (เกิด-แก่-เจ็บ-ตาย) ร่วมสมัย

มกราคม 2539 - 19 กุมภาพันธ์ 2539

เป็นกิจกรรมที่ใช้ภาษา-เหตุผลเป็นสื่อ เพื่อแสวงหา "รูปทรงความคิด" จากมวลชน เกี่ยวกับคำถามทางวัฒนธรรมร่วมสมัย เช่น

- **ทำไมต้องปฏิรูปการเมือง?**
- **ทำไมต้อง ธรรมิกสังคมนิยม หรือ เสมศึกษาลัย?**
- **ท่าทีพุทธศาสนากับสังคมร่วมสมัย?**
- **ทางออกอย่างไรต่อปัญหาโสเภณี ยาเสพติด คนชรา โรคจิต อาชญากรรม ฯลฯ ในสังคม?**
- **ทำไม "กีฬา" กลายเป็นกิจกรรมยอดนิยมของมวลชน?**
- **ทำไมวัฒนธรรมที่ส่งเสริม "ตัวตน" จึงรุ่งเรืองในสังคมปัจจุบัน?**
- **โลกและโรคของสังคมข้อมูลข่าวสาร?**
- **วิทยาศาสตร์ เทคโนโลยี วัตถุนิยม เป็นซาตานหรือพระเจ้า?**
- **วิสัยทัศน์ใหม่การจัดวางสังคมอย่างไร?**

ประกอบด้วยปาฐกถาจากนักคิดของสังคม ; สนทนาโต๊ะกลมจากตัวแทนกลุ่มต่างๆ ; ฝึกอบรมเชิงปฏิบัติการ ; นิทรรศการข้อมูล ; สำรวจสถิติทัศนคติของมวลชน ฯลฯ

...สนุนโดย

เทศบาลนครเชียงใหม่
สำนักส่งเสริมศิลปวัฒนธรรม มหาวิทยาลัยเชียงใหม่
คณะวิจิตรศิลป์ มหาวิทยาลัยเชียงใหม่
มูลนิธิญี่ปุ่น กรุงเทพฯ
บริษัท เงินทุนหลักทรัพย์ซิทก้า จำกัด (มหาชน)
บริษัท บางจาก จำกัด (มหาชน)
บริษัท โตชิบา (ประเทศไทย) จำกัด
ฮิลล์ไซด์พลาซ่าแอนด์คอนโดเทล 4 เชียงใหม่
ศูนย์สรรพสินค้าเชียงอินทร์พลาซ่า เชียงใหม่
เพชร โอสถานุเคราะห์

WEEK OF CO-OPERATIVE SUFFERING

January 1-7, 1996

Objective : By nature, human live in hope ; we hope for better life and happiness. Nevertheless, happiness is just something to hope for and we never get enough of it. A western notion of dualism is out of context in this circumstance since, as in general Buddhist idea, there is no seperation between happiness and suffering. Suffering is a fact of life we cannot deny. It is a collective experience.

'The Week of Co-operative Suffering' is intended to be a cultural activity by/for the mass bringing attention to the ideal that we are all captured in the pool of suffer. Within this time-space, everyone is encouraged to participate in this phenomenon.

Culturalists : Any body, any profession, any nationality can participate in this activity. FREE!!! Suggesting activities such as music by visual disabled people, contemporary experimental music, folk dance, live-poetry, pavement art, magical, forture-telling, comedy and, eventhough, SPECTATOR

Activities :

NIGHT OF CONTEMPORARY PERFORMANCE
The uses of body, gestures and dressing-up are ways of cultural expression.
NIGHT OF CONTEMPORARY LIGHT AND SOUND
The use of light and sound is cultural expression
MIDNIGHT UNIVERSITY
Discussion concerning the notion of suffering by people from all professions.
MIDNIGH MARKET
Culture for sale
BUY-SELL-DONATE YOUR COMMODITIES
art, antique, people, animal and religious articles.
DAY OF INSTALLATION ART
Presentation of visual art at various locations within Chiang Mai
CULTURAL PARTY NIGHT
Seminars on any interesting cultural topics.

MONTH OF CONTEMPORARY PROBLEMS (birth-Aging-Illness-Death)

January 8, 1996 - February 19, 1996

Objectives : These are activities that use language/intellect and logic/reason as means of communication in order to search for 'THOUGHT-FORM'. Questions on contemporary Culture present concerns such as

Why do we need political reform?
Why do we need Dhamma-Socialism and/or Seimasikhalai (Spirit in Education Movement)?
Buddhist attitude in contemporary society?
How to deal with problems of prostitution, drugs, mental-illness and crime?
Why is SPORTS the most popular activity in the mass?
Why is the ideal of SELF-CENTRE/EGO-CENTRIC so thriving in contem porary society?
Information-Technology Society and its problem. Science, technology and rialism - ailment or God?
What is the new vision for Social Installation?

Activities :
- Lectures by cultural theorists
- Round-table talks with representatives from various organizations
- Workshop
- Information exhibition
- Questionarei

หมายเหตุ NOTE

สำหรับรายละเอียด วัน-เวลา-สถานที่ ที่แน่นอนทั้งสัปดาห์ร่วมทุกข์ เดือนแห่งปัญหาร่วมสมัยและรายการอื่นๆ ที่จะเข้าร่วมเทศกาล จะจัดทำสิ่งพิมพ์เผยแพร่อีกครั้ง สามารถสอบถามข้อมูลได้ตั้งแต่วันที่ 20 ธันวาคม 2538 เป็นต้นไป ที่โทร และโทรสาร (053) 211724 (เชียงใหม่จัดวางสังคม)

Furture information concerning for both 'The Week of Co-operative Suffering' and 'Month of Contemporary Problem' as well as any other activities in this festival will be advertised later on.
More information can be obtained from December 20, 1995
by Tel./Fax.(053) 211724 (Chiang Mai Social Installation)

...์ เลียว คอง ยาม	(สิงคโปร์)
...LEOW KONG YAM	(SINGAPORE)
... นิโลฟาร์	(ปากีสถาน)
...NILOFAR	(PAKISTAN)
...ษมกิจวัฒนา	(ไทย)
...KASEMKITVATANA	(THAILAND)
...ราษฎร์จำเริญสุข	(ไทย)
...RASDJARMREARNSOOK	(THAILAND)
...บายาชิ	(ญี่ปุ่น)
...BAYASHI	(JAPAN)
... จันทรา	(อินเดีย)
...AN CHANDER	(INDIA)
...ีสุธาสินี	(ไทย)
...EE SRISUTHASINEE	(THAILAND)
... หอมทอง	(ไทย)
...CHAI HOMTHONG	(THAILAND)
...มเมอร์แซลเอล	(เนเธอร์แลนด์)
...EMMERZAEL	(NETHERLANDS)
...ดิ์ ภูธรารักษ์	(ไทย)
...SAK PHUTHARARAK	(THAILAND)
... ครอฟท์	(อังกฤษ)
...EL CROFT	(ENGLAND)
...โซเมอร์วิลเล	(ออสเตรเลีย)
...SOMERVILLE	(AUSTRALIA)
...ยามาอิเดะ	(ญี่ปุ่น)
... YAMAIDE	(JAPAN)
... ฮิโรเซ	(ญี่ปุ่น)
...HI HIROSE	(JAPAN)
... ชัฏอนันต์	(ไทย)
...K CHATANAN	(THAILAND)
...ะ นากามูระ	(ญี่ปุ่น)
...O NAKAMURA	(JAPAN)
...เล่อร์	(อเมริกา)
...LER	(USA.)
... เบเทนไรเชอร์	(เยอรมัน)
... BREITENREICHER	(GERMANY)
...แซ่เตีย	(ไทย)
...DEE SAETIA	(THAILAND)
...งควัฒนะพงษ์	(ไทย)
...GKAVATANAPONG	(THAILAND)
...นะลิขิกร	(ไทย)
...IAVANALIKIKORN	(THAILAND)
...ะ อินางากิ	(ญี่ปุ่น)

24 สุวรรณ ลัยมณี	(ไทย)
SUWAN LAIMANEE	(THAILAND)
25 ตัง ดา วู	(สิงคโปร์)
TANG DA WU	(SINGAPORE)
26 เปียโต เปลลินี	(อิตาลี)
โยลา บาร์เบสซ์	(เยอรมัน)
PIETRO PELLINI	(ITALY)
YOLA BERBESZ	(GERMANY)
27 อี.ที. (แลกเปลี่ยนความคิด)	
E.T. (Exchanging Thought)	
28 เตยงาม ศรีสุบัติ	(ไทย)
TOEINGAM SRISUBAT	(THAILAND)
29 ธาตรี โภควนิช	(ไทย)
THATREE POKAVANICH	(THAILAND)
30 วัฒนะ วัฒนาพันธุ์	(ไทย)
WATTANA WATTANAPUN	(THAILAND)
31 มณเฑียร บุญมา	(ไทย)
MONTIEN BOONMA	(THAILAND)
32 โรงเรียนฝึกหัดขับรถยนต์คุณนาวิน	(ไทย)
NAVIN DRIVING SCHOOL	(THAILAND)
33 เกรบส์ วูล์ฟกังค์	(ออสเตรีย)
KREBS WOLFGANG	(AUSTRIA)
34 อีฟวอน พาเรนท์	(แคนาดา)
YVONNE PARENT	(CANADA)
35 อากาซึกิ ฮาราดะ	(ญี่ปุ่น)
AKATSUKI HARADA	(JAPAN)
36 คมสัน หนูเขียว	(ไทย)
KOMSON NOOKIEW	(THAILAND)
37 สเวติสลาฟ ไคเซอร์	(ยูโกสลาเวีย)
SVETISLAV KAIZERI	(YUGOSLAVIA)
38 ชินโกะ ซูซูกิ	(ญี่ปุ่น)
SHINGO SUZUKI	(JAPAN)
39 เดบบาร์ พอร์ช	(ออสเตรเลีย)
DEBRA PORCH	(AUSTRALIA)
40 ตัน จิน กวน	(มาเลเซีย)
TAN CHIN KUAN	(MALAYSIA)
41 อิง ฮิว ชู	(มาเลเซีย)
ENG HWEE CHU	(MALAYSAI)
42 ยูทากะ โซเนะ	(ญี่ปุ่น)
YUTAKA SONE	(JAPAN)
43 ไฮดี้มารี ลัยมณี-เกาส์	(ออสเตรีย)
HEIDEMARIE LAIMANEE-GAUSS	(AUSTRIA)
44 อมานด้า เฮง	(สิงคโปร์)
AMANDA HENG	(SINGAPORE)
45 ฉุมพล อภิสุข	(ไทย)
CHUMPOL APISUK	(THAILAND)

47 อารามัยนี	(อินโดนี...
ARAHMAINI	(INDONE...
48 โนเอล โซเลอร์ คุยซอน	(ฟิลิปปิ...
NOEL SOLER CUIZON	(PHILIPPIN...
49 กิตติ บุญมี	(ไ...
KITTI BOONMEE	(THAILA...
50 ราเชล เจน ฟลาวเวอร์	(อังก...
บาร์บารา ดิคคินสัน	(อเมริ...
นฤมล ธรรมพฤกษา	(ไ...
ธีระวัฒน์ มุลวิไล	(ไ...
RACHEL JANE FLOWER	(ENGLA...
BARBARA DICKINSON	(U...
NARUMOL THAMMAPRUKSA	(THAILA...
TEERAWAT MULVILAI	(THAILA...
51 วันเอก จันทรทิพย์	(ไ...
WANEAK JUNTARATIP	(THAILA...
52 วัลลภ แม่นยำ	(ไ...
WALLOP MANYUM	(THAILA...
53 มาเซล เคาวสฮาล	(เยอร...
MARCEL KRAUSHAAR	(GERMA...
54 ดอริส เคาวสฮาล	(ออสเ...
DORIS KRAUSHAAR	(AUST...
55 โฆษิต จันทรทิพย์	(ไ...
KOSIT JUNTARATIP	(THAILA...
56 ไพศาล เปลี่ยนบางช้าง	(ไ...
PAISAN PLIENBANGCHANG	(THAIL...
57 ศุภชัย ศาสตร์สาระ	(ไ...
SUPACHAI SATSARA	(THAIL...
58 นพดล ถิรธราดล	(ไ...
NOPPADOL TIRATARADOL	(THAIL...
59 อินกริด เอช คลาวเซอร์	(อิ...
INGRID H. KLAUSER	(IT...
60 โยฮัน วาเกินนาร์	(เนเธอร์แล...
JOHAN WAGENAAR	(NETHERLA...
61 มารี ซีรัส	(เดนม...
MARI ZIRAS	(DENM...
62 อุทิศ อติมานะ	(ไ...
UTHIT ATIMANA	(THAIL...
63 ศูนย์ข้อมูล "เชียงใหม่จัดวางสังคม"	
หอศิลป์ปิ่นมาลา มหาวิทยาลัยเชียงใหม่	

"คอกก้า คูดเดิ้ล ดู"
วัดอุโมงค์
19 พฤศจิกายน 2538 ถึง
19 กุมภาพันธ์ 2539
20 พฤศจิกายน 2538
เวลา 10:30 น.

"Cocka Doodle Do"
U-Mong Temple
November 19, 1995 to February 19, 1996
November 20, 1995 ; 10:30 A.M.

2
หมุด นิโลฟาร์ (ปากีสถาน)
UT NILOFAR (PAKISTAN)

"ไร้รูปร่าง / รูปร่าง"
วัดอุโมงค์
21–27 พฤศจิกายน 2538

"Shapeless / Shape"
U-Mong Temple
November 21-27, 1995

3
ติ เกษมกิจวัฒนา (ไทย)
TTI KASEMKITVATANA (THAILAND)

"......................."
วัดอุโมงค์
19 พฤศจิกายน 2538 ถึง
19 กุมภาพันธ์ 2539

"Mo(nu)ment to The Third (CM.)SI."
U-Mong Temple
November 19, 1995 to
February 19, 1996

4
รยา ราษฎร์จำเริญสุข (ไทย)
YA RASDJARMREARNSOOK (THAILAND)

"ไม่มีชื่อ"
วัดอุโมงค์
19 พฤศจิกายน 2538 ถึง
19 กุมภาพันธ์ 2539

"Untitled"
U-Mong Temple
November 19, 1995 to
February 19, 1996

เทอิ โคบายาชิ (ญี่ปุ่น)
TEI KOBAYASHI (JAPAN)

"โยนี"
วัดอุโมงค์
19 พฤศจิกายน 2538 ถึง
19 กุมภาพันธ์ 2539

"YONI"
U-Mong Temple
November 19, 1995 to
February 19, 1996

6
กานจัน จันทรา (อินเดีย)
KANCHAN CHANDER (INDIA)

"หญิงสาว ผู้หญิง แม่...แล้วถัดไป?"
วัดอุโมงค์
19 พฤศจิกายน 2538 ถึง
19 กุมภาพันธ์ 2539

"ADOLESENCE WOMANHOOD MOTHERHOOD.... AND BEYOND?"
U-Mong Temple
November 19, 1995 to
February 19, 1996

7
เมธี ศรีสุธาสินี (ไทย)
MAETHEE SRISUTHASINEE (THAILAND)

"พิจารณา"
วัดอุโมงค์
19 พฤศจิกายน 2538 ถึง
19 กุมภาพันธ์ 2539

"Consideration"
U-Mong Temple
November 19, 1995 to
February 19, 1996

8
ธวัชชัย หอมทอง (ไทย)
TAWATCHAI HOMTHONG (THAILAND)

"ไม่มีชื่อ"
วัดอุโมงค์
19 พฤศจิกายน 2538 ถึง
19 กุมภาพันธ์ 2539

"Untitled"
U-Mong Temple
November 19, 1995 to
February 19, 1996

ลีน เอมเมอร์แซลเอล (เนเธอร์แลนด์)
LEEN EMMERZAEL (NETHERLANDS)

"สถานที่สำหรับการทำสมาธิ 3 แห่ง"
1. วัดอุโมงค์
2. ชั้นดาดฟ้า ศูนย์สรรพสินค้าเชียงอินทร์พลาซ่า
19 พฤศจิกายน 2538 ถึง
19 กุมภาพันธ์ 2539

"Three Places for Meditation"
1. U-Mong Temple
2. Chiang Inn Plaza (Top Floor)
November 19, 1995 to
February 19, 1996

10
สุทธิศักดิ์ ภูธรารักษ์ (ไทย)
SUTTHISAK PHUTHARARAK (THAILAND)

"ไม่มีชื่อ"
วัดอุโมงค์
19 พฤศจิกายน 2538 ถึง
19 กุมภาพันธ์ 2539

"ไม่มีชื่อ"
ริมคูเมืองด้านทิศเหนือของประตูท่าแพ
19 พฤศจิกายน 2538 ถึง
19 กุมภาพันธ์ 2539

"Untitled"
U-Mong Temple
November 19, 1995 to
February 19, 1996

"Untitled"
Beside city moat at the north side of Tha-Pae Gate
November 19, 1995 to
February 19, 1996

11
ไมเคิล ครอฟท์ (อังกฤษ)
MICHAEL CROFT (ENGLAND)

"ปัดกวาดความกลัว"
วัดอุโมงค์
19 กันยายน 2538 ถึง
19 กุมภาพันธ์ 2539

"Sweeping up Fear"
U-Mong Temple
December 15, 1995 to
February 19, 1996

แจนิส โซเมอร์วิลเล (ออสเตรเลีย)
JANIS SOMERVILLE (AUSTRALIA)

"ยังคงแนบชิดติดกับหมีโคล่า"
สุสานป่าแดง
19 พฤศจิกายน 2538 ถึง
19กุมภาพันธ์ 2539
Ⓟ 21 พฤศจิกายน 2538 : 13:00 น.

"Still Clinging to the Koala"
Pa-Daeng Cemetery
November 19, 1995 - February 19, 1996
Ⓟ November 21, 1995 ; 1:00 p.m.

13
จูนยา ยามาอิเดะ (ญี่ปุ่น)
JUN'YA YAMAIDE (JAPAN)

Ⓟ "ท่องเที่ยว: บางสิ่งที่คุณมีอยู่ในชีวิตประจำวัน"
เรือนไทลื้อ สำนักส่งเสริมศิลปะและวัฒนธรรม มหาวิทยาลัยเชียงใหม่ (ริมถนนคลองชลประทาน)
19 พฤศจิกายน 2538
★ ศิลปินผู้นี้จะเดินทางไปในสถานที่ต่างๆ ทั่วเมืองเชียงใหม่ เพื่อพบปะและแลกเปลี่ยนสิ่งของที่ใช้ในชีวิตประจำวัน

Ⓟ "TOUR: Something you have in a Daily Life"
Ruen Thai-Lua, Center for the Promotion of Arts and Culture, C.M.U. (Chonrapatan Road)
November 19 to 28, 1995
★ The artist will travel to several locations all over Chiang Mai to request and exchange of object used in every-day-life from Chiang Mai residents.

14
ซาโตชิ ฮิโรเซ (ญี่ปุ่น)
SATOSHI HIROSE (JAPAN)

"ไฟสีแดง"
1. เรือนไทลื้อ สำนักส่งเสริมศิลปะและวัฒนธรรม มหาวิทยาลัยเชียงใหม่ (ริมถนนคลองชลประทาน)
2. อาคารฮิลล์ไซด์พลาซ่า แอนด์ คอนโดเทล 4 ชั้น 4 ห้องติดกับบริษัทฟูริยัง จำกัด
19 ธันวาคม 2538 – 19 กุมภาพันธ์ 2539

"Red Light"
1. Ruen Galare, Center for the Promotion of Arts and Culture C.M.U. (Chonrapatan Road)
2. Hillside Plaza & Condotel 4 (4th Floor, Room beside Furiyang Company, Ltd.)
November 19, 1995 - February 19,1996

อนุรักษ์ ชัฎอนันต์ (ไทย)
ANURAK CHATANAN (THAILAND)

"ไม่มีชื่อ"
สวนสัตว์เชียงใหม่
19–25 พฤศจิกายน 2538

Ⓟ "Untitled"
Chiang Mai Zoo
November 19-25, 1995

16
มาซาโตะ นากามูระ (ญี่ปุ่น)
MASATO NAKAMURA (JAPAN)

"ด้านหน้าของด้านหลัง เฝ้ามองสิ่งที่กำลังเดินอยู่"
อาคารฮิลล์ไซด์พลาซ่า แอนด์ คอนโดเทล 4 (ชั้น 2, ห้อง 216)
19 พฤศจิกายน 2538 ถึง
19 กุมภาพันธ์ 2539

"FRONTSIDE OF THE BACKSIDE-Watch What's Showing"
Hillside Plaza & Condotel 4 (2nd Floor, Room 216)
November 19, 1995 to
February 19, 1996

17
ลิซ มิลเล่อร์ (อเมริกา)
LIZ MILLER (USA.)

"การเสี่ยงภัย"
อาคารฮิลล์ไซด์พลาซ่า แอนด์ คอนโดเทล 4 (ชั้น 2, ห้อง 203)
19 พฤศจิกายน 2538 ถึง
19 กุมภาพันธ์ 2539

"Venture"
Hillside Plaza & Condotel 4 (2nd Floor, Room 203)
November 19, 1995 to
February 19, 1996

18
ซัสเกีย เบเทนไรเชอร์ (เยอรมัน)
SASKIA BREITENREICHER (GERMANY)

"Rapunzel"
อาคารฮิลล์ไซด์พลาซ่า แอนด์ คอนโดเทล 4 (ชั้น 4, ห้อง 417)
19 พฤศจิกายน 2538 ถึง
19 กุมภาพันธ์ 2539

"Rapunzel"
Hillside Plaza & Condotel 4 (4th Floor, Room 417)
November 19, 1995 to
February 19, 1996

มลฤดี แซ่เตีย (ไทย)
MONLUDEE SAETIA (THAILAND)

"โปสการ์ด 253 นาฏกรรมควา
อาคารฮิลล์ไซด์พลาซ่า แอนด์
(ชั้น 4, ห้อง 417)
19 พฤศจิกายน 2538
19 กุมภาพันธ์ 2539

"Postcard 199
Hillside Plaza & Co
(4th Floor, Room 41
November 19, 1995
February 19, 1996

ต้อย อังควัฒนะพงษ์
TOI UNGKAVATANAPONG (THAIL

"นามธรรมพื้นเ
อาคารฮิลล์ไซด์พลาซ่า แอนด์
(ชั้น 4, ห้อง 417)
19 พฤศจิกายน 2538
19 กุมภาพันธ์ 2539

"Domestic Abst
Hillside Plaza & Co
(4th Floor, Room 41
November 19, 1995
February 19, 1996

เกศ ชวนะลิขิกร (ไทย)
KADE JAVANALIKIKORN (THAIL

"ไกลคือใกล้ ใก เหลือเกิน!"
เกาะกลางถนน บริเวณสี่แยกสวนดอก
19 พฤศจิกายน 2538
19 กุมภาพันธ์ 2539

"Far is Near/ Near is so Fa
Street isle at Suan D intersection
November 19, 1995
February 19, 1996

28
ยงาม ศรีสุบัติ (ไทย)
INGAM SRISUBAT (THAILAND)

"ไม่มีชื่อ"
วัดป่าเป้า
19–23 พฤศจิกายน 2538

"Untitled"
Pa-Pao Temple
November 19-23, 1995

29
ศรี โภควนิช (ไทย)
TREE POKAVANICH (THAILAND)

"รับใช้ตัวเองภาคพุทธะ"
วัดป่าเป้า
19 พฤศจิกายน 2538 ถึง
19 กุมภาพันธ์ 2539

"Self-Help : Buddhist Version"
Pa-Pao Temple
November 19, 1995 to
February 19, 1996

30
นะ วัฒนาพันธุ์ (ไทย)
TANA WATTANAPUN (THAILAND)

"เส้นทางที่ไม่คาดหมาย"
ห้าแยกบ้านฮ่อม (หมาหลง)
ชุมชนลอยเคราะห์
20 มกราคม 2538 : 17:00 น.

"Unpredictable Routes"
Ban-Hom Cross-road (Mah-long), Loy Khro Community
January 20, 1995 ; 5:00 p.m.

31
เทียร บุญมา (ไทย)
TIEN BOONMA (THAILAND)

"Body Temple"
วัดพันตอง
19 พฤศจิกายน 2538 ถึง
19 กุมภาพันธ์ 2539
ผลงานชิ้นนี้จะถูกเผาและฝังดินภายหลังจากสิ้นสุดการแสดง จึงขอเรียนเชิญทุกท่านเข้าร่วม โดยจะแจ้งกำหนดการให้ทราบต่อไป

"Body Temple"
Pan-Thong Temple
November 19, 1995 - February 19, 1996

32
โรงเรียนฝึกหัดขับรถยนต์คุณนาวิน (ไทย)
NAVIN DRIVING SCHOOL (THAILAND)

ด่วน ขอเชิญฝึกหัดขับรถยนต์
ฟรี!
19 พฤศจิกายน 2538 ถึง
19 กุมภาพันธ์ 2539
รับนักเรียนจำนวนจำกัด
ดำเนินการสอนโดย
นาวิน ลาวัลย์ชัยกุล
สนใจติดต่อได้ที่
"โรงเรียนฝึกหัดขับรถยนต์ คุณนาวิน"
138 ถ.ศรีดอนไชย
อ.เมือง จ.เชียงใหม่ 50100
โทร./โทรสาร (053) 80 85 81

URGENTLY WANTED
FREE!
People who want to learn how to drive a car
From November 19, 1995 to
February 19, 1996.
Limited amount of students.
By Navin Rawanchaikul.
Contact :
"Navin Driving School"
c/o. 138 Sridornchai Rd.
Chiang Mai 50100
Tel./Fax. (053) 81 85 81

33
เกรบส์ วูลฟ์กังค์ (ออสเตรีย)
KREBS WOLFGANG (AUSTRIA)

"Groundtaking"
บริเวณเทศบาลนครเชียงใหม่
1–19 กุมภาพันธ์ 2539

34
อีฟวอน พาเรนท์ (แคนาดา)
YVONNE PARENT (CANADA)

"รูปศีรษะ"
สะพานนวรัฐ
19 พฤศจิกายน 2538ถึง
19 กุมภาพันธ์ 2539

"Figurehead"
Navarat Bridge
November 19, 1995 to
February 19, 1996

35
อากาซึกิ ฮาราดะ (ญี่ปุ่น)
AKATSUKI HARADA (JAPAN)

"ไม่มีชื่อ"
1. บริเวณสวนสาธารณะข้างจวนผู้ว่าฯ ถนนท่าแพ
2. คูเมืองด้านทิศตะวันตกของประตูสวนดอก
19 พฤศจิกายน 2538 ถึง
19 กุมภาพันธ์ 2539

"Untitled"
1. Park near Governor's Residence, Tha-Pae Road
2. City moat at the west side of Suan-Dok Gate
November 19, 1995 to
February 19, 1996.

36
คมสัน หนูเขียว (ไทย)
KOMSON NOOKIEW (THAILAND)

"ฉันถูกควบคุม"
บริเวณสวนสาธารณะข้างจวนผู้ว่าฯ ถนนท่าแพ
19 พฤศจิกายน 2538 ถึง
19 กุมภาพันธ์ 2539

"I was Arrested"
Park near Governor's

37
สเวติสลาฟ ไคเซอร์ (ยูโกสลาเวีย)
SVETISLAV KAIZER (YUGOSLAVIA)

"ไม่มีชื่อ (สำหรับ ชมจส.)"
สวนสาธารณะข้างจวนผู้ว่าฯ ถนนท่าแพ
1 ธันวาคม 2538 – 19 กุมภาพันธ์ 2539

"Untitled (For CMSI.)"
Park near Governor's Residence
Tha-Pae Road
December 1, 1995 - February 19, 1996.

38
ชินโกะ ซูซูกิ (ญี่ปุ่น)
SHINGO SUZUKI (JAPAN)

"การติดต่ออันล้าหลัง การติดต่อของความรัก"
บริเวณสถานที่บริการโทรศัพท์สาธารณะ ศูนย์สรรพสินค้าเชียงอินทร์พลาซ่า ชั้น 1
19 พฤศจิกายน – 19 ธันวาคม 2538

"COMMUNICATION LAG COMMUNICATION LOVE"
Telephone Booth at Chiang Inn Plaza (1st Floor)
November 19 - December 19, 1995

39
เดบบาร์ พอร์ช (ออสเตรเลีย)
DEBRA PORCH (AUSTRALIA)

"ไม่มีชื่อ(สำหรับคลินิค)"
คลินิคทันตแพทย์มนตรี ถนนท่าแพ
19 พฤศจิกายน 2538 ถึง
19 กุมภาพันธ์ 2539
(จันทร์–ศุกร์ 17:00 น. – 20:00 น.)
(เสาร์–อาทิตย์ 9:00 น. – 17:00 น.)

"Untitled (For Clinic)"
Dr. Montri Dental Clinic,
Tha-Pae Road
November 19, 1995 to

40
ตัน จิน กวน (มาเลเซีย)
TAN CHIN KUAN (MALAYSIA)

"รอยยิ้ม สำหรับ คุณนักการเมือง"
ถนนท่าแพ
19 พฤศจิกายน 2538 ถึง
19 กุมภาพันธ์ 2539

"A Smile for Mr.Politician"
Tha-Pae Road
November 19, 1995 to
February 19, 1996

41
อิง ฮิว ชู (มาเลเซีย)
ENG HWEE CHU (MALAYSIA)

"ขายวัฒนธรรม"
ถนนท่าแพ
19 พฤศจิกายน 2538 ถึง
19 กุมภาพันธ์ 2539

"Culture for Sale"
Tha-Pae Road
November 19, 1995 to
February 19, 1996

42
ยูทากะ โซเนะ (ญี่ปุ่น)
YUTAKA SONE (JAPAN)

"ฉวยโอกาส"
ห้องภาพวิชัย (เยื้องประตูท่าแพ)
19 พฤศจิกายน 2538 ถึง
19 กุมภาพันธ์ 2539

"SCOOP"
Vichai Photo Shop

ไฮดี้มารี ลัยมณี–เกาส์
HEIDEMARIE LAIMANEE-GAUSS

"Who shows fe blue-colour wo in a shop-wind
ห้องภาพวิชัย (เยื้องประ
1 มกราคม – 19 กุมภา

"Who shows fe blue-colour wo in a shop-wind
Vichai Photo Shop (
Tha-Pae Gate)
January 1 - February

อมานด้า เฮง (สิงคโปร์)
AMANDA HENG (SINGAPORE)

"หายไป"
ร้านเอ็มพาวเวอร์ (เยื้อง
20 พฤศจิกายน–10 ธัน

"MISSING"
Empower Shop
(nearby Tha-Pae Ga
November 20 - Decem

จุมพล อภิสุข (ไทย)
CHUMPOL APISUK (THAILAND)

"มีชีวิต"
ร้านเอ็มพาวเวอร์ (เยื้อง
20 พฤศจิกายน – 10

"ALIVE"
Empower Shop
(nearby Tha-Pae Ga
November 20 - Decem

ลี เวน (สิงคโปร์)
LEE WEN (SINGAPORE)

Ⓟ "นีโอ–บ้าบ้า"
ลานเอนกประสงค์ ประตู
19 พฤศจิกายน 2538
เวลา 10:00 น. – 10:3

Ⓟ "Neo-Baba"

อินางากิ (ญี่ปุ่น)
AGAKI (JAPAN)

ไม่มีชื่อ"
พระสิงห์
มกราคม – 19 กุมภาพันธ์ 2539
ntitled"
a Singha Temple
uary 1, - February 19, 1996

23
งคเลอร์ (เยอรมัน)
LER (GERMANY)

kology Art"
ฟฟ้า ถนนราชดำเนิน
พฤศจิกายน 2538 ถึง
กุมภาพันธ์ 2539
kology Art"
ctric Poles
Rasddamnearn Road
ember 19, 1995 to
ruary 19, 1996

24
ลัยมณี (ไทย)
MANEE (THAILAND)

ไม่มีชื่อ"
โมงค์
พฤศจิกายน 2538 ถึง
กุมภาพันธ์ 2539
ณคิดไหมว่าสิ่งเหล่านี้
ามาจากกัญชา?"
ฟฟ้า ถนนราชดำเนิน
พฤศจิกายน 2538 ถึง
กุมภาพันธ์ 2539
ntitled"
ong Temple
vember 19, 1995 to
ruary 19, 1996
an you imagine that
of these items are
ing made from
arihuana?"
ddamnearn Road
ary 1 - February 19, 1996

ตัง ดา วู (สิงคโปร์)
TANG DA WU (SINGAPORE)

● "สังสรรค์กับคนเมือง เชียงใหม่"
■ ทางเท้าถนนมูลเมือง
▼ 19 พฤศจิกายน 2538 ถึง 19 กุมภาพันธ์ 2539
● "Meeting with the Chiang Mai People"
■ Foot Path at Moon Muang Road
▼ November 19, 1995 to February 19, 1996

26
เปียโต เปลลินี (อิตาลี)
โยลา บาร์เบสซ์ (เยอรมัน)
PIETRO PELLINI (ITALY)
YOLA BERBESZ (GERMANY)

P● "สังคมแห่งโลก"
■ บ้านส่วนตัว
เลขที่ 27/1 ถนนมูลเมือง ซอย 9
▼ 29–30 พฤศจิกายน 2538
เวลา 13:00 – 21:00 น.
★ ศิลปินทั้ง 2 ขอเชิญทุกท่านเข้าร่วมโครงงานนี้ โดยผู้ประสงค์จะเข้าร่วมขอให้นำภาพถ่ายของท่านขนาด 2" จำนวน 2 ใบ ไปด้วยตามวันและเวลาดังกล่าว
P● "Planetarian Society"
■ Private Residence
27/1 Moon Muang Rd., Soi 9
▼ November 29-30, 1995
1:00 p.m.- 9:30 p.m.
★ The artists invite all of you to join in this project. Please take 2 photographs of yourself (2 inches) with you at the scheduled time.

เชียงใหม่จัดวางสังคม ๑ - ๑

INTERNATIONAL CONTEMPORARY TEMPLE FAIR

อี.ที.

● "อี.ที."
(แลกเปลี่ยนความคิด)
■ 1. ตลาดต้นลำไย
2. ห้องแสดง
เลขที่ 27/1 ถ.มูลเมือง ซอย 9
▼ 1. 19–23 พฤศจิกายน และ 29 พฤศจิกายน – 3 ธันวาคม 2538
2. 19 พฤศจิกายน – 3 ธันวาคม 2538
เวลา 15:00 น. – 19:00 น.

ผู้ร่วมโครงการ "อี.ที."
ออล์เกิร์ลส์ (เยอรมัน) : โดโรที เอซเลอร์ ไทเกอร์ สแตงล์, เบตตี สตูร์เมอร์ เมอร์เซเดส บาร์รอส (บราซิล) : อีเลียต บาโรวิตส์ (อเมริกา) : อิงเกอ บรอสกา (เยอรมัน) : โอฮุอิ ซา (เกาหลีใต้) วอลเตอร์ ดาห์น (เยอรมัน) : ฟีลิกซ์ ดรอส์ คลอเดีย กรูนิค (เยอรมัน) : โนริโตชิ ฮิรากาวา (ญี่ปุ่น) : ฮูโก้ คักมัน (เนเธอร์แลนด์) คริสตีด ไครเกอโรสกี้ (เยอรมัน) : เจอร์เก้น ไคสเปล (เยอรมัน) เจอร์เก้น คลอเก (เยอรมัน) : รูธ คเนชท์ (เยอรมัน) : เจ โคห์ (เนรเทศจากสิงคโปร์) มาร์จา โคลู (ฟิน–แลนด์) : เฟอร์นาโด โมเลเรส (สเปน) : เอส.เอ็ม.อาร์ โมทาเมดี (อิหร่าน) : มาชิโกะ โอกาวา (ญี่ปุ่น) โฮวาร์ดีนา พินเดลล์ (อเมริกา) : เอ็ดดี้ ราเมยันโต (อินโดนีเซีย) : โร.คา.วิ (ฮังการี) ; ริตต้า รอน์คคู (ฟินแลนด์) เคาส์ สตาเอก (เยอรมัน) : ฮันส์–เยอร์ก เทาร์เชอร์ (เยอรมัน) : โทเนล (คิวบา) มาเรียนน์ ทราลาว์ (เยอรมัน) : นอร์เบิร์ต วิลลิ่ง (เยอรมัน) : เจียง จุน ซี (จีน) มหาโมดา ยาสซิน (เนรเทศจากอิริเทีย) ยายัก ยัทมากา (เนรเทศจากอินโดนีเซีย) และ อาเด็ม ยิลมาซ์ (ตุรกี)

ประสานงานโดย
เจ โคห์ (เนรเทศจากสิงคโปร์)

E.T.

● "E.T."
(Exchanging Thoug
■ 1. Ton Lam-Yai Market
2. Showroom :
27/1 Moonmuang Rd., So
▼ 1. November 19-23 and November 29 - December 3,
2. November 19, 1995 to December 3,1995
3:00 p.m. - 7:00 p.m.

PARTICIPANTS FOR "E.
ALLIGIRLS (GERMANY) : DORA ETZLER, TIGER STANGL AND BE STÜRMER ; MERCEDES BARI (BRAZIL) ; ELLIOTT BAROWITZ (U INGE BROSKA (GERMANY) ; OUHI (SOUTH KOREA) ; WALTER D (GERMANY) ; FELEX DROESE (C MANY) ; LISA FROMARTZ (USA.) ; G (EXILE FROM KURDISTAN) ; CLA GRÜNIG (GERMANY) ; NORITO HIRAKAWA (JAPAN) ; HUGO KAAG (NETHERLANDS) ; CHRIST KRIEGEROWSKI (GERMANY) ; JÜR KIERSPEL (GERMANY) ; JÜR KLAUKE (GERMANY) ; RUTH KNE (GERMANY) ; JAY KOH (EXILE F SINGAPORE) ; MARJA KOLU (FINL FERNANDO MOLERES (SPAIN) ; S. MOTAMEDI (IRAN) ; MACHIKO OG (JAPAN) ; HOWARDENA PINDELL (U EDDIE RAMEYANTO (INDONESIA) KA. WI. (HUNGARY) ; RIITTA RÖN (FINLAND) ; KLAUS STAECK (MANY) ; HANSJÖRG TAUCHERT (MANY) ; TONEL (CUBA) ; MARIA TRALAU (GERMANY) ; NORBERT W ING (GERMANY) ; JIAN JUN XI (CH MAHAMODA YASSIN (EXILE F ERITREA) ; YAYAK YATMAKA (E FROM INDONESIA) AND ADEM YIL (TURKEY)

COORDINATED BY
JAY KOH (EXILE FROM SINGAP

47
(อินโดนีเซีย)
(INDONESIA)

อกไม้ที่ตัดผ่านกัน"
านอเนกประสงค์ ประตูท่าแพ
สานป่าแดง
ดวงโมงค์
มกราคม 2539
ลา 5:30 น. เป็นต้นไป
มกราคม 2539
ลา 12:00 น. เป็นต้นไป
มกราคม 2539
ลา 17:00 น. เป็นต้นไป
tersection Flower"
ha-Pae Gate
-Daeng Cemetery
-Mong Temple
anuary 1, 1996
5:30 a.m. onwards
anuary 2, 1996
12:00 a.m. onwards
anuary 3, 1996
5:00 p.m. onwards

48
ซเลอร์ คุยซอน (ฟิลิปปินส์)
R CUIZON (PHILIPPINES)

ทอง บายัน"
าหารเพื่อสังคม)
านอเนกประสงค์ ประตูท่าแพ
ดวงโมงค์
สานป่าแดง
พฤศจิกายน 2538 : 18:30 น.
พฤศจิกายน 2538 : 11:00 น.
พฤศจิกายน 2538 : 11:00 น.
TONG BAYAN"
OOD FOR SOCIETY)
ha-Pae Gate
-Mong Temple
-Daeng Cemetery
ovember 19, 1995
6:30 p.m. onwards
ovember 20, 1995

49
กิตติ บุญมี (ไทย)
KITTI BOONMEE (THAILAND)

P● "กีตาร์กับดอกไม้ในแจกัน"
■ ลานอเนกประสงค์ ประตูท่าแพ
▼ 19 พฤศจิกายน 2538
เวลา 23:00–ตลอดคืน (ภาคหนึ่ง)
1 มกราคม 2539
เวลา 23:00 น.–ตลอดคืน (ภาคสอง)
P● "Guitar and Flower in a Vase"
■ Tha-Pae Gate
▼ November 19, 1995
at 11:00 p.m.- all night (Part I)
January 1, 1996
at 11:00 p.m. - all night (Part II)

50
ราเชล เจน ฟลาวเวอร์ (อังกฤษ)
บาร์บารา ดิคคินสัน (อเมริกา)
นฤมล ธรรมพฤกษา (ไทย)
ธีระวัฒน์ มุลวิไล (ไทย)
RACHEL JANE FLOWER (ENGLAND)
BARBARA DICKINSON (USA.)
NARUMOL THAMMAPRUKSA (THAILAND)
TEERAWAT MULVILAI (THAILAND)

P● "อิสรภาพ"
■ 1. ลานอเนกประสงค์ ประตูท่าแพ
2. โบสถ์มหาวิทยาลัยพายัพ
3. ศาลาธรรม มหาวิทยาลัยเชียงใหม่
4. ไนท์บาซาร์
5. ลานอเนกประสงค์ ประตูท่าแพ
▼ 1. 19 พฤศจิกายน 2538 : 16:00–17:00 น.
2. 24 พฤศจิกายน 2538 : 17:00–18:00 น.
3. 30 พฤศจิกายน 2538 : 17:00–18:00 น.
4. 7 ธันวาคม 2538 : 21:30–22:30 น.
5. 5 มกราคม 2539 : เที่ยงคืน
P● "FREEDOM"
■ 1. Tha-Pae Gate
2. Chapel at Payap University
3. Sala Dhamma Hall, CMU.
4. Night Bazaar
5. Tha-Pae Gate
▼ 1. November 19, 1995
at 4:00 p.m.-5:00 p.m.
2. November 24, 1995
at 5:00 p.m.-6:00 p.m.
3. November 30, 1995

51
วันเอก จันทรทิพย์ (ไทย)
WANEAK JUNTARATIP (THAILAND)

P● "เกย์"
■ ลานอเนกประสงค์ ประตูท่าแพ
▼ 19–21 พฤศจิกายน 2538
P● "Gay"
■ Tha-Pae Gate
▼ November 19-21, 1995

52
วัลลภ แม่นยำ (ไทย)
WALLOP MANYUM (THAILAND)

P● "ควาย–ควาย"
■ ลานอเนกประสงค์ ประตูท่าแพ
▼ 21 พฤศจิกายน 2538
เวลา 10:30 น. – 11.00 น.
P● "Baffalo-Baffalo"
■ Tha-Pae Gate
▼ November 21, 1995
at 10:30 a.m.-11:00 a.m.

53
มาเซล เคาวสฮาล (เยอรมัน)
MARCEL KRAUSHAAR (GERMANY)

P● "HATHAYOGA"
■ ลานอเนกประสงค์ ประตูท่าแพ
▼ 21 พฤศจิกายน 2538
เวลา 10:00 น. – 10:30 น.
P● "HATHAYOGA"
■ Tha-Pae Gate
▼ November 21, 1995
at 10:00 a.m.-10:30 a.m.

54
ดอริส เคาวสฮาล (ออสเตรีย)
DORIS KRAUSHAAR (AUSTRIA)

P● "Kasperltheater"
■ ลานอเนกประสงค์ ประตูท่าแพ
▼ 3, 10, 17 ธันวาคม 2538 และ 14, 21 มกราคม 2539 : 15:00 น.
P● "สันติภาพบนโลก"
■ ลานอเนกประสงค์ ประตูท่าแพ
▼ 17 ธันวาคม 2538
● "อำนาจของผู้ชาย"
■ ศูนย์สรรพสินค้าเชียงอินทร์พลาซ่า (ทางเท้าด้านหลังอาคาร)
▼ 19 พฤศจิกายน –11 ธันวาคม 2538
P● "Kasperltheater"
■ Tha-Pae Gate
▼ December 3, 10, and 17, 1995 and January 14 and 21, 1996 ; 3:00 p.m.
P● "Peach on Earth"
■ Tha-Pae Gate
▼ December 17, 1995

55
โฆษิต จันทรทิพย์ (ไทย)
KOSIT JUNTARATIP (THAILAND)

● "ด้วยรักและหลอกฟัน"
■ ลานอเนกประสงค์ ประตูท่าแพ
▼ 19–23 พฤศจิกายน 2538
● "ด้วยรักและหลอกฟัน"
■ Tha-Pae Gate
▼ November 19-23, 1995

56
ไพศาล เปลี่ยนบางช้าง (ไทย)
PAISAN PLIENBANGCHANG (THAILAND)

● "กระดูกชิ้นสุดท้าย"
■ ลานอเนกประสงค์ ประตูท่าแพ
▼ 19–27 พฤศจิกายน 2538
● "The Last Bone"
■ Tha-Pae Gate
▼ November 19 - 27, 1995

57
ศุภชัย ศาสตร์สาระ (ไทย)
SUPACHAI SATSARA (THAILAND)

● "พรรค (ชม.)จส."
■ ลานอเนกประสงค์ ประตูท่าแพ
▼ 19 พฤศจิกายน 2538 ถึง 19 กุมภาพันธ์ 2539
● "(CM.)Sl. Party"
■ Tha-Pae Gate
▼ November 19, 1995 to February 19, 1996

58
นพดล ธีรธราดล (ไทย)
NOPPADOL TIRATARADOL (THAILAND)

● "แกะดำกับแกะขาว"
■ บริเวณลานอเนกประสงค์ ประตูท่าแพ
▼ 19 พฤศจิกายน 2538 ถึง 19 กุมภาพันธ์ 2539
● "Black Sheep White Sheep"

59
อินกริด เอช คลาวเซอร์ (อิตาลี)
INGRID H. KLAUSER (ITALY)

● "หนทางศิลปะ"
■ คูเมืองด้านทิศตะวันออกของประตูท่าแพ
▼ 19 พฤศจิกายน 2538 ถึง 19 กุมภาพันธ์ 2539
● "Resource Art"
■ City moat at the north side of Tha-Pae Gate
▼ November 19, 1995 to February 19, 1996

60
โยฮัน วาเกินนาร์ (เนเธอร์แลนด์)
JOHAN WAGENAAR (NETHERLANDS)

● "ความน่าละอายที่ดูสดใส"
■ บริเวณรอบๆ ประตูท่าแพ
▼ 15 ธันวาคม 2538 ถึง 19 กุมภาพันธ์ 2539
● "Flowering Shame"
■ Area around Tha-Pae Gate
▼ December 15, 1995 - February 19, 1996

61
มารี ซีรัส (เดนมาร์ค)
MARI ZIRAS (DENMARK)

● "ไม่มีชื่อ"
■ ด้านหน้าตลาดและศูนย์อาหารทั่วจังหวัดเชียงใหม่
▼ 19 ธันวาคม 2538 – 19 กุมภาพันธ์ 2539
● "Untitled"
■ Entrance to all meat markets and food centres of Chiang Mai
▼ December 19, 1995 to February 19, 1996

62
อุทิศ อติมานะ (ไทย)
UTHIT ATIMANA (THAILAND)

● "ซีเกมส์คือศิลปะ"
■ สนามกีฬา 700 ปี
▼ 9–17 ธันวาคม 2538

ศูนย์ข้อมูล "เชียงใหม่จัดวางสังค
"CHIANG MAI SOCIAL INSTALLATION"
INFORMATION CENTER

■ หอศิลป์ปิ่นมาลา
มหาวิทยาลัยเชียงใหม่
▼ 19 พฤศจิกายน 2538 ถึง 19 กุมภาพันธ์ 2539
★ สถานที่จัดแสดงข้อมูลทั้งหมด ภาพถ่าย วีดีทัศน์ สิ่งพิมพ์ ฯ เกี่ยวกับกิจกรรมที่ผ่านมาของ "เชียงใหม่จัดวางสังคม"
■ Pinmala Art Gallery C.M.
▼ November 19, 1995 - February 19
(Official date and Time)
★ Location for the exhibition o the information concerning t past activities of the project "Chiang Mai Social Installati such as ; photographs, V.D.C printed matters, etc.

เทศกาลภาพยนตร์ญี่ปุ่น 1995
ด้วยความร่วมมือจาก
มูลนิธิญี่ปุ่นและมหาวิทยาลัยเชียงใ
JAPANESE FILM FESTIVAL 1995
Cooperated by
The Japan Foundation and Chiang Mai Unive

● ภาพยนตร์ยอดเยี่ยมจำนวน 16 เรื่อง มีผู้กำกับของ โชเฮ อิมามูระ เค คุ และ คาเนโตะ
■ ห้อง HB 5200 คณะมนุษยศาสตร์ มหาวิทยาลัยเชียงใหม่
▼ 19–26 พฤศจิกายน 2538
★ เข้าชมฟรี
ขอทราบรายละเอียดเพิ่มเติมพร้อมกำ ได้ที่ คณะมนุษยศาสตร์ มหาวิทยาลัย โทร. (053) 221699 ต่อ 3288 พร้อมรับสูจิบัตร (แจกในช่วงเทศกาล
● 16 Excellent films
Shohei Imamura, Kei Kumai and Kanet
■ HB 5200 Faculty of Humanities, C
▼ November 19-26, 1995
★ Admission Free
Detailed information and film sch can be obtained at the Faculty of Humanities, C.M.U. A Catalogue will be distributed during th

หมายเหตุ NOTE
● ชื่อผลงาน TITLE
■ สถานที่ SITE SPEC
▼ วัน, เวลา DATE AND

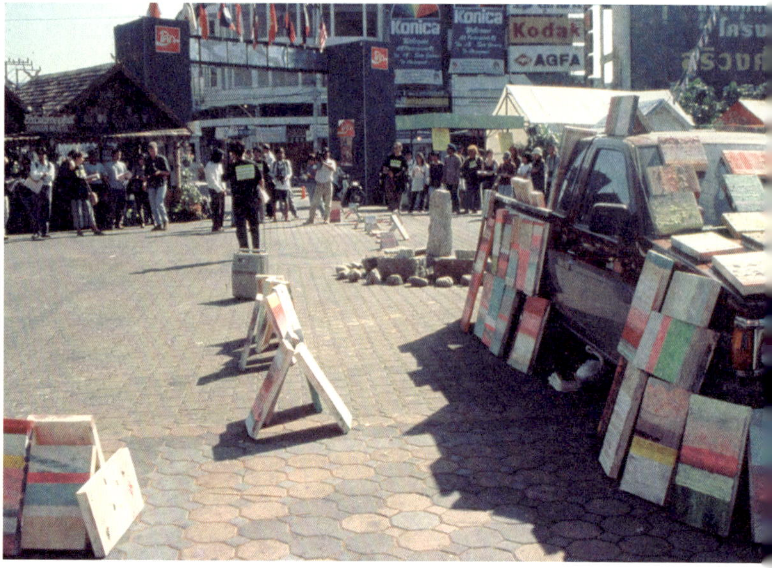

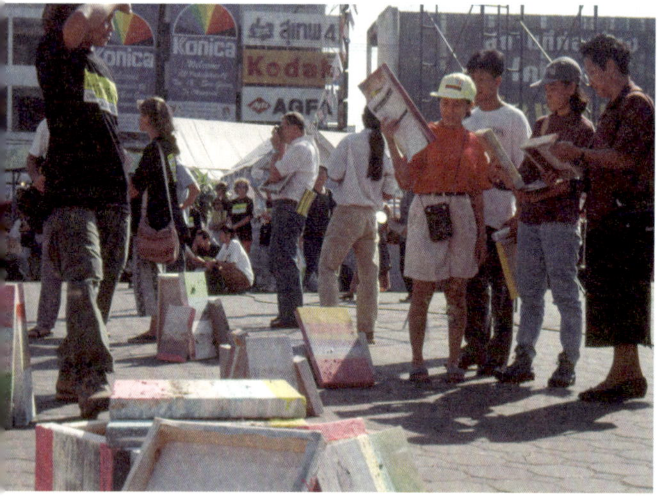

Work by Mit Jai Inn, Tha Pae Gate. As described by David Johnson in *Metro* magazine (c.1995): 'The opening morning at Tha-Pae Gate set the tone. A pick-up truck was covered in small, textured, abstract canvases by Mit Jai Inn, who was handing out 1000 originals for free, defying the perception of art as purely a saleable commodity. "Artists have the ability to make people think", he says. "And if used in the right way art can have a beneficial impact on society."' Ray Langenbach wrote at the time: '[W]e were forced to focus on our desire to acquire these works: a reflection of the emotional tenor of the art market. After a little time had passed, a rumour began to float around that the stretched canvas of the paintings had been used to wrap the bodies of eight dead men, whom Mit had collected from a Bangkok morgue and had cremated. The story goes that he then asked a monk to step on the canvas and say prayers for the men. The canvas at that point would presumably become an artefact of a holy event. He then reputedly used the canvas for the paintings, terminating the process by giving them away.'

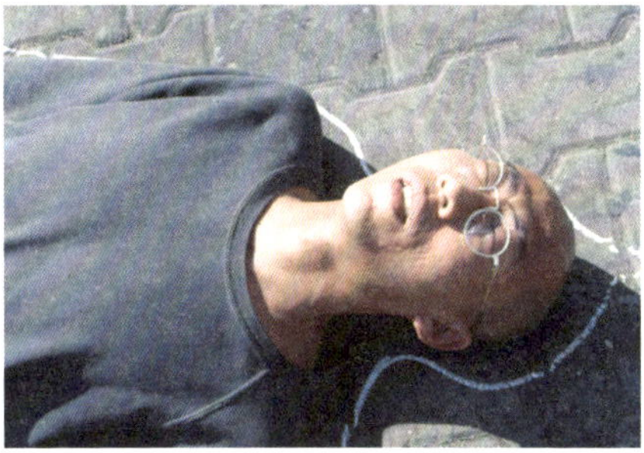

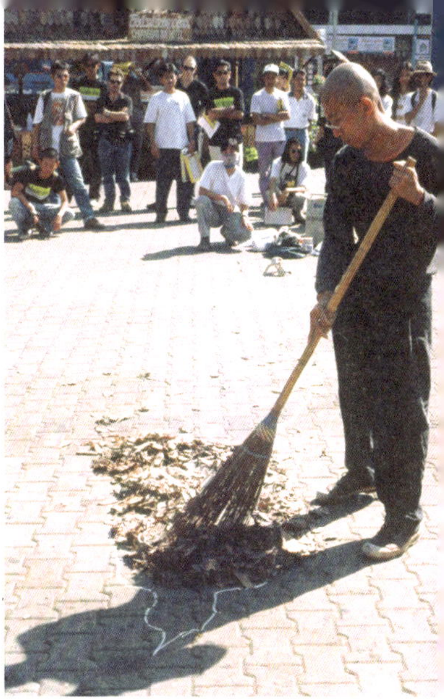

Lee Wen, *Neo-Baba*. 'Singaporean Lee Wen swept around Tha Pae Gate, chanting "Neo-Baba, you're already dead". Three times he died and was re-born. Each time, his co-performer outlined him in chalk and did the dance of death over his face with a skeleton puppet. Then Lee got up, covered the spot with leaves and lay down again. Finally, he laid seeds and funeral flowers over the body shapes, sat on the street and chewed gum. "The death doesn't only represent that of Singaporean culture", he says. "It's more about the universal death of freedom"' (*Metro*, c.1995).

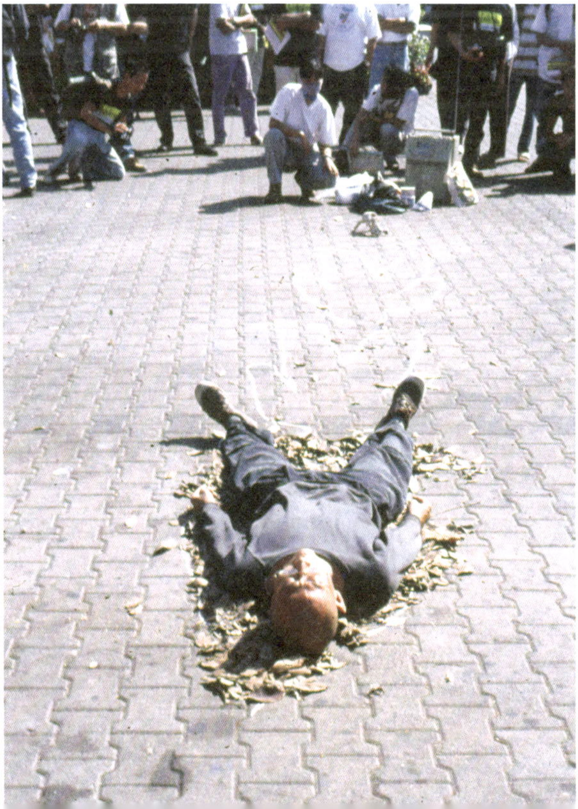

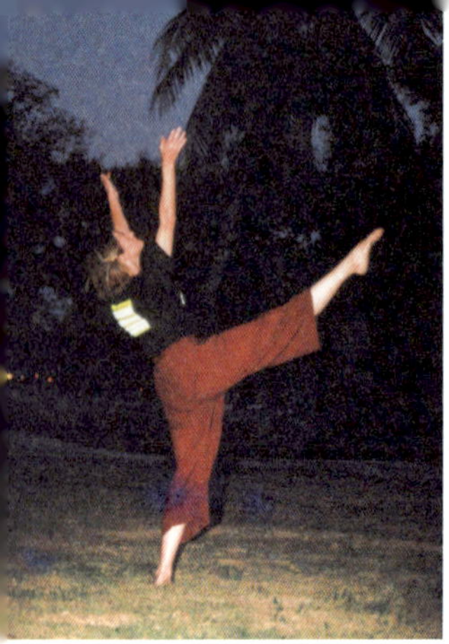

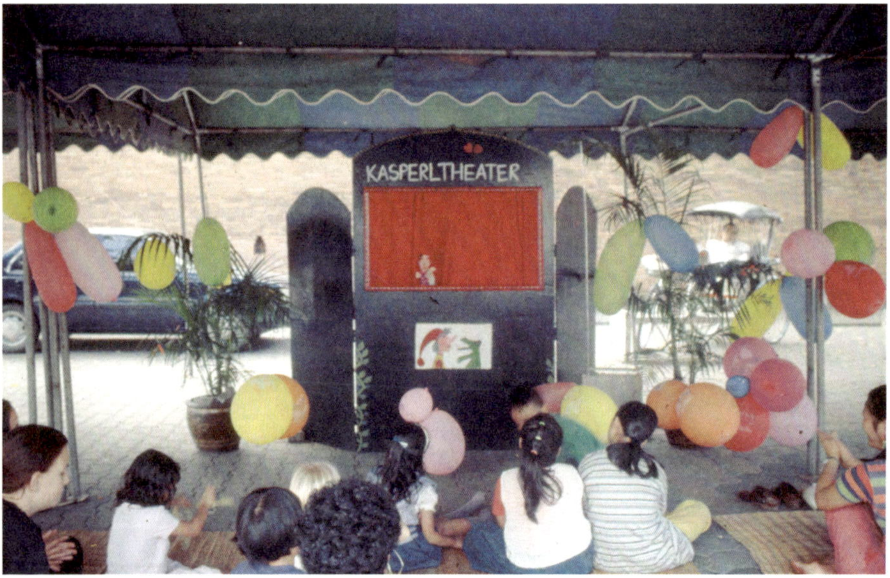

Doris Kraushaar, *Kasperltheater*.

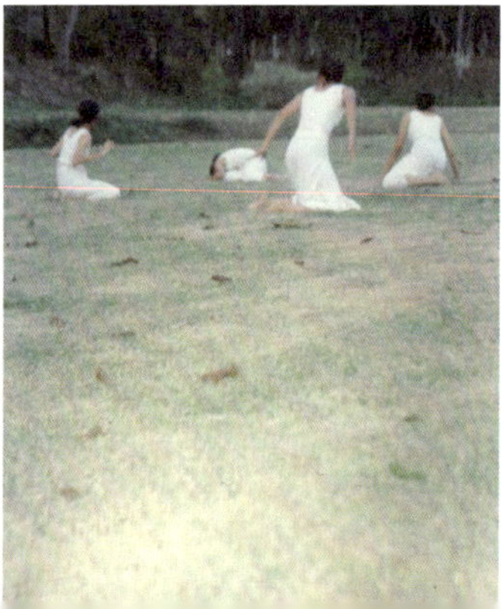

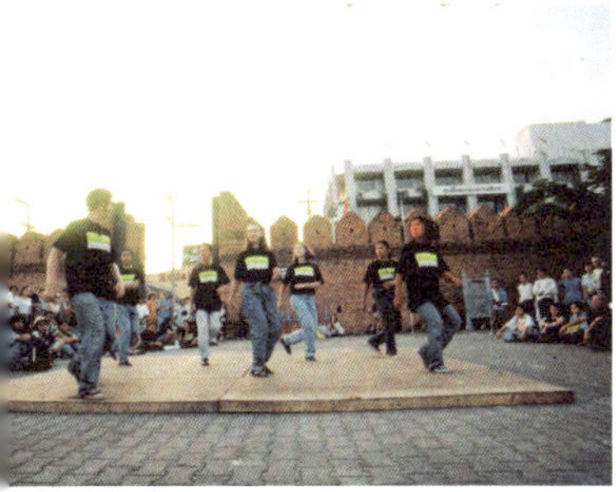

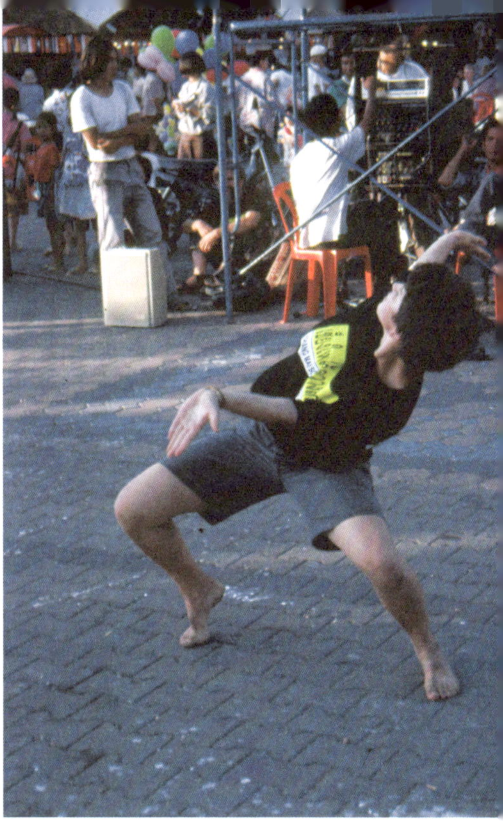

Performances at Tha Pae Gate and Chiang Mai University.

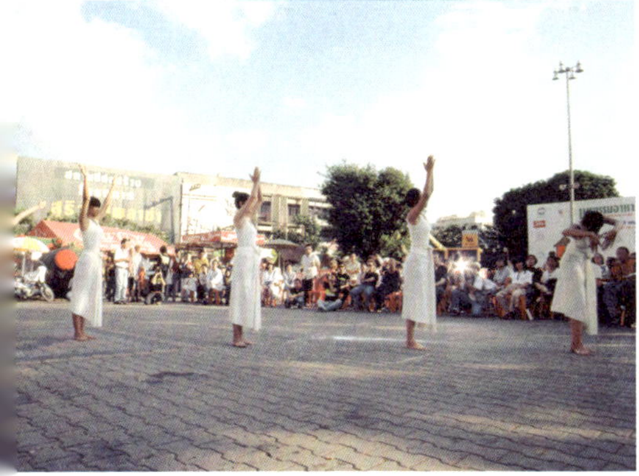

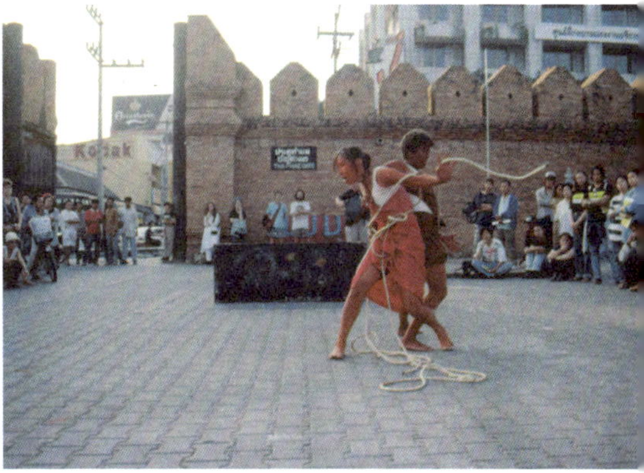

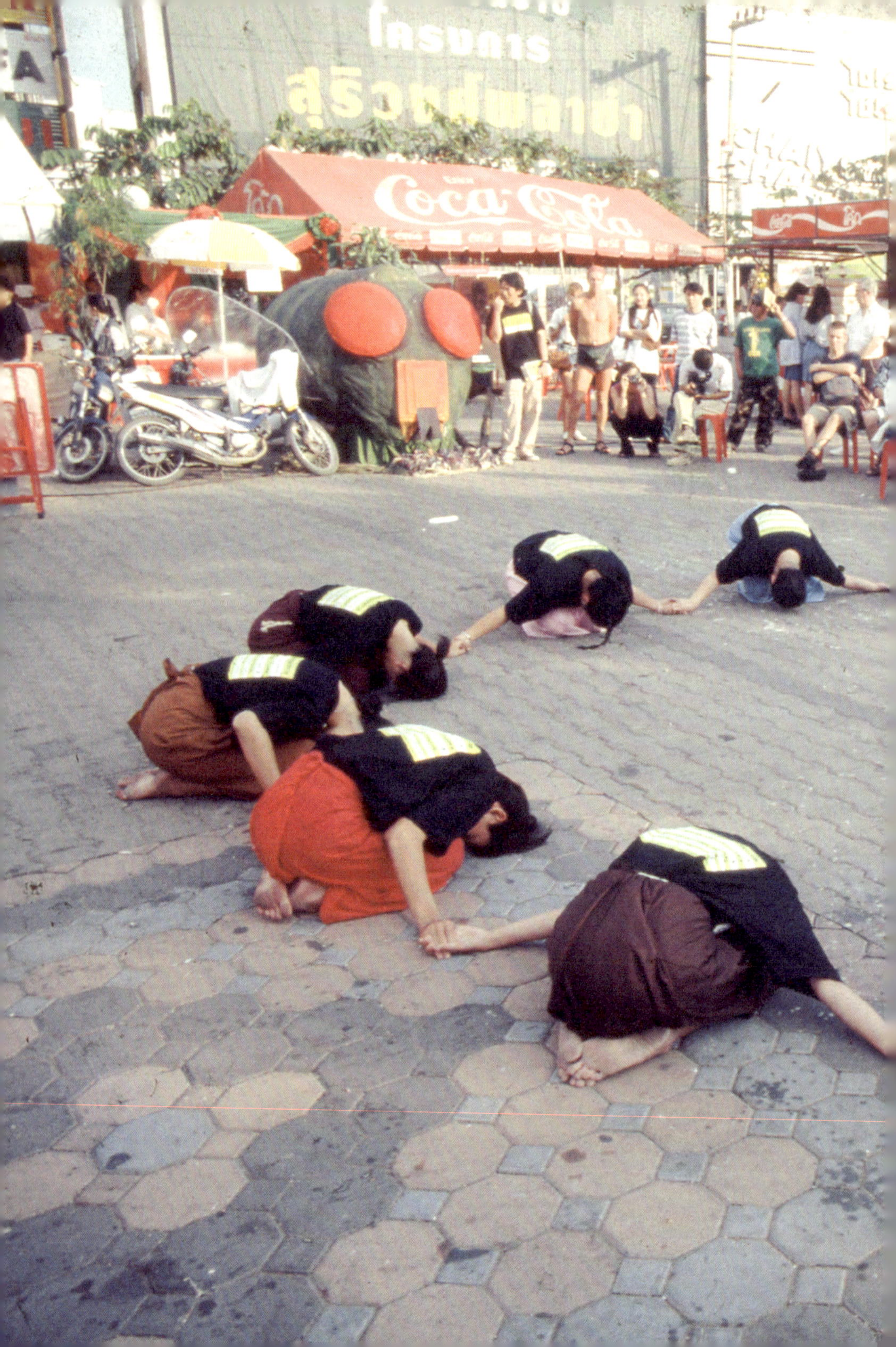
โครงการ
Coca-Cola

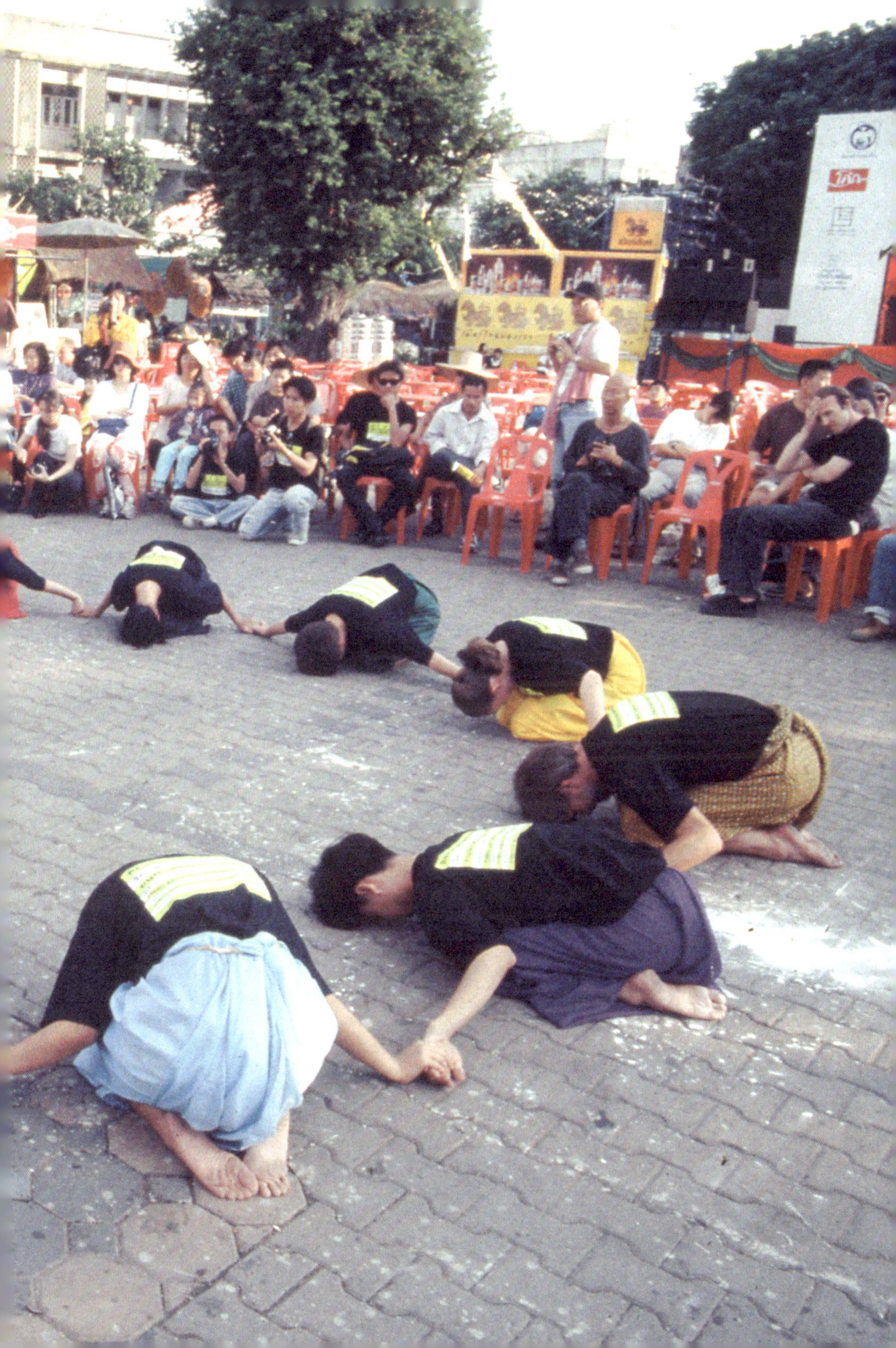

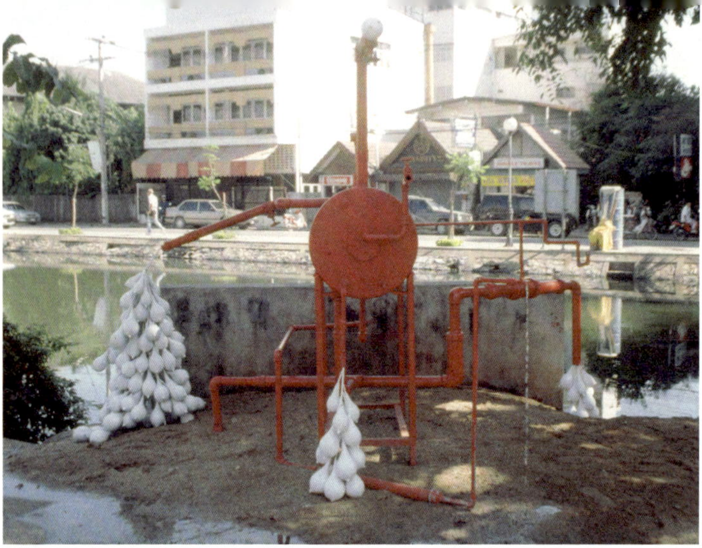

Untitled work by
Suttisak Phutararak.

Navin Rawanchaikul
acting as a guide for
visitors and participants.

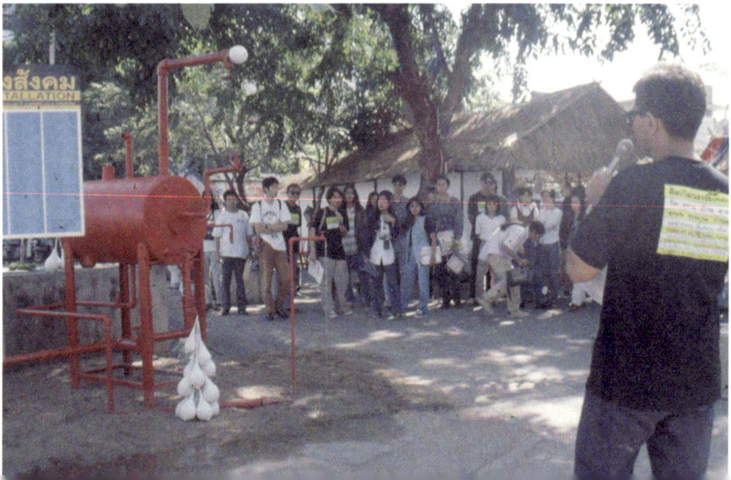

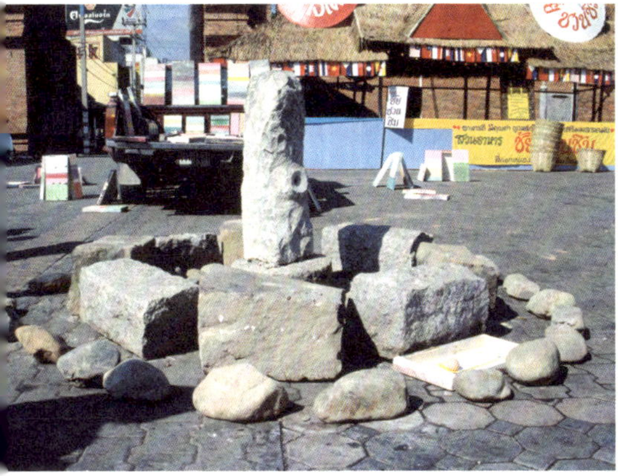

Ekachai Luadsoongnern,
Khai Nai Hin, Tha Pae Gate.

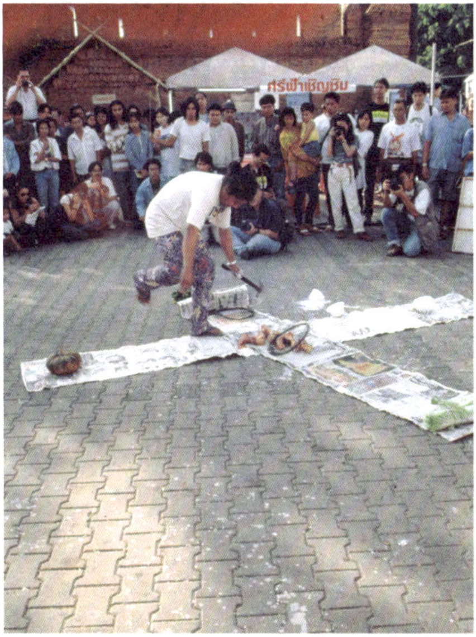

Performances at Tha Pae Gate: Paisan Plienbangchang, *THE LAST BONE* and Wunlop Manyam, *Buffalo, Buffalo* (above and left); and Ingrid H. Klauser's *Resource Art* (below).

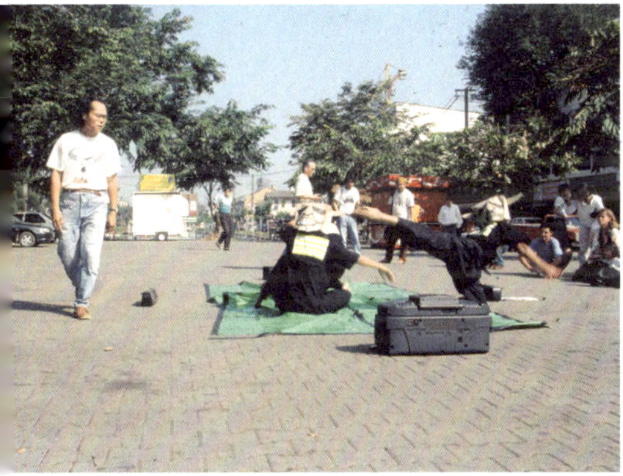

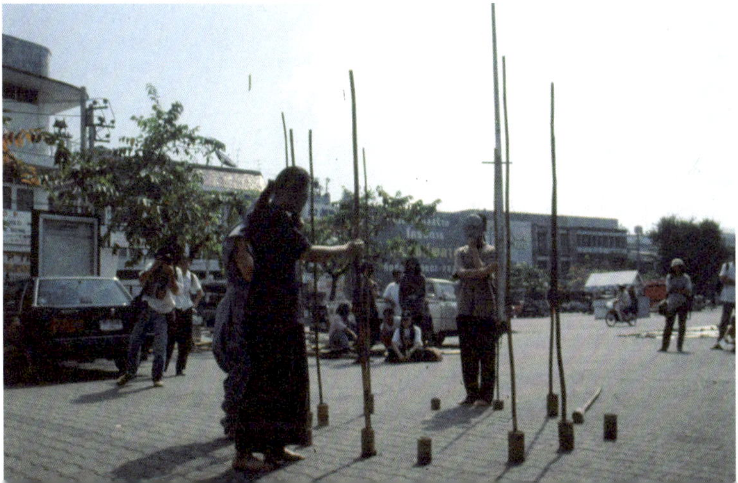

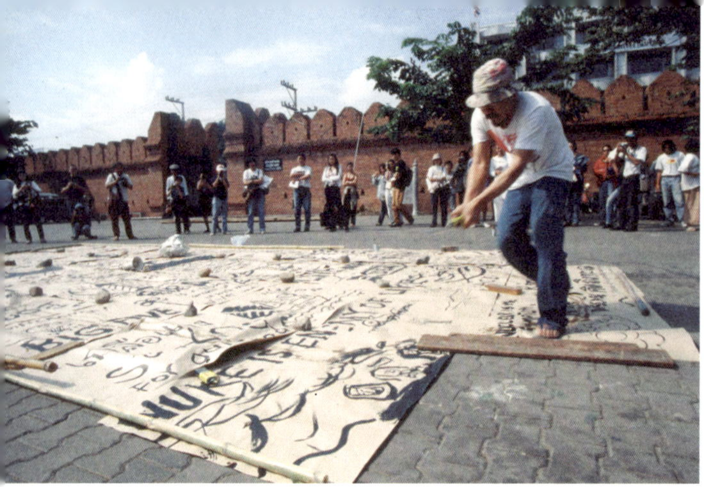

Vasan Sitthiket, *The Thai Smile*.

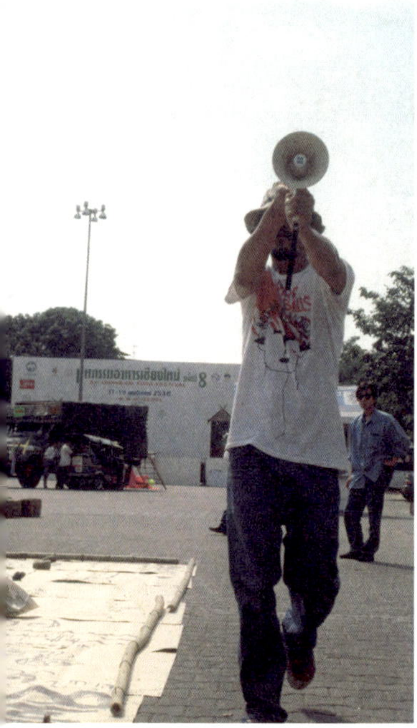

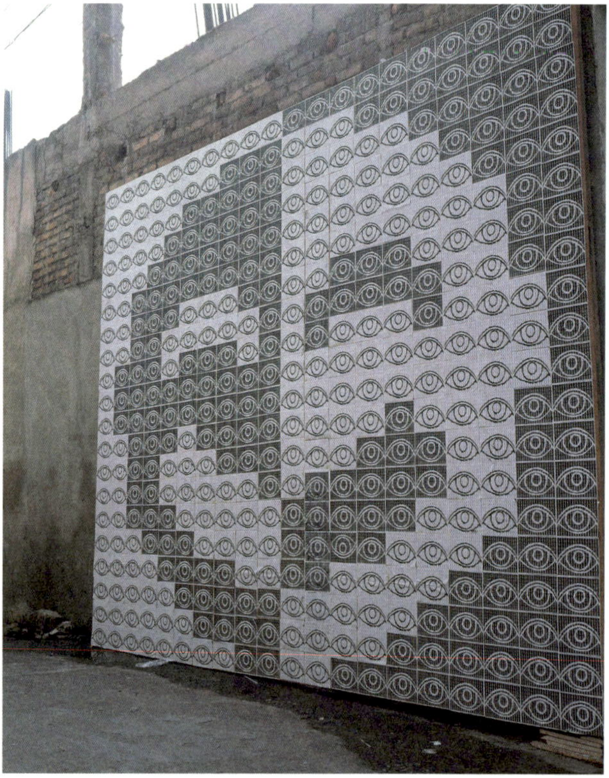

Tan Chin Kuan, *A Smile for Mr Politician*.

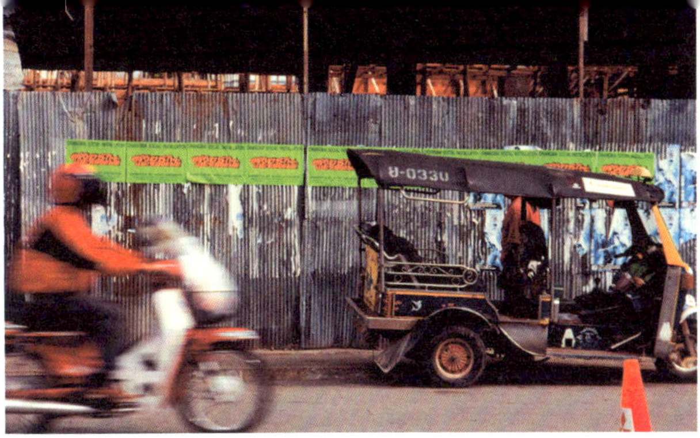

Posters promoting Kosit Juntaratip's *With Love, But Just the Sex.*

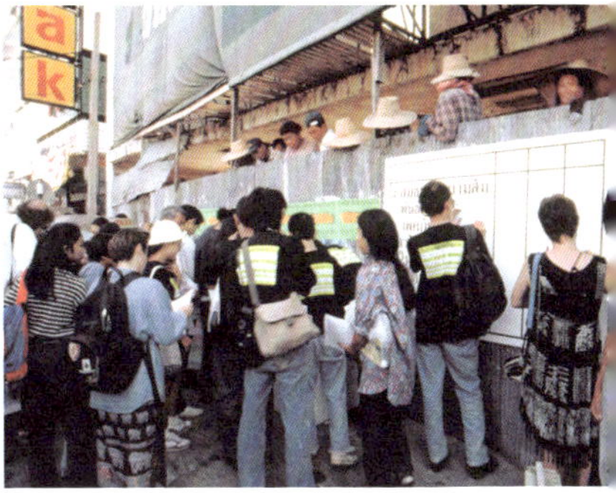

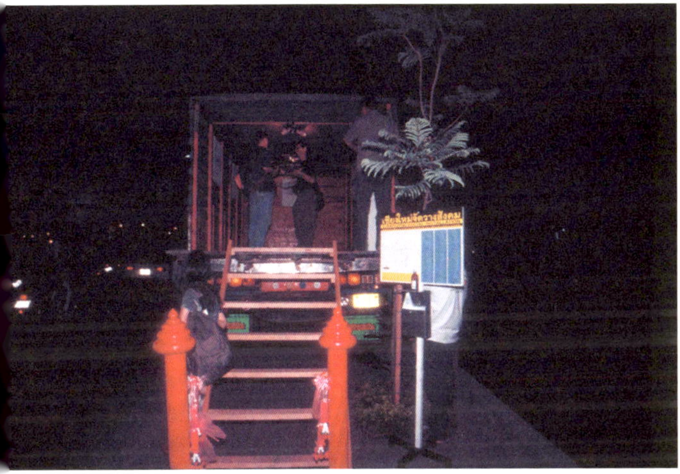

Kosit Juntaratip's *With Love, But Just the Sex.* As described by Khetsirin Knithichan and Phatarawadee Phataranawik in *The Nation* (4 December 1995): 'On the platform of a truck, the new-wave artist has hung five silk-screened canvases printed with cheeky phrases like: "mao lao sia lak, mao rak sia jai" ("too much whisky will make a person lose balance and too much love will yield sadness"), "rak mia luang, huang mia noi" ("there's love for the major wife, but a minor wife is worth possessing") and "rak luang khue ying, rakjing khue lao" ("deceitful love lies in women; the essence of true love is in whisky"). These popular sayings also appear as stickers on the exterior of [the] truck. In doing so, Kosit says he is satirizing the cultural elite who find it necessary to attend every art gallery and exhibition opening. Instead of inviting moneyed art patrons to preside over the opening ceremony of his installation, Kosit's brother and the truck owner hosted the affair. For refreshments, guests were served high-energy drinks [such as] M100, M150 and Red Bull – popular beverages among "working men" – instead [of] chilled glasses of Chablis. It's only too clear that Kosit, 25, believes art belongs to the general public, not high-society figures. "These phrases seem to promote the good side of male behaviour. For example, 'rak mia luang, huang mia noi' implies that a man can love both of his wives. But I believe every man wants to have sex with lots of women whether they love them or not."'

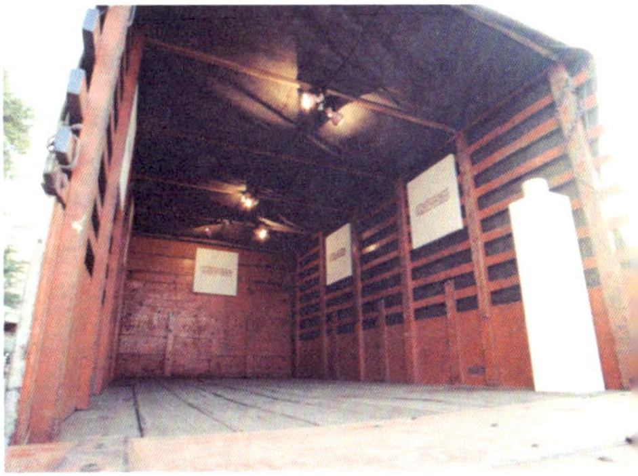

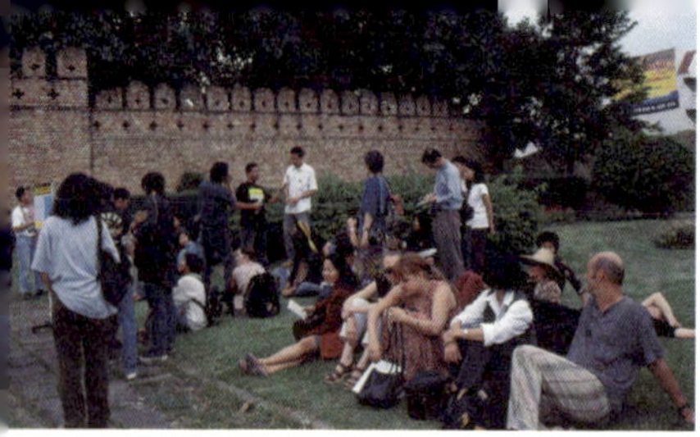

At Suan Dok Gate.

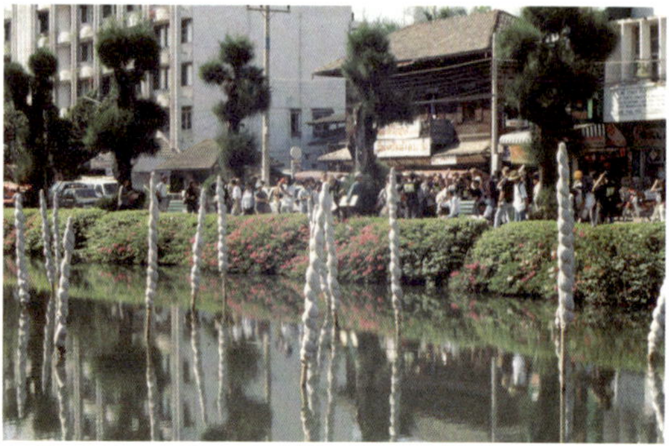

Ingrid H. Klauser, *Resource Art.*

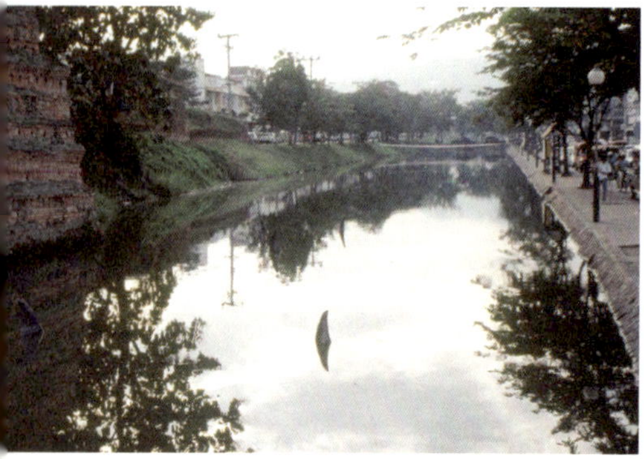

Work by Nopparat Chokchaichutikul.

Work by Akatsuki Harada.

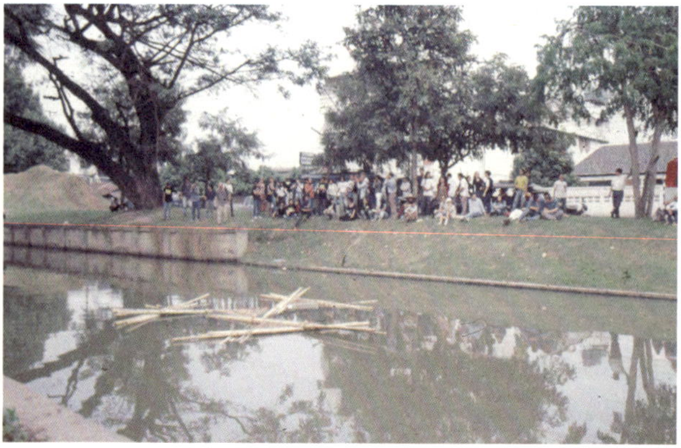

Kade Javanalikhikara,
Far is Near/Near is so Far.

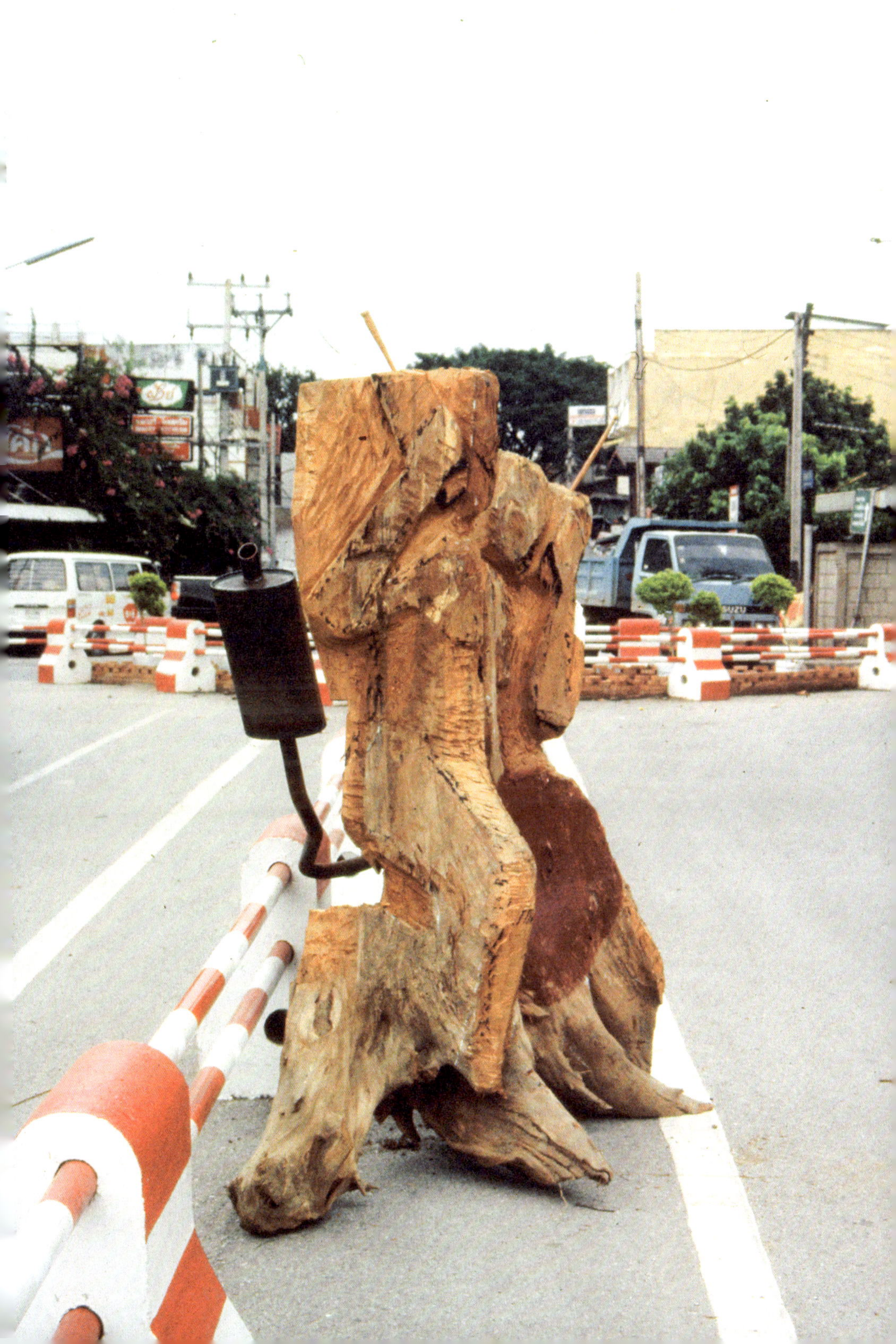

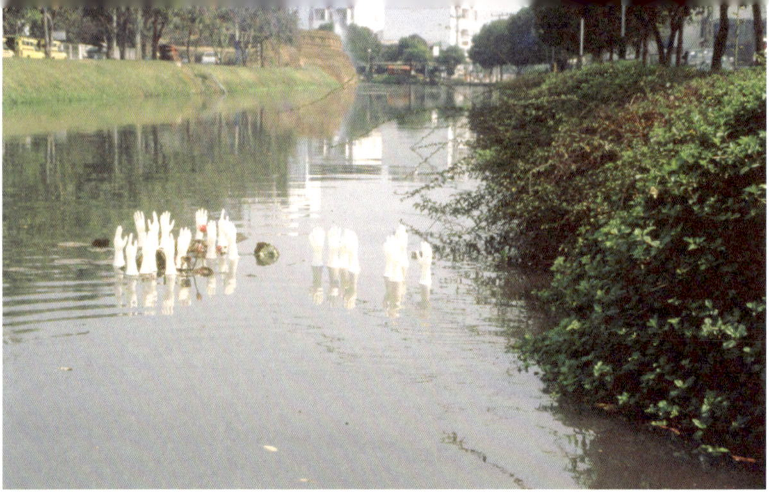

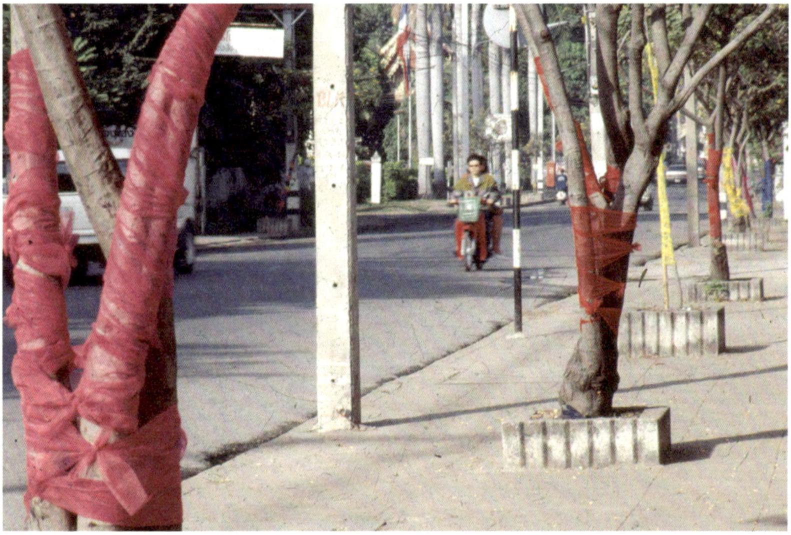

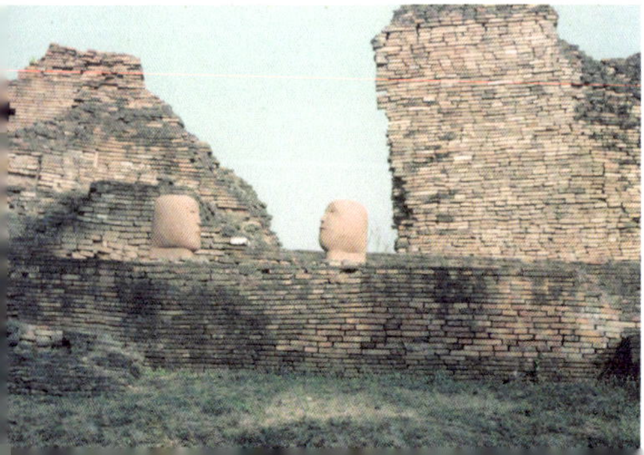

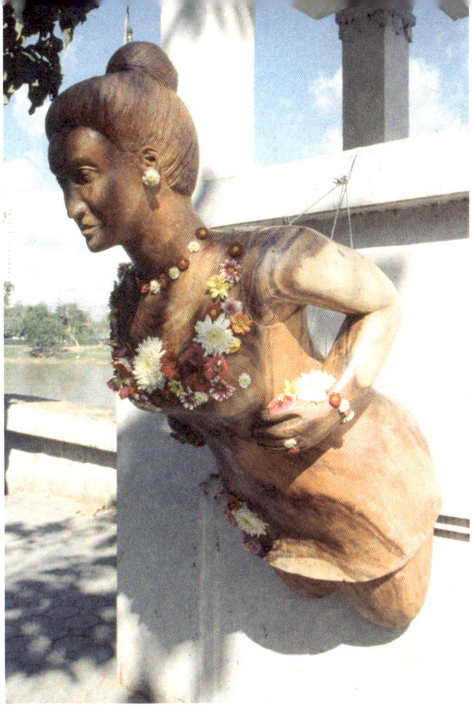

Yvonne Parent, *Figurehead*, Nawarat Bridge. '[T]his piece was made in homage to the protection these women of wood give to the world. Yvonne speaks of her work, telling me that many people have said, "I love your work, but it's just not true." Such is the forgotten strength of a figurehead, of a woman' (*Asiana*, February 1996).

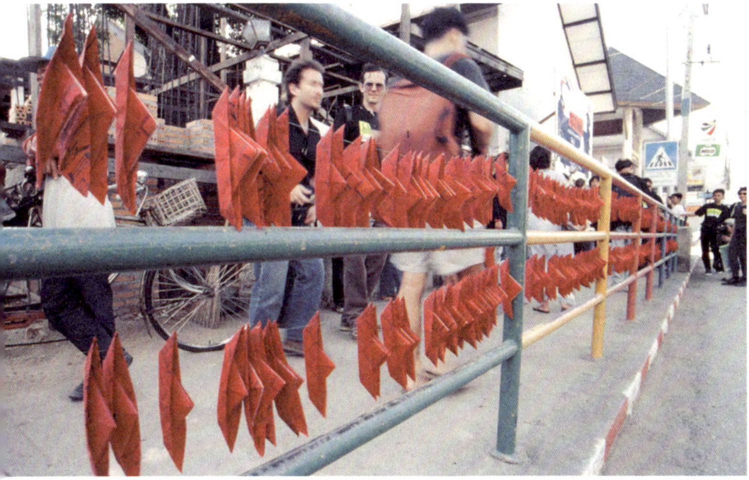

Eng Hwee Chu, *Culture for Sale*.

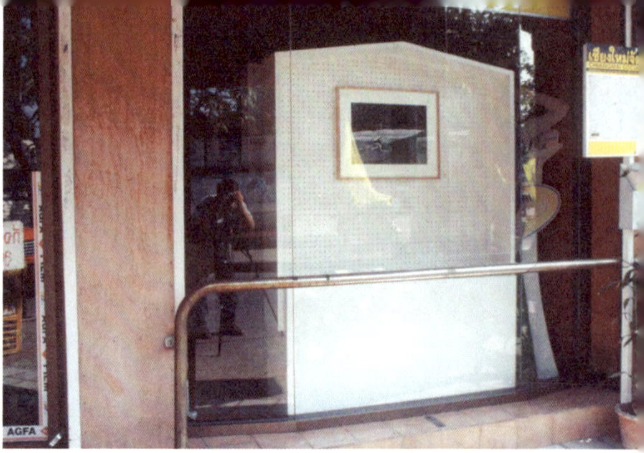

Yutaka Sone, *SCOOP*, Vichai Photolab.

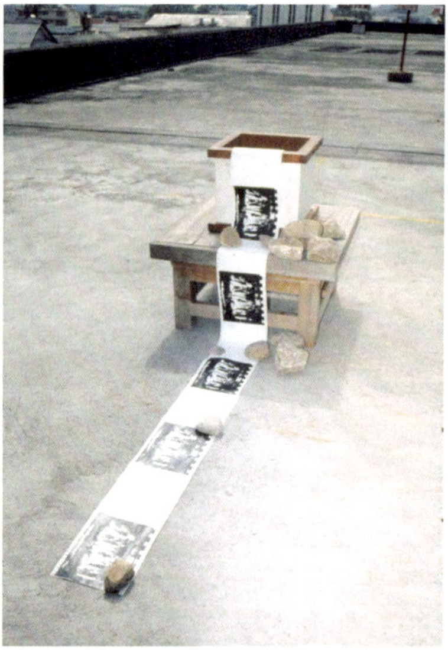

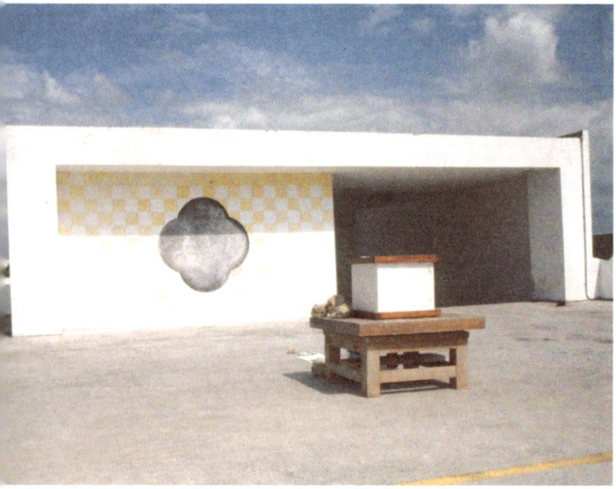

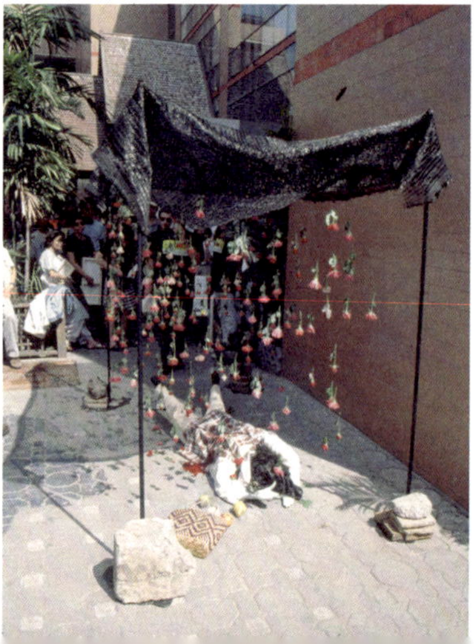

Doris Kraushaar, *Men Power*, Chiang Inn Plaza (right); Leen Emmerzael, *Three Places for Meditation*, on the roof of Chiang Inn Plaza (above).

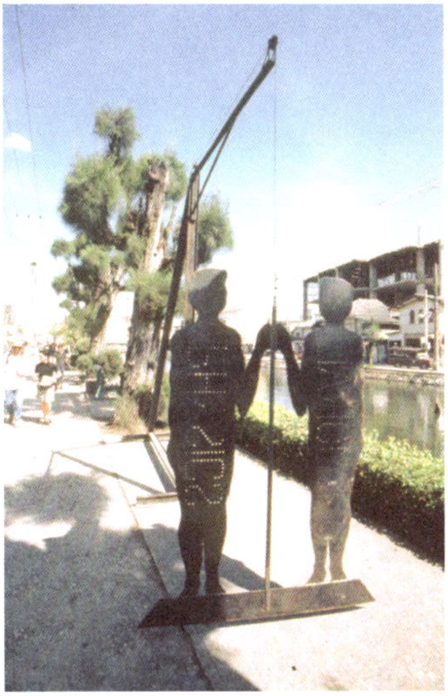

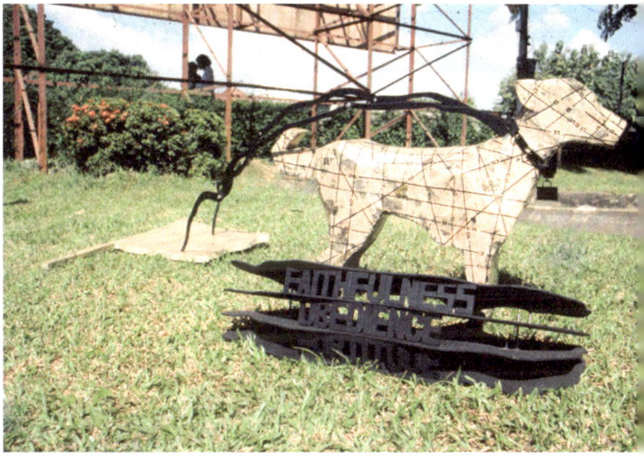

Various works including untitled work by Akatsuki Harada (left) and *I Was Arrested* by Komson Nookiew (above).

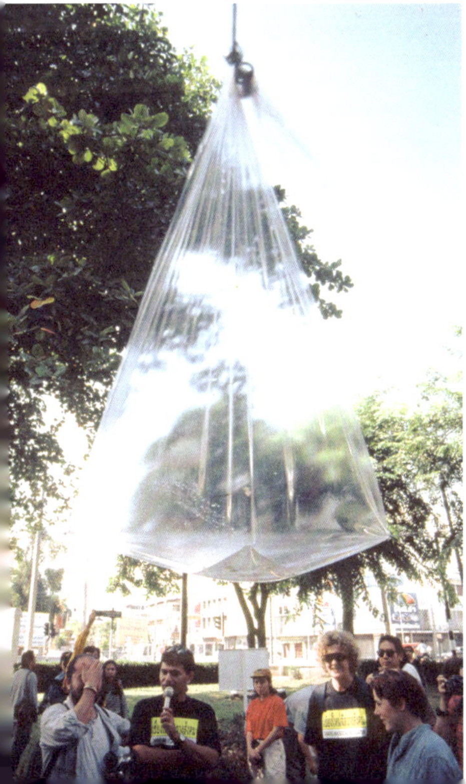

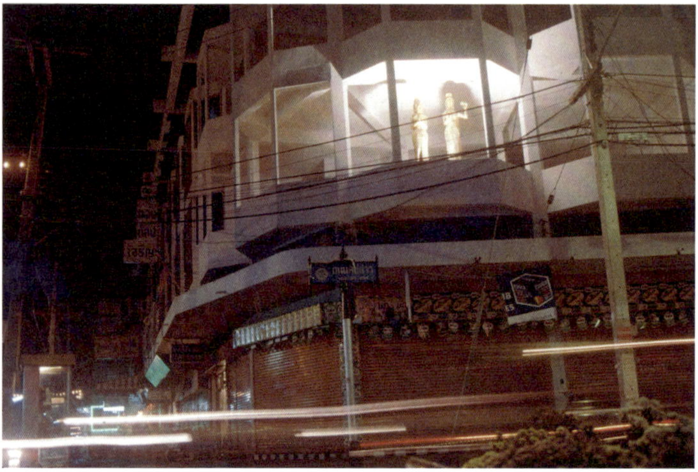

Works at Central Kad Suan Kaew department store.

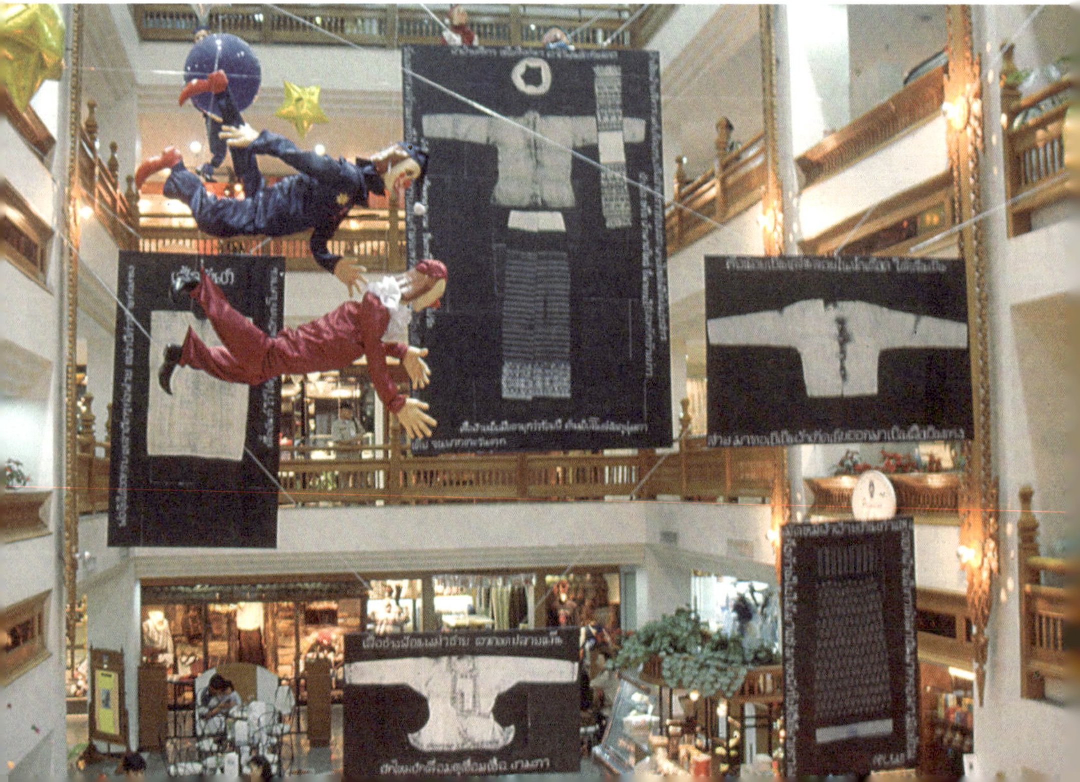

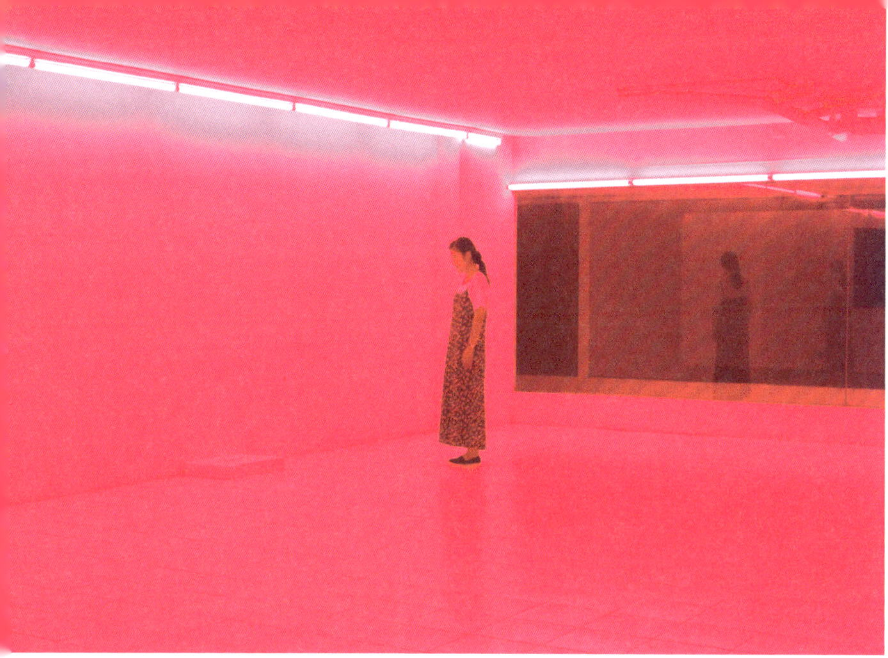

Satoshi Hirose, *Red Light*.

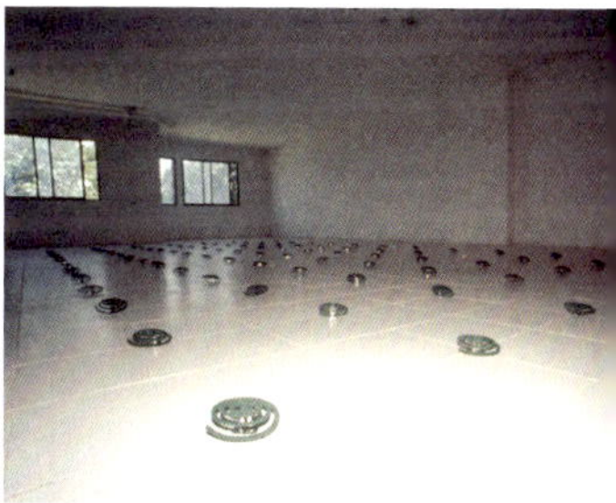

Toi Ungkavatanapong, *Domestic Abstraction*.

Masato Nakamura, *Front Side of the Back Side – Watch What's Showing*.

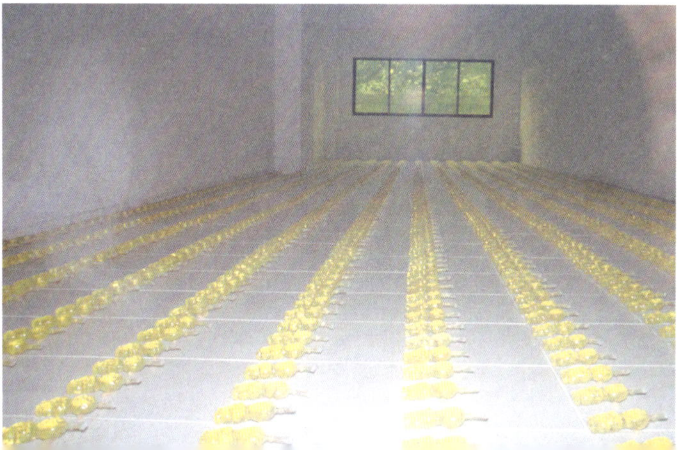

Tang Da Wu, *Meeting with the Chiang Mai People*, Moon Muang Road. 'Tang Da Wu placed wooden boards – similar to bus stops – in front of several shops. The work is entitled *Meeting With the Chiang Mai People* since the shop owners were asked to draw symbols on the boards representing products sold inside their shops. For example, a bowl of guay tiew (noodle soup) and a coffee cup appear on a board in front of a shop selling those items. "This idea came from my own direct experiences," said the artist. "Since I don't know any Thai, it's hard for me to ask local people where to buy something, even a newspaper. Language is the most important barrier. So I wanted to have a board indicating these items"' (*The Nation*, 4 December 1995).

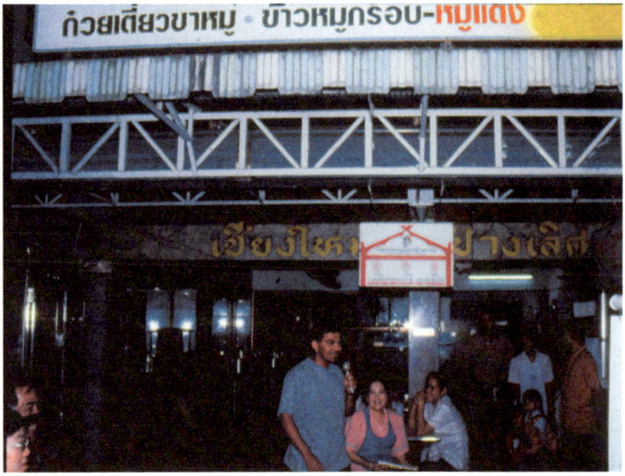

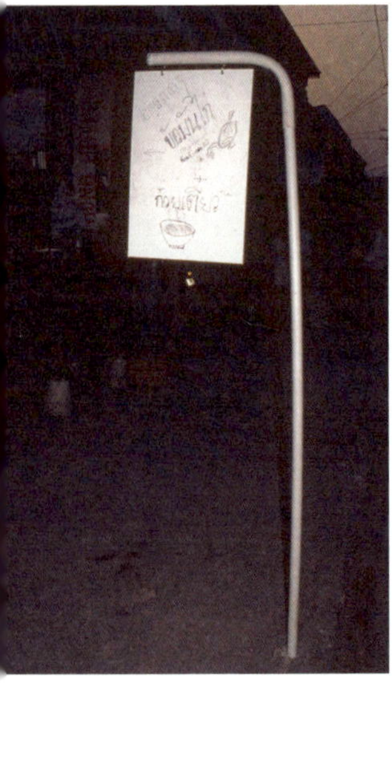

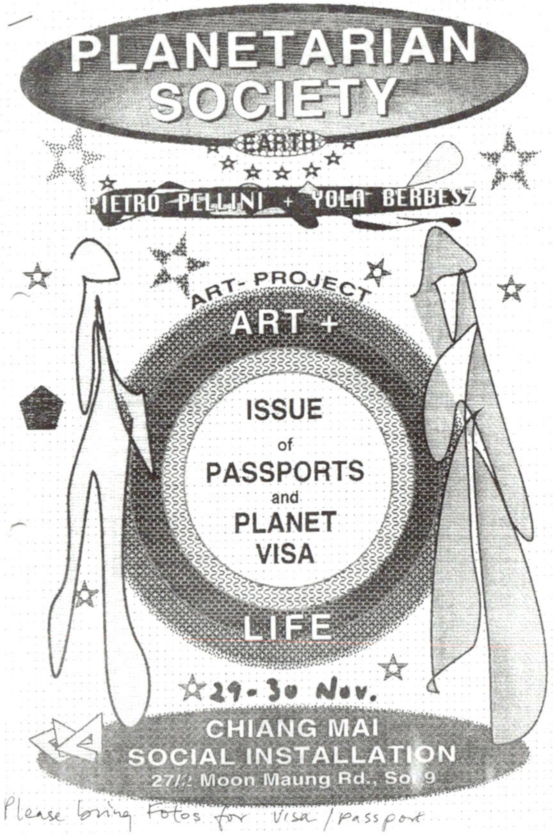

Poster for Pietro Pellini and Yola Berbesz, *Planetarian Society*.

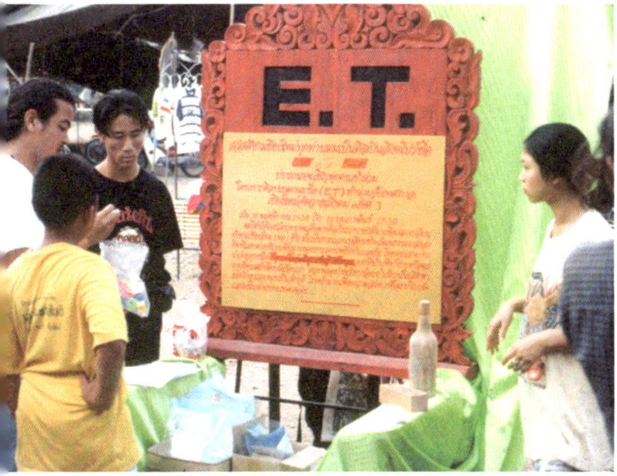

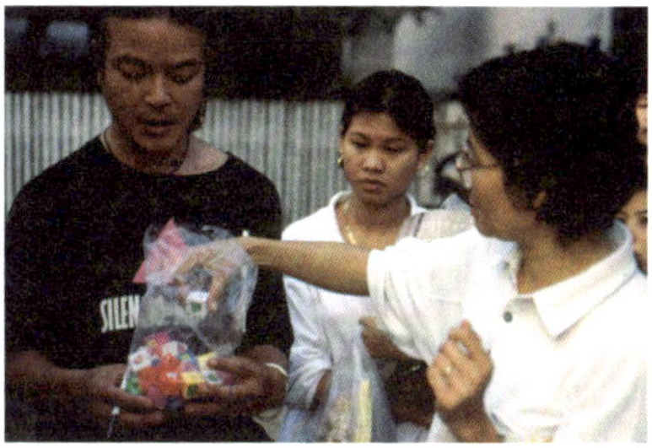

Jay Koh, *E.T. (Exchanging Thoughts)*. Koh brought objects from abroad to exchange with locals in markets around Chiang Mai.

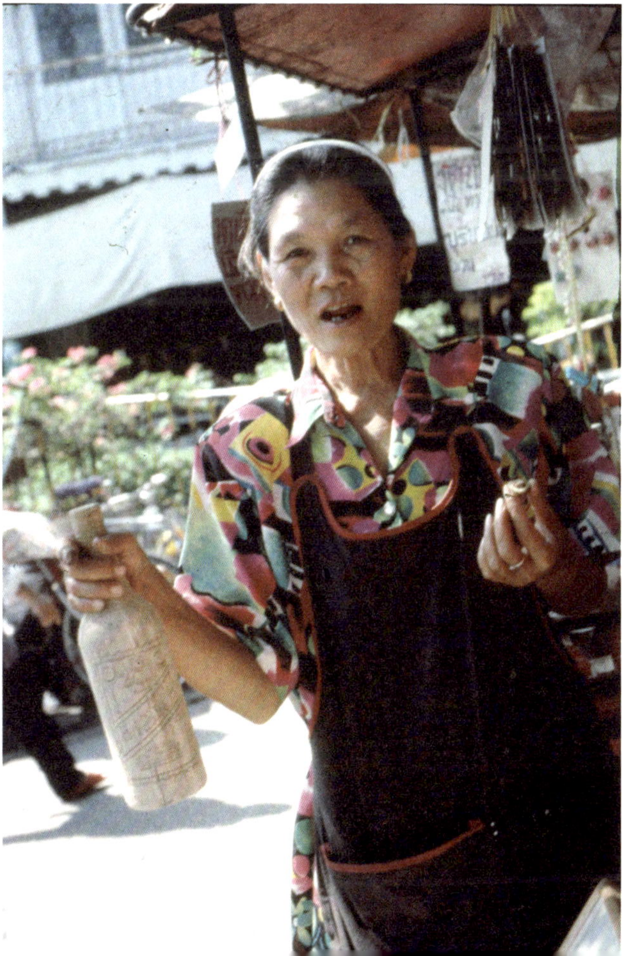

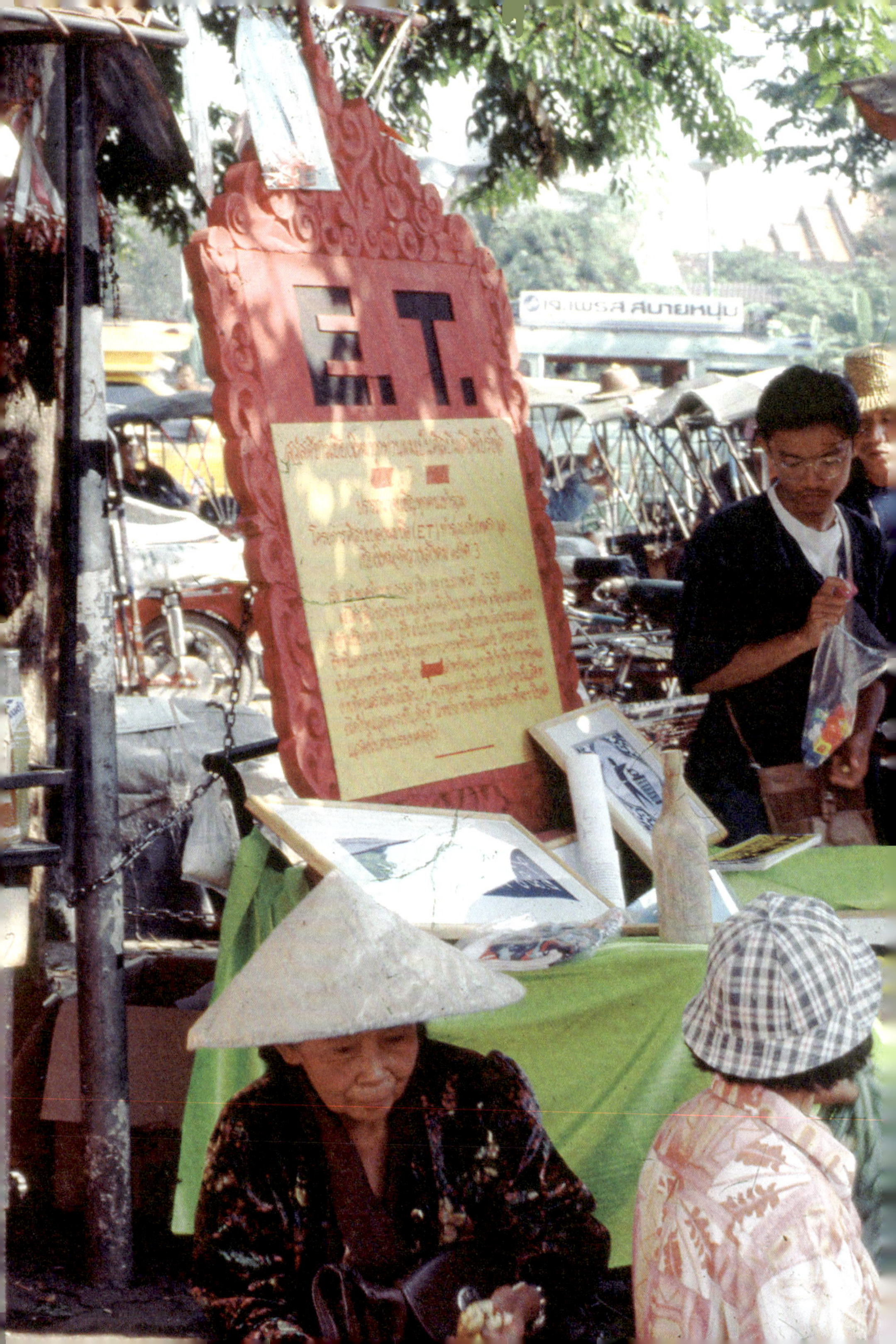
E.T.

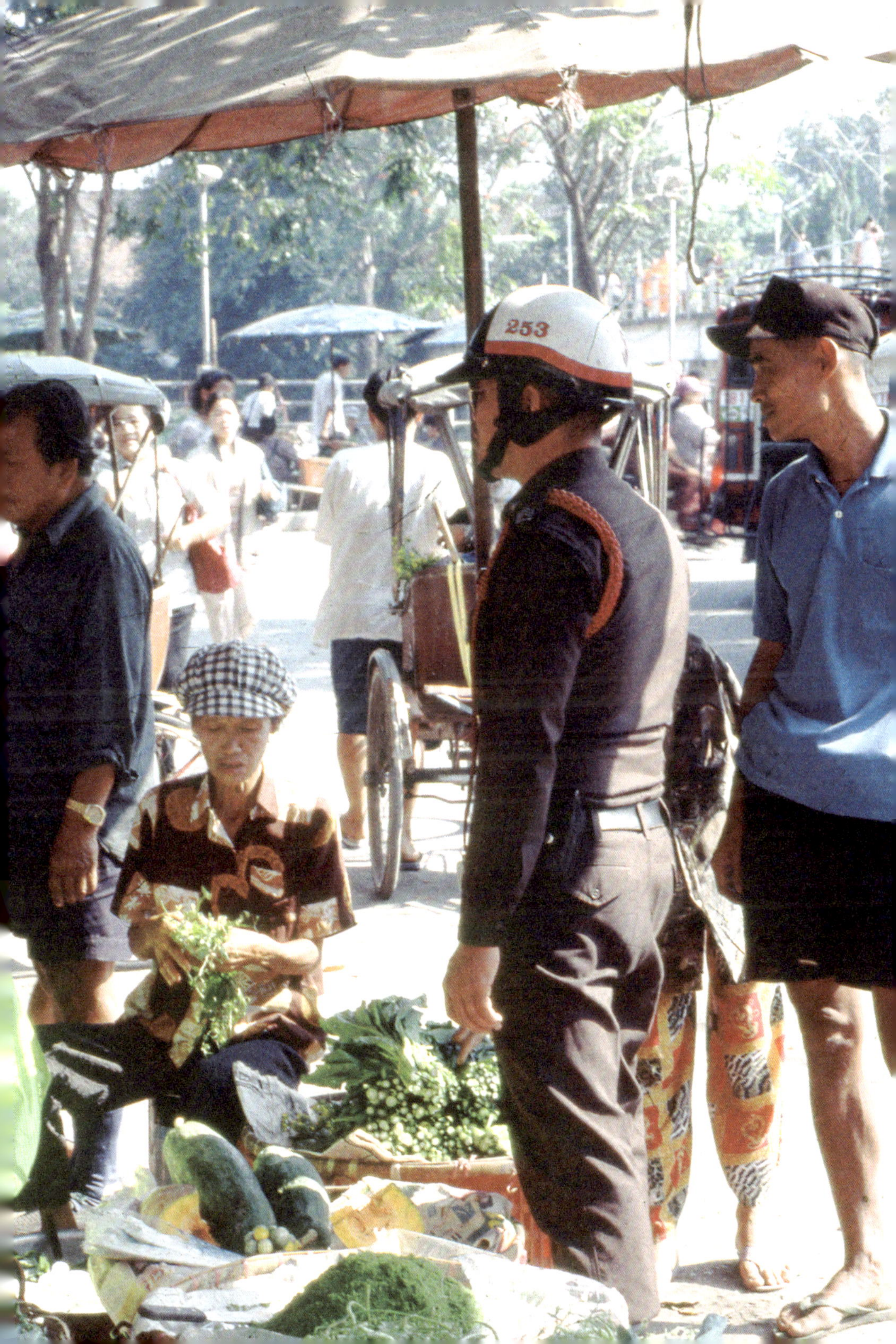
253

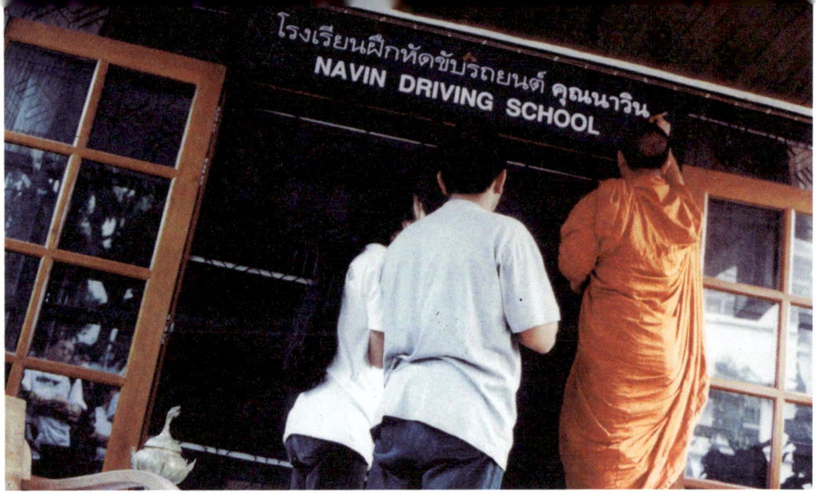

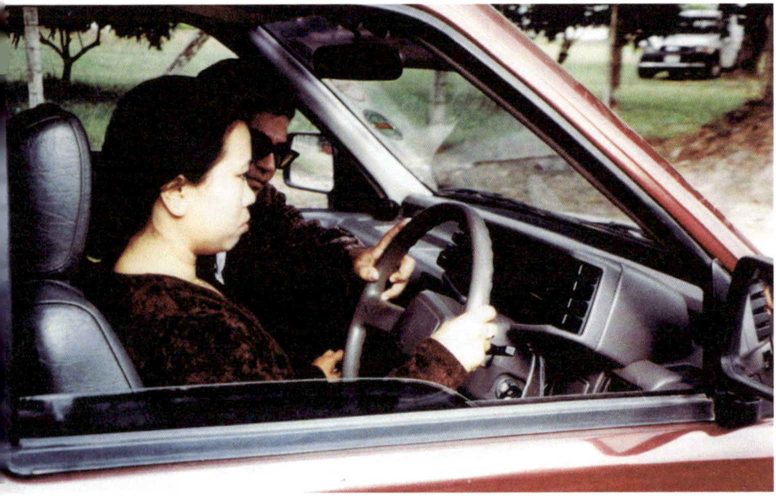

Navin Rawanchaikul 'opened a Driving School, for the purpose of "making better drivers," with the usual holy prayers by a monk said for the car and the office. The work was an explicitly non-art-art event, attended by what must have been the largest gathering of artists ever to see the opening of a driving school in the history of the world ... more than enough to transform any non-art event into high-art' (Ray Langenbach, c.1996). 'Is that art? "It's reality," explains Navin Rawanchaikul. "I'm just using a format for social, cultural expression that people can touch and experience, rather than a canvas"' (*Metro*, c.1995).

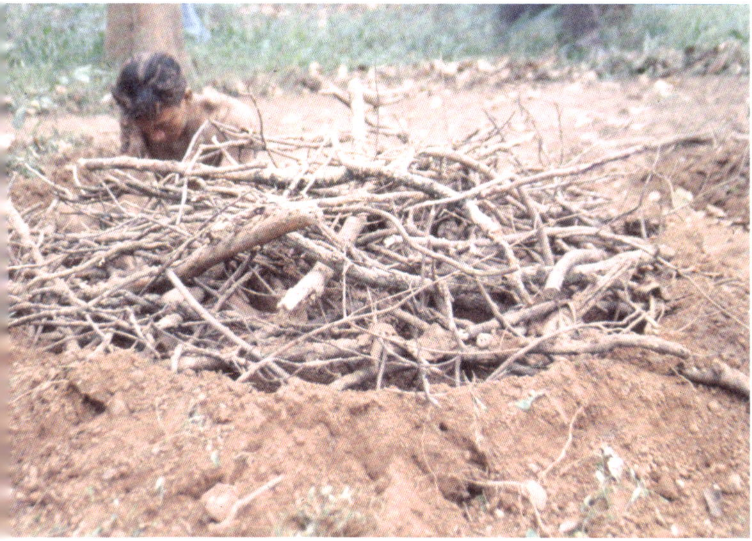

Performance by Tawatchai Homthong.

Maethee Srisuthasinee, *Consideration*. 'Maethee Srisuthasinee presented the circles of life by laying out seven circles of plaster-caste heads of decreasing size around the stupa. There was comedy at the opening as someone asked why there was the face of a head upside down in the final, smallest circle. "I didn't do it," he replied, "but I'll leave it there anyway!"' (*Waizine,* c.1995).

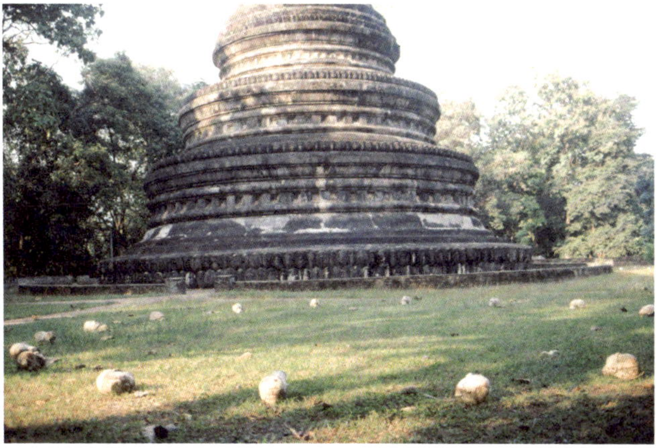

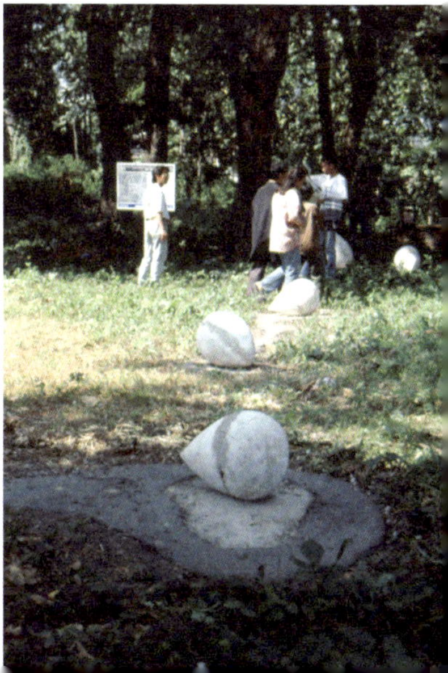

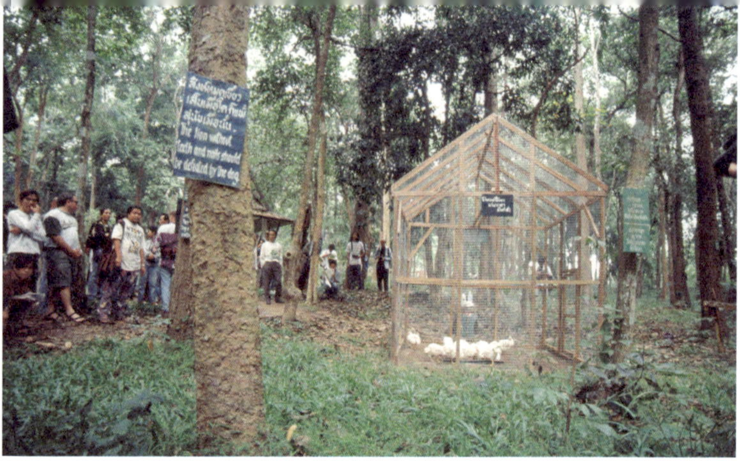

Vincent Leow Kong Yam, *Cock a Doodle Do*. 'A horrified crowd stood transfixed at Singaporean Vincent Leow Kong Yam's wire chicken hutch bearing the sign 'The Chickens are like the Teak trees in the forest'. He handed out green badges bearing the same message, whispering 'the Europeans are coming, the Americans are coming, the Asians are coming ... ', before pulling out an onlooker to hack through the sign and dig a hole to plant a tree. Then he produced a raw animal heart, sliced it up with an axe and fed it to the fowl. Monks in the audience were mesmerised when he seemed about to behead one of the chickens. Navin whispered to him please not to do it, so he handed the bird to him instead. The hutch, tree and chickens will remain until the end. Supplementing the deforestation reference, Vincent commented: 'It looks like us; the heart is the people,' adding: 'In Singapore, performance art is not recognised as an art form. You need an entertainment license to do it!' (*Metro*, c.1995).

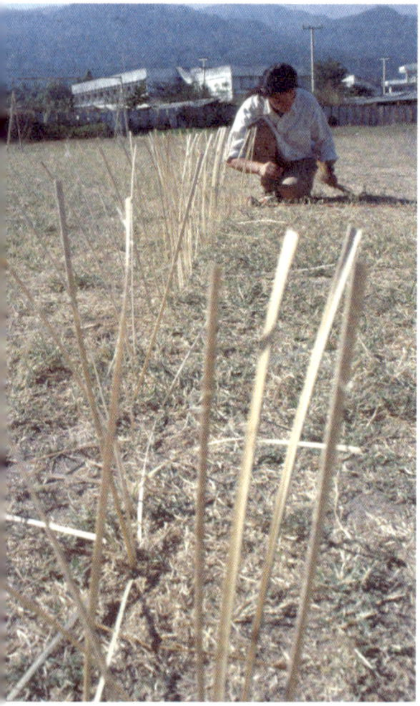

Tatsuo Inagaki performance at Faculty of Fine Arts, Chiang Mai University.

Chiang Mai University, which hosted a CMSI information centre.

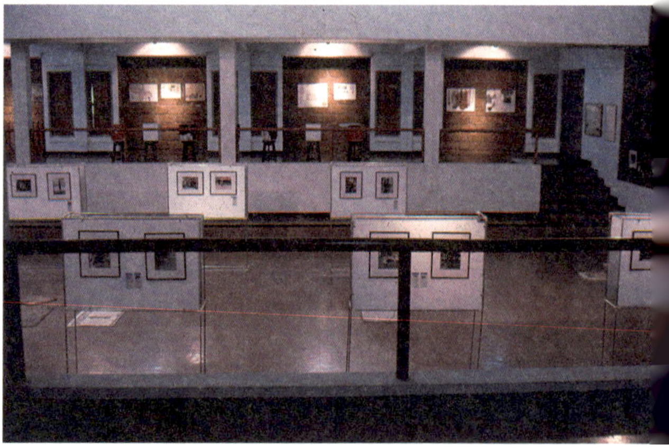

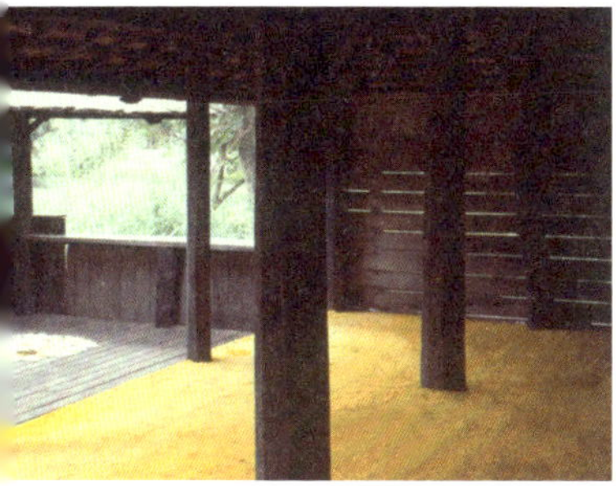

Satoshi Hirose, *Spice Room*.

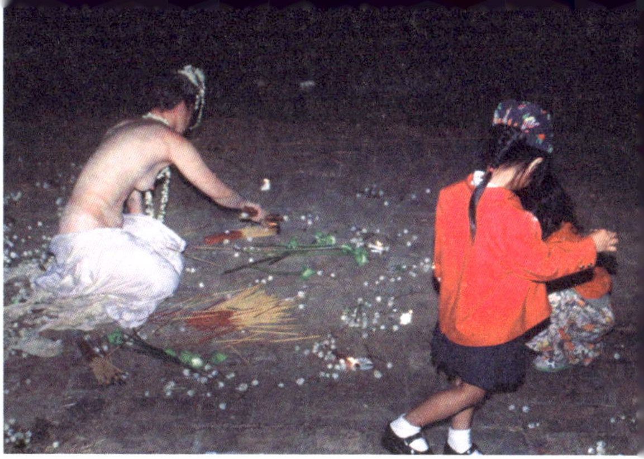

Tei Kobayashi, *Yoni*, performance at Wat Umong. 'I gave a two-hour ritual of woman in nature – a performance titled *Yoni*. She is bound to nature, birthed from nature, worshiped and bound by men, and finally returning to her original sacred state. I begin in the middle of a lake at Umong Temple with geese and ducks all around. We made boats to send the spirits off and then walked in procession to the stupa where a circumambulation and final meditation completed the work' (*Asiana*, February 1996).

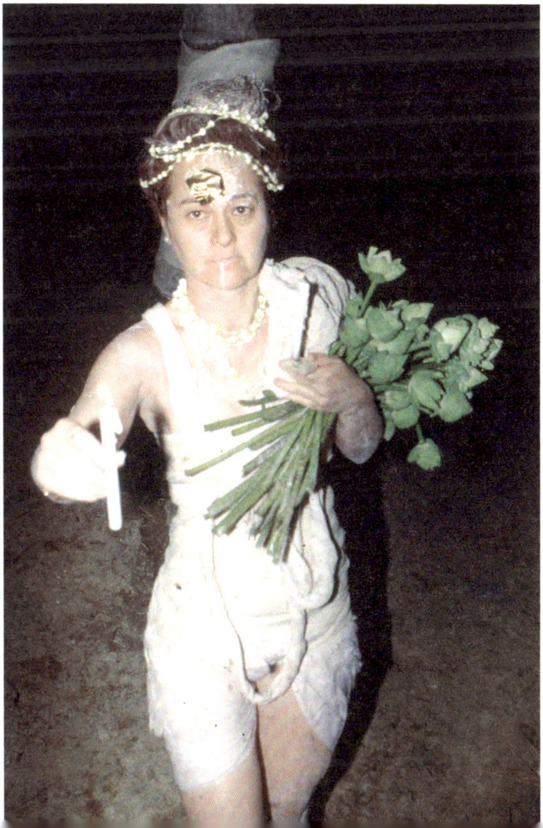

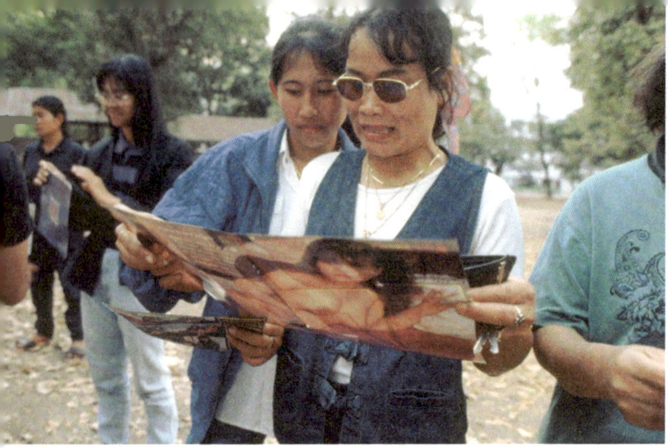

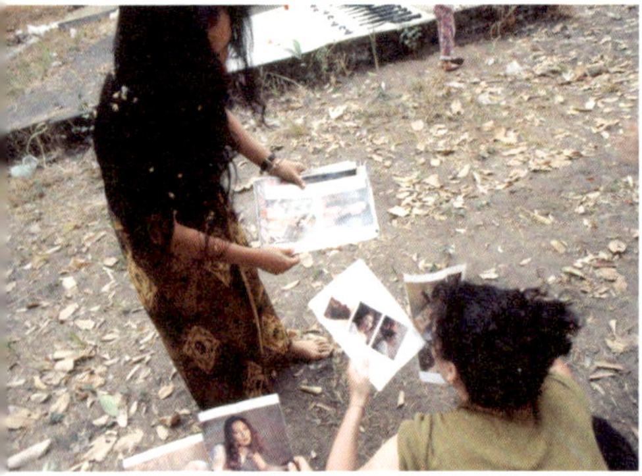

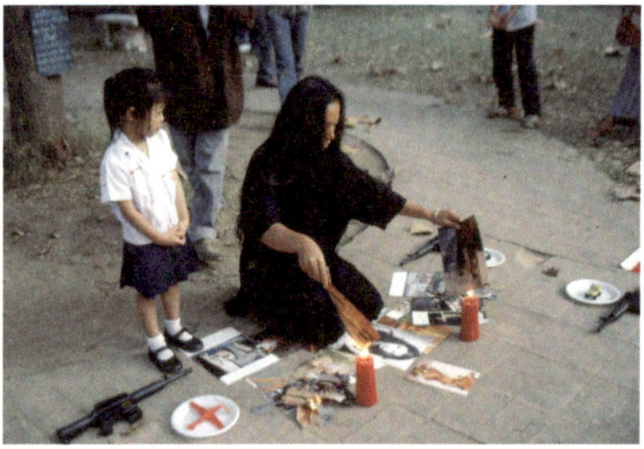

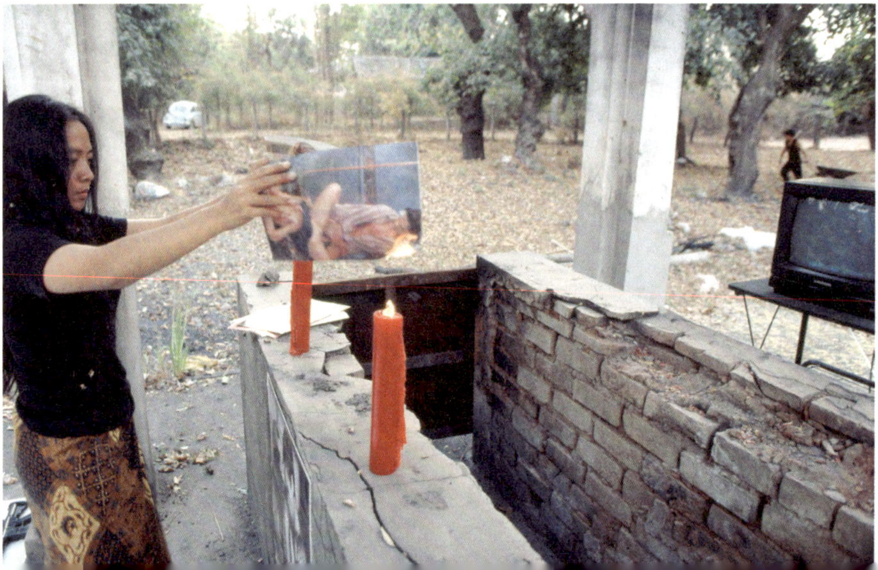

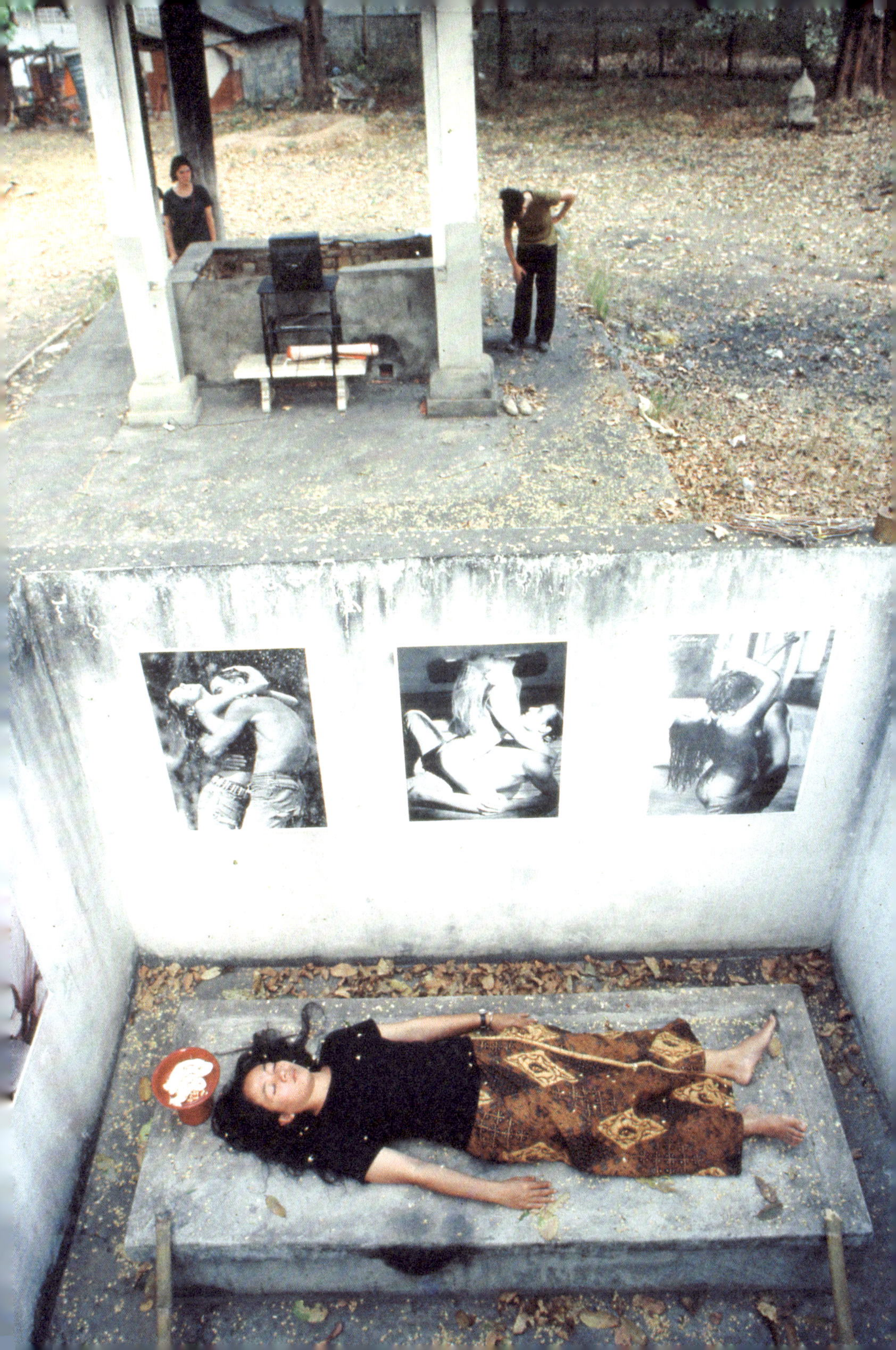

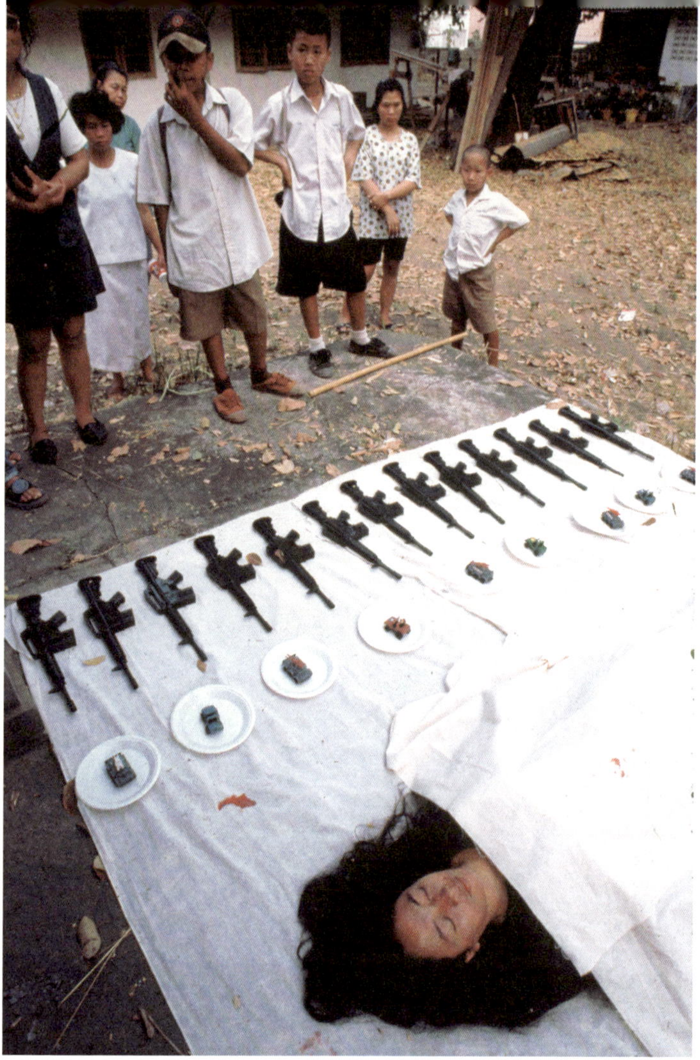

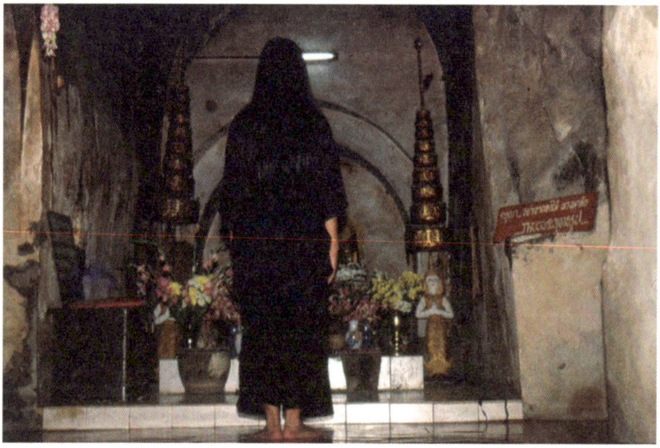

Arahmaiani, *Intersection Flower*, performance at Wat Pa Daeng cemetery.

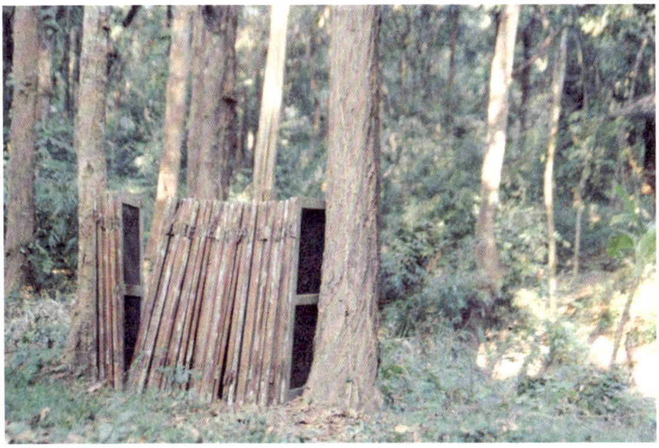

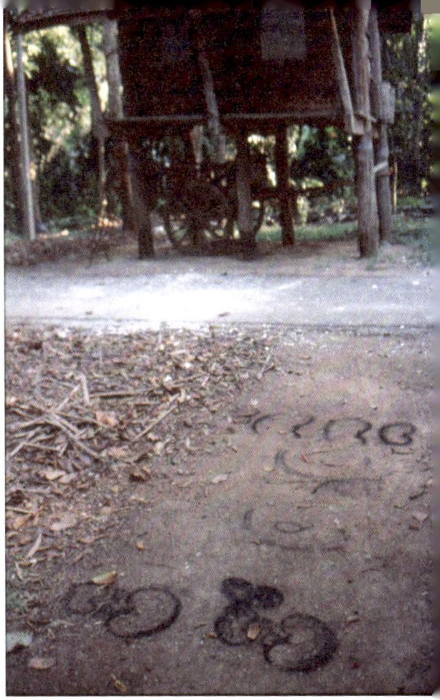

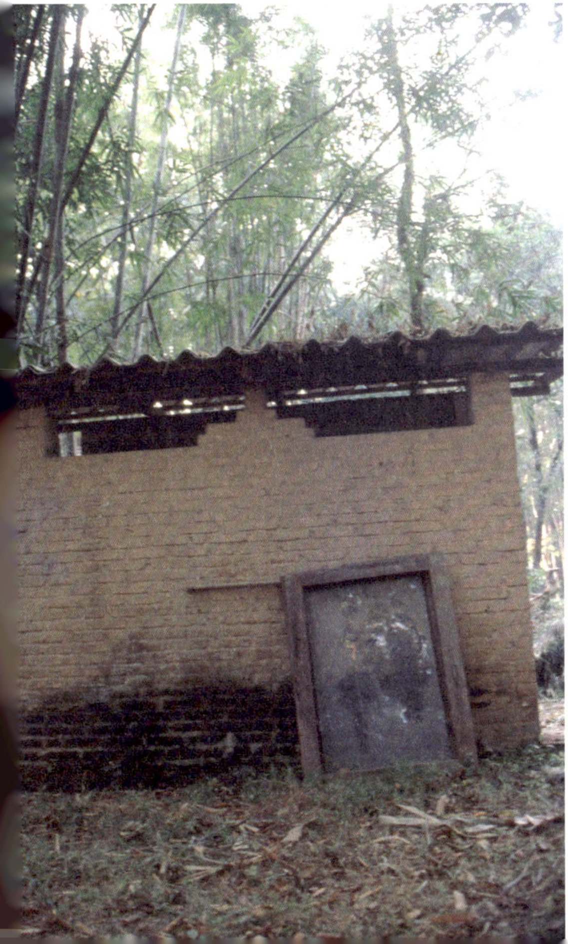

Nilofar Akmut, *Shapeless/Shape*. The artist recalls: 'I asked to perform inside the living quarters of a Buddhist monastary. I myself come from a patriarchal society where segregation is practiced and I hadn't failed to notice its prevalence in Thailand. I was given my own accommodation at a considerable distance from the monks' quarters. Each day I could hear the rhythmic Buddhist chants at their prayer meetings emitting from a dark cavernous monastery. Fasting is a common enough occurence in many tribal and religious orders. It manifests itself in different forms and cycles for various reasons. It could be undertaken for sacrificing food and thirst to a higher being or God or judgement in hell or heaven. In order to attend to a common cultural artefact, I decided to undertake a watermelon fast for ten days. Discarding its flesh, I sucked on its juices, in order to maintain my bodily functions while I tested my mental and physical limitations. As a steady pile of empty shells of watermelon gathered around my abode, I reflected on the contradictions I was creating for myself and the monks in the vicinity. They stared at me from a respectable distance and I them, whilst I meandered through their sanctified space. With no mental or physical interaction, an echo of silence was building up in my head. On my final day, a senior monk invited me to his abode to partake of a cooked meal. Neither of us spoke the same language. The echo of silence continued in my head. A moment of reflection of one's place in the circus of life.'

Janice Sommerville,
Still Klinging to the Koala.

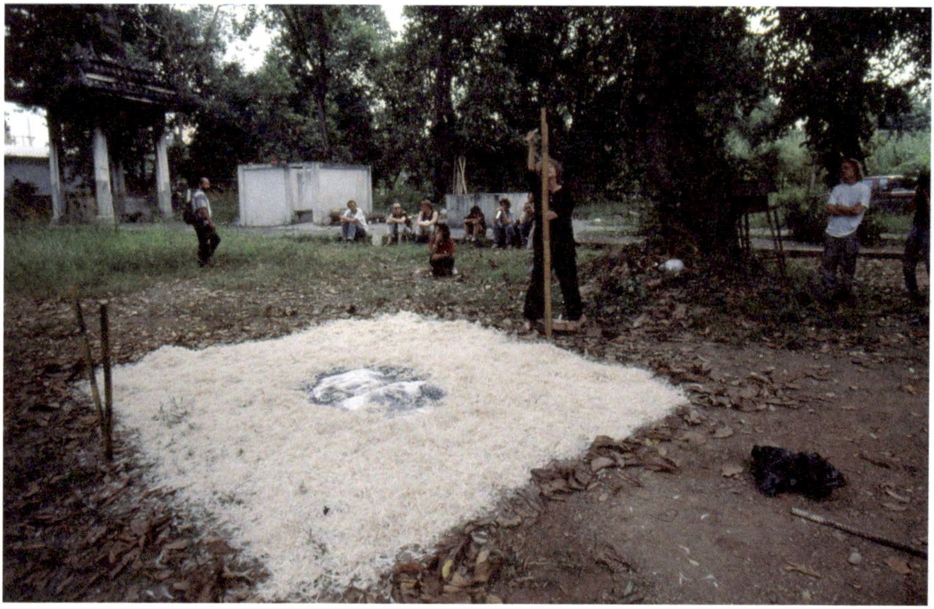

Leen Emmerzael, *Three Places for Meditation*, Wat Umong.

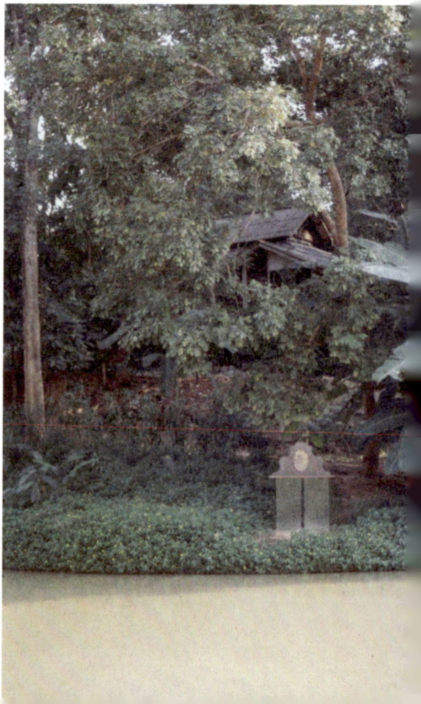

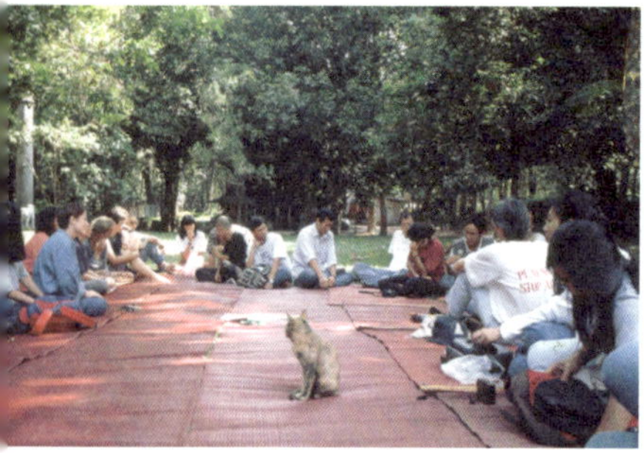

Artists' discussion at Wat Umong.

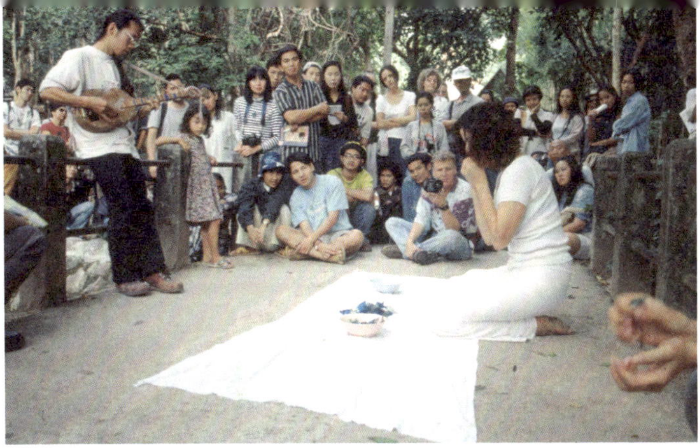

Liz Miller, *Ever Green.*

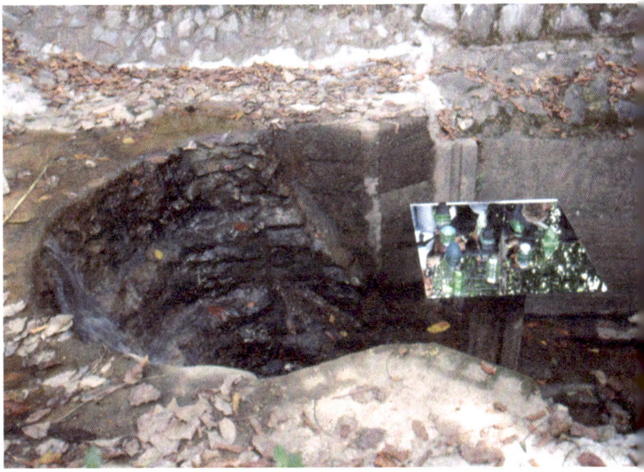

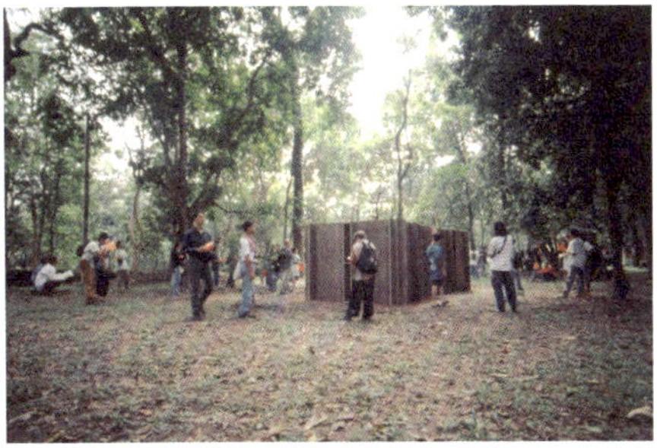

Chitti Kasemkitvatana, *Mo(nu)ment to The Third (CM)SI.*

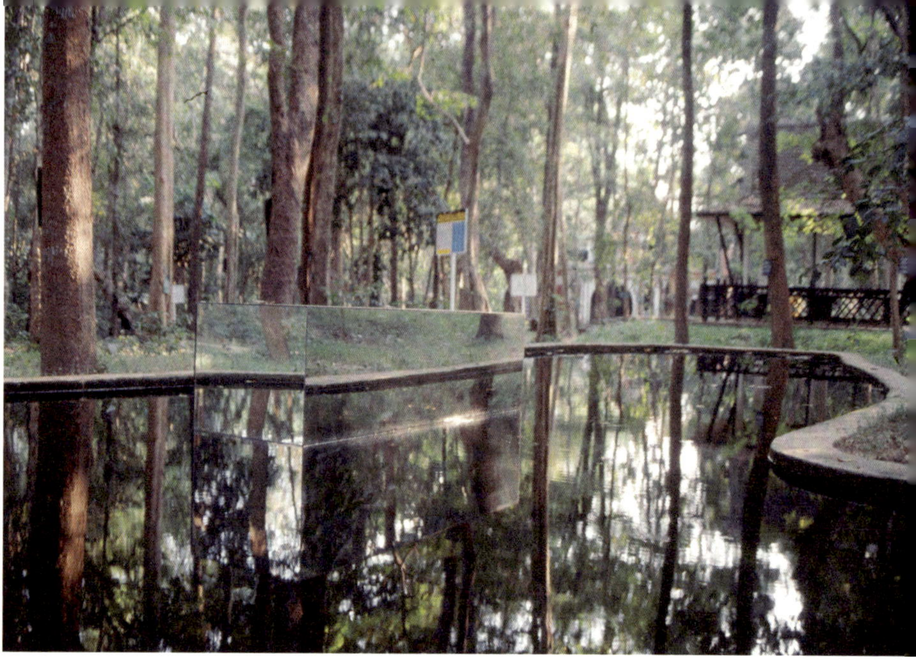

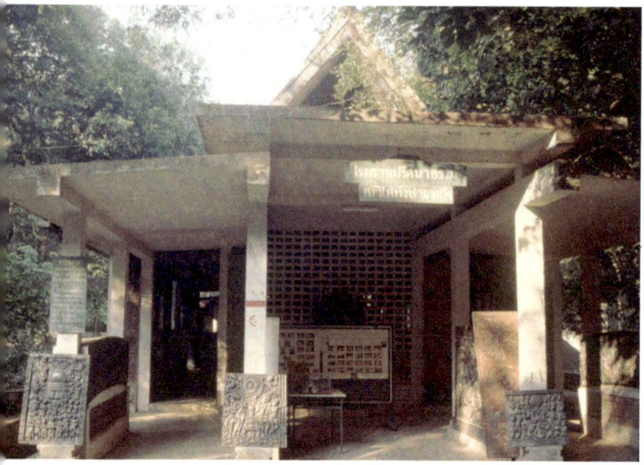

Works at Wat Umong by Araya Rasdjarmrearnsook (above) and Sutthisak Phutararak (left). 'Sutthisak Phutararak's three cabinets about the life of the prostitute – the brothel, medicine and cosmetics – flanked by two condom-shaped paintings depicting a life of hell and torment' (*Metro*, c.1995). Araya recalls that visitors 'threw stones at my work, perhaps just to see whether it was glass', and that after the opening day it 'was hit by a stone and disappeared quickly'. 'A mirrored box resembling a coffin floats in the murky waters while visitors are invited to take a look at their reflections. "This wat communes fully with nature so I decided to place a mirror, which is an industry-made thing, here. These two things [venue and object] are contrasts. I believe that even given modern lifestyles, there's still a way for people to gain deep insights into Buddhist tenets – although all things are inherently subject to change. Anyway, if we're given a chance to look at ourselves, even for a moment, we'll get to know ourselves" (*The Nation,* 4 December 1995).

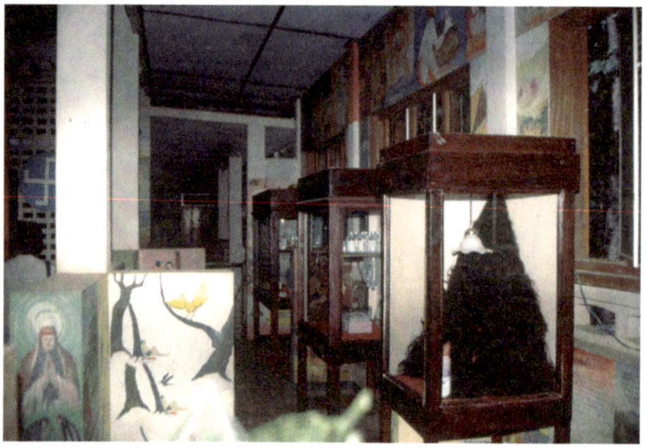

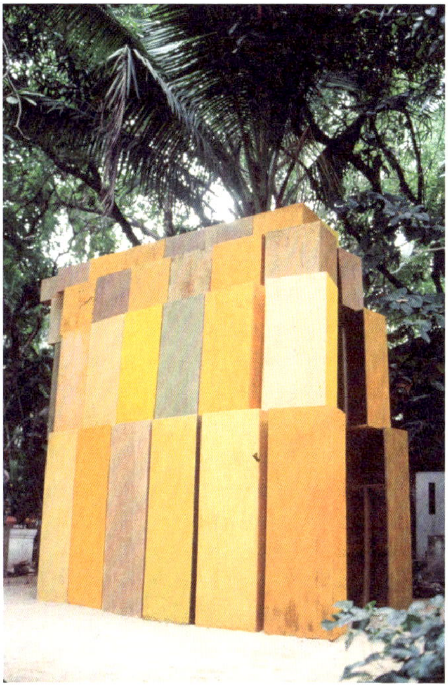

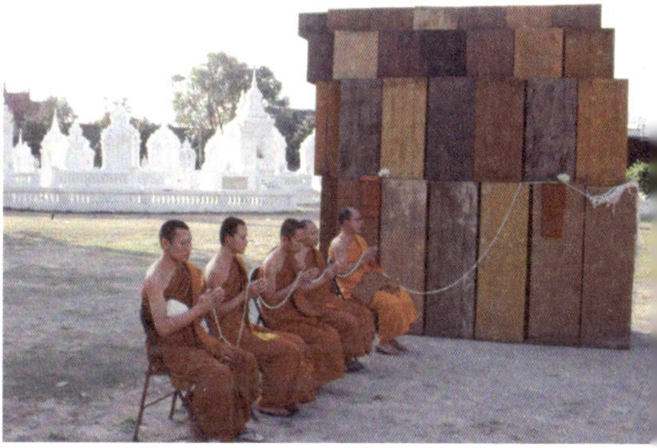

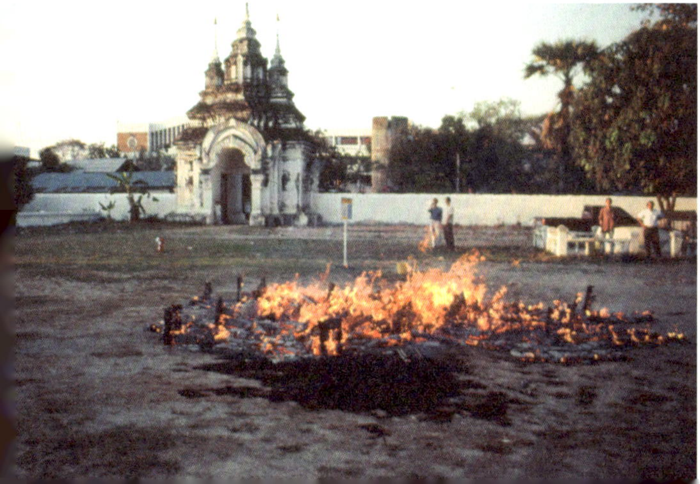

Montien Boonma, *Body Temple*, Wat Phan Tong (above left). At the end of the festival this work was relocated to Wat Suan Dok; the artist invited the monks to pray, before burning the work and burying its ashes.' Another artist who has used the coffin size and shape is Montien Boonma. The coffinlike wooden boxes are stained with various Chinese herbal medicines which take on the colour of the saffron monks' robes. These boxes are stacked precariously into the form of a stupa. One may enter the stupa, where healing, medicinal, incensed walls fill the mind and soul of the observer. One is spiritually uplifted. Montien's references to death are debilitating, yet one becomes aware of a heart filled with empathy and understanding of the precarious nature of life. One is brought to a spiritual reality' (*Asiana*, February 1996).

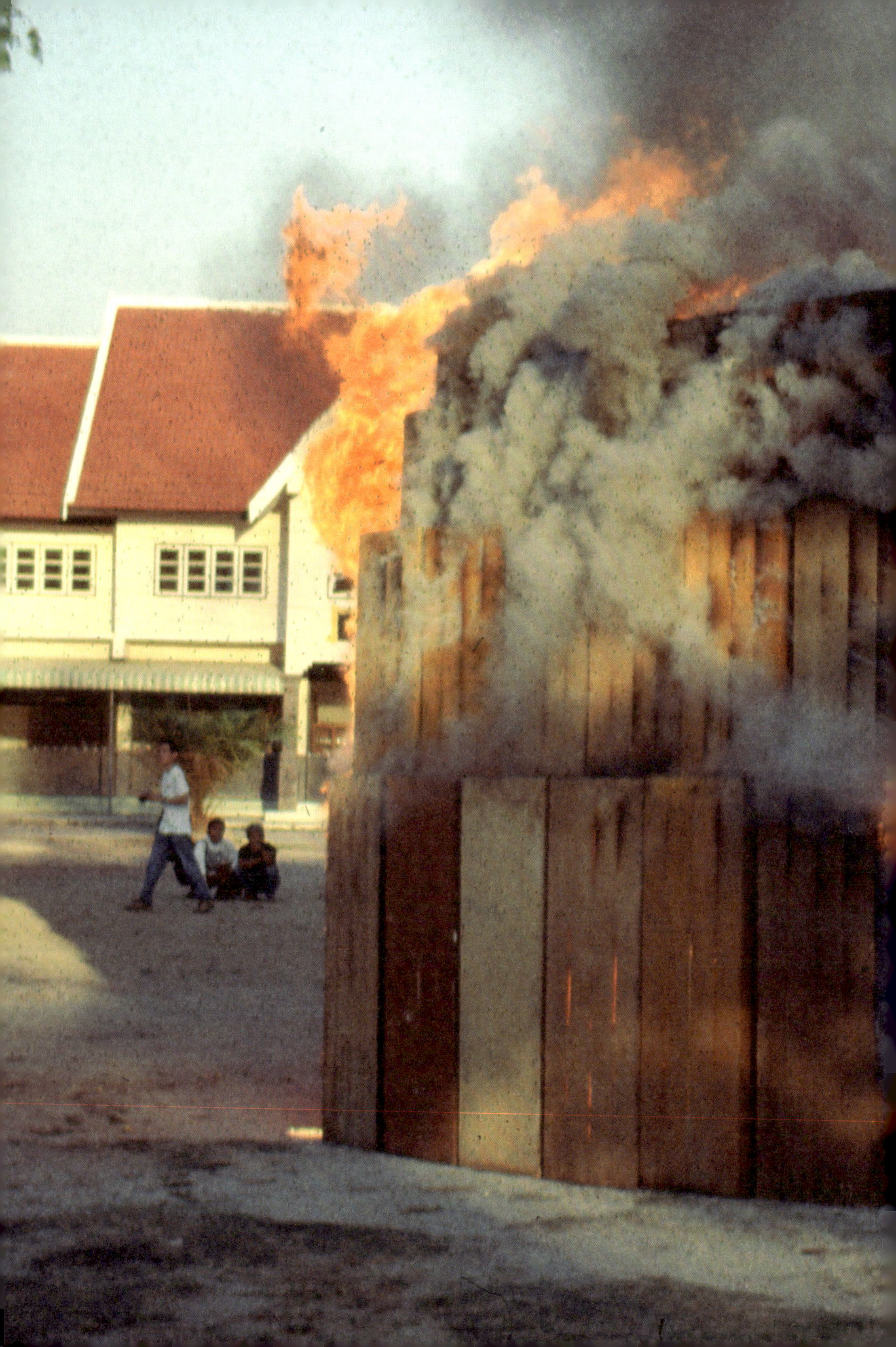

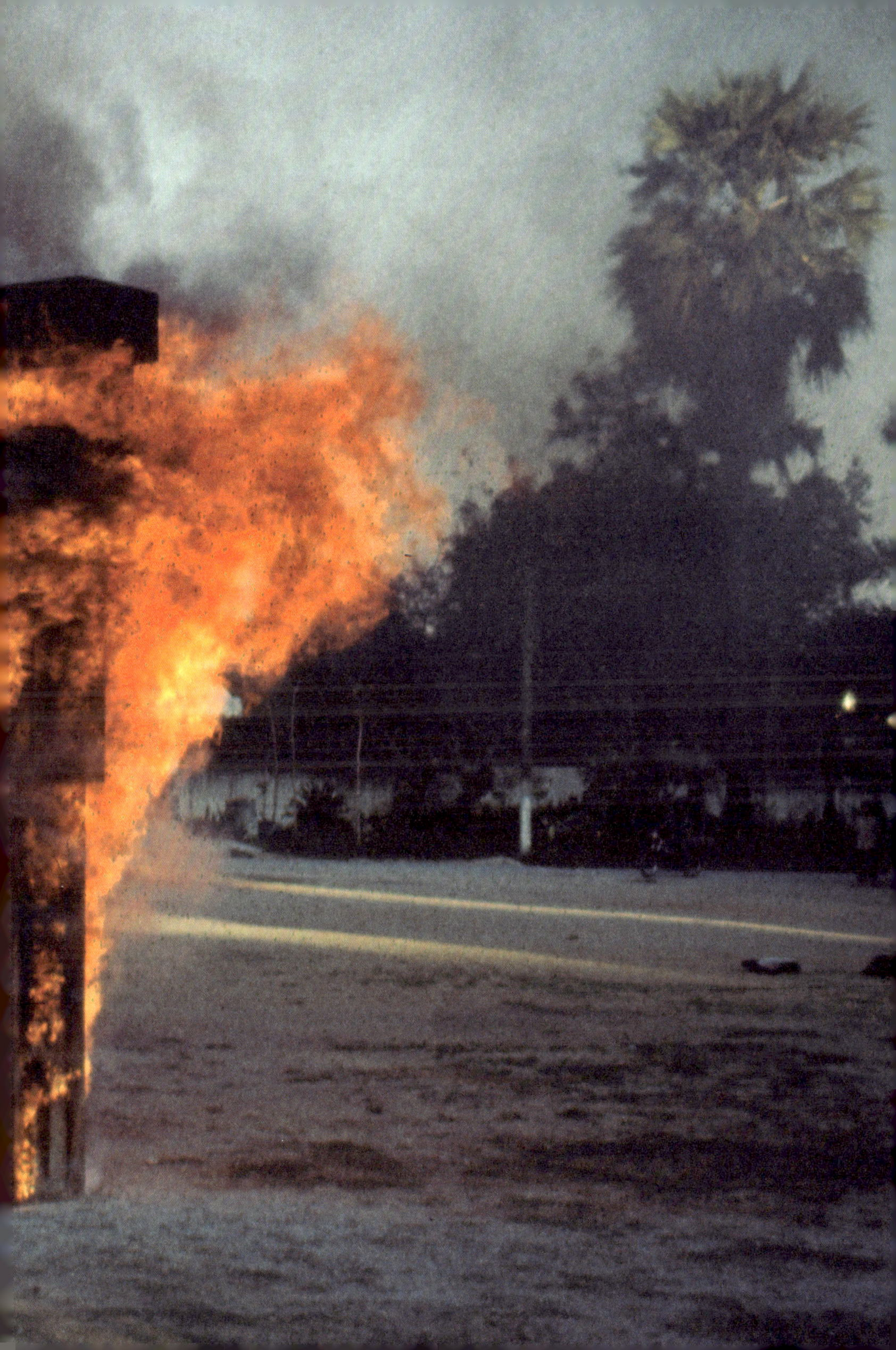

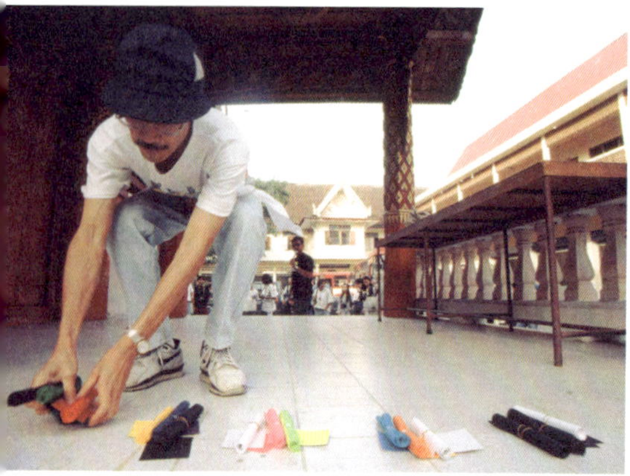

Wattana Wattanapun, *Unpredictable Routes*, performance at Wat Phra Singh.

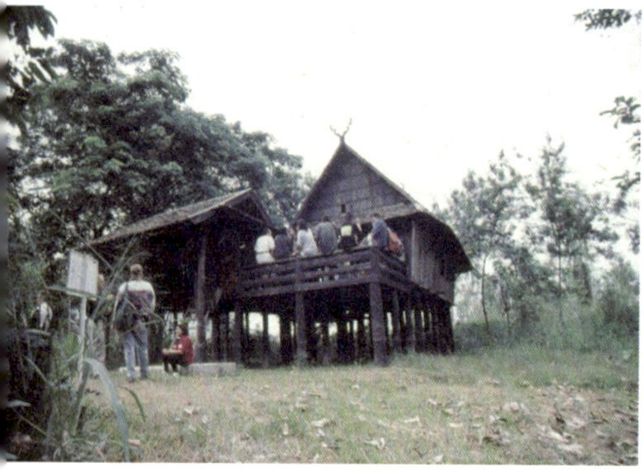

Junya Yamaide, *TOUR: Something You Have in a Daily Life*, Chiang Mai University.

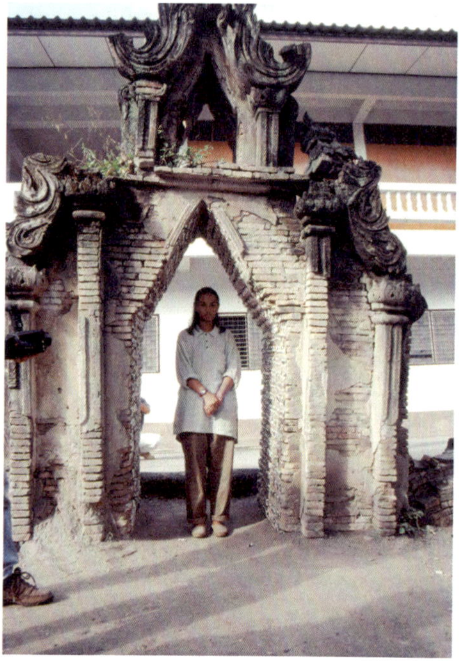

Toeingam Srisubut, *Self-Help Buddhist Version*. 'Critical exchange is encouraged by the organisers, and prompted one lively forum of debate at Wat Pa-Pao, prompted by the work by Toeingam Srisubut, a young Thai woman whose installation is made up of unlit half burnt candles stuck to the inside of the entrance to the temple's pagoda. At the opening of the installation, a young girl solemnly stood in the entrance. The foreign women artists there immediately leapt on it as a comment on the inequality of women in religion, with one lady at one point shouting at another, "don't you mean it's the vagina!", referring to the symbolism of the entrance' (*Metro*, c.1995.). 'Feminist observers spoke in reference to gender, the powerlessness of woman in society, and the role she serves or doesn't serve in this Buddhist society. This work is an undeniably quiet yet poignant statement on woman, yet the artist herself seems indifferent to its sociopolitical connotations, or perhaps she is simply too clear about the issues. She denied a feminist stance and simply said, "It's just an idea of art which works in its own right"' (*Asiana*, February 1996).

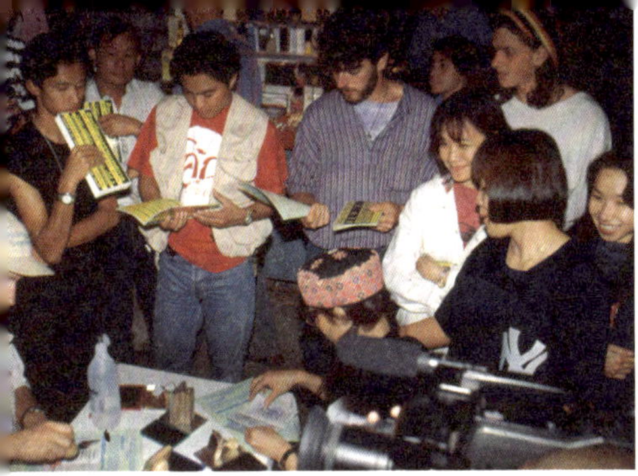

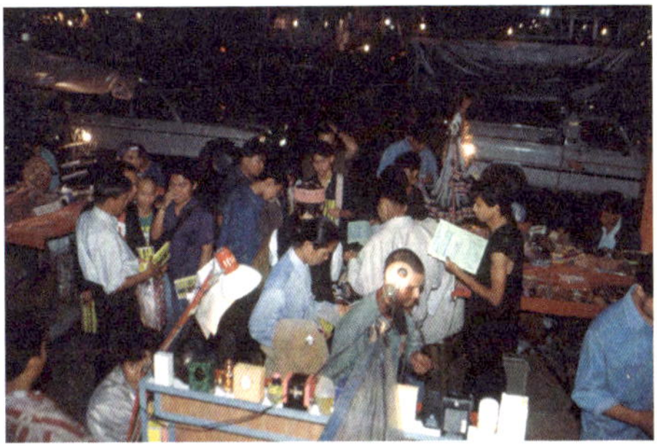

Pietro Pellini and Yola Berbesz, performance
at Chiang Mai night bazaar.

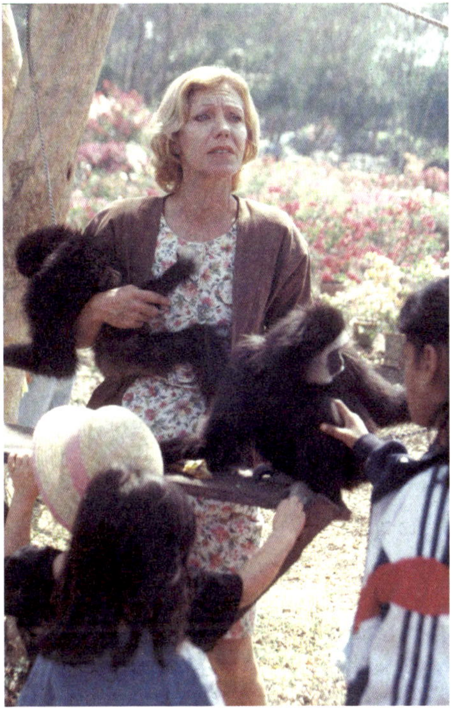

Work by Mari Zirus, Chiang Mai Zoo.

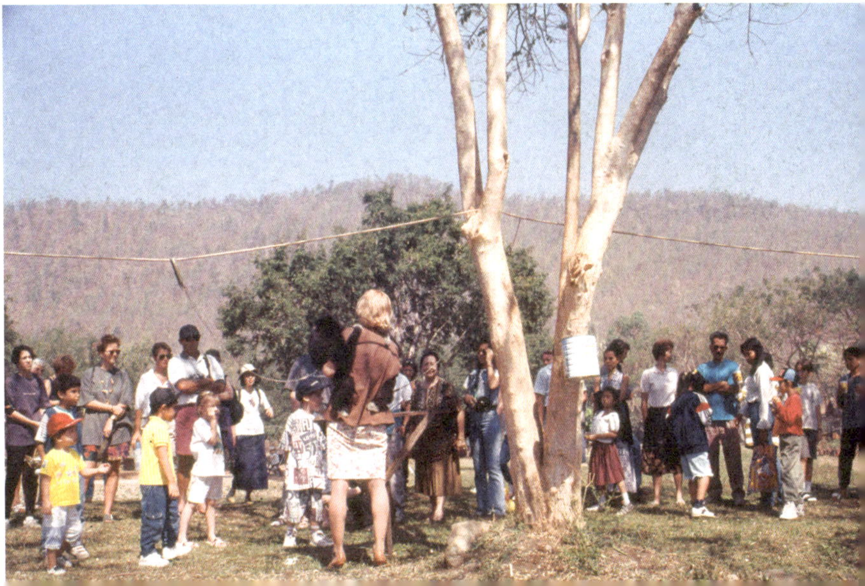

Week of Cooperative Suffering
1–7 January 1996

Week of Cooperative Suffering

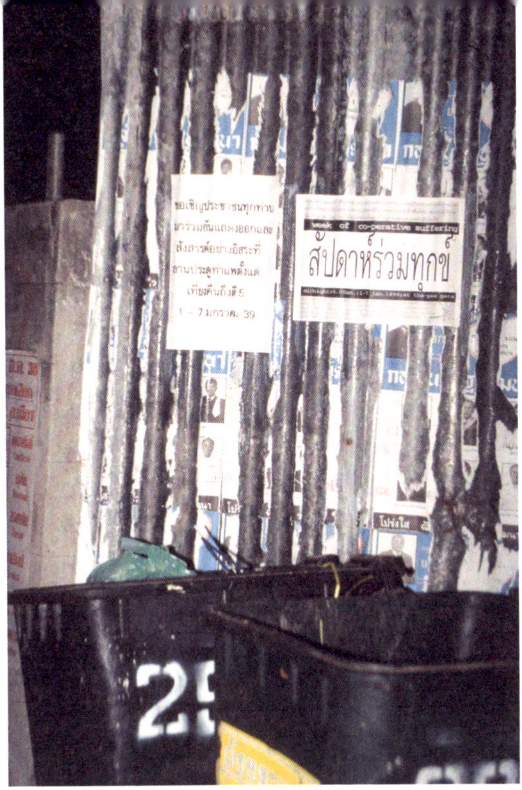

The second Week of Cooperative Suffering took place as part of the third edition of CMSI; posters were put up around Chiang Mai to publicise it.

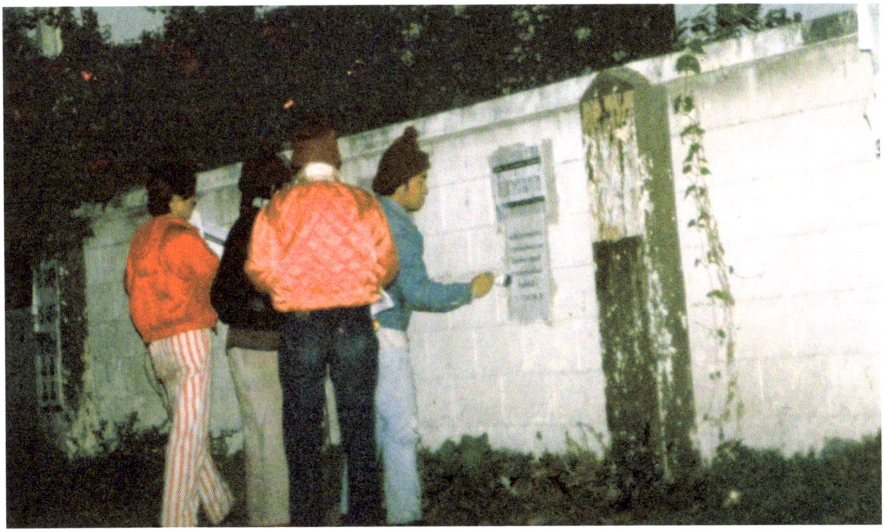

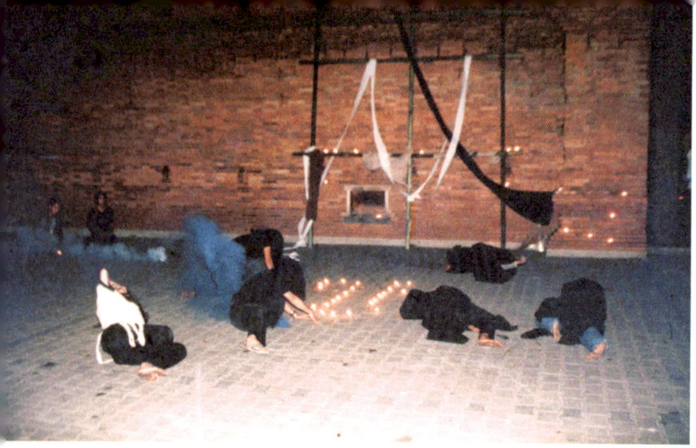

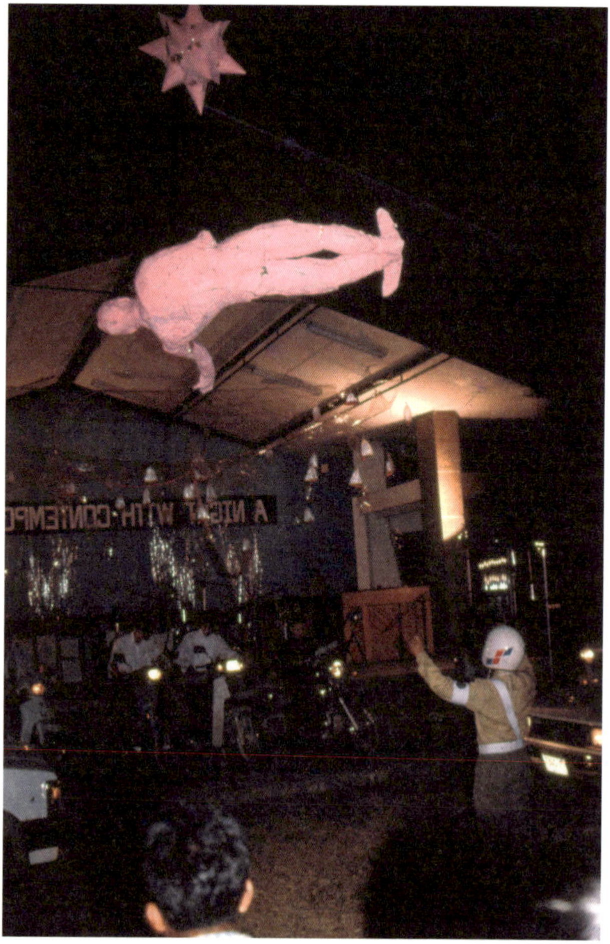
A NIGHT WITH CONTEMPO

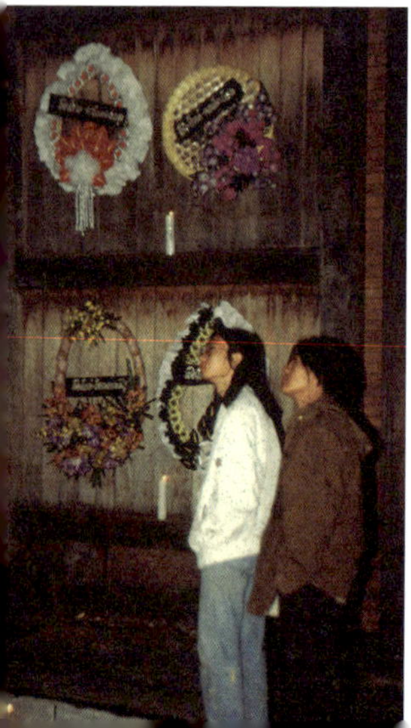

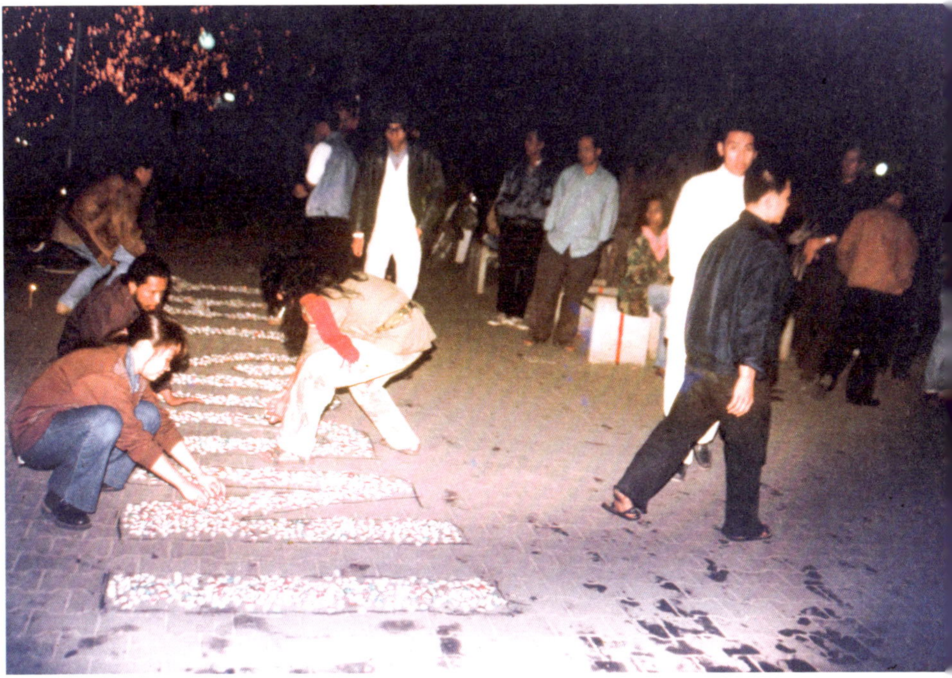

A participatory artists' project spelling out the word 'nature', Tha Pae Gate.

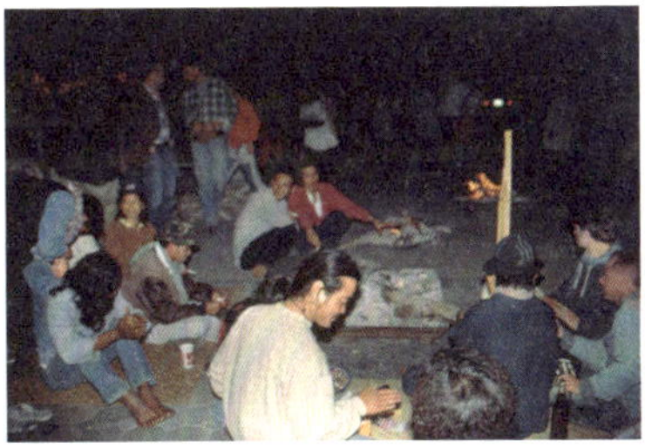

Culture and art market, Tha Pae Gate. 'At the midnight market that was held the night of January 4 I was impressed that the income from the artwork being sold was being donated to the children of the northern village to replenish their schools. I bought beautiful hand-printed cotton bags which were donated for the children of a school where some students of Chiang Mai University are helping by providing supplies as well as their own cooperation in building and teaching' (*Asiana*, February 1996).

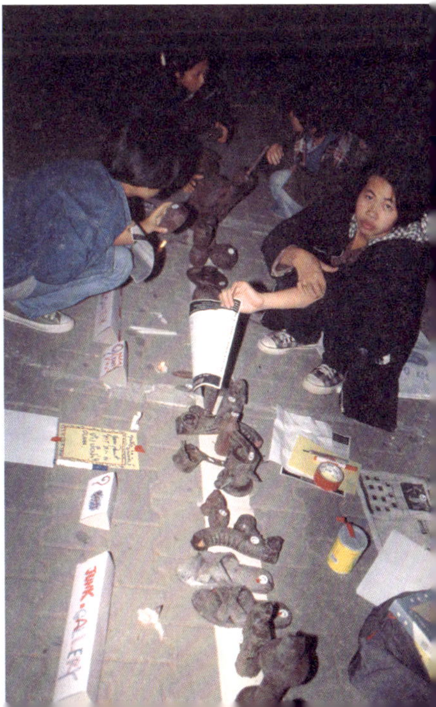

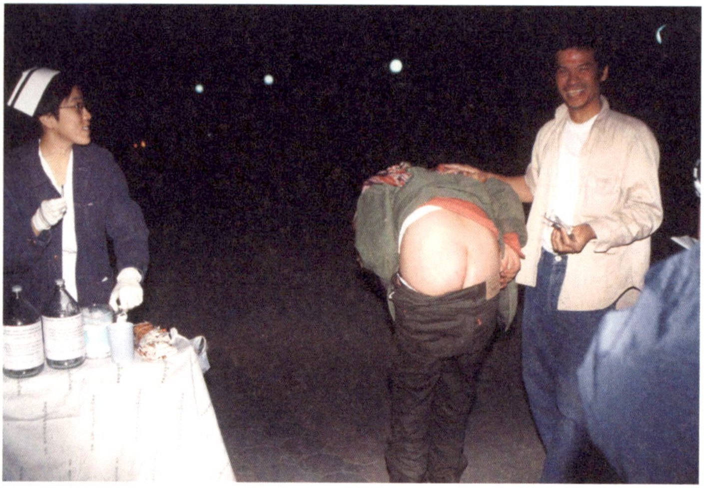

A nurse offering injections of 'anti-cultural immune deficiency vaccine'.

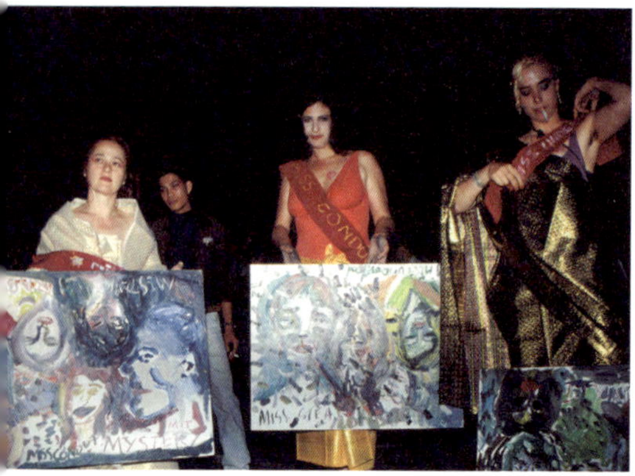

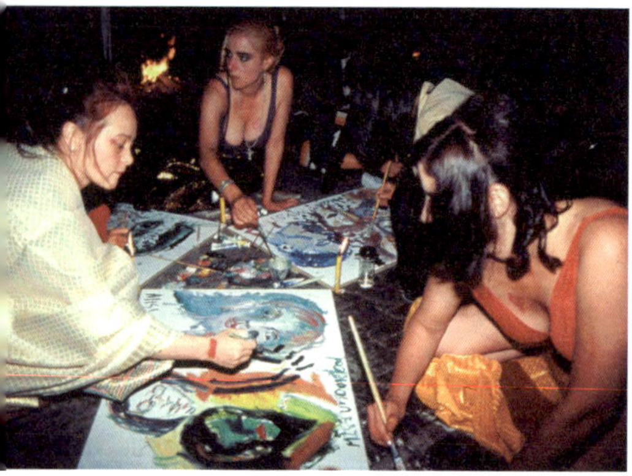

Beauty Contest, a performance by Liz Miller and friends.

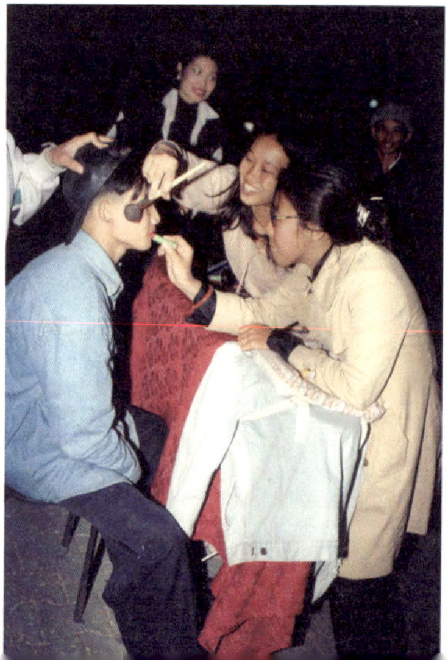

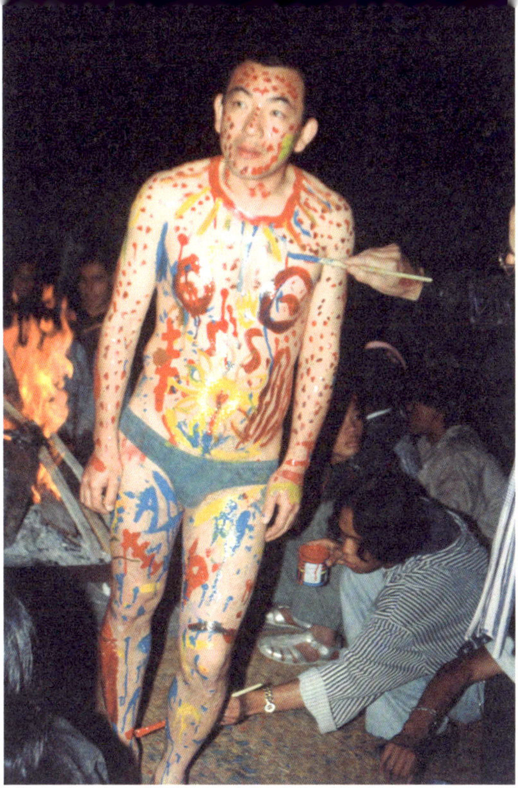

Performance by Jian Jun Xi.

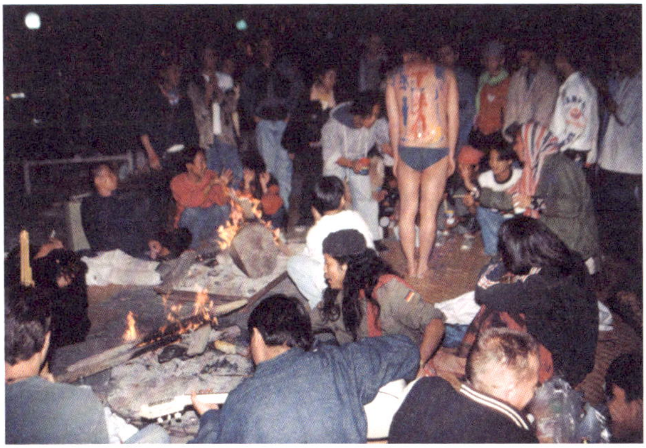

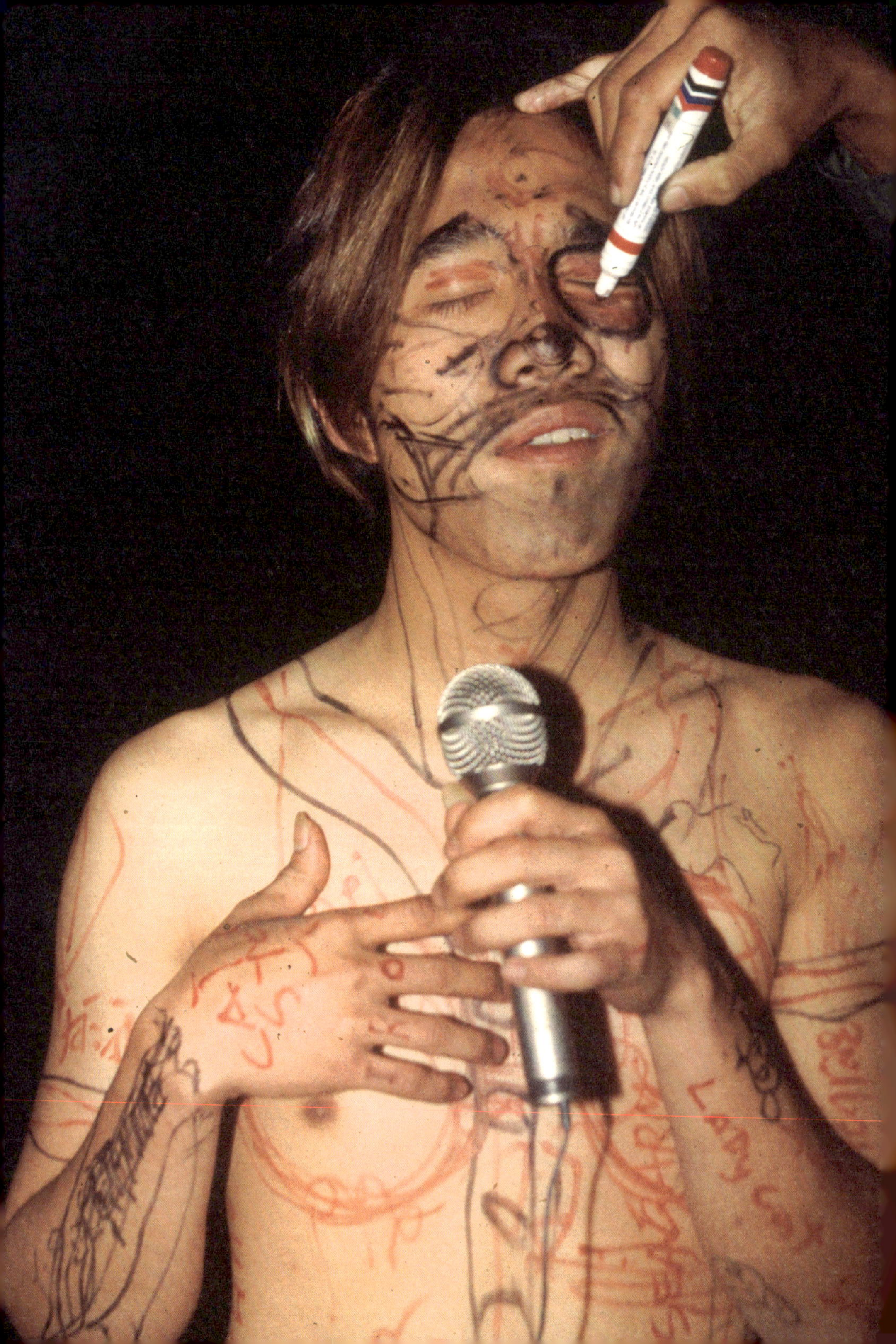

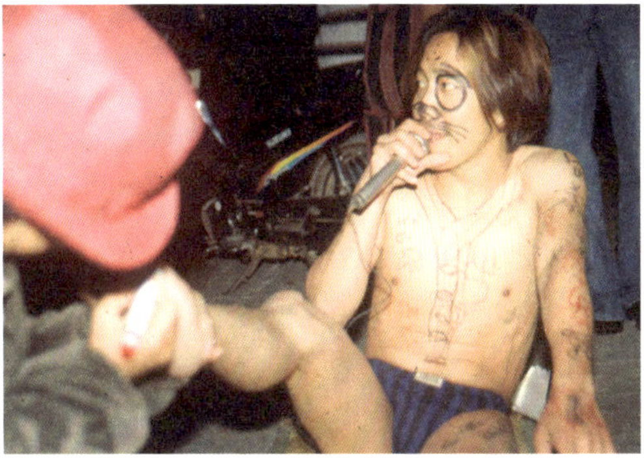

Performance by Sunya Suntivet.

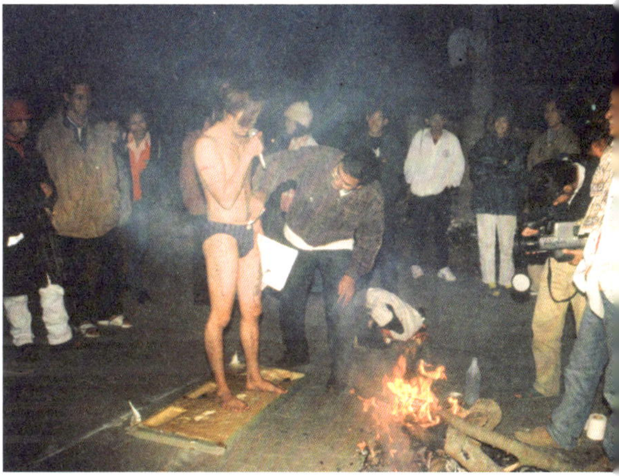

At Tha Pae Gate, an 'installation of blocks of ice filled with kerosene and lit was an intense work that spattered the center of town around Tha Pae Gate with fire and ice. The blocks burst and fire filled the air. The danger was obvious, but everything was accepted as an experiment in reality. "Inner warmth, outer chill", stated the artist, Kristana Soonthornpuk, summarizing what her social installation represented' (*Asiana*, February 1996).

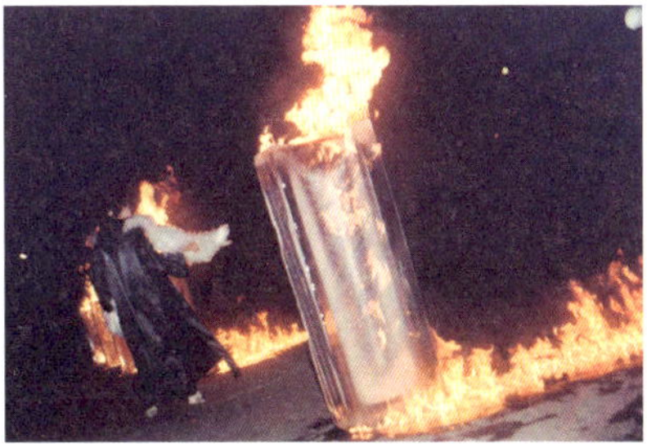

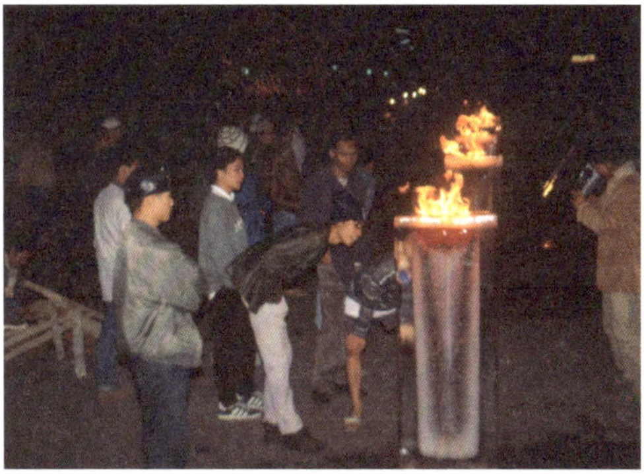

A performance by Chiang Mai University Humanities students.

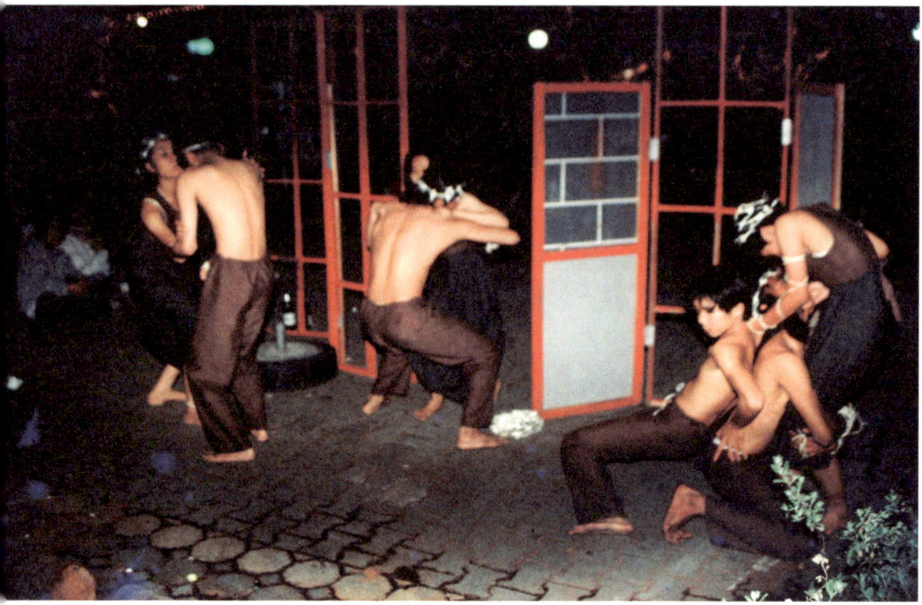

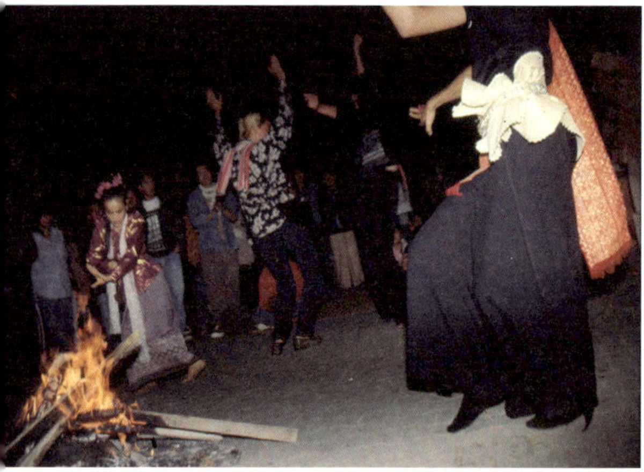

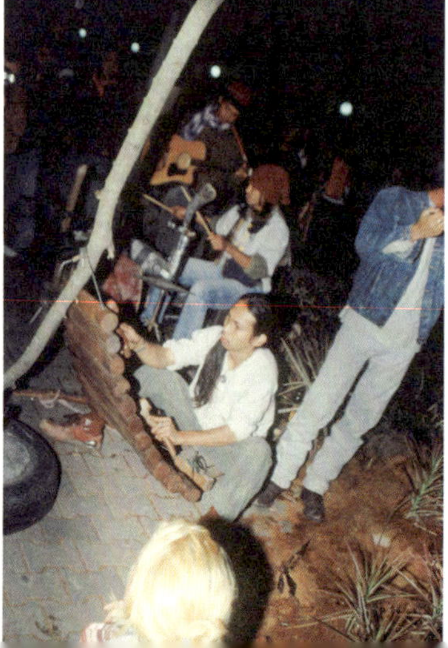

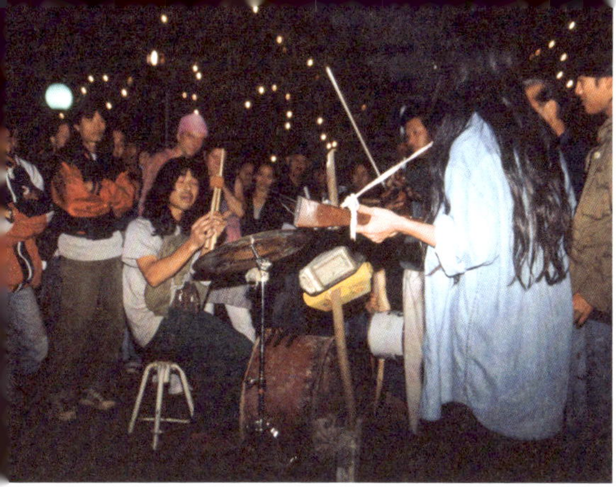

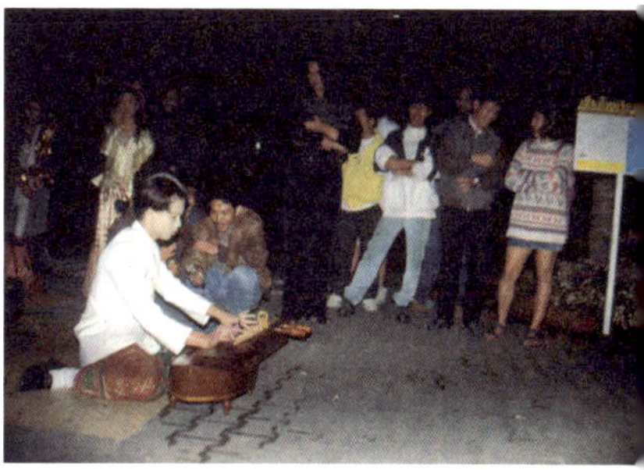

Musical performances, dance party and various other artistic interventions during the second Week of Cooperative Suffering.

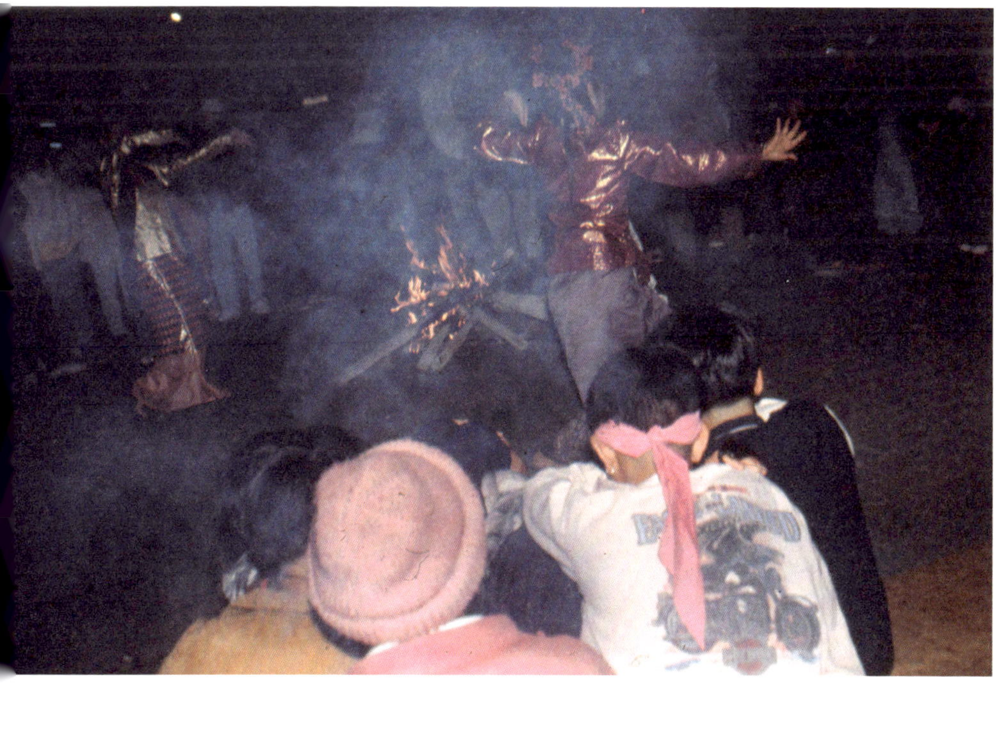

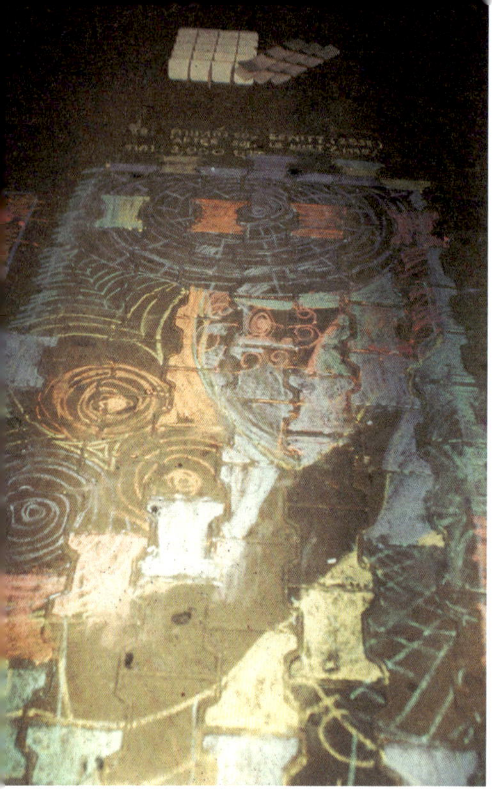

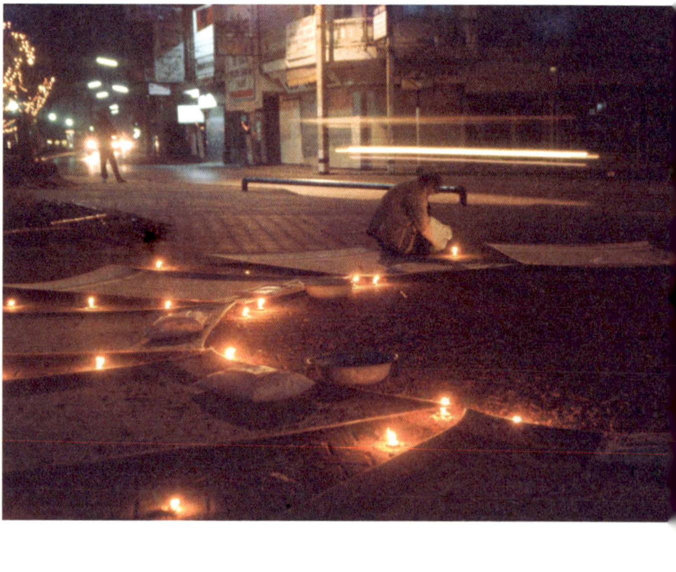

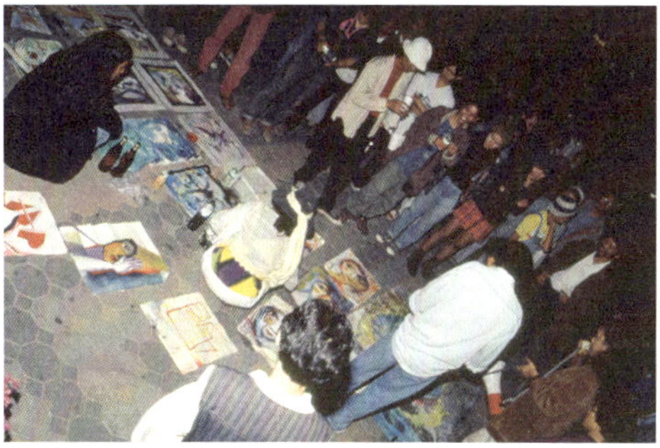

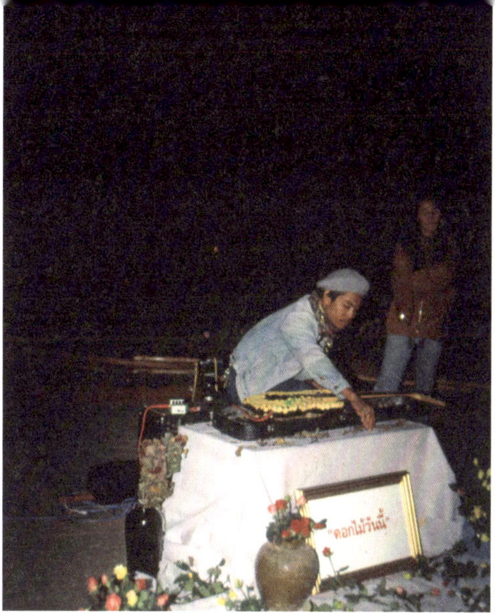
"ดอกไม้วันนี้"

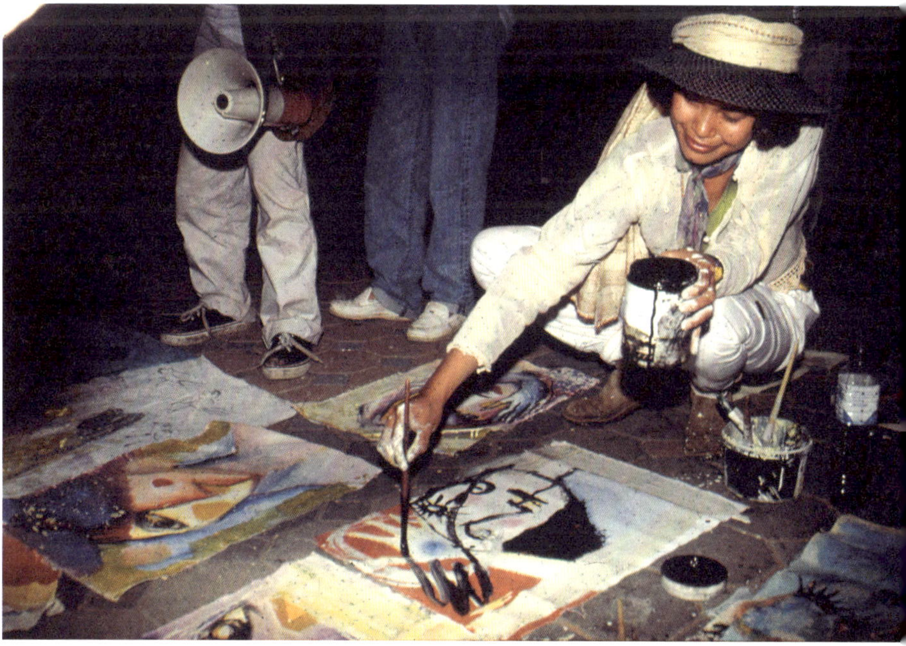

Week of Cooperative Suffering
1–7 January 1997

Week of Cooperative Suffering

1 Jan	NIGHT OF CONTEMPORARY PERFORMANCE
2 Jan	**DAY OF INSTALLATION**
3 JAN	MIDNIGHT MARKET
4 JAN	MIDNIGHT...ENLIGHTENMENT
5 Jan	MIDNIGHT UNIVERSITY
6 Jan	*MIDNIGHT UNIVERSITY*
7 Jan	NIGHT OF CONTEMPORARY LIGHT AND SOUND

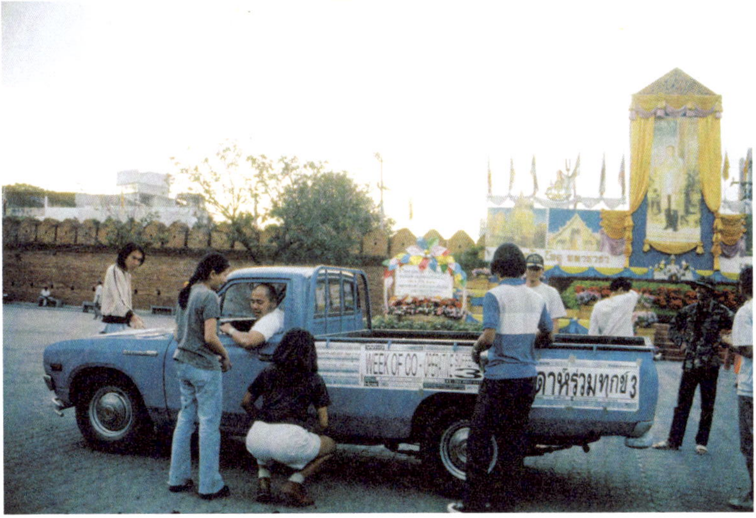

Truck promoting the third Week of Cooperative Suffering, driven by Michael Shaowanasai.

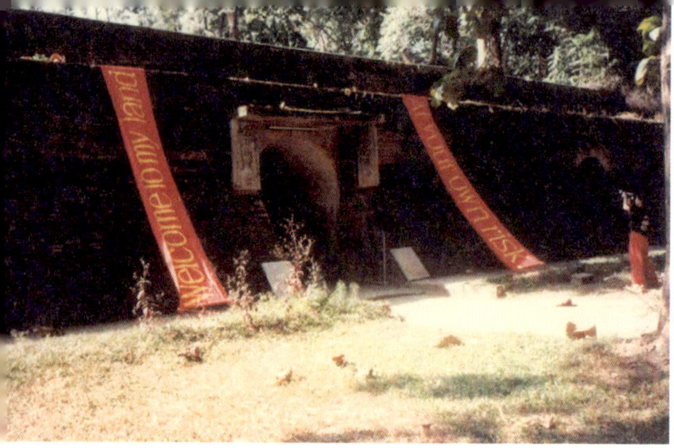

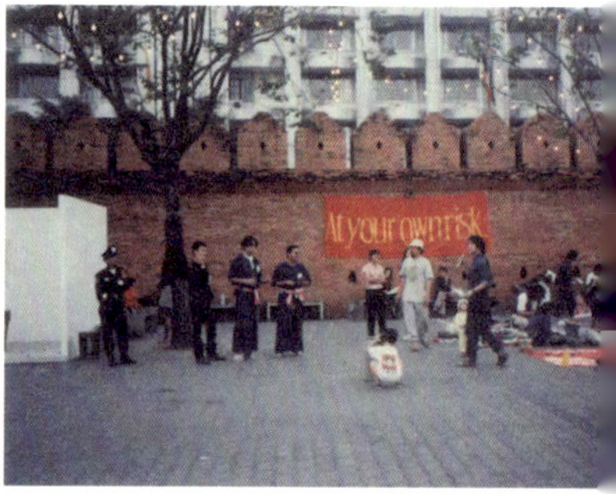

Michael Shaowanasai's *At Your Own Risk* featured texts on red banners hung around Tha Pae Gate.

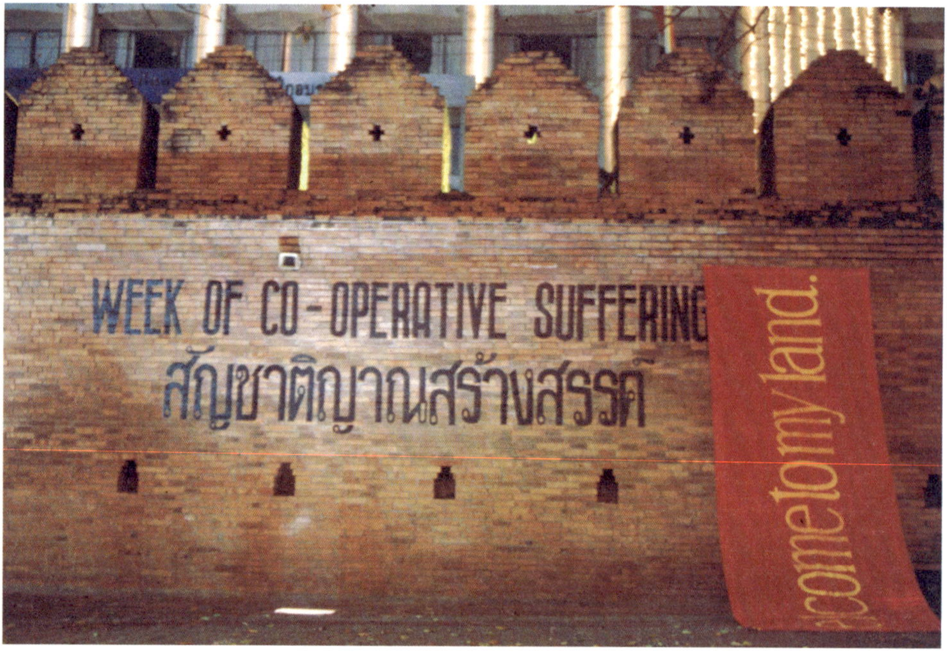

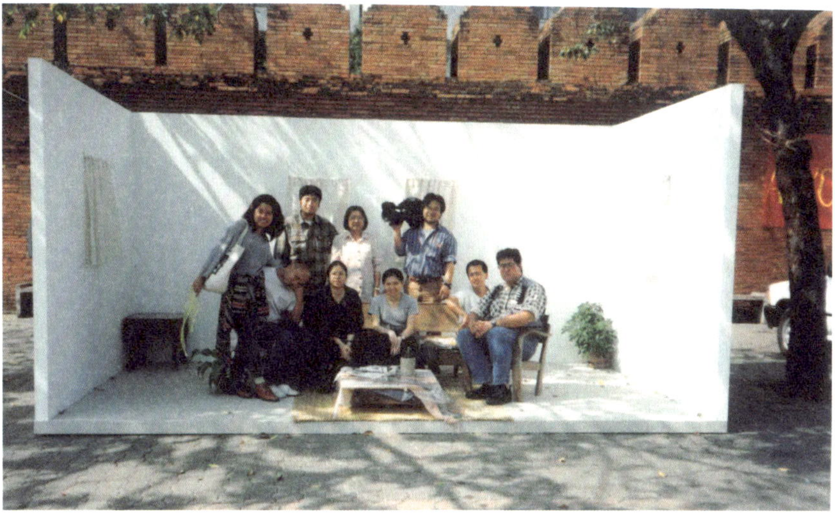

Performance by Michael Shaowanasai.

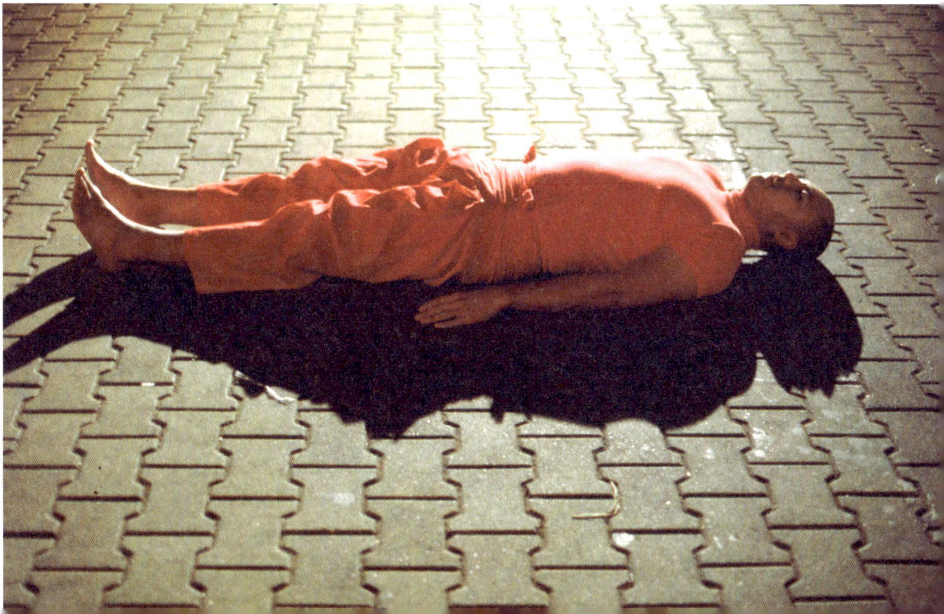

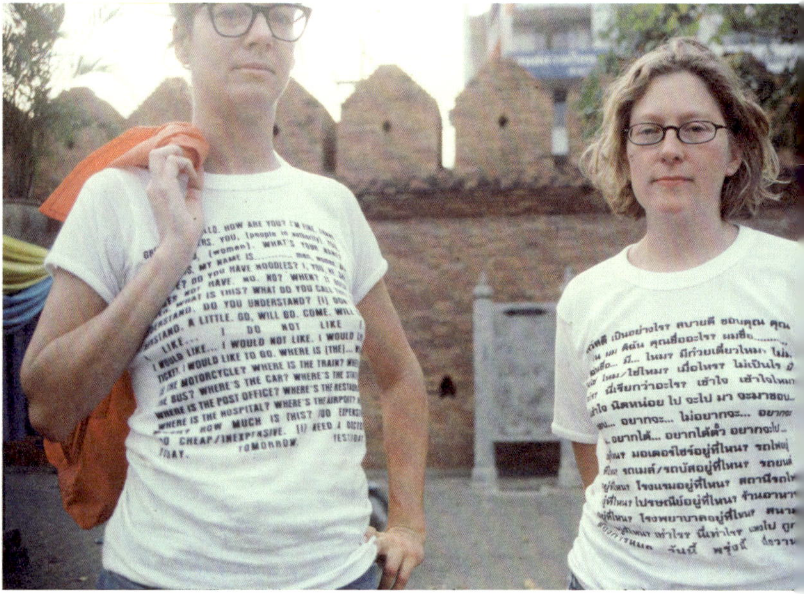

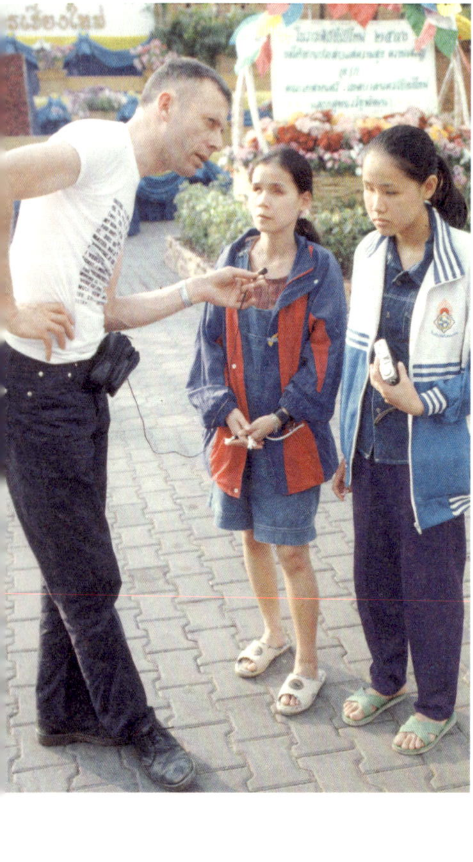

Works by Fiona Banner (above) and Johnny Spencer (left) as part of a group project titled 'Backpacker' (see p.60; other participants were David Blamey, Cornford & Cross, Bridget Smith, Roman Vasseur, Richard Wentworth, Ian Whittlesea and Jian Jun Xi). Blamey recalls: 'Fiona Banner had T-shirts made in English and Thai that extrapolated a list of texts found in an "emergency situation" language translation guide'; and 'Johnny Spencer arranged to be shown around the city by two blind girls. The insights revealed to him went far beyond anything that could be seen.'

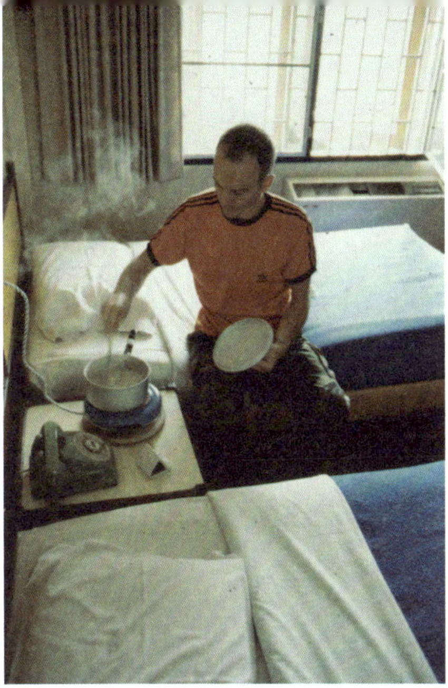

Work by David Blamey. He recalls: 'I withdrew from the event almost completely by locking myself in a businessman's hotel room and living off a week's groceries that I brought with me from London in my hand luggage. The ritual practice of cooking on a gas stove smuggled into the hotel became a meditation on cultural identity, survival, dislocation and globalisation – the most pressing sociocultural phenomenon being discussed at the time. My activities were only made public via an announcement card in Thai that described what was going on.'

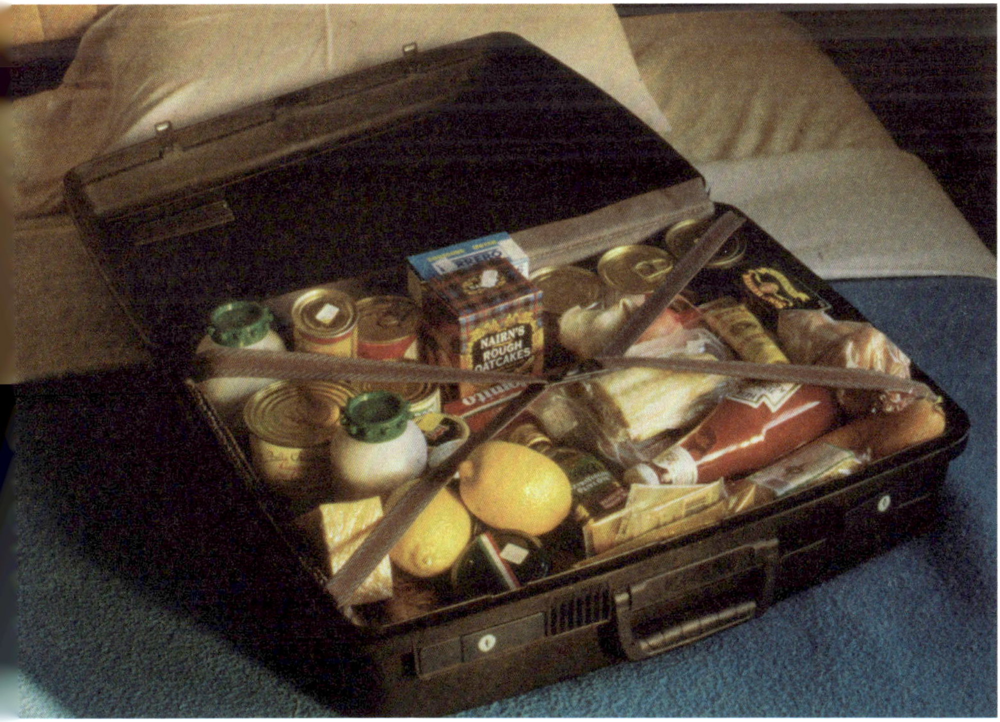

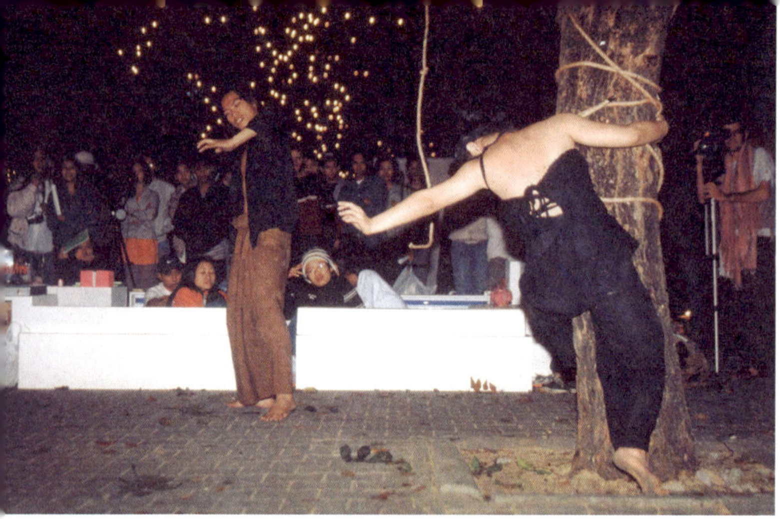

Performance by Makhampom theatre group.

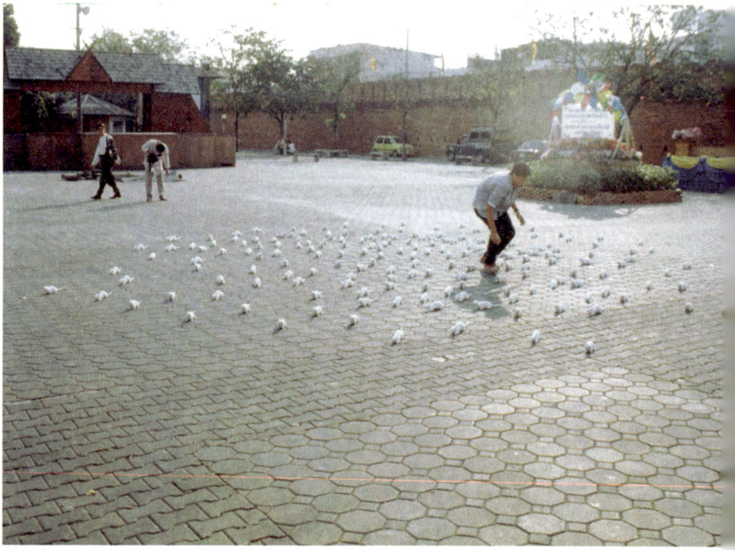

Supachai Satsara, *Rat*.

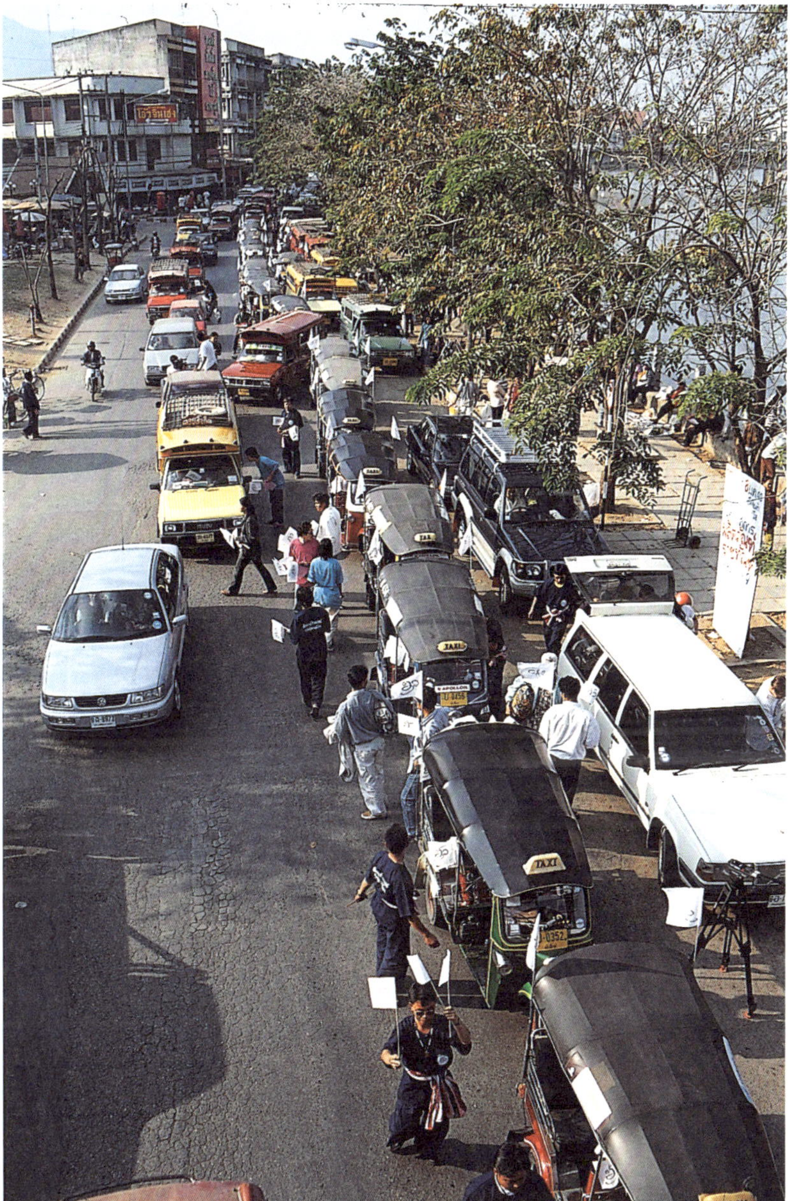
TAXI
TAXI
TAXI

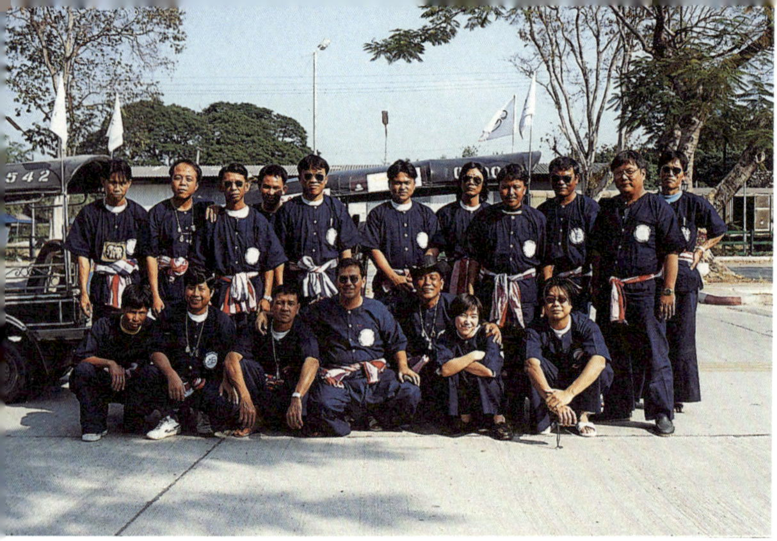

Navin Rawanchaikul, *Navin Cooperative Society Event 'Sap-Da-Ruam-Tuak, Tuk-Tuk-Kaon-Muang'* (*The Week of Cooperative Suffering, The Local Tuk Tuk Drivers*), in collaboration with Rirkrit Tiravanija and twenty tuk tuk drivers.

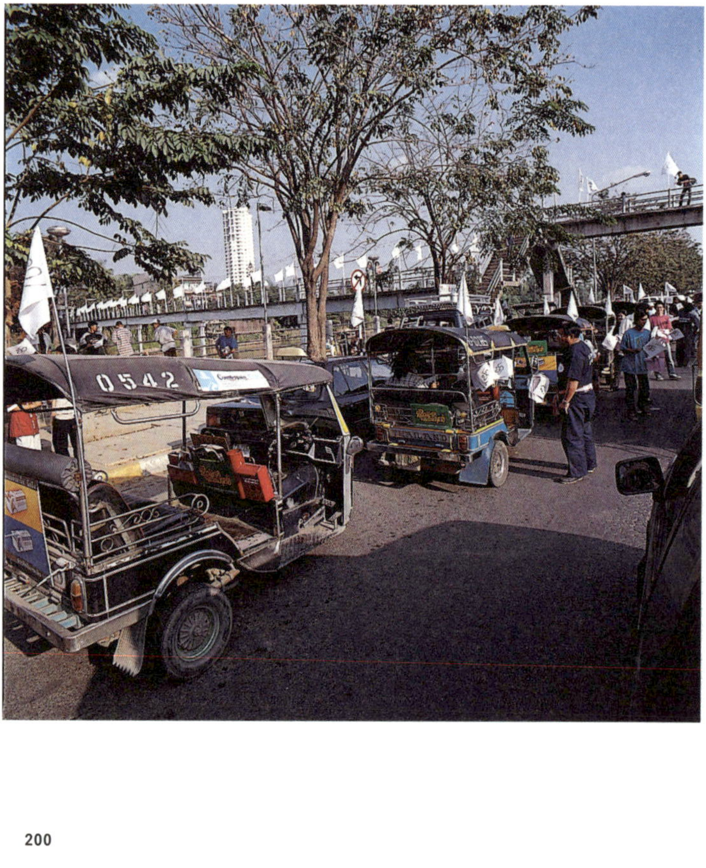

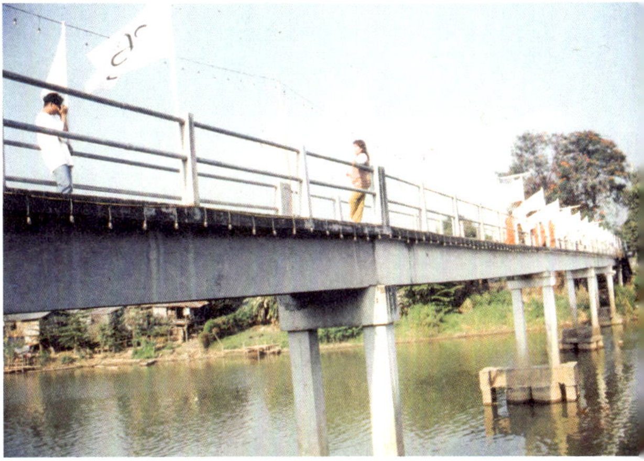

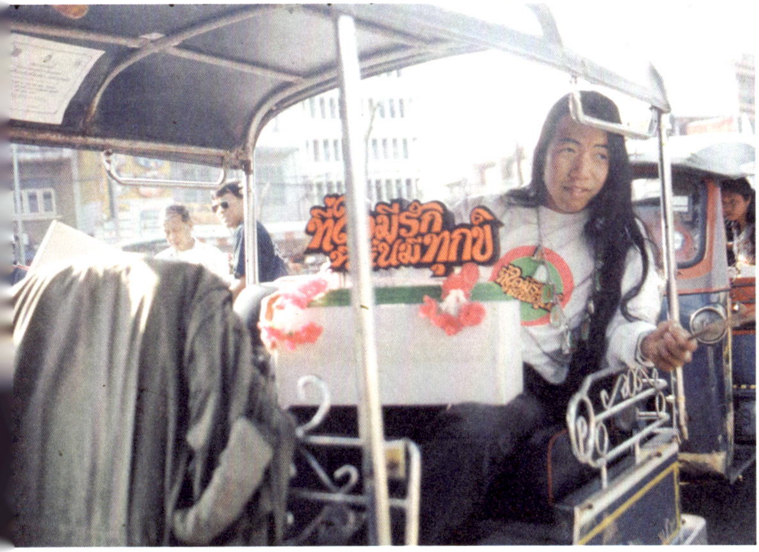

Kosit Juntaratip with his work.

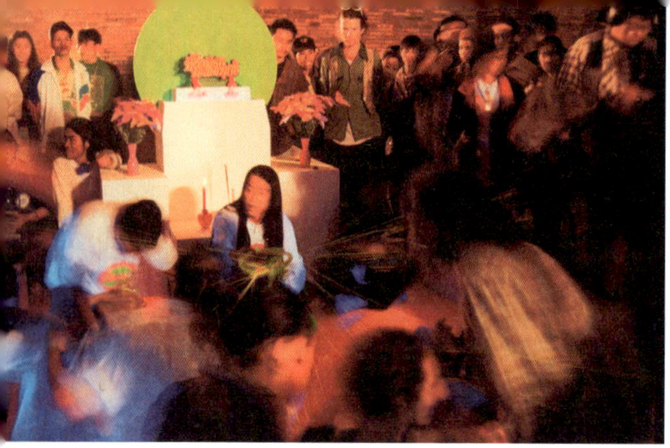

Kosit Juntaratip, *Where There is Love.*

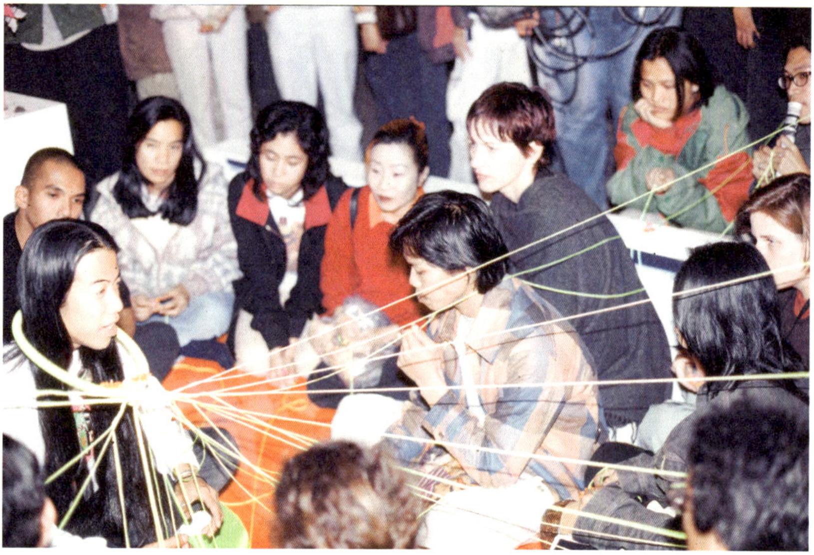

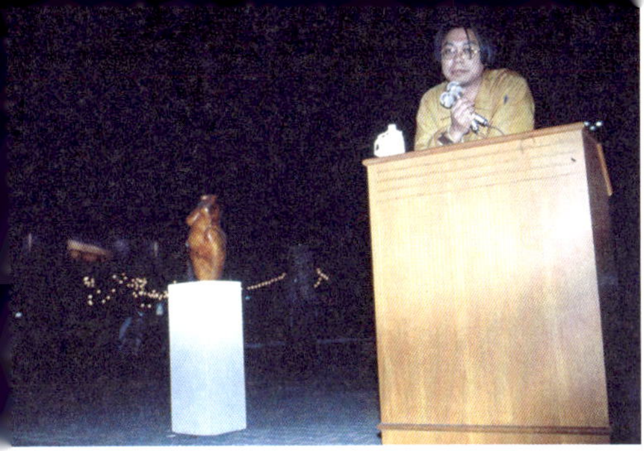

Rirkrit Tiravanajia speaking at the third Week of Cooperative Suffering.

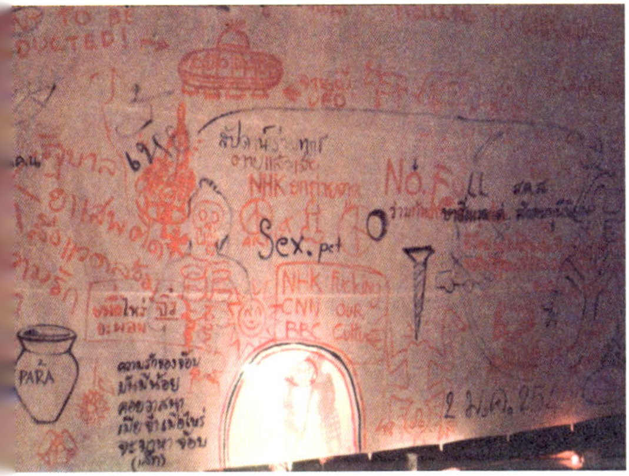

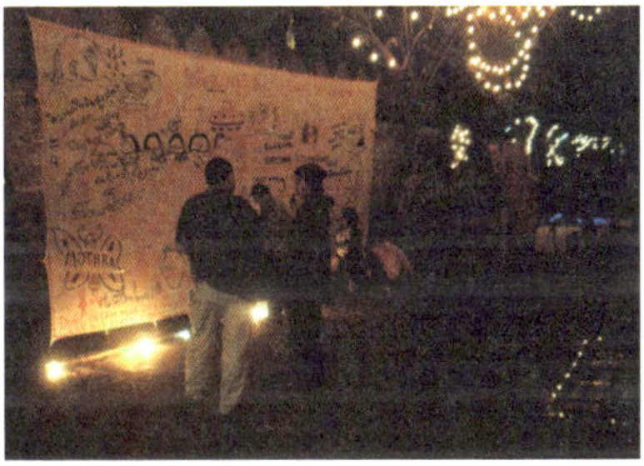

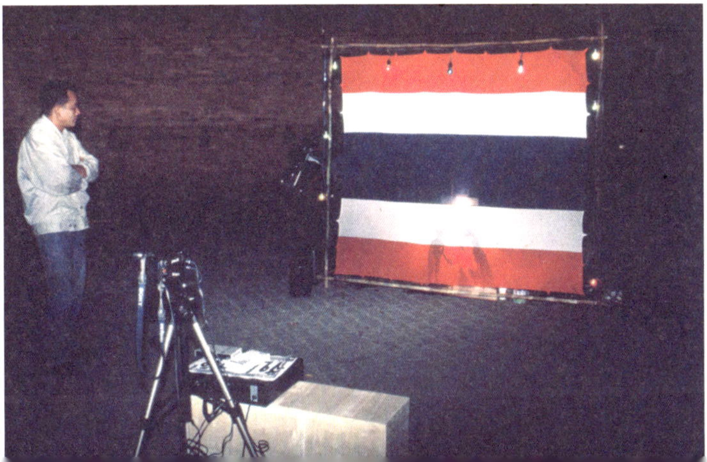

Works and performance by Vasan Sitthiket.

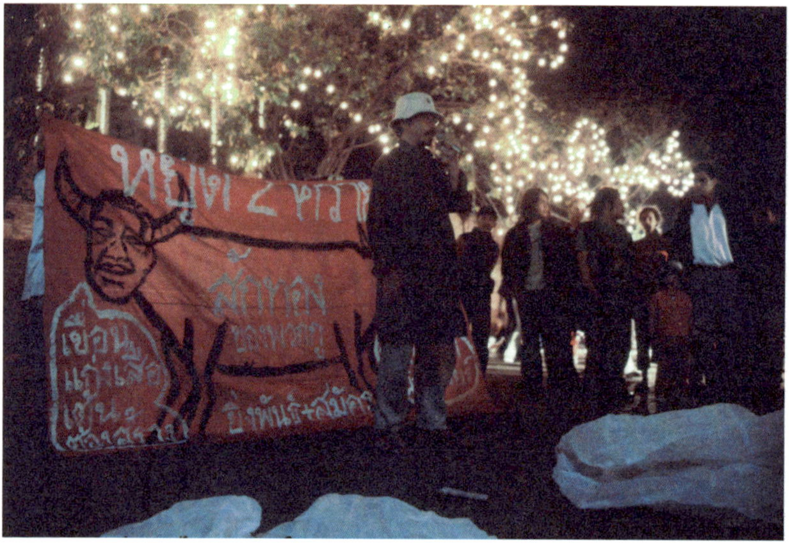

Works and performance by Vasan Sitthiket.

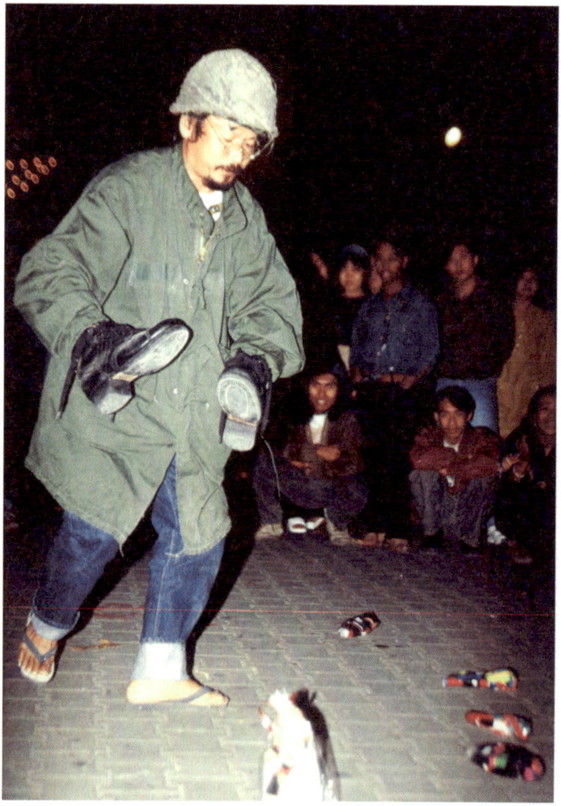

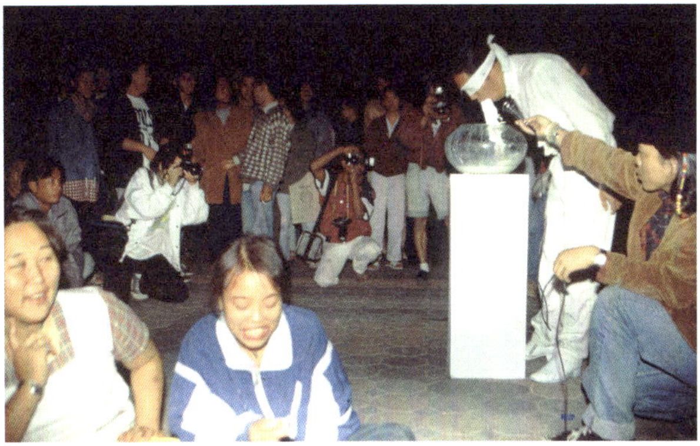

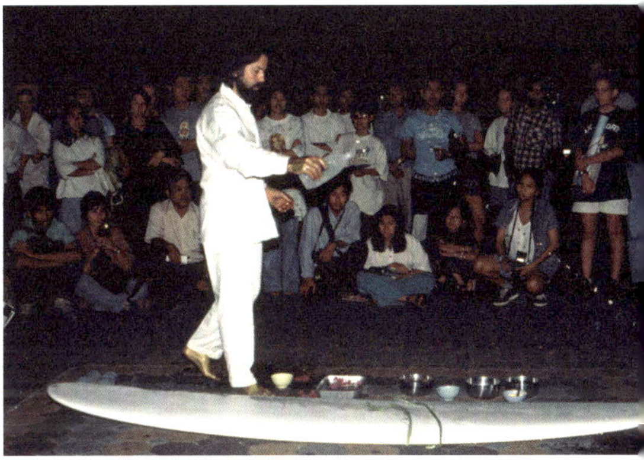

Performance by Rolf Hinterecker.

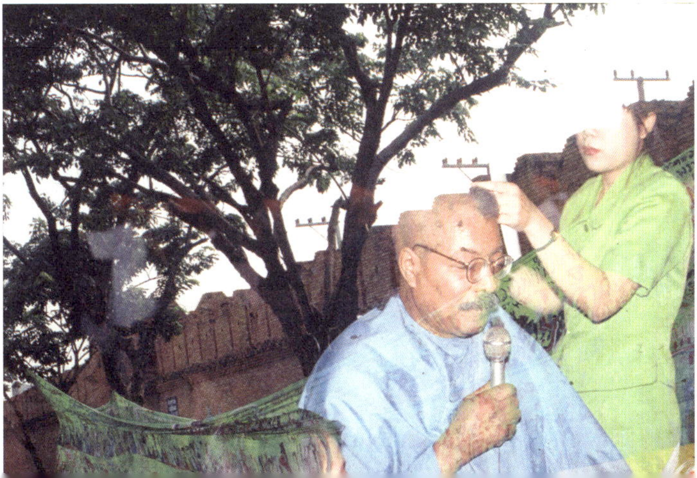

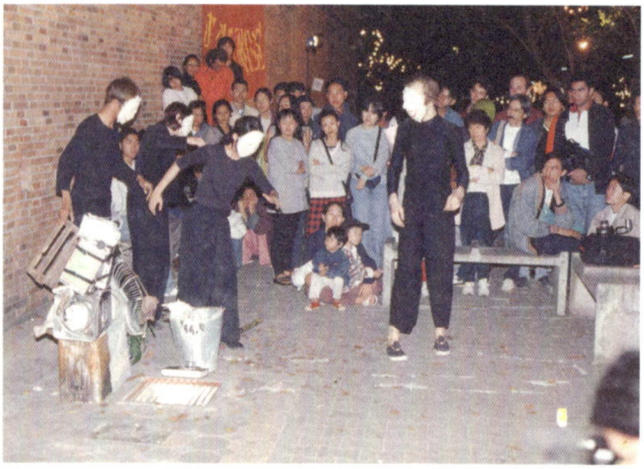

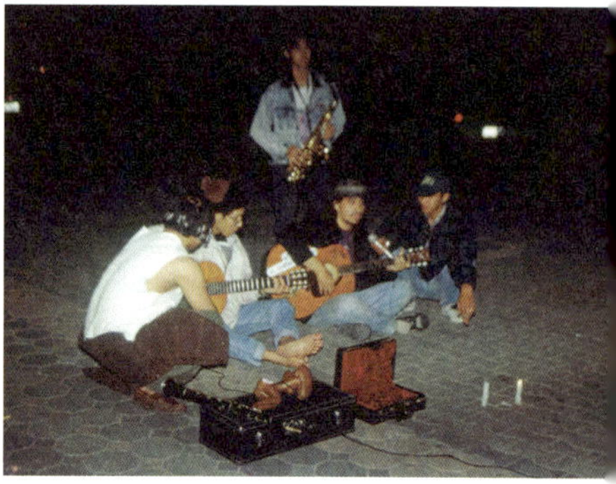

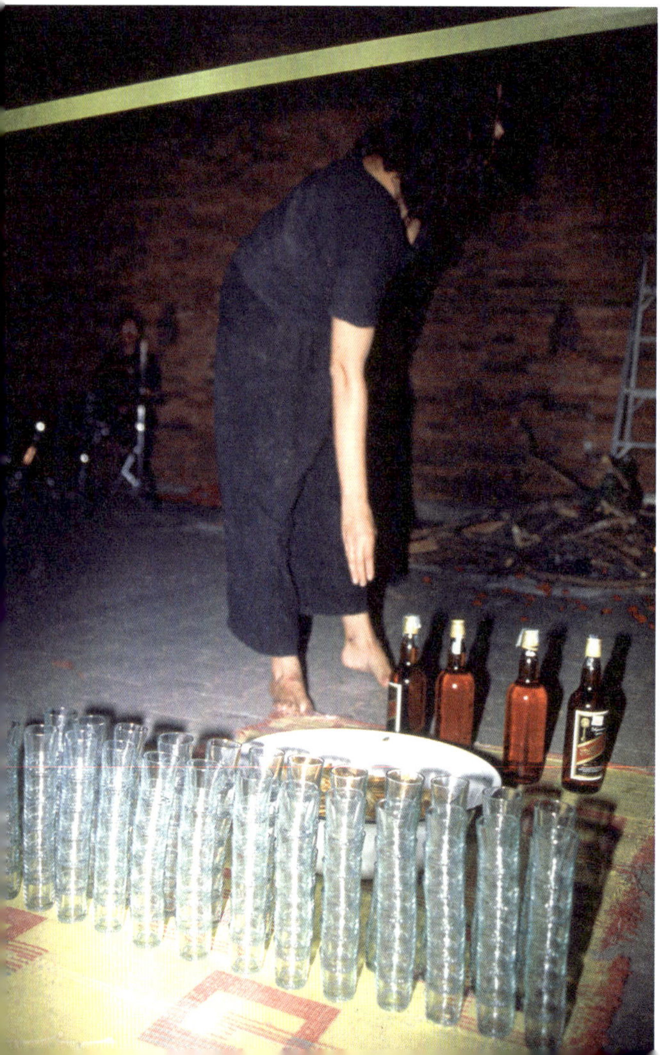

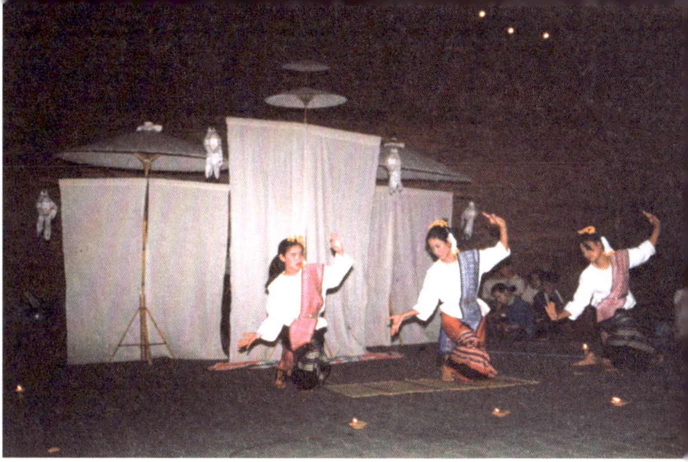

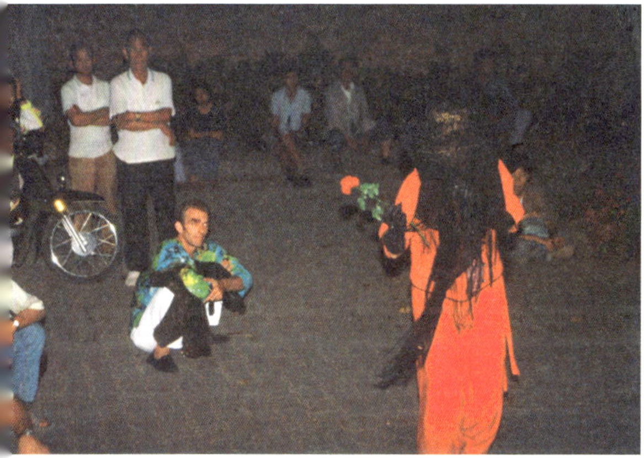

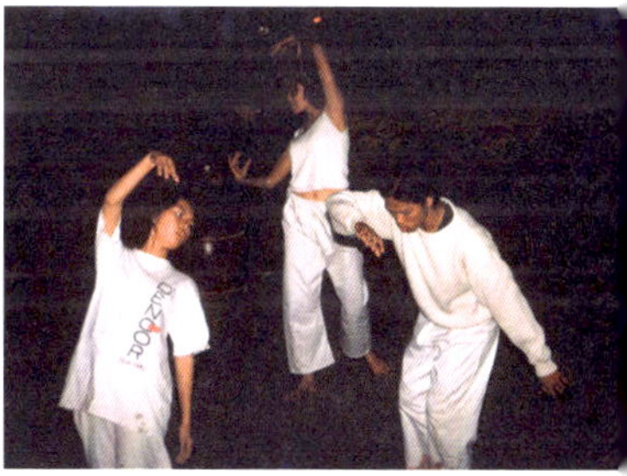

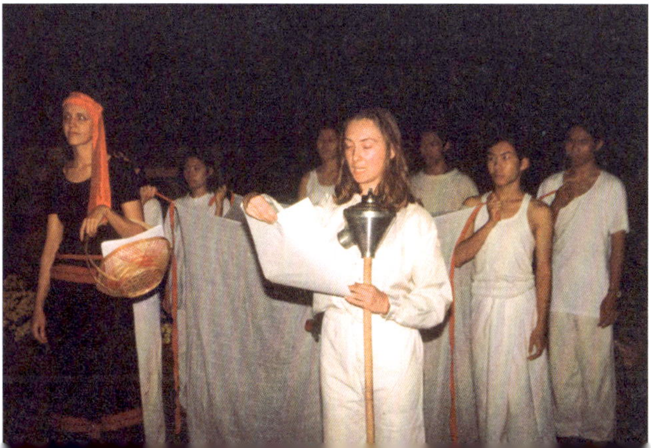

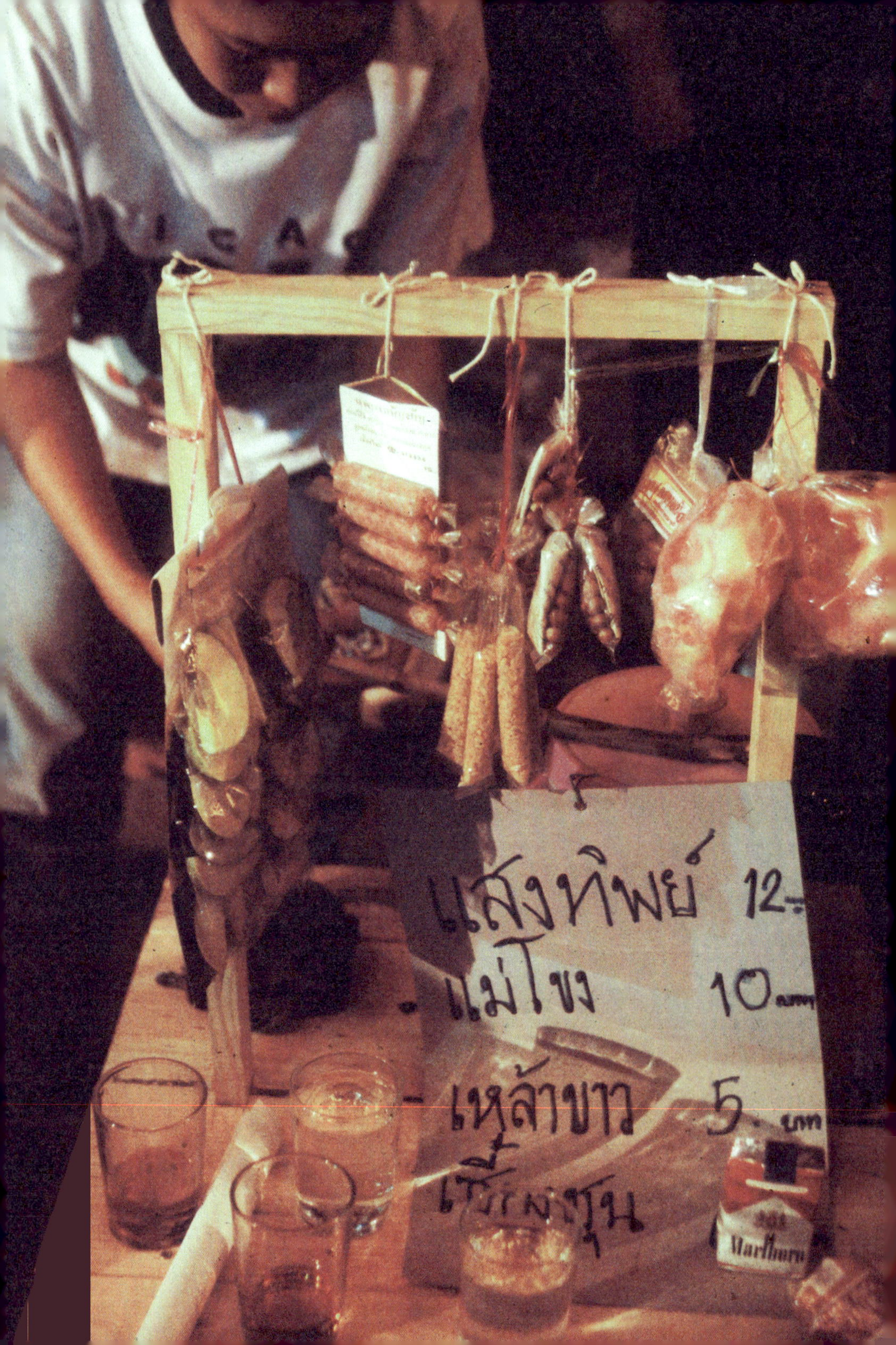
แสงทิพย์ 12
แม่โขง 10
เหล้าขาว 5
Marlboro

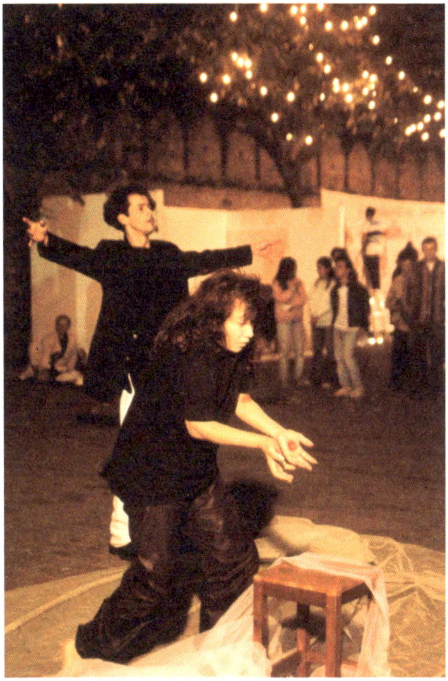

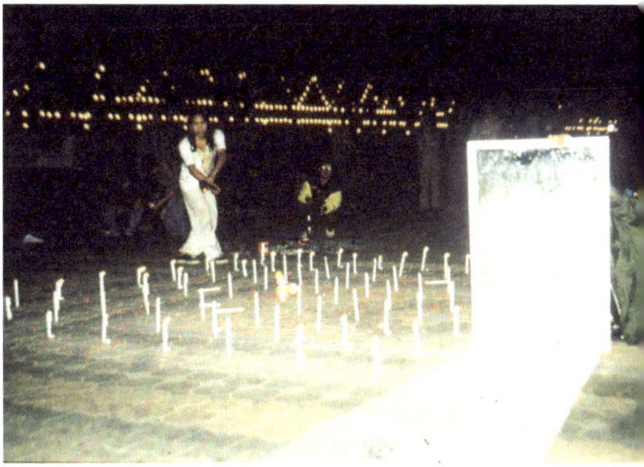

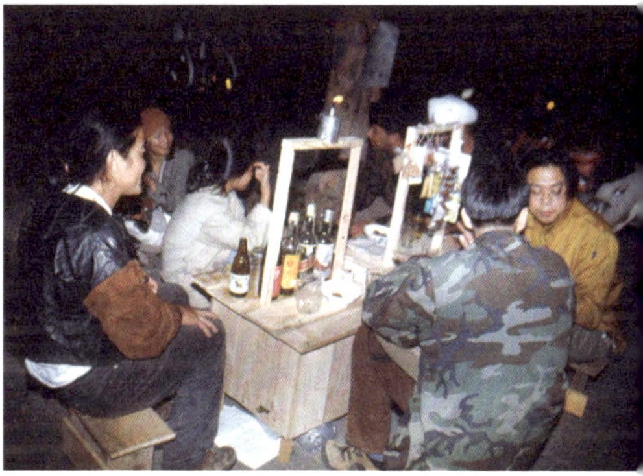

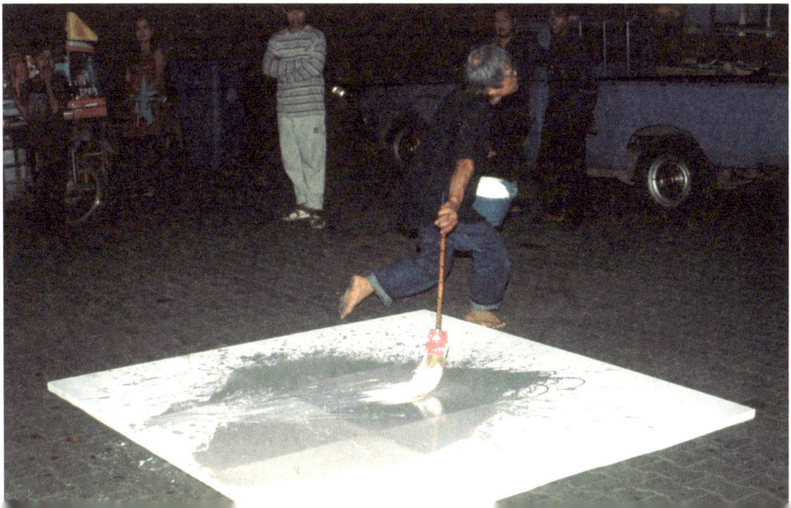

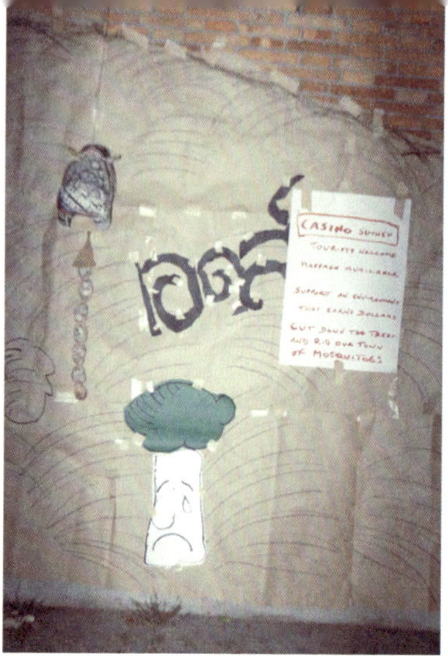
CASINO

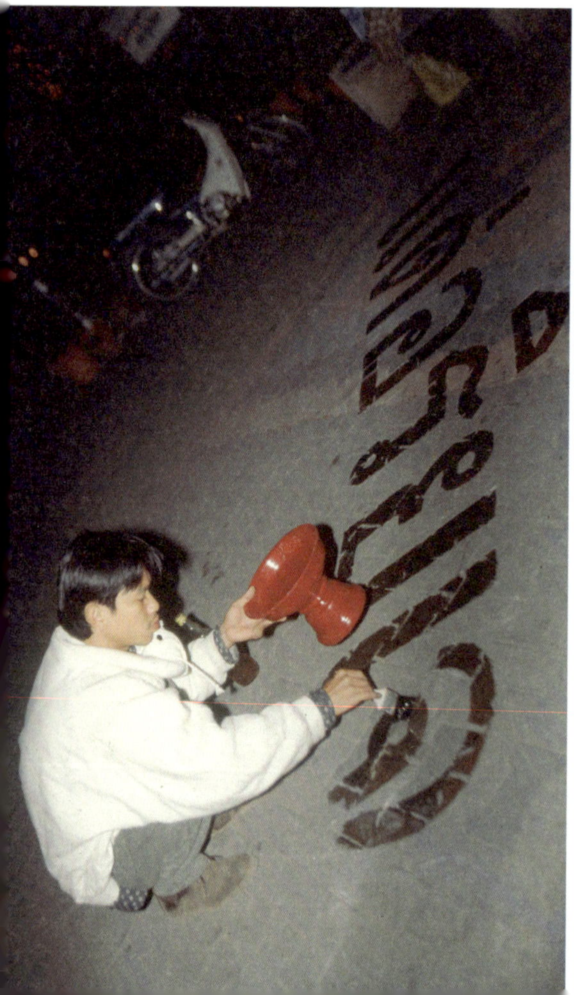

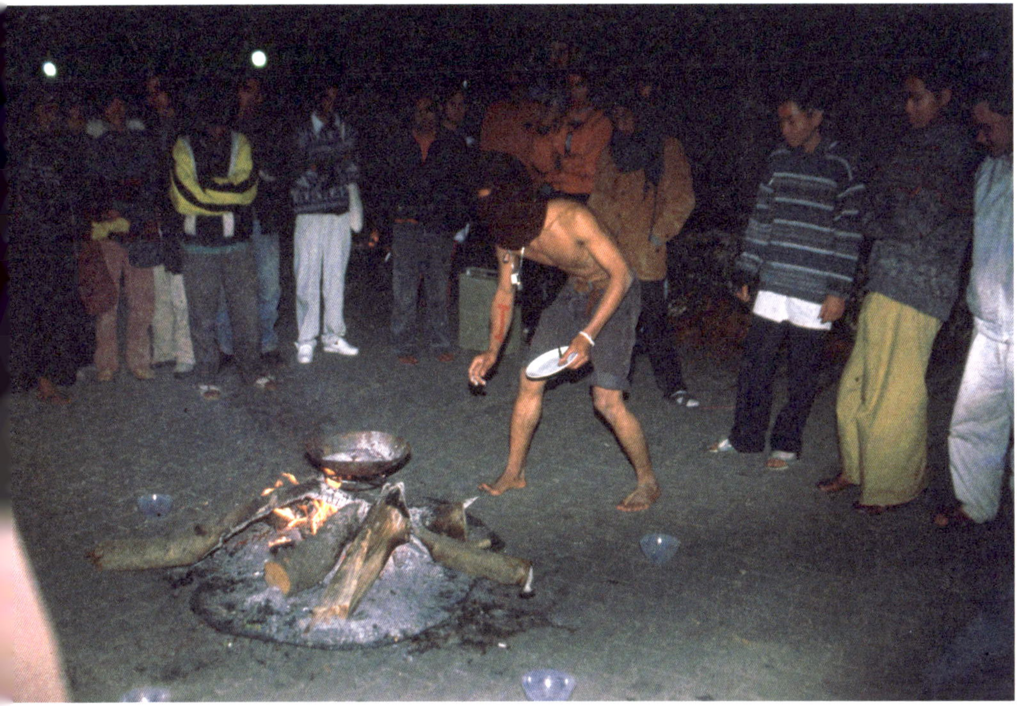

Various performances and
interventions at Tha Pae Gate.

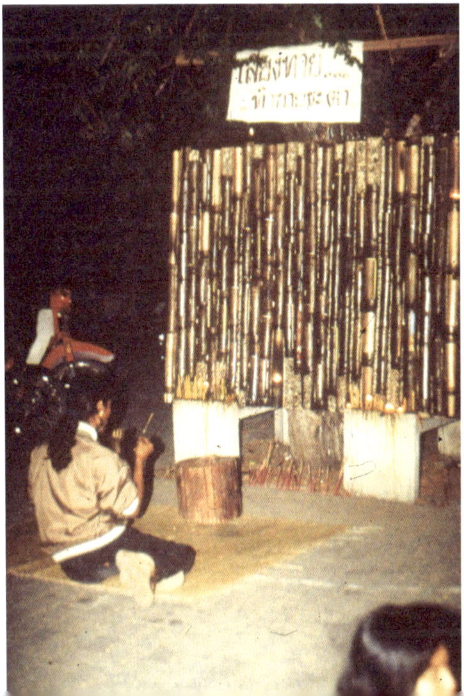

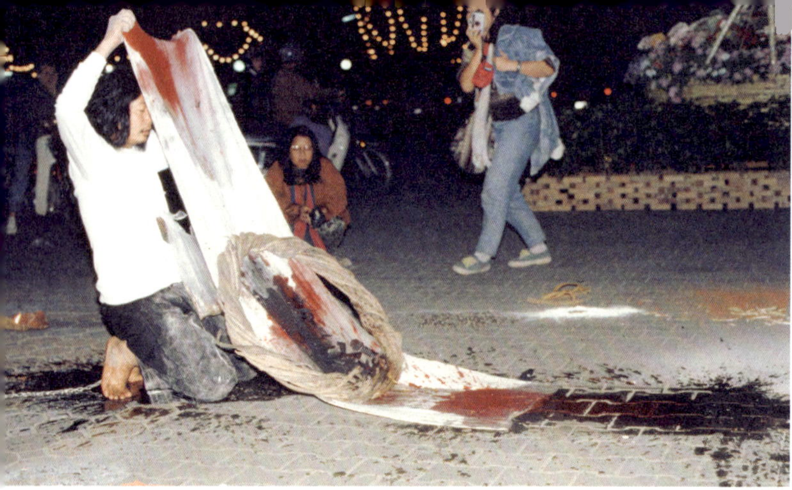

Performances by Paisan and
Mongkol Plienbangchang.

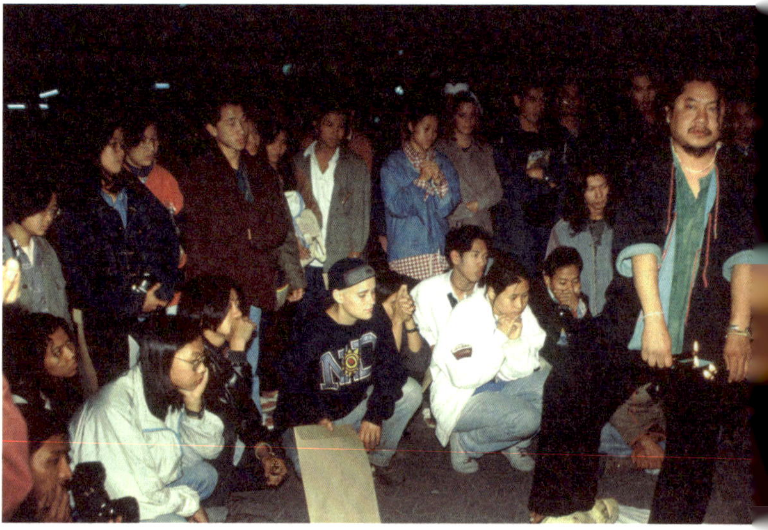

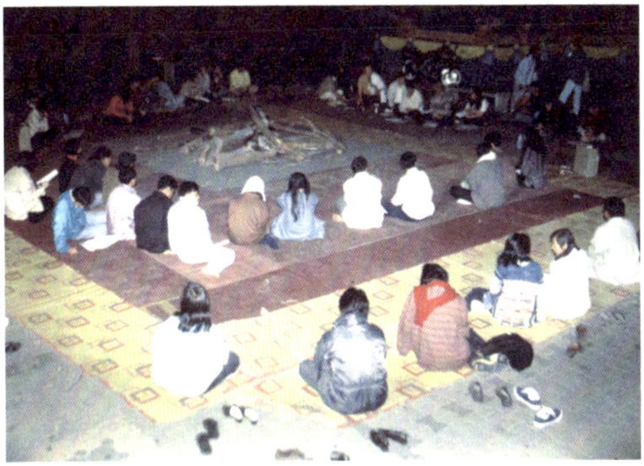

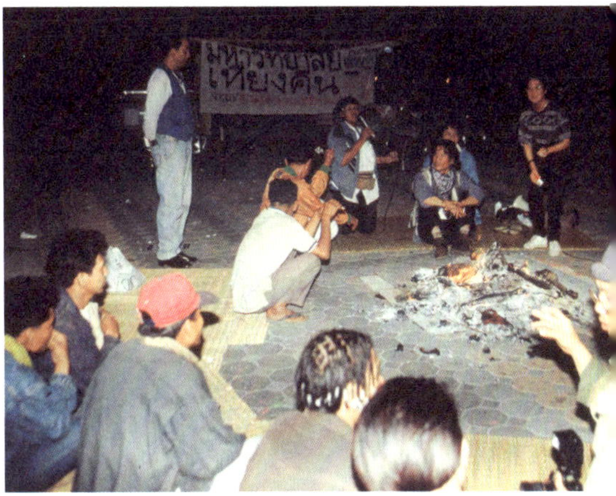

Midnight University at the Week
of Cooperative Suffering.

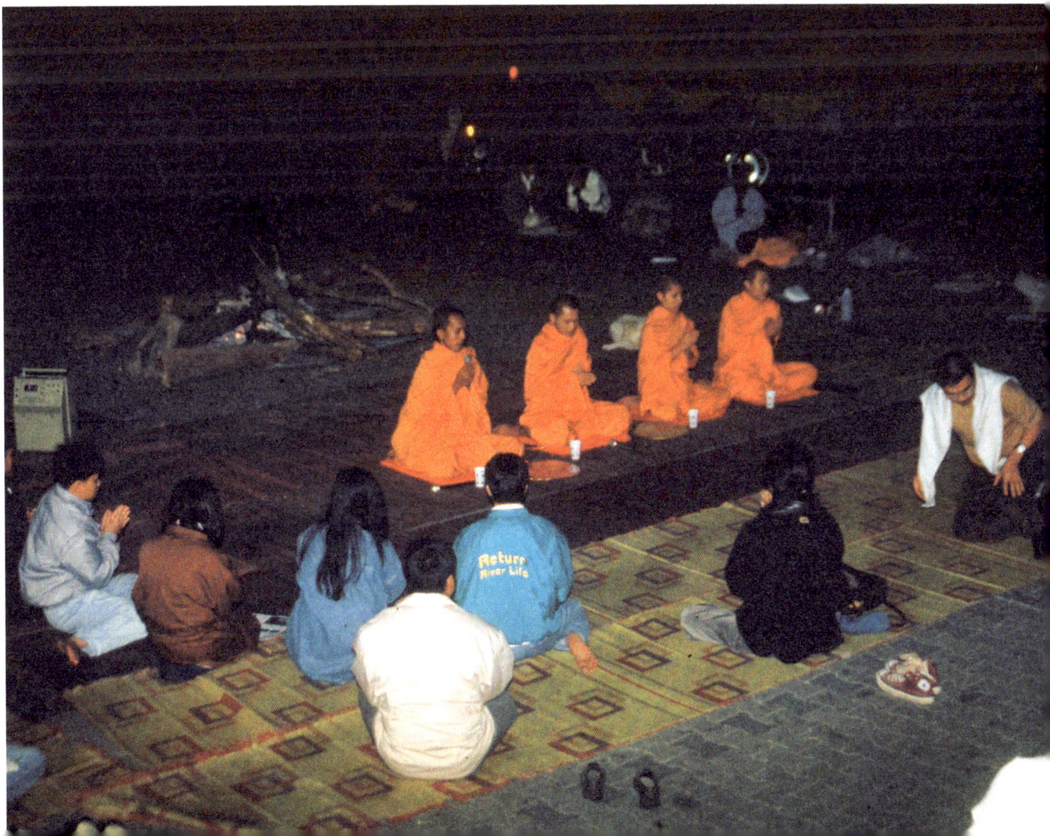

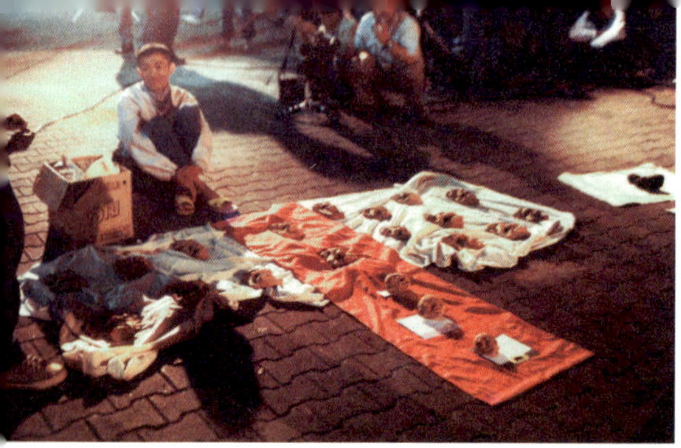

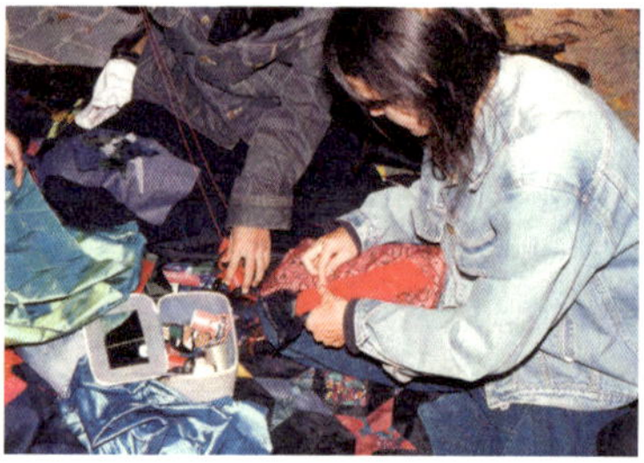

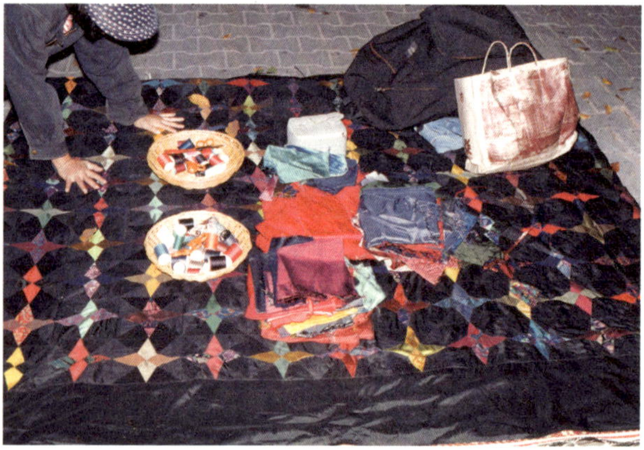

Culture and art market.

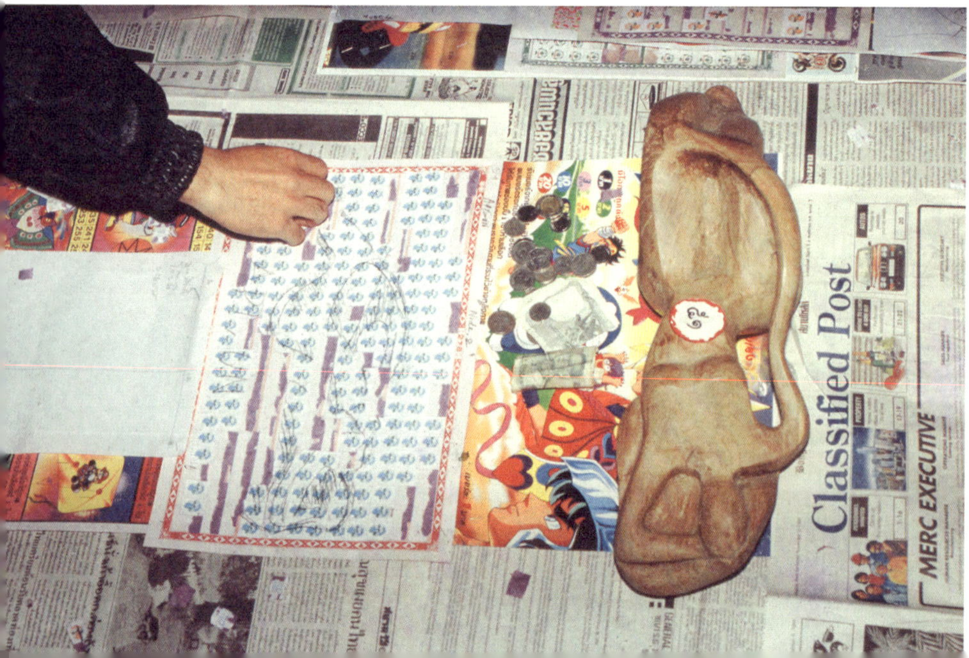

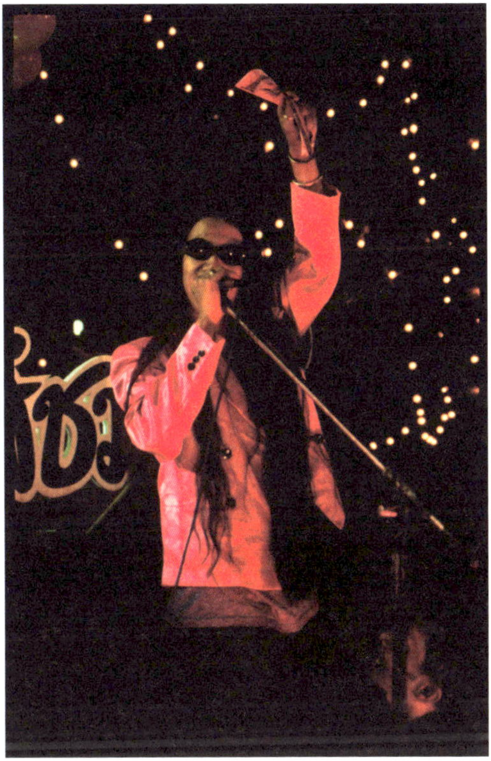

Kosit Juntaratip, *Love Dancing Party*.

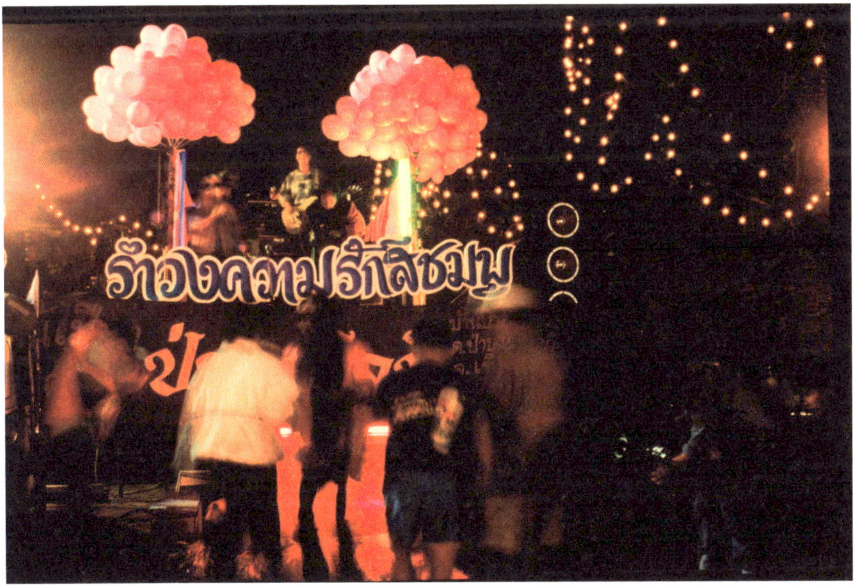

‘Chiang Mai Social Installation: Fourth Art and Cultural Festival: Temples, Cemeteries, Private-Residences, Public Buildings, Streets, Bridges, Walls, Rivers and Canals, Open Spaces’

‘Chiang Mai Social Installation: Fourth Art and Cultural Festival: Temples, Cemeteries, Private-Residences, Public Buildings, Streets, Bridges, Walls, Rivers and Canals, Open Spaces’

December 1997–January 1998

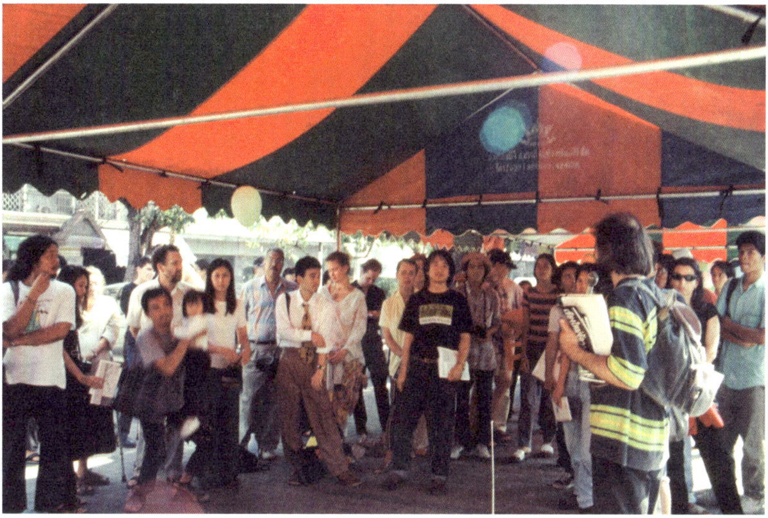

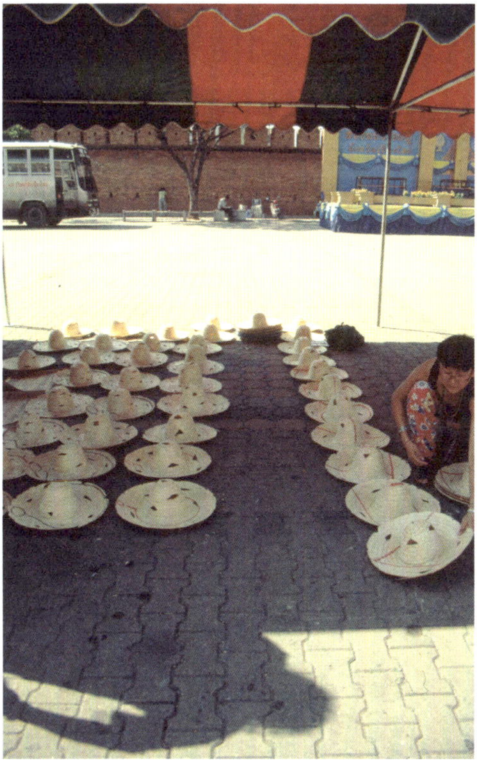

Main tent and information centre for the festival, Tha Pae Gate.

1 Tha-Pae Gate / ช่วงประตูท่าแพ
ORIS KRAUSHAAR
EFFREY BAILEY
IZ MILLER
AY LANGENBACH
กษรี สุวรรณศร/ยศวดี ฉายมณี/มรกต ยศธำรง
งคล เปลี่ยนบางช้าง
ชาญ สระศรีสม&เนติลักษณ์ ใบบัว
ญญา สันติเวส
มพงษ์ ทวี
EN PATTERSON (UA.)
CAROLA WILLBRANDT (UA.)
RANK KOLLGES/VOLKER HAMANN (UA.)
KARIN MEINER & MANFRED HAMMES (UA.)
ISA CIESLIK (UA.)
PARZIVAL POERSCH (UA.)
VOLKER HAMANN (UA.)

2 วัดอุโมงค์ / Wat U-mong
ฤษณา สุนทรภัค
บุญเกิด แก้วดี
ธีระพงศ์ บุญจันทร์ดะ
ฤษฎินันท์ ปินวัฒนากุล
วัฒนะ วัฒนาพันธุ์
สุธรรม แก้วตาทิพย์
ภูกชัย ลิ่มประสิทธิอิสระ
ENNO STAHL (UA.)

3 Wat Chat Yot / วัดเจ็ดยอด
AKATSUKI HARADA

4 Wat Thoong-Yoo / วัดทุงยู
ANNE ROCHETTE

5 FACULTY OF FINE ART/คณะวิจิตรศิลป์ มช.
DEBRA PORCH
PIETRO PELLINI (ITALY) / YOLA BERBESZ
โครงงาน ลานสรรพสินค้าวัฒนธรรม มช.

6 the Night Bazaar/ตลาดไนท์บาซ่า
ROBERT PETERS

7 the Good View Bar&Restaurant/ร้านเดอะกู๊ดวิว
QING QING CHEN
สุดศิริ ปุยอ๊อก

8 ถนนราชดำเนิน / Ratchdamneon Rd.
จักรพันธ์ ศรีเพชร&วิสิฐ จันมา

9 สำนักส่งเสริมศิลปวัฒนธรรม มช.
The Center for Promotion Arts and Culture CMU.
ธีรนารถ แซ่เตียว

10 โรงเรียนสอนคนตาบอดภาคเหนือ ถ. อารักษ์
Blindness Tranning School
ยศสรัล ไชยดวงแก้ว/ธนัญญา บุญยังและเพื่อนๆ

11 จากวัดอุโมงค์ถึงสี่แยกโรงแรมรินคำ
From Suthep Rd. to Nim Man Hemin Rd.
อุดม ฉิมภักดี

12 Wat Phra-Singh / วัดพระสิงห์
SUSANNE HEIMES (UA.)

13 Wat Chieng Mun / วัดเชียงมั่น
BARBARA ELLMERER (UA.)

14 In the city / บางแห่งในเมือง
สกนธ์ เพ็ชรศรี
อังกฤษ อัจฉริยโสภณ
JOSIE CAVALLARO
GABY LUDWIG (UA.)
KNOPP FERRO (UA.)
MARIANNE TRALAU (UA.)
ROLAND KERSTEIN (UA.)
ROLF HINTERECKER (UA.)
RUTH JAGER (UA.)

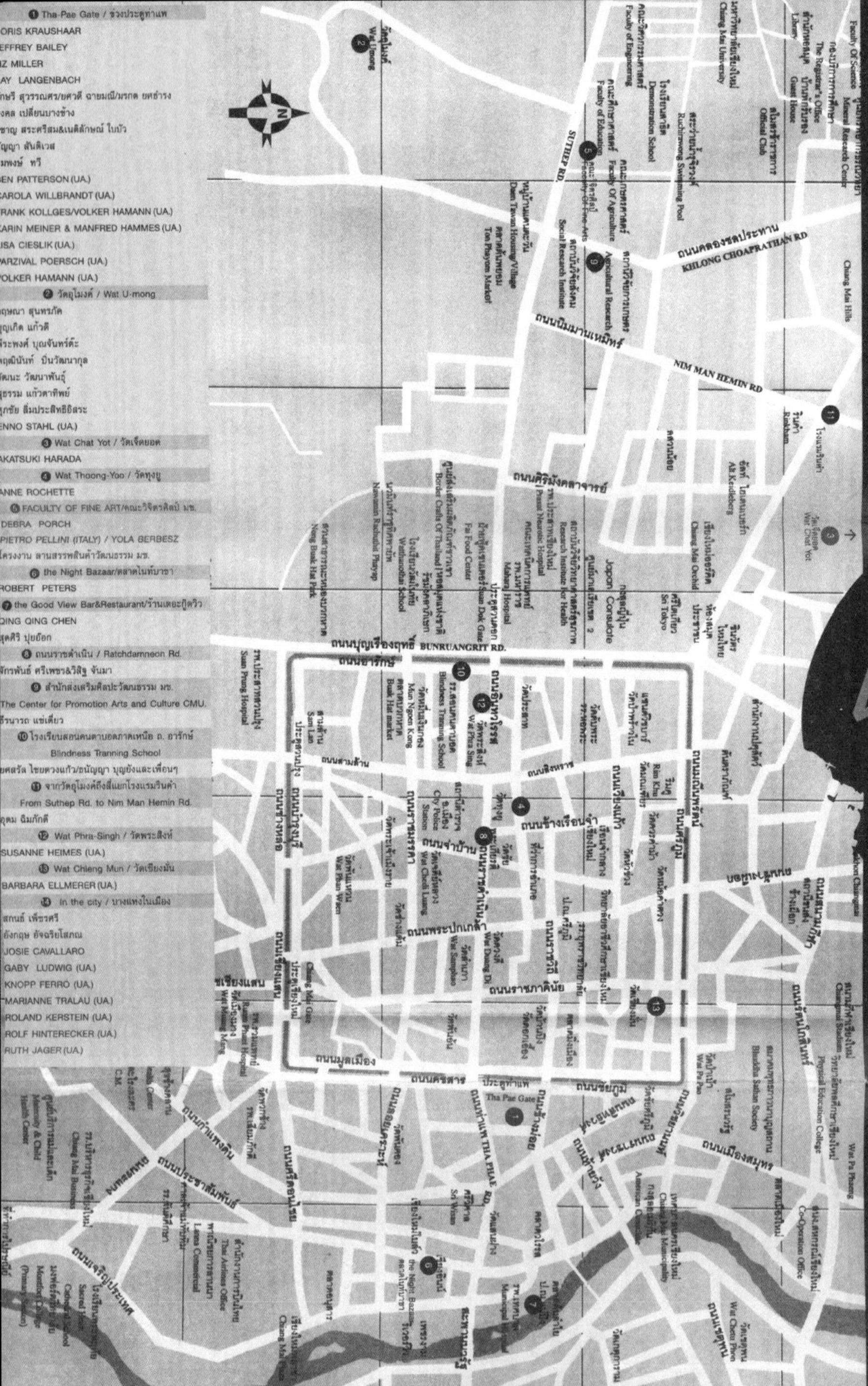

4 th
ครั้งที่

ศิลปวัฒนธรรมเทศกาล ART AND CULTURAL F

วัด สุสาน บ้าน อาคาร ถนน สะพาน กำแพง แม่น้ำลำคลอง พื้นที่ว่าง ครั้ง

FOURTH ART AND CULTURAL FESTIVAL: TEMPLES,CEMETERIES,PRIVATE-RESIDEN
PUBLIC BUILDINGS, STREETS, BRIDGES, WALLS, RIVERS AND CANALS, OPEN SPA

CHIANGMAI SOCIAL INSTALLATION

เชียงใหม่จัดวางสังคม

ร่วม :"เชียงใหม่จัดวางสังคม" คณะวิจิตรศิลป์ มหาวิทยาลัยเชียงใหม่ 50200 โทร. / โทรสาร (053)21172

SS : "CHIANGMAI SOCIAL INSTALLATION" C/O FACULTY OF FINE ARTS CHIANGMAI UNIVERSITY, CHIANGMAI 50200 THAILAND. TEL/FAX.(6653)2117

วาคม 2540 - 7 มกราคม 2541 ณ จังหวัดเชียงใหม่

mber 1, 1997 - January 7, 1998 At Chiang Mai THAILAND

"SOCIAL INSTALLATION :...open for all disciplines in society, that want to "rouse" an atmosphere and stimulate activities on a Contemporary Cultural level,...NATURAL VALUE :...where people present creative activities together;...where we respect, acknowledge and exchange each other's point of view....it is a form of "cooperative consciousness" CONTEMPORART VISION :...encourages works and activities that deal with originality, creativity...be likened to "Social Consciousness" CULTURAL LOCATION :...the function of existing locations...will be altered into locations, for cultural expression...CULTURALISTS & INTER-EXPRESSION :...everybody has the potential to be a Culturalist. Any activity, any topic, any means of expression...can become a creative activity that contributes to social installation."

(Editing from 7 COLLECTIVE PRINCIPLES FROM FRIENDS)

• The Chiang Mai Social Installation (CMSI)is a group of people that organizes activities concerning "Human relations" as a contribution to the creation of a more balanced culture in the context of free-market, capitalistic contemporary society. CMSI is a project that seriously attempts to form a counterweight, to stimulate "Cultural activities",to co-operate in humbleness, in the hope that contemporary society will develop towards a mixed cultural activities /capitalistic society.

• Working method of CMSI :The festival, CMSI is a search for the 3 basic values (1) HUMAN SPIRIT during the 'Week of co-operative Suffering'; to create a "co-operative Spirit-form". (2)ART ACTIVITIES ; to create a "co-operative Art-form". (3) THOUGHTS ; to create a "co-operative Thought-form".

• CMSI aims at organizing a yearly social installation which could be a model for all levels of society all over the world. This should function as a social consciousness, through a process of "installation", rather than "occupation", of a lasting and continuous society-model, with complete participation of the people, which we see as the foundation for the development of a natural unified society.

นิยาม "ศิลปะกิจกรรม" ในฐานะเครื่องมือสร้างวัฒนธรรมชุมชน

*" **จัดวางสังคม** : เชียงใหม่จัดวางสังคม เป็นเทศกาลประจำปี... เพื่อ"ปลูก" กิจกรรม สาระ และบรรยากาศทางวัฒนธรรมร่วมสมัย...**คุณค่าธรรมะ**...คุณค่าที่มนุษย์นำเสนอกิจกรรมสร้างสรรค์ร่วมกัน...นำมาแสดงออกปฏิสัมพันธ์ร่วมกัน... ได้เรียนรู้แลกเปลี่ยน...ความคิดความเชื่อซึ่งกันและกัน...เป็นรูปทรงแห่ง "สหกรณ์จิตวิญญาณ" **วิสัยทัศน์ทางสังคม** :...ส่งเสริมผลงานและกิจกรรมที่แสดงความคิดริเริ่มสร้างสรรค์...จากทุกคนและทุกศาสตร์...เป็น"สติของสังคม"เป็นกลไก...พัฒนาระบบวัฒนธรรม...ให้มี...ชีวิตยืดหยุ่น...การแก้ไขสังคมวัฒนธรรม...เป็นไปเองตามธรรมชาติ **วัฒนธรรมสถานร่วมสมัย :** ทุกๆ พื้นที่...จะถูกเปลี่ยนบทบาทเดิม...มาทำหน้าที่ใหม่ เป็นพื้นที่เพื่อการแสดงออกทางวัฒนธรรม...**นักวัฒนธรรม** :..."ประชาชนทุกคนมีศักยภาพเป็นนักวัฒนธรรม" ...ทุกกลวิธีการแสดงออก...ที่ดำเนินอยู่ในสังคม สามารถกลายเป็น กิจกรรมสร้างสรรค์ เพื่อการจัดวางสังคม"*

(ตัดตอนมาจากบทแถลงการณ์ในอดีต "7 สาระรวบรวมจากเพื่อน")

•"เชียงใหม่จัดวางสังคม" (ชมจส) เป็นความพยายามของคนกลุ่มหนึ่ง ที่จัดกิจกรรมเกี่ยวข้องกับ "การสร้างความสัมพันธ์ในหมู่มนุษย์" ในนาม "วัฒนธรรม?" โดยความคาดหวังที่จะเห็นสังคมทุนนิยมร่วมสมัย ซึ่งเป็นสังคมที่เน้นคุณค่าทางเศรษฐกิจ พัฒนาอย่างมีดุลยภาพกับกิจกรรม หรือ "คุณค่าทางวัฒนธรรม ?" โดยวางนโยบายรูปแบบของกิจกรรมเป็น 3 ลักษณะ (ก)สร้างค่านิยมการมีส่วนร่วม วัฒนธรรมชุมชน กัลยณมิตรทางวัฒนธรรม (รูปทรงของจิตวิญญาณ) (ข)เน้นศิลปะกิจกรรมสาขาต่างๆ และกิจกรรมทางวัฒนธรรมจากทุกๆ ศาสตร์ (รูปทรงของศิลปะวัฒนธรรม) (ค)เน้นการเสวนา แลกเปลี่ยนทางปัญญา (รูปทรงของปัญญา)

• ครั้งนี้ เชียงใหมจัดวางสังคม ครั้งที่ 4 ในประเด็น "ความจน" (กรณีศึกษาสังคมไทยยากจนเพราะการเมือง?) อะไรคือนิยามและเหตุปัจจัยของความจน ? เมื่อไม่มีเงินเป็นพื้นฐาน กิจกรรมทางวัฒนธรรมในนาม ชมจส จะเกิดได้อย่างไร? อะไรคือคุณภาพของศิลปะหรือกิจกรรมทางวัฒนธรรม? ความจนกับวัฒนธรรมเกี่ยวข้องกันอย่างไร? ฯลฯ ล้วนเป็นบริบทแห่งคำถาม สำหรับเทศกาลในครั้งนี้

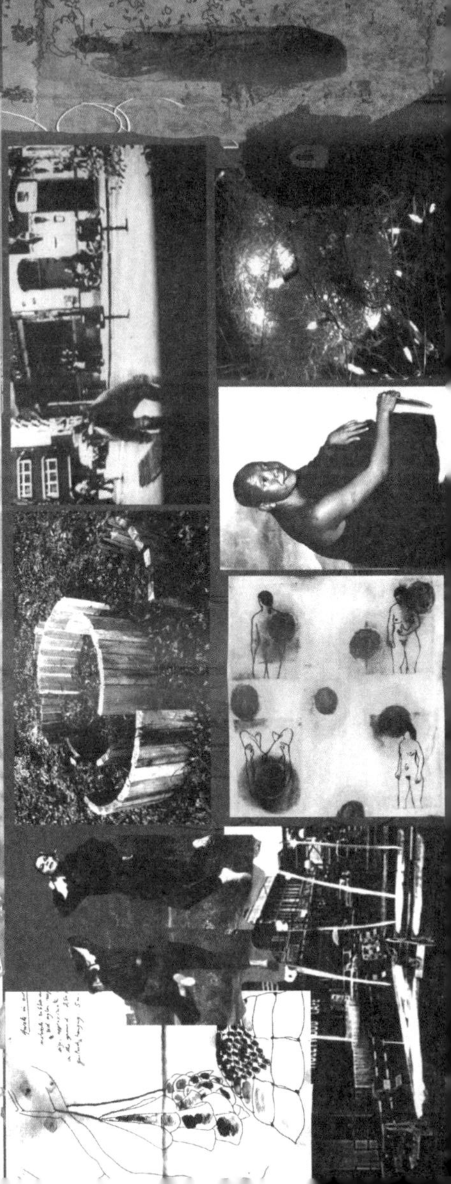

Wat Chai Yot / วัดไชยยศ
- December 1-16, 1997 / วันที่ 1-16 ธันวาคม 2540
- I want to restore the identity of refuse rubber, give them one more chance to recall there connection with the earth before they descends into ashs and dust.

ANNE ROCHETTE (FRANCE)
- "Awake in our sleep" (Installation)
- Wat Thoong Yoo / วัดทุงยู
- December 1-30, 1997 / วันที่ 1-30 ธันวาคม 2540
- Using rubber (a material produced by Thailand in large quantities), before it becomes industrially processed, I looked for a meditative image of an alert state of consciousness.

Sponsored by The Association Française pour l' Action Artistique

DEBRA PORCH (AUSTRALIA)
- "Veil" (Installation)
- at the women's Toilets of the Faculty of Fine Arts & the Faculty of Humanity / ห้องน้ำผู้หญิง คณะวิจิตรศิลป์ คณะมนุษยศาสตร์ มช.
- December 2-30, 1997/ วันที่ 2-30 ธันวาคม 2540
- There are many storytellers amongst us. Histories are passed on. The invisible women are exchanging stories and histories, they are whispering

DORIS KRAUSHAAR (AUSTRIA)
- "The step" (Performance)
- Tha-Pae Gate / ประตูท่าแพ
- December 2, 1997 , 6.00 PM.
- เฉพาะวันที่ 2 ธันวาคม 2540 เวลา 18.00 น.
- two people are seperated. A wall (Ego) is between them.There is a door in the wall (love) But it is small ! So after a while fighting between themselves,they saw a bigdoor (love) to come together and overcome thewall (Ego)

JEFFREY BAILEY (AUTRALIA)
- "Theatre SetforThailand" (Sculpture/Installation)
- Tha-Pae Gate / ลานประตูท่าแพ
- December1-16,1997/วันที่ 1-16 ธันวาคม 2540
- Theatre set for Thailand is a conceptual metaphore of absurdist theatre implanted at Tha-Pae Gate

- The side of canal in the city / ริมคูเมือง
- December 1-3, 1997 / วันที่ 1-3 ธันวาคม 2540

LIZ MILLER (USA)
- "Shift" (Installation)
- Tha-Pae Gate / ประตูท่าแพ
- December 2-16, 1997/ วันที่ 2-16 ธันวาคม 2540
- I Want to use the structure of the wall and An element of suprise to convey an idea of awareness of the current socio-economic and political changes in Thailand. I also want to maintain a sense of humor.

RAY LANGENBACH (USA)
- "The Performance Indoctrination" (Performance)
- Tha-Pae Gate / ประตูท่าแพ
- December 15, 1997 / วันที่ 15 ธันวาคม 2540

ROBERT PETERS (USA)
- "International Relations" (Installation)
- the Night Bazaar/ บันไดทางขึ้นในตลาดไนท์บาซาร์
- December 1-30,1997 /วันที่ 1-30 ธันวาคม 2540
- This project explores the relationship between "outside visitor" and their hosts. It will be located at sites in Chiangmai where Thai culture engages these "visitors"("Visitors") includes individuals as well as material and symbo(lic culture). The proposed site is the Night Bazaar. The work is comprised of textual observations that delineate the above relationship.

QING QING CHEN (CHINA/AUSTRIA)
- "Human being & nature" (Performance/Installation)
- The side of the Good View Bar&Restaurant / ริมแม่น้ำปิงร้านเดอะกู๊ดวิว
- December 1, 1997 6.00PM.
- เฉพาะวันที่ 1 ธันวาคม 2540 เวลา 18.00 น.
- To show my love for the natural environment and bring to attention the issue of environment pollution

กฤษณา สุนทรภักดิ์
(KRITSANA SOONTHORNPAK)
- "รัก โลภ โกรธ หลง"(ศิลปะจัดวาง) "Love Needy Angry" (Installation)
- สวนสมุนไพร วัดอุโมงค์ / Wat U-mong

พึงรู้เท่าทัน

จักรพันธ์ ศรีเพชร & วิสิฐ จันมา
(CHAKKAPAN SRIPET & VISIT JANMA)
- "ชั่วขณะหนึ่ง" (ศิลปะจัดวาง) "Once up on a time" (Installation)
- เสาไฟฟ้าจากประตูท่าแพถึงหน้าวัดพระสิงห์ Ratchdamneon Rd.
- วันที่ 2-30 ธันวาคม 2540 / December 2-30, 1997
- ระลึกถึงการมีสติของตนเองที่ได้รับประสบการณ์จากภายในวัดเคลื่อนย้ายความรู้สึกเหล่านั้นออกมาสู่ สถานที่สาธารณะอันวุ่นวาย เร่งรีบในเมืองใหญ่

จักษรี สุวรรณศร / ยศวดี ฉายมณี /มรกต ยศธำรง
(JAKSAREE SUVANASARA / YOSAWADEE CHAYMANEE / MORAGOT YOSTAMRONG)
- "ศิลปะเด็กกับจัดวางสังคม" (ศิลปะกิจกรรม) "Children-Art & social Installtation"(Art Activity)
- ลานประตูท่าแพ / Tha-Pae Gate
- 3 ธันวาคม 2540 / December 2-30, 1997

ธีรนารถ แซ่เตี่ยว (TEERANAT SA-DIAW)
- "คนงาม" (ศิลปะจัดวาง) "Nice girl" (Installation)
- สำนักส่งเสริมศิลปะวัฒนธรรม มช. /The Center for Promotion Arts and Culture CMU.
- 2-30 ธันวาคม 2540 / December 2-30, 1997
- วัฒนธรรมไทย การแสดงออกเรื่องทางเพศเป็นสิ่งควรปิดกั้น ก่อให้เกิดความกดดันที่ต้องปฏิบัติตนเพื่อวัฒนธรรม โดยฝืนธรรมชาติพื้นฐาน ของมนุษย์

บุญเกิด แก้วดี (BOONKERT KAEWDEE)
- "ฉันรักวัฒนธรรม 700 ปี" (ศิลปะจัดวาง) "I love Chiang Mai culture (700 years ago)" (Installation)
- ลานเจดีย์ วัดอุโมงค์ / Wat U-mong
- 2-30 ธันวาคม 2540 / December 2-30, 1997
- เชียงใหม่? ถ้าไม่มี 700 ปี ก็ไม่มีคุณค่าคุณค่าอยู่ที่คน

พีระพงษ์ บุญจันทร์ตะ
(PHEERAPHONG BOONJANTA)
- "ไม่มีชื่อ" (ประติมากรรมสื่อประสม)
- วัดอุโมงค์ / Wat U-mong
- 2-30 ธันวาคม 2540 / December 2-30, 1997

(PRETTINUN PINWUTTANAKUL)
- "ไข่ลอย" (ศิลปะจัดวาง) "Can eggs float" (Installation)
- วัดอุโมงค์ / Wat U-mong
- 2-30 ธันวาคม 2540 / December 2-30, 1997
- การร่วมกันของวิทยาศาสตร์ แบบพื้นฐานกับศิลปะ

มงคล เปลี่ยนบางช้าง
(MONGKOL PLIENBANGCHANG)
- "ฉลองชัย ไอเอ็มเอฟ" (การแสดง) "Let s' Celebrate IMF Land" (Performance)
- ลานประตูท่าแพ / Tha-Pae Gate
- วันที่ 2 ธันวาคม 2540 / December 2, 1997

ยศสรัล ไชยดวงแก้ว / ธนัญญา บุญยัง และเพื่อนๆ
YOTSARUN CHAIDOUGKEAW / THANUNYA BOONYONG AND FRIENDS
- "โครงงานมิติมืด" (ศิลปเหตุการณ์) "Project of the blindness"(Art-Event)
- โรงเรียนสอนคนตาบอดภาคเหนือ ถ. อารักษ์ Blindness Tranning School
- เฉพาะวันที่ 2 ธันวาคม 2540 เวลา 16.00 น. December 2, 1997, 4.00PM.
- เปลี่ยนแปลงความเคยชินของการรับรู้ศิลปะจากความรู้สึกที่ปิดกั้น จะทำให้มนุษย์ตั้งประสาทสัมผัสส่วนอื่นๆ มาใช้

วัฒนะ วัฒนาพันธุ์
(WATTANA WATTANAPUN)
- "เข้า-ออก" (ศิลปะจัดวาง) "Entrance-Exit" (Installation)
- ซอยวัดอุโมงค์ / Soi Wat U-mong
- 14 ธันวาคม 2540 (ขอรายละเอียดเพิ่ม) December 14, 1997

วิชาญ สระศรีสม & เนติลักษณ์ ใบบัว
(WICHARN SARASRISOM & NETILUCK BAIBOU)
- "กีฬาในบริบทศิลปะ" (การแสดง) "Sport in the Art context" (Perfromance)
- ประตูท่าแพ / Tha-Pae Gate
- เฉพาะวันที่ 6 ธันวาคม 2540 เวลา 20.00-01.00 น. December 6, 1997, 8.00 PM. to 1.00 AM.
- เรามักประมาทอยู่กับสิ่งที่เป็นความสุข ความชอบสิ่งอันเป็นที่รักเสมอ ในขณะเดียวกันก็พยายามกลบเกลื่อนสิ่งไม่พึงปรารถนาต่างๆ ดังนั้น ความทุกข์ จึงกลายเป็นเพื่อนแท้ของมนุษย์ตลอดกาล

- (ถนนท่าแพ) (การแสดง/ศิลปะจัดวาง) "Follow me" (Performance/Installation)
- ทางม้าลายในอำเภอเมือง เชียงใหม่ Pedestrian crossing in the city
- 1-3 ธันวาคม 2540 / December 1-3, 1997
- คนที่เดินข้ามทางม้าลายเป็นประจำ ครั้งหนึ่งเขาได้มีโอกาสเดินข้ามทางม้าลายปูด้วยเสื่อสาน เสื่อยางเพื่อการหวลรำลึกถึงสิ่งดีๆ ในชีวิต

สัญญา สันติเวส (SANYA SANTIVES)
- "อยากรู้อะไรจากพระเจ้า โปรดถาม" "If you want to know something from God, just ask" (การแสดง) (Performance)
- ประตูท่าแพ / Tha-Pae Gate
- 2 ธันวาคม 2540 / December 2, 1997

สมพงษ์ ทวี (SOMPONG TAWEE)
- "ความเงียบ ความว่าง ความมืด" (การแสดง) "Quiet Emptiness Dark" (Performance)
- ประตูท่าแพ / Tha-Pae Gate
- 1 ธันวาคม 2540 / December 1, 1997
- มนุษย์โลดแล่นไปท่ามกลางสิ่งสมมุติมานาประการ เราพยายามสะโกนแต่ก็เป็นความเงียบ พยายามเพิ่มให้เต็มแต่ก็ว่างเปล่า พยายามพัฒนาสติปัญญา แต่สังคมบริโภคก็ตดันให้โลกภายในมืดมน

สุดศิริ ปุยอ๊อก (SUDSIRI PUI-OUK)
- "สดทุกวัน" (ศิลปกิจกรรม) "Every Day fresh" (Performance)
- ร้านกู๊ดวิว / The Good View
- 1 ธันวาคม 2540 / December 1, 1997
- สังคมปัจจุบัน "เพศหญิง" เป็นเรื่องของบริโภคนิยม ผู้หญิงเป็นผู้ผลิต ผู้บริการ ทำให้เกิดคำถามว่าผู้หญิงควรวางตัวอย่างไร

สุธรรม แก้วตาทิพย์
- "ธรรมชาติ" (ศิลปจัดวาง/การแสดง) "Nature" (Installation/Performance)
- วัดอุโมงค์ / Wat U-mong
- 2 ธันวาคม 2540 / December 2, 1997

ศุภชัย ลิ้มประสิทธิอิสระ
(SUPCHAI LIMPRASITISSARA)
- "ทัศนศิลป์และบทกวี" (ศิลปะจัดวาง) "Visual Art&Poetry" (Installation)
- ห้องสมุดวัดอุโมงค์/ In the Library at Wat U-mong
- 2-30 ธันวาคม 2540 / December 2-30, 1997

(ANGKRIT AJCHARIYASOPHON)
- "เบญจศีล" (ศิลปะ...) "The Five Percepts "(Installation/Performance)
- จุดต่างๆ เขตอำเภอเมือง เชียงใหม่ In the city of Chiang Mai
- 1-3 ธันวาคม 2540 / December ...
- ศีล 5 ช่วยคุณได้

อุดม ฉิมภักดี (UDOM CHI...
- "โดนัทส่งออก"(การแสดง) "Import of Donuts"
- เฉพาะวันที่ 2 ธันวาคม 2540 เว... December 2, 1997, 3.00 PM.
- จากวัดอุโมงค์ถึงสี่แยกโรงแรมริน... From Suthep Rd. to Nim M...
- มนุษย์ทุกเผ่าพันธุ์มีวัฒนธรรม... อาหารเป็นของตนเอง ...แต่การโฆษณา...ทำให้มนุษย์เปล... ที่เหมาะสมกับวิถีชีวิตตนเอง

Co-ordinated by

ULTIMATE AKADEMIE

Sponsored by Goethe Institut BANGKOK

THE ULTIMATE AKADEMIE IS A PROJECT WHICH WAS FOUNDED IN COLOGNE, GERMANY BY LISA CIESLIK & AL HANSEN THE VISION IS AN EXPERIMENTAL ACADEMY OPEN FOR ALL KINDS OF CONTEMPORARY ART... IN AN OPEN TENT AT THA-PAE GATE CHIANG MAI THAILAND ......IS INVITED TO JOIN THE PROJECT..........."EVERYBODY IS PROFESSOR ON ITS OWN. EVERY PROFESSOR IS A STUDENT".....ALL KIND OF ART ARE WELLCOME....THE VISION OF SOCIAL INSTALLATION (CMSI) AS A PROCESS AMONG CREATIVE PEOPLE WE ARE IN OPERATION EVERYDAY FROM 1.00- 8.00 PM. DECEMBER 1-16, 1997 ....EVERY EXTENTON IS POSSIBLE AND PART OF THE CONCEPT. ....

ANJA IBSCH (GERMANY)
- "The Purpose of Hygiene" (Installation)
- Tha-Pae Gate / ประตูท่าแพ December 2-30, 1997 / วันที่ 2-30 ธันวาคม 2540
- "One Kiss" (Performance) December 1 and 2, 1997 วันที่ 1 และ 2 ธันวาคม 2540 เวลา 18.00 น.

BARBARA ELLMERER (SWITZERLAND)
- "Eyewash" (Painting/Installation)
- Wat Chieng Mun / วัดเชียงมั่น December 1-16, 1997 / วันที่ 1-16 ธันวาคม 2540 (ขอรายละเอียดเพิ่ม)

KEN PATTERSON (USA/GERMANY)
- "Incitus-decided" (Performance)
- Tha-Pae Gate / ประตูท่าแพ December 3-16, 1997 / วันที่ 3-16 ธันวาคม 2540 (ขอรายละเอียดเพิ่ม)
- He will decide on the spot which kind of work he will do.

CAROLA WILLBRANDT (GERMANY)
- "State Of Suspence" (Performance/Installation)
- Tha-Pae Gate / ประตูท่าแพ December 3, 1997 / วันที่ 3 ธันวาคม 2540

ENNO STAHL (GERMANY)
- "Voice Garden" (Acoustic Installation)
- Garden of Wat U-mong / วัดอุโมงค์
- December 2, 1997 / วันที่ 2 ธันวาคม 2540
- An installation with 8 walkman in the garden of Wat Umong

FRANK KOLLGES / VOLKER HAMANN (GERMANY)
- "Thai Intermission Orchester" (Sound Art)
- Tha Pae Gate and Different sites in the city ประตูท่าแพและที่ต่างๆ ในเมือง
- December 3-16, 1997 / วันที่ 3-16 ธันวาคม 2540 (ขอรายละเอียดเพิ่ม)

GABY LUDWIG (GERMANY)
- "Banner of the trees in the wind" (Painting-Performance/Installation)
- The Tree on Bumrung Buri Rd.
- December 3-16, 1997 / วันที่ 3-16 ธันวาคม 2540

KARIN MEINER & MANFRED HAMMES (GERMANY)
- "Connected" (Performance/Painting)
- Tha Pae Gate / ประตูท่าแพ
- December 3-16, 1997 / วันที่ 3-16 ธันวาคม 2540 (ขอรายละเอียดเพิ่ม)
- A joint venture among artists and musicians.

KNOPP FERRO (AUSTRIA)
- "Bait Field" (Performance/Installation)
- Corner of Rajwithi Road & Mun Muang Road มุมของถนนราชวิถีและถนนมูลเมือง
- December 3-16, 1997 / วันที่ 3-16 ธันวาคม 2540 (ขอรายละเอียดเพิ่ม)
- Thin swinging steel poles and mirrors

LISA CIESLIK (GERMANY)
- "Consume Realism" (Poster)
- Tha-Pae Gate / ประตูท่าแพ
- December 12-16, 1997 วันที่ 12-16 ธันวาคม 2540 (ขอรายละเอียดเพิ่ม)
- Poster with flyers and advertising

MARIANNE TRALAU (GERMANY)
- "Red Cloth" (Installation)
- different places in the city / ที่ต่างๆ ในเมือง
- December 12-16, 1997 วันที่ 12-16 ธันวาคม 2540 (ขอรายละเอียดเพิ่ม)
- A piece of red cloth will be installed every

PARZIVAL POERSCH (GERMANY)
- "The Golden Middle Course of the Golden West" (Performance)
- Tha-Pae Gate / ประตูท่าแพ
- December 12-16, 1997 วันที่12-16 ธันวาคม 2540(ขอรายละเอียดเพิ่ม)
- Everyday material is sprayed golden

PIETRO PELLINI (ITALY)
YOLA BERBESZ (GERMANY)
- "Electronic World Shrine" (Internet)
- "http://www.asa.de/e-world-shrine" (homepage) e-mail: "e-world-shrine@dom.de"
- December 1-16, 1997/ วันที่ 1-16 ธันวาคม 2540
- An Internet Project of the Planetarian Society

ROLAND KERSTEIN (GERMANY)
- "Video Installation in a Rikshaw" (Performance/Video Art)
- he will drive around the city เขาจะขี่สามล้อถีบรอบเมือง
- December 12-16, 1997 วันที่ 12-16 ธันวาคม 2540

ROLF HINTERECKER (AUSTRIA)
- "a global affair" (Object/Performance)
- On Traffic Islands in the city เกาะกลางช้างถนนในเมือง
- December 3-16, 1997 วันที่ 3-16 ธันวาคม 2540 (ขอรายละเอียดเพิ่ม)

RUTH JAGER (GERMANY)
- "Untitled" (Painting)
- Somewhere on Electricity collums เสาไฟฟ้าในเมือง
- December 12-16, 1997 วันที่ 12-16 ธันวาคม 2540(ขอรายละเอียดเพิ่ม)

SUSANNE HEIMES (GERMANY)
- "Bound Space Bound" (Performance/Dance)
- Garden of Wat Phra-Singh / วัดพระสิงห์
- December 12-16, 1997 วันที่ 12-16 ธันวาคม 2540(ขอรายละเอียดเพิ่ม)

VOLKER HAMANN (GERMANY)
- "Who Tried" (Performance)
- In the city of Chiang Mai / ในเมืองเชียงใหม่
- December 3-16, 1997 วันที่ 3-16 ธันวาคม 2540 (ขอรายละเอียดเพิ่ม)

โครงงาน ลานสรรพสินค้าวัฒนธรรม มช.

ระหว่าง วันที่ 17-19 ธันวาคม 2540
เวลา 16.00-22.00 น.

ณ ลานหน้าคณะวิจิตรศิลป์ มหาวิทยาลัยเชียงใหม่

•"ทุกๆคนคือพ่อค้าและผู้บริโภคในขณะเดียวกัน" ดังนั้นใครใคร่ ขาย-ขาย ใครใคร่ ซื้อ-ซื้อ ใครใคร่แสดงออกทางทัศนศิลป์ ดนตรี ละคร ฯลฯ แสดง ใครใคร่เพียงมาเดินดู สนทนากับผู้คนแปลกหน้า ร่วมนำสินค้ามาขาย ฯลฯ เลือกบทบาท เพื่อการ มีส่วนร่วมได้ โดยเสรี เน้น "วัตถุ" "กิจกรรม" ที่เกี่ยวข้อง กับในนาม "ศิลปะวัตถุ" "วัฒนธรรมวัตถุ"ที่สามารถซื้อขายได้จริง ในราคามิตรภาพ นอกเหนือการแลกเปลี่ยนทางนามธรรม

(รับผิดชอบโดย สงกรานต์ สุดจอม)

THE JAPAN FOUNDATION
This Brochure Sponsored by Japan Cultural Center, BANGKOK

สัปดาห์ร่วมทุกข์
ในบริบทความจน

WEEK OF COOPERATIVE SUFFERING

เริ่มวันที่ 1-7 มกราคม 2541 ณ ลานประตูท่าแพ
JANUARY 1-7, 1998
AT PHA-PAE GATE CHIANG-MAI, THAILAND

- **ELLEN BECKERMAN (USA)** "Dream" (Performance)
- **KEIKO SEI (JAPAN)** "Untitled" (Installation)
- **KRISTINE SCHOEDER (GERMANY)** "Untitled" (Installation)
- **LEE WEN (SINGAPOPE)** "Untitled" (Performance)
- **MANUEL LUTGENHORT & RIHARD ZIDKA (GERMANY)** "Untitled" (Performance/Installation)
- **MICHAEL BIELICKY (CZECH)** "Untitled" (Installation)
- **MILOS VOJTECHOVSKY (CZECH)** "Untitled" (Installation)
- **ตรา แสงแข** "มนุษย์สีแดง" (การแสดง)
- **ณัฐพล บัวฮ่ำ** "ไม่มีชื่อ" (การแสดง)
- **ดำรงค์ จารุธรอุไร** "เที่ยวใจ" (ศิลปะจัดวาง)
- **เติมศักดิ์ ขจรเกียรติพาณิช** "แบทแมนกับโรบิน" (ศิลปะจัดวาง)
- **นฤมล ธรรมพฤกษา** "ฮะแซ่ง ไทยแลนด์" (การแสดง)
- **ปัญญา ศรีเดชี** "ไม่มีชื่อ" (ศิลปะจัดวาง)
- **พรทิพย์ มงคลแสงสุรีย์ และ สมาพร คล้ายวิเชียร** "ไม่มีชื่อ" (ศิลปะจัดวาง)
- **พิเชษฐ วงศ์จันทรสม** "โลก โรค ภาษรมณ์" (ประติมากรรม)
- **ไพศาล เปลี่ยนบางช้าง** "การทำลายล้างใหม่" (การแสดง)
- **สราวุธ ทองคำภา** "ประติมากรรมจิตสำนึก" (ศิลปะจัดวาง)
- **สุริยันต์ โกสะแหน่**

REALITY IS NOT ART, ILLUSION IS NOT ART, ART IS IN BETWEEN, IT MAKES US REALIZE THAT EVERYTHING IS BEING BY US.PLEASE DO NOT BE NEGLIGENT ?

ความจริง ไม่ใช่ศิลปะ ความลวง ไม่ใช่ศิลปะ ศิลปะอยู่ระหว่างกลาง

Sanya Santives, *If You Want Something from God, Just Ask*, performance.

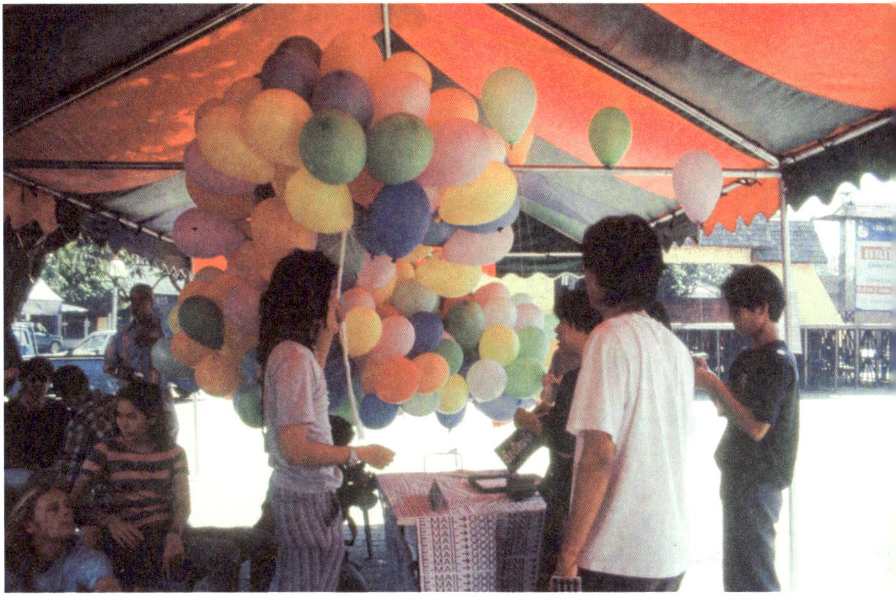

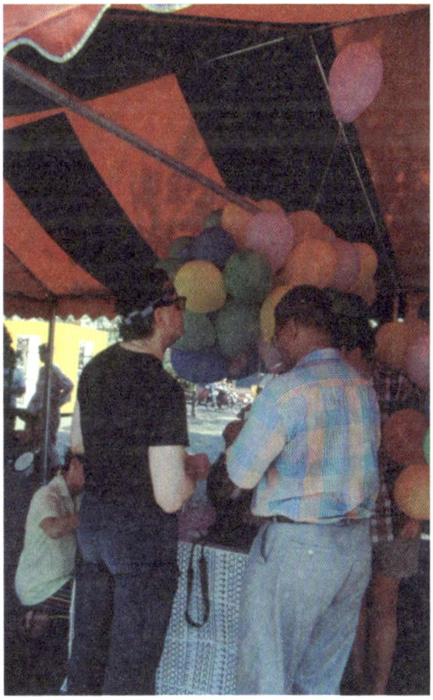

Work by Ben Patterson. Rolf Hinterecker recalls: 'He bought ten one-way cameras and then he asked ten rickshaw drivers to document their day driving and waiting in their job. After one day they all brought the cameras back and he developed the pictures and [hung] them in an installation on ropes in the open tent.'

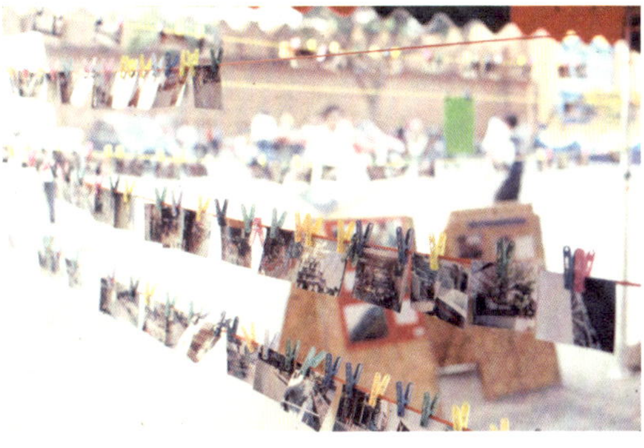

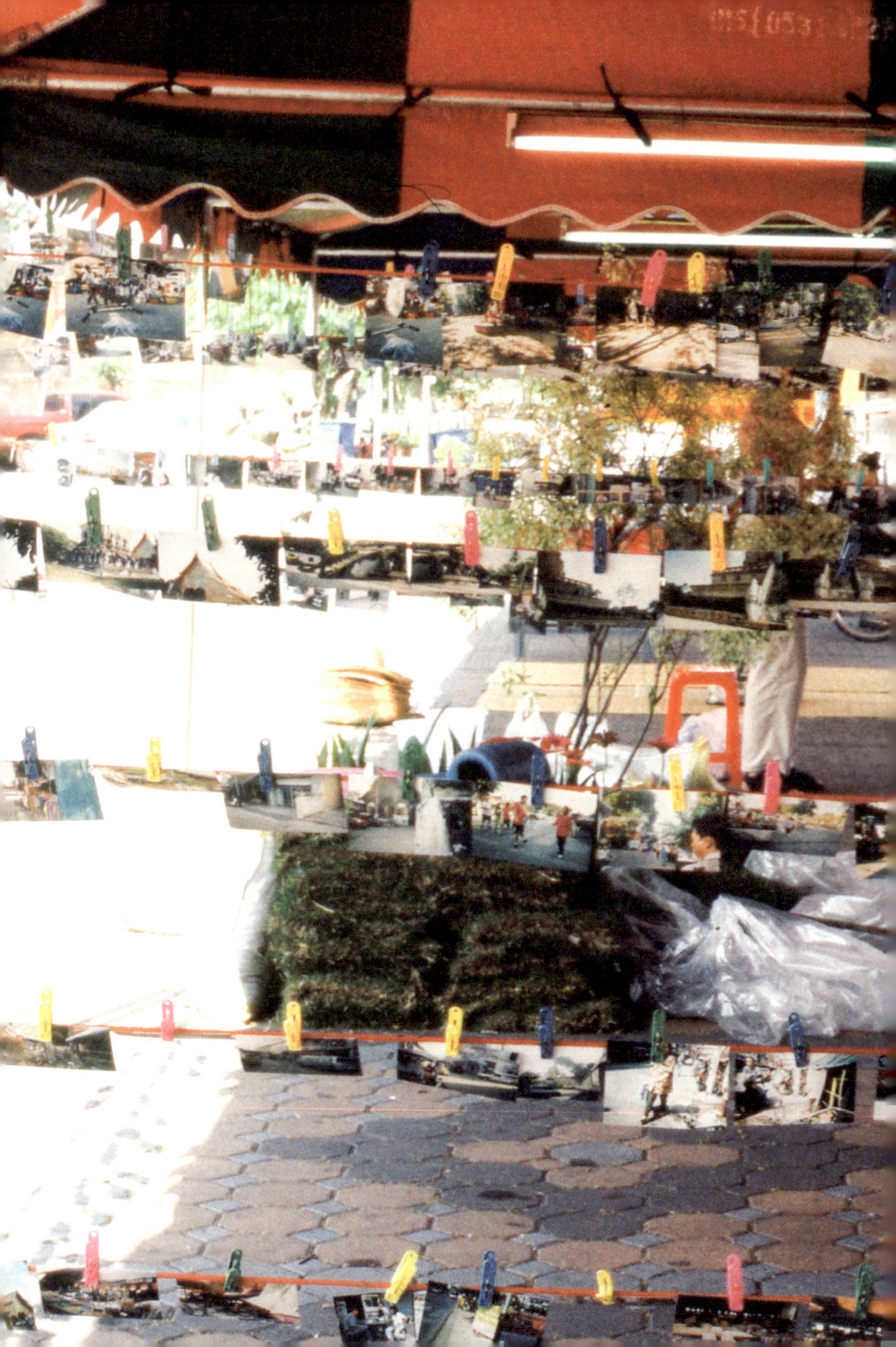

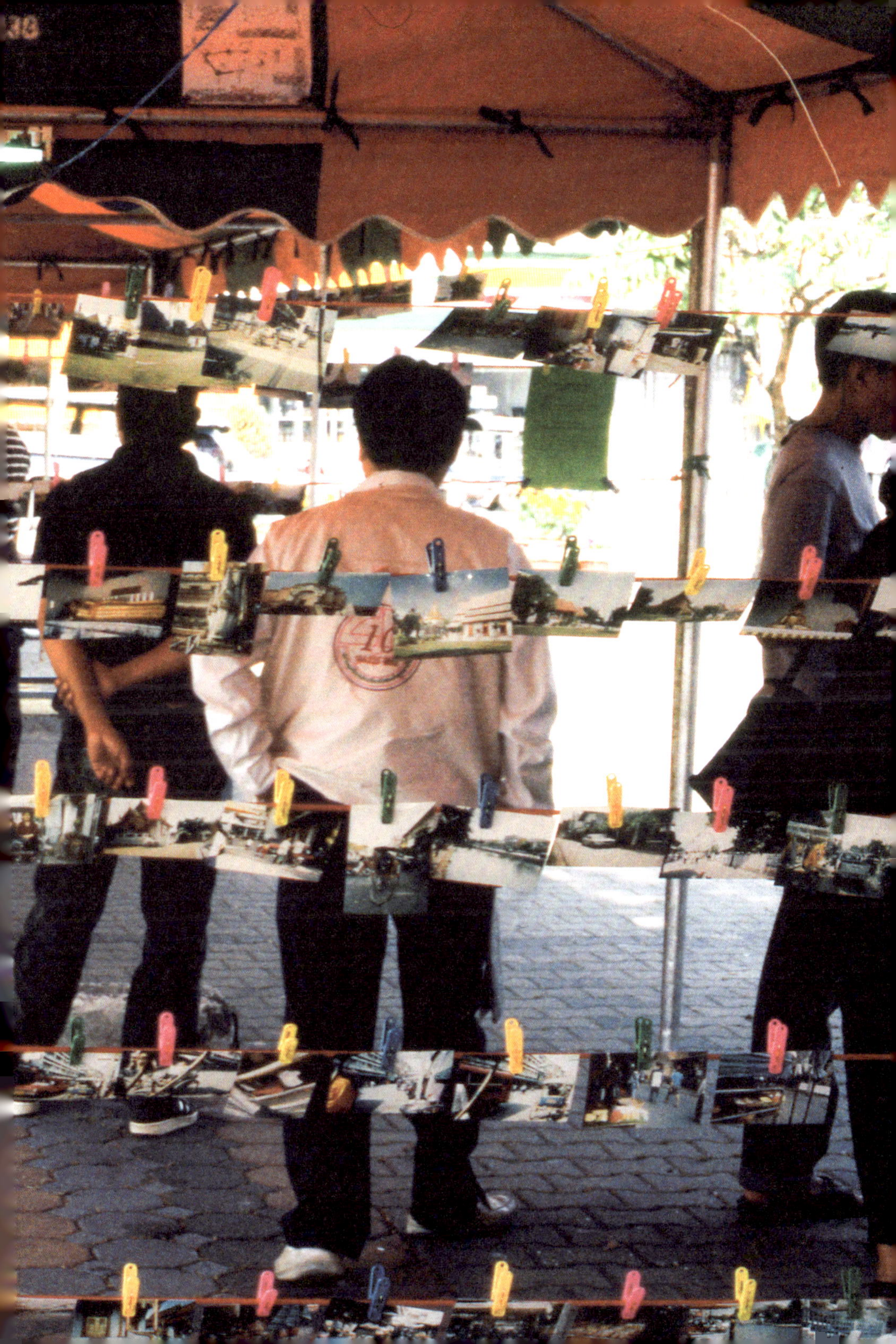

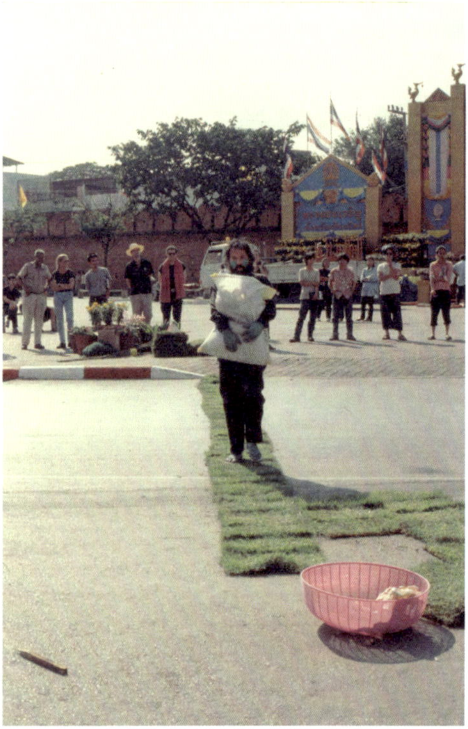

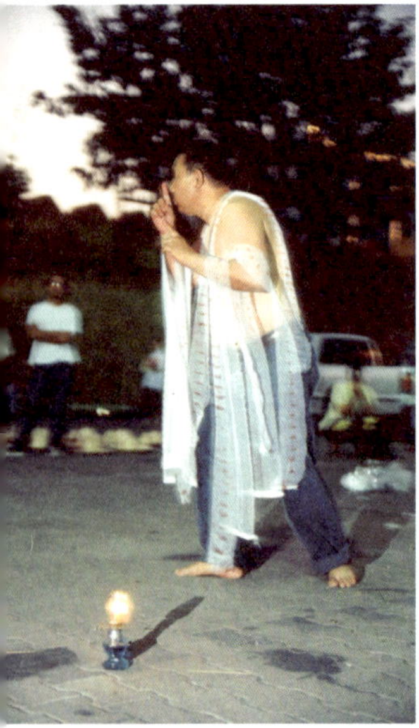

Performances at Tha Pae Gate. Rolf Hinterecker, *A Global Affair* (above); Sompong Tawee, *Quiet Emptiness Dark* (left); and Mongkol Plienbangchang, *Let's Celebrate IMF Land* (below).

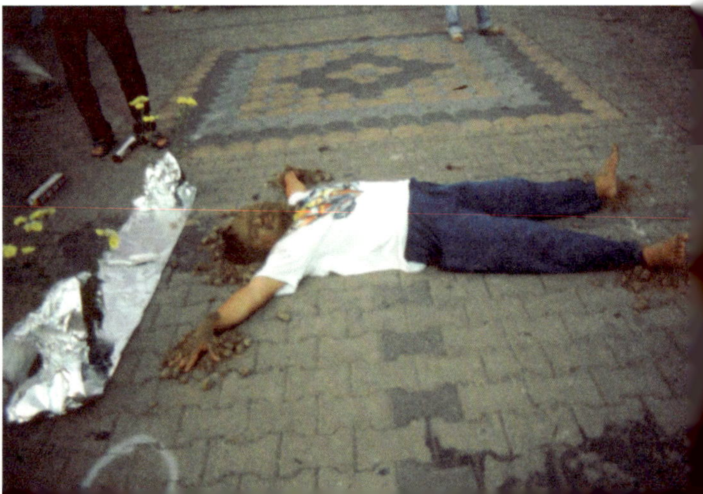

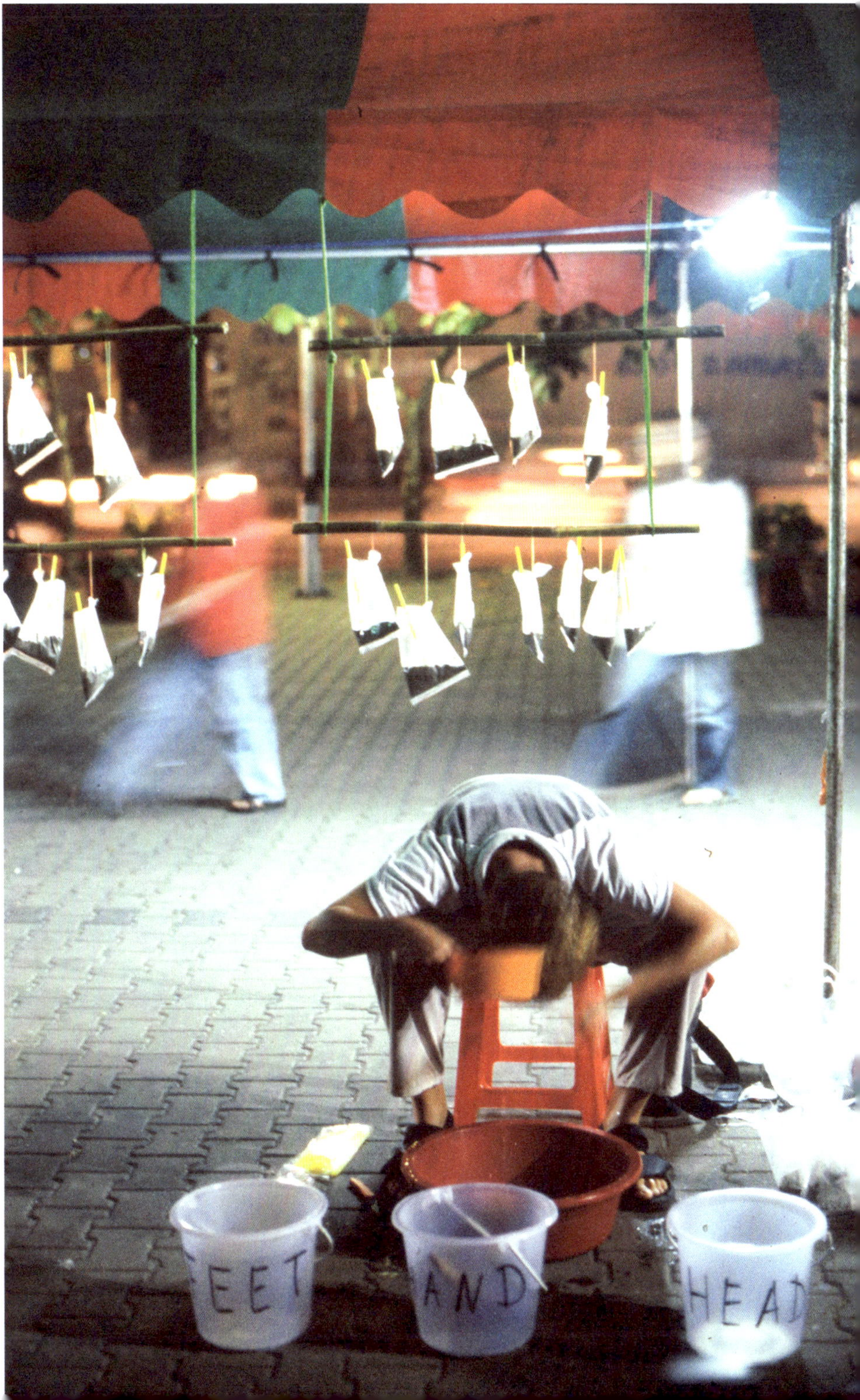
FEET
AND
HEAD

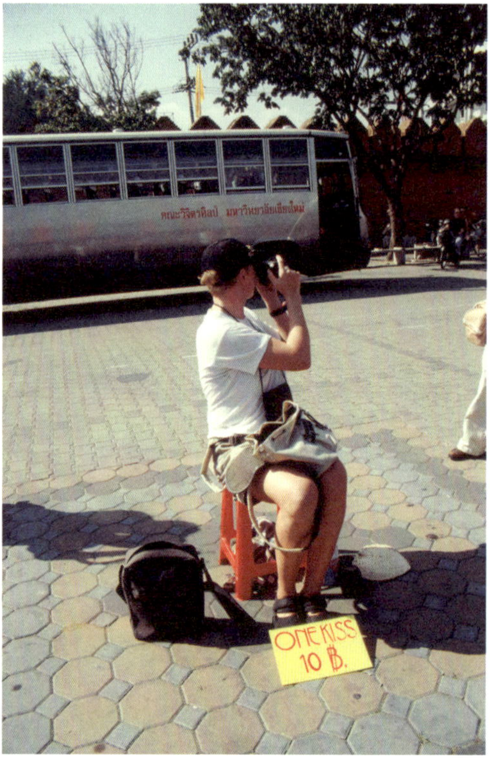

Anja Ibsch, *One Kiss*.

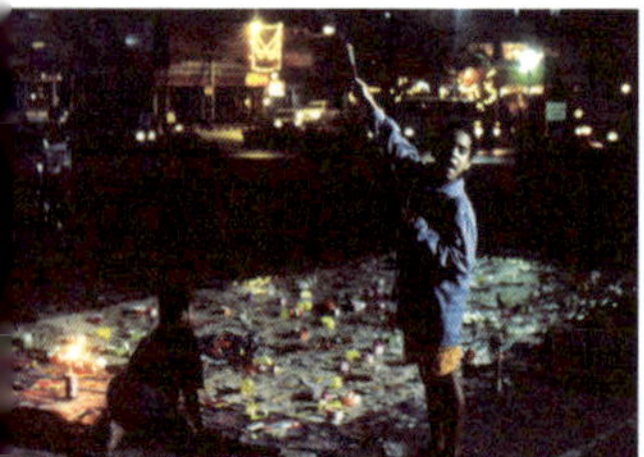

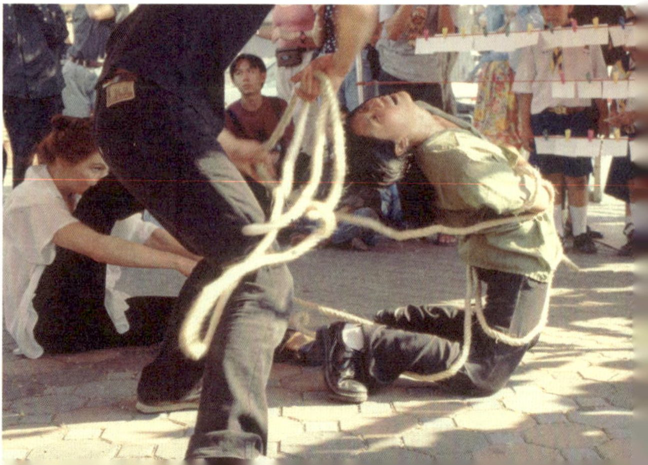

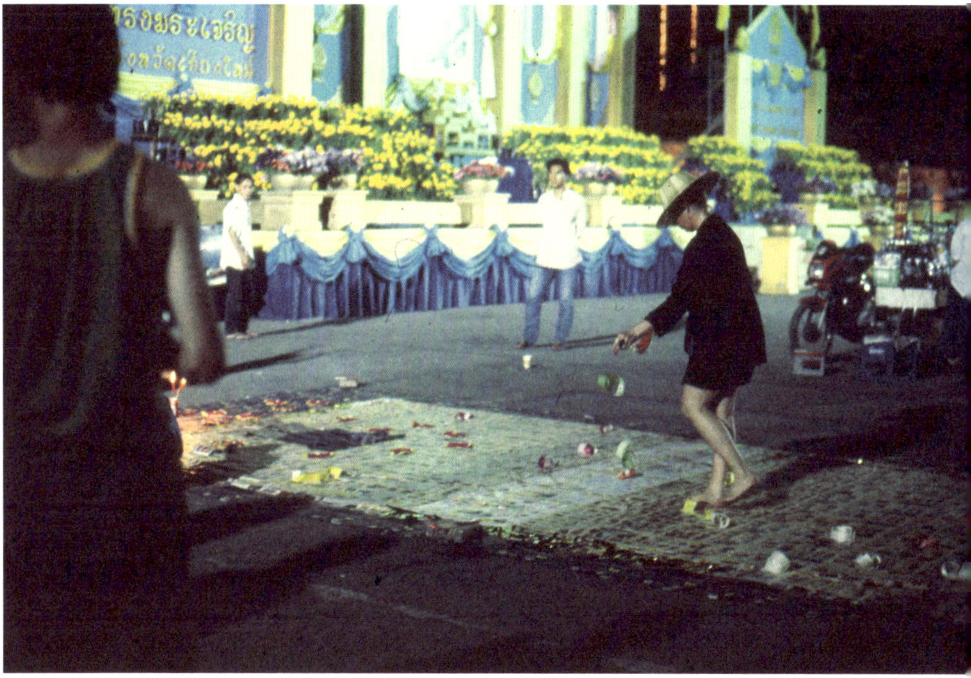

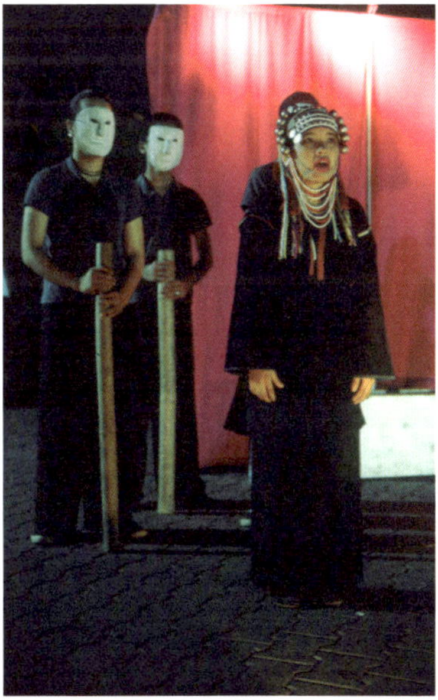

Various performances and interventions at Tha Pae Gate.

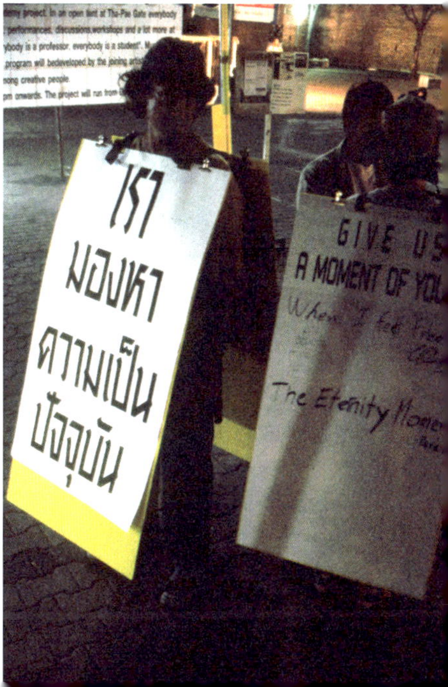

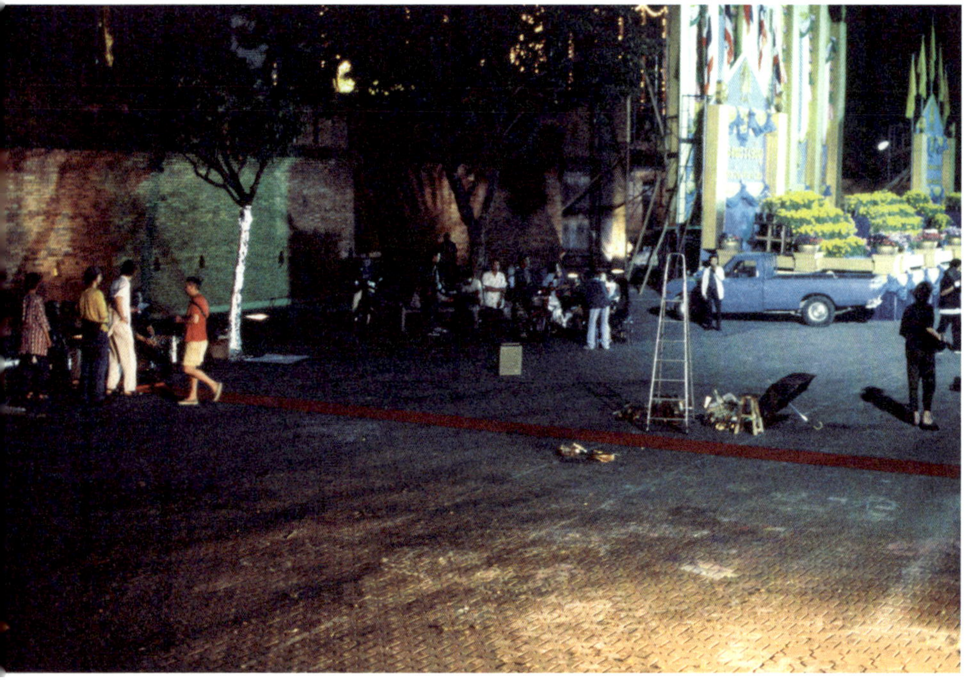

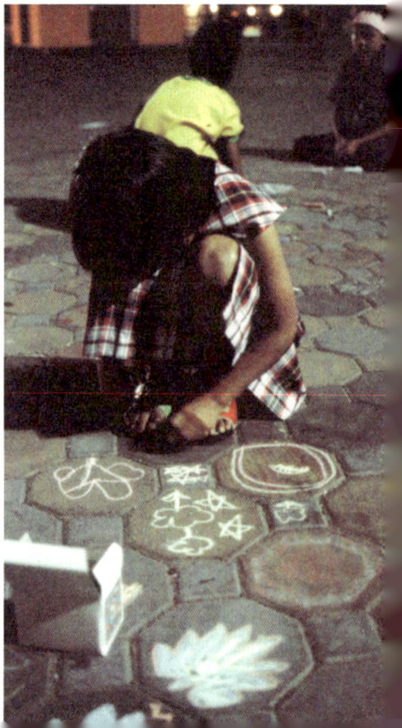

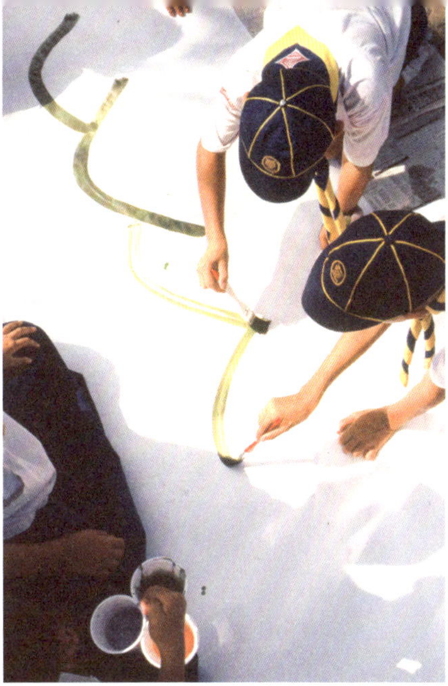

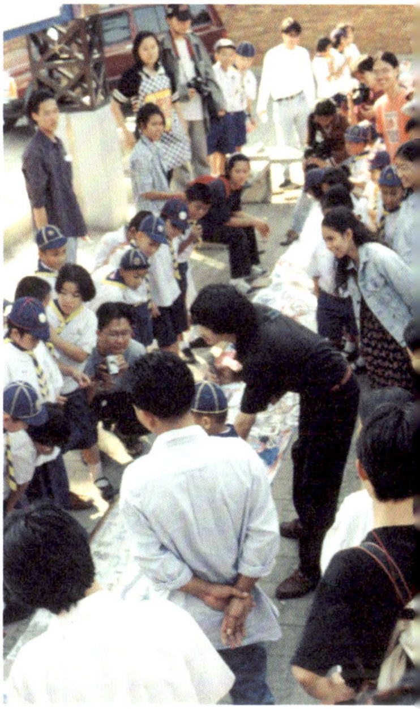

Jaksaree Suvanasare, Yosawadee Chaymanee and Moragot Yostamrong, *Children-Art & Social Installation*.

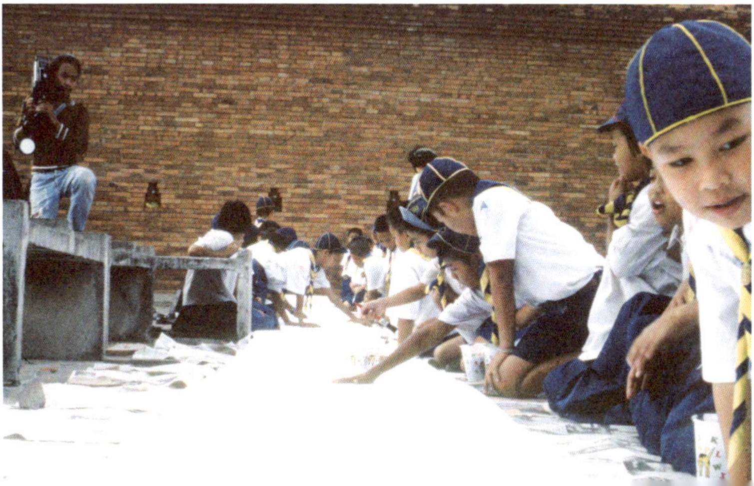

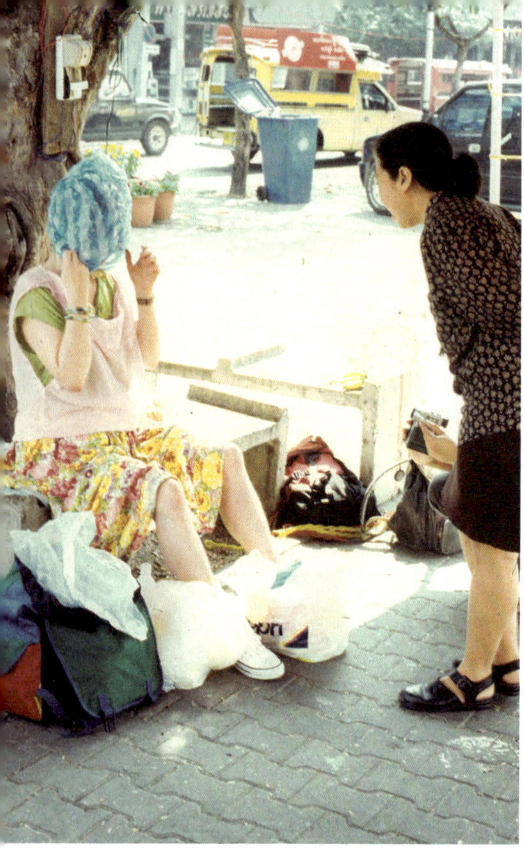

Carola Willbrand, *State of Suspense*.

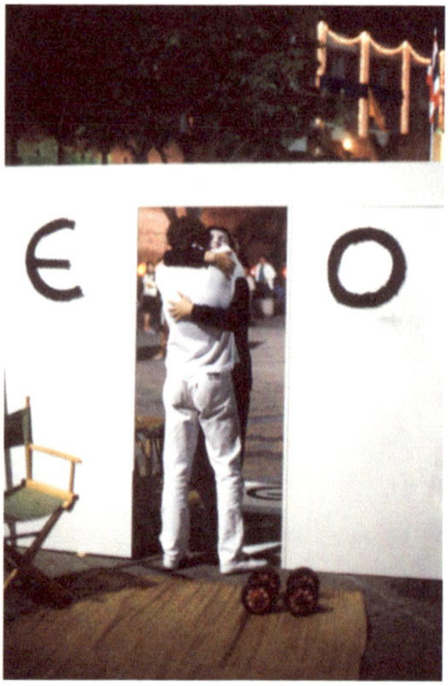

Doris Kraushaar, *The Step*, performance.

Frank Köllges,
Thai Intermission Orchestra.

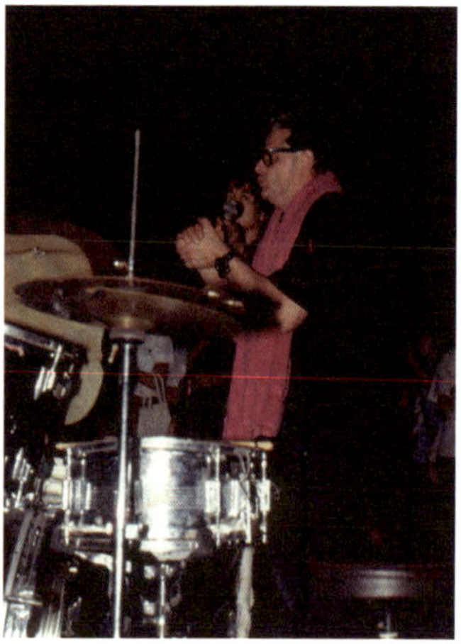

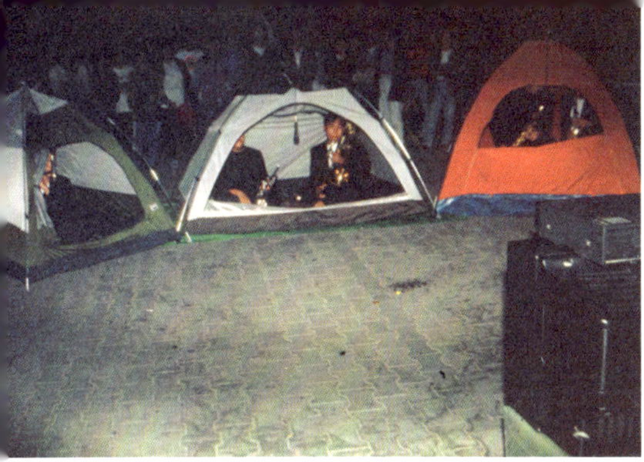

Noppadol Tirataradol, *5 Composers 5 Musicians*.

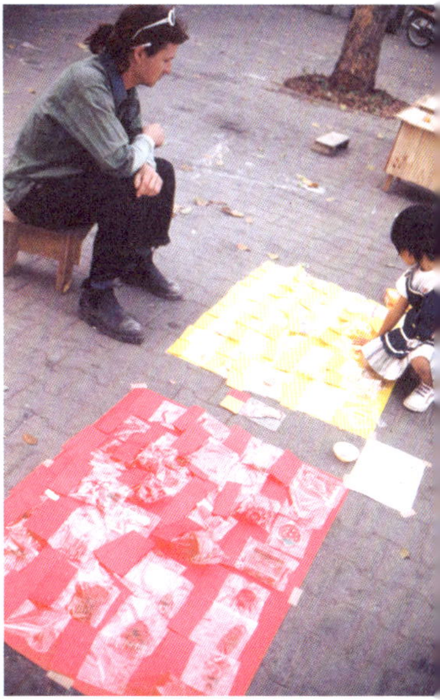

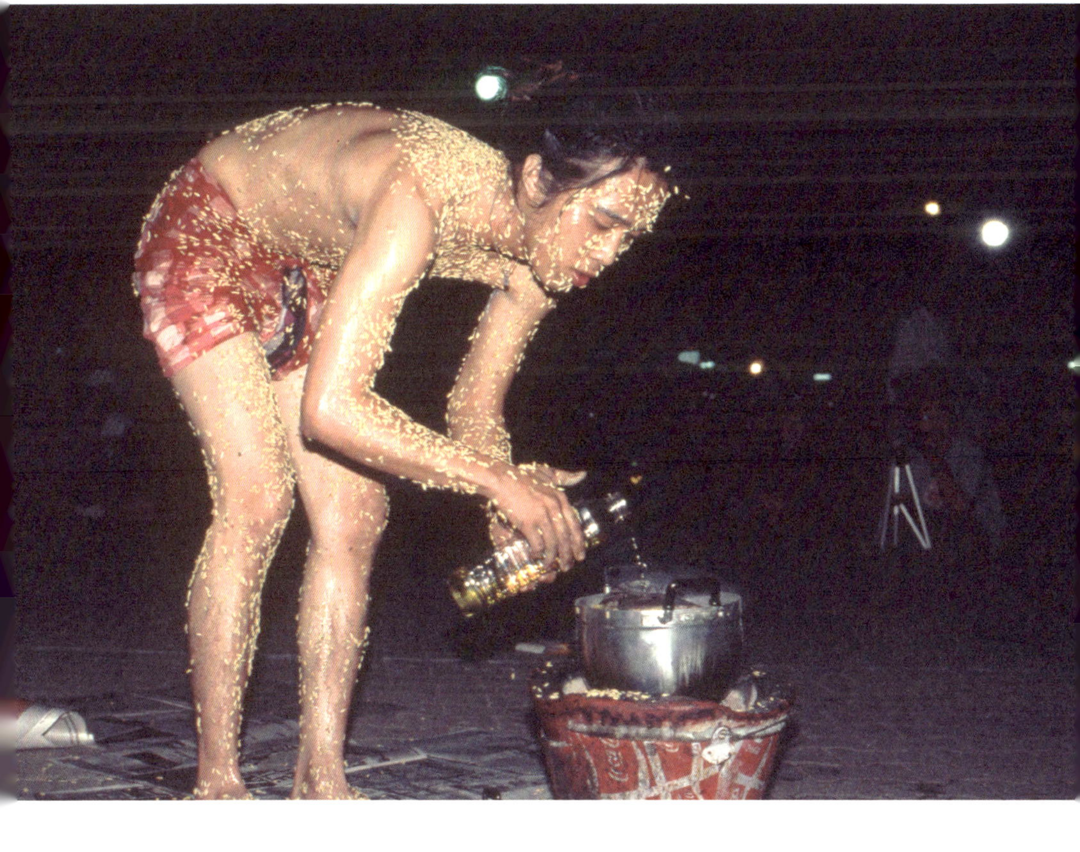

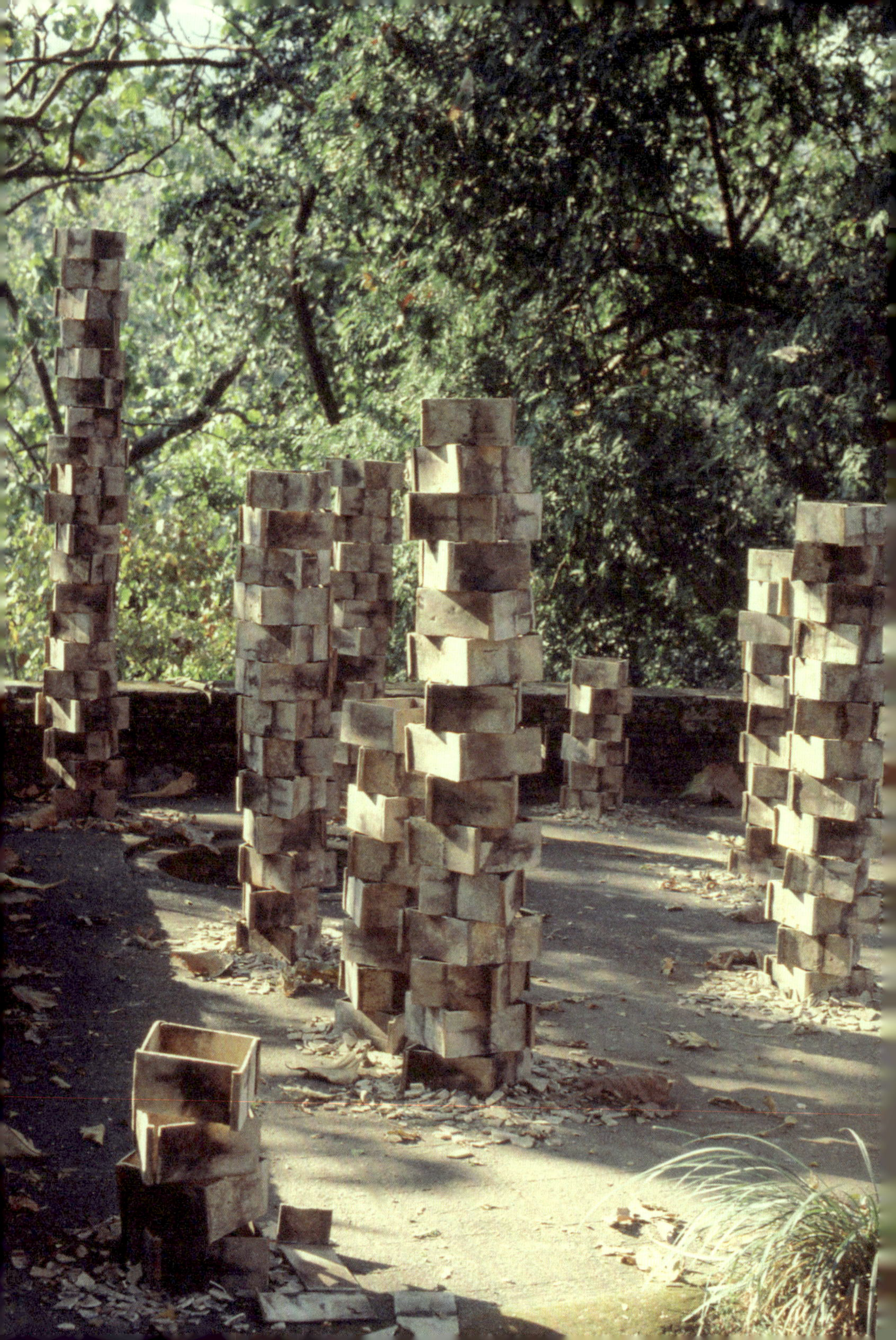

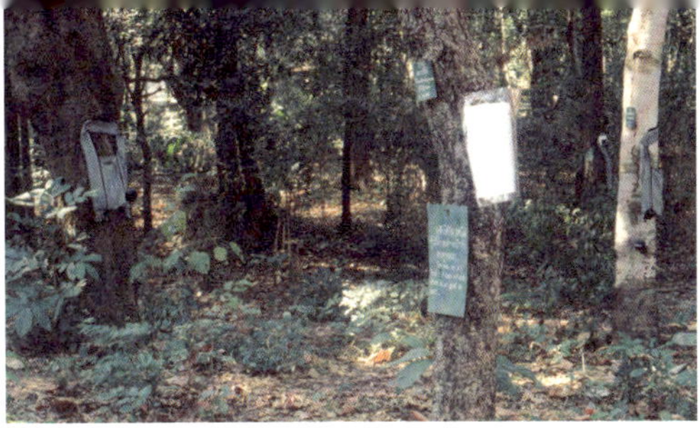

Enno Stahl, *Voice Garden,* Wat Umong.

Kritsana Soonthornpak,
Love Needy Angry.

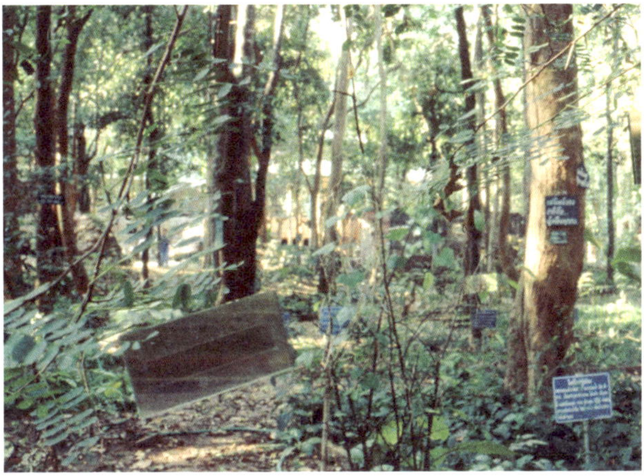

Work by Preeraphong Boomjanta.

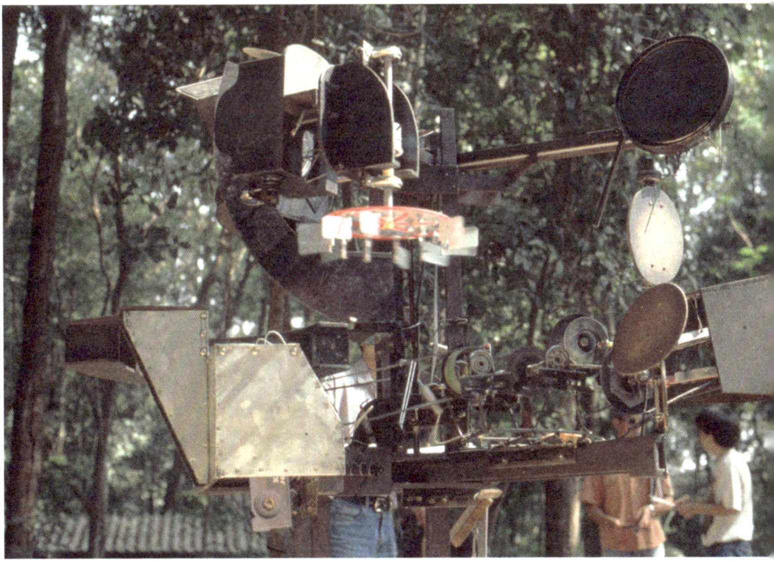

Luka Boonkerd Kaewdee, *I Love Chiang Mai Culture (700 Years Ago).*

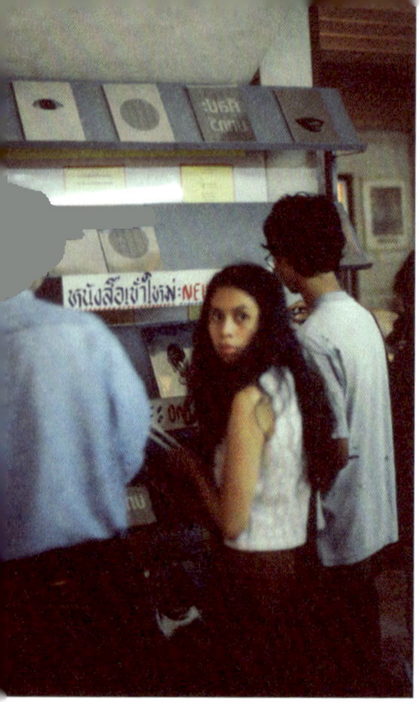

Supachai Limprasitissara, *Visual Art & Poetry*, library at Wat Umong.

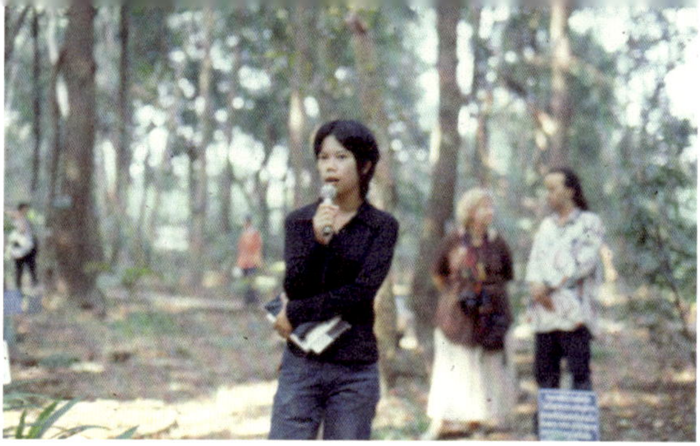

Guide at Wat Umong (above) and Prettinun Pinwuttanakul, *Can Eggs Float* (below).

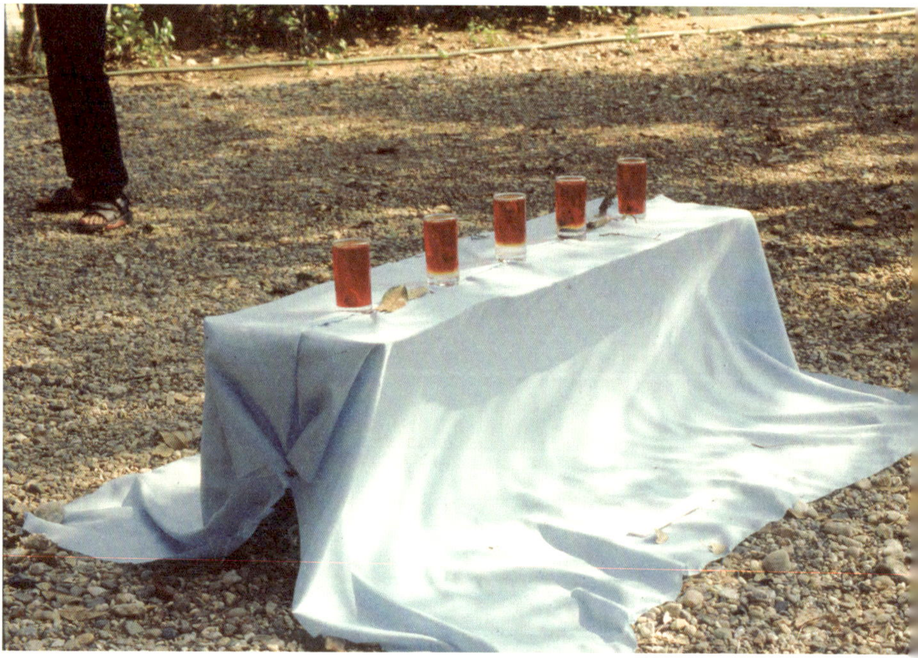

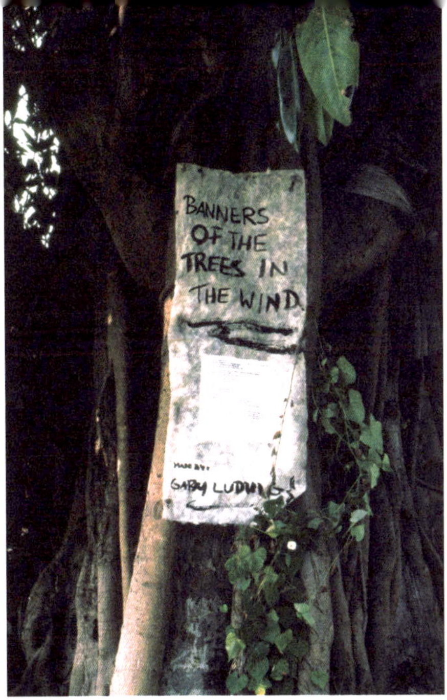

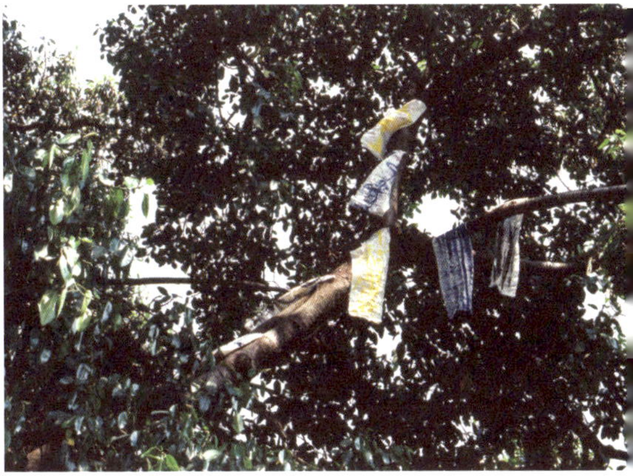

Gaby Ludwig, *Banner of the Trees in the Wild*, Bumrung Buri Road.

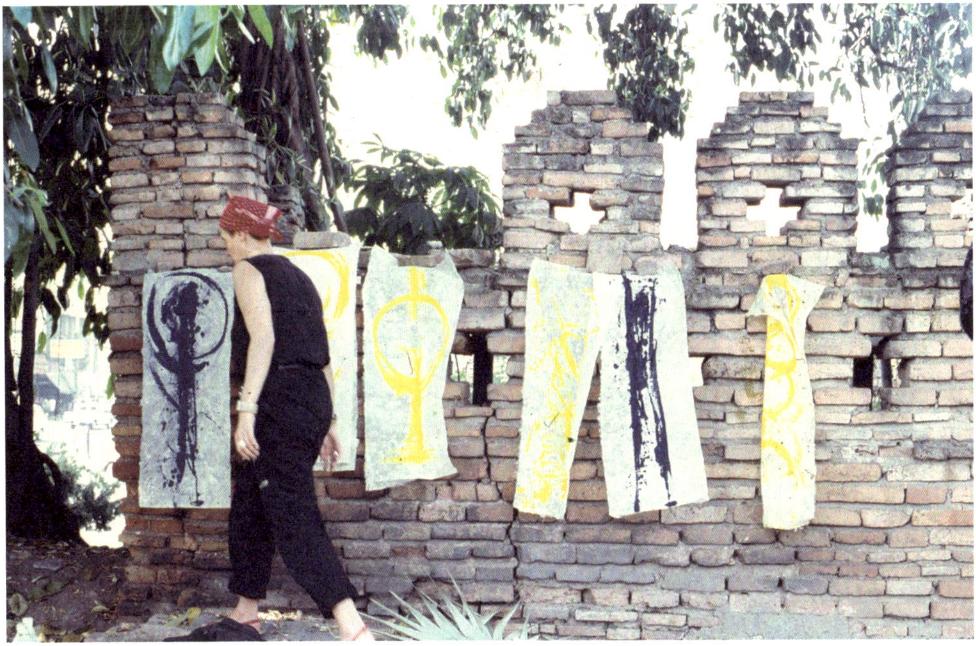

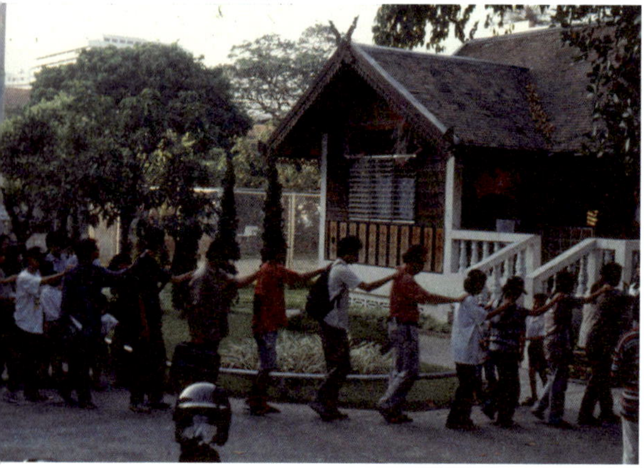

Yotsarun Chaidougkeaw, Thanunya Boonyong and others, *Project of Blindness*.

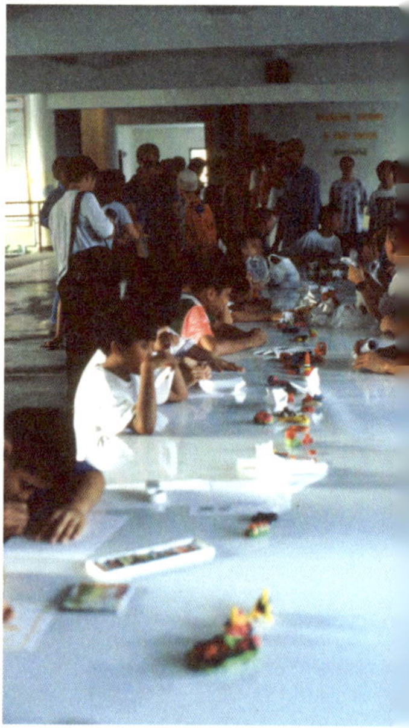

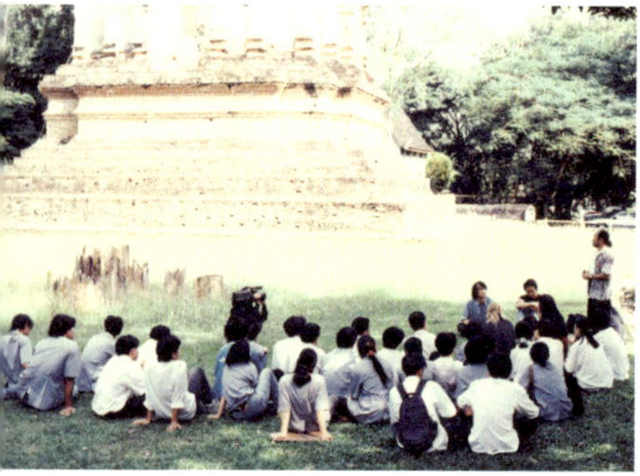

Akatsuki Harada, *Memory of the Earth* (below) and the artist speaking about the work (left), Wat Chet Yod.

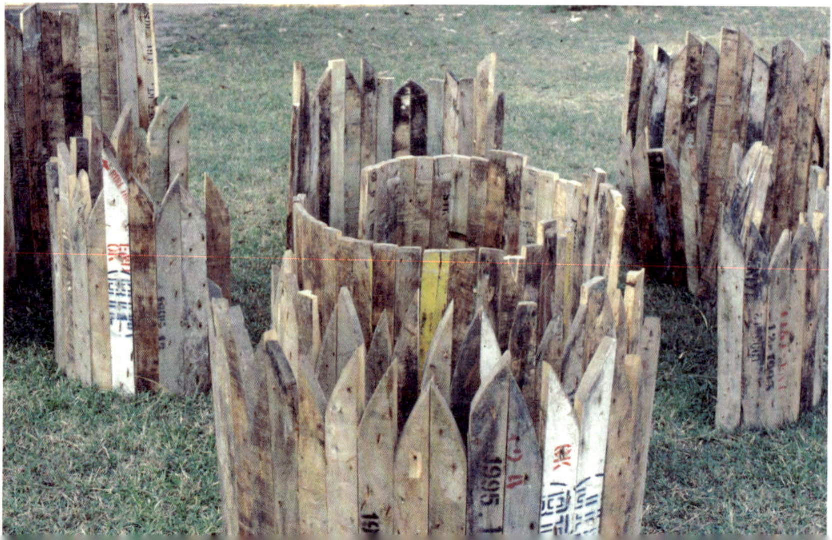

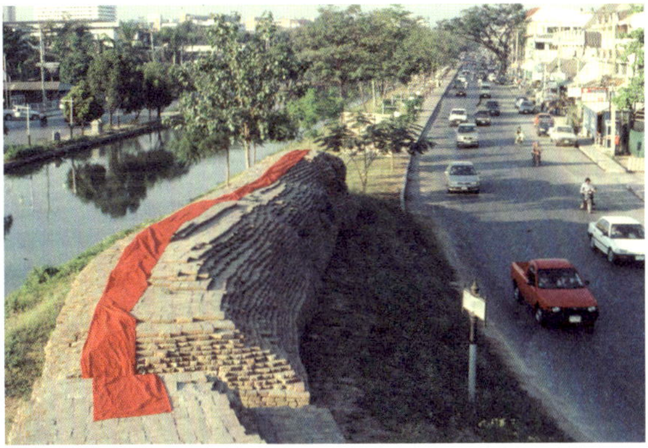

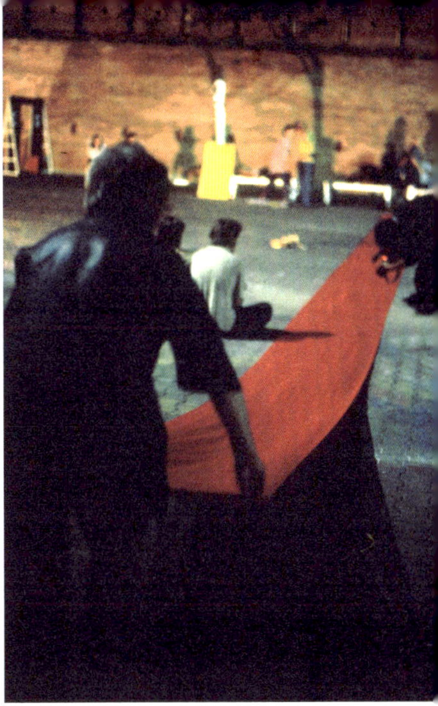

Marianne Tralau, *Red Cloth*, the old city wall at Jaeng Hua Lin (above) and Tha Pae Gate (right).

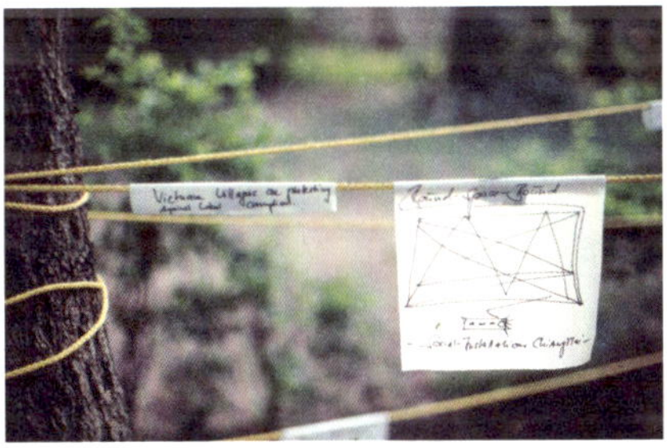

Anne Rochette, *Awake in Our Sleep,* Wat Tung Yu.

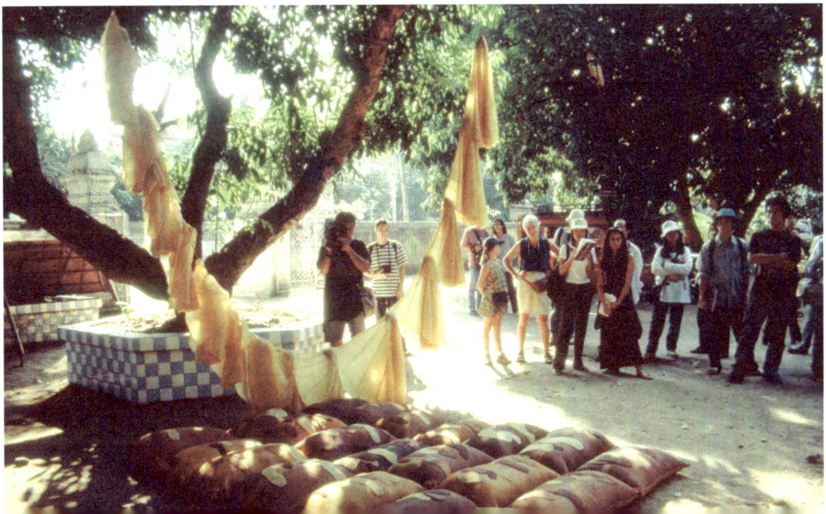

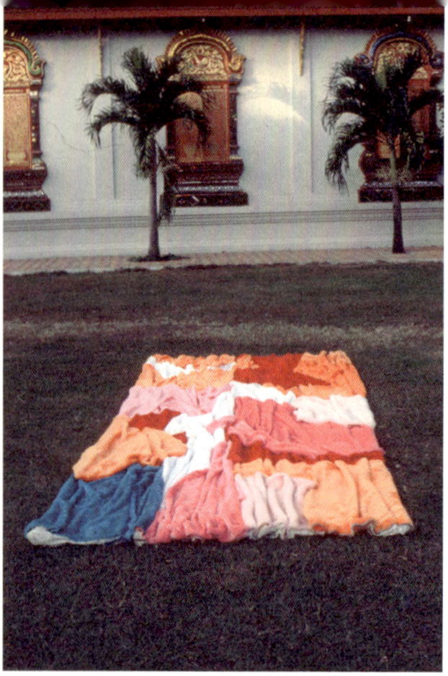

Barbara Ellmerer, *Eyewash*, Wat Chiang Man.

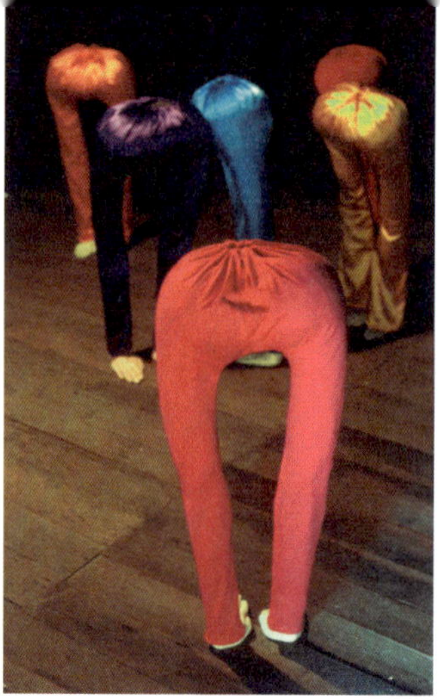

Teeranat Sa-Diaw, *Nice Girl,* Chiang Mai University.

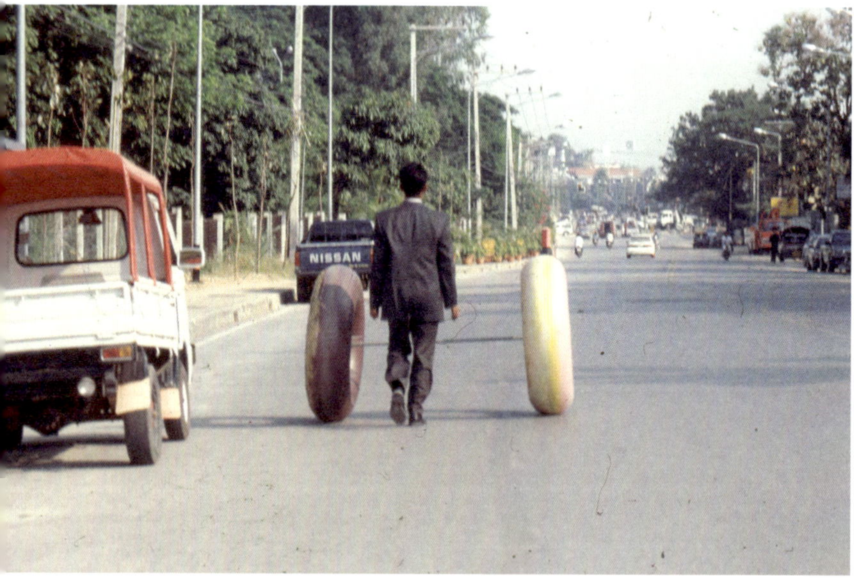

Udom Chimpakdee, *Import of Donuts*, performance from Nimmanhemin Road to Huay Kaew Road (near a branch of Dunkin' Donuts).

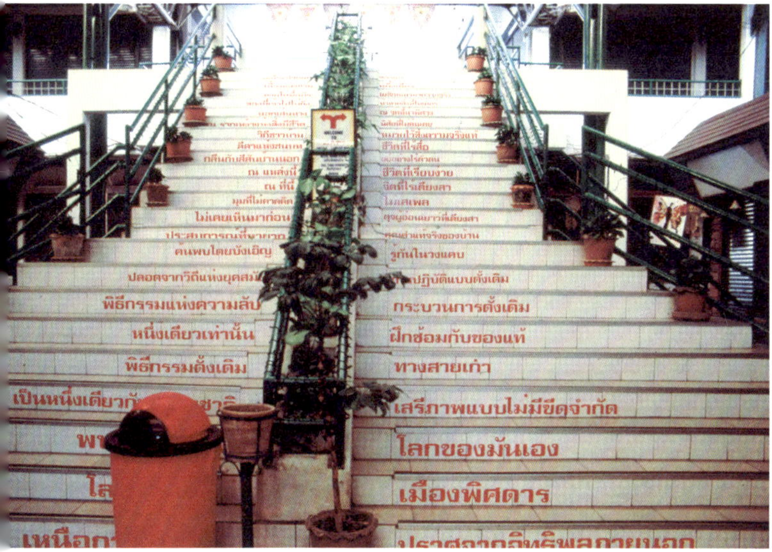

Robert Peters, *International Relations*, Chiang Mai night bazaar.

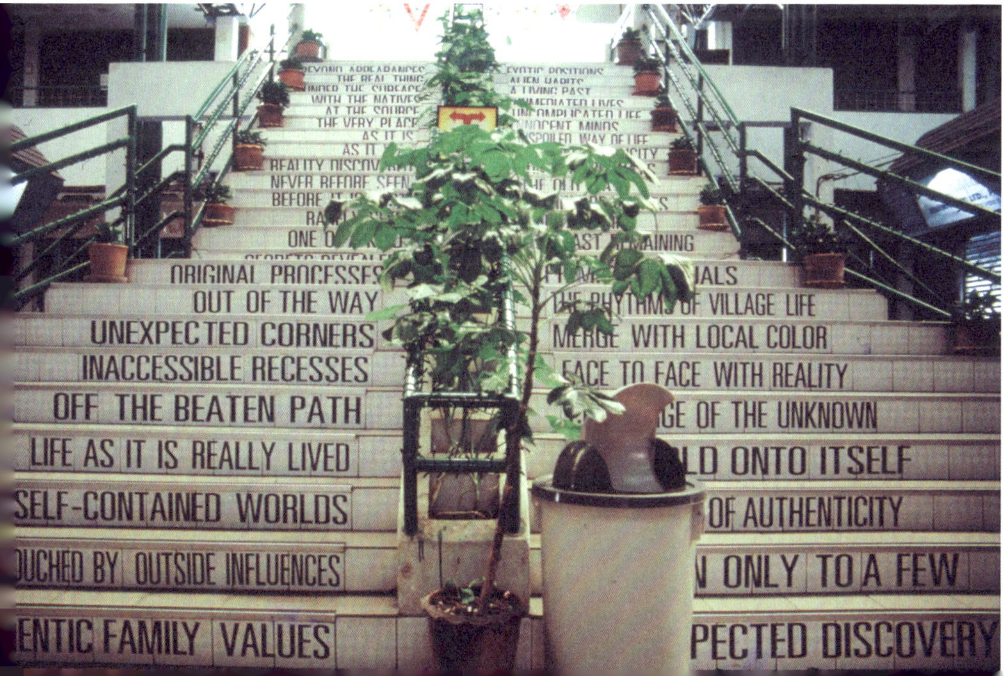

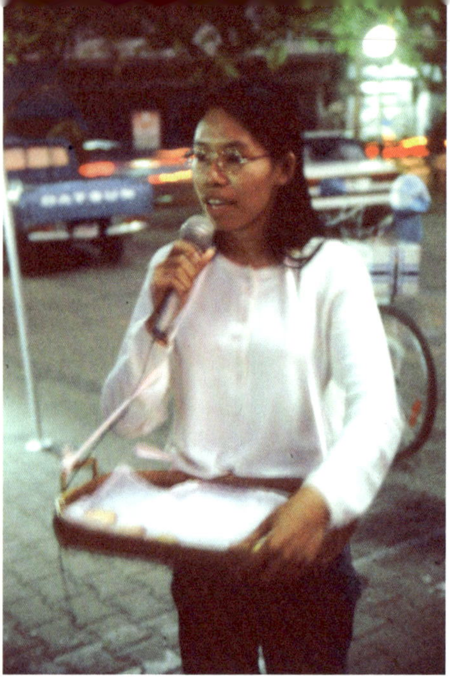

Sudsiri Pui-Ock, *Every Day Fresh*, performance at Good View restaurant.

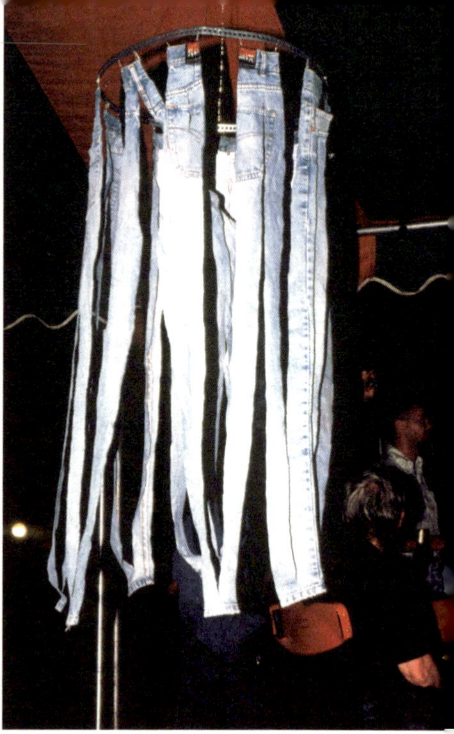

Work by Parzival (Frank Poersch), Tha Pae Gate.

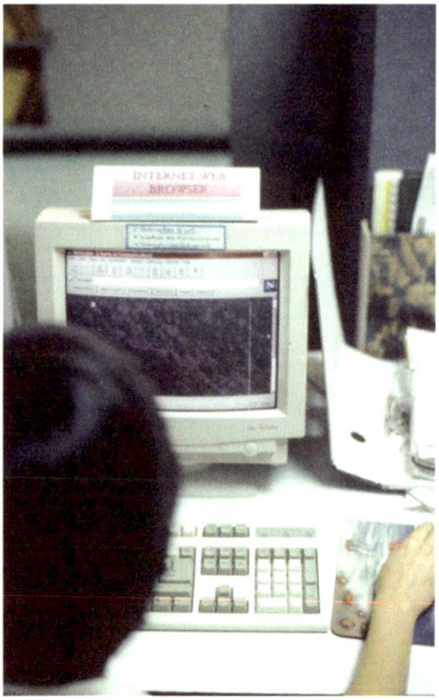

Pietro Pellini and Yola Berbesz, *Electronic World Shrine*.

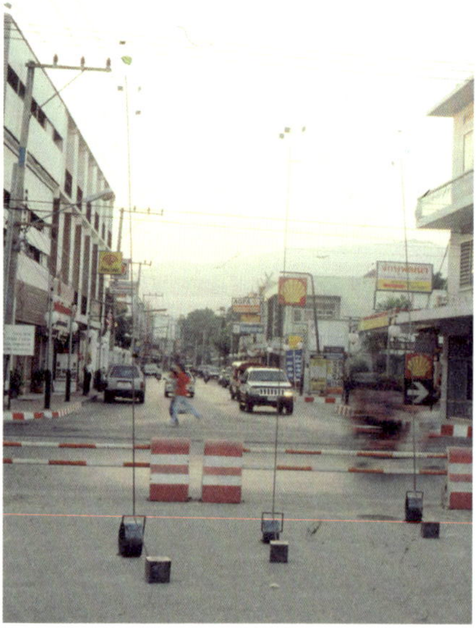

Knopp Ferro, *Bait Field*, corner of Ratvithi Road and Moon Muang Road.

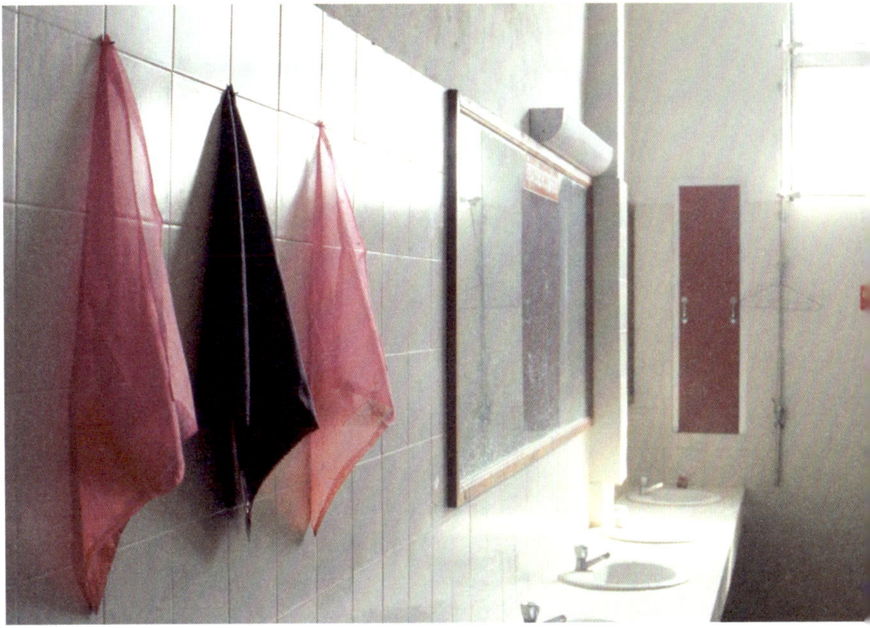

Debra Porch, *Veil*, installation in the women's toilets at the Faculty of Fine Arts and Humanities, Chiang Mai University.

Ultimate Open Akademie, Tha Pae Gate.

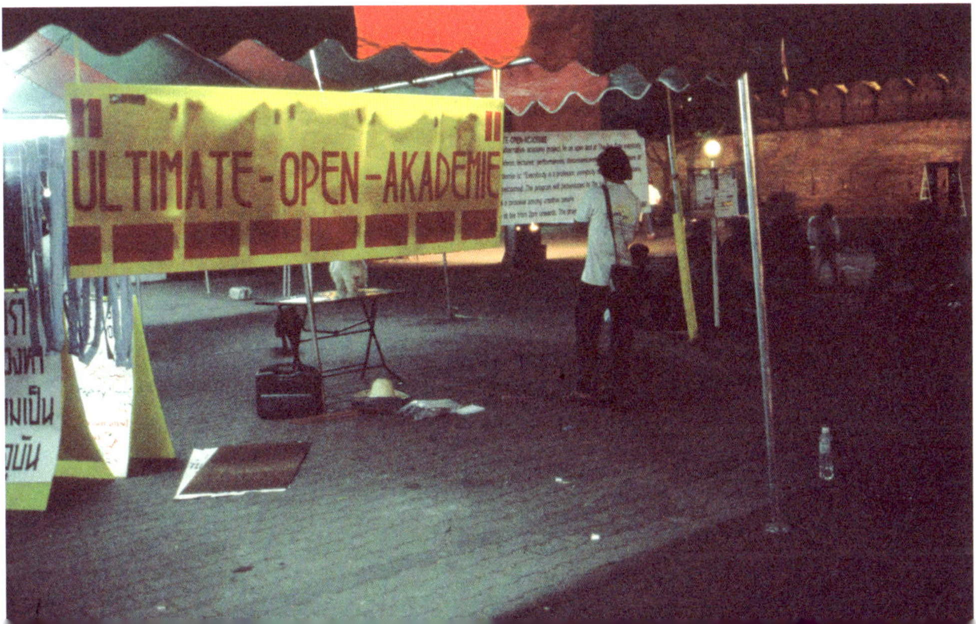

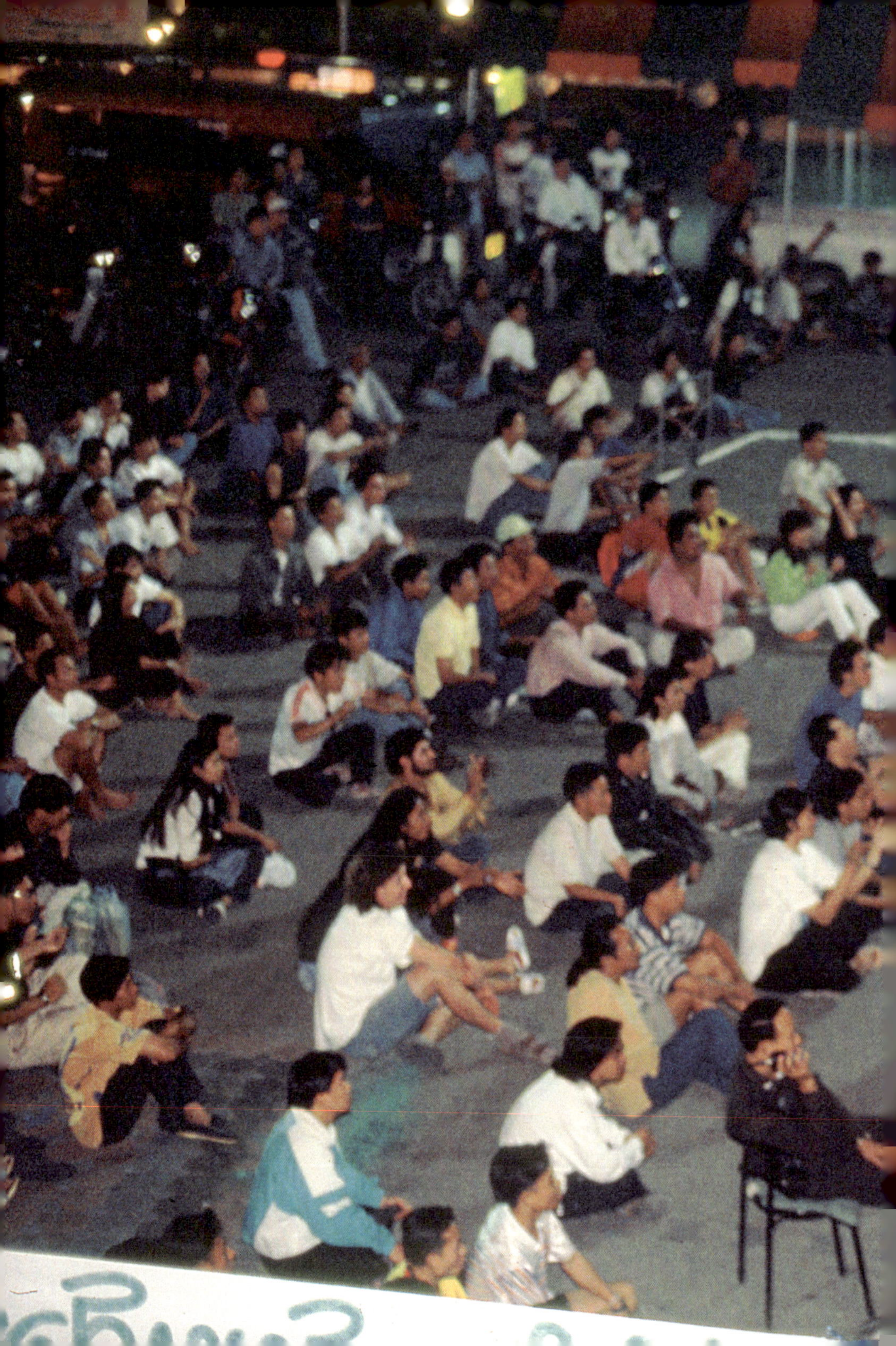

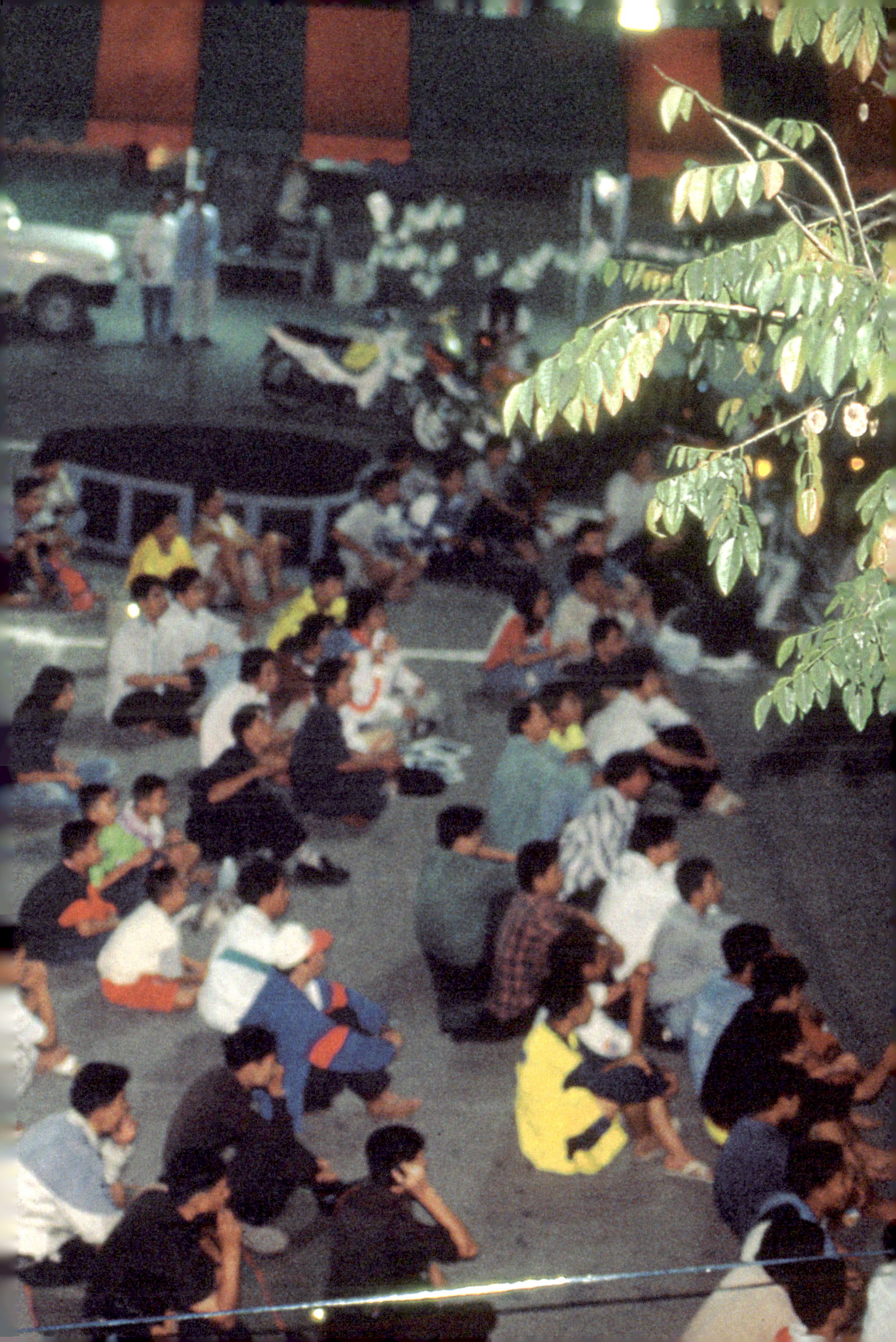

Chiang Mai: Looking Back at the Nineties[1] — Rosalind C. Morris

One might say that Chiang Mai's eternally recurring predicament is that of the 'new city' rediscovering its origins. Its name appears to have been its destiny from the beginning.

In the early nineties, when I first went to Thailand to conduct research (I had been visiting the country since the mid-eighties), Chiang Mai was a self-consciously 'emergent city', confident but also ambivalent. The most common description I heard from the people I knew – intellectuals as well as teachers, chefs, shopkeepers and ritual practitioners – was of transformation. Chiang Mai, they said, was radically unlike what it had been a generation or even a decade before. And of course, that was true. It's remarkable to think about how rapid and profound the city's transformation was after the end of the US wars in Southeast Asia – wars that played a significant part in enabling the modernisation that people were referencing, although they rarely, if ever, mentioned those wars and Thailand's place in the US imperial project.

The 'new' Chiang Mai was full of novelty, its forms and spaces mutating with the terrifying velocity of a retrovirus. That the city was a scene of the unfolding HIV/AIDS epidemic is sometimes forgotten in histories written about Chiang Mai and its place in the broader struggle for popular democracy. This catastrophe is important in any account of the decade, and it may partly account for the fact that much of the neo-traditionalism that would emerge in the nineties paired a nostalgia for the premodern with an ethos of temperance, and a suspicion not only of prostitution but of the erotics that saturated the commodity sphere in every domain.

Construction was visible everywhere – on the skyline, filled with cranes and the skeletal frameworks of new buildings; on the main thoroughfares leaving the old city; and on billboards announcing new real estate developments and advertising the aesthetics of genteel suburban life. Often, change was referenced in a wistful tone, with nostalgia for a less commodity-filled, more sedate urban existence. But by no means was this always the case. I recall interviewing women over the age of seventy about their experience of recent history, and hearing from them an exuberant affirmation of the conveniences now available, most especially automotive transport to and from the wats (temples), and labour-saving devices like washing machines. And they had little understanding of, and perhaps even less patience for, the adoration of tradition and antiquities that was gripping Chiang Mai.

There was at that time a powerful interest in Lannathai, the kingdom and epoch established by King Mengrai in the late thirteenth century, with Chiang Mai as its centre. More or less contemporary with Sukhothai, it preceded both the Burmese invasions of the north and the subsequent rise of the Ayutthaya and then Bangkok-based empires. Interest in Lannathai anchored a critical and regionalist counter-discourse arrayed against the Bangkok-centred, Siamese nationalism of the state. The discourses about Lannathai were being authored by people outside of Chiang Mai as well, and they involved a resignification of Chiang Mai's spatial and temporalised 'marginality'. What in nationalist historiography had been deemed backward, primitive or peripheral *vis-à-vis* the modernism of the Siamese state acquired the aura and virtue of the originary: firstness and purity were its values. An aesthetic of the ruin and a love of patina were expressive of Lannathai nostalgia in the cultural domain. It was not incidental that a lot of discourse about Lannathai was appearing in the context of critical and art historical writing, for example in the pages of the journal *Silapa Watthanatham* (Arts and Culture). There was a certain affinity between historiography and collecting in the project.

In my mind, few places seemed more eligible for Walter Benjamin's description of the modern era as one in which it is possible to 'find a new beauty in what is vanishing' than Chiang Mai – albeit more among the (middle-)ageing elite than the restless youth who would soon be surfing the Web and entering emerging virtual communities of popular uprising.

The critical intellectual ambition of those who were advocating a recovery of Lannathai history and identity was, it seemed to me then (as now), ironically compatible with the increasing touristification of Chiang Mai. A huge source of Thailand's new wealth, tourism was the object of deep ambivalence, and not a little resentment. Chiang Mai was, to borrow a phrase from André Malraux, becoming a 'museum without walls'. But whereas for Malraux this museum was an internal one – in the imagination, comprised of the world's art and supported by photographic reproductions – Chiang Mai was transforming itself into a 'to-be-photographed' space. I have written about this at some length, but I think the great energy of self-discovery that was at the heart of the Lannathai movement (if one may call it that) was inseparable from a pervasive tendency to self-objectification and an equally pervasive obsession with self-documentation.[2] Chiang Mai was giving itself to be seen – by others. It was being staged for others, including those from Chiang Mai who were themselves being and feeling estranged by the historical transformations afoot.

The interventions of Chiang Mai Social Installation (CMSI) partook of these transformations but also worked against them. CMSI's situation-specific installations, aimed at the provocation and participatory engagement of urban dwellers, worked against the contemplative, interiorising drive expressed in Malraux's concept. The emphasis on the social dimension of the intervention is crucial in this respect. The entire urban space of the city was becoming a forest of images, whose emblem might be the trees of postcards that adorned so many street corners, shop windows and airport kiosks. CMSI's work was also somewhat ironic; its own self-conscious and self-monumentalising gestures referred participants to the space of encounter as much as the locus of history. Just as postmodernism may be seen in some contexts to precede modernism, in the absence of a strong museological tradition CMSI introduced forms of installation and participatory art that elsewhere were organised *against* and *in the aftermath* of more conventional forms of museology (although, again, the museological impulse linked to collecting and self-objectification was

—

[1] This text was written in response to questions by David Morris and David Teh, February–March 2018.
[2] See my *In the Place of Origins: Modernity and Its Mediums in Northern Thailand*, Durham, NC: Duke University Press, 2000.

everywhere). But above all, they were resisting the reduction of Chiang Mai to a venue for the staging (and selling) of authenticity in the form of display-value.

Emerging cultural politics, based in concerns for things local, were ambivalent too. On the one hand, the emphasis on and interest in the pre-Siamese past risked a re-valorisation of aristocracy and feudality. Yet, intentionally or not, images and accounts of the *cao*s (feudal princes who joined but did not surpass Rama V in popularity as cult objects) also worked to recall sovereign and, on occasion, insurrectionary pasts. This provided a kind of affective reservoir, which was ready to be mobilised against the restoration of military authority, initially in solidarity with democracy activists in Bangkok.

The art scene was small but, as I recall, vibrant. One could feel a gathering force, born of the contradictions in Chiang Mai at that time and, despite some frustration, clearly on the verge of release. The emerging art, including that which was not directly inspired by the recovery of the past, and by craft renewal especially, was often engaged with questions that arose from it, including concern for the environment (we did not yet speak in the idiom of climate change). Water and deforestation were issues of special relevance in the still heavily agricultural province, and I recall a couple of powerful installations that took on the problems of environmentalism and contamination, drawing upon but radically transforming the Buddhist-inspired conservationism also in the air – but not yet formalised and/or appropriated as a monarchical project of alternative development).

It was in that context that I first met Montien Boonma, in about 1992. I was immediately struck by the sense that he was a powerful and yet modest dissident voice in that space. His works were commenting upon such contradictions, mobilising the materials of apparently traditional cultural forms and, without defacing them, resignifying them. The monochromatic sculptural works, fabricated from the materials of everyday (agricultural) life, at once gestured to the figuration of the rural/urban or traditional/modern divide, and ironised them. They were, to me, quite unprecedented in the Thai art scene. So were his quiet provocations about Buddhism and its instrumentalisation in modern Thailand. Significantly, he had been working in the late 1980s at Chiang Mai University, an epicentre of critical discourse about such changes and developments. He was then, as I think he remains now, an inspirational figure for young artists.

That was before artists like Rirkrit Tiravanija and Kamin Lertchaiprasert undertook their own activist work on issues of environmental pedagogy in the form of The Land Foundation, established around 1998. By then, shortly after the debilitating financial crisis of 1997, Chiang Mai was deeply imbricated in a complex web of transnational movements, and it was acquiring a self-consciously cosmopolitan identity in contrast to the assertive regionalism of the decade's early years. Many people in the cultural scene were mobile and claimed residencies and affiliations in many places. And Thai artists – in New York, London and elsewhere – were beginning to think of the city as a place in which to make and to think about art and cultural politics, and they began to return to Chiang Mai. A number of galleries opened. Abroad, international art festivals were taking up Thai artists, and Thai cinema was beginning to make its mark.

Moreover, cultural revival was not limited to the restitution of tradition. It was also a project of translation and especially self-translation for a more international, English-speaking audience. Throughout the nineties, the publication of modernist Thai fiction under the imprint of Thai Modern Classics, an initiative of the Bangkok-based Chaiyong Limthongkul Foundation, was symptomatic of this double desire to assert the accomplishments of Thai artists (in this case writers) and to demonstrate the presence of modernist aesthetic trajectories within Thailand, precisely by bringing them into English, and thus to an international readership (or, in the case of the visual arts, into the world of biennales). One can see in this double desire the force of recognition, the desire to be seen and known from without. This was not unrelated to the transformation of the mass media in Thailand at the time. Nor can it be separated from the political events of the decade, especially of its early years.

My sense of those first years, even now, more than 25 years later, is one of excitement, of things flowing and moving – before they were cauterised by trauma. Between the beginning and final years of the nineties, the country was riven by catastrophic events: brief, nearly utopian flashes of self-organisation followed by terrifyingly violent repressions of democratic movements. The return of military rule, in the form of the junta led by Suchinda Kraprayoon in 1991, was, of course, quickly followed by the democratic protests and retaliatory massacres of May 1992 ('Black May'). Many people have observed that the democracy movements, largely middle class in their composition, were enabled by cell phone technology. This was certainly true in Bangkok, where hundreds of thousands of calls were made from the centre of protest, at Sanam Luang Park, on any given day. But it was also true throughout the country, and Thailand's insurrectionary experiment with such technology foreshadowed what would occur throughout the region, and especially in the Philippines, where, some years later, texting and crowdsourcing would be the very medium of opposition for the People Power II movement. Indeed, a genealogy of social media protests of the new millennium, from the various Springs of the Arab and Persian worlds to the Orange Revolution of the Ukraine, ought to extend to, if not commence in, Thailand in the early nineties.

Although there was satellite television at the time of the first Democracy Protests in 1992, Thai censors were able to interrupt the transmission of news – thus not only blinding the population to the events in Bangkok but momentarily severing the solidarities that had emerged in the midst of and despite the regionalism that had taken route in the north of the country. Initially, news got out by virtue of the actual physical transport of video cassettes, and through the efforts of those who carried them and mediated them for the publics that assembled to hear messages otherwise travelling in the form of rumour. 'We will be your media' was a phrase spoken by activists.[3]

That slogan resonated with the logic of spirit mediumship I was studying at the time. And the fact that northern Thai activists mobilised ritual theatre – in the form of public cursings carried out by charismatic spirit mediums – redoubled the resonance. The potency of these 'traditional' gestures for modern audiences was

—

[3] See my 'Representations: Locality and the Spirit of Democracy', chapter 7 in *ibid.*

not lost on Bangkok's activists, who were quick to mobilise this previously local signifier in their arsenal of anti-dictatorial practices. I place 'traditional' in quotes because tradition had itself been radically reformed under the influence of new media technologies, and especially the gradual appropriation of photographic technologies by ritual practitioners. What had been prohibited in the ritual sphere in an earlier era had, by the nineties, become an integral aspect of ritual performance, and spirit mediums, like everyone else, were documenting their activities, anticipating a future in which they would be seen from afar.

Reflecting on this complex oppositional theatre, and on the doubling of mediatic strategies, which led not to a displacement of old forms of mediation but rather to their intensification and extension, made me rethink my own research – although it took me some years to fully grasp the significance of what I was seeing in Chiang Mai. I began to think that the potentialities for what we now consider to be modern forms and orientations were being retrospectively discovered in premodern traditions. This is not quite the same thing as saying that those traditions anticipated or intuited what was to come. It is rather a way of recognising the ceaseless and retrospective writing of history as the origin of the present and not merely as that which is chronologically prior.

Among the many things going on in this double mediation was a transformation of the relation between the local and, for lack of a better phrase, the foreign. To a certain extent, the art scene had to catch up to this fact of Thai life in order to make a break within its own development, and to realise itself as a set of practices both grounded in prior traditions and productive of unprecedented visions and formulations.

Thailand in the nineties was a place in which simulation and the simulacrum had a particularly powerful place. It was known elsewhere as the marketplace of imitations, with the night markets of Bangkok and Chiang Mai especially famous for rip-offs of brand-name commodities. In the visual art world, modernism itself was spoken of in these terms – as derivative if not imitative. In the world of commodities, however, this sense of the ersatz was not itself a liability. The foreign could be valorised so long as it was made in Thailand. The work of the aesthetic domain required and produced something else, namely the discovery and generation of foreignness – something new and as yet unknown – within and as a property of things Thai. It needed to (and in some cases, did) produce or affirm an internal difference and a possible way of becoming other in ways that were not contained or domesticated by discourses of regional or historical specificity.

To look at this period in this way is to acknowledge that there was something enormously generative in the experience of 'connection' that was being facilitated by new and rapidly metamorphosing media technologies – and indeed by the valorisation of 'connectivity' that accompanied them. But it would be wrong to think that the mere fact of such connection enabled the transmission of ideas and that the gradual entry into and exposure to networks of festivals and biennales were, in themselves, determinant of the changes that would occur in the cultural and specifically artistic work of the new millennium. I do not mean to say that the emergence of a so-called cosmopolitan aesthetic sensibility was itself the function of being inserted into a global web of artists, galleries, museums and prizes. It's difficult to even speak of these histories without making recourse to the very language, which is say the metaphoricity, of that media-technological and financial-institutional development. But 'the web' and the concept of connection that accompanies it are metaphors as much as they are aspects of a technological support system. What happened in the nineties, seen now from the second decade of the new millennium, must be understood in this way: as the realisation and transformation of relations between the local and the foreignness within, and not merely as exposure to things from afar.

Of course, such transformations are always resisted. In the period of the military dictatorship in the early nineties, democracy activists were regularly disparaged as being manipulated by third-hand forces, foreign elements, anti-Thai conspirators. Militant nationalism continually resurfaces in Thailand, and even political opposition must generally cloak itself in the language of fidelity to the nation's ostensibly traditional institutions (although these were consolidated in their present form quite recently, via constitutional amendments).[4] Thai artists have had to negotiate that demand with delicacy.

What has been described, in an especially felicitous phrase, as the 'ambient transnational contemporaneity'[5] of the festival circuit today is perhaps best understood as the flip side of the regionalist domestication of alterity that I have described with reference to Lannathai. I think the ambient transnational contemporaneity of those circuits (again the language of the network) is afflicted by the loss, or at least the muting, of the foreign – of thinking that, whatever its forms, is new, unprecedented, inventive even to the point that its effects are unrecognisable. This is what I mean by 'foreign'.

Work that is understood to be 'parochial' does not move or signify in those international festival contexts. At the same time, there is, in the same contexts, often a compensatory privileging of identity, of work that signifies itself as the expression of a non-generalisable mode of being (whether racial, national or sexual, or whether understood as a function of historically traumatic events). A certain danger arises, however, when a claim is made that work must be grounded in experience, and that this experience must be linked to an exclusive identity. The danger is that of domestication, of limiting not what can be said but what can be imagined. I do not say that this is always the case, only that it is a threatening possibility. Artists from minoritised categories and spaces in the Global South understand this domestication as the demand that they limit their discourse to their 'own issues', and that they signify themselves for others in terms of their ascribed identity. For this reason, because regionalism is one of the names of identity, there is much to be learned from a reflection on Chiang Mai in the nineties, in all the aspects that I have described above – and more besides.

—

[4] See Benedict R. O'G. Anderson, 'Studies of the Thai State: The State of Thai Studies', in Eliezer Ayal (ed.) *The Study of Thailand: Analyses of Knowledge, Approaches and Prospects in Anthropology, Art, Economics, History and Political Science*, Athens, OH: Ohio University Center for International Studies, 1978, pp.193–247.

[5] D. Morris and D. Teh, correspondence with the author, February 2018.

Perhaps one of the most interesting dimensions of the regionalist phenomenon, and one that is revealed with particular clarity in Chiang Mai's recent history, is the fact that regionalism cannot be understood in terms of a pure opposition to – or even a dialectical relation with – locality or globality. There are relative scales of regionalism, and dynamic relations of vertical integration as well as contraction, which are complexly related to even broader movements. On the one hand, the regionalism of the Lannathai movement constituted a movement away from, or a withdrawal from, nationalist and what can be called internal colonialist histories and tendencies. Its directionality was inward, its scale was diminishing, its circumference was narrowing. At the same time, Chiang Mai was integrated into and played an important role in Southeast Asian regionalisms that emerged in and through media-technological developments at the time – via cellular telephony and cinematic circuits of distribution, in the movement of capital (and its crises), in the spread of particular forms of democratic protest as well as populist authoritarianism.

The processes of re-regionalisation that occurred in Chiang Mai were taking place at the same time that other regionalisms were emerging: in Europe, for example, following the fall of the Berlin Wall; in the Middle East, as a result of militarised conflict. One way to understand this is as part of the reformation of interstate dynamics in the aftermath of the collapse of the Soviet Union and the entire bloc system of geo-politics, as well as in the rise of new kinds of internationalism (such as Islamic internationalism, which has had a special force in Thailand's southern provinces). Southeast Asian regionalism was and remains fragile. The conflict between Thailand and Cambodia over the temple complex at Preah Vihear demonstrates this, as does the ongoing struggle for recognition on the part of Thailand's Muslim residents (not unrelated to the struggles of Rohingya in Myanmar). In Chiang Mai, as elsewhere, the complexity of the regionalist phenomenon was linked to greater integration into an increasingly integrated global sphere, including the artistic sphere, on the one hand, and a sense of refusal or disavowal *vis-à-vis* the social demands being made by global capital, on the other. Groups like CMSI were in some ways a product of this tense vacillation, and they expressed simultaneously a desire for access to centres of power and influence and a refusal to be the mere object of consumerist desire emanating from the metropolitan centres of the Global North.

The artistic movements of the nineties share something with the activist, democratically oriented politics of the time; both were born in a space of fantastical economic growth, and then transformed (in different ways) in the aftermath of the financial crisis of 1997. It's difficult to know how much the trajectories of these spheres – the activist and the artistic – can be understood in local terms. The ironic autonomisation of the artistic sphere in the new millennium is profoundly different from that which was imagined as a definitive attribute of the aesthetic in classical Enlightenment philosophy. The autonomy one sees now, if it may be called that, is a function of market forces as much as it is an ideal of contemplative or critical distance. More and more Thai artists move in international circuits of recognition and display, and they are part of a global community whose discourses are shaped by co-inhabitation of a realm defined by its relative freedom from purely parochial concerns, and from material need. Globally speaking, they are part of a relatively autonomised world defined by the growing distance and intensifying inequality between classes of people who either do or do not have access to waged labour, mobility and educational opportunity. Let me put this a little differently: the people who enjoy autonomy now are those who are most advantaged in or adept at negotiating the global economy. This is as true in the cultural sphere as in the economic. And this is related to the forms of political discourse that we see everywhere – including in Chiang Mai and in Thailand more generally.

Democratic politics around the world have been hijacked by populist ressentiment, and they are increasingly subordinated to fantasies of ethnic purification, territorial self-containment and economic nationalism. In many places, the idea of political representationalism has given way to the adoration of the leader as the singular and emblematic *embodiment* of national sovereignty. Thailand is no exception, although it has its peculiarities in the unique form of its sacralised military-monarchical alliance.

But this may be where, once again, an analysis of media and artistic practice can provide some real insight. The doubled rise of media technologies and media capital since the nineties and of artistic communities and forms that valorise connectivity are perhaps coextensive with the rise of the new populisms – despite the fact that much contemporary art is explicitly engaged in a critique of those populisms. New political movements on the left and the right make use of media forms first visible in Thailand in the early 1990s. And such techno-mediatic forms get used to express an ironic aspiration for more immediacy, less bureaucracy and more locally oriented causes (often to the exclusion of foreigners). Though the claim of installation art was and is partly against this overdetermined connectivity, it nonetheless enabled its rise in places like Chiang Mai. In the critical urbanist intervention, there is an effort to make the situation of the encounter a source not of illumination but of éclat, a flash or brilliant effect that is felt as much as seen.

It is possible that such moments are increasingly difficult to generate in cities that have domesticated so many of the techniques and forms that CMSI pioneered. Improvisational gallery spaces are increasingly indistinguishable from pop-up stores, just as crowdsourced happenings are an occasion for profit-making as much as politically dissident gatherings. Every era must invent its insurrectionary practice and know that what emerges as the self-consciously newest form will likely become outmoded more quickly than that which preceded it. The form of appearance of our accelerating times is obsolescence. The premodern persists in the present; this much is a truism of modernist aesthetic theory. But obsolescence is the process by which the new enters into history, not as ruin but as the discarded and the unfashionable. Modernity might well be the point of intersection and visibility between the premodern and the discarded. In the nineties, the idea of social installation art was an effort to both recognise and evade this fatality within the mediatised world. It remains to be seen what it can become as those forces intensify.

It has been a number of years since I was in Chiang Mai. I am not in a position to judge the work being done by its young artists today, but I often hear people say that the city is changing, that it is unlike what it was two decades ago, and that, in fact, it is an entirely new place. I wouldn't recognise it, they tell me. Hearing this, I am gripped by an odd sensation. It is not quite an uncanny feeling, but I have heard these lines before. And, now, I believe them to be true, once more.

Art's Potentiality Revisited: Araya Rasdjarmrearnsook's Late Style and Chiang Mai Social Installation — May Adadol Ingawanij

This article takes its cue from Simon Soon's proposal to return to Chiang Mai Social Installation (CMSI) by assembling archival fragments and memories in order to narrate the festival as potentiality rather than actuality.[1] It juxtaposes CMSI with a reading of the late style of Araya Rasdjarmrearnsook – a canonical if not globally familiar figure in Southeast Asian contemporary art, best-known for her series of video installations presenting her reflexively feminine performances of communicating with corpses (1997–2005). 'Late style' is a nomenclature borrowed from Edward Said which will be used here to explore Araya's intermedial artistic practice of the past decade or so.[2] In making a montage of Araya's commentary on CMSI, in which she was a participant and exhibiting artist, and her recent
p.258
exhibition-project 'An Artist is Trying to Return to "Being a Writer"' (2017/18),[3] my intention is to create an ensemble of otherwise dissociated moments. Assembling the details of these different moments of artistic practice enables us to return to the question of art's potentiality and to route its genealogy through Cold War and post-Cold War Thailand – conjunctures not usually associated with the fostering of artistic autonomy.

Then and now

Araya has said that shortly before the first edition of the festival in 1992 she had just returned to her home country to work as a lecturer at the Faculty of Fine Arts at Chiang Mai University (CMU), having completed a postgraduate art degree in Germany. She was, at that point, the only female lecturer in a traditionally structured, mostly artistically conservative faculty.[4] Not being part of the 'boys' club' of managers, as she puts it, and living alone in a dormitory, her daily routine consisted of going to campus to teach and make art at the faculty's studio facilities. For leisure, instead of afterwork drinking sessions, she would go out for an ice cream with fellow artist and lecturer Montien Boonma. Her involvement with the CMSI festivals was partly due to this experience of marginalisation, and also to her friendship with students, including the locally networked Navin Rawanchaikul, a coordinator of CMSI (who would become a well-known contemporary artist internationally). She now casts her experience of participating in the first few years of the festival as being swept up by a youthful initiative. She recognises its energy as transgressive of the academic strictures of modern art in Thailand, and she notes that there was an unspoken understanding amongst CMSI's instigators of a need to make space for broader conceptions of artistic practice than those petrified within the hierarchical structure and provincialism of the country's fine arts academia.

Araya did indeed produce works for exhibition in the first few iterations of CMSI,
pp.174 and 273
for instance a site-specific sculpture that was a human-size coffin-shaped box

—

[1] See Simon Soon, 'Images Without Bodies: Chiang Mai Social Installation and the Art History of Cooperative Suffering,' *Afterall*, issue 42, Autumn/Winter 2016, pp.36–47.

[2] See Edward Said, *On Late Style*, London: Bloomsbury, 2006. Said's reflection on this topic is itself a form of interlocution with Theodor Adorno's articulation of it.

covered with mirrors and floating on a pond situated within the large grounds of a temple. Yet, when asked to speak on how she took part in the festival, Araya seems less interested in recalling the chronology of works she contributed than in telling an amusing anecdote about how the mirror sculpture was made useful by viewer-participants who turned it into the target of a stone-throwing game. To hear her tell stories now of CMSI is not so much to catch remnants of memorable artists' works and performances. Instead, Araya recalls that as a female artist-participant with her own car she spent considerable time chaperoning guests from the airport to their campsites or installations across the city, and to and from big nightly parties held at a local illustrator-writer's house. In her description of CMSI's beginnings, the mode of involvement that came into being during the festival's germination was an improvisatory one with local roots in agricultural labour and ritual – *long khaek*.[5]

Along with taking part in the festival both as an artist and as a labourer, Araya was an early chronicler of CMSI. In the 1990s, she was most known in Thailand as a writer of feminine fiction and a columnist for newspapers and magazines that projected, at that point, a globalising and liberalising image; these were edited or owned by figures linked to Thailand's October Generation, associated with anti-military uprisings in the 1970s. Araya wrote a column on CMSI for *Krungthep thurakij* in November 1995, shortly after the third iteration of the festival. During the 1990s, this Thai-language newspaper's arts and culture section was the leading publication platform for news and articles on non-traditional arts. The playful title of Araya's piece roughly translates as 'Soft and Hard News from Chiang Mai Social Installation',[6] and in it she writes wittily pointed vignettes from the field, presenting eight short scenes that communicate those artistic and interpersonal ideals made possible to experience in an unprecedented way in the city during the festival. She emphasises CMSI's reliance on a voluntaristic ethos and the goodwill of participating artists, who came from far and wide at their own expense to contribute wide-ranging artworks, installations, performances, walkabouts, talks and happenings in spaces remote from the global art market and institutional circuit. She notes the discrepancy between the city administration's investment in Chiang Mai's litter-free appearance and those spatial and social forms given temporary material presence during the festival, such as a colourful, well-made children's climbing frame placed in a public park, or another installation that placed a cluster of trees on the large empty ground outside a newly built modern art museum.

At the same time, in her vignettes Araya does not refrain from slyly injecting snapshots of chance eruptions and awkward moments symptomatic of the gaps between CMSI's improvisatory ethos; its aspirations toward autonomy, open-

—

[3] 'Sinlapin kamlang phayayaam klub pai pen naak khien / An Artist is Trying to Return to "Being a Writer"', 100 Tonson, Bangkok, 28 June 2017–14 January 2018.

[4] Araya Rasdjarmrearnsook, interview with Manuporn Luengaram and May Adadol Ingawanij, 21 July 2017.

[5] The etymology of *long khaek* is an act of agricultural labour exchange, when villagers would take turns working on each other's land during planting and harvesting seasons. The term is now used idiomatically in two senses: it may refer to voluntary acts of collective endeavour; more disturbingly, it may refer to gang rape.

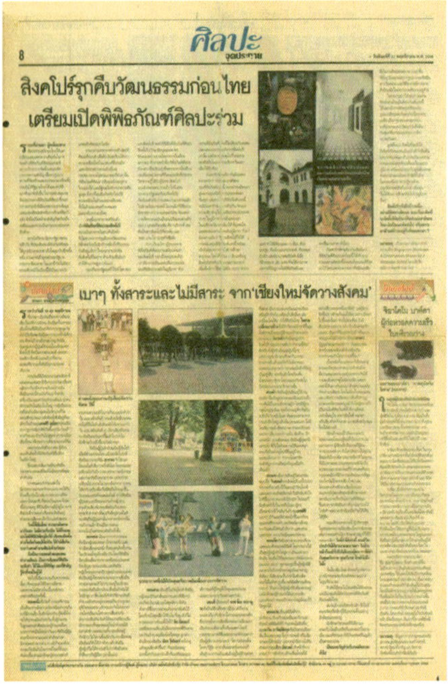
8

ศิลปะ

สิงคโปร์รุกคืบวัฒนธรรมก่อนไทย เตรียมเปิดพิพิธภัณฑ์ศิลปะร่วม

เบาๆ ทั้งสาระและไม่มีสาระ จาก'เชียงใหม่จัดวางสังคม'

Araya Rasdjarmrearnsook,
'Soft and Hard News from
Chiang Mai Social Installation',
in *Krungthep thurakij jood prakai*,
27 November 1995

ended processes, deterritorialisation and horizontality; and the persistent reality of cultural insularity, social hierarchy and mismatched expectations brought to bear on intercultural encounters. In an exquisitely toned anecdote, she tells of an embarrassed exchange between Navin and a participating feminist artist who had flown in from Pakistan. Arriving at the airport, where Navin was waiting to pick her up, the artist immediately asked to be taken to meet the city's leading feminists. According to Araya's mischievous rendition, her question had the young male organiser somewhat rattled. Smiling sheepishly, he replied: 'There might be some, uh, we might be able to find some.'[7]

Two decades later, Araya makes the important point that the festivals' ad hoc, counter-institutional energy could not have sustained itself beyond a few years.[8] To have persisted with the kind of improvisational brio with which they had started, which appropriately embodied the fleeting potentiality of becoming, would have led to an ossification of improvisational gestures, and to the formulaic repetition of an informal ambient. According to Araya, CMSI came into being at a moment in which the core organisers were not especially familiar with the figure of the contemporary art curator. Nevertheless, once the festivals began to grow in size and

—

[6] Araya, 'Bao bao thang sara lae mai mee sara jaak "chiang mai jad wang sangkhom"', *Krungthep thurakij jood prakai*, 27 November 1995, p.8.

[7] *Ibid.*

[8] Araya, interview with Manuporn and May Adadol, 21 July 2017.

international visibility, they had to institutionalise, to accept having a director or curator to oversee the process of settling into a large-scale arts event. Or it had to stop. The textual archive of CMSI has a poetic symmetry. Another article by Araya, 'A narrative of an event that has just come to an end', published in the journal of CMU's Faculty of Fine Arts, chronicles the ending of CMSI the previous year.[9]

Returning to CMSI in this manner, by drawing on Araya's assessment of the festivals and her more recent recollections, opens up a few possible paths for thinking about artistic potentiality with, or against, existing narratives of the CMSI festivals. The figuring of female presence, and the frictions that come into view by following the latent trail of engendered participation hinted at in Araya's recollection, contrasts somewhat with the seeming absence of interest in the gendering of artistic agency in existing testimonies about CMSI's life and afterlife. The need to consider women's experiences and participation in any future historiography of CMSI, and perhaps more significantly to read the discursive figuring of female presence in and around the festival, might be highlighted by juxtaposing Araya's narratives above with a curious tale by the artist-provocateur Mit Jai Inn, one of the festival's instigators.[10] This thought-provoking detail is part of his recollection of CSMI's perhaps most famous happening, the pilgrimage around the city during the Week of Cooperative Suffering, when participants were physically assembled into a congregation and bound together by rope. The group was then taken on a walkabout through Chiang Mai's legitimate and illicit spaces, with the additional conceit that they had to carry a large stone without putting it down at any point. Women appear in Mit's memory akin to the figure of the primitive spectator in early cinema, so crucial to film's self-mythologisation as a techno-aesthetic medium of modernity: the uninitiated bodies in front of the screen who screamed and fled in pleasure and terror in response to the novel sight of a speeding train approaching them for the first time. Making up a good half of the assembled and bound bodies, many women, Mit claims, entered a brothel and saw what went on there with their own eyes for the first time.

Ending and lateness

The other suggestive if counter-intuitive direction for thinking about the question of the potentiality of CMSI would be to pause over the relatively early ending of the festival series.[11] As Araya recollects, CMSI could have expanded into a regularly held citywide arts festival, or it could have stopped. And rather than assume that all endings signal decline or defeat, we might instead, following Giorgio Agamben, associate the capacity or potentiality of an event or a thing not with the execution of action and the exercise of will and intention, but with the non-execution of that which could have been done. The gesture of stopping is not necessarily a symptom of disillusionment or exhaustion. As a capacity that persists in not doing, the gesture signals the possibility of the festival to embody transformation aligned to open-ended process, autonomy and horizontality. This implies the contingency of that possibility's future return irrespective of CMSI's

—

[9] Araya, 'A narrative of an event that has just come to an end', *Journal of Fine Arts*, vol.1, no.1, 2000, pp.14–16.

[10] Mit Jai Inn, interview with Gridthiya Gaweewong and Penwadee Nophaket Manont, 10 February 2015.

achievements, underachievements, or the tensions or irresolvable contradictions manifested in its brief chronology of actualisation.

Around twenty-five years after CMSI's first appearance, the context for Araya's solo exhibition 'An Artist is Trying to Return to "Being a Writer"' was her reaching official retirement age from CMU at sixty. Shortly before, she had been belatedly granted a professorship, after several unsuccessful applications to a committee consisting of arts bureaucrats who remained loyal to officialdom's conservative nationalist conception of fine arts and ethical taste. In the last decade or so of her tenure at the Faculty of Fine Arts, she successfully campaigned to validate, in the face of hostility from other senior academics, an undergraduate curriculum in multidisciplinary arts characterised by a pedagogical worldliness that remains unusual in Thai universities' fine arts departments, the majority of which classify according to medium. In Araya's artistic practice, intermediality is a consistent yet constantly evolving feature. While still an undergraduate, the artist found herself in a miniature media storm when she was awarded a national art prize for a print work she made by copying a photograph.[12] Her retirement exhibition, as its title suggests, continued to play on intermedial movements and transitions, involving a simultaneously visual, audiovisual and textual process; a gallery installation of newly made artworks and a non-gallery mode of exposure and circulation; and a durational event and performance of production and presentation.

Araya turned the show's six-month duration into a writing deadline, met in the form of a book at the exhibition's end, poetically titled *Phud kerd ma laa raam* (very roughly, 'a nascence to bid farewell').[13] 'An Artist is Trying to Return to "Being a Writer"' opened with an almost entirely empty space save for a carved wooden sign displaying the title. Over time, elements accumulated in it: sculptures made of wood, fibreglass, fabric and 3D-printed figures of the artist's naked, aged body, as well as video pieces. One of these, *The Cruel,* is a re-enactment of Thai-language attacks and criticisms that the artist has received, and it features a number of her male students in the multidisciplinary arts programme dressed up retro-style in the denim-and-long-hair look of the October Generation of male modern artists. They recite speeches drawn verbatim from academic committee reports explaining the rationale for rejecting Araya's application for promotion, and these scenes alternate with textual quotations of negative Thai-language judgments of her art. While Araya herself did not attend the opening party, several Araya lookalikes sporting wavy, salt-and-pepper wigs were there. The artist made her appearance at the exhibition some months later, attending but not speaking at the conversation to launch her book.

Phud kerd ma laa raam is the story of the three ages of the existential and artistic being of a powerless female, Laileeya; it is an ambiguous object with the deceptive

—

[11] See S. Soon, 'Images Without Bodies', *op. cit.*

[12] See Araya, '*Kane krai krai kor rak*', in *Phom pen sinlapin*, Bangkok: Matichon, 2005, pp.93–101.

[13] Araya, *Phud kerd ma laa raam,* Bangkok: 100 Tonson Gallery, 2018. As an object-form the book's purpose and function is multiple, and somewhat unclear. It was not actively placed in the market for a Thai-language fiction readership; and it is a catalogue of the

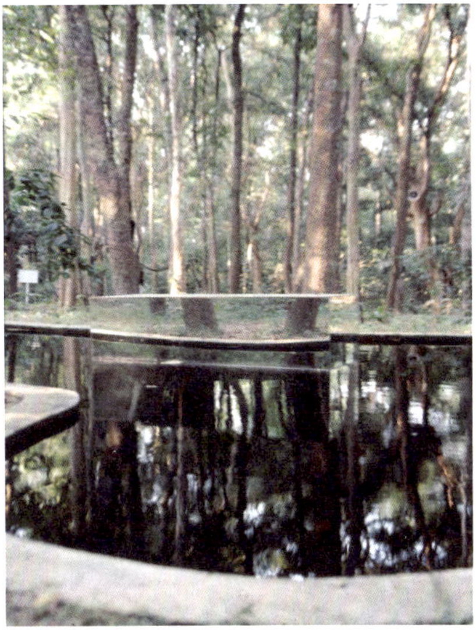

Araya Rasdjarmrearnsook, untitled work installed at Wat Umong as part of the third Chiang Mai Social Installation, 1995–96
Courtesy the artist, Uthit Atimana and Gridthiya Gaweewong

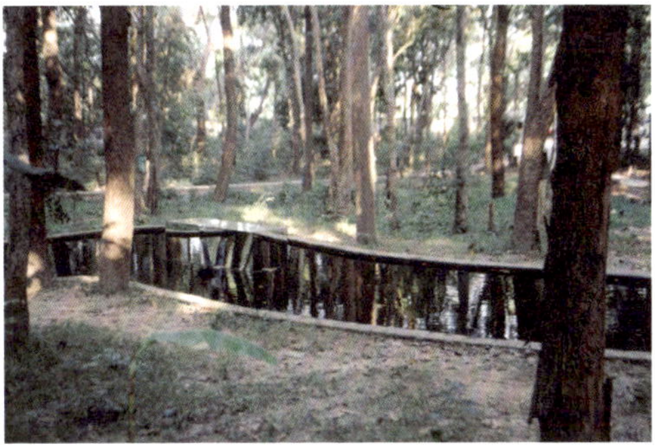

first appearance of an autobiography.[14] Scenes, events and spaces narrated in excessively photorealist detail, such as the interior of the wooden house after the death of the toddler Laileeya's mother, or the grown artist's activity of dressing up female corpses in beautiful costumes, signal a process of writing as *remediation* of Araya's past artworks. Its prose might be described as a kind of Thai-language baroque: ultra-feminine and excessively ornamental in its rhyming poetics; indulging in an anachronistic recuperation of feminine Thai-language writing that evokes, and exceeds, the stylistic sensibility of mid-twentieth-century women's literary magazines. Forced to part in early childhood from her biological and surrogate mothers, the verbal portrait presents the girl as if she is a hungry ghost in the family house, moving amongst objects and fixtures whose animistic liveliness relate to her with an intimacy denied by her father and stepmother. Laileeya the young woman learns to exercise agency through artistic endeavour, excelling as an artist within national institutional and ideological frameworks, but eventually turning her back on such values. Laileeya the middle-aged, single female artist moves to a remote place and turns her house into a sanctuary for stray dogs. She finds herself becoming more creaturely; the bond with her rescued dogs becomes life itself. The weight of the human world overwhelms her and makes her yearn for death. She is ostracised by those officially upholding national art institutions. She

—

works displayed in the gallery exhibition, with images and information on the works occupying a marginal place as a kind of appendix.

[14] In a recent class, which we co-taught at the CMU multidisciplinary arts programme in April 2018, the art historian Sayan Daengklom described the prose of the book as almost unreadable. Over the last decade or so, Sayan has been producing extraordinary Thai-language deconstructive poetics as a form of critical interlocution with Araya's artistic practice, published in the journal *Aan / Read*.

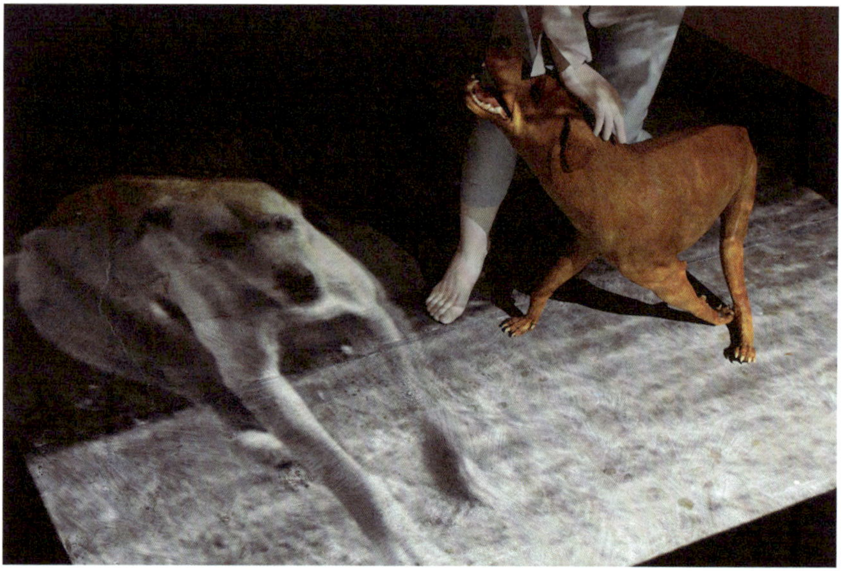

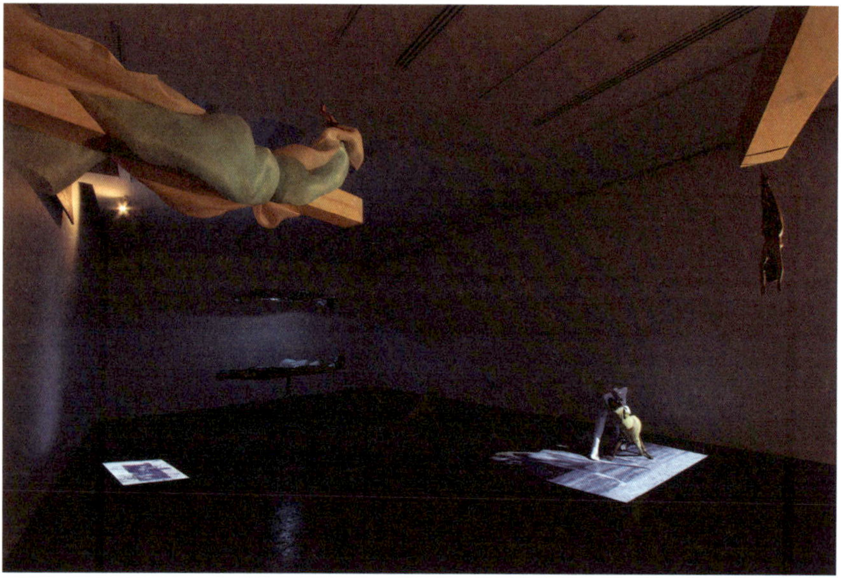

Installation views, Araya Rasdjarmrearnsook, 'An Artist is Trying to Return to "Being a Writer"', 100 Tonson Gallery, Bangkok, 2017–18
Courtesy 100 Tonson Gallery and the artist

seeks to accumulate her psychiatric examination records, the purpose of which is ambiguous. She may be looking for a way to continue to live less painfully, or she is gathering the required paperwork for an assisted-suicide hospice in Switzerland. She may be planning to exercise autonomy in ending her life, or she may be making an art project from the temporality and event of dying.

Paying attention to the excessive intermedial playfulness of 'An Artist is Trying to Return to "Being a Writer"' opens up ways of thinking about potentiality in relation to CMSI and this phase of Araya's artistic practice, and, importantly, via an understanding of the stylistic and aesthetic particularity and promise of lateness. Said's posthumously published book on late style describes a particular kind of energy that propelled certain canonical artists, such as Ludwig van Beethoven or Luchino Visconti, to acquire new idioms in their twilight years. Rather than continuing to produce artistic works characterised by the kinds of transcendental maturity and serenity that signal the culmination of a lifetime's aesthetic achievements, these are artists who departed into 'a sort of deliberately unproductive productiveness'.[15] The aesthetic idioms and experiential power of their late works are not characterised by resolution but by intransigence, irreconcilability and lack of unity. The lateness of late style goes hand in hand with untimeliness, and with the presence of death. The irresolvable and the anachronistic are its sources of energy, as well as a curious sense of being in the present – acutely aware of it, yet apart from it.[16]

A Buddhist cliché anoints the reaching of retirement as a watershed moment in life, the point at which a person is meant to have attained spiritual maturity, serenity and the beginning of the process of renunciating worldly struggle and attachment. By contrast, within the world created by 'An Artist is Trying to Return to "Being a Writer"', Araya's assembling and imbrication of divergent languages, mediums, processes and conventions of symbolic materialisation create a dispersive and exaggeratedly unfixed time-space for entanglement with the exhibition's becoming, which might be encapsulated in the Thai word *khwaeng*.[17] This word is roughly translatable as a duration and a state of becoming unhinged. Consistent with the dispersive characteristics of an exhibition of which a book of fiction forms a part, the intermediality of *Phud kerd ma laa raam* implies a dynamic of entangling the reader in *khwaeng*. In a late chapter, a trial of sorts takes place: the artist faces judgment from those with whom she is 'karmically entangled' – institutional-academic figures recalling those in *The Cruel* and also the corpses Laileeya has involved in her installations.[18] Laileeya says nothing in self-defence, but is grateful to sense the presence at the trial of the creatures she has rescued and cared for. Ultimately, the accusers and judges deny the female artist the request to end her life, and they pass the verdict for her to continue a living death in compensation for the karmic wrongs that have accrued as a result of her artistic practice. Following this, in the book's third and final part, the late phase of Laileeya's life is described in proximity with death via a short scene of violence. Laileeya takes the frailest,

—

[15] E. Said, *On Late Style, op. cit.*, p.7.

[16] See *ibid.*, p.24.

[17] With thanks to the artist Jedsada Tangtrakulwong for drawing my attention to the significance of this word for Araya's artistic and pedagogical practice. Conversation with the author, July 2017.

most abject of the injured dogs to be put down. The act, says the narrator, undoes the portrayal of Laileeya as someone who can justifiably accuse others of making her life one of suffering through their acts of abandonment and emotional cruelty, their exercising of group power in judging her art as a debasement of principles of beauty and morality. The fiction seems to end with the aged Laileeya exercising the negative capacity of human sovereignty by denying life. With an effect of *mise en abyme* that echoes many of her installations and performances, Araya implicates the seemingly autobiographical female subject of the fiction and entangles the reader-participant in the same executionary agency as the trial's accusers and judges.

Yet, there is another twist. In its book-object form, the interval between the seeming ending of the fiction and the catalogue listing of the artworks displayed at the 100 Tonson exhibition is occupied by a short text, '*Lang karn khien*', or 'After the Writing'. It describes a conversation between a Western curator and 'a woman', which takes place in an old Chiang Mai restaurant favoured by Araya. They encircle each other in an exchange that slowly becomes at once an intimate talk between old friends about their respective ways of enduring psychic pain, and a courtship between artist and curator as they explore the possibility that the woman might, just might, be able to propose to him a new artwork carrying out her assisted suicide as part of the project he is curating in the next few years. This text, occupying the interval within the book, is both outside and inside the world of fiction; it is indeterminately art and life, actual and virtual autobiography. The old woman can continue to live and she can end her life. The old woman can not make art and live, and she can make art and not live.

The curious afterlife of 'art for life'

Military dictatorship returned to Thailand in 2014, and with it the neo-feudalist capture, in the name of Thai-ness and political morality, of the agency to imagine collective forms of life or what passes for life. In the country's artistic and literary spheres, the present crisis has brought into sharper focus the curious afterlife of the conception of art's heteronomy pertaining to a vernacular vanguardist tradition with genealogical links to the radical struggles of the socialist intelligentsia during the Cold War.[19] Distilled into the slogan 'art for life', this tradition was in some ways a vernacularisation of the Maoist conception of the artistic avant-garde that conceived of the artist as part of a masculinist intellectual class in an underdeveloped society, with the artist-as-revolutionary-agent's responsibility being to serve the people by educating them. Its conceptualisation of the social function and authority of the modern artist might be thought of as a minor tradition, in the Deleuzian sense, parallel to the dominant models of the modern artist as state client, and the modern/contemporary artist as the charismatic figure of Buddhist renunciation and agential causation so provocatively theorised by David Teh in his recent book on the contemporaneity of Thai contemporary art.[20]

—

[18] This reading of the chapter is inspired by Sayan Daengklom's commentary in our co-taught CMU class.

[19] The best book on this subject remains Kasian Tejapira's Benjaminian historicisation of the circulation of Marxist ideas in Cold War Thailand via market mechanisms and translation. See his *Commodifying Marxism: The Formation of Modern Thai Radical Culture, 1927–1958*, Kyoto and Melbourne: Kyoto University Press and Trans Pacific Press, 2001.

Although the history of leftist political struggles in Thailand is a short one of defeat and relatively swift co-optation, it casts a surprisingly long shadow over the task of historicising modern and contemporary art and aesthetic practices. An important issue that still awaits in-depth critical and art historical exploration concerns the afterlife of the ideals and conventions of 'art for life'; in other words, the somewhat surprising persistence of the vernacular vanguardist's programmatic notion of the social purpose of art and the role of the artist as leader and educator of the people in an underdeveloped society, and across contemporary fields of artistic and aesthetic practices. The residue or perhaps even the allure of 'art for life' has persisted to a degree somewhat out of keeping with the limited extent of the actualisation of socialist political organisation, or the embedding of socialist values concerning relationality, reproduction and the conception of the good life during the Cold War decades of active leftist struggles in Thailand.

Indeed, in the present moment of political crisis, one of the most curious aspects of the fascistic aestheticisation of politics to legitimise royalism and non-elected political leadership is the spectacular co-optation of songs, slogans and audiovisual set pieces associated with 'art for life'. The reanimation of the aesthetic and symbolic idiom of this vanguardist tradition is, strangely enough, the currency of affective mobilisation of reactionary protest platforms that, in the past decade or so, have been complicit in creating affects and rhetoric amenable to royalism and military dictatorship, justified as an effective mode of opposition to a mass electoralism that has to be prevented at whatever cost. We might call this particular mode of the reanimation of Cold War vanguardism a 'zombie' turn: a spectacular mobilisation of the artist-activist persona, visual aesthetics and programmatic symbolic actions of the previous era, which styles itself, in a hyper-visible idiom, as a transformative force for life. Yet, this zombie mode of the aestheticisation of politics moves and aligns itself with the deep state, and with the authoritarian politics of the military-industrial-entertainment complex.

In tandem with the zombification of the vernacular vanguardist tradition of artistic heteronomy is a melancholic disposition. This tends to be embodied by the liberal and self-identified progressive artists and intellectuals who first came to political awareness in their late teens or early twenties, during the moment of the Black May uprising against military dictatorship in 1992. The severity of the political crisis of this past decade has led to a loss of emotional and intellectual bearing, the paralysing effect of which is perhaps most devastatingly experienced among the generation now reaching middle age. Previously, in the triumphant aftermath of that uprising, coupled with the vertiginous sensation of change fostered by rapid urbanisation and global integration, they could recognise themselves as youthful heirs to a genealogy of transformative promise connecting 1992 with the uprising of 1973 and the massacre of 1976. Many romanticised the struggles and personas of male artists, poets and writers of the Cold War leftist generation. Even those who had no particular inclination to find a voice by hero-worshipping the country's minor canon of leftist artists and intellectuals nevertheless continued to inhabit the residue of vernacular vanguardism in an important sense. The works and ideas

—

[20] David Teh, *Thai Art: Currencies of the Contemporary*, Cambridge, MA: The MIT Press, 2017, pp.109–43.

produced during the 1990s and 2000s by liberals and self-identified progressives of this Black May generation did not, in most cases, replicate the forms, moods and genres stemming from those produced under the nomenclature of 'art for life'. Importantly, the conception of the role and authority of artists as cultural and societal leaders nevertheless remained a powerfully affecting assumption of entitlement. That confidence of somehow inheriting the vanguardist prerogatives of the previous era has been, belatedly, shattered.

The exhaustion of a residual tradition of vernacular vanguardism provides an overdue opening to revisit the dialectics of artistic potentiality and political capacity. This essay's experiment in juxtaposing CMSI with Araya's late artistic practice is a preliminary effort to create a thought object with which to return to this question via another route, without succumbing to melancholy or to farcical replication of the idiom of the heteronomy of another era. Approaching CMSI in this manner refracts the historiographic narrative of the festival from one that would, at the domestic level, imply its value as grounded very much in the past tense, in the autonomous execution of youthful improvisatory actions impelled by the liberalising political energy of the time. It would also place less emphasis on the historiographic significance of the festival as a beginning, and namely on its recent accrual of art historical status as a point of origin for Southeast Asian regional contemporary art. Juxtaposing CMSI with Araya's late style shadows the festival with such key phrases as 'ending' and 'estrangement from its present'. In this regard, and perhaps above all, the sense of possibility and of a capacity to be recuperated from CMSI in the here and now lies in the 'unproductive productiveness' of its early ending.

In parallel, conceptualising Araya's late style in adjacency with CMSI encourages thinking about the autonomy of her artistic practice in a more complex register than the existing mode of valuing her practice as a female conceptualist artist condemned to isolation and lesser visibility in a patriarchal art world and society.[21] Those characteristics of Araya's late style – its reflexive excesses, anachronistic and ultra-feminine performativity, and intermediality as processes of unhinging – partially intersect with CMSI's experimentations with non-art and with heterogeneous chronotopes of artistic practice and participation. As with the counterintuitive possibility of CMSI's ending, Araya's aesthetics of lateness and feminine potentiality is both dissociated from and speaks strongly to its politically zombified present. In a time of exhaustion and the unravelling of the fiction of art's social purpose and artistic agency, Araya's late practice is explicitly grounded in powerlessness and creatureliness, and in a studied scepticism regarding the social and political agency of artists and artworks. Yet, in seemingly retreating once again to the domain of the personal, or that which is implicitly feminised, her late practice is a mode of artistic practice whose acknowledgement of the artist-author's impending death nevertheless affirms life's intransigence and irreconcilability by suspending the distinction between art and life, the time of living and the time of dying, rather than by formulating the indistinctness of art and life to be transmitted to society by the socially engaged artist. Perhaps most importantly, the lateness of

—

[21] For an important reading of Araya's work as an erotics of feminist intimacy, see Arnika Fuhrmann's book *Ghostly Desires: Queer Sexuality and Vernacular Buddhism in Contemporary Thai Cinema*, Durham, NC: Duke University Press, 2016.

Araya's late style speaks to its estranged present, and not by associating artistic potentiality with authoritative action and transformative agency, and emphatically not with Buddhist withdrawal. It is a late style that does no more and no less than affirming an inexhaustibility of a capacity to remain unreconciled with the present, figured as an indeterminate capacity to do and equally to not do.

It seems appropriate to end this essay by sketching a related point of departure. Another way to use CMSI as an archival source and an art-historiographic-theoretical thought object is to repeat the question of how historically rooted forms of gender identities and power, and of agencies linked to sexual difference, inform and shape modern and contemporary art practices and values in Southeast Asia. Here, art historian Eileen Legaspi-Ramirez's work on women's roles and activities in exhibition-making history in the modern Philippines creates an important opening for long-overdue research and critical discourse.[22] While informal, grass-roots modes of producing, circulating and facilitating contemporary art in and beyond Southeast Asia are fast becoming identified as a key characteristic of the region's contemporary art and its basis of valorisation, an overlooked question is how gender and/or sexual difference constitute a determinant in the emergence, and the sustenance or otherwise, of contemporary art's counter- or alter-institutional networks, platforms and durations.

One way to proceed with CMSI's fragmented archives and histories in this respect would be to compare the figure of the artist-as-organiser that was emergent during the festival with both the historical and present-day models of facilitators and instigators of artistic practices and artistic mobility within non-official networks and institutions of art. And here, a speculation worth entertaining would be to consider a differential genealogy of agency, comparing the masculine vanguardist model of artist-as-organiser with what might be conceptualised as the matriarchal model of artistic potentiality. While the acknowledged instigators of CMSI seemed enabled by the residual presence of vanguardism in post-Cold War Thailand, their self-professed renunciation of artistic authorship of the festival triangulates interestingly with another trajectory embodied and developed by women in the Cold War era and since. These are women who have assumed important, sometimes influential, but most often overlooked roles in facilitating artistic production – whether as wives, patrons, curators, producers, administrators or archive keepers. The idea of the matriarchal here borrows Ashley Thompson's deconstructive reading of sexual difference and sovereignty in Angkorean Buddhist statehood to cast the matriarch as both the embodiment of power and the condition of possibility for male sovereignty.[23] We may wonder how such women, and their activities and modes of accumulating aura and exercising agency, constitute the condition of possibility for artistic autonomy: a reserve of resistant, evasive, perhaps even anarchistic potential; a 'matriarchal' practice yet to be named.

—

[22] Eileen Legaspi-Ramirez, 'Art on the Back Burner: Gender as the Elephant in the Room in SEA Art History', presented at the symposium 'Gender in Southeast Asian Art Histories', University of Sydney, 11–13 October 2017.

[23] Ashley Thompson, *Engendering the Buddhist State: Territory, Sovereignty and Sexual Difference in the Inventions of Angkor*, Abingdon: Routledge, 2016.

A Changing World: Phases of the Installative in Southeast Asia — Patrick D. Flores

When the artist-curator Raymundo Albano travelled to Fukuoka, Japan in 1980 to curate the Philippine section at the first Asian Art Show,[1] he brought with him loose-leaf materials on his project 'Art of the Regions'. It was important for Albano to speak about the region at an event that styled itself as a gathering on and for Asia. In his mind, the region was a place beyond the privileged capital of Manila, around which modern and contemporary art orbited, inevitably settling at the Cultural Center of the Philippines, where Albano was curator of the museum and other spaces. The region meant to the south and north of Manila, respectively to Los Baños in Laguna and to Baguio in the Cordillera.

Albano was to be disappointed. He had wanted to represent the Philippines with works involving the ephemeral, but he was discouraged by the organisers, who prescribed certain rules on presentation and conservation, for example 'No plant materials'. This prompted Albano to ask:

> *Why, for instance ... is the show so organized within a highly Western mold when it should be Asian? Then one questioned why works had to be expensive objects. Then one questioned why works had to be transported one week before the opening and nothing is left to chance. Then one questioned why it was called a 'festival' and it was only a painting and sculpture exhibition. Then one questioned why such contemporary art had to be so bound within highly predictable rules.*[2]

This commentary, or cycle of questions, is instructive in many ways, and particularly germane in evoking not only the place of region in the contemporary but also the valence of the contemporary as an existing modality of gathering deemed distinct from the exhibition. In Albano's estimation, the festival was organically, if not inalienably, *installative.*

By foregrounding these anxieties, Albano took to task the exhibitionary format of the Western modern museum and its display methods. Second, he spoke of how the expensive object of art was the central artefact of an exhibition largely of paintings and sculpture that described itself as a 'festival'. He was invested in the idea of the festival as an expressive event not so much about the exhibition of objects as the installation or performance of a world that, in his words, was 'suddenly turning visible'.[3] Lastly, he challenged the 'highly predictable rules' according to which the contemporary was made to play out, which consequently negated the element of chance. He thought that contemporary art should be treated 'like artists did it, like artists brought the works together – no diplomats, no bureaucrats, just

—

[1] Held at the Fukuoka Art Museum, 1–30 November 1980.

[2] Raymundo Albano, 'Dateline: Fukuoka', *Philippine Art Supplement*, vol.2, no.1, January–February 1981, p.12.

[3] R. Albano, 'Development Art of the Philippines', *Philippine Art Supplement* vol.2, no.4, July–August 1981, p.15.

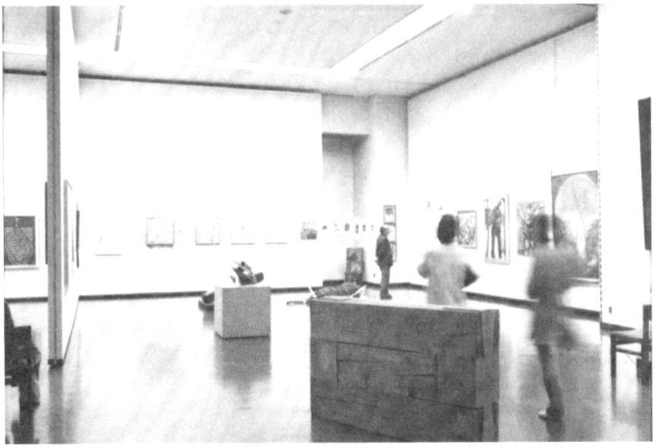

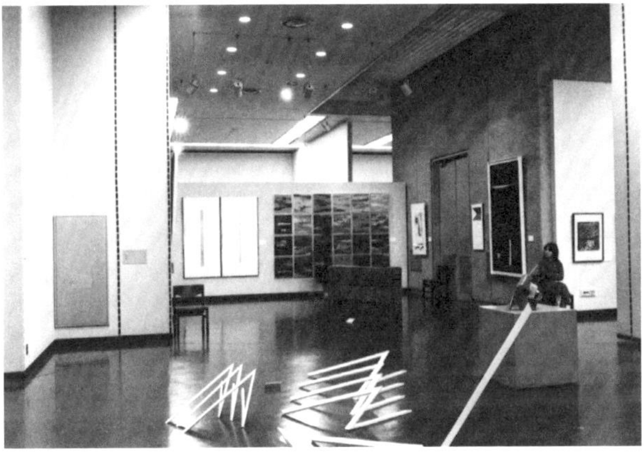

Installation views, Philippine section of the first Asian Art Show, Fukuoka Art Museum, 1980
Courtesy Fukuoka Art Museum

people knowing the problems of art … which is to take risks, to be not too cold, to make things complicated, to create an aura of things casually placed there, like nothing's real and nothing's permanent – very contemporary.' In spite of the Asian Art Show's constraints, Albano contended that in the Philippine section 'the unconventional arrangement of the works and their strange variety worked for charmingly uneven effects. If there is restlessness as well as fun, it is because the works themselves jolted for individual attention. Curator Obigani [Akio] of the Museum recognized the fact that it was the most contemporary entry.'

Such restlessness and unevenness confounded the audience at Fukuoka. According to Albano, 'it was difficult for them to receive installations as they did not know how much it meant to Filipinos until they saw the slide presentation of exhibitions here. It did not occur to them that being contemporary was dealing with virtually untested, unknown realms of evidences that would lead to further understanding of ourselves.'[4] For him, installation was some kind of

—

[4] R. Albano, 'Dateline: Fukuoka', *op. cit.*, pp.12–13.

a laboratory in which art itself and the Philippine as a category of distinction were simultaneously conceptualised in the field of the contemporary. Hence his insistence on the contemporary as a kind of breeding ground or hothouse of an event. Whether carnivalesque or psychopolitical, events 'represent breaks and discontinuities; they open up *new spaces for action*'.[5]

A year after the foray at Fukuoka, Albano wrote an essay on installation, describing it as the Philippine creative agent's intrinsic urge, honed since childhood and inflected in everyday life. Yet while installation might be enlivened by local histories, the term was transacted through the vocabulary of the Western modern. Imbricated in the context of developmental art, the installative aesthetic was an unfolding experiment. It testified to an environment assertively being primed by the post-independence Southeast Asian nation state to become democratic and developing, indeed destined to secure its rightful place in the international economic and political order. According to this agenda, to be original in the post-colony was a fraught but ultimately necessary posture. In Albano's retrospective view on installations in the Philippines since 1968: 'It may be that our innate sense of space is not a static perception of flatness but an experience of mobility, performance, body-participation, physical relation at its most cohesive form.' This take rehearsed the Philippine installative *Kunstwollen* as 'akin to *fiestas* and folk rituals, from all our ethnic groups'.[6]

Construing the region as both Southeast Asia and the Philippine province, and therefore not national, was a way to contract the international without being beholden to the Western. Installation was a vital idiom or device in this strategy. It was to the installative that Albano would turn, at least in part, in curating the Philippine representation in Fukuoka. Perhaps to skirt the constraints of resources and museum protocols, he asked the artist Ileana Lee to carry out a masking tape work within the exhibition space. Lee taped her dotted lines – strips of the tape uniformly cut – on the floor, wall and ceiling to delineate space within space. In the history of Asia-focussed exhibitions at Fukuoka, this was arguably the first installation work in which the specificity of site, medium and technique responded to the conceptual problematics of contemporary art, on the one hand, and to the exigencies of local participation in an international event, on the other. Furthermore, Lee's affirmation of herself as a woman artist in the male-dominated art world of Japan and most of Asia was germinal. For a woman artist to plot out a parasitic space in a museum and to then embody her wandering presence without the tumescent artifice of the art object was not merely an exploit; it sowed an all-over atmosphere.

With the practice of Albano as a cipher, certain theoretical entry points open up into the domain of installation, and into thoughtfulness about and attentiveness to installation as an idea and an initiation in Southeast Asia. Albano intimated that internal transformations within sculptural form were extending into something

—

[5] Byung-Chul Han, *Psychopolitics: Neoliberalism and New Technologies of Power*, New York: Verso, 2017, p.77, emphasis in original.
[6] R. Albano, 'Installations: A Case for Hangings', *Philippine Art Supplement*, vol.2, no.1, January–February 1981, p.3.

else. He characterised the 'new sculpture' as resistant to being ensconced as either monument or object on a base as prescribed by custom. 'New sculpture' assumed the tendency of the material: 'spreading, hanging, stretching, laying down arbitrarily'. Such emancipation was made possible by a range of methods Albano marked as rudimentally significant, and he drew signals from the 'total visual installation' of Philippine artist Junyee's *Wood Things* (1981): 'dry leaves attach to the floor, dry branches hang from the ceiling and float in mid air. Colored lights heighten strange illumination of the work, shadows spread patterns throughout the room ... the fact that a sculptor no longer depends on gravity alone changes attitudes towards the concept of art itself.'[7] The ways by which art is captured in art historical taxonomies were unsettled: 'What is permanently in art: the object? What is sculpture? Or can sculpture borrow from theater, landscape architecture and science?'[8] In the same year, Junyee coordinated with several artists the project Los Baños Site Works, in which, 'like extensions of nature', the works 'sprouted from the ground, floated in the air, surrounded an area, dangled from branches'. It was for him an 'encounter with nature on a halfway ground between the mountain and the city'.[9] According to Albano, the work of Junyee goes a step further than Roberto Chabet's *Bakawan* (*Mangrove*, 1974) – a 'tri-dimensional drawing of lines' evoked by a grid of pieces of mangrove wood hanging from the ceiling, set against a white ground, seen through the glass of a closed door – because it implicates an environment.[10]

In many ways, this performative and provocative act of de-posing sculpture elicits a foundational mutation within the materiality of art and the sociality of its reception. And this troubled the doxic underlying the hegemonic stature of the museum, the object and the habitus of the beholder in Southeast Asia. The 1972 and 1974 Modern Art Society exhibitions in Singapore may offer a case in point. In the 1972 sortie, Cheo Chai-Hiang submitted an entry to disrupt the protocols of 'participation', as art historian Seng Yu Jin has recounted: 'someone would draw *5' x 5' (Singapore River)* according to Cheo's instructions, rendering the making of the work collaborative as opposed to solitary. In particular, Cheo's emphasis on the process over the finished work privileged the thought process (ideas and concepts) over the finished work usually associated with painting.'[11] To some extent, in according primacy to interaction and process as foils to the formalism of the object, the proposition prefigured Ileana Lee's taping action at Fukuoka. As a critique of the institutions of modern art, this was clearly a conceptualist manoeuvre. In 1974, Tang Da Wu participated in the same forum with the work *Sculpture*. Involving 'clear plastic bags filled with what appears to be boxes ends

---

[7] *Ibid.*

[8] R. Albano, 'Junyee's Woodland Fantasy', *Philippine Art Supplement*, vol.2, no.3, May–June 1981, p.5.

[9] Junyee, 'A Halfway Ground: Los Baños Site Works', *Philippine Art Supplement*, pp.2, 7.

[10] R. Albano, 'Junyee's Woodland Fantasy', *op. cit.* The description of *Mangrove* is drawn from Albano's notes, available at https://cdn.aaa.org.hk/_source/digital_collection/fedora_extracted/18287.pdf (last accessed on 3 April 2018).

[11] Seng Yu Jin, 'Rejection-Proof: Contestations of the "New" (新) in the Modern Art Society Exhibition of 1972', in *Contemporary Modern: Modern Art Society 50th Anniversary Commemoration,* Singapore: Modern Art Society Singapore, 2014, pp.36–45.

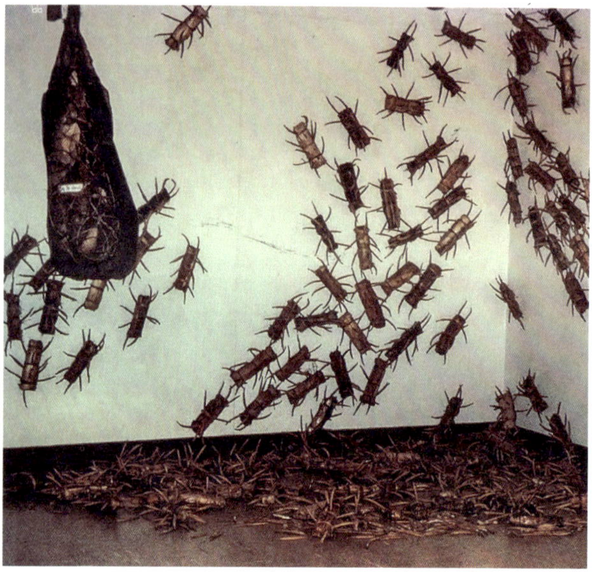

Installation view, Junyee, *Wood Things* (1981), Cultural Center of the Philippines
Courtesy Jorge B. Vargas Museum and Filipiniana Research Center

suspended from above', it was described further as 'an organic form with tentacle-like armatures stretching out onto the floor with strings used to tie its ends'.[12]

In this extension of the sculptural into something beyond its field, concerns relating to form and to social and cultural contexts take up residence. For instance, Redza Piyadasa, while studying at Hornsey College of Art in London (1963–67), questioned the dichotomy between painting and sculpture as an index of the basis of the order of things in the Western art world and its art historical systems. It is at this point that he became drawn to painted sculptures and the unease created by Constructivism, Minimalism and Conceptual Art. In 1974, in the exhibition 'Towards a Mystical Reality' at Dewan Bahasa dan Pustaka in Kuala Lumpur, Piyadasa and fellow artist Sulaiman Esa brought together instinct and reflexivity to collectively initiate and document experience. In carefully choreographing found objects – from pieces of hair to half-filled Coca-Cola bottles – the artists endeavoured to emplace both viewer and sensible life in a renewed, or perhaps revised, scenario of phenomenological interest. As Piyadasa asked, 'How do we perceive reality? Do you do so in the physical sense, at the first level, in an empirical sense? Or do you do so within cultural frames?'[13]

In Indonesia in 1975, Jim Supangkat attached an image of the head of Ken Dedes, queen of the Rajasa dynasty that prevailed during the Singhasari and Majapahit eras, to the torso and extremities of a modern-day woman with fulsome bosom,

[12] *Ibid.*
[13] 'Piyadasa in Conversation with T.K. Sabapathy', in *Piyadasa: An Overview 1962–2000*, Kuala Lumpur: National Art Gallery, 2001, p.116.

wisps of exposed pubic hair and smeared red lipstick. In doing so, Supangkat threatened the traditions of modernist sculpture and civilizational statuary both, as well as the nation state imaginary – for the regime of Muhammad Suharto, then President, looked to the Majapahit dominion for ideological continuity. This defilement, as it were, loosened up sculpture's armature, making it a matter of play, as in the work of Napoleon Abueva in the Philippines or Inson Wongsam in Thailand. In 1955–56, during his studies at the Cranbrook Academy of Art outside of Detroit, Abueva made sculptures largely of wood (cherry or jackfruit) and meant to float on water, for example *Baby Moses*, *Fish Forms* and *Three Kings* (or *Crossing the River*). At the end of the decade, when he was teaching at the University of the Philippines Diliman, he crafted a chariot to ride around the campus. In 1974, Inson did a series of sculptures that invited 'viewers to feel and touch the smooth surface of the carving'. Earlier, from 1966–74, he had been in New York, where he 'designed several projects related to environmental art, as well as space and underwater sculptures'. He also 'planned to build abstract sculptures in space for viewers to see from a satellite and also a submarine-like construction inhabited with fish'. Inson also staged happenings – burning wood in the park or urinating on ice blocks 'outside a supermarket to make the outline of an elephant'.[14] In 1974, in Bangkok, he threw a bundle of Thai baht bills soaked in ink into the Chao Phraya River.

Another artist releasing sculpture out into the open was David Medalla of the Philippines, who hurled it into another constellation. His 'MMMMMMM … Manifesto', published in the eighth issue of *Signals* magazine in 1965, is a deft and ethereal mixture of so-called art and so-called science. At its crux is sculpture, and Medalla begins with the line 'I dream of the day when I shall create sculptures that breathe, perspire, cough, laugh, yawn, smirk, wink, pant, dance, walk, crawl … and move among people as shadows move among people'. He contemplates the existence of a 'flower-sculpture … its petals curled like the crest of a tidal wave approaching the shore', and of 'missile-sculptures … on their way from our galaxy to the Spiral Nebula'.[15] His machines of all kinds – bubble, mud, sand – further articulated the auto-figuration of sculpture beyond its stature as fine art and modernist totem, and the kinetic sculpture he made in London after migrating there, between 1961–67, became seminal in the global art scene.

In summary, this idea of sculpture as a contact zone between tradition and whatever lies beyond would lead to enhancing the intersubjective faculties of installation: first, via a reiteration of the strategic dichotomy between collective doing and individualist intellection; second, through a redistribution of the agency of the collective and of the individual so that both participate in the production of reception; and third, perhaps, through the interlocution of artist, audience and artistic practice, the heightening of the level of cogent relationality. Central to such articulations of the installative – as relationality activated by multiple forces – was a search for well-being that prompted artists to move into the realm

—

[14] Apinan Poshyananda, *Modern Art in Thailand: Nineteenth and Twentieth Centuries*, New York: Oxford University Press, 1992, p.126.

[15] David Medalla, 'MMMMMMM … Manifesto', in Jessica Lack (ed.), *Why Are We 'Artists?': 100 World Art Manifestos*, New York: Penguin Classics, 2017, p.95.

of the rural, broadly conceived, or the *lieu de mémoire* of tradition. The rural was coveted as a source of local knowledge in opposition to the urban, understood as the locus of alienation and the fragmentation of human integrity. Critique of the city intersected with the animus of the countryside and the prospective healing of the autonomous albeit increasingly anomic self. The 'earth' became the ground for performativity.

In 1970, Junyee did *Balag*, a trellis or shelter made from bamboo strips through which people could 'pass underneath, reach the top grid, and tie onto this object pieces of paper or board on which there were protests, poetry, love notes to their partners, quotations, fruits, candies'. For the artist, this was both *domus* and *demos*, a plea against the modern and the colonial, and at the work's opening event there was live music as well as poetry read to evoke 'a raw open democracy ... opposed ... to the posh and often exclusive art openings that took place at ... the then very elite Luz Gallery'.[16] Almost a decade later, at the National Museum Art Gallery in Singapore, Tang Da Wu presented *Earth Work* (1979), an assembly of material traces and other documentation of his 'land art interventions, earth installations and mineral pigment drawings'. According to curator Charmaine Toh, the exhibition 'was not only the earliest recorded instance of land art in Singapore, but also a literal intervention into the Permanent Exhibition of NMAG. Key works were placed on the floor, right in the middle of the gallery space, surrounded by paintings in the National Collection.'[17]

In the early 1980s, rooted in 'his desire for a rustic environment far from the buzzing urban-based consumer culture of Bangkok', Chalood Nimsamer was cultivating a practice centred on what might be retroactively designated 'environmental art', in other words, outdoor sculptures as well as assemblages at his residence. *Suan Pratima* (*Sculpture Garden*, 1982), *Green Sculpture Project* (1982) and *Rural Sculpture 4/2525* (1982) involved 'found objects (logs, bamboo, cloth, cans, and plastic bags)' from all sorts of Thai social gatherings and rituals, reflecting his exposure to the pedagogy of sculptor Silpa Bhirasri, who emphasised Thai values in relation to temple life among monks.[18] Chalood's *Muthri* (1982) is exemplary, evincing an 'atmosphere of smoke, water, grass, and trees that can be seen from far away', in the words of the artist. 'I have a unique habit of hanging things. I hang everything. Rural people do that. They hang and stick things around their houses. ... Anything can be hanged.'[19] This method of hanging figures is delineated in Raymundo Albano's writing on installation as a 'case for hangings'.[20]

Later in Thailand, Montien Boonma would sharpen the ties between spirituality and sympathy for the earth. In *A Changing World No. 2* (1982), 'rows of bulbous

—

[16] Jose Tence Ruiz, *Wood Things*, Manila: National Commission on Culture and the Arts, 2016, p.146.
[17] Charmain Toh, 'Notes on Tang Da Wu's *Earth Work*', in *Earth Work 1979 – Tang Da Wu* (exh. cat.), Singapore: National Gallery Singapore, 2016, p.11.
[18] Apinan, *Modern Art in Thailand: Nineteenth and Twentieth Centuries*, *op. cit.*, p.211.
[19] Quoted in Ochana Poonthongdeewatthana, *Chalood's Mural Painting – Retrospective* (exh. cat.), Bangkok: Bangkok Art and Culture Center, 2013, p.125.
[20] R. Albano, 'Installations: A Case for Hangings', *op. cit.*, p.2.

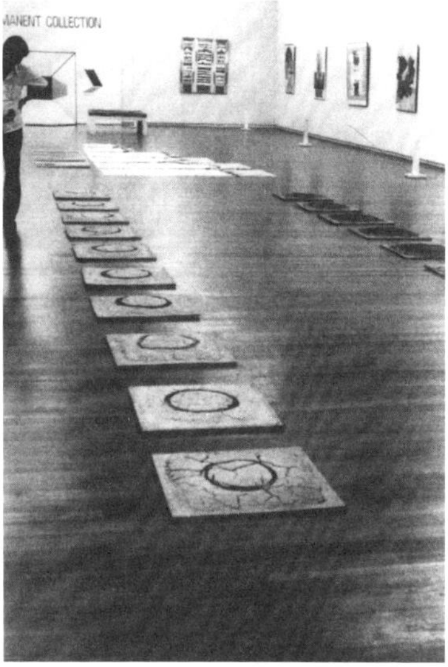

Installation view, Tang Da Wu, 'Earth Work', with his *The Product of the Sun and Me* (1979), National Museum Art Gallery, Singapore, 1980

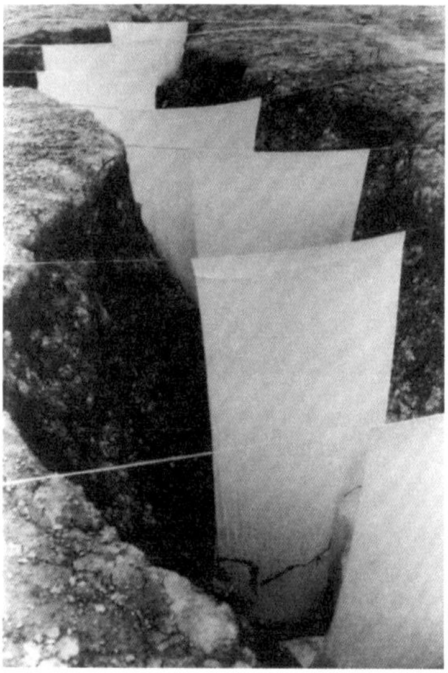

Tang Da Wu, *Gully Curtains* (1979), oil and mineral pigment on cloth, at its original site in Ang Mo Kio, Singapore
Collection of the National Gallery Singapore

aluminum rivets and screws are placed like metal corn in a plantation'. In the Ladkrabang District of the suburbs of Bangkok, Montien 'began to explore environmental art in the context of Thai ways of life', contrasting the natural landscape with the industrial commonplace, portrayed as 'alien growth and altered states'.[21] It may well have been in this artist's work that beliefs around the sacred and the ethical imperative to defend the earth from pillaging tapped into a shared wellspring. A cosmopolitan animism encouraged reciprocities between the material and the immaterial and reared, in the long haul, what David Teh has called 'Arte Povera-inspired folk conceptualism' and the 'rural vernacular'.[22] According to Thai art historian-curator-artist Apinan Poshyananda, Joseph Beuys's practice was an important inspirationå for Montien, as it had been for Tang Da Wu. Together with beliefs linked to Buddhism, Montien was able to contrive his own bricolage, in works done in Paris that 'consist of branches inserted into containers, improvised materials used for symbols of spirit houses', including *La Maison d'éspirit* (1987), *L'Espace d'éspirit* (1987) and *La Boîte mystique* (1987).[23]

—

[21] Apinan, *Montien Boonma: Temple of the Mind* (exh. cat.), New York: Asia Society, 2003, p.14.
[22] David Teh, *Thai Art: Currencies of the Contemporary*, Singapore: National University of Singapore Press, 2017, p.63.
[23] Apinan, *Montien Boonma: Temple of the Mind, op. cit.,* p.16.

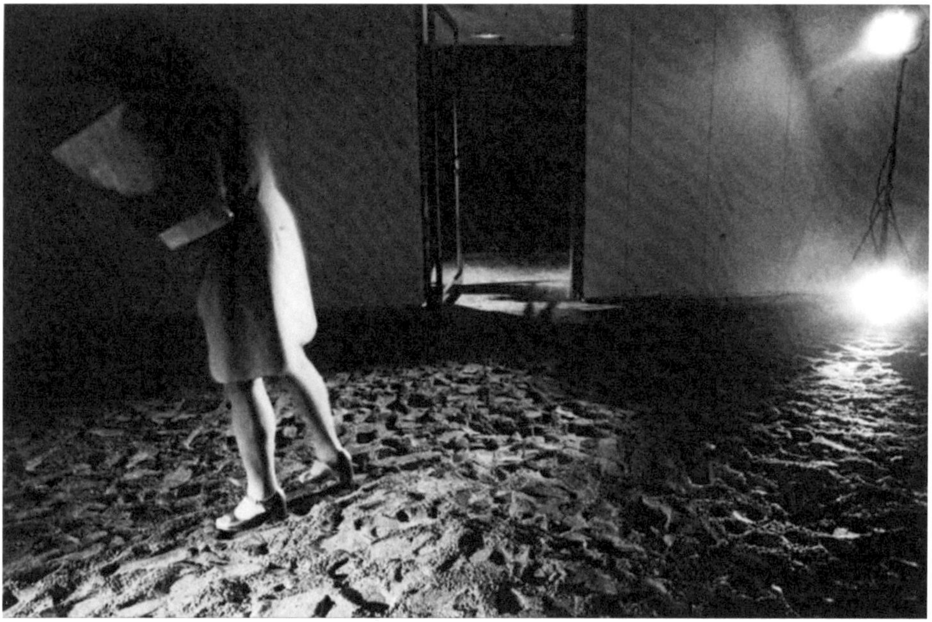

Raymundo Albano, *Step on the Sand and Make Footprints* (1974), Cultural Center of the Philippines, 1970s

While the latter examples reference the countryside and the provincial as a realm distinct from the city and the urban, there had been responses to the installative that sought to harness its capacity as ever-circulating in interaction with the technologies of mass society. Through printed matter a more copious space could be charted and forms replicated for what was imagined as a mass audience. In 1974, for instance, Albano submitted to the Tokyo Biennale of Prints a blueprint for a work to be titled *Step on the Sand and Make Footprints*, which he later described as 'a piece of paper with instructions to spread enough sand for four people to step on. It was the only floor piece in the show. They said it qualified because a foot print is ... a print.'[24] The Thai artist Prawat Laucharoen did cognate experiments that 'explored the potentials of "print in space"'. For example, in 1981, in collaboration with the American artist Dennis Oppenheim, he carried out the installation *Launching Station*: 'various chemicals and missiles were "launched" onto three large printing plates over a period of many hours. ... Prawat attacked the metal plates with ferric chloride and nitric acid. Drips of acid running in streaks and blotches were regarded as evidence of the process of creativity by chance.'[25]

—

[24] R. Albano, in 'Interview', *Sunburst*, March 1975, p.8.
[25] Apinan, *Modern Art in Thailand*, *op. cit.*, p.209.

A corollary to this reprographic tendency was artists' fascination with the concrete and, coextensively, Pop art. Artists identified with the group Gerakan Seni Rupa Baru Indonesia (Indonesian New Art Movement) reflected on the problematic of the former in a 1975 exhibition. According to GSRB stalwart Jim Supangkat, 'The conception of "concreteness" talks about the physical involvement of observers, meaning that if we cannot make a dialogue with the awareness of the observers, we disturb their physical condition. And here the distance between the observers' actual world and the imaginary world of a work is eliminated.'[26] The critic Sanento Yuliman insisted on the physicality of the materials themselves in writing on GSRB's Anyool Soebroto and Bachtiar Zainoel, artists creating 'things out of things', using colours that 'shake up our optics'.[27]

It was through the concrete that a sense of confoundedness was instilled in the viewer, and this made the artist decisively consider risk as a defining aspect of facture. This confoundedness could take numerous forms: surprise or confusion as to why ordinary, commonplace, industrial, reprographic materials were part of an artwork (for example, appropriated plastic or glass instead of canvas); disorientation brought about by the configuration of the work, based on purportedly incompatible components (a replica of an ancient goddess, a drawing of a naked woman in jeans, an actual bird cage on a painted canvas); alarm over the absence of typical painting or sculpture, their traces reorganised, diminished and disfigured, replaced by a lack of refinement or a distressed, unpolished veneer; or provocation by the pressure to figure out and make sense of this new theatre or locale of phenomena in space, and the assignment of themes such as 'sadism'. From this affective habitus came the propensity towards assemblage and installation in works by FX Harsono, Jim Supangkat, Nanik Mirna and Siti Adiyati. These artists might spread works on the floor (Harsono and Adiyati), juxtapose anachronistic images and objects (Supangkat's *Ken Dedes*, 1975), or make environments (Supangkat's *Kamar Ibu Dan Anak* (*A Room of a Woman and Her Baby*), *Baby's Room* and *Birth Event* (all 1975)).

Concrete itself was referenced as alternative or even resistant material that displaced revered substances of the academic establishment. Even so, it was valorised by favored architects of Southeast Asian nation states invested in the internationalist agenda as well as political figures keen to explore the material's relational potential. For instance, Leandro Locsin, who designed many buildings for Philippine First Lady Imelda Marcos, thought of concrete as a natural material. Marcos also supported the musique concrete-influenced experiments of the musicologist José Maceda, who encouraged performative gestures via sonic assemblage in works such as *Casettes 100* (1971) and *Ugnayan* (1974).

This interest in the tactile may have contributed to a wider conversation on Pop art. The new style's ability to break down hierarchies of high and low resonated with critiques of colonial and academic systems and their diminishment of the

—

[26] Jim Supangkat, 'Keinginan Berkomunikasi', *Kompas Daily*, 9 September 1975.

[27] Sanento Yuliman, 'Perspektif Baru', in *Pengantar dalam Katalog Pameran Seni Rupa Baru Indonesia 1975*, Jakarta: Taman Ismail Marzuki, 1975; reprinted in J. Supangkat (ed.), *Gerakan Seni Rupa Baru Indonesia*, Gramedia: Jakarta, 1979, pp.96–98.

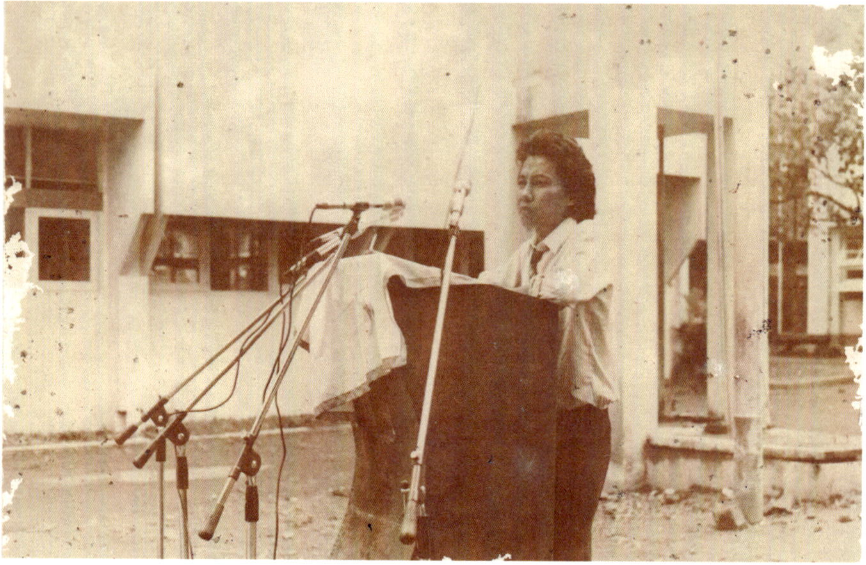

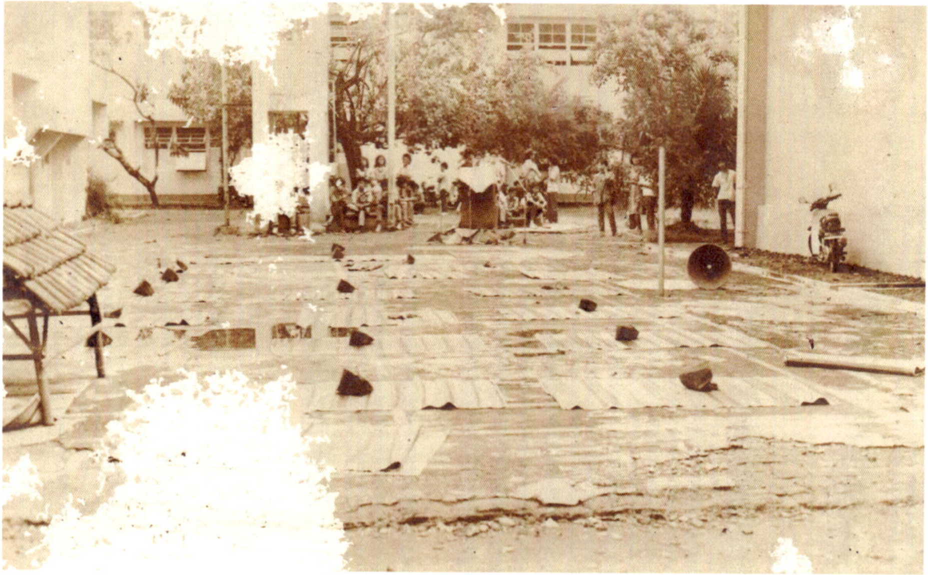

Moelyono, *Kesenian Unit Desa* (*Art in the Village*, 1985), Indonesia
Courtesy Indonesian Visual Art Archive (IVAA), Hyphen — and the artists

significance of mass culture. The source of the stigma was surely aesthetic, and it was through an aesthetic response that the repressed would be recovered conceptually and critically. Kamol Tassananchalee, who relocated from Thailand to Los Angeles in 1969, tried to 'move away from the notion of high, autonomous art' by using photocopied images from art history and 'freely mixing garish and artificial colors in his subjects related to folk and traditional national popular cultures'. For *Mojave Desert* (1979–80), he 'sprinkled over 100 meters of color pigments on the dried, cracked soil of a desert'. In 1985 in Bangkok, Apinan Poshyananda exhibited *How to Explain Art to a Bangkok Cock*, a heady combination of video, installation and performance – 'an elaborate pastiche of historical vanguards from da Vinci to Yves Klein and Joseph Beuys'. Two years hence, he made *Blue Laughter*, in which 'television sets forming part of the work served … their normal function' while 'as a sculpture presenting the video-recorded performance of the artist'. It was a mélange 'flung at the feet of the Silpakorn establishment, modernist and neotraditionalist alike'.[28]

Finally, the performative would inevitably inflect efforts to harness techniques of installation to elude museological space and art world affectation. Emblematic in this schema was David Medalla as prolific producer of narratives and relations (in Spanish, *relación* is the word for both). *Stitch in Time* (1968) is a well-known project that dwelt, under the auspice of cooperative stitching, on the interplay between free time and skilful toil. But what perhaps best condensed such performativity was Medalla's contribution to the exhibition 'Fluxattitudes', in 1992. Guy Brett has recalled that Medalla, true to eccentric and queer form, 'irked some by declining to do what was expected of a Fluxus artist, or to set up some participatory proposition'. He went the other way and 'used the room consecrated to him to install and continue working on a large, allegorical oil painting. This was no conceptual or ironic pose … but an activity in which he took a sincere delight.' And the result was something that could not be captured by art world episteme: 'The room was always crowded with people fascinated by the age-old, but today unusual, sight of an artist, on a stepladder, at work on an unfinished painting, all the while conversing on the many conundrums of the connection between art and everyday life.'[29]

Besides Medalla's interventions, Paiboon Suwannakudt's, Moelyono's and Santiago Bose's works underscore community-making in their intricate relationships with local cultures and cultural politics. Paiboon, for instance, while primarily a mural painter in Thailand, was involved in dance and theatre as a designer, performer and playwright. In Indonesia in 1985, Moelyono set up *Kesenian Unit Desa* (*Art in the Village*) and in a badminton court spread 'twenty-two woven mats. … On each … was a traditional banana-lead plate containing a handful of soil with seeds of cassava, corn and water spinach.'[30] This was meant to parody the state's Village Unit Co-operatives, also known as KUD, in Bahasa Indonesia, and the project clarified Moelyono's ideas on art that was 'aware' and 'virtuous', and immersed in 'community'.

—

[28] Apinan, *Modern Art in Thailand, op. cit.*, p.207.

[29] Guy Brett, *Carnival of Perception: Selected Writings on Art,* London: Institute of International Visual Arts, 2004, p.88.

Bose's installations of 1978 around the Igorots, a northern Philippine ethnic community, stemmed from his interest in their art, how 'they carve' and 'gather things that they find at random and put them together in their houses'.[31] Artist Jimmie Durham, detecting a shamanistic persona in Bose, has stressed his outsider, ludic charisma in recounting how he 'built his own huge anti-radar tower from bamboo, vines, and leaves' in Baguio, and how, in 1979, he designed and made sets for Francis Ford Coppola's film *Apocalypse Now*.[32] Bose's involvement in organising communities through his practice eventually led to performances and the institution of an artist guild and international festival in Baguio in the late eighties.

All this takes us back to Albano's contemplation of the festival and the folk. It is worth noting that techniques of assemblage or bricolage are key to the morphology of improvised Philippine forms. The post-War shanty became a basis of modernist Cubist form in painting, while the *jeepney*, used for public transport and forged from Willys Jeeps brought to the region by the US military, is a salient generative form that demystifies the colonial inheritance. Such refunctioning of inherited modernity has set off relays of connections to eventually give rise to new social forms, as may be discerned in Paiboon's mural cohort; Moelyono's community project; Bose's festival; and Medalla's copious commitments to the politics and poetics of communing, namely Artists for Democracy (1974–77), Exploding Galaxy (1967–68) and the London Biennale (first held in 1998).

This essay began with Raymundo Albano attempting to come to terms with the international. It will end with the interlocution of two critics who have also helped shape the discourse of installation in Southeast Asia: theorist Geeta Kapur, from India, and pioneering curator Julie Ewington, from Australia, an organiser p.45 of the Asia Pacific Triennial of Contemporary Art (APT) in Brisbane, which presented many groundbreaking installations from the region beginning in 1993. Their thoughts have faceted more acutely the angle of the local as it implicates that which exceeds it and which, in turn, it reinscribes.

Ewington reasons that installation as a form speaks to an array of anxieties and options – 'immediacy, working with specific sites, the excitements of combining disparate materials, working collaboratively and, not unimportantly, economy, if local materials are used'. In this welter of possibilities, the Southeast Asian artist is able to re-enlist 'materials familiar from social life', and this is the reason some examples of installation in Southeast Asia are referred to as 'indigenous'. And Ewington points out the converse as well, that such installation demonstrates the 'successful indigenization of imported cultural practice', a notion that she complicates in venturing that 'in installation art notions of authenticity are made to cohabit with invention, and the figments of the past with aspirations

—

[30] Sumartono, 'The Role of Power in Contemporary Yogyakartan Art', in Melissa Larner (ed.), *Outlet: Yogyakarta within the Contemporary Indonesian Art Scene*, Yogyakarta: Cemeti Art Foundation, 2001, p.29.

[31] Santiago Bose, 'Ethnic Foragings', in Krip Yuson (ed.), *Espiritu Santi: The Strange Life and Even Stranger Legacy of Santiago Bose*, Quezon City: Water Dragon, 2004, p.144.

[32] Jimmie Durham, 'A Shaman Hits the Island', in K. Yuson (ed.), *Espiritu Santi*, *op. cit.*, p.69.

for the future'.[33] Transposed to the Australian milieu, the politics of authenticity and invention merge with feminist and ecological ethics. Ewington intuits this through an appraisal of works by Australian women artists Bonita Ely, Joan Grounds and Judy Watson among others who have integrated the personal and the political as they work on 'the raw matter of the universe'.[34]

Geeta Kapur scrupulously remarks on the possible materialist critique of installation to excite a space for the postcolonial contemporary. She specifically probes the deep strata of Vivan Sundaram's installation *History Project* (1998), described by Homi K. Bhabha as 'a haunting of the Victoria Memorial with the archival montage of the history of Bengal (1847–1947)'.[35] Kapur inserts the history of installation into Sundaram's work, first by citing texts by Hal Foster and Boris Groys, and then by rewriting the 'provenance' of said history. In revisiting Groys, she spins the problematic of the freedom, or emancipatory strain, thought to inhere in the installative. According to her, in installation 'the act of production and the act of presentation are the same, thus offering the perfect experimental terrain for revealing and exploring the ambiguities that lie at the core of the liberal notion of freedom'.[36] Kapur characterises the genealogy of installation as 'heterodox', pointing to the following as 'junctions': Dada and Constructivism; Minimalism and Arte Povera; conceptual art and institutional critique. From these vectors emerge 'political possibilities' for installation that may, in fact, render it preeminently hospitable to the postcolonial and enable it to materialise its promise to 'stage a cultural mise-en-scène and actualize praxis'.[37] It might be productive to strongly position this reflection on the installative in Southeast Asia by teasing out a strand from Kapur's marginalia on the history of installation in the international contemporary. From the articulations of the practice presented here, a horizon can at last be configured.

The installative sought to reclaim a sense of nature or a local moral ground on which a distinct practice could find its ecology. This was to be made complex by postcolonial critique of the occupation of territory and displacement of culture, and by reinvestment in a compromised but prevailing environment.

In relation to this sense of nature and its vital critique of the colonial, the installative laboured to mediate the entire gamut of modernity's impedimenta – art, museum, nation state, heritage, academy, culture, realism, capital, institution, the international. This mediation became a vehicle for a differential practice that invariably rested on reflexivity, materialist or cosmological revaluation, epistemic shift, intense translation and the reinstitution of the social.

—

[33] Julie Ewington, 'Five Elements: An Abbreviated Account of Installation Art in Southeast Asia', in *Art Studies 03: Shaping the History of Art in Southeast Asia*, Tokyo: The Japan Foundation Asia Center, p.36.
[34] J. Ewington, 'In the Wild: Nature, Culture, Gender in Installation Art', in Adam Geczy and Benjamin Genocchio (ed.), *What is Installation?: An Anthology of Writings on Australian Installation Art*, Sydney: Power Publications, 2001, p.49.
[35] Homi K. Bhabha, 'Foreword', in *Vivan Sundaram: History Project*, New Delhi: Tulika Books, 2017, p.9.
[36] Geeta Kapur, 'Monument as Bricolage', in *Vivan Sundaram*, *op. cit.*, p.69.
[37] *Ibid.*, p.107.

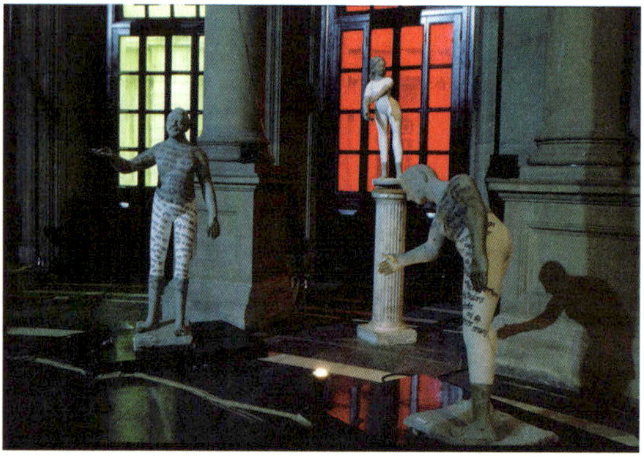

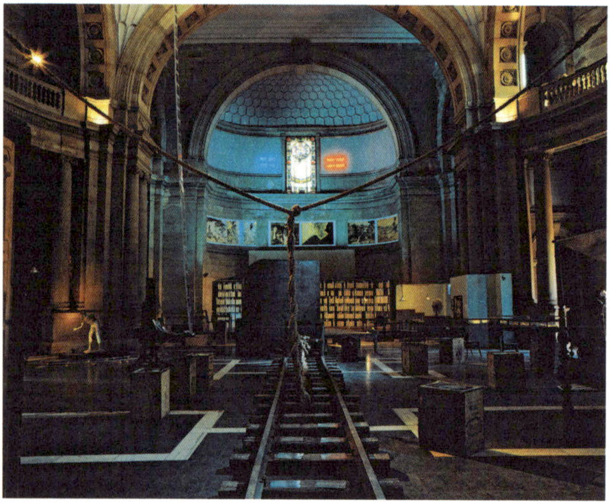

Installation views, Vivan Sundaram, *History Project* (1998), Victoria Memorial Museum, Kolkata
Courtesy the artist

Finally, the Southeast Asian installative expressed the desire of the artist to convene an art world, or a relational or transpersonal world of art, by creating conditions for people to assemble along the various axes of dissent, development, nationalism and solidarity. This would find a watershed at the Chiang Mai Social Installation in the 1990s, in which the social and the installative converged in a phrase to instantiate an exceptional event of gathering. Whatever it was that stirred up the energy to come together, the installative strove to summon a formation and, in the process, to be always-already and ever-formative: a public sphere, a civil society, a ritual, a festival, a common passage to a changing world.

Authors' biographies

Patrick D. Flores is Professor of Art Studies at the Department of Art Studies at the University of the Philippines, which he chaired from 1997 to 2003, and Curator of the Vargas Museum, Manila. Flores was one of the curators of 'Under Construction: New Dimensions in Asian Art' (The Japan Foundation Forum and Tokyo Opera City Art Gallery, 2000) and 'Turns in Tropics: Artist-Curator' (as part of 'Position Papers', 7th Gwangju Biennale, 2008), co-curator of 'South by Southeast. A Further Surface' (Times Museum, Guangzhou, 2016), curator of the Philippine Pavilion at the 56th Venice Biennale in 2015, and a member of the advisory board for the exhibition 'The Global Contemporary: Art Worlds After 1989' (ZKM | Center for Art and Media, Karlsruhe, 2011). His publications include *Painting History: Revisions in Philippine Colonial Art* (1999), *Remarkable Collection: Art, History, and the National Museum* (2006), *Past Peripheral: Curation in Southeast Asia* (2008) and the 'Contemporaneity and Art in Southeast Asia' special issue of *Third Text* (co-edited with Joan Kee, 2011). On behalf of the Clark Institute and the Department of Art Studies of the University of the Philippines he convened the 2013 conference 'Histories of Art History in Southeast Asia' in Manila. Flores has also held positions as a Visiting Fellow at the National Gallery of Art in Washington DC (1999), an Asian Public Intellectuals Fellow (2004), a grantee of the Asian Cultural Council (2010), a member of the Guggenheim Museum's Asian Art Council (2011 and 2014), and a Guest Scholar at the Getty Research Institute in Los Angeles (2014). He was recently appointed Artistic Director of the 2019 Singapore Biennale.

May Adadol Ingawanij is Reader at the University of Westminster, where she co-directs the Centre for Research and Education in Arts and Media (CREAM). She is writing a book titled *Contemporary Art and Animistic Cinematic Practices in Southeast Asia*. Her publications include 'Exhibiting Lav Diaz's Long Films: Currencies of Circulation and Dialectics of Spectatorship' (in *Aniki: Portuguese Journal of the Moving Image*, 2017), 'Long Walk to Life: The Films of Lav Diaz' (in *Afterall*, 2015), 'Animism and the Performative Realist Cinema of Apichatpong Weerasethakul' (in *Screening Nature: Cinema Beyond the Human*, Berghahn Books, 2013), *Glimpses of Freedom: Independent Cinema in Southeast Asia* (co-edited with Benjamin McKay, Cornell University Press, 2012) and 'Aesthetics of Potentiality: Nguyen Trinh Thi's Essay Films' (forthcoming). Her recent curatorial projects include 'Lav Diaz: Journeys' (London Gallery West, 2017), 'On Attachments and Unknowns' (Sa Sa Bassac, Phnom Penh, 2017) and 'Comparing Experimental Cinemas' (Srishti School of Art, Design and Technology, Bangalore, 2014).

David Morris is a writer, researcher and editor at Afterall. His work explores different approaches to artistic research, education and exhibition, with a focus on experimental, collective and interdisciplinary practices. He is co-editor, with Sylvère Lotringer, of *Schizo-Culture: The Event, The Book* (Semiotext(e)/The MIT Press, 2014). Other recent publications include *Wendelien van Oldenborgh: Amateur* (co-edited with Emily Pethick and Wendelien van Oldenborgh; Sternberg Press/The Showroom/If I Can't Dance, 2016) and *Anti-Shows: APTART 1982–84* (co-edited with Margarita Tupitsyn and Victor Tupitsyn; Afterall Books, 2017). He teaches at University of the Arts London.

Rosalind C. Morris is Professor of Anthropology at Columbia University. Her early scholarship focussed on the social history of modernity in Southeast Asia and the place of media technology in its development, and included the book *In the Place of Origins: Modernity and its Mediums in Northern Thailand* (2000). More recently, she has been writing about the lives and afterlives of extractive industries in southern Africa. Traversing these fields of inquiry, her work addresses questions of the relationships between value and violence; aesthetics and the political; the sexualisation of power and desire; and the history of social theory. A frequent collaborator with South African artists, Morris is also a poet and a librettist. Her documentary film *We are Zama Zama* will be released in 2019.

David Teh is a curator and Associate Professor at the National University of Singapore, specialising in Southeast Asian contemporary art. His curatorial projects include 'Unreal Asia' (55. Internationale Kurzfilmtage Oberhausen, 2009), 'Video Vortex #7' (Yogyakarta, 2011), 'TRANSMISSION' (Jim Thompson Art Center, Bangkok, 2014) and 'Misfits: Pages from a Loose-leaf Modernity' (Haus der Kulturen der Welt, Berlin, 2017). He is a co-curator of the 12th Gwangju Biennale (2018). Teh's writings have appeared in journals including *Afterall*, *ARTMargins*, *Third Text* and *Theory, Culture and Society.* His book *Thai Art: Currencies of the Contemporary* was recently published by The MIT Press. Teh is also a director of Future Perfect, a gallery and project platform in Singapore.

Selected bibliography

The most significant archive of Chiang Mai Social Installation is that of Uthit Atimana, recently digitised as part of an initiative led by Gridthiya Gaweewong and sponsored by Asia Culture Center, Gwangju. Ray Langenbach's video documentation of the 1995–96 CMSI, as well as subsequent performance and art festivals in the region, is part of The Ray Langenbach Archive of Performance Art, held by Asia Art Archive. CMSI was a focus of the symposium 'Regions of the Contemporary: Transnational Art Festivals and Exhibitions in 1990s Southeast Asia', 5–7 November 2016, University of Melbourne, co-organised by Afterall and the School of Culture and Communication, University of Melbourne as part of the research process for this book: see https://www.afterall.org/events/regions-of-the-contemporary (last accessed on 4 September 2018).

The Artists Village, 20 Years On (exh. cat.), Singapore: Singapore Art Museum and The Artists Village, 2009

Apinan Poshyananda, *Modern Art in Thailand: Nineteenth and Twentieth Centuries*, Singapore: Oxford University Press, 1992

Apinan Poshyananda, *Behind Thai Smiles: Selected Writings, 1991–2007*, Bangkok: Office of Contemporary Art and Culture, 2007

Pandit Chanrochanakit, 'The Negotiation of Approaches: From Chiang Mai Social Installation and Asiatopia to Contemporary Southeast Asian Art', presentation at 'Continuous Horizons: Contemporary Art for Asia', Asia Society Hong Kong Center, 11 January 2014

John Clark, *Asian Modernities: Chinese and Thai Art Compared, 1980 to 1999*, Seattle: University of Washington Press, 2011

Patrick D. Flores, *Past Peripheral: Curation in Southeast Asia*, Singapore: National University of Singapore Museum, 2008

Patrick D. Flores, 'The Exhibition as Historical Proposition', *Yishu: Journal of Contemporary Chinese Art*, vol.13, no.2, March–April 2014, Asia Art Archive special issue 'Sites of Construction: Exhibitions and the Making of Recent Art History in Asia', pp.103–04

Gridthiya Gaweewong and Manuporn Luengaram (ed.), *An Anthology of Southeast Asian Modern and Contemporary Art*, Bangkok: Office of Contemporary Art and Culture, 2016

Joan Kee and Patrick D. Flores (ed.), 'Contemporaneity and Art in Southeast Asia', special issue, *Third Text*, vol.25, no.4, 2011

Iola Lenzi (ed.), *Concept, Context, Contestation: Art and the Collective in Southeast Asia* (exh. cat.), Bangkok: Bangkok Art and Cultural Centre Foundation, 2014

Rosalind C. Morris, *In the Place of Origins: Modernity and Its Mediums in Northern Thailand*, Durham, NC: Duke University Press, 2000

T.K. Sabapathy, 'Developing Regionalist Perspectives in Southeast Asian Art Historiography' (1996), in Melissa Chiu and Benjamin Genocchio (ed.), *Contemporary Art in Asia: A Critical Reader*, Cambridge, MA: The MIT Press, 2011, pp.47–61

Jeffrey Say and Seng Yu Jin (ed.), *Histories, Practices, Interventions: A Reader in Singapore Contemporary* Art, Singapore: Institute of Contemporary Arts, Singapore and Lasalle College of the Arts, 2016

Thasnai Sethaseree, 'Overlapping Tactics and Practices at the Interstices of Thai Art', unpublished doctoral thesis, Chiang Mai University, 2011

Simon Soon, 'Images Without Bodies: Chiang Mai Social Installation and the Art History of Cooperative Suffering', *Afterall*, issue 42, Autumn/Winter 2016, pp.37–47

Nora A. Taylor and Boreth Ly, *Modern and Contemporary Southeast Asian Art: An Anthology*, Ithaca, NY: Cornell Southeast Asia Program Publications, 2012

David Teh, 'Obstacles to Exhibition History: Institutions, Curatorship, and the Undead Nation State', in Paul O'Neill, Mick Wilson and Lucy Steeds (ed.), *The Curatorial Conundrum: What to Study? What to Research? What to Practice?*, Cambridge, MA: The MIT Press, 2016, pp.26–38

David Teh, *Thai Art: Currencies of the Contemporary*, Cambridge, MA: The MIT Press, 2017

Thongchai Winichakul, *Siam Mapped: A History of the Geo-Body of a Nation*, Honolulu: University of Hawaii Press, 1994

Seng Yu Jin, 'The Primacy of Exhibitionary Discourses: Contemporaneity in Southeast Asian Art, 1992–2002', in T.K. Sabapathy (ed.), *Intersecting Histories: Contemporary Turns in Southeast Asian Art* (exh. cat.), Singapore: Nanyang Technological University, 2012

Picture credits

All artworks © the artists

Unless noted below, all images from the archive of Uthit Atimana and courtesy Uthit Atimana and Gridthiya Gaweewong (pp.50–243)

Courtesy Navin Production Co., Ltd. (pp.164 and 199–201)

Courtesy Tan Chin Kuan (p.150)

Courtesy and © Satoshi Hirose. Photography: Masato Nakamura (pp.159 and 167)

Text credits

Texts referenced pp.86–243 are as follows. All other quotations are taken from interviews for this publication.

Chanyaporn Chanjaroen, 'Art is a Temple', *The Nation*, 19 January 1993

Khetsirin Knithichan, 'Turning Galleries Inside Out', *The Nation*, 29 November 1993

Chanyaporn Chanjaroen, 'Art to Bump Into', *Bangkok Post*, 15 December 1993

Khetsirin Knithichan and Phatarawadee Phataranawik, 'But is it Art?', *The Nation*, 4 December 1995

David Johnson, 'Earth Works', *Metro*, c.1995, copy held by Uthit Atimana

'Future of Chiang Mai Social Installation' / 'Chiang Mai Social Installation, What Next?', *Wai* [zine], issue 2, c.1996

Tei Kobayashi (writing as T.J. McGuire), 'A Week of Suffering in Chiang Mai', *Asiana*, February 1996

Ray Langenbach, early draft of 'Through the Keyhole: The third Chiangmai art and culture festival', *ArtAsiaPacific*, vol.3, no.3, 1996

Araya Rasdjarmrearnsook, 'A narrative of an event that has just come to an end', *Journal of Fine Arts* (Chiang Mai University Faculty of Fine Arts), vol.1, no.1, 2000, pp.14–16

Mit Jai Inn interviewed by Simon Soon, 2 February 2014

Acknowledgements

Afterall would like to thank the authors, artists and photographers for their contributions to this book.

For support in the research process that led to this publication we are additionally grateful to: Angkrit Ajchariyasophon; Riksa Afiaty; Nilofar Akmut; Apinan Poshyananda; Arahmaiani; Araya Rasdjarmrearnsook; Atikom Mukdaprakorn; David Blamey; Chanon Kenji Praepipatmongkol; Chumpon Apisuk; John Clark; Pamela Corey; Anthony Gardner; Charles Green; Gridthiya Gaweewong; Nigel Helyer; Rolf Hinterecker; Koh Nguang How; Kade Javanalikhikara; Kamin Lertchaiprasert; Ingrid H. Klauser; Tei Kobayashi; Jay Koh; Kosit Juntaratip; Ray Langenbach; Vera Mey; Mit Jai Inn; Varsha Nair; Hammad Nasar; Navin Rawanchaikul; Narumol Thammapruksa; Roger Nelson; Alfred Pawlin; Phaptawan Suwannakudt; Rirkrit Tiravanija; Claire Roberts; Grace Samboh; Santiphap Inkong-ngam; Simon Soon; Enno Stahl; Alec Steadman (2015 Asia Art Archive researcher-in-residence); Russell Storer; Supachai Satsara; Sutthirat Supaparinya; Alia Swastika; Erika Tan; Tawatchai Puntusawasdi; Thanom Chapakdee; Thasnai Sethaseree; Thatree Pokawanich; Thepsiri Sooksopa; Uthit Atimana; Chương-Đài Võ; Carola Willbrand; and Seng Yu Jin.

The *Exhibition Histories* series has been generously supported by the Academy of Fine Arts Vienna; Asia Art Archive; Central Saint Martins, University of the Arts London; the Center for Curatorial Studies, Bard College; MUDAM Luxembourg, Musee d'Art Moderne Grand-Duc Jean; the National Lottery through Arts Council England; and Van Abbemuseum, Eindhoven. For her support of the project from the outset the editors would like to thank Marie-Claude Beaud.

ARTS COUNCIL ENGLAND

Index

Please note that Chiang Mai Social Installation editions and related events are listed on the contents page.

Note on Thai spelling and usage:
This book follows the convention of referring to Thai persons by given name rather than family name. For transliterated names and terms it follows the general rule of adopting spellings that are most likely to advance the understanding of readers who are unfamiliar with Thai language and custom.